T0340015

Multiteam Systems

*An Organization Form for Dynamic
and Complex Environments*

ORGANIZATION AND MANAGEMENT SERIES
Series Editors

Arthur P. Brief
University of Utah

Kimberly D. Elsbach
University of California, Davis

Michael Frese
University of Lueneburg and National University of Singapore

Ashforth (Au.): *Role Transitions in Organizational Life: An Identity-Based Perspective*

Bartel/Blader/Wrzesniewski (Eds.): *Identity and the Modern Organization*

Bartunek (Au.): *Organizational and Educational Change: The Life and Role of a Change Agent Group*

Beach (Ed.): *Image Theory: Theoretical and Empirical Foundations*

Brett/Drasgow (Eds.): *The Psychology of Work: Theoretically Based Empirical Research*

Brockner (Au.): *A Contemporary Look at Organizational Justice: Multiplying Insult Times Injury*

Chhokar/Brodbeck/House (Eds.): *Culture and Leadership Across the World: The GLOBE Book of In-Depth Studies of 25 Societies*

Darley/Messick/Tyler (Eds.): *Social Influences on Ethical Behavior in Organizations*

DeCremer/van Dick/Murnighan (Eds.): *Social Psychology and Organizations*

Denison (Ed.): *Managing Organizational Change in Transition Economies*

Dutton/Ragins (Eds.): *Exploring Positive Relationships at Work: Building a Theoretical and Research Foundation*

Earley/Gibson (Aus.): *Multinational Work Teams: A New Perspective*

Elsbach (Au.): *Organizational Perception Management*

Garud/Karnoe (Eds.): *Path Dependence and Creation*

Harris (Ed.): *Handbook of Research in International Human Resource Management*

Jacoby (Au.): *Employing Bureaucracy: Managers, Unions, and the Transformation of Work in the 20th Century, Revised Edition*

Kossek/Lambert (Eds.): *Work and Life Integration: Organizational, Cultural and Individual Perspectives*

Kramer/Tenbrunsel/Bazerman (Eds.): *Social Decision Making: Social Dilemmas, Social Values and Ethical Judgments*

Lampel/Shamsie/Lant (Eds.): *The Business of Culture: Strategic Perspectives on Entertainment and Media*

Lant/Shapira (Eds.): *Organizational Cognition: Computation and Interpretation*

Lord/Brown (Aus.): *Leadership Processes and Follower Self-Identity*

Margolis/Walsh (Aus.): *People and Profits? The Search Between a Company's Social and Financial Performance*

Messick/Kramer (Eds.): *The Psychology of Leadership: Some New Approaches*

Miceli/Dworkin/Near (Aus.): *Whistle-Blowing in Organizations*

Nord/Connell (Aus.): *Rethinking the Knowledge Controversy in Organization Studies: A Generative Uncertainty Perspective*

Pearce (Au.): *Organization and Management in the Embrace of the Government*

Multiteam Systems

An Organization Form for Dynamic and Complex Environments

Edited by

Stephen J. Zaccaro

George Mason University
Fairfax, Virginia

Michelle A. Marks

George Mason University
Fairfax, Virginia

Leslie A. DeChurch

University of Central Florida
Orlando, Florida

Routledge
Taylor & Francis Group

LONDON AND NEW YORK

First published 2012 by Routledge

2 Park Square, Milton Park, Abingdon, Oxfordshire OX14 4RN
52 Vanderbilt Avenue, New York, NY 10017

Routledge is an imprint of the Taylor & Francis Group, an informa business

First issued in paperback 2019

Copyright © 2012 Taylor & Francis

All rights reserved. No part of this book may be reprinted or reproduced or
utilised in any form or by any electronic, mechanical, or other means, now
known or hereafter invented, including photocopying and recording, or in
any information storage or retrieval system, without permission in writing
from the publishers.

Notice:
Product or corporate names may be trademarks or registered trademarks,
and are used only for identification and explanation without intent to
infringe.

ISBN: 978-1-84872-869-1 (hbk)
ISBN: 978-0-367-86579-5 (pbk)

I dedicate this volume to my students—past and present—for
their passion and curiosity about leadership and teams, and to my
wife, Gail, who teaches me every day the value of team work.

Stephen J. Zaccaro

To Steve and John, with whom the MTS adventure began.

Michelle A. Marks

To the multiteam systems in which I am embedded—

To my mentors and students, for their intellectual
stimulation in advancing our understanding of MTSs.

To Cameron and Maddy for their constant reminder of
the practical value of MTSs in our daily lives.

Leslie A. DeChurch

Contents

Series Foreword

Multiteam systems are two or more teams that interface directly and interdependently in response to environmental contingencies toward the accomplishment of collective goals. Such collaborations across traditional team and organizational boundaries are now commonplace but ill understood. Zaccaro, Marks, and DeChurch have gone a long way toward filling this void in knowledge by bringing together *the* experts in this volume. Chapters flesh out the multiteam systems construct and address the variety of forms they take. Other chapters address how they should be composed, led, and developed, and their members linked. Importantly, still other chapters attend to the methodological and theoretical challenges that remain to be met in the study of multiple-team systems. We anticipate that when readers turn that last page, they too will count themselves among the knowledgeable. Obviously, we are pleased to welcome Zaccaro, Marks, and DeChurch to our series.

Arthur Brief
Kim Elsbach
Michael Frese
Series Editors

Acknowledgments

We want to acknowledge and thank several people and their organizations for helping us with the achievement of this book. First, the workshop that inspired this book was funded by contract from the U.S. Army Research Institute (ARI, Contract # W91WAW-07-C-0047) to the University of Central Florida. This contract also funded in part our efforts in preparing this book. We thank Shawn Burke, Melisa Grzanich, and Eduardo Salas at UCF for coordinating the workshop. We also thank Jay Goodwin and Linda Pierce from ARI for their support of this work. The people at UCF and ARI created a scholarly environment for us and a disparate group of scientists to explore and ask the right questions about multiteam systems. They also supported this book as a first step in answering those questions. We are grateful for their encouragement.

We want to thank Art Brief for adding our book to the Taylor & Francis/ Routledge *Series in Organization and Management*. We are proud to be included in this scholarly set of contributions. We also want to thank Anne Duffy for her patience, persistence, and encouragement in helping this book to emerge. She connected us with Art Brief, and brought to our collaboration a long history of working with scholars in the organizational psychology and management domains. We are grateful for that experience. We also want to thank Erin Flaherty, Andrea Zekus, and Iris Fahrer for their editorial assistance at different stages of this project.

We want to thank the chapter authors. Many of you showed up at the workshop, some with a healthy skepticism, to challenge us, and to discuss and argue with each other about multiteam systems. We were delighted to see these conversations expand in sessions at several professional conferences, and we appreciated your growing excitement about this concept. We also greatly enjoyed reading your chapters. You have given us much to think about. Finally, we want to thank John Mathieu, not only for providing the concluding chapter, but also for working with us on the taxonomy of multiteam system attributes described in the first chapter, and for continuing to encourage our ideas and research about multiteam systems. He has been a longtime friend, collaborator, and research mentor to all of us.

About the Editors

Stephen J. Zaccaro is a professor of psychology at George Mason University, Fairfax, Virginia. He received his PhD in social psychology from the University of Connecticut. He is also an experienced leadership development consultant. He has written over 100 journal articles, book chapters, and technical reports on group dynamics, team performance, leadership, and work attitudes. He has authored *The Nature of Executive Leadership: A Conceptual and Empirical Analysis of Success* (2001), and coedited three other books: *Occupational Stress and Organizational Effectiveness* (1987); *The Nature of Organizational Leadership: Understanding the Performance Imperatives Confronting Today's Leaders* (2001); and *Leader Development for Transforming Organizations* (2004). He has also coedited special issues of *Leadership Quarterly* (1991–1992) on individual differences and leadership, and a special issue for *Group and Organization Management* (2002) on the interface between leadership and team dynamics. He serves on the editorial board of *Leadership Quarterly*, and is an associate editor for the *Journal of Business and Psychology* and *Military Psychology*. He is a fellow of the American Psychological Association, Divisions 14 (Society for Industrial and Organizational Psychology) and 19 (Military Psychology).

Michelle A. Marks is an associate professor of management in Mason's School of Management, George Mason University. She earned her undergraduate degree from James Madison University and her MS and PhD in industrial/organizational psychology from George Mason University. She also currently serves as associate provost for graduate education at George Mason University. Prior to her faculty appointment at George Mason, Dr. Marks was an assistant professor at Florida International University. She has authored and delivered more than 75 peer-reviewed journal articles and national conference research presentations. She studies leadership development and teamwork in organizations. In 2006, Dr. Marks won the George Mason University Teaching Excellence Award, and in 2008 she won the Executive MBA Professor of the Year award. She teaches courses in leadership, organizational behavior, global business, and change management in executive, MBA, and undergraduate programs. Dr. Marks is a member of the editorial board of the *Journal of Applied Psychology* and a board member of the Interdisciplinary Network for Group Research.

Leslie A. DeChurch is an assistant professor of organizational psychology at the University of Central Florida. Dr. DeChurch's research interests include team and multiteam system effectiveness, leadership, and conflict and negotiations. Her research has appeared in the *Journal of Applied Psychology*; the *Leadership Quarterly*; the *Journal of Applied Social Psychology*; *Small Group Research*; *Human Factors*; *Group Dynamics: Theory, Research, & Practice*; and the *International Journal of Conflict Management*. Dr. DeChurch is a consulting editor at the *Journal of Applied Psychology* and the *Journal of Business and Psychology*; her research has been funded by the National Science Foundation and the Army Research Institute for the Social and Behavioral Sciences. Dr. DeChurch earned a BS (1996) in environmental science from the University of Miami, and MS (2000) and PhD (2002) degrees in psychology from Florida International University.

Contributors

Juliet R. Aiken
Department of Psychology
University of Maryland
College Park, Maryland

Kevin R. Betts
Department of Psychology
North Dakota State University
Fargo, North Dakota

C. Shawn Burke
Institute for Simulation and
    Training
University of Central Florida
Orlando, Florida

Corinne Coen
Weatherhead School of
    Management
Case Western Reserve University
Cleveland, Ohio

Stacey Connaughton
Department of Communication
Purdue University
West Lafayette, Indiana

Noshir Contractor
Department of Industrial
    Engineering and Management
    Science
Department of Communication
    Studies
Northwestern University
Evanston, Illinois

Robert B. Davison
The Eli Broad Graduate School of
    Management
Michigan State University
East Lansing, Michigan

Leslie A. DeChurch
Department of Psychology
University of Central Florida
Orlando, Florida

Daniel Doty
Department of Psychology
University of Central Florida
Orlando, Florida

Peter J. M. D. Essens
TNO Human Factors
Soesterberg, the Netherlands

Debra J. Ford
School of Nursing
University of Kansas Medical
    Center
Kansas City, Kansas

Gerald F. Goodwin
Office of Basic Research
U.S. Army Research Institute
    for the Behavioral and Social
    Sciences
Arlington, Virginia

Paul Hanges
Department of Psychology
University of Maryland College
College Park, Maryland

Verlin B. Hinsz
Department of Psychology
North Dakota State University
Fargo, North Dakota

John R. Hollenbeck
The Eli Broad Graduate School of
    Management
Michigan State University
East Lansing, Michigan

Ruth Kanfer
School of Psychology
Georgia Institute of Technology
Atlanta, Georgia

Matthew Kerry
School of Psychology
Georgia Institute of Technology
Atlanta, Georgia

Joann Keyton
Department of Communication
North Carolina State University
Raleigh, North Carolina

Dave Luvison
H. Wayne Huizenga School of
    Business and Entrepreneurship
Nova Southeastern University
Ft. Lauderdale, Florida

Michelle A. Marks
Office of the Provost
School of Management
George Mason University
Fairfax, Virginia

John Mathieu
School of Business
University of Connecticut
Storrs, Connecticut

Mark Mortensen
INSEAD
Fontainebleau, France

Michael Boyer O'Leary
McDonough School of Business
Georgetown University
Washington, DC

Marshall Scott Poole
Department of Communication
University of Illinois
    Urbana-Champaign
Urbana, Illinois

Joan R. Rentsch
Industrial/Organizational
    Psychology Program
Department of Management
The University of Tennessee
Knoxville, Tennessee

Christian Resick
LeBow College of Business
Drexel University
Philadelphia, Pennsylvania

Andrew Schnackenberg
Weatherhead School of
    Management
Case Western Reserve University
Cleveland, Ohio

Marissa L. Shuffler
ICF International & Institute for
    Simulation & Training
University of Central Florida
Orlando, Florida

David G. Smith
DRDC Toronto
Toronto, Ontario, Canada

Faye L. Smith
Craig School of Business
Missouri Western State University
St. Joseph, Missouri

Rhetta L. Standifer
Department of Management and
    Marketing
University of Wisconsin–Eau
    Claire
Eau Claire, Wisconsin

Melissa J. Staniewicz
Industrial/Organizational
    Psychology Program
Department of Management
The University of Tennessee
Knoxville, Tennessee

Sjir Uitdewilligen
Faculty of Psychology and
    Neuroscience
Maastricht University
Maastricht, the Netherlands

Mary J. Waller
Schulich School of Business
York University
Toronto, Ontario, Canada

Elizabeth A. Williams
Department of Communication
Purdue University
West Lafayette, Indiana

Anita Williams Woolley
Tepper School of Business
Carnegie Mellon University
Pittsburgh, Pennsylvania

Stephen J. Zaccaro
Department of Psychology
George Mason University
Fairfax, Virginia

Section I

Introduction

1

Multiteam Systems: An Introduction

Stephen J. Zaccaro
George Mason University

Michelle A. Marks
George Mason University

Leslie A. DeChurch
University of Central Florida

Over the last 2 decades, the operating work environment has become exceedingly more challenging and complex (Ilgen & Pulakos, 1999). To wit, communication and information technology has grown exponentially, increasing the pace, scope, and scale of work (Hesketh & Neal, 1999). Such technology has also increased the globalism and geographic dislocation of organizational work (Ireland & Hitt, 1999). Because of the global reach of today's business, and the increasing immediacy afforded by current technology, strategic issues, problems, and implications have greater interconnectivity across organizational boundaries. Traditional organizational forms have been typically insufficient to respond effectively to such changes. Accordingly, a number of different organizational forms that complement more conventional structures have emerged, including matrix and virtual organizations, as well as cross-functioning and ad hoc project teams.

One of these forms includes different kinds of collaborations that can exist across traditional team and organizational boundaries. Such cross-boundary collaborations have been observed in the past, of course, in the face of large-scale crisis events that require the interdependent responsiveness of multiple agencies (e.g., see response to Hurricane Katrina; Moynihan, 2007). The collectives formed from such requirements do not resemble traditional organizations or large-scale teams. Nor do such collectives reflect more recent forms such as team-based organizations, virtual organizations, or matrix organizations. Instead, current environmental challenges have increasingly given rise to a form of aggregation that includes tightly coupled constellations of teams, where the different teams may possess very different core missions, expertise, structures, norms, and operating procedures to the collective effort. However, the performances of such constellations reflect the kinds of integrated and interdependent actions typical of more traditional teams and organizations.

Mathieu, Marks, and Zaccaro (2001) defined these kinds of organizations as *multiteam systems* (MTSs), and argued that they represented a relatively new collective form that has emerged as adaptive responses to the aforementioned environmental challenges. Thus, they noted that "MTSs are usually formed or develop naturally to deal with highly turbulent environments that place a premium on the ability to transform work units and to respond rapidly to changing circumstances" (Mathieu et al., 2001, p. 290). They also asserted that existing organizational or team theories and models do not provide sufficient means of understanding the processes and dynamics of MTSs. Accordingly, they cited the need to recognize and study such collectives in the organizational sciences. Since the publication of Mathieu et al. (2001), several other studies, both empirical and conceptual, have been published that have provided some insight into MTSs (e.g., Coen, 2006; DeChurch & Marks, 2006; DeChurch & Mathieu, 2009; Hoegl & Weinkauf, 2005; Liu & Simaan, 2004a, 2004b; Liu, Simaan, & Cruz, 2003; Marks, DeChurch, Mathieu, Panzer, & Alonso, 2005; Marks, Mathieu, & Zaccaro, 2004; Mathieu, Cobb, Marks, Zaccaro, & Marsh, 2004; Standifer & Bluedorn, 2006). Other studies have examined specific types of MTSs, such as incident command systems (Moynihan, 2007), multisystem coordination in space missions (Caldwell, 2005), multi-unit human–robot systems (Hsu & Liu, 2005), and joint venture teams and other kinds of business alliances (Johnson, Korsgaard, & Sapienza, 2002; Marks & Luvison, 2008). MTSs have also been the subject of several conference papers and symposia at recent annual meetings of the Society for Industrial and Organizational Psychology (e.g., Burke, DeChurch, Salas, & Goodwin, 2008; DeChurch, 2010; DeChurch & Burke, 2009; DeChurch & Marks, 2008; DeChurch et al., 2010; Marks et al., 2010; Wooten et al., 2009), Human Factors and Ergonomics Society (e.g., Dean et al., 2008), Academy of Management (e.g., DeChurch, 2006), and Interdisciplinary

Network for Group Research (e.g., DeChurch, Burke, & Salas, 2009; DeChurch & Resick, 2006; Lyons et al., 2008).

In June 2008, a conference sponsored by the U.S Army Research Institute brought together several scholars to explore in more detail the concept of MTSs. This conference highlighted the necessity for an expanded and deeper focus on the nature of MTSs that (a) describes these organizational forms more fully, (b) builds conceptual frames that can guide research on such forms, and (c) begins developing tools to improve the study of MTSs. The purpose of this book is to respond to these needs. This book contains a series of chapters that expand prior conceptual frames of MTSs, defining in more detail the compositional and linkage attributes that characterize such units. It also explores how such systems emerge and develop, as well as the methods for studying MTSs. The intent, therefore, is to establish and nurture a strong conceptual and methodological foundation that can guide future research and practice with MTSs.

In this first chapter, we provide a summary of the core concepts that define MTSs. We then provide a listing of characteristics and dimensions that distinguish different forms of MTSs. We conclude with a brief summary of the major sections and chapters of the book.

MULTITEAM SYSTEMS: CORE CONCEPTS

In this section, we elucidate some core concepts that define MTSs, and distinguish them from other kinds of teams and organizations. We are summarizing ideas and concepts offered by Mathieu et al. (2001), Marks et al. (2004), and DeChurch and Mathieu (2009). We refer readers to those sources for greater details.

Mathieu et al. (2001) defined MTSs as follows:

> Two or more teams that interface directly and interdependently in response to environmental contingencies toward the accomplishment of collective goals. MTS boundaries are defined by virtue of the fact that all teams within the system, while pursuing different proximal goals, share at least one common distal goal; and in doing so exhibit input, process and outcome interdependence with at least on other team in the system. (P. 290)

The above definition indicates several core parameters that distinguish MTSs from other types of collectives in organizations. Regarding composition, Mathieu et al. (2001) noted that although they can include as few as two component teams, MTSs are typically larger in size than most teams but smaller than their embedding organizations. Perhaps one of the more important and interesting features regarding membership, however, is that the boundary of the MTS can cross the boundaries of multiple organizations—that is, an MTS can be composed of tightly coupled teams that are themselves members of different organizations. Mathieu et al. (2001) distinguished between MTSs embedded entirely within an organization (called *internal MTSs*) and those composed of teams from different embedding organizations (called *cross-boundary MTSs*). In the latter, there exists a significant degree of interdependence among component teams, even as they are integrated within other systems. Such MTSs confront complexity of a magnitude greater than their wholly internal counterparts because they need to integrate demands not only from the environmental context common to all of the component teams, but also from their respective and different embedding organizations. Mathieu et al. (2001) noted that with internal MTSs, influences from the external environment are more likely to be filtered through characteristics of the embedding organization such as its goals, strategies, culture, norms, values, and reward systems. Accordingly, internal MTSs are likely to have more shared value, motivational, and cognitive systems than cross-boundary MTSs.

Although the notion of cross-boundary MTSs may resonate more intuitively as a unique organizational form, internal MTSs can appear to resemble other forms of collectives within organizations (Mathieu et al., 2001). For example, most, if not all, organizations above a certain size are structured as a system of interlocked departments and units, each with clearly defined functions (i.e., "subsystems"; Katz & Kahn, 1978). Such subsystems can be characterized as "functional groupings of individuals based on a purpose within the organization" (Mathieu et al., 2001, p. 292). However, an MTS can include and integrate multiple functions that would be the purview of separate subsystems in a traditional organization. More importantly, an MTS is fundamentally a team-based collective, where each of its members belongs to one of the component teams. In many organizations, units are not organized as teams, and members may not be engaged in activities that require the collaborative integration of teamwork. Even when these organization units are organized as teams (cf. Mohrman, Cohen, & Mohrman, 1995), they are more loosely coupled than in MTSs, without the level of interdependence in the latter that is described below. Collective or joint activity by traditional organizational units typically takes the form of coaction, or pooled interdependence, and sometimes sequential interdependence, where one team may hand its work products off to another team for subsequent additions (see Thompson [1967] and Tesluk, Mathieu, Zaccaro, and Marks [1997] for descriptions of different types of interdependence within teams—in the present discussion, these are extended to the collective activity of multiple teams). MTSs are typically characterized more by what Tesluk et al. (1997) summarized as reciprocal or intensive interdependence, where component teams may exchange work products back and forth, or work in close and intense collaboration to accomplish shared goals.

Mathieu et al. (2001) described other collectives associated with traditional organizations that can have overlapping characteristics with MTSs. These include "subassemblies" (Simon, 1962), matrix organizations (Knight, 1976), and task forces (Hackman, 1990). To this list, we would add distributed teams (Jarvenpaa, Knoll, & Leidner, 1998; Mittleman & Briggs, 1999) and top management groups or executive teams (Hambrick, 1994; Mohrman et al., 1995; Mohrman & Quam, 2000). Subassemblies are organizational units that typically have more autonomy from a parent organization than most traditional units; thus, they share this quality in part with MTSs (Scott, 1998). However, unlike MTSs, such units are structured around specific functions, and they are not necessarily organized as a collection of teams with the level of interdependence that characterizes MTSs. Matrix organizations use teams staffed by members drawn from multiple and different functional units (Davis & Lawrence, 1977). They share with MTSs their quicker responsiveness to turbulent environments and their cross-boundary membership. However, teams in matrix organizations are still loosely coupled if at all, and also do not exhibit the degree of interdependence found in MTSs. Task forces are ad hoc groups that also come together and respond with a significant degree of autonomy to a set of objectives provided by higher levels of an organization (Hackman, 1990). However, like cross-functional project teams, task forces are limited in tenure to the duration of a single project and do not typically function as a collection of teams (Sundstrom, McIntrye, Halfhill, & Richards, 2000).

MTSs also share some characteristics with two other organizational forms—virtual teams and top management teams in team-based organizations. Virtual or distributed teams are composed of members that do not work together in the same geographic or temporal space (Jarvenpaa et al., 1998; Mittleman & Briggs, 1999). Thus, like component teams in MTSs, members of virtual teams may be embedded within different contexts and have multiple environmental demands. Component teams in MTSs are also often dispersed geographically and temporally. However, unlike MTSs, virtual teams are single units not strongly coupled to other teams, and they typically reside under single organizational umbrellas.

MTSs resemble team-based organizations, especially at the top of such organizations where the managers of such teams are themselves organized into a team. Mohrman and Quam (2000; see also Mohrman et al., 1995) defined *team-based organizations* as ones in which a team represents the key unit that "delivers products or service of value to the customer. Ideally the team is relatively self-contained and contains the various skills and knowledge sets necessary to carry out its task with minimal external intervention" (p. 21). Mohrman and Quam noted that teams in such organizations are embedded within functional business units. They also indicated that the work of such teams can become interdependent with that of other teams, and therefore mechanisms promoting lateral integration and coordination emerge. In such instances, these systems begin to resemble internal MTSs. We would note, however, that in many team-based organizations, teams still operate mostly independently of one another, linking primarily through managerial processes. They tend to stay within the boundaries of single business units, and do not typically cross organizational boundaries. Thus, although MTSs reflect a type of team-based organization, they retain a number of unique features that distinguish them from other types of such organizations.

Perhaps the most distinguishing feature of MTSs, aside from their cross-boundary membership, lies in their high level of reciprocal or intensive functional interdependence not only within but also *across* component teams. Mathieu et al. (2001, p. 293) defined such interdependence as "a state by which entities have mutual reliance, determination, influence, and shared vested interest in processes they use to accomplish work activities." This mutuality is encoded within the goal hierarchies that direct the activities of the MTS. As noted in the definition of MTSs, component teams (a) have different proximal goals, but (b) share at least one distal goal. The goals of the entire MTS, then, are organized in a hierarchy, where each component team goal is at the lowest level, and the goal or goals common to all teams are at the highest level (Mathieu et al., 2001). For example, Mathieu et al. (2001) described the proximal and distal goals of an MTS responding to a severely injured accident victim. This MTS is composed of a firefighting unit, an EMT unit, a surgical team, and a recovery team. The ultimate or distal goal of this MTS is, of course, survival of the patient. However, the firefighters and the EMTs have the proximal goals of (a) extracting and stabilizing the injured motorist, and (b) transporting him or her to the hospital, while continuing emergency care. Once at the hospital, the surgical team is responsible for the next-level goal of repairing the patient's injuries. After the surgery, the recovery team administers to the patient toward survival and full recovery. Note that all of the component teams contribute to the distal goal of patient recovery, but each component team has responsibility for a different proximal goal within the goal hierarchy (Mathieu et al., 2001).

According to Mathieu et al. (2001), such goal hierarchies have several features that are relatively standard across different types of MTSs: (a) MTS goal hierarchies have a minimum of two levels; (b) goals at higher levels entail greater interdependent actions among more component teams than goals at lower levels, (c) the superordinate goal at the apex of the hierarchy rests on the accomplishment by component teams of all lower order goals; (d) higher order goals are likely to have a longer time horizon than lower order goals; and (e) goals vary in their priority and valence; this clarification of goal ordering and priority is a crucial element of MTS effectiveness. As two or more component teams share responsibility for a goal, the quality of interteam action processes becomes more strongly related to the overall success of the MTS (Marks et al., 2005).

What forms of functional interdependencies characterize the actions of component teams working on a common goal? Mathieu et al. (2001) specified three such forms—input, process, and outcome interdependence. They defined *input interdependence* as the sharing by component teams of human, informational, technological, material, and financial resources. Such interdependence also reflects the common environmental challenges that require an integrated response from multiple component teams. Thus, in Mathieu et al.'s (2001) example of an emergency response MTS, "the firefighters and EMTs share inputs such as rescue equipment and face common challenges at the accident scene. Elsewhere, the surgical and recovery teams share resources in terms of facilities, supplies, space, etc. at the hospital" (p. 295).

Process interdependence pertains to the degree of interteam interaction that is required during the completion of goals specified by the MTS mission (Mathieu et al., 2001). Here, component teams share several functions necessary for effective collective action, including boundary spanning and environmental sense making, task ordering and tactical planning, communicating key information, the timing and coordination of sequential and synchronous actions, and the monitoring and backup of MTS actions (cf. Marks, Mathieu, & Zaccaro, 2001). The integration of component team activities can take the form of sequential interdependence, where one component team (or set of teams) accomplishes a task and hands the next step in proximal goal attainment to another part of the MTS (Mathieu et al., 2001). Thus, in the aforementioned emergency response MTS, the firefighters needed to first ascertain the safety of the damaged vehicle and begin cutting part of it away before the EMTs could attend to the victim.

Reciprocal interdependence occurs when there are cyclical accomplishments of proximal goals by separate component teams (Tesluk et al., 1997). For example, DeChurch and Mathieu (2009) described a firefighting MTS composed of fire suppression, ventilation, and search and rescue units. The fire suppression and search and rescue teams will often act in reciprocal interdependence: The fire suppression unit clears the way for the search and rescue teams to enter the site; and, once on site, the latter teams relay information back to the fire suppression teams to assist in their subsequent operations.

Intensive forms of process interdependence represent another type of integrated activity that can be observed in the emergency response and firefighting MTSs (Mathieu et al., 2001). Such interdependence occurs when the actions of component teams need to be integrated in such a manner that they transpire in simultaneous (or rapidly sequential and reciprocal) collaboration (Tesluk et al., 1997). Thus, in the emergency response MTS, once the vehicle is deemed (or made) safe to enter, the firefighters and EMTs must work closely together to extract the accident victim from the care and stabilize that individual for subsequent travel to the hospital. In the firefighting MTS DeChurch and Mathieu (2009) noted that the actions of the ventilation team needed to be carefully synchronized with those of both the fire suppression and search and rescue teams. The ventilation team controls airflow along which fire and smoke will also flow; therefore, the creation of these airflows needs to occur with knowledge of and coordination with the actions of the other teams so as to not overly impair their activities (DeChurch & Mathieu, 2009).

The third form of functional interdependence that occurs within MTSs refers to *output interdependence*, or the degree to which the outcomes (benefits, costs) for component teams depend upon the goal accomplishments of other teams in the MTS (Mathieu et al., 2001). Although all component teams share the common outcome defined by the superordinate goal at the apex of the MTS goal hierarchy, according to Mathieu et al. (2001) the successful accomplishment of more proximal goals will depend upon the goal outcomes at still lower levels. Obviously, in the emergency response MTS described earlier if the actions of the EMTs and firefighters are not successful in extracting and stabilizing the victim, the surgery team cannot accomplish its goal of patient repair. Thus, although input and process interdependence occur in the accomplishment of particular proximal goals, outcome interdependence resides in the linking of proximal goal accomplishment across the MTS goal hierarchy.

An MTS constitutes subsets of component teams acting interdependently to accomplish at least one proximal goal, with all acting in concert toward a superordinate distal goal. However, the joint and separate actions of component teams can become quite complex in their interdependence. For example, component teams may be responsible for multiple goals within the goal hierarchy, and have to work interdependently with other teams at different times in an MTS performance episode (Mathieu et al., 2001). Thus, one component team may work with another team to meet one proximal goal, but need to work with still another team in accomplishing a second goal, either at the same proximal level or at a higher level in the goal hierarchy. Likewise, goal accomplishment by one team may require intensive interaction with another team at one point in the performance episode, but sequential interdependence with the same team or another team at a different point. Thus, the interactive dynamics among component teams can shift significantly in accomplishing distal goals.

As we have noted, this degree of interdependence in the goal-directed processes of component teams provides one of the key defining features of MTSs, especially when such teams come from different parent organizations. Teams in more traditional organizational forms rarely exhibit the kinds of integration within goal hierarchies that we have described for MTSs. The level of integration within an MTS does not, however, blur the boundaries and unique character of individual teams. Mathieu et al. (2001;

see also DeChurch & Mathieu, 2009) noted that component teams will likely have different functions, proximal goals, and temporal cycles in their own performance episodes. We would add that such teams may differ in terms of their core values, compositional attributes, domains of expertise, leadership structures, behavioral norms, historical cultures, and internal climates. Individual team members are likely to have a greater identification with their component teams than with the MTS as a whole (DeChurch & Mathieu, 2009). Rather than a detriment, we would argue that such diversity actually represents a core strength of the MTS, allowing it to bring a complex variety of skills, knowledge, and functions to the solution of challenges from its correspondingly complex environment.

We would also submit that such diversity, valued in most MTSs, points to another feature that distinguishes this type of collective from more traditional organizational teams, or even from large teams with multiple subunits. Teams and organizations generally operate effectively by establishing significant pressures toward uniformity among their members (Festinger, 1950; Katz & Kahn, 1978) that foster regulated and common beliefs and behaviors. Members who stay within the team or organization develop shared expectations about the goals of the collective, ways of behaving, accepted beliefs and attitudes, and perceptions of outside individuals and teams. In MTSs, such pressures exist only around the points of interdependent actions related to common proximal goals. Otherwise, component member teams of an MTS are often free to exhibit significant degrees of diversity around the core attributes that define them. This quality of MTSs suggests that different kinds of influence dynamics may operate in such systems than in more traditional teams and organizations. The antecedents of intrateam processes within an MTS may be very different from the antecedents of interteam processes. Likewise, the regulatory processes that promote organized and integrated activities around distal goals in the MTS goal hierarchy may in turn be distinct from those processes around proximal goals.

A TYPOLOGY OF MTS CHARACTERISTICS

We have described to this point the features that are generally standard in most MTSs and that distinguish them from other forms of collectives.

However, there are also a number of attributes that define and separate different types of MTSs. In this section of the chapter, we present several of the characteristics and dimensions along which MTSs may differ. We have classified these attributes into three sets, labeled *compositional attributes*, *linkage attributes*, and *developmental attributes*. Table 1.1 indicates the more specific MTS qualities that are grouped into each set.

Compositional Attributes

Compositional attributes include the overall demographic features of the MTS, as well as the relative characteristics of component teams. The most surface attributes of the MTS pertain to the *number* of component teams in the MTS, as well as the total *size* of the MTS in terms of individuals who compose these teams. After Mathieu et al. (2001), we have stated that an MTS can operate with as few as two component teams. We have not put an upper limit of the size of the MTS, but we suspect that too many component teams would make the MTS unwieldy and less able to respond effectively to the environmental challenges for which it was formed. When MTSs are small in terms of number of component teams, goal hierarchies are likely to be flatter and interteam interactions are likely to be more integrated. As the number of teams in the MTS increases, proximal goals are more likely to become unique to subsets of component teams, and overall interdependence across the MTS may begin to exhibit more complex patterns. For example, interteam processes may become less important among some of the component teams that do not share proximal goals. Some teams may exhibit sequential or reciprocal interdependence, whereas others interact intensively. The size of the component teams, which reflects the total number of individuals in the MTS, can have similar effects on the interaction dynamics among component teams. Larger teams may contain subunits, which themselves interact at different levels of interdependence with other component teams (or their subunits). Leadership processes and norm dynamics also may become more complex with increases in both the number of component teams and the numbers of individuals comprising them.

As we noted earlier, MTSs can also be distinguished by the *boundary status* of the component teams. Internal MTSs are composed of teams that are members of the same organization; external MTSs have teams from different organizations (Mathieu et al., 2001). This difference in boundary

TABLE 1.1

Dimensions of Multiteam System (MTS) Characteristics

Compositional Attributes

Number: Number of component teams within the MTS

Size: Total number of individual members across teams

Boundary status: Component teams come from single organization (internal) versus multiple organizations (external or cross-boundary)

Organizational diversity: In a cross-boundary MTS, the number of different organizations represented among the component teams

Proportional membership: In a cross-boundary MTS, the percentage of teams from different organizations

Functional diversity: Degree of heterogeneity in the core purposes and missions of component teams

Geographic dispersion: Co-located or dispersed component teams

Cultural diversity: Degree to which component teams come from different nations or cultures

Motive structure: Degree of commitment of each component team to the MTS; the compatibility of team goals and MTS goals

Temporal orientation: Level of effort and temporal resources expected of each component team

Linkage Attributes

Interdependence: Degree of integrated coordination (e.g., input, process, outcome) among members of different component teams

Hierarchical arrangement: Ordering of teams according to levels of responsibility

Power distribution: The relative influence of teams within the MTS

Communication structure

    Network: The typical patterns of interteam communication

    Modality: The modes of communication (e.g., electronic, face-to-face, or mixed) that occur across component teams

Developmental Attributes

Genesis: The initial formation of an MTS as either appointed or emergent

Direction of development: From emergent to formalized; an evolution from an early formal state

Tenure: The anticipated duration of the MTS

Stage: The stage of MTS development from newly formed to mature

Transformation of system composition

    Membership constancy: Fluidity versus constancy of component teams as members

    Linkage constancy: Fluidity versus constancy of linkages among component teams

---

status can have significant influences on MTS performance requirements and processes. External teams are likely to face greater task and social complexity than internal teams. Task complexity can derive from the levels of information load, information diversity, and information change in the extant environment (Campbell, 1988; Schroder, Driver, & Struefert, 1967). MTSs form in response to turbulent environments (Mathieu et al., 2001), so they are likely to have to operate under high task complexity; however, this complexity will likely be still higher for external MTSs, with attendant consequences for MTS dynamics, where component teams are responding to multiple environments. As suggested by Mathieu et al. (2001), internal MTSs are more likely to be buffered from the full blast of environmental turbulence by their parent organizations.

Social complexity refers to the scope, scale, diversity, and dynamism of stakeholders in the MTS's environment (Bentz, 1987; Zaccaro, 2001). Again, external MTSs composed of teams from different organizations, each with its own constellation of constituents, are likely to have to confront greater social complexity than their internal counterparts. These differences have implications not only for the degree of integration processes that would be required for success, but also for the level of cognitive and social capacities required of leaders and members of the MTS (Zaccaro, 2001).

The boundary status of the MTS can also reflect two finer distinctions among component teams—*organizational diversity* and *proportional membership*. The former refers to the number of different organizations that are represented within the MTS. Higher numbers of organizations can raise the level of social complexity facing MTS members. *Proportional membership* refers to the number of teams in a cross-boundary organization that come from the same parent organization. For example, Marks et al. (2004) described a joint military airborne strike force MTS that was composed of seven component teams—two from Coalition Forces, two from Naval Forces, and three from the Air Force. In this MTS, the Air Force has proportionately higher representation than other organizations. In the emergency response MTS described by Mathieu et al. (2001), two teams were from the county government and two from the hospital, providing an equal proportion. Disparity in proportional representation may have consequences for influence dynamics within the MTS, as well as for the kinds of norms and other regulatory mechanisms established to organize MTS activities (e.g., Lau & Murnighan, 1998, 2005).

The utility of an MTS to address environment challenges resides in part in its ability to bring together teams with different core functional expertise to effectively address a particular problem. Although most MTSs are likely to contain teams having different core functions, they can still range in how much *functional diversity* is represented among the component teams. Functional diversity in teams has been associated with a greater range of cognitive perspectives that can be applied to different team problems (Bantel, 1993; Wiersema & Bantel, 1992). However, diversity can also result in greater conflict and less social cohesion (O'Bannon & Gupta, 1992). Greening and Johnson (1997) found that moderate functional diversity in top management teams helped organizations manage crises better; these effects were reversed, however, as functional diversity reached higher levels. The degree of functional diversity in MTSs may have similar consequences.

MTSs may also be distinguished by *geographic location*, or the degree to which component teams are co-located, partially dispersed (where some teams are co-located, whereas others are geographically dispersed), or fully dispersed. The literature on virtual teams highlights a number of problems that arise when team members are dispersed (Cramton, 2001; Jarvenpaa & Leidner, 1999). These include difficulties in communication, trust building, and member coordination. These kinds of difficulties can become magnified in MTSs where component teams are located in different physical settings, especially when these component teams operate at different temporal schedules. When cross-boundary MTSs include teams that extend over national boundaries, then geographic dispersion may also reflect another MTS dimension, *cultural diversity*, or the degree to which component teams come from different national cultures.

The mix in motive structures among component teams is another compositional factor that can distinguish MTSs. The *motive structure* within an MTS refers to the degree of compatibility between team and MTS goals, with attendant consequences for strength of the team's commitment to the MTS. Some component teams may have shared responsibility for only a single proximal goal in the MTS goal hierarchy, whereas others may have responsibility for multiple proximal goals within an MTS's performance episode. Moreover, the distal goals in the MTS may be indifferent to, or even partially conflict with, the core mission and goals of one or more component teams. For example, MTSs associated with U.S and NATO efforts in Afghanistan may have as distal goals to "extend the authority of the Afghan central government, promote and enhance security, and facilitate humanitarian relief and reconstruction operations" (Dziedzic & Seidl, 2005, pp. 1–2). These MTSs will likely be composed of Army combat forces, Army civil affairs units, Red Cross and other humanitarian units, and mixes of applicable international and nongovernmental organizations. For the sake of parsimony, we can divide teams from these organizations into civilian and military teams. The following is a description from Dziedzic and Seidl of the kinds of conflicts that can characterize an MTS with a mixed and complex motive structure:

> There are fundamental differences in the way the civilian assistance community and military leaders conceive of a secure environment. The military emphasizes national security, public order, and force protection—all of which are enhanced by assertively addressing and reducing sources of threat. Civilian assistance providers, on the other hand, equate security with ensuring that belligerents do not perceive them as a threat. (P. 2)

Dziedzic and Seidl (2005) described how even the goal of providing "humanitarian assistance" to locals may be perceived differently by teams from each type of organization in the MTS. They noted,

> Humanitarian organizations seek to alleviate suffering without regard for the aid recipient's affiliation with any of the parties to a conflict. When military units in a combat provide "humanitarian-type" relief, it is typically associated with political objectives. For military forces confronting an insurgency, it may be a matter of military necessity to ensure that assistance is provided to displaced civilians and that civic action projects are undertaken to cultivate popular support and increase force protection. When the focus shifts from humanitarian assistance to reconstruction, the salient concerns that arise are the blurring of civil and military roles and interference with each other's efforts. (P. 2)

Thus, an MTS composed of military and civilian units in such settings can reflect mixed-motive structures that result in more complex interteam processes than MTSs where the core missions of component teams are more compatible with each other and with the distal goal of the MTS. As incompatibility in team motive structures increases, members of teams, although committed to a proximal goal, may be less committed to the overall goal hierarchy of the MTS. Thus, if the distal goal in a joint military–civilian MTS is security and force protection, component teams from humanitarian organizations may have less commitment to such goals. Indeed, Dziedzic and Seidl (2005) noted that in such MTSs in Afghanistan "civilian assistance providers insist that they cannot allow their efforts to be perceived as part of a campaign plan of a belligerent force" (p. 2). Alternatively, if the distal goal in such MTSs becomes providing reconstructive aid, then any combat component units could lessen their commitment to all but their particular proximal goals.

The motive structure may be associated with the last compositional attribute in Table 1.1, *temporal orientation*. This refers to the level of effort and time expected to be devoted by component teams to the goals of the MTS. In some MTSs, all teams are expected to provide comparable personnel and temporal resources to goal accomplishment. In others, some teams are expected to provide disproportionally more, or less, of such resources.

Compositional attributes will arguably be a significant driving force on the interteam dynamics within MTSs. They may also influence the attachments of team members to the overall MTS, and of teams to each other. Recent work in the team composition literature has emphasized how certain demographic patterns can produce faultlines in teams that can in turn foster subgroups and coalitions within them (Lau & Murnighan, 1998, 2005). Similar processes can occur in an MTS. For example, a faultline can form when (a) there exists some diversity in MTS compositional attributes (e.g., national origin, parent organization, motive structure, geographic colocation, or core function), or (b) component teams possessing one or more compositional attributes align more strongly with teams having similar attributes than with teams with different characteristics. As with teams, strong aligning faultlines in MTSs can foster perceptions of ingroup–outgroup status, less interteam communication, greater interteam conflict, and less overall cohesion (Hogg & Terry, 2000; Lau & Murnighan, 2005; Thatcher, Jehn, & Zanutto, 2003). Thus, compositional attributes have important consequences for MTS effectiveness—we believe this represents a particularly important avenue for future MTS research.

Linkage Attributes

The different kinds of linking mechanisms that connect component teams serve as other ways of distinguishing MTSs. We have already noted that MTSs can vary in terms of the degree of *interdependence* required of its component teams to meet collective goals. All MTSs exhibit some level of interdependence in the interactions among their teams. We regard this as a necessary condition that makes MTSs different from more traditional organization forms. However, in some MTSs, some or all of their teams may coact in patterns of sequential or reciprocal interdependence, whereas in others the component teams are required to engage intensively with one another. These differences in the levels of required interdependence will have significant consequences for the amount of interteam processes necessary for MTS effectiveness (Marks et al., 2005).

Two other related linkage attributes include the hierarchical arrangement of component teams and the power distribution among them. *Hierarchical arrangement* refers to the ordering of teams within the MTS according to their levels of responsibility for goal attainment. Some teams could be responsible for only a single proximal goal, whereas others could be required to manage and accomplish multiple proximal goals. The latter teams may also need to address goals at different levels of the MTS goal hierarchy. This requirement gives them more responsibility for coordinating goal accomplishment at these multiple levels.

Power distribution refers to the relative influence that component teams have within the MTS. Some teams by virtue of their higher placement in a hierarchical arrangement would likely have more power than those at lower levels with fewer goal responsibilities. Teams may also gain disproportionate power within an MTS because of their larger size, their functional centrality to the core mission of the MTS, and/or their appointment by parent organizations as having authority and prime responsibility for MTS decisions. Both hierarchical arrangement and power distribution will likely influence the patterns of communications and interactions among the component teams.

MTSs may also be distinguished by their normative communication structures, specifically their dominant communication networks and communication modalities. In team research, *communication networks* refer to the structured patterns of interaction flow in a collective (Leavitt, 1951; Shaw, 1964, 1978). Such patterns can be fully decentralized, where all members communicate with all other members; fully centralized, where all members communicate to and through a single member; and various combinations of patterns between these extremes (Shaw, 1964). Communication networks have significant consequences for task efficiency—centralized networks yield greater efficiency on simple tasks, whereas decentralized ones are better for more complex tasks where information saturation may be higher (Shaw, 1964). Also, when members are in more central positions in a network, they report greater satisfaction and commitment than members in more peripheral positions (Eisenberg, Monge, & Miller, 1983; Lovaglia & Houser, 1996). Similar kinds of effects may accrue in MTSs with different communication structures. Also, MTSs may vary in terms of *communication modality*, or the degree to which communication occurs primarily face-to-face, electronically, or a mix of the two. This attribute would be specifically tied to the degree of geographic diversity in the MTS, with dispersed component teams more likely to communicate electronically (Griffith & Neale, 2001; Kirkman & Mathieu, 2005). Research on dispersed teams indicates that teamwork in such teams may often be less efficient and effective than in their co-located counterparts (Cramton, 2001). We would expect similar kinds of issues in MTSs where component teams need to communicate electronically.

Developmental Attributes

The final category of attributes that can be used to distinguish different types of MTSs includes those characteristics pertaining to their developmental dynamics and patterns. For example, MTSs can differ in terms of their *genesis*, or their mode of initiation. Some MTSs may be appointed or created by leaders or superordinate executive committees from parent organizations. These leaders would establish the mission parameters and the distal goals of the MTS. Other MTSs may emerge from the collective initiative of several teams that would eventually comprise the MTS. In these types of MTSs, the proximal and distal goals would likely emerge from negotiations and interactions among the component teams. Thus the MTS's mode of initiation can have a determinative influence on how its missions, goal hierarchy, and perhaps other structural elements emerge as well.

Although an MTS may begin as an appointed or emergent entity, it may change as component teams pass through subsequent performance episodes. Thus, the *direction of development* in an MTS may begin as it emerges informally or on an ad hoc basis in response to a crisis or national incident; however, it may then become more formalized as a relatively permanent guard against similar future events. Indeed, some MTSs composed of national security agencies and civilian relief organizations that emerged in the immediate aftermath of the terrorist attacks on September 11, 2001, become formalized by subsequent government actions. Other MTSs may have a different developmental path, where they are formally planned in outline to anticipate possible emergencies or crises, but actually evolve in membership and linkages when these events do occur.

MTSs may also differ in terms of their expected duration, or *tenure*, and their *stage* of development. Models of group development describe the stages or processes that such collectives go through in becoming mature and effective systems (and, in some cases, dissolving when their mission expires) (Chang, Duck, & Bordio, 2006; Gersick, 1988; Tuckman, 1965). These stages reflect processes of moving from relative member independence to effective interdependence through the resolution of disagreements or incompatible member agendas, and the development of normative or social regulatory systems (Tuckman, 1965; Tuckman & Jensen, 1977). MTSs as collectives will likely go through similar processes as they become mature systems. A particular MTS developmental stage also may determine the efficiency of its interteam processes (cf. Kozlowski, Gully, McHugh, Salas, & Cannon-Bowers, 1996).

As MTSs develop and move through performance episodes, they may also experience changes in composition and linkages among component teams. The remaining two attributes in this set pertain to such *transformation of system composition. Membership constancy* refers to the fluidity versus constancy of component team membership in the MTS. MTSs can typically be relatively stable in terms of their membership. However, in highly turbulent environments, when strategic challenges are constantly changing, then MTSs operating in such contexts may well change their component team membership on a fairly regular basis (cf. Mathieu, Maynard, Rapp, & Gilson, 2008, p. 463, on such transitions within teams). In such instances, new teams would be required to become quickly integrated into existing MTS norms, structures, and procedures. Models of team member socialization suggest that this entry process would entail reciprocal evaluation and commitment processes, where new members and the existing team evaluate each other for potential gains versus costs of membership, and, as gains outweigh cost, commit to each other (Moreland & Levine, 1982). Moreland and Levine (1982) suggested that this evaluation and commitment process is a dynamic one that can change at various stages of new member socialization, integration, and perhaps removal from the team. We expect that a comparable process, albeit a more complex one, may occur when new component teams are recruited and socialized into an existing MTS.

Even if MTS membership is constant, the nature of the ties and interdependencies among component teams may shift as MTSs develop across performance episodes. Thus, MTSs can differ according to their *linkage constancy*. Some MTS maintain fairly steady hierarchal arrangements, power and communication structures, and patterns of interdependence. However, in more turbulent and dynamic environments, MTSs may be required to display considerable adaptability in the coordinating structures among component teams. Recent research on team adaptation has emphasized how teams adjust their role structures and task-related relationships among members as operating environments change (LePine, 2003; Stagl, Burke, Salas, & Pierce, 2006). LePine (2003) emphasized that such role structure adaptation is particularly important for teams that are required to make decisions in different situations over extended periods of time. He noted that "production teams involved in long linked and continuous flow processes, surgical teams, flight crews, and command and control teams do not have the time to stop and plan a rational response to an unexpected change that makes their established role structure inappropriate … these teams must be capable of adapting on the fly to be effective" (p. 28). We have described briefly in this chapter (see also Chapters 2 and 3) several examples of MTSs that contain just these kinds of teams. LePine's admonishment about teams in such settings applies as well to MTSs. We have noted the arguments of others that MTSs are an adaptive response by organizations to a complex and turbulent environment (DeChurch & Mathieu, 2009; Mathieu et al., 2001). Accordingly, we expect that role structure adaptation, or adjustments in other kinds of linking arrangements, will be a particularly important developmental attribute in effective MTSs.

We have described three sets of attributes that we believe distinguish different types of MTSs. Such a classification is important as a driver of future research on MTS processes and effectiveness. In our discussion, we have noted only briefly how MTS attributes might influence MTS processes. We believe a simple model of MTS effectiveness might look like the one in Figure 1.1, where compositional, linkage, and developmental attributes serve as antecedents of different intrateam and interteam processes. The effects of these attributes on overall effectiveness would be mediated by these processes. We expect that future

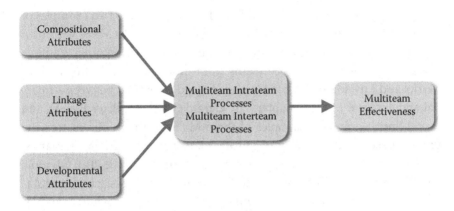

FIGURE 1.1
A model of multiteam system effectiveness.

MTS research will lead to specifications of more complex versions of this model.

One purpose of this book is to foster a deeper exploration of these attributes and their influences on MTS processes and outcomes. Accordingly, three of its sections correspond to these three sets of attributes. We turn now to a broader overview of this book and its contents.

AN OVERVIEW OF THIS BOOK

We noted earlier that in June 2008, a conference sponsored by the U.S. Army Research Institute (ARI) brought together several scholars to explore in more detail the concept of MTSs. Early research on MTSs and the discussions at that ARI conference have highlighted the necessity for an expanded and deeper focus on the nature of MTSs. We can identify five needs that are, in turn, reflected in the approach and contents of this book. First, at the ARI conference, scholars interested in MTSs argued for more detail and elaboration on the features that distinguish MTSs from other conventional and unconventional organizational forms. This suggests a need to define more firmly what the boundaries of MTSs are, and what kinds of systems are excluded by these boundaries. Thus, the present chapter provides definitional material on the nature of MTSs. The next two chapters provide examples of such systems from multiple domains.

In Chapter 2, Michelle Marks and Dave Luvison describe two examples of MTSs from the business world. The first example refers to MTSs within an organization responsible for launching new products; the other example is a strategic alliance between teams from different organizations. Thus, Marks and Luvison offer descriptions of—and a contrast between—internal and external MTSs. Chapter 3 by Gerald Goodwin, Peter Essens, and David Smith provides examples of three MTSs in the public sector. The first of these is a description of railway management in the Netherlands, the second of public safety arrangements in Canada for the 2010 Olympic and Paralympic Games, and the third of security force assistance and stabilization operations in the U.S. military. This chapter provides examples of MTSs within different nations, as well as a multinational or multicultural MTS.

The second need driving this book reflects the fact that MTSs raise the focus from individuals to component teams as the unit of analysis; accordingly, research questions abound in terms of the compositional properties of unit teams and the MTS as a whole. For example, we have noted that the overlapping and complex goal structures of the component teams reflect a range of competing motivational processes—component teams have commitments to stakeholders and constituents that can both support and contrast with the commitments made to the MTS. Likewise, component teams in an MTS have multiple attachments, including to their home organization, which can create complex social identities. We have also noted that when particular component teams have greater commonality (in terms of function, values, and cultures) with each other than with other component teams, deleterious faultlines can develop in the MTS.

These complex and interesting issues form the basis for several chapters in Section II of this book. Chapter 4 by Ruth Kanfer and Matthew Kerry examines motivation processes that may operate in MTSs. They define *motivation* as reflecting goal-directed processes, including goal choice, goal accomplishment, and particularly the allocation of resources across multiple goals. In MTSs, individuals and teams are faced with choices to allocate resources to self, team, and MTS goals. Kanfer and Kerry provide elucidation of some of the issues and concerns related to such choices.

The nature of MTSs often means that members can belong simultaneously to multiple collectives—their parent organizations, their teams, the MTSs, and, in rare cases, multiple teams within the MTS. The remaining three chapters in Section II of this book are concerned with different aspects of this multiple-membership quality of MTSs. Chapter 5 by Stacey Connaughton, Elizabeth Williams, and Marissa Shuffler examines social identity issues that can arise from several compositional attributes of MTSs, including boundary status, and the multiple forms of diversity that can exist in such entities. *Social identity* refers to the derivation of an individual's self-image in part from his or her social memberships (Tajfel & Turner, 1986). The presence of diversity within the MTS can hinder the emergence of an MTS-level social identity. Thus, an interesting question concerns how a collective social identity necessary for effective MTS functioning emerges from—or is thwarted by—members' multiple memberships; also of interest is how a collective identity contributes to MTS-level processes and conflict resolution, especially in MTSs with high levels of diversity. The chapter by Connaughton et al. provides some insight into these and related questions. Chapter 6 by Michael O'Leary, Anita Woodley, and Mark Mortensen describes in more detail the potentially complex nature of multiple team memberships (MTMs) within MTSs, including how MTMs can influence learning and productivity. The final chapter in Section II, by Joann Keyton, Debra Ford, and Faye Smith, introduces a variant of MTSs called the *representative MTS*. In such forms, "individuals from different organizations form teams to problem solve for a third-party organization" (Keyton et al., Chapter 7, this volume p. 174). This chapter also associates communication, collaboration, and identification linkage processes to multiple compositional attributes of representative MTSs.

The third need driving this book pertains to the interrelationships and linkages among the component teams. The effectiveness of MTSs will derive mostly from the ability of component teams to integrate their actions successfully in response to the kinds of environmental events that instigated their formation. Although much work has been completed on the attributes that promote effective interdependence and coordination within teams (see review by Mathieu et al., 2008), the findings of such research do not translate easily and isomorphically to the MTS level. Thus, a series of chapters in Section III of the book will focus on the linking mechanisms, such as communication dynamics, leadership, and between-team action processes, that promote effective MTS performance. Chapter 8 by Marshall Poole and Noshir Contractor considers MTSs as an ecosystem of networked individuals and groups, in which links depend upon the nature of the work and goals addressed by the network. Joan Rentsch and Melissa Staniewicz outline in Chapter 9 the various kinds of cognitive similarity configurations that promote effective coordination in MTSs. Chapter 10 by Stephen Zaccaro and Leslie DeChurch explores the leadership functions within and between teams in an MTS that can enable its effectiveness. They also describe the different forms that leadership can take within MTSs.

The first three chapters in Section III offer greater understanding of the processes that foster collaboration among teams in an MTS. However, the presence of multiple forms of diversity in most MTSs suggests a greater likelihood of conflict among units. Chapter 11 by Verlin Hinsz and Kevin Betts explores the nature of such conflicts, and offers remedial strategies. Finally, the various forms of linkages within the MTS, and the differences in the nature of these linkages among alternate types of MTSs (e.g., external versus internal MTSs), suggest multiple forms of boundary-spanning processes that may operate in such organizational forms. The final chapter of this section, by Robert Davison and John Hollenbeck, provides a framework for conceptualizing different types of boundaries and boundary-spanning activities within MTSs.

Chapters on how MTSs emerge and develop in response to environmental contingencies form the fourth section of this book. Component teams need to derive coordination patterns, as well as the capacity to maximize their adaptability as events change. Chapter 13 by Sjir Uitdewilligen and Mary Waller examines how MTSs form, respond to dynamic environmental contingencies, and then disband; their description of these processes is provided within the backdrop of the Port of Rotterdam in the Netherlands. Their chapter, as well as others in this volume, emphasizes the complexity that confronts MTSs, and the concordance between such complexity and their emergent structures. Chapter 14 by Rhetta Standifer, explores the temporal synchrony of component team actions, and how teams develop their coordinating structures in a manner that maximizes their degree of responsive adaptability as organizational forms.

The final section of the book focuses on the need to examine and discuss the kinds of tools and strategies needed to study MTSs. Many researchers have commented on the unique challenges in research on organizations and groups, as well as the strategies needed to conduct such research. These challenges may increase exponentially when studying MTSs. Chapter 15 by Juliet Aiken and Paul Hanges highlights the challenges in conducting research on MTSs, and suggests some methodologies from the domain of complexity science. The chapter by Corinne Coen and Andrew Schnackenberg describes the nature of MTSs as complex systems, including the use of computational simulations to study them. Chapter 17 by Christian Resick, Shawn Burke, and Daniel Doty examines the challenges of conducting experimental or lab-based research on MTSs. The final chapter in the book, by John Mathieu, integrates this material with the rest of the book's content and summarizes key topics and questions for future research in this area.

Our hope is that the chapters in this book accelerate the burgeoning interest and research in MTSs as new organizational forms. As operating environments for today's organizations become increasingly more complex, and as multi-organizational collaborations become more necessary to meet such complexity, we expect that MTSs will grow in number, becoming a more standard organizational form. If researchers simply try isomorphic application of existing models of team or organizational processes to understand MTS processes, we believe such efforts would be insufficient and perhaps misleading. We hope that the contributions by the various scholars in this book will provide new pathways to understanding the MTS as an evolving organizational form.

REFERENCES

Bantel, K. A. (1993). Strategic clarity in banking: Role of top management team demography. *Psychological Reports, 73,* 1187–1201.

Bentz, V. J. (1987). *Explorations of scope and scale: The critical determinant of high-level effectiveness* (Technical Report No. 31). Greensboro, NC: Center for Creative Leadership.

Burke, C. S., DeChurch, L. A., Salas, E., & Goodwin, G. F. (2008, April). Modes of coordination in multiteam systems. In G. Grote & R. A. Roe (Chairs), *Team Coordination in High-Risk Environments.* Symposium conducted at the meeting of the Society for Industrial and Organizational Psychology, San Francisco, CA.

Caldwell, B. S. (2005). Multi-team dynamics and distributed expertise in mission operations. *Aviation, Space, and Environmental Medicine, 76*(6), Sec. II, B145–B153.

Campbell, D. J. (1988). Task complexity: A review and analysis. *Academy of Management Review, 13,* 40–52.

Chang, A., Duck, J., & Bordio, P. (2006). Understanding the multidimensionality of group development. *Small Group Research, 37,* 327–350.

Coen, C. A. (2006). Seeking the comparative advantage: The dynamics of individual cooperation in single vs. multiple team environments. *Organizational Behavior and Human Decision Processes, 100,* 145–159.

Cramton, C. D. (2001). The mutual knowledge problem and its consequences for dispersed collaboration. *Organization Science, 12*, 346–371.

Davis, S. M., & Lawrence, P. R. (1977). *Matrix.* Reading, MA: Addison-Wesley.

Dean, C., MacMillan, J., Bennett, W., Jr., Merket, D., Salas, E., Zaccaro, S. J., et al. (2008, September). *Challenges in teams-of-teams training and assessment.* Panel presentation at the 52nd annual meeting of the Human Factors and Ergonomics Society, New York.

DeChurch, L. A. (2006, August). Defining the challenge of leadership in multiteam systems. In L. A. DeChurch & C. J. Resick (Chairs), New Directions in Team Leadership Research. Symposium conducted at the meeting of the Academy of Management, Atlanta, GA.

DeChurch, L. A. (Chair) (2010, April). Multiteam imperatives for leadership and organizations. Symposium presented at the 25th annual conference of the Society for Industrial and Organizational Psychology, Atlanta, GA.

DeChurch, L. A., & Burke, C. S. (Co-Chairs) (2009, April). Multiteam systems: Exploring an emerging organizational form. Symposium presented at the meeting of the Society for Industrial and Organizational Psychology, New Orleans, LA.

DeChurch, L. A., Burke, C. S., & Salas, E. (2009, July). A multiteam perspective: Coordination within and across teams. In R. Rico (Chair), New Trends in Team Coordination. Symposium conducted at the meeting of the Interdisciplinary Network for Group Research, Colorado Springs, CO.

DeChurch, L. A., & Marks, M. A. (2006). Leadership in multi-team systems. *Journal of Applied Psychology, 91*, 311–329.

DeChurch, L. A., & Marks, M. A. (2008, April). Leader mental models and multiteam system effectiveness. In L. A. DeChurch & M. A. Marks (Chairs), Leading the Team, and Above. Symposium conducted at the meeting of the Society for Industrial and Organizational Psychology, San Francisco, CA.

DeChurch, L. A., & Mathieu, J. E. (2009). Thinking in terms of multiteam systems. In E. Salas, G. F. Goodwin, & C. S. Burke (Eds.), *Team effectiveness in complex organizations: Cross-disciplinary perspectives and approaches* (pp. 267–292). New York: Taylor & Francis.

DeChurch, L. A., & Resick, C. J. (2006, July). *Task interdependence in multiteam systems: Examining differences in critical leader functions.* Paper presented at the meeting of the Interdisciplinary Network for Group Research, Pittsburg, PA.

DeChurch, L. A., Resick, C. J., Doty, D. A., Murase, T., Jiménez, M., Mathieu, J. E., et al. (2010, April). Examining leadership in complex network environments. In L. A. DeChurch (Chair), Multiteam Imperatives for Leadership and Organization. Symposium conducted at the meeting of the Society for Industrial and Organizational Psychology, Atlanta, GA.

Dziedzic, M. J., & Seidl, Col. M. K. (2005). Provincial reconstruction teams and military relations with international and nongovernmental organizations in Afghanistan (Special Report No. 147). Washington, DC: U.S. Institute for Peace. Retrieved from http://www.usip.org/resources/provincial-reconstruction-teams-military-relations-international-and-nongovernmental-organ

Eisenberg, E. M., Monge, P. R., & Miller, K. I. (1983). Involvement in communication networks as a predictor of organizational commitment. *Human Communication Research, 10*(2), 179–201.

Festinger, L. (1950). Informal social communication. *Psychological Review, 57*, 271–282.

Gersick, C. J. G. (1988). Time and transition in work teams: Toward a new model of group development. *Academy of Management Journal, 31*(1), 9–41.

Greening, D. W., & Johnson, R. A. (1997). Managing industrial and environmental crises: The role of heterogeneous top management teams. *Business and Society, 36,* 334–361.

Griffith, T. L., & Neal, M. A. (2001). Information processing in traditional, hybrid, and virtual teams: From nascent knowledge to transactive memory. In B. Staw & R. Sutton (Eds.), *Research in organizational behavior* (Vol. 23, pp. 379–421). Stamford, CT: JAI.

Hackman, J. R. (1990). *Groups that work and those that don't.* San Francisco: Jossey-Bass.

Hambrick, D. C. (1994). Top management groups: A conceptual integration and reconsideration of the team label. In B. M. Staw & L. L. Cummings (Eds.), *Research in organizational behavior* (Vol. 16, pp. 171–214). Greenwich, CT: JAI.

Hesketh, B., & Neal, A. (1999). Technology and performance. In D. R. Ilgen & E. D. Pulakos (Eds.), *The changing nature of performance: Implications for staffing, motivation, and development* (pp. 21–55). San Francisco: Jossey-Bass.

Hoegl, M., & Weinkauf, K. (2005). Managing task interdependencies in multiteam projects: A longitudinal study. *Journal of Management Studies, 42*(6), 1287–1308.

Hogg, M. A., & Terry, D. J. (2000). Social identity and self-categorization processes in organizational contexts. *Academy of Management Review, 25*(1), 121–140.

Hsu, H. C., & Liu, A. (2005). Multiagent-based multi-team formation control for mobile robots. *Journal of Intelligent and Robotic Systems, 42,* 337–360

Ilgen, D., & Pulakos, E. (1999). Employee performance in today's organizations. In D. R. Ilgen & E. D. Pulakos (Eds.), *The changing nature of work performance: Implications for staffing, motivation, and development* (pp. 1–20). San Francisco: Jossey-Bass.

Ireland, R. D., & Hitt, M. A. (1999). Achieving and maintaining strategic competitiveness in the 21st century: The role of strategic leadership. *Academy of Management Executive, 13*(1), 43–57.

Jarvenpaa, S. L., Knoll, K., & Leidner, D. E. (1998). Is anybody out there? Antecedents of trust in global virtual teams. *Journal of Management Information Systems, 14*(4), 29–64.

Jarvenpaa, S. L., & Leidner, D. E. (1999). Communication and trust in global virtual teams. *Organization Science, 10*(6), 791–815.

Johnson, J. P., Korsgaard, M. A., & Sapienza, H. J. (2002). Perceived fairness, decision control, and commitment in international joint venture management teams. *Strategic Management Journal, 23,* 1141–1160.

Katz, D., & Kahn, R. L. (1978). *The social psychology of organizations* (2nd ed.). New York: Wiley.

Kirkman, B. L., & Mathieu, J. E. (2005). The dimensions and antecedents of team virtuality. *Journal of Management, 31,* 700–718.

Knight, K. (1976). Matrix organization: A review. *Journal of Management Studies, 13,* 111–130.

Kozlowski, S. W. J., Gully, S. M., McHugh, P. P., Salas, E., & Cannon-Bowers, J. A. (1996). A dynamic theory of leadership and team effectiveness: Developmental and task contingent leader roles. *Research in Personnel and Human Resources Management, 14,* 253–305.

Lau, D. C., & Murnighan, J. K. (1998). Demographic diversity and faultlines: The compositional dynamics of organizational groups. *Academy of Management Review, 23,* 325–340.

Lau, D. C., & Murnighan, J. K. (2005). Interactions within groups and subgroups: The effects of demographic faultlines. *Academy of Management Journal, 48*(4), 645–659.

Leavitt, H. J. (1951). Some effects of certain communication patterns on group performance. *Journal of Abnormal and Social Psychology, 46,* 38–50.

LePine, J. A. (2003). Team adaptation and postchange performance: Effects of team composition in terms of members' cognitive ability and personality. *Journal of Applied Psychology, 88,* 27–39.

Liu, Y., & Simaan, M. A. (2004a). Noninferior Nash strategies for multi-team systems. *Journal of Optimization Theory and Applications, 120*(1), 29–51.

Liu, Y., & Simaan, M. A. (2004b). Noninferior Nash strategies for routing control in parallel-link communication networks. *International Journal of Communication Systems, 18,* 347–361.

Liu, Y., Simaan, M. A., & Cruz, J. B., Jr. (2003). An application of dynamic Nash task assignment strategies to multi-team military air operations. *Automatica, 39,* 1469–1478.

Lovaglia, M. J., & Houser, J. A. (1996). Emotional reactions and status in groups. *American Sociological Review, 61*(5), 867–883.

Lyons, R., Jiménez, M., Burke, C. S., DeChurch, L., Salas, E., & Goodwin, J. (2008, July). Understanding the coordinative mechanisms in multiteam systems: A historiometric analysis. Poster presented at the meeting of the Interdisciplinary Network for Group Research, Kansas City, MO.

Marks, M. A., DeChurch, L. A., Mathieu, J. E., Panzer, F. J., & Alonso, A. A. (2005). Teamwork in multi-team systems. *Journal of Applied Psychology, 90*(5), 964–971.

Marks, M. A., & Luvison, D. (2008, April). Understanding leadership in multiteam alliances. Paper presented at the 23rd annual meeting of the Society for Industrial and Organizational Psychology, San Francisco, CA.

Marks, M. A., Mathieu, J. E., Hollenbeck, J. R., DeChurch, L. A., Zaccaro, S. J., & Goodwin, G. F. (2010, April). A discussion of current research on multiteam systems. Panel discussion presented at the 25th annual meeting of the Society for Industrial and Organizational Psychology, Atlanta, GA.

Marks, M. A., Mathieu, J. E., & Zaccaro, S. J. (2001). A temporally based framework and taxonomy of team processes. *Academy of Management Review, 26*(3), 356–376.

Marks, M. A., Mathieu, J. E., & Zaccaro, S. J. (2004). Using scaled worlds to study multi-team systems. In S. G. Shiflett, L. R. Elliot, E. Salas., & M. D. Coovert (Eds.), *Scaled worlds: Development, validation, and applications* (pp. 279–296). Burlington, VT: Ashgate.

Mathieu, J. E., Cobb, M. A., Marks, M. A., Zaccaro, S. J., & Marsh, S. (2004). Multiteam ACES: A research platform for studying multiteam systems. In S. G. Schiflett, L. R. Elliott, E. Salas, & M. Coovert (Eds.), *Scaled worlds: Development, validation and applications* (pp. 297–315). Burlington, VT: Ashgate.

Mathieu, J. E., Marks, M. A., & Zaccaro, S. J. (2001). Multiteam systems. In N. Anderson, D. Ones, H. K. Sinangil, & C. Viswesvaran (Eds.), *International handbook of work and organizational psychology* (pp. 289–313). London: Sage.

Mathieu, J. E., Maynard, M. T., Rapp, T., & Gilson, L. (2008). Team effectiveness 1997–2007: A review of recent advancements and a glimpse into the future. *Journal of Management, 34,* 410–476.

Mittleman, D., & Briggs, R. O. (1999). Communication technologies for traditional and virtual teams. In J. R. Katzenbach (Ed.), *The work of teams* (pp. 246–270). Boston: Harvard Business Press.

Mohrman, S. A., Cohen, S. G., & Mohrman, A. M., Jr. (1995). *Designing team-based organizations: New forms for knowledge work.* San Francisco: Jossey-Bass.

Mohrman, S. A., & Quam, K. (2000). Consulting to team-based organizations: An organizational design and learning approach. *Consulting Psychology Journal: Practice and Research, 52,* 20–35.

Moreland, R. L., & Levine, J. M. (1982). Socialization in small groups: Temporal changes in individual-group relations. In L. Berkowitz (Ed.), *Advances in experimental social psychology* (Vol. 15). New York: Academic Press.

Moynihan, D. P. (2007). *From forest fires to Hurricane Katrina: Case studies of incident command systems.* Washington, DC: IBM Center for the Business of Government. Retrieved from www.businessofgovernment.org/report/forest-fires-hurricane-katrina-case-studies-incident-command-systems

O'Bannon, D. P., & Gupta, A. K. (1992, August). The utility of homogeneity versus heterogeneity within top management teams: Alternate resolutions of the emerging conundrum. Paper presented at the annual meeting of the Academy of Management, Las Vegas, NV.

Schroder, H. M., Driver, M. J., & Streufert, S. (1967). *Human information processing.* New York: Holt, Rinehart & Winston.

Scott, W. R. (1998). *Organizations: Rational, natural, and open systems.* Saddle River, NJ: Prentice Hall.

Shaw, M. E. (1964). Communication networks. *Advances in Experimental Social Psychology, 1,* 111–147.

Shaw, M. E. (1978). Communication networks fourteen years later. In L. Berkowitz (Ed.), *Group processes.* New York: Academic Press.

Simon, H. A. (1962). The architecture of complexity. *Proceedings of the American Philosophical Society, 106,* 467–482.

Stagl, K. C., Burke, C. S., Salas, E., & Pierce, L. (2006). Understanding adaptability: A prerequisite for effective performance within complex environments. In C. S. Burke, L. G. Pierce, & E. Salas (Eds.), *Understanding adaptability: A prerequisite for effective performance within complex environments.* Amsterdam: Elsevier.

Standifer, R. L., & Bluedorn, A. C. (2006). Alliance management teams and entrainment: Sharing temporal mental models. *Human Relations, 59,* 903–927.

Sundstrom, E., McIntyre, M., Halfhill, T., & Richards, H. (2000). Work groups: From Hawthorne studies to work teams of the 1990s and beyond. *Group Dynamics: Theory, Research, and Practice, 4*(1), 44–67.

Tajfel, H., & Turner, J. C. (1986). The social identity theory of inter-group behavior. In S. Worchel & L. W. Austin (Eds.), *Psychology of intergroup relations* (pp. 7–24). Chicago: Nelson-Hall.

Tesluk, P., Mathieu, J. E., Zaccaro, S. J., & Marks, M. A. (1997). Task and aggregation issues in analysis and assessment of team performance. In M. T. Brannick, E. Salas, & C. Prince (Eds.), *Team performance assessment and measurement: Theory, methods, and applications.* Mahwah, NJ: Lawrence Erlbaum.

Thatcher, S. M. B., Jehn, K. A., & Zanutto, E. (2003). Cracks in diversity research: The effects of diversity faultlines on conflict and performance. *Group Decision and Negotiation, 12,* 217–241.

Thompson, J. D. (1967). *Organizations in action.* New York: McGraw-Hill.

Tuckman, B. W. (1965). Developmental sequences in small groups. *Psychological Bulletin, 63,* 384–399.

Tuckman, B. W., & Jensen, M. A. C. (1977). Stages of small group development revisited. *Group and Organization Studies, 2,* 419–427.

Wiersema, M. F., & Bantel, K. A. (1992). Top management team demography and corporate strategic change. *Academy of Management Journal, 35,* 91–121.

Wooten, S., Doty, D., Murase, T., Burke, C. S., DeChurch, L. A., & Pierce, L. (2009, April). A taxonomy of platforms for MTS research: A critical review. In W. Bedwell & F. J. Panzer (Chairs), Research on Teams and Multiteam Systems: Selecting Game-Based Research Platforms. Symposium conducted at the meeting of the Society for Industrial and Organizational Psychology, New Orleans, LA.

Zaccaro, S. J. (2001). *The nature of executive leadership: A conceptual and empirical analysis of success.* Washington, DC: APA Books.

2

Product Launch and Strategic Alliance MTSs

Michelle A. Marks
George Mason University

Dave Luvison
Nova Southeastern University

This chapter details two examples of MTSs in business environments. Though both are organizational MTSs, they differ in purpose, configuration, and operation of MTSs, as well as in the fact that one example is intraorganizational whereas the other example is interorganizational. These business examples illuminate the high prevalence of MTSs in today's workplaces. We describe the purpose and the structural characteristics of the MTSs, illustrate how the MTSs operate and change over time, and then categorize them based on the typology dimensions presented in Chapter 1.

PRODUCT LAUNCH MTS

MTSs are fundamental structures in our workplaces today. The product launch activities for a large, high-technology company offer a good example of the way in which complex MTSs can operate within a single firm. This process involves all of the activities required to take a product from the development stage through the initial introduction and growth stages of its sales cycle. Such an endeavor, especially for a firm that offers a product incorporating a combination of hardware and software components such as a network communications vendor, involves numerous coordination points across multiple teams. When a firm brings a new product to the market, it has a number of high-level objectives, including increasing revenues, capturing market share, redefining an existing product category, or establishing market and technological leadership. A successful launch will not only establish that product's presence in the market but also increase the overall value of the firm. Consequently, these distal goals offer a number of reasons why the various teams associated with the launch will benefit from effective coordination of their activities.

Nevertheless, each of the teams can have proximal goals that are more salient than the larger distal goal of the firm, and these differences can create mixed-motive conflict among the teams. For example, the hardware and software development teams may be most interested in creating a product that incorporates the latest complex technology, but the inclusion of these features can interject difficulties that can delay the product's release, thereby conflicting with marketing teams' objectives of releasing a viable product ahead of the firm's competitors. Manufacturing teams are typically preoccupied with simplifying the production process and reducing the firm's costs of goods, but the additional features in the advanced product may complicate the manufacturing process and increase costs. Sales teams are likely to seek advantages over their competitors, so the incorporation of advanced features can provide them with a leg up. On the other hand, these complex features can also drive up the cost of the product, forcing them to sell it at a higher price point and possibly lengthening their sales cycle. The use of a cutting-edge hardware technology may create increased demands on the software teams to write more sophisticated code to take advantage of that technology's features. Similarly, that new technology may require the use of new diagnosis and service techniques that can create additional pressures on the teams supporting the product installed in the field. Consequently, the decision to incorporate advanced technology may be beneficial to the firm in the long run, but it will be necessary to ensure that all of these team-level objectives are successfully reconciled if the launch process is to be successful in achieving its ultimate, distal goals.

Scenario Description

Figure 2.1 shows the various teams that make up this product launch MTS. Six functional units participate in this example; within each are

Intrafirm MTS: High Tech Firm Product Launch Teams

| Project Manager |

HW Development Manager	SW Development Manager	Mfg & Ops Manager	Product Manager	Sales Manager	Support Services Manager
Architecture	Architecture	Manufacturing Operations	Marketing Communication	District Sales	Field Support
Development	Development	Procurement	Training	Regional Sales	Technical Support
Quality Assurance	Quality Assurance	Logistical Operations		Inside Sales	
Documentation	Documentation				
Hardware	**Software**	**Production**	**Marketing**	**Sales**	**Support**

FIGURE 2.1
Intrafirm MTS: High-tech firm product launch teams.

a number of teams that are involved in the overall process. An overall project manager will have responsibility for coordination of the various activities conducted by these functional units. Each unit is headed by a functional manager overseeing this product launch. Because a complex technical product is generally a combination of both the physical hardware and the software used to control its operation, both hardware and software functions within the firm are involved. Each group will involve a number of discrete component teams having specific roles in the development process: architecting the hardware and software solution, developing the actual device and controlling software, testing and performing quality assurance on the respective components, and documenting the end technical features and operations of each component. (*Note*: Depending upon the size or development philosophy of the firm, some or all of these functions can be consolidated. For this example, we have assumed the operations of a large firm to better highlight the interdependencies between teams.) Production of the product will be handled by the manufacturing and operations unit, which will be composed of discrete teams responsible for actual production, procurement, and logistical operations (e.g., warehousing and shipping).

Consumer-facing activities will be the responsibility of the marketing, sales, and support functions. Efforts within the marketing unit are typically managed by the product manager, who maintains the overall development "roadmap" for the product. Other teams within marketing that will be involved in the launch will include *marketing communications*, which is responsible for advertising and public relations activities; and *training*, which will be involved with product training for the sales and support organizations. Sales teams will include district and regional teams (including international sales areas) in the field as well as telephone-based inside sales teams. Support will be provided through pre-sales field support teams that will augment the sales teams' efforts or technical support teams that will be responsible for maintenance and resolution of customers' problems after they have purchased the product.

In order to more easily understand the interrelationships among the various teams involved in this product launch, it is best to isolate three specific phases of the process: *development, launch coordination,* and *ongoing sales.* This breakdown highlights the teams that are most active during each of these respective stages. Figures 2.2 through 2.4 lay out the functional units and representative component teams that make up this product launch MTS at each phase of the product launch.

Development Phase

Development activities involve the design and development of the physical equipment and supporting software that make up the product. This phase begins when specifications for the new product are frozen for the upcoming release and ends when the product is actually released to manufacturing. During this phase, the bulk of the interaction occurs between the hardware and software development teams; development teams from each function

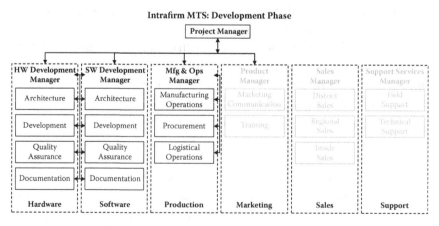

FIGURE 2.2
Intrafirm MTS: Development phase.

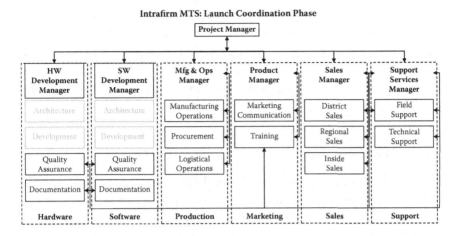

FIGURE 2.3
Intrafirm MTS: Launch coordination phase.

coordinate with the respective architecture groups to finalize the design of the product and later to integrate their component parts. Quality assurance teams work concurrently with the development teams to test product components and code modules, and then in tandem to verify the integrated product. In the meantime, documentation teams have been working along with the development and testing groups to ensure that reference materials for the product will be available at the time of product release.

Throughout the development phase, the product manager has been involved to ensure that these activities are congruent with the overall

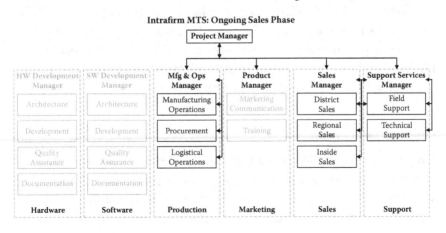

FIGURE 2.4
Intrafirm MTS: Ongoing sales phase.

objectives and plans for the product. The product manager also interacts with manufacturing operations to ensure that special production requirements for the product, such as retooling or the purchase of mission-critical production machinery, and logistical needs are properly anticipated. Procurement requirements and relationships with external suppliers are also negotiated during this time.

Launch Coordination Phase

Launch coordination begins 6 to 12 months in advance of formal product release with planning activities (e.g., production levels and sales forecasts) in order to coordinate the levels of materials to be ordered and inventoried, production schedules, and revenue and expense budgets. These forecasts are ultimately coordinated between the product manager and the manufacturing, procurement, and logistical operations teams to ensure that purchasing teams and production operations teams have provided the appropriate resources to manufacture the product. Similarly, separate operations teams devoted to packaging the product (i.e., hardware, software media, documentation, and other materials that make up the final shipping version) coordinate with the respective teams to ensure that all the materials come together in a coordinated fashion and that logistical issues concerning finished goods storage and distribution are scheduled.

An important set of pre-release activities involves the creation of marketing communications materials and public relations efforts by the marketing communications team. Similarly, the training organization coordinates education efforts for the sales force and support functions in order to prepare them for customer contact. The launch coordination phase generally ends 2 to 3 months after release when the marketing communications team concludes launch promotion events.

Ongoing Sales Phase

Ongoing sales activities involve the long-term interaction with customers and distribution channels. In this phase, the district, regional, and inside sales teams engage in sustained sales activities in the market supported by field support and technical teams operating in both pre- and postsales roles. These efforts will generally continue until the product manager has decided to terminate the product. At the same time, internal technical support teams not only support the field teams but also interact with the development groups to report product anomalies and/or convey product fixes back out to the field teams. Finally, sales forecasts are relayed back to manufacturing and operations in order to ensure proper levels of production over time.

Standard Features of the MTS

The product launch MTS has the definitional features of all MTSs, including integrated, patterned actions that occur within a constellation of teams acting to achieve the collective, superordinate goal of successfully launching a new product. The network of teams involved in a product launch has come together to respond to the demands placed on companies to contend globally in a highly competitive global marketplace. It is precisely the adaptive, swiftly collaborative actions among specialized units within a larger system that enable organizations to compete globally with new products, and this is especially true in technology industries that are characterized by their dynamism.

The teams within a product launch MTS have input, process, and output interdependencies. *Input interdependence* occurs throughout the three phases of this MTS's life. During the development phase of the project, the hardware and software teams are highly dependent on the input elements of other team members. For example, the resource availability of each team influences the others' timelines as well as the overall project schedule. Similarly, hardware and software specifications dictate each others' feature requirements. Such input interdependence continues during the launch coordination phase (e.g., product feature and documentation information helps define the training team's curriculum) and ongoing sales phase (e.g., sales leads generated by an inside sales team determine field sales team account targeting and follow-up schedules).

Process interdependence is also a prominent feature of these MTSs. For example, quality assurance test processes need to interact with hardware and software development team processes to ensure that bug fixes are scheduled, implemented, and retested. During the launch coordination phase, a number of teams, including marketing, sales, production, and operations, need to coordinate their respective processes into a cross-team forecasting process. Similarly, during the ongoing sales phase the production team coordinates with procurement and operations team processes to ensure that manufacturing is prepared to produce adequate quantities of product.

Output interdependence, the extent to which outcomes of team members depend on the performance of others, occurs in a number of notable ways for a product launch MTS. For example, delays caused by development teams can affect the manufacturing schedules of the production team, the competitiveness of the marketing team's strategy, and the ultimate quantity of products that can be sold by the sales teams. Of course, weak performance by any team at any step in the process will have an effect on the overall MTS's success. If sales teams significantly fall below sales expectations, it will result in inventory management challenges for the production and operations teams, and, if severe enough, could signal that the organization should not develop future versions of the product, possibly redefining the need for some of the development teams.

Unique Attributes of This MTS

Compositional Attributes

There are a number of features of this type of MTS that are noteworthy. First of all, the compositional attributes reflect the scale of operations for a major high-technology firm, and they ensure that the MTS in this example will be large in terms of the number of teams as well as the number of participants. In this example, Figure 2.1 describes six functional units, each containing several teams with differentiated purposes. This is an example of a large and diverse MTS that has a *large number of component teams, some with many members.* The MTS represents many functions across the component teams, indicating *significant functional diversity.* Some component teams have large numbers of members. The implication in large MTSs is that some component teams, such as the hardware and software development teams, may be highly interdependent with each other, the quality assurance team, and the documentation team, yet would have little direct interaction with other teams, such as manufacturing or sales. The firm will launch the product globally, creating not only a *broad geographical dispersion* but also the need to deal with a *significant level of cultural diversity.* Nevertheless, all of the teams making up the MTS operate within the same organizational boundary, so they have *low organizational diversity.* More importantly, because all the teams are ultimately working toward the same organizational goal of increasing shareholder value, their goal hierarchies at the highest level are highly congruent. However, as was explained above, the proximal objectives of the respective teams will differ sufficiently to create conflicts among the teams, indicating a *significantly complex motive structure*. Component teams in a product launch MTS spend a significant percentage of their efforts focused on launch-related goals and activities, representing an MTS with *a strong temporal orientation*.

Linkage Attributes

A product launch MTS can also be described in terms of linking mechanisms that explain the way component teams coordinate their actions. The component team interdependencies in this example are *largely serial between phases*, but *within each stage of the product launch cycle they reflect a high level of reciprocal interdependence* (Thompson, 1967). For example, quality assurance teams will pass findings back and forth to the development teams on a continuous basis during the development phase in order to complete the product. During the launch coordination phase, the marketing communication and training teams will work actively with the sales organization to bring them up to speed on the product while the various teams in the production function will interact to ensure that sufficient product will be available by the time the product is ready to sell. During the ongoing sales phase, field and inside sales teams will coordinate their actions intensively in order to develop leads into closed sales, and the field sales and field support teams will need to coordinate on pilot projects. On the other hand, most efforts between stages will tend to pass serially. For example, once the hardware and software teams have completed development of the product and the product is being sold, they will transfer their focus to development activities for the next generation of products. Similarly, once manufacturing and operations teams have produced the new product, they will retain contact with the sales and marketing organizations to ensure that forecasts are translated into correct production levels, but the process will be less dynamic unless major changes in demand or production problems are encountered.

As is suggested in Figures 2.1 through 2.4, the teams operating in a product launch MTS exist in discrete functional units that have similar status within the firm. These teams exist at something of a peer level within this example, and each is likely to report up to a senior or general manager that represents the function at the top management team level. Consequently, various teams may have some ability to influence other teams within their functional unit (e.g., the manufacturing team may be able to dictate some specifications to the procurement group), but these teams are likely to have little influence over teams in other functions (e.g., the sales teams cannot define the development timeline for the hardware and software teams). As a result, this MTS has *low hierarchy* and *fairly equal power distribution* because component teams do not differ significantly in their ability to influence the activities of the MTS. It should also be noted that the project manager coordinating this project, though he or she may oversee the actions of the respective teams in the MTS, is unlikely to have a high degree of positional power over the respective teams or the various functional units, Consequently, task-based conflict among the teams, such as disagreement over scheduling priorities, must either be resolved among the respective team leaders or be escalated to their functional leaders or senior management.

This product launch MTS operates as a *fairly decentralized communication network* in that interteam communication occurs directly among team members rather than through centralized boundary spanners. For example, members of the quality assurance team will often work directly with hardware and software team members to debrief on test results or discuss approaches to crucial issues. Similarly, manufacturing team members will likely coordinate directly with procurement team members to discuss specific purchase specifications just as field sales reps will coordinate customer calls directly with their field support team members. As a result, the *communication modality* of this MTS is highly varied, with a high level of face-to-face contact that is augmented by technologically enhanced modes (e.g., email, phone, or video-conference), especially during project stages having critical deadlines.

Developmental Attributes

Because large firms sustain their competitive advantage by continually releasing new products, *the structure and interactions represented by this type of MTS are formally created within the organization* and repeated with each new product release cycle. Consequently, even though the launch process profiled here may only be *active for a period of 6 to 12 months*, it is one that is *continually repeated over time for new product*. Because new product release cycles are ongoing, the *MTS represents a mature process with linkages exhibiting a high level of constancy.* However, *over time there is likely to be a high level of fluidity of team membership* due to turnover in the various groups involved.

DRUG DEVELOPMENT ALLIANCE MTS

Drug development collaborations between a large pharmaceutical firm and a smaller biotech company display many of the characteristics that differentiate an alliance MTS. Like the product launch MTS, the drug development alliance involves numerous coordination points across a number of teams. Unlike the product launch, however, those team interdependencies occur both within and across organizational boundaries.

It is very common for pharmaceutical firms to create alliances with other pharmaceutical firms, biotechnology companies, and universities in order to gain access to the science that can be developed into future drugs. However, the process of drug discovery and development is a lengthy one that is marked by a slow and intricate approval process by the U.S. Food and Drug Administration (FDA) as well as a high probability that the product will not be found to be efficacious. Consequently, there are many challenges that must be managed in order to keep this type of MTS on track.

A typical scenario for these MTSs is for a larger pharma company to partner with a smaller biotech. In these relationships, the smaller firm generally brings access to promising compounds or genomic science that can be mutually developed and taken through the clinical trial process with the pharmaceutical firm. Given that this process is navigated successfully, the larger pharmaceutical partner will generally manage the follow-on commercialization process involving manufacturing and distribution (though some biotech partners looking to develop their own channels may retain rights to directly sell the finished drug in specifically identified markets). Because instances where the pharmaceutical firm directly manages the commercialization phase are internally controlled and not a cross-boundary MTS, this example profiles only the development and clinical trial process.

The high-level, distal objective of this collaboration is the development and sale of a successful drug, and both firms benefit from the endeavor. Even though the large pharma firm will manage the commercialization and sale of the drug, the biotech partner is often able to share in those revenues by way of ongoing royalties from those sales. Additionally, the biotech firm is generally able to enjoy milestone payments from the pharmaceutical firm for each stage of the development process it is able to successfully deliver. This shared-risk, shared-reward environment provides an effective mechanism to align the objectives of the two firms and incent them to work toward a marketable product.

Even in this environment, there is ample opportunity for mixed-motive conflicts among the various teams involved in the development process. At the most basic level, the scientific teams involved in the actual drug development process are likely to feel more bound to the sometimes serendipitous nature and timelines of basic research than the marketing teams wishing to expedite the drug's ultimate release. Similarly, scientists at the biotech may be more interested in discovering ways in which their research can be leveraged to develop other drugs that are outside of the alliance's focus, whereas the scientists at the pharma will wish to focus the biotech's development schedule on the compounds that are identified in the alliance agreement. Although both partners are aware of the importance of meeting the strict criteria of the FDA's approval process in their clinical trials, there are liable to be different interpretations of the criteria by teams within each firm. These conditions create conflicts that, unlike a scenario such as the intrafirm product launch MTS described in this chapter, can be very difficult to resolve because the cross-boundary nature of the alliance means that there is not unity of command by a single firm. Instead, issues are governed by either the terms of the specific alliance agreement or the ability and willingness of the two firms to cooperate.

Scenario Description

Figure 2.5 shows the three types of component teams that operate in an alliance: *executive management, alliance management,* and *support.* Executive management teams are a form of management team (Cohen & Bailey, 1997) that has responsibility for determination of organizational direction, partner selection, terms of agreement, and ongoing alliance

Alliance MTS: Pharmaceutical Drug Development

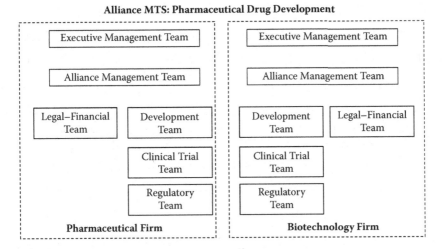

FIGURE 2.5
Alliance MTS: Pharmaceutical drug development.

governance. Alliance management teams operate in the manner of self-managing work teams (Cohen & Bailey, 1997) and are responsible for the coordination and delivery of the designated operational outcomes of the alliance. Support teams have responsibility for functions that augment the creation of the relationship or facilitate the delivery of alliance outcomes (e.g., legal, financial, and sales teams). These correspond to the activities carried out by parallel or project teams (Cohen & Bailey, 1997); negotiation, commission, design, and production teams (Devine, 2002); and advice teams (Stewart, Manz, & Sims, 1999). Figure 2.5 depicts the interrelationships among these three types of teams.

The teams that participate in formal alliances, such as a pharmaceutical drug development alliance, consist of two general phases: activities that lead up to the creation of the alliance agreement, and those that follow and involve the operationalization of the agreement. The pre-agreement phase is composed of three distinct stages: *identification*, *investigation*, and *negotiation*. During identification, the pharmaceutical firm's business development group, a support team that works on behalf of the executive management team, scans the universe for potential partner firms that have the scientific capabilities in the required therapeutic area (e.g., Klee, 2004). Once a viable partner candidate is identified, executive management and support teams representing scientific, finance, and legal functions (Mascarenhas & Koza, 2008) coordinate the flow of information

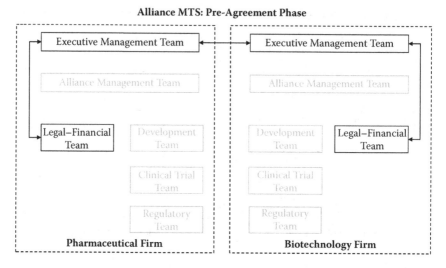

FIGURE 2.6
Alliance MTS: Pre-agreement phase.

between the two firms in order to probe and assess each other's fit (Das & Teng, 2002; Ring & Van de Ven, 1994). Given that the expectations of the respective firms are met, the executive management team or its representatives then finalize mutual goals and negotiate the formal terms of the alliance agreement. Figure 2.6 shows the team interrelationships occurring during the pre-agreement phase.

There is a brief *handoff stage* between the pre- and post-agreement phases during which control of the alliance transfers from the executive management team that oversees the negotiation activities to the alliance management team that manages execution activities. The handoff stage is important from an MTS perspective because it reflects (a) that a new type of team is introduced into the alliance, (b) that the activity of the alliance switches from strategic negotiation between the two firms to operational planning within the individual firms, and (c) that control for the alliance is passed from an executive-level team to a team operating at a lower level in the organizational hierarchy. Figure 2.7 maps the team interrelationships that make up the handoff phase.

The post-agreement phase is also divided into three stages: *integration, implementation,* and *transformation.* During integration, the alliance management teams and the support teams from development and clinical functions responsible for implementing the relationship are introduced

Alliance MTS: Handoff Phase

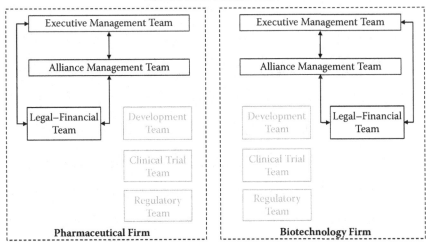

FIGURE 2.7
Alliance MTS: Handoff phase.

to each other and begin to plan their joint agenda. During implementation, the participating teams from development and clinical operations will focus on executing those plans in order to deliver the intended results of the relationship. The alliance will ultimately reach a point of transformation where the development and clinical teams will disengage because they have either successfully developed the target drug or, conversely, failed one of the stages in the clinical trial process. In some cases, the joint activity between the two firms will cause them to identify additional areas in which they can collaborate; when this occurs, the control of the alliance is transferred back to executive management teams who engage in pre-agreement activities aimed at developing a new set of goals (Ring & Van de Ven, 1994). Figure 2.8 depicts the team interactions that occur during the post-agreement phase.

Unique Attributes of This MTS

As described above, alliance MTSs have the defining features of all core MTSs, including a network of teams structure, interdependence among component teams, and collective goal hierarchies. Yet the alliance MTS can be further categorized using the MTS attributes typology.

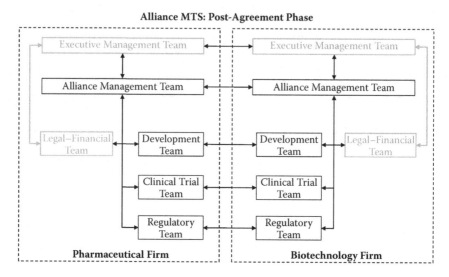

FIGURE 2.8
Alliance MTS: Post-agreement phase.

Compositional Attributes

The first distinguishing feature of this type of MTS is seen in its compositional attributes. This type of MTS has a *small number of teams* when compared to the MTS described in the "Product Launch MTS" section of this chapter, and there is a tendency for the *number of members per team to be comparatively small* given the specialized nature of this type of work. On the other hand, there are a number of areas in which this MTS exhibits a high level of diversity, with the most salient factor being the *cross-boundary nature of this system because the alliance is created through the collaborative efforts of two different firms.* Additionally, the teams involved in this type of MTS are not typically co-located, so the component teams need to deal with a *high level of geographic dispersion* and, in cases when the partnering firms are in different countries, *high cultural diversity* across the teams.

Most noteworthy, however, is the moderate to high level of *functional diversity* exhibited by this type of MTS. As was described in this chapter, the purpose of executive management teams is to create favorable relationships for their firms and monitor them to ensure that they achieve that objective. Alliance management teams' primary purpose is to manage the implementation process, which calls for a high degree of coordination.

However, because of the mixed-motive aspects of the various teams participating in the alliance, their mission also requires them to manage both cognitive and affective conflict. Support teams often serve specialist roles in the alliance in areas such as legal, operations, clinical trial, and scientific functions. However, these purposes can often be in conflict, such as when scientific and clinical trial teams disagree over the correct approach to use in structuring an upcoming trial.

The motive structure for the teams participating in this type of MTS is highly varied. Many of the teams involved in pre-agreement activities, such as the business development, finances, and legal teams, are generally focused on maximizing the value to be captured by their respective firms. There are likely to be competing objectives between the firms, so the respective teams will exhibit different motivations. Similarly, there can be differences between the motives of the scientific and commercialization teams conducting the exploratory research in terms of the target market for the drug (Abboud, 2005). By the same token, *the temporal orientations of the various teams are likely to differ* as the scientific teams can be more prone to expect a protracted exploration process than marketing teams, who are looking to bring the new drug to market quickly. The orientations of the clinical trial teams, who are focused on ensuring the validity of their trials, can likewise be in opposition to those of the marketing teams, who are looking to move the product to commercialization.

Linkage Attributes

A second feature of this type of MTS is its *high level of reciprocal interdependence.* The development and clinical trial teams continuously exchange data in order to determine how to qualify potential drug compounds, set up the tests for the clinical test trials, and evaluate findings of those tests. Although the relationships among the various development and clinical trial teams will tend to be among peer-level teams, the governance structure set up to oversee the alliance creates various executive steering committees that will interact with these teams in a hierarchical relationship. Although the teams will periodically meet for review sessions and governance meetings, they are generally not co-located so their typical mode of communication will be virtual and highly reliant on electronic methods.

The power relationship among the teams participating in this MTS will vary by life cycle stage. Pre-agreement negotiations are likely to be influenced by the asymmetries between the larger, well-financed pharma firm and the smaller biotech that seeks access to its finances and distribution channels. Post-agreement activities, on the other hand, can potentially reverse this relationship as the biotech's science can give it more influence over the nature of the drugs that can actually be produced (de Rond & Bouchikhi, 2004).

Over the course of the entire alliance MTS life cycle, there is a clear *hierarchical arrangement* among the teams, but that distinction will become blurred during the integration and implementation stages of the relationship. Because the alliance fundamentally represents a firm-level commitment between the pharma and biotech, the decision to create the relationship is typically formed at the highest levels of the two organizations and held in place with a formal contract and governance structure. Consequently, executive management teams continue to exert ultimate control over the alliance process and direct specific actions of the alliance management and support teams. However, it should be noted that such hierarchical ordering is often less salient during the integration and implementation stages because the frequency of executive management team involvement lessens (and, in some cases, can become nonexistent). Hence, between governance committee review meetings, the peer-level alliance management and support teams often operate in a nonhierarchical context. As might be expected, such switching between hierarchical and nonhierarchical contexts has the tendency to create an uneven *power distribution* among these teams.

Because the teams participating in the alliance MTS are usually housed in their respective offices, *communication modality* is highly reliant on asynchronous forms of communication such as email and voicemail. Unless provision has been made for periodic face-to-face meetings, even synchronous modes of communication for teams operating across firm boundaries will tend to be less informal and direct (e.g., telephone calls or conference calls) than for teams operating within a firm. As a result, alliance MTSs often operate through highly structured *communication networks* characterized by scheduled meetings (e.g., weekly, monthly, or quarterly) and dissemination of information as coordinated by the alliance management team.

Developmental Attributes

Alliance *MTSs are highly formalized*; the teams' members are selected based on the scientific requirements for the specific compounds being tested for development. However, *these teams will tend to remain in existence for a protracted period of time*, or at least as long as the product successfully completes the various clinical trial phases. *Membership will generally be constant*, especially among the scientists on the development teams, and the *linkages among the teams within each phase will remain intact throughout the phase.*

In summary, this chapter offers a detailed illustration of two different types of organizational MTSs and how the Chapter 1 typology can be used to classify elements of MTSs. Although the product launch cycle and alliances have been studied extensively in business journals, neither entity has been described in the organizational form of an MTS. Highlighting the compositional, linkage, and developmental attributes of these entities has value in illustrating the collaborative complexities of both units with the intention of focusing a more behavioral lens on the networks of teams that enact organizational alliances and launch products. This chapter has detailed how these collectives are distinct from traditional team and organizational classifications, calling for a more rigorous study of MTS composition, norms, structure, processes, and outcomes to answer emerging research questions about MTS design and execution.

REFERENCES

Abboud, L. (2005, April 27). How Eli Lilly's monster deal faced extinction—but survived. *Wall Street Journal*, p. A1.

Cohen, S. G., & Bailey, D. E. (1997). What makes teams work: Group effectiveness research from the shop floor to the executive suite. *Journal of Management, 23*(3), 239–290.

Das, T. K., & Teng, B.-S. (2002). The dynamics of alliance conditions in the alliance development process. *Journal of Management Studies, 39*(5), 725–746.

de Rond, M., & Bouchikhi, H. (2004). On the dialectics of strategic alliances. *Organization Science, 15*(1), 56–69.

Devine, D. J. (2002). A review and integration of classification systems relevant to teams in organizations. *Group Dynamics: Theory, Research, and Practice, 6*(4), 291–310.

Klee, K. (2004). Lilly's prescription for growth. *Corporate Dealmaker*, 12–20.

Mascarenhas, B., & Koza, M. P. (2008). Develop and nurture an international alliance capability. *Thunderbird International Business Review, 50*(2), 121–128.

Ring, P. S., & Van de Ven, A. H. (1994). Developmental processes of cooperative interorganizational relationships. *Academy of Management Review, 19*(1), 90–118.

Stewart, G. L., Manz, C. C., & Sims, H. P., Jr. (1999). *Team work and group dynamics.* New York: Wiley.

Thompson, J. D. (1967). *Organizations in action: Social science bases of administrative theory.* New York: McGraw-Hill.

3

Multiteam Systems in the Public Sector

Gerald F. Goodwin
U.S. Army Research Institute for the Behavioral and Social Sciences

Peter J. M. D. Essens
TNO—The Netherlands

David Smith
Defence Research & Development—Canada

Throughout government organizations, and the public sector more broadly, there are numerous examples of multiteam systems (MTSs). Although some of these are ad hoc in nature (e.g., the system of teams that emerged in responding to Hurricane Katrina), others are more permanent and intentionally structured (e.g., the National Counter Terrorism Center, combining teams from intelligence and law enforcement agencies with a singular focus). Importantly, these systems of teams—or a reasonable facsimile thereof—exist in numerous organizations, often in the "middle management" layers where coordination between multiple agencies and organizations is a critical point of failure. Here we attempt to provide an array of examples of governmental and public sector multiteam systems operating in a variety of contexts—specifically, railway management in the Netherlands, public safety in Canada for the 2010 Olympic and Paralympic Games, and security force assistance and stabilization operations from a U.S. military perspective. Through these descriptions, we hope to provide a sense of the richness and complexity of multiteam systems as they exist in the public sector as well as some of the particular challenges faced in these types of organizations.

Following the general structure and key facets of multiteam systems described in Chapter 1 (Zaccaro, Marks, & DeChurch, this volume), we have structured these descriptions in terms of component teams, tasks, goals, nature of interdependence, and other relevant team and multiteam attributes. The description of the component teams within the system addresses the nature of each team and its sourcing organization, the functions to be performed, and temporal aspects of the team. The tasks and goals include those of the multiteam system as a whole (e.g., maintain public safety and security at the Winter Olympics), those of the individual component teams, as well as the relevant goals of the sourcing organizations—which may often conflict with those of the multiteam system in important ways. The nature of interdependence is addressed in terms of shared resources, common environmental conditions, interteam and intrasystem interaction requirements, and outcome interdependencies. Finally, other notable attributes of the multiteam systems and component teams are discussed, including notable core values and norms of behavior, domains of expertise, aspects of the team or multiteam history, leadership structures, fluidity of personnel, membership, and structural linkages, among other notable features.

OPERATIONAL CONTROL CENTER RAIL, THE NETHERLANDS

The explosive growth of transportation demand in our networked societies has led to complex highway and railway systems. To keep up with the demand, several strategies are applied such as extending roads and tracks, optimizing their use by spreading peak demands, and increasing and maintaining the transit capacity per time unit. Substantial control systems—automated, human operated, and distributed—have been developed to manage day-to-day operations, to respond to variations in demand, and to mitigate effects of disturbances in the traffic flows. In such complex systems, many parties are involved in managing operations. Usually these are regionally organized, and local sites are often best equipped to solve local problems. In high-density networks, local problems easily spread out to supraregional levels, making decision making and coordination between the diverse, distributed organizations complex and slow. However, in these conditions intensive interactions, sharing of information, and fast decision making are required. For the railway system in the Netherlands, an Operational Control Center Rail[1] (OCCR) concept has been developed. The parties critical in national rail network calamity management are brought together in one working environment but retain full independence. This collective has the typical characteristics of a multiteam system (Mathieu, Marks, & Zaccaro, 2001), being characterized by high interdependency that requires the parties to trade off their individual goals in order to achieve the collective goal.

Background

In the Netherlands, the railway system handles about 6,000 passenger trains and 400 freight trains daily, and is the most intensely used rail network of Europe (Ramaekers, de Wit, & Pouwels, 2009). Since 2003, ProRail is the main network manager and is tasked by the government to provide adequate network capacity, manage infrastructures, and fairly and impartially distribute the capacity among the parties that request it. The largest nationwide people transporter is Netherlands Railways (NS), and there are various small regional transport companies operating particular routes. Most freight transport (75%) is transit oriented, mainly using network corridors, with Germany as a main destination. Rail freight transport is growing in importance for transshipment from the main harbor areas. The ambition of the ministry and transporters is to achieve a 50% capacity growth in 2020 (Minister of Transport, Public Works and Water Management, 2007).

The density of use of the transport systems in the Netherlands has reached such a sensitive point that local disturbances easily spread through the network. Yearly there are on average 60,000 disturbances requiring some level of adjustment of the preplanned timetable; 3,000 are classified as calamities (from a diversity of sources: infrastructure and matériel, fires, collisions, environmental conditions, people, security alerts, and computer systems). *Calamities*, operationally defined as a disruption of train service longer than 30 minutes, often cumulate delays in the network. Disturbances and calamities are controlled by four interacting controllers' networks: the *control square* comprising two levels of traffic control and transportation control.

The control square model critically failed to handle the calamity of April 6–7, 2005, in Utrecht, which became the turning point in the organization of handling calamities. Utrecht, in the center of the Netherlands, is the largest rail intersection in the Netherlands: It has both west-east and south-north rail lines, and it transits 100,000 to 200,000 passengers every day. In the early evening at the peak of rush hour, the train process control system came to a halt with a complete loss of situation awareness, stopping all trains in Utrecht and the wider surroundings. Later that evening, the control system was brought to life again. The next morning, the same problem recurred, and an estimated 100,000 passengers could not travel or were stuck at the stations. Although the system was up again within hours, trains could not move immediately due to overcrowded platforms at diverse stations. Moreover, it took significant time to get trains and train personnel to the right positions. By 11:00 a.m., the situation was under control, with trains moving in all directions, and gradually the system got back to normal (Minister of Transport, Public Works and Water Management, 2005).

Post hoc analysis of the calamity showed that the cause of the problem was a broken circuit board of the train process control system, which resulted in errors and alarms in other systems. Besides the technical problem, a deeper, structural problem was the inadequacy of the whole process of handling calamities. The existing working model for the prior 25 years required too many steps and forced parties to make decisions sequentially. A faulty train at a platform—not really a serious calamity—required some 28 telephone calls, 14 direct communications, and the involvement of at least 18 persons from multiple organizations and units (Montanus, 2008). In the words of a rail network specialist, "Often network situations change faster than the involved parties can communicate and act." It was concluded that the working model that developed over the years failed to match the increased complexity and dynamics of the network.

Top management realized that a new working model was needed, rather than the standard bureaucratic response of better procedures, better communication technologies, and better performance contracts between the parties. Intensive workflows require synchronous, tightly linked communications (Bell & Kozlowski, 2002). To achieve that in turbulent conditions with high-risk consequences, expertise and authority should be so closely coupled that decision making can be comprehensive and fast. The concept of a shared control room emerged—the Operational Control Center Rail— where representatives of all relevant parties are present and can contribute their part to the resolution of network calamities. However, just co-locating the relevant parties would not resolve the problem. A collaboration concept is required that provides some formal backing for how to organize interactions, information exchange, leadership, and decision making. A collaboration concept was developed (te Brake, Rakhorst-Oudendijk, de Bruin, & Punte, 2008) based on team effectiveness literature (e.g., Essens et al., 2005), concepts of team-based design of command centers (e.g., Essens et al., 2004; Punte & Post, 2004; Rakhorst-Oudendijk, te Brake, & Essens, 2007), and multiteam systems concepts discussed in the literature (DeChurch & Marks, 2006; Mathieu et al., 2001). Below, we will describe the OCCR concept and its development with reference to conceptual MTS attributes.

Development of the OCCR as an MTS

The development of the OCCR concept considered the collaboration processes and related aspects, the collaborative working environment, and the internal and external representation of decisions and processes of the OCCR. Emphasis here is placed on the collaboration processes and related aspects, while acknowledging critical aspects of the collaborative working environment and representation of the decisions and processes of the OCCR.[2]

An important choice in the development of the OCCR concept was to involve not only the four directly involved internal parties of ProRail but also the users of the rail network, the transporters. This was not a self-evident choice. There is a built-in tension between the provider of the network, a monopoly position that is government appointed, and the users of the network. Tension arises, for instance, when there is an infrastructure failure (e.g., a malfunctioning switch that delays trains); customers will then first blame the transporter, not the provider. In past years, some transporters publicly accused ProRail of not providing adequate infrastructure. Some transporters filed legal complaints with the Netherlands Competition Authority due to ProRail not providing them timely capacity (Netherlands Competition Authority [NMa], 2008), or due to ProRail asking too high compensation for use of the network (NMa, 2009). Negative sentiments and skepticism (in the sourcing organizations) are serious obstacles in the development of collaboration between parties and compete with the operational insight that only intense collaboration can enable improvement of the management of a complex system.

Major contributions to the OCCR are from two organizations: the network management organization, ProRail, and the main people transporter, Netherlands Railways, both with four teams, both about equal in size. Other participants, currently, are four rail construction and maintenance contractors and one regional transporter (remote). The freight transporters are not represented at the moment. There are 10 parties involved (if we take the contractors as one). Five component teams are distinguished: Four are from ProRail; Netherlands Railways has chosen to represent its internal teams as one component; the contractors are linked to a ProRail team, and the regional transporter can link virtually if required. Each component team has a representative—a *director*—who interacts with other directors and represents the team's interests in consultation and decision meetings. An independent person—the *national coordinator rail* (NCR)—is responsible for the alignment of all processes in the OCCR and stimulates the interteam interactions, but has no role inside the teams. These parties, except the regional transporter, will be co-located at a physical location and operate 24/7. A virtual OCCR will be set up to involve the smaller, regional parties to keep them informed and participate in the decision making when required. The OCCR has almost a hundred workplaces.

The collaboration concept of the OCCR is based on two main supporting concepts: organizational awareness and shared situational awareness, and teamwork and leadership. The basic concept is that there is intensive and continuous interaction between the specialists of the parties (see Figure 3.1).

To realize effective interaction and communication—a networked organization—the specialists of each team should not only have knowledge and understanding of their own roles, responsibilities, competencies, procedures, and processes (Cannon-Bowers, Salas, & Converse, 1993), but also have insight in the other parties' roles, responsibilities, procedures, and

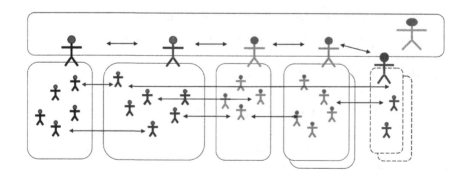

FIGURE 3.1
Sketch of a multiteam system configuration of the OCCR, with co-located and remote partners (dashed box).

processes. In addition, it is also critical to have understanding of the other parties' perspectives in their decision making and their stakes in solutions to the problem, as well as the sensitivities and emotions that implicitly may drive their choices (Essens & Van Loon, 2008). Shared situational awareness has its basis in sharing information augmented with interpretations and projections of the development of the situation (Endsley, 1995). Every team will have its own perspective, and part of the problem-solving process is to bring those perspectives on impact of the situation and possible solution approaches together. It is assumed that with well-developed organizational awareness and an interaction-rich social network, a high level of shared situational awareness will be established and maintained most effectively.

The type of leadership evoked substantial discussions between the major parties, in particular concerning the authority of the leader. The participating organizations do not want to see their independence limited by another organization having the authority to impose decisions on them. Therefore, a hierarchical structure with an integral responsible leader does not fit an OCCR, despite the need for fast decision making. A form of shared or distributed leadership is chosen in which the directors influence each other in order to find solutions to the shared problem (Pearce & Conger, 2003). The directors will receive the responsibility to actively seek to resolve issues in collaboration and take shared responsibility for the decisions taken. That means that they should not only defend their own position to minimize their costs in a shared-solution approach, but also balance this with the interests of the partners. For the role of the leader of the team of directors, several options were discussed. It was realized that when decision making stalls between the directors and instant response is required, one person should have the mandate to take a decision. Given the required impartiality, this is preferably not one of the directors in a form of *primus inter pares* (first among equals). Rather an independent, but domain-expert, person would be better qualified to lead and facilitate the directors' meeting. The lead person in the OCCR is the national coordinator rail. The NCR represents as point of contact the OCCR in the outside world. Inside, the NCR chairs the directors' meetings but has no hierarchical authority. The only mandate is to enforce an end decision if the directors do not arrive at a timely decision. The directors and the NCR share the responsibility for the decisions of the directors' meeting. A second crucial role of the NCR is the role of impartially facilitating collaboration and connecting the parties that often have different and sometimes conflicting interests. It is not sufficient to assume that hammering out the shared goal is sufficient to make conflicts go away. The burden or cost of resolving a calamity is typically not equally distributed, and to find each other somewhere "in the middle" is usually not possible. For instance, a quick-fix repair of a broken switch may result in less passenger dissatisfaction and claims (for the people transporter), but doubles the repair effort and associated costs (for the network provider). Costs may also include employee satisfaction, reputation, costumer appreciation, and income. The NCR should maintain the longer term perspective and seek to balance costs and burden. The role of the NCR is to facilitate and stimulate the relational processes of the directors to achieve and maintain agreement in the collective's overall goals, remain willing to balance his or her own goals with other directors' goals and the collective goal, and align the component teams' knowledge and work processes (Drath et al., 2008). To achieve this, the NCR should have a deep understanding of each of the parties' motives, intentions, ambitions, and values.

An additional consideration of the OCCR collaboration concept is the arrangement of parties and workplaces in the operational center. This should facilitate the interaction between the directors, the teams, and the individual workers in the center. An open arrangement is chosen, with the directors and their teams clustered such that direct visual contact is possible within teams and between teams. Link analysis of who interacts with whom is just a starting point for an arrangement. Learning by doing is the development perspective that is also adopted by the OCCR for the arrangement of workplaces. During operations, one may discover new requirements; moreover, new partners may come in and affect the arrangement. Workplaces are generic for easy reallocation and scaling up and down during day and night shifts. Information walls around the workspace provide shared awareness of network status. The center is planned to be an open space, with no cubicles or cells; the directors will be sitting with their teams, but located at the gangway so that they are in visual reach of each other.

Tasks and Goals

The primal goal of the OCCR is to recover rail transport services from complex disturbances in minimal time and with minimal costs. A secondary goal is to develop network optimization concepts. The OCCR strategy is (a) to, in a timely fashion, detect disturbances that have the potential to grow from local to regional and national effect; and (b) to collaboratively, with all parties, decide on an integral solution approach.

In the OCCR, five component teams from the two main sourcing organizations are distinguished with their specific proximal goals. The primary goal of the National Traffic Management team is to reschedule and reallocate pathways to the transporters in order to recover from disturbances to the planned schedule with minimal impact on network services. The primary goal of the Incident Management back office and Traffic Information team is to provide timely process alarms and reports during calamities, and to provide information to internal and external organizations. The Rail ICT management team's main function is to be the central service desk, and their primary goal is to resolve ICT problems. The Infrastructure Management team has a primary goal to connect or disconnect electrical power to train routes and repair energy services as soon as possible and as well as possible. Maintenance and repair of rail infrastructure are tasked to this team's main contractors. Finally, the Netherlands Railways has a primary goal to recover as soon as possible to the normal train schedule with minimal burden and delay for passengers.

The goals of the sourcing organizations, although overlapping with those of the component teams, differ somewhat from those of the OCCR. ProRail has an overall goal to provide a reliable rail network, fast recovery from disturbances, sufficient transport capacity, and safe and efficient train pathways to transporters that request rail capacity. Competition regulations require that decision making on transport capacity is done transparently and impartially. Netherlands Railways has an overall goal to provide accurate and reliable train service, improve social safety, continue passenger growth, and become more cost-effective. Accuracy of service (< 5% delay) is a primary performance indicator used by public perception and action groups. In the past, both organizations competed publicly for rail customer satisfaction by attributing rail disturbances to the other party. With both parties in the OCCR, it is expected that this will be limited or disappear.

Interdependence

The specialization and responsibility of the diverse parties in managing the complex rail network have created a highly interdependent system. The way the system was organized has shown not to be effective in calamity situations. The OCCR is the materialization of how to deal with the input, process, and outcome interdependencies between the involved parties. The OCCR is intended to provide a better model for dealing with the interdependencies more quickly and to higher, mutual satisfaction. The OCCR applies an intensive collaboration model where parties immediately connect and collectively focus on the steps that have to be taken.

The OCCR provides a shared facility with centralized information, designed to foster direct interaction between specialists over the component teams. The design of the control room is set up for intensive intercomponent and intracomponent team interactions. High process and outcome interdependency has driven the development of the OCCR. However, the parties protect their independence in matériel and finances and are tenants of the OCCR facility.

Interaction between the component teams is formalized at the level of the component team directors, and guided by the NCR. When a calamity emerges, the process is first to establish the criticality of the situation. Trade-off choices, balancing costs and efforts between the parties, will usually be discussed in the NCR–directors' meetings. If virtually linked parties are involved, the NCR will take care that they are able to contribute in the trade-off discussion. The OCCR will address network-wide and corridor impacts of disturbances and coordinate with the regional and local elements of their sourcing organizations to execute the planned actions, monitored at a distance by the OCCR. Central coordination is done where necessary. In a so-called bathtub model for handling complex disturbances, the first step is to bring the rail network system down to a "stable disturbed" situation, then in a second step use the time to repair infrastructure, create free train paths, take care of passengers, arrange alternative transportation, and in a final step gradually bring the system up to normal service. This model requires highly interdependent parallel and connected actions of the parties involved.

As is apparent in the short listing of the parties' goals, there is an inherent tension between infrastructure goals and transport goals. As indicated above, the components' cost–benefit trade-offs may differ, and short-term solutions may benefit one but cost the other more. The sourcing organizations have (public) key performance indicators, and contracts or obligations that limit or at least affect the freedom of choice in a collective trade-off discussion. The decisions have to be explained not only inside the OCCR, from directors to their component teams, but also (afterward) in the sourcing organizations in two ways: upward to higher management levels (in particular the sounding and steering boards) and downward to the decentralized, not interconnected, execution levels where choices may not always seem logical. The NCR and the directors will be closely monitored by the participating parties on how well they operate in this tense domain.

Other Attributes

Despite all the differences between the main sourcing organizations, on the work floor there is still a reminiscence of an earlier shared rail culture when they belonged to one organization (i.e., before 1995). At the first OCCR pilot (2008), some participants reported this to be an emotional moment of good old times. However, the differences between the component teams are still substantial. For instance, one organization has kept the more directive, top-down leadership culture of the past, whereas the other organization is less hierarchical and more open for information from the bottom up. Size differences may create another complexity in the OCCR. The two main sourcing organizations have about the same number of people on the floor of the OCCR, but are represented four to one at the directors' level. Their size is also a concern for smaller parties in terms of not being taken seriously enough. This may be even more problematic when that party is remotely located, due to costs of being present 24/7 in the OCCR. Part of the role of the NCR is to watch out for single-party dominance, and also to ensure that small parties have a stake in the solution approach. The level of interaction of the diverse component teams supported by a shared working place may blur the boundaries of the teams and create a new identity, thereby putting the sourcing organizations at a further distance. Working in the OCCR has already generated high expectations, and is regarded as the top of a growth path in one's career from regional to national to OCCR.

Summary

The OCCR is a complex collective of diverse, independent, yet interdependent parties united in the common goal to recover as quickly and robustly as possible from network disturbances and to optimize network services. They are highly interdependent on several layers: in their goal achievement and in execution. In most solution approaches, trade-off choices have to be made that most often result in the uneven optimization of proximal goals. In execution, the timing and quality of the actions by the execution levels of the sourcing organizations are crucial.

Fast decision making is often thought to require a strong leader with authority and responsibility to choose between options. In the OCCR, this would violate the parties' requirement (and perception) of independence. The leadership role in the OCCR does not easily fit a leader–follower paradigm where decision authority stays with the leader. It is assumed that a shared leadership model plus a facilitating, impartial leader (*coordinator*) will be more effective in the end. The coordinator should encourage and stimulate teamwork and support the team climate in a facilitative and connecting style (Hirst, Mann, Bain, Pirola-Merlo, & Richter, 2004; Pirola-Merlo, Härtel, Mann, & Hirst, 2002). This quality of connecting leadership may be a crucial quality in high-cost operations. Even in military coalition operations, a classical hierarchical context with diverse parties from different sourcing organizations and countries, a commander cannot simply impose his or her authority on these parties, but has to take a connecting approach and bring the parties together in sharing the burden of dangerous operations (Essens & Van Loon, 2008).

From the review of the OCCR's compositional attributes and the underlying competing interests, it can be seen that there are many faultlines with opportunities for conflict to develop, such as between the teams, between a director and his or her team, or between the team and its sourcing organization. A crucial role in managing potential tensions between teams and between OCCR and its sourcing organizations is given to the coordinator. The development of the OCCR will provide valuable insight into the development of a robust MTS, in particular the roles of leadership, the intragroup and intergroup balance, and perceptions in the sourcing organizations. The intention of the OCCR to learn and improve provides a unique opportunity to gather longitudinal operational data on these dimensions. A long-term study plan is in place to follow its development.

TASK FORCE PHOENIX

For much of the last decade,[3] the U.S. military and NATO forces have been engaged in military operations that have entailed an approach combining traditional military campaigns with stability and security operations and security force assistance under the broad rubric of *counterinsurgency*. This broad focus has led the military to adapt its organizational approach to include and incorporate partner organizations—nongovernmental organizations (e.g., the International Red Cross and Médecins Sans Frontières [Doctors Without Borders]), other governmental organizations (e.g., the U.S. Agency for International Development and U.S. Department of Agriculture), and local and national organizations of host nations (e.g., the Afghan National Police). Moreover, in most of these operations multiple national military units have been combined under either the NATO umbrella or other international agreements. In understanding this complex web of relationships and partnerships, it may be useful to focus on a military headquarters unit, which often serves as a primary coordination point among these disparate partners.

A traditional military headquarters is typically organized in a fairly robust, hierarchical organization with a command team and a small number of staff sections (see Figure 3.2). Within this structure, the staff sections function as a multiteam system inside the headquarters organization. Each staff section has a set of goals that it alone is pursuing within the broader goals of the headquarters organization. The staff sections are inherently interdependent to varying degrees, and this interdependence will vary to some extent depending on the specific activities of the headquarters organization and ongoing operations. For example, the operations and intelligence sections are typically highly interdependent based on the information requirements and availability within each section. The operations and logistics sections have a moderate level of interdependence as the logistics section provides matériel and transportation support for the operational units—which is one factor that is accounted for in planning and executing operations. Similarly, the personnel section is relied

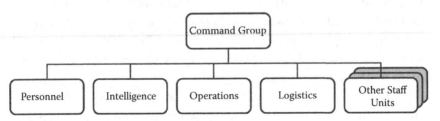

FIGURE 3.2
Structure of a military headquarters.

upon by the operations section to ensure that adequate, qualified personnel are available for operations, whereas the logistics section assists in ensuring that personnel are transported in and out of the operational theater in a timely manner. This type of military structure is prototypical of most military organizations throughout the world. However, in the current operational environment the integration of military capabilities with those of other organizations has been required in order to accomplish the broader national security goals of the United States and other nations.

The national security objectives of the United States and other Western nations for the last decade and more have broadly expressed the goal of reducing conditions that have led to the terrorist attacks against national interests at home and abroad. In pursuit of those objectives, an approach combining military capabilities and other international development capabilities has been adopted that generally falls under the label of a *whole of government approach* (or a similar title depending on the specific nation in question). From a U.S. military standpoint, such an approach is typically labeled *stability operations* and/or *security force assistance*. The goal of this approach is simply to provide assistance to national governments so that they can provide for the security and safety of the populace and assist in the development of critical infrastructure and systems that will permit those governments to maintain secure and stable internal conditions on their own in the future. Such an approach, as indicated by the *whole of government* label, is hardly the purview of the military—or any national agency—alone. It requires the integrated efforts of many governmental organizations, including those of the host nation. Although ultimate achievement of this goal is beyond the purview of military and security-focused organizations, in order to maintain some level of simplicity in this example only the military and security organizations involved will be included. However, it should be clearly acknowledged that the capabilities and activities of the vast number of development-focused governmental and nongovernmental organizations (e.g., the U.S. Agency for International Development, the Afghanistan Relief Organization, and Médecins Sans Frontières) are critical to achieving secure, safe living conditions in developing countries.

Task Force Phoenix is an organizational concept connecting the efforts of outside military units (e.g., U.S. and allied military units), other governmental organizations (e.g., U.S. police training units), host nation security forces (e.g., national military and police organizations), and local police and public safety organizations (e.g., city or province police forces). None of these organizations "owns" or is "in charge of" Task Force Phoenix, yet all are striving toward the overarching goal of improving the security of the local populace.

Working at a provincial level, the primary host nation organizations are the national military and police and the local police force (i.e., city police departments). External organizations either coordinate efforts with their corresponding host nation counterparts, or work directly with them in support and mentoring roles. The central U.S.–Allied military coordination point is a brigade headquarters, organized generally as indicated in Figure 3.2. However, in addition to the primary staff sections as noted, there is also a staff section dedicated to the training and development of host nation military organizations, as well as a team of specialists interacting directly with the populace to identify key problem areas (e.g., an inability to open a market bazaar due to risks of attack) and solution paths. Of particular note within the U.S.–Allied military are the teams assigned the task of training and mentoring their host national counterparts. These teams serve as the primary interface between the U.S.–Allied military units—which operate in coordination with, but independently of, the host nation military—and the host nation military forces. The training teams are attached to specific host nation military units—sharing living spaces, working spaces, and meals. The teams serve as both teachers and mentors, as well as the critical liaison to U.S.–Allied military units to obtain operational and logistical support as necessary.

In addition to the military personnel are teams of law enforcement officers from other agencies (e.g., the DEA and FBI) working with their host nation counterparts to develop the capabilities and procedures for a predictable system of laws and justice to be enforced. Thus, the Task Force Phoenix multiteam system represents a set of two parallel sets of organizations—one military and one law enforcement—combining efforts among the external U.S.–Allied organizations and the host nation organizations (see Figure 3.3).

Tasks and Goals

As noted previously, the overarching goal of the multiteam system is improving the security of the local populace. Within the system, the military units have a primary goal of lowering levels of militant violence

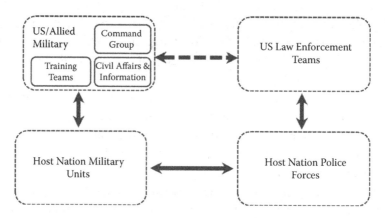

FIGURE 3.3
Task Force Phoenix component security organizations.

directed at the local populace to a point where more traditional law enforcement organizations can assume responsibility for providing for the safety and security of the populace. Military tasks within this multiteam system entail locating militants intending to act violently against the local populace or representatives of the government, proactively removing identified threats of violence, and responding to significant acts of violence in concert with law enforcement. The police and law enforcement units have the primary goals of enforcing local and national laws and prosecuting those who break them. Additionally, the host nation organizations have primary responsibility for action, whereas the U.S., Allied, and other external organizations primarily act in support of the host nation units—although they may act independently in some circumstances. The U.S. and Allied units provide support in terms of logistics, transportation, and technical capabilities that the host nation has not yet developed to sufficient capacity. Most importantly, the U.S.–Allied units provide mentoring and training to host nation units to develop the host nation's capability to operate effectively on its own.

Interdependence

In large part, the host nation and U.S.–Allied units are highly interdependent with each other within each of the military and law enforcement groupings. The U.S.–Allied units are largely restricted to acting with and through their counterpart host nation units, while providing critical support and mentoring to the host nation units. However, the host nation units are notably dependent on the U.S.–Allied units for critical support capabilities (e.g., logistics, transport, surveillance, forensic, and other technical capabilities) while developing their own capabilities of these types. The U.S.–Allied units also provide critical teaching and mentoring of their counterparts in order to develop the necessary human skills and capabilities to achieve their goals. Across the military and law enforcement groupings, there is also critical interdependence, though this is focused primarily between the host nation units. The military units provide a capability to respond to and suppress violence that law enforcement units do not possess. Conversely, the law enforcement units—specifically, the host nation's law enforcement units—possess the sole ability to arrest and prosecute individuals breaking laws. Thus, although all military units may detain individuals and collect criminal evidence, only the host nation police may actually formally make arrests and use the collected evidence to prosecute the detained individuals. When the military units do not follow appropriate law enforcement procedures in these activities, detained individuals are often set free—often frustrating the achievement of the goals of suppressing violence directed at the populace, the host nation government, and U.S.–Allied personnel. Because the U.S.–Allied units work directly with their host nation counterparts, there is less interdependence between the U.S.–Allied military and law enforcement units as well as between the U.S.–Allied military units and host nation law enforcement.

Other Attributes

There are a plethora of additional factors complicating the effective functioning of Task Force Phoenix, including cultural norms and values, organizational values, technological capabilities, sources of power, and fluidity within the multiteam system. Perhaps the most salient of these are the differences in cultural norms and values as U.S. and Allied personnel work with host nation personnel from other areas of the world. The centrality of religion and religious law and observance in daily life in Islamic nations is a stark contrast to most Western nations. In many Western nations, respect and personal power are derived from demonstrated capability and expertise, whereas in other nations and cultures these factors are more associated with personal associations, friendship networks, and familial affiliation. There are also significant differences in the respect, trust, and position power accorded to similar positions across cultures and nations.

Less salient, but in some ways more pervasive, are the differences in organizational cultures between the military and law enforcement organizations. These include fundamental differences in perspective regarding, for lack of a better term, *bad guys*. At a fundamental level within the law enforcement community, bad guys are to be arrested and brought to justice under the law. Within the military community, bad guys are to be defeated—killed or otherwise harmed so as to remove their ability to fight. Other organizational factors are also salient in terms of understanding how they interact within a larger system of teams, including organizational technologies and structure. On the whole, military organizations throughout the world tend to utilize significantly more advanced technology than their host national counterparts—to communicate, for reconnaissance and surveillance, and to plan and execute their primary tasks. This great disparity in technological sophistication and reliance can create significant obstacles in timely and sustained communication. Additionally, there are notable differences between the military and law enforcement communities in structure—although both seem quite similar in their reliance on hierarchical structures. Military organizations are almost uniformly national assets, rather than local or regional. Law enforcement, conversely, has both national and local organizations—that often are not closely tied and may maintain a somewhat antagonistic relationship.

Finally, within multiteam systems such as Task Force Phoenix, a significant challenge is the fluidity of membership—teams and personnel—with much of the dynamic occurring on the U.S.–Allied teams. U.S. and Allied personnel policies create a situation where personnel turnover within the particular teams occurs regularly, as well as the component teams from the United States and Allies rotating in and out every 12–16 months. This approach to personnel rotation creates notable challenges when working with host national teams that rely heavily on personal relationships for building functional capabilities.

Summary

The multiteam systems exemplified by Task Force Phoenix perform one of the most difficult sets of tasks in the spectrum of warfare—rebuilding and stabilizing a nation post conflict. The challenges faced by these teams are daunting, and have been notoriously difficult in the semicooperative operational environments of recent conflicts. Beyond the relatively simple challenges of smooth coordination within the system, additional challenges of differing, and sometimes conflicting, cultures and organizational norms add complexity. However, although the system and challenges are complex, they are addressable and can be overcome, and the organizational sciences focusing on understanding the nature and effectiveness of multiteam systems will aid in developing solutions to address the challenges.

INTEGRATED SECURITY UNIT: 2010 WINTER OLYMPICS AND PARALYMPICS, VANCOUVER, CANADA

In 2010, Canada hosted the Winter Olympic and Paralympic games (on February 12–28 and March 12–21, respectively). The games were held in two main areas: Vancouver and Whistler, British Columbia. Security during the games was considered the top domestic priority for the Canadian Department of National Defence, with more than 4,000 Canadian Forces (CF) personnel committed to the broader security force. Providing security to the Olympic Games was a large-scale operation, with a budget of approximately CDN$900 million. British Columbia has approximately 36,000 emergency services personnel, with approximately 13,000 in Vancouver. The number of security personnel was augmented during the games so that on any given day an estimated 8,500 security personnel were deployed.

The Royal Canadian Mounted Police (RCMP), Canada's federal-level police force, was the lead agency in charge of security. Because the RCMP also acts as the provincial police force for British Columbia, it is very familiar with the region. As part of the security plan, the RCMP led an organization called the Integrated Security Unit (ISU), which integrated security groups at the federal, provincial, and municipal levels. The ISU was an effort to coordinate the various units into a coherent security organization able to handle multiple levels of threat in a timely and effective fashion. The ISU was composed of member teams and individuals from the RCMP, City of Vancouver Police Department, West Vancouver Police Department, and Canadian Forces.

The operational headquarters of the CF component of Canadian domestic security is called Canada Command and is located in Ottawa, Ontario. In order to help secure the Olympics, the CF created a new task force (Joint Task Force Games, or JTFG) with headquarters in Victoria, British Columbia. JTFG also had officers co-located within the various ISU operations centers. The Canadian Forces contributed land, air, and maritime resources to the overall security portfolio. The challenge was to bring together, in a coordinated effort, the capabilities of several preexisting security and public safety teams, which include police, military, and civilian groups at multiple levels of government. These teams differed in their procedures, organizational cultures, and methods and also had various levels of understanding of one another's capabilities. To help these teams work together more effectively, the Canadian government organized and executed a series of exercises that included government departments and security organizations simulating responses to various threats.

The ISU fits the definition of an external multiteam system (MTS). The ISU was a very complex organization with multiple goals that were all aimed at planning, enabling, and conducting security during the Olympic Games. Because the organization was very vast and complex, we will focus on the operational arm of the ISU.

Component Teams

The operational arm of the ISU consisted of six command centers. Four of these command centers were primarily led by the RCMP: the Theatre Command Center (TCC), the Vancouver Area Command Center (VACC), the Whistler Area Command Center (WACC), and the Olympic Marine Operations Center (OMOC). Two were CF led: the Games Joint Operations Center (GJOC) and the Air Support Operations Coordination Center (ASOCC). A seventh center, the Provincial Regional Operations Center (PREOC), was run by the British Columbia Provincial Government (Emergency Management B.C., specifically), and although it was not considered part of the ISU it was expected to act in a coordinated manner.

Tasks and Goals

The goal of the ISU was to provide for public safety and security at the Olympic venues located in the Vancouver and Whistler areas during the

2010 Vancouver Olympics and Paralympics. This, of course, is the distal or large-scale goal of the entire MTS. The various teams within the operational arm of the ISU had more specific goals, including managing security in specific regions, air support, traffic, and emergency medical response. The teams all attempted to achieve their proximal goals while informing the other teams of the critical changes in their environment, all the while keeping the larger scale goal of overall security at the forefront. The ISU had two main tasks: (a) to maintain situation awareness of security and safety issues that arose during the games, and (b) to respond to any incidents where assistance was required. The venue commands operated fairly independently of the VACC, WACC, or TCC unless additional resources are required. Requests for military or other specialized assistance went from the venues to the VACC and the WACC, who then could pass on the request to the TCC (who had access to CF resources). The teams also needed to interact in order to maintain situation awareness.

Interdependence

The six command centers were highly interdependent because they represented the entire resource pool for security assets immediately available during the games. The high-level command at the TCC needed to maintain awareness of the current environment (any safety and security incidents or potential problems) as well as maintain awareness of the security resources available. Hence situation awareness was a major process that required interdependence. Other processes requiring interdependence include coordinated responses to incidents, operational planning, the transfer of command authority, and public affairs.

Because military resources were poised to support the TCC, the TCC needed to be involved if such resources were required. Similar coordination needed to occur for resources to be transferred across regions (from Vancouver to Whistler, for instance). Hence, in order for the ISU's mission to be successful, the component teams had to act in a coordinated manner; failure to do so could have led to an over- or underuse of available resources.

The teams comprising the ISU were interdependent at all three of the levels described in Chapter 1: input, process, and outcome. They were interdependent at an input level in that the teams needed to share information, personnel, and resources. They were also interdependent at the process level as they had to produce a coordinated response and assist one another in order to accomplish their goals. Finally, they were interdependent at an output level because their actions were intended to maintain security and effectively respond to events.

Team and MTS Attributes

The ISU operational command centers shared the same goals (maintaining peace, safety, and security). However, the team consisted of at least three distinct cultures: military, police, and civilian. The military and police have related cultures, in that both are expected to sometimes be placed in harm's way; they differ, however, on several dimensions. One of the major differences is that military goals are based on defense and security (but much less on public safety) and require large pieces of specialized military equipment. Although police goals include safety and security, they are more oriented toward prosecuting criminals and monitoring for crime. Not only is there a difference in the cultures of each organization, but also there is a gulf in expertise. Military members are not necessarily familiar with the strategies and tactics used in policing, and most police have little experience working with military assets. Hence, the ability of each team to be able to understand the others' capabilities and processes was critical. Each organization, however, shares similar cultural and linguistic backgrounds because they all operate as Canadian government organizations.

Each team employed several liaison officers to coordinate with other teams and other government teams represented outside of the ISU operations centers (e.g., Canada Command and NORAD). Therefore, there was a great deal of functional diversity both between and within teams. As noted in Chapter 1, a positive benefit of functional diversity is the possibility of bringing more cognitive perspectives to a problem, but it can also create greater conflict and less social cohesion.

The ISU was a planned (as opposed to ad hoc) MTS to manage security during the Olympic Games. In order to develop the teams effectively, a series of exercises (command post, live play, and tabletop) occurred and continued until shortly before the beginning of the games. These exercises were important events in the development and training of the ISU teams and the testing of their systems.

CONCLUSIONS

Across these three examples of multiteam systems in the public sector, a number of common themes can be identified. In each case, a larger organization (often a federal government) has made a conscious and intentional effort to construct the multiteam system as a means of dealing with the complexity inherent in the overarching environment and problem space. Just as organizations adopt a team (versus individual) approach to better enable effective responses to larger and more complex problems, they may also adopt a multiteam system approach in response to additional layers of complexity. These approaches allow for bringing additional resources and skill sets into play for effectively managing these complex tasks, but also create significant challenges for communication and coordination among individuals and teams.

Additionally, in each case the multiteam system has created a structure that increases the ease and directness of communication at the tightest couplings between teams. In the OCCR and ICU examples, this involved the creation of command centers housing critical teams together, whereas the Task Force Phoenix example utilized training teams co-located with host nation units to serve as direct mentors and as liaisons to U.S.–Allied units. Interestingly, in light of the current push toward virtualness, each of these examples has adopted a strategy of colocation at the most critical junctures between teams and organizations. Although this is reflective in part of differences in technological capabilities for communication and coordination purposes, it likely also reflects a fundamental perception that direct, face-to-face communication and coordination are easier or more effective in some way. From a scientific perspective, this highlights the challenges associated with virtual organizational models and the need for research to better understand and improve the effectiveness of virtual modes of collaborative work.

Another common feature of these examples is the intentional creation of a "united front" or single face for public perception. In the OCCR example, the purpose was to address a perceived public need to eliminate ongoing public accusations and finger pointing among the parties involved and refocus efforts on addressing the root problems. In the Task Force Phoenix example, the broader intent was to build public trust and faith in the host nation organizations, ultimately enabling the drawdown and exit of the external organizations. All reflect a public desire of public services to work effectively and a general public perception of governments as a unitary whole. However, this also has the benefit of creating a larger—multiteam system level—organizational identity that helps serve to draw in the member teams and organizations and better align them with the overarching goals of the system. Developing and managing multiple organizational identities simultaneously comprise a ripe and particularly challenging domain for research, and investigation of multiteam systems provides a useful venue for this type of investigation.

Each of these examples of multiteam systems in the public sector highlights the governmental objective of providing for the public good. Although these examples focus primarily on public safety and security concerns, there are numerous other examples of public sector multiteam systems that deal with other aspects of governmental operations (e.g., public health and economic concerns). Moreover, each of these examples intentionally drew boundaries that excluded the discussion of other organizations relevant to higher order goals beyond the multiteam system described. It is important for the reader to recognize that even with the complexity inherent within the problems focused on here, there are additional layers of complexity that each of these multiteam systems must cope with external to its particular definition. From a research perspective, it is often difficult to clearly define the boundaries of a multiteam system due to the complex web of interrelationships and goals. However, a bright focus on specific goals may aid in clarifying what teams are "in" and what teams are "out" of the multiteam system, as well as further enabling robust research to be conducted in this paradigm.

DISCLAIMER

The opinions expressed in this chapter represent those of the authors and do not represent the official opinions or positions of the governments of the United States, Canada, or the Netherlands, or the authors' employing organizations. Certain aspects in the exemplars described have been omitted for national security and public safety reasons. Although these exemplars are therefore incomplete in some ways, the descriptions provided should convey to the reader the critical complexities inherent in multiteam systems as they exist in the public sector.

NOTES

1. As the OCCR is still in its starting-up phase (after being initially operational in October 2009), no behavioral or performance data are currently available. The information presented here is mainly based on interviews with the principal OCCR project leader (M. Menkhorst – 3MC), sourcing organization documents, and the TNO OCCR analysis and design report (te Brake et al., 2008).
2. For additional information on the collaborative working environment and strategic representation of decisions and processes, please see te Brake et al. (2008).
3. The name *Task Force Phoenix*, although adopted numerous times in current operations in the Republic of Iraq and the Islamic Republic of Afghanistan, is used here simply as a useful moniker for a prototypical organization engaged in stabilization and security force assistance operations. The description provided here is not specific to any current or past U.S. organization or that of any other country.

REFERENCES

Bell, B. S., & Kozlowski, S. W. J. (2002). A typology of virtual teams: Implications for effective leadership. *Group Organization Management, 27*, 14–49.

Cannon-Bowers, J. A., Salas, E., & Converse, S. A. (1993). Shared mental models in expert team decision making. In N. J. Castellan, Jr. (Ed.), *Individual and group decision making: Current issues* (pp. 221–246). Hillsdale, NJ: Erlbaum.

DeChurch, L. A., & Marks, M. A. (2006). Leadership in multiteam systems. *Journal of Applied Psychology, 91*, 311–329.

Drath, W. H., McCauley, C. D., Palus, C. J., Van Velsor, E., O'Connor, P. M. G., & McGuire, J. B. (2008). Direction, alignment, commitment: Toward a more integrative ontology of leadership. *Leadership Quarterly, 19*(6), 635–653.

Endsley, M. R. (1995). Toward a theory of situation awareness in dynamic systems. *Human Factors, 37*(1), 32–64.

Essens, P. J. M. D., Punte, P. A. J., Vermeer, J., Vogel, H., Weitenberg, A. J. M., & Zoutendijk, A. (2004). *Integrale Servicecentrale—Specificatie eisen voor technische systemen* [Integral Service center: Specifications requirements for technical systems]. Delft: TNO-TPD.

Essens, P. J. M. D., & Van Loon, T. (2008). *Cultural Challenges in Joint and Combined Command: A Military Leader's Perspective: Proceedings of the NATO RTO Human Factors and Medicine Panel (HFM) Symposium on Adaptability in Coalition Teamwork, Copenhagen, Denmark, 21–23 April 2008* (NATO report RTO-MP-HFM-142-KN2). Brussels: NATO.

Essens, P. J. M. D., Vogelaar, A. L. W., Mylle, J. J. C., Blendell, C., Paris, C., Halpin, S. M., et al. (2005). *Military command team effectiveness: Model and instrument for assessment and improvement* (NATO RTO HFM-087 TP/59). Brussels: NATO.

Hirst, G., Mann, L., Bain, P., Pirola-Merlo, A., & Richter, A. (2004). Learning to lead: The development and testing of a model of leadership learning. *Leadership Quarterly, 15*, 311–327.

Mathieu, J. E., Marks, M. A., & Zaccaro, S. J. (2001). Multiteam systems. In N. Anderson, D. Ones, H. K. Sinangil, & C. Viswesvaran (Eds.), *International handbook of work and organizational psychology* (pp. 289–313). London: Sage.

Minister of Transport, Public Works and Water Management. (2005). *Answers to the congressional committee for Transport, Public Works and Water Management on the disturbance in the control system of ProRail of April 6 and 7, 2005*. The Hague: Author.

Minister of Transport, Public Works and Water Management. (2007). *Actieplan 'Groei op het spoor' 2020* [Action plan: Growth of rail transport 2020]. The Hague: Author.

Montanus, H. (2008, May 27). Het Vierkant op de schop [The control square model reorganized]. Presentation by Head Transport Direction Netherlands Railways. Retrieved from http://www.vhsonline.nl

Netherlands Competition Authority (NMa). (2008). *NMa annual report 2007*. Amsterdam: Author. Retrieved from http://www.nmanet.nl

Netherlands Competition Authority (NMa). (2009). *NMa rail monitor*. Amsterdam: Author. Retrieved from http://www.nmanet.nl

Pearce, C. L., & Conger, J. A. (Eds.). (2003). *Shared leadership: Reframing the hows and whys of leadership*. Thousand Oaks, CA: Sage.

Pirola-Merlo, A., Härtel, C., Mann, L., & Hirst, G. (2005). How leaders influence the impact of affective events on team climate and performance in R&D teams, *Leadership Quarterly, 13*(5), 561.

Punte, P., & Post, W. (2004). *Ontwerp en evaluatie Joint Operations Room LPD-2* [Design and evaluation of Joint Operations Room LPD-2] (TNO Report). Delft: TNO-TPD.

Rakhorst-Oudendijk, M. L. W., te Brake, G. M., & Essens, P. J. (2007). *Inrichting Gemeenschappelijke Ops-room voor DTO, JCG en C2000* [A common operations room for DTO, JCG and C2000]. (TNO Report) Delft: TNO-TPD.

Ramaekers, P., de Wit, T., & Pouwels, M. (2009). *Hoe druk is het nu werkelijk op het Nederlandse spoor? Het Nederlandse spoorgebruik in vergelijking met de rest van de EU-27* [How busy is the Netherlands rail network really? Utilization of the Netherlands rail network in comparison with the rest of the EU countries]. The Hague: Statistics Netherlands.

te Brake, G., Rakhorst-Oudendijk, M., de Bruin, R., & Punte, P. (2008). *Een samenwerkingsconcept en inrichtingsvoorstel voor het OCCR* [A collaboration concept and layout for the OCCR] (TNO-DV-2008-C401). Delft: TNO-TPD.

Section II

Compositional Attributes

4

Motivation in Multiteam Systems

Ruth Kanfer
Georgia Institute of Technology

Matthew Kerry
Georgia Institute of Technology

Motivation is arguably one of the most important determinants of team and multiteam effectiveness. In this chapter, we discuss motivation theory and research in the context of teams and multiteam systems (MTSs). We begin with a description of motivation at the individual level of analysis, and then briefly review theory and research that extend the study of motivation to the team context. Next, we discuss motivation in the context of multiteam systems. In particular, *we examine the person and situation factors that affect motivation for interteam teamwork and motivation for communications, cooperation, and coordination behaviors between members of different teams.* In the final section, we identify gaps in the research regarding motivation in team and multiteam contexts and suggest potentially fruitful directions for future research.

MOTIVATION AT THE INDIVIDUAL LEVEL OF ANALYSIS

Strictly speaking, *motivation* refers to the internal and external forces that affect the initiation, direction, intensity, and persistence of goal-directed action (Pinder, 1998). Over the 20th and early 21st centuries, the scope of motivation theory and research has expanded beyond the study of person and situation determinants of behavioral intentions (i.e., goal choice) to include the regulatory processes by which individuals accomplish goals (i.e., goal pursuit) (see Kanfer, 2010). In contemporary work on motivation theory and research, *motivation* is a general term used to refer to the internal and external forces that affect both goal choice and goal pursuit. In settings characterized by the simultaneous pursuit of multiple goals, *motivation* often refers to the internal and external forces that affect the individual's allocation of personal resources, including time, effort, social capital, and information, across tasks and goals (Kanfer & Ackerman, 1989).

Motivational Determinants: Internal Forces

Internal forces, driven by biology, affect, and cognitive processes, represent the most frequently studied class of motivational determinants. Biological processes (e.g., fatigue), affect-driven action tendencies (e.g., sensitivity to threat of punishment), motives (e.g., achievement or affiliation), and cognitions (e.g., expectancies or self-efficacy) influence behavior and performance through their effects on motivational processes. Internal determinants of motivation may further be distinguished in terms of the pathway by which they exert their influence: through cognitively mediated mechanisms or through fast, nonconscious processes. Individual differences in sensitivity to threat and punishment (Gray, 1987), for example, refer to the strength of nonconscious action tendencies away from events and environments that are perceived to be unpleasant or involve potential loss. These affectively tinged motive tendencies influence what an individual notices in the environment, the goals that he or she adopts, and/or the regulatory strategies used to accomplish those goals. Other nonconscious influences on motivation include individual differences in implicit motives for achievement, power, and affiliation (McClelland, 1987). In contrast to explicit motives that are cognitively mediated and consciously accessible, implicit motives operate without conscious attention to affect behavioral tendencies during action episodes. The inclusion of nonconscious processes and implicit motives as determinants of motivation and behavior is relatively new, and the precise manner in which these person factors affect different parts of the motivation system is still unclear.

Most work on motivation theory and research focuses on explicit internal forces that can be directly measured through self-report or testing. Individual differences in cognitive abilities, personality traits, motives, interests, and values represent relatively stable person attributes that influence motivation and behavior in settings that permit expression of the ability, trait, or attribute. An extensive body of research provides support for the mediating role of motivation in the relationship of nonability traits, interests, and values with behavior and performance (Chen & Chiu, 2009; Guzzo, 1979; Nygard, 1981). Individual differences in nonability traits, values, and interests also tend to influence motivation at multiple points in the motivational system. Conscientiousness, for example, has been shown to influence the difficulty of the goal adopted as well as the self-regulatory strategies that are used during goal pursuit (Barrick & Mount, 1991; Locke & Latham, 2006).

As noted previously, contemporary theories conceptualize the motivation system as comprised of two interrelated subsystems: (a) goal choice, and (b) goal pursuit. *Goal choice* pertains to the psychological processes involved in evaluating different goals and courses of action, and adopting an outcome goal and action plan. In contrast, *goal pursuit* involves the psychological processes through which individuals accomplish goals to which they are committed. During goal pursuit, individuals monitor their behavior for the purpose of evaluating their goal progress and regulate their cognitions, affect, and behavior to promote goal accomplishment.

Recent theory and research on these two subsystems have focused on the differences in cognitive processing and orientation in each motivational system, and the influence that the purpose of an individual's goal has on information processing and the self-regulatory activities that are used in goal accomplishment. Gollwitzer (1990, 2003) suggested that the two motivational systems involve different mind-sets associated with different ways of processing information. According to Gollwitzer (2003), during goal choice individuals employ a deliberative mind-set that emphasizes seeking accurate, unbiased information and using that information to evaluate different goal options. Following goal choice, however, Gollwitzer asserts that an individual's mind-set shifts from deliberation to implementation, or to selective attention to information that supports goal accomplishment. Studies by Gollwitzer (Gollwitzer & Kinney, 1989; Taylor & Gollwitzer, 1995) and others (e.g., Armor & Taylor, 2003; Webb & Sheeran, 2008) provide support for Gollwitzer's formulation and show that individuals who hold a deliberative mind-set are more attentive to negative goal-related information than individuals who hold an implementation mind-set. Further, individuals who hold an implementation mind-set report stronger illusions of control, increased self-efficacy, and more optimistic outcome expectations about goal accomplishment than individuals who hold a deliberative mind-set.

Other recent work on motivational processing focuses on the purpose of goal adoption. Theorizing by Deci and Ryan (1985), Dweck (1986), Nicholls (1984), and Higgins (1998) argues that individuals who adopt a goal for the purpose of learning, mastery, enjoyment, or satisfaction of intrinsic motives engage in different, more effective patterns of self-regulation than individuals who adopt a goal in order to demonstrate or prove one's competency, or for other extrinsic reasons. Findings obtained to test different formulations provide convergent evidence for the positive role that learning or mastery goal orientation plays in motivation and performance. However, there are mixed results with respect to whether goals adopted for the purpose of demonstrating competency or for other extrinsic reasons exert a negative influence on motivation and performance.

Motivational Determinants: External Forces

Events, conditions, and information that are generated external to the individual influence motivation in multiple ways. Task-related variables, such as difficulty and complexity, influence motivation through their impact on explicit psychological variables, such as performance expectancy, as well as through their impact on implicit motive activation during goal pursuit. Other external variables that refer to the social environment, such as coworker and leader communications, influence motivation through their effects on the individual's affective state as well as through their effects on the individual's perception of prevailing behavior–outcome contingencies with respect to intrinsic and extrinsic outcomes, including social relations.

External forces may also be organized in terms of their conceptual proximity to the immediate action setting. Distal external factors, such as the societal culture and the individual's professional identity, are posited to influence performance indirectly through their effects on beliefs, goal preferences, values, and interpretation of events (Triandis, 1979). Features of the organization and one's work unit, such as climate, influence performance through their effects on the norms an individual holds for work-related behaviors (Chatman & Flynn, 2001) and expectations about rewards and disincentives for particular actions (Beersma et al., 2003) Task or job demands are often considered the most proximal external influences on motivation and performance. Job characteristics, such as challenge, complexity, and variety, influence affective states such as enjoyment, boredom, and sense of competence (Oldham & Hackman, 1980).

The multiplicity of situation factors and the absence of a valid taxonomy for organizing different features of the work environment have made it difficult to know how features of the environment affect motivation and performance. Mischel (1968) proposed the concept of situational strength as a means of calibrating the extent to which the environment influenced behavior. Mischel argued that strong situations, in which the goals, procedures, and constraints and consequences of performance are unambiguous, reduce the impact of variability in internal forces on motivation and behavior. In contrast, weak situations allow for stronger effects of internal forces on motivation and performance. Recently, Meyer and his colleagues (Meyer, Dalal, & Bonaccio, 2009; Meyer, Dalal, & Hermida, 2009) have proposed a four-dimensional conceptualization of situational strength: clarity, consistency, consequences, and constraints. Recent meta-analytic findings by Meyer, Dalal, and Hermida (2009) provided support for the notion that individual differences in personality traits exert a significantly stronger effect on performance in situations characterized as having lower levels (weaker) of situational strength. Evidence for how different dimensions of situational strength may affect motivation processes remains an empirical question.

Summary

Investigations of work motivation at the individual level of analysis provide a strong foundation for the study of motivation in the multiteam context. Theory and research on the determinants of goal choice and goal pursuit suggest that individual differences in personality traits, motivational or goal orientation, and self-regulatory strategies play an important role in determining task performance, beyond that of cognitive abilities alone. Recent investigations have focused on the influence of situational forces on motivation, in terms of both the social conditions that affect goal choice and the situational features that interact with implicit motives and action tendencies.

To date, however, most research in work motivation has looked at the impact of the team and the social context on the individual. More recently, research on teamwork and team performance has started to extend motivational formulations to the team level, and to explore cross-level influences between individual-level and team-level motivation. However, as will be discussed in the "Motivation in and of Teams" and "Motivation in

Multiteam Systems" sections of this chapter, motivational formulations at the team and multiteam levels require consideration of additional issues, such as cross-level influences, spontaneous motivated behaviors, and motivational conflicts arising from the conflicting demands associated with intraindividual needs, team demands, and multiteam system goals.

MOTIVATION IN AND OF TEAMS

Beyond the external factors described in this chapter, teams exert distinct influences on the motivation of their members. Team members also exert influence on team-level processes that govern the direction, intensity, and persistence of the team's behavior as a whole. Over the past few decades, team researchers have focused increasing attention on the behaviors and activities of team members and their leaders that support individual and team-level performance (e.g., Baker, Salas, King, Battles, & Barach, 2005; Chen & Kanfer, 2006; Chen, Kanfer, DeShon, Mathieu, & Kozlowski, 2009; Marks, Mathieu, & Zaccaro, 2001; and see Mathieu, Maynard, Rapp, & Gilson, 2008, for a review).

Teamwork Processes and Motivation

A unique feature of contemporary research on teams pertains to the use of multilevel frameworks and methodologies for examining not just individual-level and team-level performance but also the cross-influence that individuals and teams exert on each other. Several multilevel frameworks for understanding teamwork processes and motivation and performance in teams have been proposed, including models by Chen and Kanfer (2006); Kozlowski and Klein (2000); and Deshon, Kozlowski, Schmidt, Milner, and Wiechmann (2004). These formulations have stimulated numerous studies directed toward identifying basic team-level motivation processes that contribute to team performance over time. Marks et al. (2001) proposed a dynamic, three-dimensional model of teamwork processes similar in several ways to individual-level models of motivation. In the Marks et al. (2001) model, *team transition processes* refer to the cognitive and planning activities performed by team members before and between performance episodes, including, for example, mission analysis, goal formulation, and strategic planning. The second set of team-level processes, called *action processes*, refers to activities that take place during goal pursuit, including, for example, team-level monitoring, coordination, and adjustment of team member behaviors and team-level goals.

Marks et al. (2001) also posited a third set of unique team-level processes, that is, team-level processes directed toward the management of social, interpersonal interactions among team members. This third set of interpersonal processes operates during both the transition and action phases. Team-level regulatory activities in this dimension focus on modulating team member conflicts, supporting team member motivation, and helping team members manage the affective demands of task work. Results of a recent meta-analysis by LePine, Piccolo, Jackson, Mathieu, and Saul (2008) provide empirical support for the Marks et al. (2001) formulation, and show a significant positive relationship between these processes, team performance, and team member satisfaction.

In 2006, Chen and Kanfer proposed a complementary motivational model of individual and team-level processes. Extending individual-level motivation formulations, Chen and Kanfer proposed a parallel and homologous relationship between individual and team-level motivation processes and performance. As shown in Figure 4.1, the Chen and Kanfer model follows the Marks et al. (2001) model by delineating two primary team-level motivation processes: goal choice and goal striving. Similar to Marks et al. (2001), Chen and Kanfer described team-level goal generation processes as those involving goal choice and planning activities. With

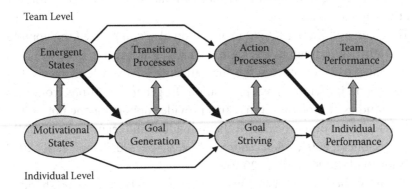

FIGURE 4.1
An integrative model of individual and team motivation. (Modified from Chen & Kanfer, *Research in Organizational Behavior*, 27, 223–267, 2006).

respect to the team-level action processes in the Marks et al. (2001) model, Chen and Kanfer posited a functionally homologous set of goal-striving processes directed toward monitoring team performance; evaluating team performance and progress relative to the team goal; and understanding team reactions, including team-level efficacy judgments.

Chen and Kanfer (2006) did not posit a third dimension of processes pertaining to the management of interpersonal dynamics, but rather focused on two other aspects of the common framework. First, Chen and Kanfer proposed a distinction between ambient and discretionary external (contextual) forces that influence both individual-level and team-level motivation (Hackman, 1992). *Ambient influences* on teams and their members include factors such as the physical condition in which the team and its members perform (Hackman, 1992). An important characteristic of ambient influences is their exogenous origin and their impact on all team members. In contrast, *discretionary forces* represent external factors that are not experienced in a uniform way by the team and all of its members. One example of discretionary stimuli (that exert an external influence on one member of the team but not another or at the team level) is when a leader admonishes a specific team member. Ambient and discretionary stimuli are posited to influence motivation through their effects on both team-level emergent states and individual-level motivational states. In addition to these external influences on motivation at both the individual level and team level, Chen and Kanfer (2006) also noted that internal forces (i.e., individual differences in personality traits) also exert a direct effect on individual-level motivational states, but not team-level motivation processes.

The Chen and Kanfer (2006) formulation also emphasized the homologous nature of individual-level and team-level motivation processes, and proposed cross-level effects for the influence of team-level motivation processes on individual-level motivation. In general, findings from multilevel studies of motivation in teams provide support for the notion that the architecture of motivation at the individual and team levels is similar (Chen & Bliese, 2002; Chen, Thomas, & Wallace, 2005; Chen et al., 2002; DeShon et al., 2004; Gibson, 2001).

Recent studies also indicate important cross-level effects, as might occur when a team-level emergent state (e.g., team efficacy) exerts influence on individual team member motivation and performance. Chen et al. (2009), for example, examined the impact of motivational variables at the team level on individual-level motivation. As expected, they found that team efficacy exerted a significant positive influence on activities during goal execution. In addition, however, team efficacy had a positive indirect influence on individual behavior through its effects on self-efficacy. That is, emergent states at the team level affected not only team-level action processes but also individual-level motivation and behavior. The demonstration of cross-level effects on motivation in the team context indicates a critical pathway in the process by which teams affect individual performance (Chen & Kanfer, 2006).

In the Chen and Kanfer (2006) model, team-level goal processes are proposed to exert cross-level effects on the direction of team member attention and intensity of effort; however, team-level goals may or may not specify *how* personal resources should be allocated. Team-level processes establish team-level goals, such as winning a sports competition, creating a new market slogan, or developing a new curriculum. These team-level outcome goals direct team member attention and provide information to team members about the general intensity of effort that is likely to be required for team-level goals to be accomplished.

Summary

Over the past decade, research and theory on team processes have burgeoned (see Mathieu et al., 2008). The Marks et al. (2001) model and associated research provide support for homology between individual-level and team-level performance processes, and Chen and Kanfer (2006) further link these processes to motivational phenomena. Findings by Chen et al. (2007, 2009) have also begun to delineate the cross-level pathways by which team-level activities affect individual-level motivational processes. From a motivational perspective, however, it is also important to consider how team member dispositions affect team-level motivation.

Team Member Attributes and Motivation in and of Teams

Chen and Kanfer (2006) pointed out that cross-level motivational influences do not singularly determine either individual or team performance. As noted above, individual differences in motives, knowledge, skills, and abilities also exert a direct influence on individual-level motivation and behavior. To date, the bulk of research in this area has focused on the impact of person attributes on interpersonal dynamics and behaviors that contribute to the disruption of team performance, including, for example, team member conflict (De Dreu & Weingart, 2003), lack of cooperation and low levels of helping behavior, the absence of a shared mental model, and deficits in team member motivation (e.g., Tesluk & Mathieu, 1999). Studies in this paradigm have examined the effects of surface-level team composition variables (e.g., race, age, and gender) on interpersonal teamwork and team performance (Hackman, 1987). For example, Wegge, Roth, Neubach, Schmidt, and Kanfer (2008) examined the relationship between surface-level person characteristics, such as age and gender, and team performance using Byrne's (Byrne & Griffitt, 1971) similarity–attraction theory and Tajfel and Turner's (1979) intergroup social identity theory. In this study, salient differences in surface-level person attributes were proposed to promote the development of different social identities and, in turn, social motives for different patterns of interpersonal communication and helping within the team. Wegge et al. found that greater variability in surface-level characteristics, such as age and gender, was negatively related to team performance. These findings suggest that the importance of surface-level composition variables on team-level performance is likely to occur as a consequence of how these composition variables affect patterns of communications during task performance.

Recent approaches have extended the study of team composition influences to the effects of deep-level composition variables, such as psychological traits and attitudes. In a meta-analysis of the relationship between deep-level team composition variables and team performance, Bell (2007) obtained support from field study findings for the positive relationship between team-level deep-level composition variables and team performance. Bell also found that team member personality and interests can influence team performance. Although interpersonal team member dynamics are the most likely mediator of the relationship between team member traits and team-level performance, there has been surprisingly little work done on the role of the interpersonal dynamics through which traits gain their influence on team and inter-team processes. Porter et al. (2003) examined the impact of team characteristics on one form of team-relevant interpersonal behavior, namely, engaging in behaviors that provide backup support for another team member. They found multiple interaction effects, such that team members high on extraversion and conscientiousness requested and received more backup behavior when the need for backup was perceived to be legitimate compared to team members low in these traits. Also, regardless of the legitimacy of need for backup behavior, team members who were high on emotional stability provided more backup to others than those low in emotional stability. Porter et al. showed that increasing levels of backup behavior were associated with higher levels of team performance. These findings suggest that team member trait variables influence both the initiation and receipt of task assistance from others. More research on the relationship between team member attributes and other positive interpersonal behaviors, such as coordination and planning, will help map the pathways by which interpersonal behaviors affect team performance.

Situational and Ambient Influences on Motivation in and of Teams

Individual and team-level motivation and performance may also be affected by the situational factors and ambient stimuli that characterize the performance setting. As discussed below, multiteam systems per se represent a potentially powerful ambient feature of the work environment that can have direct effects on individual-level and team-level motivation. In disasters, for example, the failure of teams tasked with rapid restoration of communications may directly curtail team-level coordination and support activities of rescue teams. Similarly, multiteam environments may directly affect individual team member motivation through ambient influences on goal setting, goal tenacity, and goal persistence as well as the ways in which an individual goes about accomplishing his or her role in the team.

A second situational influence on motivation in and of teams pertains to the strength of the situation (Meyer, Dalal, & Bonaccio, 2009; Mischel, 1968). Extending previous discussion on the determinants of individual-level motivation, situational strength may also mediate the impact of team-level attitudes and other deep-level composition variables on team-level motivation processes and team performance. In established and cohesive teams, situational strength is likely to be high due to role clarity and consistency. In the interstitial space between teams, however, situation strength is likely to be low because such interactions often occur spontaneously during performance and are typically not governed by the team. As a consequence, individual differences in conscious and nonconscious person attributes are likely to exert greater influence on motivation to initiate and sustain cross-team member exchanges.

MOTIVATION IN MULTITEAM SYSTEMS

Multiteam systems refer to socioemotional action structures in which teams with different cultures, norms, values, skill sets, and goals operate interdependently in the pursuit of a common goal (see Marks, DeChurch, Mathieu, Panzer, & Alonso, 2005; Zaccaro, Marks, & DeChurch, Chapter 1, this volume). Multiteam systems can be found in military, business, and health care settings, including, for example, teams of teams organized for disaster relief, new product development, space missions, and patient care. The use of multiteam systems has steadily increased over the past few decades as scientific and technological, sociopolitical, and economic changes have enabled governments and organizations to quickly bring together specialized teams for the accomplishment of complex goals.

In a seminal article, Marks, Mathieu, and Zaccaro (2001) described many of the important contextual features and task characteristics that distinguish multiteam systems from single teams. They suggest that multiteam systems are more vulnerable to performance derailment when communication networks among members of different teams are sparse or nonexistent. Support for this notion can be found in retrospective analyses of multiteam system effectiveness in response to crises such as Hurricane Katrina (Moynihan, 2008), in military missions such as the provincial reconstruction initiative in Afghanistan (2002–2005; Perito, 2005), and in the health care system (Institute of Medicine, 1999) that emphasize the deleterious effects of poor interteam communications, low levels of cooperation among members of different teams, and interteam conflict. In this section, we describe the motivational issues involved in poor interteam communications and the motivational forces that affect interteam member interactions.

High levels of process interdependence in multiteam systems require that members are also proficient in establishing and maintaining positive cross-team communications. However, as noted previously, the context in which these communications develop and stabilize is often quite different from the single-team performance context. In contrast to the single-team context, where situational strength is often high, situational strength in interteam and cross-team member communications is often low. As a consequence, individual-level motivation processes should play a larger role in interteam communications and in cross-team member cooperation and conflict.

Interteam Communications

From a motivational perspective, poor interteam communications represent a failure in system-level regulatory control, comparable to a failure in self-control at the individual level of analysis. At the team level, the allocation of individual and team resources to team task performance affords more attractive, reliable, and immediate rewards than allocation of resources to the development of interteam communications. In high-urgency environments, for example, the high-performance demands of the medical transport team to keep the patient alive may reduce time and effort for communicating with the waiting hospital medical team. Individual and team policies that direct resources toward team task accomplishment typically yield higher levels of team performance, and offer team members intrinsic rewards such as pride in team performance and a sense of competency. In medical transport, for example, close teamwork that successfully keeps the patient alive during transit is a powerful team and team member reward. In contrast, interteam communications are often time-consuming and can divert critical resources away from team-level performance. In the demanding medical transport team environment, team performance is likely to suffer when a member of the team redirects his or her attention to communications rather than immediate task performance. In addition, the successful development of interteam communication processes also typically offers few immediate or tangible rewards at either the team or individual level. Although teams and their members often acknowledge the importance of multiteam communications, there are typically no rewards (and may even be negative consequences) associated with diverting one's attention away from immediate task performance and toward communications with the hospital medical team. As a consequence, all other things being equal, in the absence of a specific intervention to reward such "off-team task" activities, teams and their members can be expected to allocate most or all resources toward team performance rather than toward interteam communication activities.

In the longer term, however, such team-level allocation policies hinder multiteam system performance by underfunding the development of interteam communications that are necessary for multiteam system performance. Over time, the cost of team-first resource allocation strategies on the multiteam system is also likely to exert a negative impact on the team, as interteam coordination problems impede team performance. The factors that contribute to this regulatory control problem are discussed in greater detail in the next section.

Why Teams Favor Within-Team Resource Allocation Policies

One of the most fundamental influences on how teams formulate resource allocation policies relates to the way that multisystem goals are articulated. In many instances, multisystem goals are articulated with respect to an outcome, but fail to specify the advantages (to teams) associated with interteam communication or the methods by which teams can effectively interface to achieve the all-team goal. Explicit multiteam system goals, such as saving a patient's life, for example, imply cooperation and communication between teams of physicians and nurses, but do not specify the way that teams and team members are to work together for goal accomplishment or the reward structure for such behaviors. When multiteam goals do not reward or articulate the benefits of proactive interteam communication for the *team*, teams are unlikely to construe such activities as part of their performance mandate. As a consequence, the allocation of team resources to communication activities is likely to be problem based, for example, when the engineering team runs into a problem during construction of a prototype and needs assistance from the development team. When teams do not foresee the need for assistance from other teams during goal planning, interteam communications are more likely to occur during the later action phase of team performance. Attempts to establish communications in goal pursuit during the action phase are also likely to have a greater negative impact on team performance, such as when the engineering team must stop its activities until it gets information from the development team.

Even when multisystem goals clearly articulate the need and rewards associated with interteam communications, teams may be reluctant to allocate critical resources that are needed for high levels of team performance to activities that do not directly and immediately contribute to team performance. Teams may also perceive that interteam communication activities will increase overall resource demands and overtax team members. In multiteam environments, effective team performance is often dependent on the rapid generation of goals and action plans, and the implementation of well-practiced action processes to manage team member activities. A team of firefighters, for example, typically comes to the multiteam environment with well-practiced strategies for rapid goal planning and explicit, well-trained, and efficient strategies for coordinating action to accomplish the goal. The inclusion of interteam communication activities may hamper goal planning and disrupt well-practiced strategies for action management. For example, team differences in composition, culture, identity, and behavioral norms may slow interteam communications and delay team goal planning. Interteam communication activities may also reduce available resources that can be devoted to team performance processes and increase team member stress, such as when an individual responsible for monitoring progress in the control of a fire must also communicate with police teams about roads that must be closed.

The third and perhaps most important motivation for the failure to allocate resources beyond team performance pertains to the strong intrinsic and extrinsic rewards associated with within-team resource allocations. Both teams and team members benefit from resource allocations that increase team performance. At the team level, high levels of team performance contribute to extrinsic rewards, such as recognition from others. High levels of team performance may also contribute to intrinsic rewards or outcomes associated with performance enjoyment, such as increased team cohesion, and helping behaviors (e.g., backing-up behaviors) that also promote sustained performance. At the individual level, team-first resource allocation policies that contribute to team performance promote self-efficacy, a sense of competency, and satisfaction of affiliation and achievement motives. As a consequence, effective incentives for teams and individuals to allocate resources to activities that do not directly contribute to team performance must be clear, immediate, and of high value to the team and/or individual.

Recent empirical evidence for the importance of reward structure to team and individual resource allocation policies is provided by Pearsall, Christian, and Ellis (2010) in a study investigating the influence of different reward structures on team member resource allocation policies within a team. Pearsall et al. found that the use of hybrid rewards—contingent on *both* individual and team-level performance outcomes—yielded more effective resource allocation information policies, reduced declines in effort, and resulted in higher levels of performance than the use of either individual or shared rewards. These findings suggest that simultaneous team and individual rewards for interteam communications may be useful in overcoming the natural barriers to time and effort directed beyond team performance. Similarly, research by Crown and Rosse (1995) showed that the introduction of both group-centric individual goals as well as group goals increased overall team performance in an interdependent task. Moreover, Crown and Rosse (1995) also showed that combining both group goals and group-centric individual goals interacted with respect to their effects on effort. The results from these studies that utilized a "fusion" structure of rewards and goals to increase overall team performance are encouraging for potential adaption in the MTS environment.

Goal Orientation and Interteam Communications

Team-level goals develop in the context of broader multisystem goals. As noted previously, multisystem goals are often ill defined with regard to the rewards and processes involved in effective interteam communications. In some cases, however, there are few extrinsic rewards for interteam communications and support behaviors. Nonetheless, the perceived purpose associated with the multiteam system goal may operate as an important determinant of team willingness to incorporate interteam processes in team-level goal formulation and action planning.

Findings in the individual performance literature indicate that people who adopt approach-oriented or learning orientations to goal accomplishment employ different self-regulatory strategies than people who adopt avoidance-oriented or performance orientations to goal accomplishment (e.g., Dweck & Leggett, 1988). Extending this analysis to the team level, Gully and Phillips (2005) suggested that a team's goal orientation may exert cross-level effects on individual-level motivation and performance. Specifically, they suggest that teams that adopt learning goal orientations may be more likely to develop situated team task goals and employ more inclusive action processes than teams that adopt a performance orientation to goal accomplishment. Indirect support for this notion is provided by findings obtained by LePine (2005) and Porter (2005) on the effects of goal orientation on team processes and performance. Porter found that teams with a *learning goal orientation* (operationalized as the mean goal orientation of individuals comprising the team) engaged in more backing-up behaviors than teams that held a performance goal orientation. LePine (2005) found that teams composed of members who held a learning goal orientation were more successful in adapting to an unexpected problem during performance than teams composed of individuals holding a performance goal orientation. They also noted that teams with members high in performance orientation communicated more about the team goal than individuals high in learning goal orientation. These findings suggest that understanding the leader, task, and contextual determinants and the within- and cross-team behavioral consequences of different team-level goal orientations in the multiteam system context is the next logical step in this stream of research.

Cross-Team Member Interactions

As discussed previously, team-level variables represent an important influence on team member propensity to engage in cross-team member interactions. For example, we would expect that individuals who are members of strong, cohesive teams that explicitly discourage interteam interactions will be less likely to initiate and engage in interteam interactions, and report more negative experiences when such interactions take place. Members of cohesive teams are likely to also express more negative attitudes toward other teams than individuals who are members of less cohesive teams or persons in teams that explicitly endorse cross-team member interactions.

Beyond cross-level effects of strong team-level variables, however, there are potentially important similarities and differences in the context in which within-team and cross-team member interactions occur. Similar to within-team interactions, many cross-team interactions are discretionary and occur as a joint function of propinquity and individual propensities. For example, individuals who are high in extraversion are more likely to initiate and enjoy conversation with a stranger eating at the same table than individuals low in extraversion. When members of different teams come into proximity, an individual's traits and skills are likely to be the most important determinants of the initiation, frequency, and content of cross-team member interactions. Research to examine the influence of different personality traits (e.g., neuroticism) on cross-team interactions in different contexts is needed to evaluate this hypothesis.

Another similarity in within-team and cross-team contexts pertains to the factors that motivate social interaction. Both within teams and across teams, individuals often initiate interaction with others for the purpose of requesting assistance in accomplishing specific tasks. For example, police officers may ask emergency medical technicians (EMTs) to provide assistance in clearing an area when there are no other police officers available to assist. Similarly, EMTs may ask police officers to provide information about the most efficient methods of evacuation. Similar to the team context, direct cross-team member requests for assistance may be more rapid and efficient than team-to-team requests for assistance.

However, there are also a number of important psychological differences between the within-team and cross-team interaction contexts. Within a team, interactions typically occur among team members who share a common work culture and environment (relative to members of other teams). Interactions within a team typically conform to shared behavioral norms and conventions. Task-driven interactions within a team are often oriented toward information sharing for the purpose of common goal accomplishment. In contrast, cross-team member interactions often occur in unfamiliar environments and involve interactions in which behavioral norms and values may be only partially developed and shared. For example, although all members of the interprofessional team may share a common norm for how to begin conversation, internalized professional norms regarding the appropriate way to raise questions or express disagreement with others may greatly differ among interprofessional team members.

Opportunities for conflict resolution are also often quite different in within-team versus cross-team contexts. Within a team, conflicts between team members are often readily detected and may be legitimately resolved by other team members. In multiteam systems, however, cross-team member interactions often occur "offline" and beyond formal team-based channels for conflict resolution. In interteam interactions, misunderstandings that generate negative affective states in one or more parties are likely to go unresolved, unnoticed by team leaders, or ignored by others until the intensity of the conflict creates a clear impediment to interteam cooperation. Among physicians and social workers, for example, repeated interactions in which a physician expresses little regard for a patient's concern (a core value in social work) may strengthen a social worker's negative stereotype of physicians, and ultimately lead the social worker to refuse to share valuable patient information with any physician. The absence of regular mechanisms for conflict resolution in the cross-team context suggests that greater attention be given to methods that facilitate the early identification and remediation of cross-team member conflicts.

As Weiss and Cropanzano (1996) suggested, social interactions involve affectively charged events or episodes that afford intrinsic and extrinsic rewards. Opportunistic cross-team interactions may be intrinsically motivated and associated with the pleasure derived from the interaction per se. Other potential intrinsic rewards include increased feelings of affiliation, competence, control, or power that are experienced during or after the interaction. Extrinsic rewards for cross-member interactions include those outcomes that provide the individual with information or resources useful for attainment of individual or team-level goals, such as learning where to obtain materials that are critically needed by the team, or the protocol for indicating appreciation in the other team's culture. Of course, cross-member interactions may also result in negative outcomes, including the instigation of negative emotions such as anger, fear, or feelings of incompetence. Anticipation of negative outcomes may inhibit an individual's initiation of cross-member interactions despite situational favorability.

To date, little is known about which traits are most closely associated with the initiation and maintenance of cross-team interactions. However, research findings on the determinants of backing-up behavior within teams suggest several traits, action tendencies, and contextual factors that may be important determinants of cross-team member interactions (Barnes, Hollenbeck, Wagner, DeRue, & Nahrgang, 2008; McIntyre & Salas, 1995; Porter, 2005; Porter et al., 2003). Porter et al. examined backing-up behavior among individuals in four-person groups performing a high-fidelity command-and-control simulation. They found that individuals high in extraversion were more likely to seek help from other team members than individuals low on extraversion. Porter et al. also found that conscientious and extraversion interacted with the perceived legitimacy of helping requests, such that persons high in conscientiousness or extraversion tended to request help only when such help was appropriate. The Porter et al. findings are consistent with research findings in the cultural intelligence literature that indicate that extraversion is positively associated with motivation for cross-cultural interactions and adjustment. In the context of cross-team member behavior, these findings suggest that individuals high in extraversion may be more likely to initiate interactions and to seek assistance from individuals in other teams than persons low in extraversion. Therefore, it is reasonable to ask extraverts to serve as the linking members to other teams. Further research is needed, however, to understand the form, content, and pattern of helping requests in cross-team member interactions.

Communications among individuals in different teams, such as a request for assistance, set in motion relationships that unfold over time and offer the opportunity for further cooperation between the parties as well as expectations of reciprocity. Again, evidence on the factors that affect relationships within a team may be fruitfully extrapolated to understand the determinants and consequences of behavior in cross-team member interactions. In the context of a single team, Harrison, Price, Gavin, and Florey (2002) examined college student teams performing a class project over a 4-month period. As expected, Harrison et al. found that over time and repeated collaboration, the salience of surface-level differences declined. However, deep-level differences in values were not significant, but deep-level attitudes related to team task meaningfulness and outcome importance increase in salience over time.

The Harrison et al. (2002) findings are particularly relevant to the multiteam context, where differences in surface-level characteristics, such as uniforms, language, and behavior patterns, are typically the most salient features in initial cross-team interactions. Although the Harrison et al. findings must be generalized with caution to the multiteam system environment and cross-team interactions, the results are provocative with respect to understanding cross-team relationships over time. Specifically, the Harrison et al. findings suggest three pivotal determinants of successful cross-team member relations: (a) repeated collaborative interactions, (b) a shift to a shared perspective regarding the salience and valence of attitudes associated with the accomplishment of multiteam system goals, and (c) the effective modulation of deep-level variables (e.g., values) that may create conflicts and negative affective reactions that divert attention away from multiteam system goals. It may also be that different traits and action tendencies drive the initiation of cross-team member interactions and the development of these interactions into viable relationships over time. For example, extraverts may successfully initiate cross-team interactions but may encounter difficulty in maintaining the relationship over time if they lack sufficient skill in recognizing and modulating emotions that arise during interactions.

Preparatory Strategies for Facilitating Cross-Member Interactions

There is a widespread belief that cross-cultural and cross-team interactions are less frequent and less effective when individuals lack sufficient information about the other individual's world, including culture, values, and behavioral norms. A similar notion suggests why cross-training is often recommended and implemented (e.g., Volpe, Cannon-Bowers, Salas, & Spector, 1996). In the expatriate domain, organizations have increasingly sought to facilitate expatriate adjustment to new cultures and practices by providing individuals with cultural information and training in cross-cultural interactions (Fiedler, Mitchell, & Triandis, 1971). Consistent with theories of skill acquisition, cross-cultural interaction training is posited to enhance interaction outcomes by providing individuals with greater skill in managing communications and emotions during cross-cultural exchanges. The training approach has also become quite popular in the health care professions, where interprofessional teams are used with increasing frequency in patient care to reduce medical errors and improve patient care. With the increased use of interprofessional teams, many medical schools and nursing programs have incorporated interprofessional team training into their curricula (Alonso et al., 2006). In these programs, individuals are encouraged to become more knowledgeable about other relevant professional cultures (e.g., in nursing or medicine) and associated communication patterns prior to working in a high-stakes interprofessional team environment (Robertson et al., 2009). Although preparatory cultural training appears beneficial in the avoidance of interactions that generate negative affective states, less is known about how such training affects the initiation of cross-team interactions.

FUTURE DIRECTIONS

Research on motivation in and of teams has burgeoned during the past decade. Findings to date suggest a functional homology between motivational mechanisms at the individual and team levels, and provide support for the Marks et al. (2001) model of transition and action processes. Multilevel research on team motivation also indicates important cross-level effects between motivational mechanisms at the individual and team levels, and provides initial support for the Chen and Kanfer (2006) model of motivation in team contexts.

Motivation at the individual level for performance in the multiteam system environment is complex and overdetermined. Attributes of the multiteam system goal, team composition variables, team-level action strategies used to accomplish the team goal, individual differences in personality traits and skill competencies, and situational strength all play a role in determining interteam member interactions.

Recent work on the role of motivation in interteam communications and cross-team member interactions has drawn from individual-level theories that emphasize the way that an individual's goals affect goal choice and goal pursuit. In this chapter, we suggest that the utility of these motivational formulations may be further enhanced by taking into account unique features of multiteam systems. Specifically, we note that communication behaviors of interest (i.e., interteam and cross-team member communication) most often occur in a psychological and situational space that is quite different from the psychological processes and environment in which teams and team members perform their primary tasks. Interteam communications are often ill defined in multiteam system goals and insufficiently rewarded compared to the intrinsic and extrinsic incentives associated with within-team resource allocation policies. Safeguards for preventing misunderstandings and deescalating affectively driven conflicts in cross-team member interactions do not typically exist. Rather, the negative outcomes of such communications reported to other team members are likely to be more salient and influential in attitude formation than outcomes of a positive nature. The high resource costs associated with engaging in effective interteam and cross-team member interactions tend to lead teams and their members to exclude these domains in early goal generation and action processes. Finally, unlike the positive orientation taken to achieve high levels of performance in the pursuit of team task goals, motivation and performance in the domain of interteam and cross-team member interactions are often problem driven rather than solution focused. Taken together, in the absence of proactive design efforts, motivation on average for team performance activities and within team interactions is likely to be stronger than motivation for interteam and cross-team member interactions.

At the same time, our motivational analysis suggests that interteam and cross-team member communications are driven by different forces. Interteam communications rely on goal conceptualizations and reward structures that promote team and individual resource allocation to activities beyond team performance. In contrast, cross-team member interactions are likely to be importantly influenced by person traits, action tendencies, and emotion-related skills. As observers of multiteam systems have often commented, team member competencies in interteam and cross-team member interactions do not appear to be highly related to factors that predict technical job performance.

Team member traits and skills may also promote high levels of cross-team member communications even when interteam communications are poor. Based on this review, we suggest two potentially promising areas for future research on motivation in multiteam systems.

The Impact of Ambient and Discretionary Stimuli on Team-Level Goal Generation and Action Processes

The way in which multiteam system goals influence team-level goals and action processes remains poorly understood. Research is recommended to understand the relationship between multiteam system goals, multiteam system climates (ambient stimuli), and leader behaviors (discretionary stimuli; see DeChurch & Marks, 2006) and their respective effects on team-level goal orientation with respect to scope (e.g., interteam communications) and direction (e.g., promotion vs. prevention; Crowe & Higgins, 1997). In the health care system, for example, *patient-centered care* can be conceptualized as an effort to establish a multiteam system climate that subordinates team-level goals and practices to superordinate goals that promote interteam cooperation and increased cross-team member interactions.

In the multiteam system environment, leaders play a major role in the interpretation and implementation of reward structures to promote goal accomplishment (Marks et al., 2005). Leaders inform and motivate team members through direct and indirect communication channels. In a multiteam system, team leaders may motivate interteam communications and opportunistic cross-team member interactions by disseminating knowledge about other teams that increases the perceived utility of interteam communications, fosters cross-team knowledge, and/or encourages the development of a broadened team identity. Leader behaviors that encourage learning and promotion-oriented team goal orientations may further encourage cross-team member interactions. Leaders may also increase motivation for interteam communications by assigning interteam communication tasks in pairs that contain a highly skilled communicator and a less skilled communicator. The relative efficiency of different leader strategies to increase interteam and cross-team member interactions will require further study.

Trait, Interest, and Skill Determinants of Motivation for Cross-Team Member Interactions

Our motivational analysis suggests that individual differences in nonability traits and skills play a major role in the initiation and success of cross-team member interactions. Scattered findings in the team and expatriate motivation literature suggest that individual differences in select personality traits, interests, and emotion recognition and regulation skills figure prominently in an individual's motivation and performance in interactions with persons who are different from those of one's referent culture. Findings in the team literature also suggest that the factors that influence the initiation of cross-team member interactions may be distinguished from the factors that influence the subsequent development of more binding social relations (e.g., Harrison et al., 2002). Research to further examine the influence of person and temporal factors on the form and intensity of cross-team member interactions in both strong and weak situations will likely have important practical implications for staffing and task assignments.

At the broadest level, most people who work in multiteam systems agree with the notion that cooperation and communication between teams and across members of different teams enhance multiteam system performance. The problem arises in action, as individuals respond individually and collectively to experienced and perceived gains and losses associated with different resource allocation policies and reward or incentive structures. Incentive structures and resource scarcity often support the development of team-first resource allocation policies, even when such policies are known to contribute to team performance problems over time. What is less well known are the factors and interventions that may be effective in mitigating these trends and promoting sustained allocation of resources toward interteam and cross-team member inter-actions and cooperation. Hopefully, the analysis presented in this chap-ter will stimulate new streams of inquiry to help answer the question of how best to promote and reward interteam communication and cooper-ation as well as cross-team member relations in high-risk work settings.

REFERENCES

Alonso, A., Baker, D. P., Holtzman, A., Day, R., King, H. B., Toomey, L. M., et al. (2006). Reducing medical error in the military health system: How can team training help? *Human Resources Management Review, 16,* 396–415.

Armor, D. A., & Taylor, S. E. (2003). The effects of mindset on behavior: Self-regulation in deliberative and implemental frames of mind. *Personality and Social Psychology Bulletin, 20,* 86–95.

Baker, D. P., Salas, E., King, H., Battles, J., & Barach, P. (2005). The role of teamwork in the professional education of physicians: Current status and assessment recommenda-tions. *Joint Commission Journal on Quality and Patient Safety, 31*(18), 185–202.

Barnes, C. M., Hollenbeck, J. R., Wagner, D. T., DeRue, D. S., & Nahrgang, J. D. (2008). Harmful help: The costs of backing-up behavior in teams. *Journal of Applied Psychology, 93,* 529–539.

Barrick, M. R., & Mount, M. K. (1991). The big five personality dimensions and job perfor-mance: A meta-analysis. *Personnel Psychology, 44*(1), 1–26.

Beersma, B., Hollenbeck, J. R., Humphrey, S. E., Moon, H., Conglon, D. E., & Ilgen, D. R. (2003). Cooperation, competition, and team performance: Toward a contingency approach. *Academy of Management Journal, 46*(5), 572–590.

Bell, S. T. (2007). Deep-level composition variables as predictors of team performance: A meta-analysis. *Journal of Applied Psychology, 92,* 595–615.

Byrne, D., & Griffitt, W. (1971). Interpersonal attraction. *Annual Review of Psychology, 24,* 317–336.

Chatman, J. A., & Flynn, F. J. (2001). The influence of demographic heterogeneity on the emergence and consequences of cooperative norms in work teams. *Academy of Management Journal, 44*(5), 956–974.

Chen, C. C., & Chiu, S. F. (2009). The mediating role of job involvement in the relationship between job characteristics and organizational citizenship behavior. *Journal of Social Psychology, 149*(4), 474–494.

Chen, G., & Bliese, P. (2002). The role of different levels of leadership in predicting self and collective efficacy: Evidence for discontinuity. *Journal of Applied Psychology, 87,* 549–556.

Chen, G., & Kanfer, R. (2006). Toward a systems theory of motivated behavior in work teams. *Research in Organizational Behavior, 27,* 223–267.

Chen, G., Kanfer, R., DeShon, R. P., Mathieu, J. E., & Kozlowski, S. W. J. (2009). The moti-vating potential of teams: A test and extension of Chen and Kanfer's (2006) model. *Organizational Behavior and Human Decision Processes, 110,* 45–55.

Chen, G., Kirkman, B. L., Kanfer, R., Allen, D., & Rosen, B. (2007). A multilevel study of leadership, empowerment, and performance in teams. *Journal of Applied Psychology, 92*, 341–346.

Chen, G., Thomas, G., & Wallace, C. (2005). A multilevel examination of the relationships among training outcomes, mediating regulatory processes, and adaptive performance. *Journal of Applied Psychology, 90*, 827–841.

Chen, G., Weber, S. S., Mathieu, J. E., Bliese, P. D., Payne, S. C., Born, D. H., et al. (2002). Simultaneous examination of the antecedents and consequences of efficacy beliefs at multiple levels of analysis. *Human Performance, 15*, 381–410.

Crowe, E., & Higgins, E. T. (1997). Regulatory focus and strategic inclinations: Promotion and prevention in decision-making. *Organizational Behavior and Human Decision Processes, 69*(2), 117–132.

Crown, D. F., & Rosse, J. G. (1995). Yours, mine, and ours: Facilitating group productivity through the integration of individual and group goals. *Organizational Behavior and Human Decision Processes, 64*, 138–150.

DeChurch, L. A., & Marks, M. A. (2006). Leadership in multiteam systems. *Journal of Applied Pscychology, 91*, 311–329.

Deci, E. L., & Ryan, R. M. (1985). *Intrinsic motivation and self-determination of behavior.* New York: Plenum.

De Dreu, C. K. W., & Weingart, L. R. (2003). Task versus relationship conflict and team effectiveness: A meta-analysis. *Journal of Applied Psychology, 88*, 741–749.

DeShon, R. P., Kozlowski, S. W. J., Schmidt, A. M., Milner, K. R., & Wiechmann, D. (2004). Multiple goal feedback effects on the regulation of individual and team performance in training. *Journal of Applied Psychology, 89*, 1035–1056.

Dweck, C. S. (1986). Motivational processes affecting learning. *American Psychologist, 41*, 1040–1048.

Dweck, C. S., & Leggett, E. L. (1988). A social-cognitive approach to motivation and personality. *Psychological Review, 95*, 256–273.

Fiedler, F. E., Mitchell, T., & Triandis, H. C. (1971). The culture assimilator: An approach to cross-cultural training. *Journal of Applied Psychology, 55*, 95–102.

Gibson, C. B. (2001). Me and us: Differential relationships among goal-setting, training, efficacy, and effectiveness at the individual and team level. *Journal of Organizational Behavior, 22*(7), 789–808.

Gollwitzer, P. M. (1990). Action phases and mind-sets. In E. T. Higgins & R. M. Sorrentino (Eds.), *Handbook of motivation and cognition* (Vol. 2, pp. 53–92). New York: Guilford Press.

Gollwitzer, P. M. (2003). Why we thought that action mind-sets affect illusions of control. *Psychological Inquiry, 14*(3–4), 261–269.

Gollwitzer, P. M., & Kinney, R. F. (1989). Effects of deliberative and implemental mind-sets in the control of action. *Journal of Personality and Social Psychology, 59*, 1119–1127.

Gray, J. A. (1987). The neuropsychology of emotion and personality. In S. M. Stahl, S. D. Iversen, & E. C. Goodman (Eds.), *Cognitive neurochemistry* (pp. 171–190). Oxford: Oxford University Press.

Gully, S. M., & Phillips, J. M. (2005). A multilevel application of learning and performance orientations to individual, group, and organizational outcomes. In J. Martocchio (Ed.), *Research in personnel and human resources management* (Vol. 24, pp. 1–52). Greenwich, CT: JAI/Elsevier Science.

Guzzo, R. A. (1979). Types of rewards, cognitions, and work motivation. *Academy of Management Review, 4*(1), 75–86.

Hackman, J. R. (1987). The design of workteams. In L. Hoch (Ed.), *Handbook of organizational behavior* (pp. 315–342). Englewood Cliffs, NJ: Prentice Hall.

Hackman, J. R. (1992). Group influences on individuals in organizations. In M. D. Dunnette & L. M. Hough (Eds.), *Handbook of industrial and organizational psychology* (Vol. 3, pp. 199–267). Palo Alto, CA: Consulting Psychologists Press.

Harrison, D. A., Price, K. H., Gavin, J. H., & Florey, A. T. (2002). Time, teams, and task performance: Changing effects of diversity on group functioning. *Academy of Management Journal, 45*, 1029–1045.

Higgins, E. T. (1998). Promotion and prevention: Regulatory focus as a motivational principle. In M. P. Zanna (Ed.), *Advances in experimental social psychology* (Vol. 30, pp. 1–46). New York: Academic Press.

Institute of Medicine. (1999). *To err is human: Building a safer health system*. Washington, DC: National Academy Press.

Kanfer, R. (2010). Work motivation: Theory, practice, and future directions. In S. W. J. Kozlowski (Ed.), *The Oxford handbook of industrial and organizational psychology*. New York: Oxford University Press.

Kanfer, R., & Ackerman, P. L. (1989). Motivation and cognitive abilities: An integrative/aptitude-treatment interaction approach to skill acquisition. *Journal of Applied Psychology—Monograph, 74*, 657–690.

Kozlowski, S. W. J., & Klein, K. J. (2000). A multilevel approach to theory and research in organizations: Contextual, temporal, and emergent processes. In K. J. Klein & S. W. J. Kozlowski (Eds.), *Multilevel theory, research, and methods in organizations: Foundations, extensions, and new directions* (pp. 3–90). San Francisco: Jossey-Bass.

LePine, J. A. (2005). Adaptation of teams in response to unforeseen change: Effects of goal difficulty and team composition in terms of cognitive ability and goal orientation. *Journal of Applied Psychology, 90*, 1153–1167.

LePine, J. A., Piccolo, R. F., Jackson, C. L., Mathieu, J. E., & Saul, J. R. (2008). A meta-analysis of teamwork processes: Tests of a multidimensional model and relationships with team effectiveness criteria. *Personnel Psychology, 61*, 273–307.

Locke, E. A., & Latham, G. P. (2006). New directions in goal-setting theory. *Current Directions in Psychological Science, 15*(5), 265–268.

Marks, M. A., DeChurch, L. A., Mathieu, J. E., Panzer, F. J., & Alonso, A. (2005). Teamwork in multiteam systems. *Journal of Applied Psychology, 90*, 964–971.

Marks, M. A., Mathieu, J. E., & Zaccaro, S. J. (2001). A temporally based framework and taxonomy of team processes. *Academy of Management Review, 26*, 356–376.

Mathieu, J. E., Maynard, M. T., Rapp, T. L., & Gilson, L. L. (2008). Team effectiveness 1997–2007: A review of recent advancements and a glimpse into the future. *Journal of Management, 34*, 410–476.

McClelland, D. C. (1987). *Human motivation*. New York: Cambridge University Press.

McIntyre, R. M., & Salas, E. (1995). Measuring and managing for team performance: Lessons from complex environments. In R. A. Guzzo & E. Salas (Eds.), *Team effectiveness and decision-making in organizations* (pp. 9–45). San Francisco: Jossey-Bass.

Meyer, R. D., Dalal, R. S., & Bonaccio, S. (2009). A meta-analytic investigation into the moderating effects of situational strength on the conscientiousness-performance relationship. *Journal of Organizational Behavior, 30*, 1077–1102.

Meyer, R. D., Dalal, R. S., & Hermida, R. (2009). A review and synthesis of situational strength in the organizational sciences. *Journal of Management, 36*, 121–140.

Mischel, W. (1968). *Personality and assessment*. New York: Wiley.

Moynihan, D. P. (2008). Learning under uncertainty: Networks in crisis management. *Public Administration Review, 68*(2), 350–361.

Nicholls, J. (1984). Conceptions of ability, subjective experience, task choice, and performance. *Psychological Review, 91*, 328–346.

Nygard, R. (1981). Toward an interactional psychology: Models from achievement motivation research. *Journal of Personality, 49*(4), 363–387.

Oldham, G. R., & Hackman, J. R. (1980). Work design in organizational context. In B. M. Staw & L. L. Cummings (Eds.), *Research in organizational behavior* (pp. 247–278). Greenwich, CT: JAI.

Pearsall, M. J., Christian, M. S., & Ellis, A. P. J. (2010). Motivating interdependent teams: Individual rewards, shared rewards or something in between? *Journal of Applied Psychology, 95*, 183–191.

Perito, R. (2005). The U.S. experience with provincial reconstruction teams in Afghanistan: Lessons identified (Special Report No. 152). Washington, DC: U.S. Institute of Peace.

Pinder, C. C. (1998). *Work motivation in organizational behavior*. Upper Saddle River, NJ: Prentice Hall.

Porter, C. O. L. H. (2005). Goal orientation: Effects on backing up behavior, performance, efficacy, and commitment in teams. *Journal of Applied Psychology, 90*, 811–818.

Porter, C. O. L. H., Hollenbeck, J. R., Ilgen, D. R., Ellis, A. P. J., West, B. J., & Moon, H. (2003). Backing up behaviors in teams: The role of personality and legitimacy of need. *Journal of Applied Psychology, 88*, 391–403.

Robertson, B., Schumacher, L., Gosman, G., Kanfer, R., Kelly, M., & DeVita, M. (2009). Simulation-based crisis team training for multidisciplinary obstetric providers. *Simulation in Healthcare, 4*(2), 77–83.

Tajfel, H., & Turner, J. C. (1979). An integrative theory of intergroup conflict. In W. G. Austin & S. Worchel (Eds.), *The social psychology of intergroup relations*. Monterey, CA: Brooks-Cole.

Taylor, S. E., & Gollwitzer, P. M. (1995). Effects of mindset on positive illusions. *Journal of Personality and Social Psychology, 4*, 141–185.

Tesluk, P. E., & Mathieu, J. E. (1999). Overcoming roadblocks to effectiveness: Incorporating management of performance barriers into models of work group effectiveness. *Journal of Applied Psychology, 84*, 200–217.

Triandis, H. C. (1979). Values, attitudes, and interpersonal behavior. In H. E. Howe, Jr. (Ed.), *Nebraska Symposium on Motivation* (pp. 195–258). Lincoln: University of Nebraska Press.

Volpe, C. E., Cannon-Bowers, J. A., Salas, E., & Spector, P. E. (1996). The impact of cross-training on team functioning: An empirical investigation. *Human Factors, 38*(1), 87–100.

Webb, T. L., & Sheeran, P. (2008). Mechanisms of implementation intention effects: The role of goal intentions, self-efficacy, and accessibility of plan components. *British Journal of Social Psychology, 47*, 373–395.

Wegge, J., Roth, C., Neubach, B., Schmidt, K., & Kanfer, R. (2008). Age and gender diversity as determinants of performance and health in a public organization: The role of task complexity and group size. *Journal of Applied Psychology, 93*(6), 1301–1313.

Weiss, H. M., & Cropanzano, R. (1996). An affective events approach to job satisfaction. In B. M. Staw & L. L. Cummings (Eds.), *Research in organizational behavior* (Vol. 18, pp. 1–74). Greenwich, CT: JAI.

5

Social Identity Issues in Multiteam Systems Considerations for Future Research

Stacey L. Connaughton
Purdue University

Elizabeth A. Williams
Purdue University

Marissa L. Shuffler
University of Central Florida

Our purpose in this chapter is to consider social identity issues in multiteam systems (MTSs). This is a theoretically interesting and practically important topic for a host of reasons. First, individuals in MTSs have multiple memberships, that is, multiple groups to which they belong. For instance, individuals working in an MTS belong to their component team as well as the larger multiteam system. Each individual belongs to at least one organization, and he or she may belong to a specific functional and/or professional unit as well. In addition, MTSs are often composed of teams from several organizations. Although each of these social entities (team, organization, or MTS) may be trying to achieve the same overarching goal, it may also have competing distal goals, thus, perhaps, putting these multiple identities in tension. Second, shifting identities may be experienced in MTSs. That is, at different times individuals may enact different identities and as such may make decisions based on different values or goals.

To illustrate these points, consider the case of one type of multiteam system—provincial reconstruction teams (PRTs). PRTs are joint civilian–military systems designed to manage security and rebuild regions in unstable nations such as Afghanistan and Iraq (Feickert, 2006). The goals of PRTs are deceivingly straightforward; some PRTs may organize a medical clinic, and others may provide support to build a school. Although these are seemingly clear-cut and attainable goals, in unstable nations they can prove to be quite challenging. Often times, achieving these goals requires a high degree of coordination among members of multiple teams, including military units from various nation-states, nongovernmental organizations (NGOs), and local governments. Each of these collectives constitutes a necessary team within the MTS. Ensuring that each component team understands its roles, goals, and interdependencies is key, as coordination and communication are essential to the safety and well-being of everyone involved.

A specific example of one PRT's experiences highlights several issues related to social identity within MTSs. The mission of this particular PRT was to offer medical aid to civilians within the town of Musa Kehl, Afghanistan (Rietjens, 2008). Successful accomplishment of this mission required the coordination of Dutch military, NGO, and local health center staff members. Although PRT members successfully developed a plan, gathered supplies, and arrived at the local health center, one important piece of information was not communicated—that is, no one in the local community was told that the PRT would be available with this aid. Once this omission was recognized, however, PRT members immediately set out on foot throughout the town to notify local residents of the medical aid. In less than an hour, approximately 50 children and adults gathered outside the facility. As a result of the quick coordination between members of the PRT, and their ability to effectively communicate this message to the intended constituents, over 150 patients were seen and assisted that day.

What prompted these PRT members to respond so quickly and in this manner? In answering this question, one might imagine a host of possibilities related to social identity. Was it that the PRT members were also from the region and thus identified with the local community, recognized the urgent need for medical care, and understood how to effectively get word out about medical aid? Was it that they saw themselves as medical personnel who had a professional obligation to treat patients? Or, perhaps, was it that they identified with the overall goal of the PRT and wanted to achieve this goal however possible? Which of these identities (a local member of the community, a medical professional, or a PRT member) was more salient for the PRT when it made the decision to behave in the way that it did? Did these various identities somehow work together? How did these identities lead to effective coordination and execution of the PRT's mission? As this example begins to illustrate, it is critical to understand issues related to social identities and identifications in an MTS context, for they can begin to help unravel motivations for human behavior and the ways in which relationships among various component teams are forged and/or maintained.

Because multiteam systems constitute a relatively new context for study, very little has been written or tested regarding the role of social identity in such systems (DeChurch & Mathieu, 2009). However, we can draw from some of the initial research that has been done in this area as well as related theory and empirical work to begin to understand why social identity is relevant to the MTS context and therefore must be considered. Social identity has been a construct of interest for many years in a range of disciplines (e.g., psychology, communication, and management), and therefore what is already known regarding its influence can be leveraged to initiate our understanding in this new context. Two well-established bodies of literature that cross disciplines—teams and culture—also inform this chapter. For one, the name of the phenomenon under study—*multiteam systems*—suggests that we consider the extent to which MTSs are like other kinds of teams or whether they are different, a question we take up later in the chapter. Doing so requires that we examine the teams literature. In addition, as the PRT example suggests, MTSs are constituted by individuals and teams from various kinds of cultures. As we will discuss, putting the culture literature in conversation with the literature on social identity leads to important questions. Another area of study that informs theorizing about social identity in MTSs is the literature on social identity in distributed teams. *Distributed teams* have been defined as groups in which members' communication is often constrained by geographic and/ or temporal dispersion, and is often mediated through electronic communication technology; these teams' permanence varies according to task demands (Zaccaro, Ardison, & Orvis, 2004). Many MTSs share these components of dispersion, mediated communication, and duration. Therefore, the extant research on distributed teams allows us to advance questions concerning social identity antecedents, processes, and outcomes in MTSs.

In an effort to explore these issues and begin to theorize about the relationships between social identity and MTSs, we first offer an overview of social identity theory (SIT). We then consider the role of social identity in MTSs and organize our discussion along four facets of the MTS definition that are particularly relevant. Within each definitional feature, we advance questions and, when appropriate, propositions that future researchers should consider. Table 5.1 provides a summary of these research questions and propositions, divided out by the four facets of MTSs as well as some general issues of interest relevant to understanding social identity in MTSs. We conclude the chapter by offering an alternative way of examining identity issues in MTSs based on structuration theory as well as note some methodological and conceptual considerations when conducting research in this area.

SOCIAL IDENTITY THEORY

Social identity theory was developed as a theory of intergroup relations and tensions. SIT posits that individuals define themselves by the groups in which they perceive membership. For SIT researchers, the self-concept tends to constitute two dimensions: (a) a *personal identity*, which consists of such individual characteristics as attributes, traits, interests, and competencies; and (b) a *social identity*, which includes salient group features. In the words of Tajfel and Turner (1986), social identity constitutes "those aspects of an individual's self-image that derive from the social categories to which he [or she] perceives himself [or herself] as belonging" (p. 16). Further consideration of these potential social categories begins to shed light on how SIT is related to multiteam systems. These social categories may include gender, age, racial and/or ethnic groups, religious affiliation, organizational membership, or other cohorts, all of which may be classifications relevant to MTS members. SIT suggests that these social classifications serve two purposes: (a) to enable an individual to define him- or herself in the social environment; and (b) to help the individual to define others and define themselves to others in that social environment. SIT conceives of social groups as comparative and relational. Indeed, according to Tajfel and Turner, "They [social groups] define the individual as similar to or different from, as 'better' or 'worse' than, members of other groups" (p. 16). SIT holds that although many of these social categories are categorical (e.g., female, Chinese, or an employee of IBM), the extent to which the individual identifies with each category can vary.

Researchers in several disciplines have drawn upon social identity theory to understand relationships between a member and a collective.

TABLE 5.1

Social Identity in MTSs: Future Research Questions

Research Area	Questions (RQ) and Propositions (P)
Component Team Issues	
RQ 1.	How does an MTS create a sense of shared identity among various component teams?
RQ 2.	Do team members identify with the MTS?
P 2a.	The degree to which team members experience interdependence, common goals, feelings of ownership, team consistency, and differentiation will influence the extent to which team members identify with the MTS.
RQ 3.	What group serves as a reference group from which MTSs differentiate themselves?
RQ 4.	Which identities are most salient for members of the MTS?
RQ 5.	What influences whether an identity becomes salient or not in MTSs?
P 5a.	Saliency of MTS identity will correlate with the degree to which team members experience interdependence.
P 5b.	When system goals and component team goals mirror one another, individuals will not have to choose to privilege one identity over another.
RQ 6.	How do MTSs capitalize on and overcome challenges rising from heterogeneity?
MTSs that establish MTS-level norms, rules, and languages derived from those of the component teams will perform better than MTSs without such commonalities.	
Cross-Boundary Issues	
RQ 7.	Who determines the boundaries of an MTS?
RQ 8.	Do various component teams and team members have different perceptions of these boundaries?
RQ 9.	How do these boundaries facilitate and constrain work processes for MTSs?
P 9a.	MTSs that have little reciprocal interdependence will have clearer system boundaries.
RQ 10.	What are the relationships among social identities and shifting cultural mosaic tiles in MTSs?
RQ 11.	How do these factors work together to influence MTS outcomes?
P 11a.	MTS component teams who perceive commonalities among their identities (e.g., common mosaic tiles) will have better outcomes than MTSs who do not perceive such similarities.
RQ 12.	How are cultural differences enacted in MTSs?
RQ 13.	Under what conditions do cultural differences adversely affect identification with an MTS as well as other MTS processes and outcomes?
P 13a.	Cultural faultlines in MTSs will negatively impact team processes and outcomes.

(continued)

TABLE 5.1 (continued)

Social Identity in MTSs: Future Research Questions

Research Area	Questions (RQ) and Propositions (P)
P 13b.	Cultural faultlines in MTSs will lead to reduced cross-functional processes, negatively impacting overall MTS performance.
RQ 14.	What effects do cultural differences have on the performance of MTSs?
P 14a.	MTSs whose members identify more with the MTS culture as opposed to their component team culture will be more successful in achieving MTS-level goals.
P 14b.	MTSs whose members identify more with their component team culture as opposed to their MTS culture will be less successful in achieving MTS-level goals.

Goal Hierarchy and Goal Accomplishment Issues

RQ 15.	Are component teams and/or subteams aligned with the overall MTS goal?
RQ 16.	If so, how is that alignment accomplished and maintained?
RQ 17.	If not, what are the consequences for MTS processes and outcomes?
P 17a.	A lack of goal alignment between MTS and component team goals will negatively impact MTS processes and outcomes.
RQ 18.	What is the relationship between the degree of goal alignment and the dual identity of MTS members with the MTS and their component teams?
P 18a.	The more aligned MTS and component team goals are, the less identity tension MTS members will experience.
RQ 19.	What are the consequences of team members identifying with different goals along the goal hierarchy?
P 19a.	Team members who more strongly identify with the MTS will choose to accomplish MTS-level goals over component team goals when these goals are in competition.
P 19b.	Team members who more strongly identify with their component team will choose to accomplish component team–level goals over MTS goals when these goals are in competition.

Process Interdependence Issues

RQ 20.	Is a shared social identity important when there is sequential interdependence?
RQ 21.	Is a shared social identity important when there is reciprocal interdependence?
RQ 22.	Does having a shared MTS identity moderate the relationship between MTS members' differences (in information processing and role-specific knowledge) and MTS processes?
P 22a.	Having a cohesive MTS identity will decrease the negative impact of MTS members' differences on team processes.

TABLE 5.1 (continued)

Social Identity in MTSs: Future Research Questions

Research Area	Questions (RQ) and Propositions (P)
RQ 23.	How is conflict enacted in MTSs, and what is its relationship to shared identity?
P 23a.	Shared identity in MTSs will moderate the relationship between conflict and MTS outcomes, such that for MTSs whose team members more strongly identify with one another, conflict will have a reduced impact on MTS outcomes.
RQ 24.	How is conflict resolved in MTSs, and to what extent is shared identity used to resolve conflict?

Overarching Issues

What are other relevant perspectives that inform identity in MTSs?

What are the methodological challenges of examining social identities in MTSs?

Is social identity experienced differently for MTS members than team members?

SIT has been used as a theoretical framework guiding organizational and group research, particularly in examining identification (Ashforth & Mael, 1989; Dutton & Dukerich, 1991; Dutton, Dukerich, & Harquail, 1994; Scott, 1997; Scott et al., 1999). In one of the foundational works on this topic, Ashforth and Mael defined *social identification* as "the perception of oneness with or belongingness to some human aggregate" (p. 21). Researchers utilizing SIT have often examined *organizational identification*, a specific form of social identification (Ashforth & Mael, 1989), and they have underscored three factors that may influence an individual's organizational identification: (a) a positive informational involvement with another member (Dutton & Dukerich, 1991; Dutton et al., 1994), (b) the nature of organizational socialization behaviors (Bullis & Bach, 1989, 1991), and (c) tenure with an organization (Barker & Tompkins, 1994).

Yet in complex organizations—and, we argue, in multiteam systems— organizational identification is not the only type of identification that may occur. Indeed, as Ashforth and Mael (1989) contended, social identity may actually be composed of "disparate and loosely coupled identities" (p. 22). Thus, multiple identifications are possible and even likely. Researchers have examined the multiplicity of identities and identifications, specifically in work on multiple identification targets (sources). Guided by SIT, Scott, Corman, and Cheney (1998) argued, for example, that four targets are especially salient to for-profit organizational members: individual, work group, organization, and occupation. Those targets and others may be working together in a complex manner (Scott et al., 1999). These multiplicities of identifications and identities are especially important because of their potential influences on how individuals make decisions (Cheney, 1983a, 1983b; Tompkins & Cheney, 1985), both for the team and for the MTS.

Social Identity and Multiteam Systems

> Multiteam systems are two or more teams that interface directly and interdependently in response to environmental contingencies toward the accomplishment of collective goals. MTS boundaries are defined by virtue of the fact that all teams within the system, while pursuing different proximal goals, share at least one common distal goal; and in so doing exhibit input, process, and outcome interdependence with at least one other team in the system. (Mathieu, Marks, & Zaccaro, 2001, p. 290)

This definition has four distinct elements that may have implications for and be influenced by individuals' social identities: (a) MTSs have two or more component teams, (b) MTSs cross boundaries, (c) a goal hierarchy exists within MTSs, and (d) interdependence exists amongst these teams. In the following sections, we consider each of these elements within the context of existing research and then posit questions and propositions for future research to consider in regard to social identity in MTSs. Before we examine each feature and its relationships to social identity issues, it is important to recognize that we cover some of these elements in more detail than others. This is not to suggest that those features that receive more attention in this chapter are more important to MTSs than are the other elements, but merely that we find more robust linkages between some features of MTSs and notions of social identity.

Two or More Component Teams

A primary aspect of MTSs is that they are composed of two or more component teams (Mathieu et al., 2001). One example of these MTS component teams can be found in the joint task force (JTF) teams established to provide aid to individuals following Hurricane Andrew in 1992 (Bessler, 2008). Hurricane Andrew was one of the most devastating hurricanes to hit the U.S. coast, displacing countless individuals from their homes and requiring an urgent national response. The JTFs that responded to the crisis were composed of component teams responsible for the rescue, evacuation, and medical treatment of casualties. Each component team possessed expertise and training in particular areas, such as medical doctors and emergency medical technicians (EMTs) in one component team and firefighters in another team. Even within these teams, subteams were likely to occur, as those within the medical team may have broken into smaller groups to treat different patients. However, all team members were working toward the overarching MTS goal of rescue, evacuation, and treatment.

As we can see from this example, it is very likely that the individuals within these component teams may have different social identities, as these teams often serve interdependent yet separate purposes and their members may range widely in terms of their backgrounds (DeChurch & Mathieu, 2009). In addition, each of these component teams has its own goals and reasons for existence (component team identities). Moreover, each component team may have subteams as well. Given this variation on multiple levels, a question arises:

Research Question 1: How does an MTS create a sense of shared identity among various component teams?

Drawing from relevant literature on distributed teams, there are several factors that promote a shared identity among team members. These include "interdependence, common goals, feelings of ownership, low turnover, and differentiation" (Mortensen & Hinds, 2001, p. 231). The first two elements identified by Mortensen and Hinds (interdependence and common goals) echo features of the definition of MTSs advanced by Mathieu and colleagues (2001). In fact, part of building a team identity is reliance on other team members (or, in the case of MTSs, reliance on other component teams) to achieve a shared goal. In addition, Mortensen and Hinds (2001) pointed to feelings of ownership (i.e., do team members believe they have ownership over their project and its goals?), low turnover (i.e., is membership on the team relatively stable?), and differentiation. *Differentiation* can be thought of in terms of how the team positions itself in relation to other groups (Tajfel & Turner, 1986). However, with MTSs the possibility exists that individuals may identify with either their team or the MTS (or, as Scott et al. [1999] would argue, perhaps another target such as their organization or occupation). The degree to which an individual sees his or her identity as being with a particular subgroup influences the larger team (Gibson & Vermeulen, 2003). Based on this discussion, we pose the following questions and proposition:

> Research Question 2: Do team members identify with the MTS?
>
> Proposition 2a: The degree to which team members experience interdependence, common goals, feelings of ownership, team consistency, and differentiation will influence the extent to which team members identify with the MTS.
>
> Research Question 3: What group serves as a reference group from which MTSs differentiate themselves?

As alluded to previously, individuals often shift between multiple identities (Ashforth & Mael, 1989; Cheney, 1991; Scott et al., 1998). In MTSs, a potential additional identity (i.e., system identity) may exist for team members to call upon when making decisions. The questions and proposition become as follows:

> Research Question 4: Which identities are most salient for members of the MTS?
>
> Research Question 5: What influences whether an identity becomes salient or not in MTSs?

Hogg and Terry (2000) explained that various identities become salient because they are appropriate given the situation. However, Hogg and Terry were also quick to point out the influence of social interaction on an individual's assessment of which identity is appropriate. That is, a particular identity not only becomes salient based on the situation, but also comes to the fore as a result of interactions with others. In the MTS context, this suggests that when interacting with other system team members, the MTS identity may become more or less salient based on the interactions that the member has with other system team members. Similarly, scholars have highlighted the importance of proximity for identity salience. For example, Barker and Tompkins (1994) pointed to the increased influence that team identification may have over organizational identification because individuals work in the team each day. Similarly, Scott's (1997) examination of a dispersed organization revealed that participants identified most strongly with their "local" target. For MTSs, this suggests that if system team members work frequently on system initiatives or with other system members, the system identity may become more salient. This implies that the level of interdependence, which will be discussed later in this chapter, may have a strong influence on whether MTS identity is salient. Hence, we offer the following propositions:

> Proposition 5a: Saliency of MTS identity will correlate with the degree to which team members experience interdependence.

It is also important to note that although this chapter's discussion about identities may imply that multiple identities are always in competition, and although several studies have highlighted tensions between multiple identities (DiSanza & Bullis, 1999; Tompkins & Cheney, 1985), Scott (1997) pointed out that these multiple identities may also be compatible. Thus,

> Proposition 5b: When system goals and component team goals mirror one another, individuals will not have to choose to privilege one identity over another.

Another relevant consideration is the homogeneity or heterogeneity of component team members. In the literature on distributed teams, for instance, it is often assumed that distributed teams are less homogeneous in composition based on their physical dispersion. Diversity of team members may arise from cultural differences or differences in functional areas (Mortensen & Hinds, 2001, 2002). The heterogeneity of team members makes it more difficult to foster a shared identity (Mannix, Griffith, & Neale, 2002) and can increase conflict among team members (Hinds & Bailey, 2003). In MTSs, team members may also come from a variety of organizations, all of which have unique cultures, thus increasing heterogeneity. For example, when responding to a car crash, an MTS composed of police, firefighters, and EMTs may emerge. Although team members from these three organizations may all have the same MTS-level goal of saving lives, it is very likely that they will also have their own norms, rules, and even languages. Such differences, if not addressed upfront, may lead to critical breakdowns in communication and coordination within the MTS. Thus, we ask and conjecture,

Research Question 6: How do MTSs capitalize on and overcome challenges rising from heterogeneity?

Proposition 6a: MTSs that establish MTS-level norms, rules, and languages derived from those of the component teams will perform better than MTSs without such commonalities.

Crossing Boundaries: Internal and Multiorganizational

The definition of MTSs also opens up the possibility that teams within the MTS may share organizational affiliations or may cross different organizations. Mathieu and colleagues (2001) noted that MTSs can either be internal to one organization or cross organizational boundaries, being composed of individuals and component teams spanning multiple organizations. These potential differences can be expanded to include differences in culture, nationality, and even language, creating a very complex environment within which these MTSs must operate.

Dealing with boundary issues is not unique to MTSs, for all teams must deal with boundary issues. In distributed teams, for example, Mortensen and Hinds (2002) found that although team members often had different definitions of who was part of their team, these teams often had greater agreement on team boundaries, arguably because there is less reciprocal interdependence on distributed teams and there is a degree of novelty for distributed team members (i.e., they are "new" people to work with). We suggest that boundary issues are compounded in MTSs because boundaries must be determined not only for individual membership on teams but also for team inclusion in the MTS. Important questions, therefore, arise:

Research Question 7: Who determines the boundaries of an MTS?

Research Question 8: Do various component teams or team members have different perceptions of these boundaries?

Research Question 9: How do these boundaries facilitate and constrain work processes for MTSs?

Proposition 9a: MTSs that have little reciprocal interdependence will have clearer system boundaries.

The possibility of crossing cultural boundaries is another important consideration in MTSs. *Culture* has been defined in many ways across disciplines, and a thorough review of these is out of the scope of the current chapter (but see Chao, 2000; Erez & Gati, 2004; Sperber & Hirschfeld, 1999). Culture is a complex construct that is multifaceted and multidimensional, as illustrated through many of the current approaches to studying it (e.g., Chao & Moon, 2005; Hofstede, 1980; Sutton, Pierce, Burke, & Salas, 2006). For the purposes of the current chapter, we view *culture* as a construct that delineates individual characteristics as well as a means by which to group collectives (Chao & Moon, 2005).

As Zaccaro, Marks, and DeChurch propose in Chapter 1 of this volume, the individuals and the component teams that comprise an MTS may have wide variances in their historical culture, behavioral norms, and internal climates. Indeed, for MTSs culture can play a role in many ways, from the national diversity of members of component teams to differences in organizational cultures (e.g., Army interacting with Navy). Therefore, culture can influence component team and MTS effectiveness. This impact of culture may interact with social identity, potentially strengthening or weakening team identities as well as members' identifications with their component teams and with the MTS as a whole. This interaction may in turn impact component team and MTS performance, which can have severe consequences considering the challenging nature of MTS goals.

Culture not only has been defined in a variety of ways but also has been operationalized differently throughout the literature. Traditionally, much of the culture literature has focused on identifying dimensions of national culture, such as individualism/collectivism and power/distance, that can be used to classify different cultures given the prominence of particular attitudes and values within these cultures (e.g., Hofstede, 1984; Sutton et al., 2006). Although the use of these dimensions may be beneficial in allowing for some comparisons among individuals from various national cultures, it does not allow for some of the finer nuances of culture to be understood, and it can promote stereotyping of cultures (Connaughton & Shuffler, 2007).

A recent approach to culture that may be more advantageous in the context of social identity is Chao and Moon's (2005) cultural mosaic. This approach suggests that an individual's cultural identity is a composite set of tiles that represent geographic (e.g., natural features of a region or country), demographic (e.g., age, gender, and ethnicity), and associative (e.g., association with family, employer, and profession) facets. This view may be particularly relevant to MTSs and their component teams as it posits that culture can be perceived as being influenced by both global and local facets. Furthermore, the cultural mosaic of any given individual may vary depending upon the social situation.

The cultural mosaic perspective has implications for understanding social identity in MTSs. The demographic aspect of the cultural mosaic is driven by sociohistorical information that shapes an individual's social identity. However, these social identities may change and develop due to associative factors as individuals are introduced to and become members of different groups. Thus, team members' culture may drive their social identity during any given social situation, increasing or decreasing their connections with not only their own component team members but also their MTS as a whole. However, as team members learn more about one another, they may experience shifts in the importance of certain cultural mosaic tiles, meaning that the saliency of certain cultural values and attributes may change depending upon their interactions.

For example, a component team composed of EMT workers may have a strong social identification with one another due to the prominence of their EMT organization cultural tile, increasing their cohesion with one another but decreasing their cohesion with other MTS component teams. However, if they learn that members of another component team are from their own hometown, their identification with this component team may change and increase cohesion. We suggest that the cultural mosaic approach has implications for social identity. Thus, we ask,

Research Question 10: What are the relationships among social identities and shifting cultural mosaic tiles in MTSs?

Research Question 11: How do these factors work together to influence MTS outcomes?

Proposition 11a: MTS component teams who perceive commonalities among their identities (e.g., common mosaic tiles) will have better outcomes than MTSs who do not perceive such similarities.

Additional issues related to understanding the impact of culture on social identity in MTSs exist as a result of the way in which cultural differences manifest themselves in teams. At times, cultural differences may affect team members' abilities to identify with one another, which may impact team and MTS outcomes. As highlighted by Zaccaro et al. in Chapter 1 of this volume, faultlines may arise in MTSs when there are cultural differences (Lau & Murnighan, 2005). These faultlines can affect the social identity of MTS team members by placing increased emphasis on differences among team members, decreasing social cohesion and impeding team members from identifying with one another. Furthermore, as it is likely that these faultlines will also fall across component teams, it is possible that team members will fail to identify with other component team members. This lack of identification can in turn lead component teams to be less likely to engage in cross-functional processes, hurting the overall MTS performance. However, future research is needed to explore the exact interactions of such issues on MTS processes and performance. Therefore, we posit,

Research Question 12: How are cultural differences enacted in MTSs?

Research Question 13: Under what conditions do cultural differences adversely affect identification with an MTS as well as other MTS processes and outcomes?

Proposition 13a: Cultural faultlines in MTSs will negatively impact team processes and outcomes.

Proposition 13b: Cultural faultlines in MTSs will lead to reduced cross-functional processes, negatively impacting overall MTS performance.

Culture may influence social identity in other ways as well. For example, Gibson and Zellmer-Bruhn (2001) found that employees in different national cultures utilize differing metaphors (military, sports, community, family, and associates) to define *teamwork*. This can in turn lead to differing expectations regarding team roles, scope, membership, and objectives. Furthermore, Van der Zee and Van der Gang (2007) investigated the influence of social identity and personality on work outcomes among business students who worked together in culturally diverse teams. Their findings illustrated that for very culturally diverse teams, teams had a stronger sense of well-being if team members identified most strongly with the team itself than if team members identified most strongly with their native culture. For MTSs, such differences may have an even stronger impact on similar outcomes, as differences are prevalent not only across team members but also across component teams. Future research should address how such cultural differences at the team and MTS levels relate to overall MTS functioning and outcomes. Thus, we ask,

Research Question 14: What effects do cultural differences have on the performance of MTSs?

Proposition 14a: MTSs whose members identify more with the MTS culture as opposed to their component team culture will be more successful in achieving MTS-level goals.

Proposition 14b: MTSs whose members identify more with their component team culture as opposed to their MTS culture will be less successful in achieving MTS-level goals.

Although much of the literature looking at culture in team contexts has focused on determining the impacts of culture on team outcomes, recent work has begun to examine certain skills that may be beneficial to enhancing functioning in culturally rich teams. This literature may be applicable in terms of understanding social identity in MTSs, as the use of such skills may aid in strengthening team members' identification with one another as members of an MTS, as well as making such attachment more salient. Two sets of skills discussed in this literature, cultural competencies and frame switching, will therefore be discussed below.

Cultural competency literature may also be of interest to understanding social identity issues in MTS. Recently, researchers have begun to investigate the benefit of exploring general cultural competencies that individuals must possess in order to effectively operate in multicultural environments (Abbe, Gulick, & Herman, 2008). Abbe and colleagues have identified several such competencies, such as flexibility and self-regulation, which are advantageous to individuals working in cross-cultural environments. It is expected that individuals utilizing such skills will be able to better understand the implications of culture and predict how team members may interact given their cultural and social identities. This may prove to be advantageous to MTS members when social identification among component teams is very strong. Instead of attempting to realign the social identities of team members, enhancing their cultural competencies may provide them with the ability to understand one another and interact effectively by being flexible and adaptable to a range of cultural situations.

Another cultural perspective that may aid in understanding social identity in MTS is that of frame switching. Frame switching is the idea that individuals can alternate between different culturally based interpretive lenses in response to cultural cues (Benet-Martinez, Leu, Lee, & Morris,

2002). Frame switching is beneficial to individuals who must operate with different environments that may demand different cultural knowledge and understanding, such as an immigrant who is able to master switching between his ethnic identity with his home country and his national identity with his current country (Lehman, Chiu, & Schaller, 2004). Frame switching may be relevant to members of MTSs who may have to switch their identification frames when working across boundaries. This may be easier for MTS members who are working within one organization than those who are working across organizations, as the frames that they must switch between may not be as different from one another. However, future research is needed to better understand the potential impact of such skills.

Goal Hierarchy and Collective Goal Accomplishment

An additional aspect of MTSs that may relate to social identity is the potential conflict between team and MTS goals. Within an MTS, there exists a goal hierarchy that may or may not align (Marks, DeChurch, Mathieu, Panzer, & Alonso, 2005). Marks and colleagues examined goal hierarchy and the structure of MTSs, finding that the goal hierarchy dictates the level of teamwork process that is most important as a predictor of success. They found that when MTSs were less interdependent, within-team processes were more important, but as the need for interdependency increased, between-team processes became more critical.

This finding is pertinent to the current discussion of MTSs because the component teams within an MTS have their own goals that may or may not be exclusive to the overall collective MTS goal. For example, if a nuclear power plant is attacked by a terrorist, an MTS may emerge in order to attempt to remove the threat and restore the safety of the power plant, the collective MTS goal. This MTS may involve nuclear power plant workers trying to repair components damaged by the terrorist attack; the FBI trying to locate and arrest the terrorist, who may still be in the power plant; and firefighters attempting to evacuate the plant. Each of these component goals may align perfectly with the MTS goal, or there may be conflicts (e.g., between firefighters trying to evacuate workers and workers trying to stay to repair damaged components).

Social identity can play a role in this understanding of the goal hierarchy. If component team members cannot identify that they are a part of the MTS as a whole and must work on accomplishing their collective goal, it is possible that they may only focus on their own component team goal, thus reducing MTS effectiveness. However, if team members associate only as MTS members and identify less as members of their own component teams, these component team goals may be ignored to the detriment of both MTS and component team performance. Clearly, this dual identity has serious implications for MTSs that need to be further explored. Thus, we wonder,

> Research Question 15: Are component teams and/or subteams aligned with the overall MTS goal?
>
> Research Question 16: If so, how is that alignment accomplished and maintained?
>
> Research Question 17: If not, what are the consequences for MTS processes and outcomes?
>
> Proposition 17a: A lack of goal alignment between MTS and component team goals will negatively impact MTS processes and outcomes.
>
> Research Question 18: What is the relationship between the degree of goal alignment and the dual identity of MTS members with the MTS and their component teams?
>
> Proposition 18a: The more aligned MTS and component team goals are, the less identity tension MTS members will experience.

Not only may MTS members identify with their component teams more so than with the MTS, but also it is important to consider the extent to which they *should* identify with the MTS as a whole. This dual identity may be challenging to MTSs because not all of the MTS's collective goals may coincide with the distal goals of the individuals' team. For example, within the aforementioned JTF, a critical goal to the component teams may have been to keep all of their team members out of imminent and avoidable danger, because they needed their team members safe so that they could continue functioning as a team after the JTF was dissolved. However, if rescuing a particular civilian (which falls in line with the overall MTS goal of rescuing, evacuation, and treatment) put component team members in danger, the MTS and component team goals would be conflicting, with no easy way to resolve the conflict. Therefore, the individuals may be forced to choose between not only competing goals but also competing identities. A question then becomes,

Research Question 19: What are the consequences of team members identifying with different goals along the goal hierarchy?

Proposition 19a: Team members who more strongly identify with the MTS will choose to accomplish MTS-level goals over component team goals when these goals are in competition.

Proposition 19b: Team members who more strongly identify with their component team will choose to accomplish component team–level goals over MTS goals when these goals are in competition.

Process Interdependence

Although, definitionally, *interdependence* in the MTS context includes input, process, and outcome interdependence, we focus on process interdependence in this section. Although we do not seek to minimize the importance of the other two aspects of interdependence, we believe that process interdependence has particular relevance to issues of social identity, for it is during the MTS's coordination and communication processes that individuals have the opportunity to exercise agency and in doing so rely on their social identities. As defined in Chapter 1 of this volume, *process interdependence* refers to the degree of interaction that is required between teams to accomplish the goals of the MTS. This feature refers to exactly *how* goals are accomplished in the MTS, whether there is a sequential ordering of tasks among MTS members, or if tasks are completed in a reciprocal fashion. Sequential interdependence exists when tasks pass from one team to the next. Another way to think of this is that the output of one team is the input for the next team. Reciprocal interdependence, on the other hand, suggests that teams will need to coordinate their actions more and will need to rely on similar decision-making premises. Individuals' use of an organization's decision premises have been theorized to come in part from the degree to which individuals identify with the organization (Cheney, 1983a, 1983b; Tompkins & Cheney, 1985). Thus, it is logical to assume that the degree to which MTSs have a shared identity will influence the rules they use to make decisions. The question, however, is how important is it that there are shared rules for decision making? We wonder if this depends in part on the type of interdependence. Therefore, we pose the following questions:

Research Question 20: Is a shared social identity important when there is sequential interdependence?

Research Question 21: Is a shared social identity important when there is reciprocal interdependence?

Arguably, the most important product of shared identity is that it "can create a psychological tie between distant team members that helps them to bridge the physical and contextual distance that otherwise separates them" (Hinds & Mortensen, 2005, p. 293). That is, shared identity allows teams to overcome their geographic dispersion and their differences in culture, individual goals, and so on. This is important as individuals often bring role-specific knowledge to the team, thus creating the need for interdependence discussed in this chapter (Maznevski, 1994). Additionally, individuals process information in different ways, which allows for synergies to emerge on the team (Maznevski, 1994). The coordination of role-specific knowledge and the varying ways of processing information are perhaps the most important products of and arguments for distributed teams. In essence, distributed teams are striving to coordinate differences, and this is done, in large part, through shared identity. Within MTSs, these same processes and products may exist, but the question becomes,

Research Question 22: Does having a shared MTS identity moderate the relationship between MTS members' differences (in information processing and role-specific knowledge) and MTS processes?

Proposition 22a: Having a cohesive MTS identity will decrease the negative impact of MTS members' differences on team processes.

Finally, a large proportion of the distributed team literature that examines social identity also deals with conflict (e.g., Hinds & Bailey, 2003; Hinds & Mortensen, 2005; Mortensen & Hinds, 2001). This line of research indicates that shared identity will be associated with less conflict (Mortensen & Hinds, 2001). More specifically, shared identity reduces affective conflict, and shared context reduces task conflict (Hinds & Mortensen, 2005). We can reason that in MTSs, this pattern would also hold true. Just as shared identity among individuals allows them to understand the position of the other and therefore reduce conflict, it follows that in MTSs if the individuals share a common viewpoint and appreciate the larger context, they will be better able to rationalize the actions of other MTS members, and therefore conflict will not be as prevalent. However, because of the complex nature of MTSs, we wonder,

Research Question 23: How is conflict enacted in MTSs, and what is its relationship to shared identity?

Proposition 23a: Shared identity in MTSs will moderate the relationship between conflict and MTS outcomes, such that for MTSs whose team members more strongly identify with one another, conflict will have a reduced impact on MTS outcomes.

Research Question 24: How is conflict resolved in MTSs, and to what extent is shared identity used to resolve conflict?

OVERARCHING ISSUES RELEVANT TO IDENTITY IN MTSs

The previous sections have identified several questions specific to understanding the dynamic characteristics of MTSs that may affect—or be affected by—social identity. Other questions remain, however, that are not necessarily specific to these dynamics but instead are more overarching in nature. These questions are presented in this section, and tackle larger issues regarding alternative perspectives to SIT, methodological challenges, and one of the driving questions behind current MTS research: How are MTSs different from regular teams? Just as before, we do not present definitive answers to these questions, but instead attempt to provide an overview of why these issues are important to the study of identity in MTSs.

What Are Other Relevant Perspectives That Inform Identity in MTSs?

Beyond social identity theory, another theoretical lens through which to understand identity issues in MTSs is structuration theory. Structuration focuses on systems of human practices, or patterns of activity. In the performance of these activities, humans rely on a structure composed of rules and resources to inform their actions. *Rules* are those assumptions and foundations that individuals use when deciding how to act, whereas *resources* are "anything people are able to use in action, whether material (money, tools) or nonmaterial (knowledge, skill)" (Poole & McPhee, 2005, p. 174). Therefore, we can conceptualize systems as the combined actions of individuals who are relying on the rules of the system, the resources that the system provides, and those nonmaterial resources that they bring to the system to facilitate and inform their actions. Their actions in turn help to reproduce the system. This production–reproduction duality is a key concept surrounding structuration theory. Structure can be seen as both a medium and outcome of interaction (Giddens, 1979). That is, "[E]very action, every episode of interaction has two aspects: It 'produces' the practices of which it is a part and it 'reproduces' the system and its structure, usually in a small way, as changed or stable" (Poole & McPhee, 2005, p. 175).

Previous researchers have utilized structuration theory to understand identity and identification. The application of structuration theory to these concepts is based on the assumption that a duality exists between identity and identification (Scott et al., 1998). If we consider identification to be the process of aligning one's values and goals with those of the organization, identity then becomes the product of identification. However, we could also label identification as the type of behavior produced by identity. The duality of the two constructs is said to "account for the perceived linkage between (re)sources of identity and/or (re)presentations of identification" (Scott et al., 1998, p. 306). To clarify, organizational *identification* can be described as the act of creating our identity in an organization by internalizing organizational values and using those values to make decisions. *Identity*, on the other hand, can be described as how we define ourselves in terms of the organizations or social structures with which we choose to align and the values we use when determining what actions to take or not to take.

We can learn more about identity in MTSs from a structuration perspective if we consider it in the context of the three MTS interdependencies (i.e., input, process, and output). We see that identity is a vital part of each of these interdependencies. First, if we consider identity as an input, we are left to ponder how the identities of individuals based on their individual teams or organizations influence their actions within the MTS. That is, what rules do they depend on when acting? Next, if we consider process interdependencies, we must question how rules are formed across teams based on identities and how these rules are enacted. Furthermore, how does identity function as a resource for MTSs? Finally, we must theorize about how identity influences the outcomes of MTSs. That is, how do actions reflect the identities of the individual, the teams, and the MTS, and how do the actions of each of these in turn help to create the identities?

What Are the Methodological Challenges of Examining Social Identities in MTSs?

As researchers begin to explore the issues of social identity within MTSs, it is important to note that studying this may involve both common and unique methodological challenges. Within MTSs, there are multiple levels of analysis that must be carefully examined in order to determine if what is being measured is actually indicative of MTS-level issues, component team–level issues, or individual-level issues. Furthermore, some of the problems common to studying social identity in teams, such as the very common operationalization of culture as national instead of and/ or in addition to organizational, will also transfer to MTS research. This subsection provides just a brief overview of a few challenges that must be considered when designing social identity research for MTSs.

First, it is critical that when studying social identity in MTSs, the appropriate level of analysis is utilized for different constructs. Determining at what level to assess social identity and related constructs such as team processes and outcomes is necessary for MTSs, as social identity may impact MTSs at multiple levels and even across levels. Furthermore, once levels of analysis are determined, it is also important to note how team- or MTS-level information will be compiled or aggregated across team members. Although researchers often rely on averages to develop higher level constructs, it is important to consider that other factors, such as variance, minimums, and maximums, may also provide unique information that contributes to our understanding of these higher level variables (Smith-Jentsch, 2009). For example, it may be that an average of how much MTS members identify with their component team or MTS is less informative than the variance among members. Undoubtedly, the first step to effectively designing studies to examine social identity in MTS is to address this issue of level of analysis.

Another issue is related to the operationalization of terms such as *culture* within the teams literature. Often, although these terms can be examined through a variety of interpretations and meanings, their operationalization has a very narrow focus. For example, with respect to teams and MTS, there is much ongoing debate regarding the impact of culture on teams and when it is salient and consequential (Connaughton & Shuffler, 2007). Although there are many aspects of culture, including different levels (e.g., national, regional, and organizational), most often in respect to teams, literature and empirical studies are driven by the national level. For example, in their review of the literature of multicultural, multinational distributed teams, Connaughton and Shuffler found that a large majority of the empirical studies conducted on such teams operationalized cultural heterogeneity and homogeneity as differences or similarities in national culture or race. Although an important area of study, this limits our understanding of the role of culture to the national perspective, which may be detrimental to understanding culture on other levels, such as the organizational or regional level. This is particularly problematic for MTSs, as one of the most challenging aspects of culture to social identity may be found within differing organizational cultures. Therefore, it is important that researchers examining the relationship between social identity and culture in MTSs do not simply limit themselves to national culture but examine other aspects of culture as well.

A final issue that may be of relevance to identity within MTSs is the use of social networks as a means of analyzing how social identity changes over time. Social network research is focused on the identification of relationships and interactions among individuals and groups, and allows for the visual diagramming of relationships (Scott, 2000). Such an approach could be highly beneficial to the study of social identity within MTSs, as temporal issues such as the change in identity over time and the degree of association among component teams could be mapped using such a methodology. Certainly, it is important to consider options such as these in order to fully and accurately assess the complexity of such issues.

Is Social Identity Experienced Differently for MTS Members Than Team Members?

Perhaps one of the most intriguing questions that must be asked when exploring MTSs in terms of any issue is "How is this really different from what we already know about teams?" Although initial empirical MTS research has begun to show distinctions between MTSs and teams, such as the identification of cross-team interactions that occur only within MTSs (Marks et al., 2005), it is important to note that much of what is already known regarding teams may be applicable. Therefore, one aspect of examining social identity issues in MTSs is to first begin to tease apart the differences, if any, between how social identity impacts teams and how it is different for MTSs.

As has been reiterated multiple times throughout this chapter, there are many more unanswered questions regarding MTSs and social identity than answered ones, and extensive research is needed to further understand social identity's role in such contexts. However, this does not mean that we can simply ignore everything that is already known regarding teams, as it is quite possible that much can be transferred to MTSs. So much of the teams literature is already fraught with overlapping constructs that it can be difficult to determine what is actually known. Therefore, it is important that MTS researchers do not make similar errors by creating new terms and constructs when perfectly good ones already exist. This is not to say that new concepts should not emerge as the investigation of social identity and MTS research begins, but that instead researchers should remain cognizant of what is already known regarding teams and attempt to determine if and how MTSs differ. By doing so, we will not only improve our understanding of social identity in MTSs but also continue to advance teams research as a whole.

We tentatively suggest that identity issues in MTSs may resemble identity issues in teams and also differ slightly from them in the following ways (see Figure 5.1 for a visual representation of our argument). As in teams in general, MTSs arise out of a need for multiple parties (individuals and component teams) with varying expertise and backgrounds to work together interdependently to address a goal (Salas, Sims, & Burke, 2005). In other words, a stimulus occurs (i.e., an emergency in the MTS health context and an infrastructure need in the PRT context) that requires the

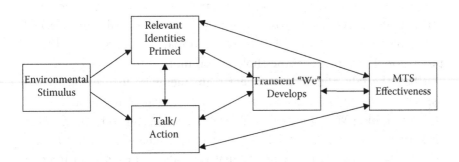

FIGURE 5.1
Proposed MTS identity model.

attention and interconnected action of multiple parties. To be sure, these parties will come to the MTS context, just as they would to the team context, with diverse demographics and experiences, and hence with varied and multiple identities.

In response to the stimulus, in the MTS context, component team members' professional identities (e.g., an EMT professional) and/or organizational or team identities (e.g., the U.S. Army) are primed and/or made salient. Again, this is not unlike what happens in teams, where multiple social identities are made salient in response to team activities, team interactions, and/or environmental factors that affect the team in some way (Salas, Stagl, Burke, & Goodwin, 2007). And, as this takes place among individuals in teams in general, talk and activities (actions) among component teams occur in response to the stimuli and come to define the team or MTS. The duration of that talk and/or those actions will vary based on the nature of the stimuli.

Where we suspect identity phenomena depart slightly from those which take place in teams relates to the following: Whereas in intact teams (and organizations) the nature of the interactions and activities defines a sense of *we* that is enduring (i.e., Albert & Whetten's [1985] definition of *organizational identity*), we are less convinced that an overall MTS identity develops in the same regard. Perhaps a temporary *we* or a transient *we* that ties component team members together has to do with the shared overarching goal or an aspect of it (not the component teams' own goals). Health care professionals in an MTS, for instance, would have in common a desire to help the patient. That common professional goal would serve to develop a momentary sense of *we* that is enacted in the activity and talk involved in assisting that particular patient. Similarly, PRT members might share the common goal of wanting to help (re)build an aspect of a country's infrastructure. That shared goal may involve aspects of their professional identities that they hold in common.

When the talk among component team members focuses on shared aspects or commonalities among their professional identities and/or on the overarching MTS goal, we would predict the MTS will be more effective. This is not to suggest that component team members will not have organizational and team identities that they also bring to each interaction. Indeed, as we mentioned in this chapter, the organizational and team identities (as well as other identities) that component team members bring to their work in the MTS may be in tension with their professional or MTS-level identities.

We might also suspect that, similar to faultline research in teams (Lau & Murnighan, 2005), component teams with strong team identities that close themselves off from and/or act superior to other component teams within the MTS will detract from the effectiveness of the overall MTS. The more permeable the team or organizational boundary (i.e., the more open the team or organization is to other MTS component team members' expertise and knowledge), the more effective the MTS. Thus, we suggest that what is "distinct" (differentiated) about a component team must be *harnessed* in terms of professional specialization as these varying sets of expertise among component teams are needed in order to achieve the overarching MTS goal, but *muted* when it comes to a component team having a strong organizational or component team identity. The enactment of strong organizational and/or team identities among component team members may threaten the MTS's effectiveness.

In posing these tentative arguments, we do so with caution. Clearly, research must be conducted first to determine if an MTS identity emerges at all and/or if MTS members believe that an overall MTS identity exists or is even necessary. Researchers need to get a better handle on these aspects of the MTS phenomenon itself. We also need to keep in mind that component team members will change, and hence relationships among component teams will undoubtedly change as well. For instance, if members of two different component teams in the MTS have had a good history of working together and have come to trust one another, removal or replacement of team members could have adverse impacts on MTS effectiveness.

CONCLUSION

Certainly, much is left to be understood regarding what impact social identity has upon MTSs, their processes, and their performance. These are important issues to address, as MTS members may have numerous identities that can drive interactions with their component team members, across component teams, and in the MTS as a whole. These interactions can in turn inhibit or promote MTS success, which, given the high-stakes nature of many such systems, justifies further study of such issues.

This chapter has accomplished its three goals. First, we have outlined the defining characteristics of MTSs and how they may require new and unique approaches to understanding social identity's role in such systems. Second, drawing upon several bodies of literature, we have identified current areas of research that may contribute to our understanding of social identity issues in MTS, including social identity theory, culture, and distributed teams. Finally, we have presented an extensive, but not exhaustive, list of questions and propositions that should be addressed in future research, as well as multiple challenges that MTS researchers should be cognizant of when conducting such research. Although social identity research in MTSs will undoubtedly be challenging, this review provides a point from which future research may depart.

REFERENCES

Abbe, A., Gulick, L. M. V., & Herman, J. L. (2008). *Cross-cultural competence in Army leaders: A conceptual and empirical foundation* (ARI Study Report 2008-01). Arlington, VA: U.S. Army Research Institute for the Behavioral and Social Sciences.

Albert, S., & Whetten, D. (1985). Organizational identity. In L. Cummings & B. Shaw (Eds.), *Research in organizational behavior* (Vol. 7, pp. 263–295). Greenwich, CT: JAI.

Ashforth, B. E., & Mael, F. (1989). Social identity theory and the organization. *Academy of Management Review, 14*, 20–39.

Barker, J. R., & Tompkins, P. K. (1994). Identification in the self-managing organization: Characteristics of target and tenure. *Human Communication Research, 21*, 247–264.

Benet-Martínez, V., Leu, J., Lee, F., & Morris, M. (2002). Negotiating biculturalism: Cultural frame-switching in biculturals with "oppositional" vs. "compatible" cultural identities. *Journal of Cross-Cultural Psychology, 33*, 492–516.

Bessler, J. (2008). Defining criteria for handover to civilian officials in relief operations (Strategy Research Project Report). Carlisle, PA: U.S. Army War College. Retrieved from http://www.dtic.mil/cgi-bin/GetTRDoc?AD=ADA479053&Location=U2&doc= GetTRDoc.pdf

Bullis, C., & Bach, B. W. (1989). Socialization turning points: An examination of change in organizational identification. *Western Journal of Speech Communication, 53*, 272–293.

Bullis, C., & Bach, B. W. (1991). An explication and test of communication network content and multiplexity as predictors of organizational identification. *Western Journal of Speech Communication, 55*, 180–197.

Chao, G. T. (2000). Multilevel issues and culture: An integrative view. In K. J. Klein & S. W. J. Kozlowski (Eds.), *Multilevel theory, research, and methods in organizations: Foundations, extensions, and new directions* (pp. 308–348). San Francisco: Jossey-Bass.

Chao, G. T., & Moon, H. (2005). The cultural mosaic: A metatheory for understanding the complexity of culture. *Journal of Applied Psychology, 90*, 1128–1140.

Cheney, G. (1983a). On the various and changing meanings of organizational membership: A field study of organizational identification. *Communication Monographs, 50*, 342–362.

Cheney, G. (1983b). The rhetoric of identification and the study of organizational communication. *Quarterly Journal of Speech, 69*, 143–158.

Cheney, G. (1991). *Rhetoric in an organizational society: Managing multiple identities.* Columbia: University of South Carolina Press.

Connaughton, S. L., & Shuffler, M. (2007). Multinational and multicultural distributed teams. *Small Group Research, 38*, 387–412.

DeChurch, L., & Mathieu, J. (2009). Thinking in terms of multiteam systems. In E. Salas, J. Goodwin, & C. S. Burke (Eds.), *Team effectiveness in complex organizations* (pp. 267–292). New York: Psychology Press.

DiSanza, J. R., & Bullis, C. (1999). "Everybody identifies with Smokey the Bear": Employee responses to newsletter identification inducements at the U.S. Forest Service. *Management Communication Quarterly, 12*, 347–399.

Dutton, J., & Dukerich, J. (1991). Keeping an eye on the mirror: Image and identity in organizational adaptation. *Academy of Management Journal, 34*, 517–554.

Dutton, J., Dukerich, J., & Harquail, C. (1994). Organizational images and member identification. *Administrative Science Quarterly, 39*, 239–263.

Erez, M., & Gati, E. (2004). A dynamic, multi-level model of culture: From the micro level of the individual to the macro level of a global culture. *Applied Psychology: An International Review, 53*, 583–598.

Feickert, A. (2006). U.S. and coalition military operations in Afghanistan: Issues for Congress. Washington, DC: Congressional Research Service. Retrieved from http://italy.usembassy.gov/pdf/other/RL33503.pdf

Gibson, C. B., & Vermeulen, F. (2003). A healthy divide: Subgroups as a stimulus for team learning behavior. *Administrative Science Quarterly, 48*, 202–239.

Gibson, C. B., & Zellmer-Bruhn, M. E. (2001). Metaphors and meaning: An intercultural analysis of the concept of teamwork. *Administrative Science Quarterly, 46*, 274.

Giddens, A. (1979). *Central problems in social theory.* Berkeley: University of California Press.

Hinds, P. J., & Bailey, D. E. (2003). Out of sight, out of sync: Understanding conflict in distributed teams. *Organization Science, 14*, 615–632.

Hinds, P. J., & Mortensen, M. (2005). Understanding conflict in geographically distributed teams: The moderating effects of shared identity, shared context, and spontaneous communication. *Organization Science, 16*, 290–307.

Hofstede, G. (1980). *Culture's consequences: International differences in work-related values.* Beverly Hills, CA: Sage.

Hofstede, G. H. (1984). *Culture's consequences: International differences in work-related values* (Cross-Cultural Research and Methodology Series). Beverly Hills, CA: Sage.

Hogg, M., & Terry, D. J. (2000). Social identity and self-categorization processes in organizational contexts. *Academy of Management Review, 25*, 121–140.

Lau, D., & Murnighan, J. K. (2005). Interactions with groups and subgroups: The effects of demographic faultlines. *Academy of Management Journal, 48*, 645–659.

Lehman, D. R., Chiu, C., & Schaller, M. (2004). Psychology and culture. *Annual Review of Psychology, 55*, 689–714.

Mannix, E. A., Griffith, T., & Neale, M. A. (2002). The phenomenology of conflict in distributed work teams. In P. Hinds & S. Kiesler (Eds.), *Distributed work* (pp. 213–233). Cambridge, MA: MIT Press.

Marks, M. A., DeChurch, L. A., Mathieu, J. E., Panzer, F. J., & Alonso, A. (2005). Teamwork in multiteam systems. *Journal of Applied Psychology, 90,* 964–971.

Mathieu, J. E., Marks, M. A., & Zaccaro, S. J. (2001). Multiteam systems. In N. Anderson, D. S. Ones, H. K. Sinangil, & C. Viswesvarin (Eds.), *Handbook of industrial, work and organizational psychology* (pp. 289–313). Thousand Oaks, CA: Sage.

Maznevski, M. L. (1994). Understanding our differences: Performance in decision making grounds with diverse members. *Human Relations, 47,* 531–543.

Mortensen, M., & Hinds, P. J. (2001). Conflict and shared identity in geographically distributed teams. *International Journal of Conflict Management, 12,* 212–238.

Mortensen, M., & Hinds, P. (2002). Fuzzy teams: Boundary disagreement in distributed and collocated teams. In P. Hinds & S. Kiesler (Eds.), *Distributed work* (pp. 283–308). Cambridge, MA: MIT Press.

Poole, M. S., & McPhee, R. D. (2005). Structuration theory. In D. K. Mumby & S. May (Eds.), *Engaging organizational communication theory and research: Multiple perspectives* (pp. 171–196). Thousand Oaks, CA: Sage.

Rietjens, S. J. H. (2008). Managing civil-military cooperation: Experiences from the Dutch provincial reconstruction team in Afghanistan. *Armed Forces & Society, 34,* 173–207.

Salas, E., Sims, D. E., & Burke, C. S. (2005). Is there "big five" in teamwork? *Small Group Research, 36,* 555–599.

Salas, E., Stagl, K. C., Burke, C. S., & Goodwin, G. F. (2007). Fostering team effectiveness in organizations: Toward an integrative theoretical framework of team performance. In J. W. Shuart, W. Spaulding, & J. Poland (Eds.), *Modeling complex systems: Motivation, cognition and social processes* (Nebraska Symposium on Motivation, Vol. 51, pp. 185–243). Lincoln: University of Nebraska Press.

Scott, C. R. (1997). Identification with multiple targets in a geographically dispersed organization. *Management Communication Quarterly, 10,* 491–522.

Scott, C. R., Connaughton, S. L., Diaz-Saenz, H. R., Maguire, K., Ramirez, R., Richardson, B., et al. (1999). The impacts of communication and multiple identifications on intent to leave. *Management Communication Quarterly, 12,* 400–435.

Scott, C. R., Corman, S. R., & Cheney, G. (1998). Development of a structurational model of identification in the organization. *Communication Theory, 8,* 298–336.

Scott, J. (2000). *Social network analysis: A handbook.* London: Sage.

Smith-Jentsch, K. A. (2009). Measuring team cognition: The devil is in the details. In E. Salas, J. Goodwin, & C. S. Burke (Eds.), *Team effectiveness in complex organizations* (pp. 491–508). New York: Psychology Press.

Sperber, D., & Hirschfeld, L. (1999). Culture, cognition, and evolution. In R. Wilson & F. Keil (Eds.), *MIT encyclopedia of the cognitive sciences* (pp. cxi–cxxxii). Cambridge, MA: MIT Press.

Sutton, J. L., Pierce, L., Burke, C. S., & Salas, E. (2006). Cultural adaptability. In C. S. Burke, L. Pierce, & E. Salas (Eds.), *Advances in human performance and cognitive engineering research* (pp. 143–173). Oxford: Elsevier Science.

Tajfel, H., & Turner, J. C. (1986). The social identity theory of inter-group behavior. In S. Worchel & L. W. Austin (Eds.), *Psychology of intergroup relations* (pp. 7–24). Chicago: Nelson-Hall.

Tompkins, P. K., & Cheney, G. (1985). Communication and unobtrusive control in contemporary organizations. In R. D. McPhee & P. K. Tompkins (Eds.), *Organizational communication: Traditional themes and new directions* (pp. 179–210). Newbury Park, CA: Sage.

Van der Zee, K., & Van der Gang, I. (2007). Personality, threat and affective responses to cultural diversity. *European Journal of Personality, 21*, 453–470.

Zaccaro, S. J., Ardison, S. D., & Orvis, K. L. (2004). Leadership in virtual teams. In D. Day, S. Zaccaro, & S. Halpins (Eds.), *Leader development for transforming organizations* (pp. 267–292). Mahwah, NJ: Erlbaum.

6

Multiteam Membership in Relation to Multiteam Systems

Michael Boyer O'Leary
Georgetown University

Anita Williams Woolley
Carnegie Mellon University

Mark Mortensen
INSEAD, France

INTRODUCTION AND DEFINITION OF MTM IN RELATION TO MTS

As defined in Chapter 1 of this volume, "An MTS constitutes subsets of component teams acting interdependently to accomplish at least one proximal goal, with all acting in concert toward a superordinate distal goal." Interdependence in MTSs can be in terms of inputs, processes, and outputs. The inputs may include human, informational, technological, material, and financial resources. Other chapters in this book address the informational, technological, material, and financial interdependence. In this chapter, we address the critical issue of *human* resource (or *membership*) interdependence. Such interdependence exists when people are concurrently members of multiple teams. Multiple team membership (MTM) can exist with or without the presence of MTSs. Figure 6.1 summarizes the contexts in which MTM and MTSs do and do not coexist.

As shown in Cell 1 of Figure 6.1, when an MTM exists in the context of an MTS, the component teams are not only interdependent in terms of their processes and outputs, but also interdependent in terms of their shared human inputs (i.e., their shared team members). For example,

		MTS	
		Yes	**No**
MTM	Yes	1. Input- (including membership), process-, and output-interdependent teams	3. Membership interdependent teams without process or output interdependence
	No	2. Input- (*but not membership*), process-, and output-interdependent teams	4. Fully independent teams

FIGURE 6.1
Relationship between an MTS and MTM.

21st-century jet airplanes are designed and built by a complex system of teams from a variety of firms. Teams responsible for the interior fittings of the plane are dependent on the teams designing the overall cabin compartment, which are in turn dependent on teams designing the fuselage. Those component teams must be well coordinated so that the work of one team feeds into the work of other teams on a timely basis. Team leaders can manage such coordination, but coordination across teams can also occur through the less formal, less hierarchical sharing of individual team members. For example, a senior engineer with expertise in new lightweight materials might be a member of the fittings, cabin, and fuselage teams. A CAD modeler might be a member of both the cabin and fittings teams and a fourth team responsible for the cockpit design. Although these overlapping members are unlikely to be formally responsible for coordinating their teams' efforts, their multiple team membership can enhance boundary spanning, cross-team communication, and coordination, possibly more effectively and fluidly than the formal interventions of leaders to coordinate the work of these subunits.

Although MTM is quite common (as we discuss in this chapter), not all multiteam systems include multiple team membership. As Davison and Hollenbeck (Chapter 12, Figure 12.4) and Zaccaro et al. (Chapter 1, this volume) note, a group of team leaders often coordinates their teams' efforts toward some superordinate goal, without any shared membership across those teams. For example, in a battlefield context, a second lieutenant would generally lead each platoon in a company, but not be members of two platoons. Coordination and collaboration across platoons would happen via discussions in the leadership team composed of the captain or major in charge of the company and two to eight second lieutenants leading each platoon. Such a context—an example of a multiteam system without any multiple team membership—is shown in Cell 2 of Figure 6.1.

MTM can also exist *outside* the context of multiteam systems (Figure 6.1, Cell 3). Teams can share members without having any superordinate goal (beyond the general success of their organization). For example, several technical experts and a senior partner might span consulting teams in three different business units. Those business units are not interdependent in terms of processes or outputs, but they are interdependent in terms of their shared members (i.e., inputs or resources). Small to medium-sized projects are generally handled by one central team, but frequently include members who do not work on any one project exclusively. In such cases, the shared members might learn from the multiple teams, and the teams might benefit from the "cross-pollination" of ideas that their shared members can provide, but coordination and collaboration would be far less important than in the military company or airplane manufacturer.

Finally, there are contexts (Figure 6.1, Cell 4) in which all teams are fully independent. In such contexts, teams share no members, and their processes and outputs are not linked. Thus, they lack both MTSs and MTM. Such so-called traditional teams form the basis of most prior research and theory, but as organizations become more complex, markets become more intertwined, and business becomes more global, such contexts are increasingly rare.

The literature on MTSs has noted the importance of input, process, and output interdependence, tending to focus on the latter two and on the role of team leaders as formal coordinating mechanisms in MTSs. Although such process and output interdependence, as well as formal leadership, are clearly critical for understanding MTSs, in this chapter we focus on the third type of interdependence and, in so doing, bring the work on MTM into more direct dialogue with the work on MTSs. We begin with a discussion of the prevalence of MTM, followed by the temporal dynamics of MTM (inside and outside multiteam systems), the managerial implications of MTM, and the ways in which our research on MTM may inform the theory and practice of MTSs, and vice versa. In that final section, we return to the contrasting contexts depicted in Figure 6.1 in which MTS exists with and without MTM, as well as contexts in which there is MTM but no MTS.

Prevalence and Examples of MTM

Examples of MTSs described elsewhere include emergency response and firefighting systems. In response to any given incident, such systems tend not to include MTM (i.e., tend not to have shared membership across component teams). For example, fire suppression and search and rescue teams do not share members, nor do surgical and recovery teams in medical MTSs. However, MTM is a common and increasingly widespread approach to organizing work.

Although MTM is mentioned frequently in the general press, we surveyed current and former full- and part-time MBA students at two universities to gauge MTM's prevalence more directly. We received 489 responses (a response rate of 72%), of whom 425 (87%) worked on project teams. Most were junior to middle-level staff members in their organizations, with an average organizational tenure of 3.2 years. Though not intended to represent the population of all employees, these respondents provided a useful sample drawn from a wide range of industries and professional occupations (Figure 6.2). Approximately 81% of those on teams worked on more than one team at a time, and many worked on several ($M = 2.75$, $SD = 3.77$).

Other surveys place the percentage of knowledge workers who are members of more than one team as high as 94.9% (Martin & Bal, 2006), and in at least one company (Intel), 28% are on five or more (Lu, Wynn, Chudoba, & Watson-Manheim, 2003). Taking these surveys together, MTM appears to be the norm for at least two-thirds of knowledge workers. This appears to be true in both the United States and Europe (Zika-Viktorsson, Sundstrom, & Engwall, 2006). Despite being common across a range of industries and occupations, MTM seems especially common (and particularly challenging) in IT, consulting, and new product development (e.g., Baschab & Piot, 2007; Milgrom & Roberts, 1992; Shore & Warden, 2007; Wheelwright & Clark, 1992).

Based on our surveys, interviews, and reading of the literature on teams, organizational design, and workplace trends, several factors appear to be driving the use of MTM as a way of organizing work. First, the prevalence of MTM seems to have grown in tandem with the growth of the knowledge work economy, in which workers are valued for their expertise (Blackler, 1995; Drucker, 1999; Mohrman, Cohen, & Mohrman, 1995), and the increased reliance on the project model (Bredin & Söderlund, 2006; Engwall, 1998; Grabher, 2002a, 2002b; Midler, 1995; Söderlund & Bredin,

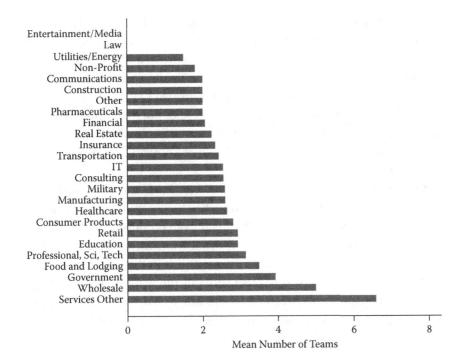

FIGURE 6.2
Multiple team membership by industry for those on at least one team (*n* = 425).

2006). Specialized expertise is best developed and leveraged in an environment in which workers can apply that experience to similar kinds of problems in a broad variety of situations, further allowing them to build on and generalize what they learn across settings (Lundin & Midler, 1998; Nobeoka, 1995; Sole & Edmondson, 2002).

Second, accompanying the rise of the knowledge economy is low unemployment for skilled workers in many parts of the United States (Bureau of Labor Statistics, 2005a, 2005b). This has led employers to create more motivating work environments to retain employees with special skills (Dychtwald, Morison, & Erickson, 2006). As one manager whom we interviewed explained, "People can work wherever they want to work. We have to make the work environment compelling. People want to work here. If you have scarce talent, you have to establish yourself and make work interesting." Another manager explained that assigning people to multiple teams made it easier to motivate them and keep their jobs interesting, because you can delicately shift them away from projects that are not working out toward a better match for their skills: "I think it is much easier to manage in a multiproject environment. If someone works for you 100% of the time, and there is a lull, then you have to find something good for them to do. But if they are on several different projects, then there is always something for them to do." In this sense, MTM is not unlike early approaches to job design (e.g., job enlargement or horizontal job loading), applied to the context of multiple teams, not just individual jobs or tasks (Chung & Ross, 1977; Griffin, 1982; Pierce & Dunham, 1976; Roberts & Glick, 1981).

Third, and finally, the shift toward flat, matrixed, and dispersed work increases the likelihood that people are asked to join multiple teams without anyone overseeing their overall schedule or commitment. A manager in one office might assign an employee to a team without realizing that she is already on three other teams for managers in distant offices. Thus, MTM prevalence appears to parallel shifts in the workforce where individuals seek greater expertise in their topic area and demand intellectually interesting work environments, as well as the increased likelihood that people work on dispersed project teams.

—————

THE RELATIONSHIPS BETWEEN MTM, LEARNING, AND PRODUCTIVITY

MTM presents both challenges and benefits to the individuals, teams, and organizations that use it as a way to organize work. In general, those benefits accrue when MTM is at moderate levels. In contrast, when MTM is too high or too low, it has the potential to trigger numerous problems. In this section, we describe the curvilinear relationships between MTM and two critical outcomes (productivity and learning) for individuals and teams. These relationships are a function of MTM's effects on time, attention, and information and are similar at both levels, but are driven by underlying mechanisms, actors, and processes that are distinct and level-specific. In particular, the team-level effects are not simply aggregations of individual-level effects. (O'Leary, Mortensen, & Woolley, in press.)

As noted earlier, we define MTM as a situation in which individuals are concurrently members of two or more teams within a given period of time. The level of MTM within a social system (i.e., within one organization or across multiple organizations) is a function of the average number of team memberships held by individual members within that same time period. To understand this definition, it is important to specify three of its key components: team, membership, and time period. *Teams* are bounded sets of individuals that work interdependently toward a shared outcome (Hackman, 2002). Team *members* share the responsibility and reward for their team's work and recognize each other as members of the team (not just consultants to it or otherwise peripheral participants in the team's work). It is also critical, when discussing MTM, to frame and bound any such discussion with respect to a context-specific *time period*. For emergency room teams, for example, MTM could be meaningfully assessed in terms of the average number of patient care teams on which doctors worked during their most recent 24–48-hour shift. For software developers, MTM would be assessed more appropriately on a weekly or biweekly basis.

Just as the time horizon over which MTM needs to be considered varies by context, so does the total amount of time people work, which we assume is relatively stable within any given work context. Acknowledging that (a) work time can clearly encroach on nonwork time; (b) individuals can shift time from one project to another; and (c) there are minor daily, weekly, or monthly variations in people's total work hours, individuals still have a limited amount of time available to work—whether it is 35–40 hours per week in some contexts or many more in others (Tischler, 2005). Thus, the time individuals dedicate to any one team must necessarily be reduced as they become members of multiple teams.

MTM affects a variety of individual and team outcomes (e.g., individual stress, work–life balance, workload, and social identity). In this chapter, we focus on MTM's relationship to productivity and learning. *Productivity* is an indicator of how effectively an individual or system converts inputs into outputs in terms of both quantity and quality (Adler & Clark, 1991). Individual productivity can be assessed with regard to a single team or in terms of an individual's average or total productivity across multiple teams. Here, we adopt the latter, broader framing. *Learning* is an indicator of the change in knowledge, routines, or behavior of an individual or team (Argote, 1999; Huber, 1991). Learning requires individual actors to "attend to, encode, store, and retrieve information that exists in the surrounding environment" (Ellis et al., 2003, p. 821). For teams, it consists of "the activities through which individuals acquire, share and combine knowledge" through their own experience and their interactions with each other (Argote, Gruenfeld, & Naquin, 1999, p. 370; Ellis et al., 2003). Thus, team learning involves search, transfer, and integration (Edmondson, 1999; Hansen, 1999). Although there is the potential for a reciprocal relationship between productivity and learning, we examine their relationship to MTM separately.

To understand MTM's effects on individual and team learning and productivity, it is critical to consider two particular mediating constructs: individual *context switching* and team *temporal misalignment*. At the individual level, individuals feel the effects of MTM most acutely when they frequently switch their focus from one team context to another. For teams, MTM's effects are felt through the mediating state of temporal misalignment, in which a lack of overlap and contiguous blocks of time in team members' schedules prevents them from focusing on one team's task and engaging in real-time idea generation, problem solving, decision making, and so on. Individual context switching and team temporal misalignment both tap into essential processes underlying how time, attention, and information are distributed (Mohrman et al., 1995; Quinn, 2005). The highest levels of productivity and learning occur with moderate levels of MTM-driven context switching and temporal misalignment.

MTM-Driven Context Switching, Productivity, and Learning

For individuals, the effects of MTM stem primarily from the costs and benefits of shifting from one team context to another. A team's context encompasses its tasks, technologies, roles, locations, and routines. In addition, each team constitutes a meaningful "symbolic domain" (Schultz, 1991), with its own distinct social definitions and meanings. Though any two teams can be more or less similar in their tasks, technologies, roles, locations, routines, and symbolic meanings, other things being equal, the more teams one is on, the more context switching one will do.

Just as team contexts may differ, so may the dynamics of the switches between them. These differences are driven by the *frequency* of the switches and the *degree of difference* between the relevant contexts. In terms of frequency, two people can have the same basic levels of MTM (e.g., they are both members of two teams concurrently), but have very different switching patterns over the course of a hypothetical week. For example, as shown

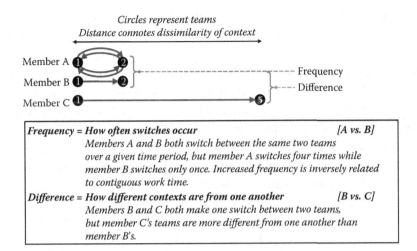

FIGURE 6.3
Characteristics of individual context switching.

with Members A and B in Figure 6.3, one might switch four times whereas the other switches only once (i.e., halfway through the week).

In addition to switching frequency, context switching is also characterized by the degree of difference among the contexts in question. One source of difference is the nature of the teams themselves. For example, the difference between two automobile design teams is likely to be far less dramatic than the difference between an automobile design team and a motorcycle marketing team. The latter two teams would be considerably different in terms of their tasks, functions, products, and so on (see Figure 6.3, members B and C, respectively). Thus, the effect of MTM-driven context switching is a function of both switching frequency and degree of difference.

Effects of MTM-Driven Context Switching on Productivity

We believe there is a curvilinear (inverted-U-shaped) relationship between context switching and individual productivity resulting from the costs of shifting attention and the competing benefits of load balancing and finding more efficient work practices. If individuals are members of multiple teams, complementary peaks and valleys in those teams' workloads may enable members to switch between teams and, thus, use their time more efficiently and effectively. When individuals are on only one team at a time, they may end up with excess slack in their schedule (if their one team has a lull in its work), which may lead them to devote more time to tasks than is truly required (Brooks, 1975). Some slack is useful. For example, *beach time* (when individuals are not assigned to projects or projects are in a lull) can provide welcome respites amidst high-intensity work (Barley & Kunda, 2004). However, if beach time persists or grows, it provokes anxiety and concern about one's value or about the organization's business viability (Yakura, 2001). MTM provides meaningful intervening work and a mechanism through which beach time can be reduced, as employees offset ebbs in one team's work with flows of another team's work. Wheelwright and Clark (1992, p. 90) witnessed this in the computer and electronics industry, and present data from one firm showing that the "percent of [engineers'] time on value-adding activities" rose from 70% to 80% as engineers added a second project. Being on multiple teams can also lead individuals to make more careful choices about how they spend their time and to develop more efficient work practices. In short, mild MTM-driven schedule pressure can help prevent work from simply expanding to fill the available time (Svenson & Maule, 1993; Waller, Conte, Gibson, & Carpenter, 2001).

Although MTM can enable load balancing and stimulate the development of more efficient work habits, the costs of MTM accrue as context switching becomes more frequent. People switch *tasks* as often as every 3 minutes (Mark, Gudith, & Klocke, 2008)—sometimes of their own accord and sometimes because they are interrupted. "Recovering" from such interruptions can consume as much as 41% of managers' time (O'Conaill & Frohlich, 1995). Although most work on interruptions has been done at the task level, it is reasonable to expect that frequent context switches also drive down productivity (DeMarco, 2002; DeMarco & Lister, 1985; Huey & Wickens, 1993)—perhaps even more than task switching because context switching can involve shifting roles, locations, and other aspects of context that go beyond the task itself. Wheelwright and Clark (1992, p. 90) observed this when the percentage of engineers' value-adding time dropped from 80% to 60% when they added a third project, to 45% when they added a fourth project, and to 35% when they were members of five projects. Aral, Brynjolfsson, and Van Alstyne (2006) found a similarly inverted-U-shaped relationship between individuals' multitasking and productivity, as has research on multiple roles (Thoits, 1986).

Thus, low levels of MTM-driven context switching can increase individual productivity by facilitating load balancing and stimulating more efficient work practices, but those benefits are offset rapidly by role conflict and overload and the time required for individuals to (a) regain focus; (b) reimmerse themselves in the people, roles, issues, and operations of another team context; (c) catch up on the work done in their absence; (d) physically relocate between team settings; and (e) shift between team-specific tools and technologies. As individuals become members of more teams, with a wider variety of tasks, roles, routines, locations, and tools, this context switching can exact considerable costs in terms of time, mental energy, and ultimately productivity.

Though relevant to all multiteaming situations, be they situated in multiteam systems or not, both the positive and negative effects of MTM are likely to be exacerbated by multiteam systems. As a key dimension of multiteam systems is their shared overall purpose, individuals involved in multiple team membership within MTSs are switching between multiple projects that are likely to be related to one another with respect to goals, schedules, and resources. The benefits of MTM-based context switching may facilitate easier switches, as the contexts of teams within MTSs are likely to be more similar than they might be in other MTM environments. As such, we expect switching costs to be lower in MTS contexts. At the same time, however, we similarly expect more extreme costs, as the teams found within an MTS context are likely to be cued to the same overall schedule and target dates—thus increasing the likelihood of multiple teams synchronously hitting points of high demand.

Effects of MTM-Driven Context Switching on Learning

As with productivity, we expect context switching to have an inverted-U-shaped relationship with individual learning. In the case of learning, the relationship is driven by the benefits of increased information variety and the costs of decreased integration time. For any learning to occur, an individual must access new information and then integrate it into his or her existing base of knowledge. Traditional job rotation usually involves *sequential* variation of work, which scholars across several disciplines have shown enhances individual learning (e.g., Allwood & Lee, 2004; Bourgeon, 2002; Eriksson & Ortega, 2006; Latham & Morin, 2005; Meyer, 1994; Ortega, 2001). The same variation and exposure to new information occur with MTM, but they happen *concurrently*, with increased opportunities to apply and integrate that new information. The MTM-driven comings and goings of team members can also enhance learning and the effort devoted to knowledge transfer and external knowledge acquisition (Kolodny, 1979; Zellmer-Bruhn, 2003).

Although concurrent exposure to new knowledge from different team contexts is likely to stimulate learning, the effect does not appear to be linear. High levels of MTM can undermine learning by introducing information that is too disparate to be integrated and by depriving people of the time needed for integration of new information. The diversity of exposure that MTM can bring is effective up to a point, but beyond that point any new information gained can be too diverse to relate meaningfully to one's existing knowledge, and too diverse for individuals to see relevant patterns in that information (Faniel & Majchrzak, 2007; Gratton & Ghoshal, 2003; Hirschfeld & Gelman, 1994). As a result, they learn less. This is consistent with prior research on other kinds of variety or diversity, which finds a similar curvilinear relationship with learning (Ancona & Caldwell, 1992; Earley & Mosakowski, 2000; Harrison & Klein, 2007). When switching occurs too frequently, it also limits people's ability to encode and retrieve knowledge (Bailey, 1989) and can be detrimental for learning (Gillie & Broadbent, 1989; Jett & George, 2003; Perlow, 1999).

As was the case with the effects of context switching on productivity within MTS contexts, we similarly expect the effects of context switching on learning to be particularly strong within MTS contexts. The shared goals of teams within MTSs imply that those team contexts are likely to be more similar than we might expect in other MTM situations. As a result, the knowledge learned in one team is likely to be more applicable to the other teams of which a given individual is also a member— thus increasing the likelihood of cross-team learning. At the same time, however, the increased overlap in contexts means that the uniqueness of information gained from multiple teams is likely to be lower than that found in unrelated teams. Thus, in the context of MTSs, the inherent relationships between the work being done in multiple teams may yield a convergence of information that is simultaneously easier to integrate and less novel.

MTM-Driven Temporal Misalignment, Productivity, and Learning

The team-level effects of MTM are driven primarily by the costs and benefits of misalignment in a team's temporal structure (Ballard & Seibold, 2003, 2004; Blount & Janicik, 2002; Orlikowski & Yates, 2002). For our purposes, a team's *temporal misalignment* is the extent to which team members do *not* have (a) overlapping work schedules, which limits their ability to work synchronously; and/or (b) temporally contiguous blocks of time to devote to the focal team's work, which introduces lags when work must be handed off from member to member. As MTM increases, so does temporal misalignment among team members. Temporal misalignment may result in greater ultimate productivity by forcing a team to find more efficient work practices. However, these benefits are likely to be short-lived and rapidly offset by increased coordination costs and lost opportunities to work synchronously.

It is important to note that schedule overlap and contiguous blocks of time are not based solely on the number of teams people are on and the percentage of their time dedicated to each. Assessing these two aspects of temporal misalignment requires knowledge of people's actual scheduling behavior and the nature of the task. Take, for example, the team in Figure 6.4.

All four members have 50% of their time dedicated to the focal team (Number 1) and 50% to a second team (Number 2). At one extreme, members B and C each spend Monday through midday on Wednesday on Team 1, and then transition to spend the rest of their time on Team 2. Thus, their schedules are 100% overlapping. At the other extreme, member A follows

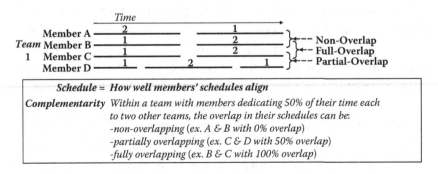

FIGURE 6.4
Example of schedule complementarity.

the opposite schedule, dedicating Monday through midday Wednesday to Team 2 and the rest to Team 1. In that case, their schedules do not overlap at all. As illustrated by member D, schedules can obviously include multiple transition points, allowing for any amount of overlap between the two extremes. Such transitions, however, also increase the number of potential misalignments and coordination overhead.

Though members A and B have no overlap in their schedules, which may constrain their ability to work on reciprocally interdependent tasks that benefit from synchronous interactions (Thompson, 1967), they do have complementary contiguous blocks of time. If they both need to do individual work toward Team 1's task, and that work is sequentially interdependent (Thompson, 1967), team member B will be able to hand off his or her portion of the task to member A with no lag. Member A's schedule allows for a clean transfer of the work. In contrast, member C may not be ready to receive the transfer because member C's schedule for the second half of the week is devoted to Team 2. Thus, temporal misalignment encompasses not only schedule overlap but also the complementary, contiguous blocks of time needed to facilitate sequentially interdependent work.

Effects of MTM-Driven Temporal Misalignment on Productivity

As MTM increases, teams are likely to become more efficient in their work. Knowing that they have small fractions of each other's time, and knowing that the coordination of that time will be challenging, team members search for ways to make their work more efficient. These practices may include more focused, structured meetings, in which teams consciously spend more time on task and less time on social, relational, or other interactions. As Fuller and Dennis (2004) noted, "The realization of misalignments or discrepant events can trigger certain activities by teams to reassess existing structures and enact new structures" (p. 2). Although there is eventually a quality–quantity trade-off, teams working under tighter time constraints do tend to produce at a faster rate (Bluedorn, Turban, & Love, 1999; Gevers, Rutte, & van Eerde, 2006; Harrison, Mohammed, McGrath, Florey, & Vanderstoep, 2003; Kelly & McGrath, 1985; Seers & Woodruff, 1997; Waller, Zellmer-Bruhn, & Giambatista, 2002). In contrast, when teams are not under some form of time pressure, they tend to use their time less efficiently and allow the work to expand to fill the time (Parkinson, 1955, 1958).

Although mild stress from MTM-driven temporal misalignment has some productivity benefits, teams can quickly reach the limits of their own efficiency-enhancing practices, and shift from being more selective in what they do to simply being less able to do it (Savolainen, 2007). Because team coordination processes are fairly fragile (Arrow, McGrath, & Berdahl, 2000), high temporal misalignment can quickly drive down productivity. Two primary mechanisms drive this negative effect on team productivity: (a) increased coordination costs (including more handoff problems between team members), and (b) decreased opportunity to work synchronously. As temporal misalignment increases, teams must devote more time to "process management" (Massey, Montoya-Weiss, & Hung, 2003) or the "overhead" (Fitzgerald & Wynn, 2004) required to find overlapping time in each other's schedules and sequence each other's work effectively given commitments beyond the focal team (Curris, Krasner, & Iscoe, 1988; Malone & Crowston, 1994; Masten, Meehan, & Snyder, 1991; Mayer, 2000; Montoya-Weiss, Massey, & Song, 2001; Olson, Teasley, Covi, & Olson, 2002). This is especially true when a team's work is highly interdependent (Wittenbaum, Vaughan, & Stasser, 1998). Limited overlap in members' schedules also requires teams to spend more time coordinating the handoffs of work from one member to another in between meetings to avoid schedule slippage (Zika-Viktorsson et al., 2006).

By contrast, when team members' schedules are aligned, they are less likely to experience slippage and can coordinate their efforts more quickly and easily (McGrath, 1991; Ocker, Hiltz, Turoff, & Fjermestad, 1995; Warkentin, Sayeed, & Hightower, 1997). The ability to work synchronously (especially in an impromptu fashion) enhances teams' productivity on complex, convergent tasks (Dennis, Fuller, & Valacich, 2008). Those synchronous interactions (especially, but not necessarily, face-to-face ones) are more evolutionarily natural (Kock, 2004) and enable fluid, interactive, intense dialogue that limits (or can correct) miscommunication, stimulates idea generation, facilitates resolution of ambiguities, fosters relationship building (Maznevski & Chudoba, 2000), and enhances productivity (Mabrito, 2006; Ruuska, Artto, Aaltonen, & Lehtonen, 2008). Not all work needs to be done synchronously, but work must be coordinated to minimize time lags between when team members are ready to hand off their part of a task and when other team members are ready to receive and begin work on that task (Gupta, 2009; Postrel, 2009). As Leroy and Sproull (forthcoming) noted, "Being fully in synch with a team and available when required is, however, likely to be much more difficult when people work on multiple teams at the same time."

Within the context of MTSs, the temporal misalignment of team members is likely to be particularly high, as the many teams within the system all share a common goal and likely share similar schedules. This increases the likelihood that interlinked teams will all need to draw heavily on their team members at the same time, creating cross-team clashes and conflicts over human resources.

Effects of MTM-Driven Temporal Misalignment on Learning

In addition to its effects on team productivity, temporal misalignment also has a curvilinear effect on team learning. The effect is driven by the benefits of unshared experience, as well as the costs of more difficult knowledge integration and shared repertoire development (Wilson, Goodman, & Cronin, 2007). Turning first to the benefits of unshared experience, *temporal misalignment*, by definition, means that team members spend time apart from one another. This time apart, in turn, increases the uniqueness of the team members' information by increasing their unshared experience. Analogous to the effect of individual-level context switching, teams gain a diversity of perspectives not only through increased diversity of experience within members but also across members. As such, a team with members who are each on one or more other teams draws not only on its own context but also on all of the contexts to which its members are exposed through their other team memberships. As noted by Lojeski, Reilly, and Dominick (2007), MTM enhances learning "because acquiring and storing knowledge among team members is not usually developed with just one group or through single projects," nor is it as likely via people's individual, non-team-based, independent work. In other words, teams with high and sustained levels of team member interactions (with low levels of external interaction) have a lower probability of retrieving new learning (Wilson et al., 2007). This is supported by a growing body of research regarding the importance of learning from external sources (Ancona & Bresman, 2007; Argote et al., 1999; Bresman, 2010; Edmondson, Bohmer, & Pisano, 2001; Tucker, Nembhard, & Edmondson, 2007; Wong, 2004; Zellmer-Bruhn, 2003).

At the same time, as Crossan, Lane, and White (1999) asserted, a critical component of effective team-level learning is integration. MTM-driven temporal misalignment can impede a team's ability to integrate the diverse knowledge it has gathered for four distinct but related reasons. First, to effectively interpret and encode the information gained by individual team members, team members must have a shared frame of reference so that they treat the information similarly (Levine, Resnick, & Higgins, 1993; Paese, Bieser, & Tubbs, 1993; Tindale, Sheffey, & Scott, 1993). Second, time outside the team is likely to generate larger pools of unique information that are likely to remain unshared (Stasser, Taylor, & Hanna, 1989; Stasser & Titus, 1985) and ultimately lost to the group (Hinsz, Tindale, & Vollrath, 1997). Third, teams lack synchronous time to carry out the actual sharing itself. As temporal misalignment in a team increases, team members have less time to interact face-to-face or voice-to-voice and have less opportunity to pool their collected information and meaningfully integrate it. Fourth, and finally, as Wilson et al. (2007) argued, relatively rare synchronous interactions hamper information retrieval and team learning. We expect this also will be true in high-MTM contexts, with their associated high levels of temporal misalignment.

Further exacerbating these negative effects are the adjustments that temporally misaligned teams are likely to make to their processes to increase the proportion of tasks that can be carried out independently. Teams that have difficulty synchronizing meeting times are likely to suffer from more communication and coordination problems (McGrath, 1991; Montoya-Weiss et al., 2001). If team members experience difficulty scheduling time to meet synchronously (whether in face-to-face or digitally mediated meetings), they will tend to structure their work so that it can be done more independently. Working in this highly independent manner, teams revert to being teams in name only, or what Hackman (1990) called "co-acting groups." This is especially problematic when MTM is present in a system of teams that are interdependent not only in terms of their membership but also in terms of other inputs, processes, and outputs.

As was the case with respect to context switching, the asynchronous nature of multiple team membership within multiteam systems affects the ability of those teams to learn. The time spent apart in multiteam systems allows for the gathering of different, novel information. To the extent that teams share similar goals and foci, as in the case of multiteam systems, the variance in that information is likely to be lower, thus resulting in smaller learning benefits.

THE CHALLENGES OF MTM

Beyond the costs and benefits of MTM for the particular teams engaged in it, MTM also poses unique challenges for managers and for the broader multiteam systems in which it may occur. In one sense, MTM is simply a dimension along which the typical level of interdependence in an MTS is increased. Where MTSs have historically been studied in terms of their outcome and process interdependence, MTM adds interdependence in terms of human inputs as well. By increasing the interdependence in an MTS and making it more complex, MTM adds a number of challenges for team leaders and managers at the system level.

Managerial Challenges Posed by MTM

Multiple team membership poses serious and unique challenges for team leaders above and beyond those found in teams lacking shared membership. Three of particular note are leaders' lack of control over their team members' time, the need to coordinate not only within but also across teams, and higher levels of stress among team members. We address each of these in turn.

First, team leaders have less control over their employees' time and efforts. In the context of fully dedicated membership, team leaders typically have knowledge of, and in some cases control over, their employees' obligations and schedules. This, however, is frequently not the case within the context of MTM, wherein team leaders have a say over only part of their employees' time. The remainder of their employees' time is under the control of either the leaders of the other teams with whom they share membership or the individual employees themselves (if they control the allotment of their time across teams). Thus, team leaders in a combined MTM–MTS context have less control over their human resources than would be the case in team settings without overlapping membership.

Second, compounding the issue, although managers in MTM contexts have less control over their human resources than do managers in non-MTM situations, they also have a greater need to coordinate those resources. The more that individual employees work on multiple teams, the more important it is that those individuals' obligations are proactively coordinated by the leaders of those multiple teams. Particularly within the context of multiteam systems, where multiple teams are working on related projects, the likelihood of conflicting obligations is high. As described in Chapter 1 (Zaccaro, Marks, and DeChurch) and in Chapter 12 (Davison and Hollenbeck), team leaders play an especially important role in MTSs. Their importance is greater still when there is MTM-driven input interdependence in the MTS.

Third, team leaders must also be aware of, and deal with, the additional stresses placed on their employees by working in MTM environments. As noted in our interviews, in addition to the typical demands of working on any team, working in multiple teams adds to overhead and coordination costs. To manage effectively in MTM environments, leaders must be sensitive to those additional demands and assist employees in dealing with them as they arise. Taken together, these challenges make managing within MTM environments more demanding than in MTSs with only process and output interdependence, and dramatically more so than in organizations with independent teams.

System-Level Challenges of MTM

Beyond the challenges facing members and leaders of particular teams, it is important to consider the dynamics of MTM at the level of the *system* of interrelated teams. In a way, MTM is a genie that—once out of the bottle—is hard to get back in. Once MTM becomes an accepted way to organize work in a given context, MTM can quickly feed on itself and spiral rapidly to higher than beneficial levels. This spiraling comes despite numerous books (especially in the innovation, R&D, and technology sectors) that bemoan the use of MTM. Shore and Warden (2007) provided just one of many examples. They wrote,

> All the team members should sit with the team full time and give the project their full attention.... Some organizations like to assign people to multiple projects simultaneously. This *fractional assignment* is particularly common in matrix-managed organizations.... If your company practices fractional assignment, I have some good news. You can instantly improve productivity by reassigning people to only one project at a time. Fractional assignment

is dreadfully counterproductive: fractional workers don't bond with their teams, they often aren't around to hear conversations and answer questions, and they must task switch, which incurs a significant hidden penalty. (p. 39)

DeMarco (2002) inveighed against MTM with similar certitude, writing, "Fragmented knowledge workers may look busy, but a lot of their busyness is just thrashing" (p. 20). In this chapter, we discussed why organizations are turning more and more frequently to MTM despite criticisms and warnings like those just quoted. In this final section, we address why organizations have a difficult time keeping MTM at healthy, moderate levels. We identify six primary reasons.

First, managers at the organizational level may not realize what is happening at the team and individual levels. Individuals are typically added to teams in a piecemeal fashion, joining additional teams as they are formed or when their particular skills are needed. In addition, teams themselves are increasingly fluid—often formed and disbanded on an as-needed basis (Cohen & Bailey, 1997; Sundstrom, McIntyre, Halfhill, & Richards, 2000). This results in what Bresnen, Goussevskaia, and Swan (2004) called a "partly indeterminate and shifting organizational terrain" (p. 1537)—one in which those managers may not have a true sense of the extent to which MTM is occurring.

Second, even when recognizing the existence of MTM, team members and managers may not have tied it to the problems it causes. Although individuals may observe negative outcomes, they do not always recognize MTM as the source of those outcomes. The stress and overwork associated with working on multiple projects with synchronized schedules are often just identified as *busy periods* or *crunch times*. Members frequently fail to recognize that this stress is a product of their teams' particular configuration.

Third, even in the face of awareness, there may also be countervailing forces that outweigh the negative effects of MTM. For example, individual team members may want the exposure, variety, and learning that they gain from being on multiple teams and be willing to trade off the costs. Teams and their managers may recognize the cost savings of sharing resources—savings that outweigh the costs of doing so. Organizations or other MTSs may view MTM as a means of ensuring commonality of focus and purpose among employees across related projects, which can be an outcome valued more highly than the process losses MTM incurs.

Fourth, in other cases, managers may accept MTM as the "nature of the beast." The people for whom MTM is especially problematic are often middle managers who are still doing some "real work" across multiple teams during the day and then must do their managerial work (e.g., performance evaluation, scheduling, and budgeting) during the evening or early morning hours. They can see MTM as a necessary condition of their intermediate status and progression to higher management ranks.

Fifth, in certain domains and cultures, there may be strong norms promoting MTM. In billable-hours cultures, for example, one of the best ways to maintain high utilization rates is to be on multiple teams. Being on only one project team can limit one's ability to be fully billable, whereas being on multiple teams provides additional flexibility and "wiggle room." Also, for senior managers, it is common to be nominally members of multiple teams and "peanut butter" their time across projects when they bill their hours.

Sixth, and finally, as we suggested earlier, MTM feeds on itself. Identifying, accessing, and combining an organization's dispersed expertise are critical for organizational success (Grant, 1996) and managers try to staff projects with the optimal set of individuals with the particular skills required by the task (Boh et al., 2007). Membership in multiple teams is a key mechanism through which information about individuals' skills and abilities is disseminated throughout the organization, highlighting those who are "star performers." As noted by Yakura (2001), individuals considered "the best" are therefore in the highest demand, consequently getting selected for multiple teams even when they don't have the bandwidth. As "the best," those people may have an even harder time saying "no" to additional team memberships because they have high levels of self-confidence and their identity as "one of the best" is tied to being able to take on anything that comes their way. Thus, by providing signals of competence, "star" individuals are likely to be more sought-after and consequently placed on multiple teams, increasing MTM.

DEALING WITH THE CHALLENGES

Despite the challenges associated with both working in and managing teams in a multiple team membership environment, MTM remains common and increasingly prevalent. It adds a dimension of interdependence and complexity to already-complex multiteam systems. To help managers foster the benefits of MTM while avoiding its key pitfalls, we highlight some of the potential levers that managers can use to reduce the negative consequences of MTM. Although we discuss these as managerial interventions, it should be noted that many can also be applied by team members themselves. To structure our discussion, we focus on those factors likely to impact context switching and temporal misalignment and highlight four basic categories of levers—those associated with team membership, task, technology, and norms.

Membership

Though not always recognized, one factor at managers' disposal is the composition of the team itself. Through manipulating membership, teams and managers can address both context switching and temporal misalignment. Although it is definitionally impossible to eliminate context switching in MTM environments, the severity of the switches that do occur can be reduced by intentionally assigning—or reassigning—employees to complementary teams. Returning to our earlier example, when looking for a brake designer for a new motorcycle, managers should consider drawing from individuals who are working on other motorcycle brakes as opposed to car or truck brakes. Beyond alignment in the context of other teams, managers can intentionally design teams to increase the complementarity in members' schedules and through that reduce temporal misalignment. By selecting team members whose other team assignments are on similar schedules, team managers increase the amount of potentially overlapping time available to the team, thereby reducing temporal misalignment.

Task

Another approach to addressing the negative consequences of MTM is through the team's task. First, changing the structure of the task with the goal of creating larger contiguous blocks of work per member will help to reduce context-switching frequency. Similarly, managers can modify task assignments to maximize the amount of time spent within the team, even if not entirely on a single subtask. Creating larger contiguous blocks can also serve to reduce temporal misalignment. Temporal misalignment can also be reduced by delaying all or part of a project until more team members will be available.

Technology

Technology can also be used to alleviate the negative effects of MTM. Communications technologies allow team members to handle problems arising in other teams quickly and remotely. By allowing team members to address concerns "from within" their focal team, this reduces the need for those individuals to switch contexts as frequently to deal with minor issues. Technologies can also allow a focal team to meet virtually when all team members cannot meet face-to-face. This allows teams to take advantage of smaller windows of time when members' schedules align but there is not enough time for all team members to physically get together.

Norms

Finally, behavioral norms and expectations also provide a mechanism for addressing some of the issues surrounding MTM. By relaxing norms demanding consensus in decision making or high levels of participation, managers can reduce the need for all team members to be present or involved in group processes. This can reduce the frequency of context switches as team members working on other teams need not return to the team as often. Norms governing work hours also provide a point of leverage, as expanding the workday or allowing more flexible work arrangements may increase the potential to find time slots that work for all or most team members.

MTM AND MTS

Having discussed the temporal and other dynamics of MTM, we now turn to the ways in which MTM does (or could) relate to MTS in both research and practice, and vice versa. To date, MTS field research has tended to focus on organizational and experimental contexts in which MTM is rare, and in some studies it is experimentally controlled away. However, MTM is common and increasingly prevalent for many of the same reasons that MTSs are increasingly common (e.g., complex, interorganizational, global business and military challenges requiring systems of teams to address them). As with process and output interdependence, the interdependence associated with MTM can exist outside MTS contexts, but many of the settings in which we have observed MTM are also multiteam systems. Thus, to understand the full range of MTSs requires understanding all three dimensions of interdependence—including input interdependence, with team members themselves being one of the most critical inputs for any team-based work. In this final section, we highlight two areas where MTM and MTS approaches might benefit one another.

First, the existing work on MTSs has focused on groups of team leaders as the primary means by which coordination across teams occurs. Team leaders as cross-team coordinators are clearly common, but MTM adds the potential for individual members to do some of the coordination as well. In a sense, MTM opens the door for a more distributed form of leadership (Ancona, Malone, Orlikowski, & Senge, 2007; Mehra, Smith, Dixon, & Robertson, 2006). Such leadership may not be as effective when projects are in an extremely high-risk, high-reliability, or highly volatile environment. Under such conditions, MTSs with MTM may still need to rely primarily on individual team leaders to coordinate multiple teams' efforts. However, even in fast-moving projects, individual team members may be able to coordinate across teams more quickly than individual team leaders could. Waiting for the relevant team leaders' schedules to overlap (i.e., depending on temporal alignment) might cause more delays in the system than allowing individual, overlapping members to address coordination questions within their range of expertise and responsibility.

Second, when teams in an MTS are linked primarily by their individual leaders, the opportunities for and likelihood of information flow across teams are necessarily constrained. Even the best intentioned and most highly skilled team leaders will not be able to share as much information as several team members with overlapping memberships would. As teams grow in size, the number of dyadic relationships grows nonlinearly. On one hand, this can cause an unmanageably large number of relationships to manage. On the other hand, it can enable the rapid, impromptu flow of information within an MTS at the level where that information can be most readily and effectively utilized.

Ultimately, the success of an MTS may depend on balancing the competing coordination costs and benefits of relying on a team leader versus using a team leader plus the overlapping team members. Furthermore, the success of an MTS is likely to depend on balancing the coordination costs and benefits with the information flow costs and benefits that result from multiple team membership within an MTS. To date, research on MTSs has rarely considered the positive or negative implications of interdependent inputs (especially human ones). Similarly, the nascent work on MTM has not yet considered the contextual constraints and opportunities that arise when MTM exists within an MTS.

CONCLUSION

Creating both costs and benefits for the members, managers, and organizations involved in it, MTM is an increasingly common reality in today's world—especially within the context of MTSs. In MTS contexts, MTM presents a significant additional layer of complexity. By binding teams together via their shared membership, there is both the potential for heightened productivity and learning, as well as the enhanced risk that both will suffer if MTM is not managed carefully and kept at appropriate levels. In MTSs, teams' contexts are likely to be more similar than in single-team systems, and, thus, switching costs are likely to be lower for those on multiple teams. However, teams in an MTS are likely to be following more similar overall schedules, and, thus, the temporal linkages and process interdependence will make MTM-driven costs more extreme. The process of learning across shared membership ties in an MTS is also likely to be easier because of the greater relevance and applicability of cross-team knowledge, but that information also risks being so similar that it becomes redundant in an MTS. In terms of temporal misalignment, MTSs are likely to enhance the overlap in workers' schedules, with a common goal or project yielding more coinciding deadlines and clashes over shared (human) resources as schedule pressures increase.

In short, MTM is a little-explored but extremely common way of organizing work—one that is especially common in multiteam systems. Such systems tend to heighten the risks and rewards of multiple team membership, providing especially good opportunities for scholars to track the curvilinearity of MTM's costs and benefits and better understand the managerial and member practices that can keep MTM at effective levels.

REFERENCES

Adler, P. S., & Clark, K. B. (1991). Behind the learning curve: A sketch of the learning process. *Management Science, 37*(3), 267–281.

Allwood, J. M., & Lee, W. L. (2004). The impact of job rotation on problem solving skills. *International Journal of Production Research, 42*(5), 865–881.

Ancona, D. G., & Bresman, H. (2007). *X-teams: How to build teams that lead, innovate and succeed.* Cambridge, MA: HBS Press.

Ancona, D. G., & Caldwell, D. F. (1992). Demography and design: Predictors of new product performance. *Organization Science, 3*(3), 321–341.

Ancona, D., Malone, T., Orlikowski, W., & Senge, P. (2007). In praise of the incomplete leader. *Harvard Business Review, 85*(2), 92–99.

Aral, S., Brynjolfsson, E., & Van Alstyne, M. W. (2006, June). Information, technology and information worker productivity: Task level evidence. Paper presented at the International Conference on Information Systems, Milwaukee, WI.

Argote, L. (1999). *Organizational learning: Creating, retaining and transferring knowledge.* Boston: Kluwer Academic.

Argote, L., Gruenfeld, D. H., & Naquin, C. (1999). Group learning in organizations. In M. E. Turner (Ed.), *Groups at work: Advances in theory and research* (pp. 369–411). Mahwah, NJ: Erlbaum.

Arrow, H. A., McGrath, J. E., & Berdahl, J. L. (2000). *Small groups as complex systems: Formation, coordination, development and adaptation.* Thousand Oaks, CA: Sage.

Bailey, C. D. (1989). Forgetting and the learning curve: A laboratory study. *Management Science, 35*(3), 340–352.

Ballard, D., & Seibold, D. (2003). Communicating and organizing in time: A meso-level model of organizational temporality. *Management Communication Quarterly, 16*(3), 380–415.

Ballard, D., & Seibold, D. (2004). Communication-related organizational structures and work group temporal experiences: The effects of coordination method, technology type, and feedback cycle on members construals and enactments of time. *Communication Monographs, 71*(1), 1–27.

Barley, S. R., & Kunda, G. (2004). *Gurus, hired guns, and warm bodies: Itinerant experts in a knowledge economy.* Princeton, NJ: Princeton University Press.

Baschab, J., & Piot, J. (2007). *Executives guide to information technology.* New York: Wiley.

Blackler, F. (1995). Knowledge, knowledge work and organizations: An overview and interpretation. *Organization Studies, 16*(6), 1021–1046.

Blount, S., & Janicik, G. (2002). Getting and staying in-pace: The in-synch preference and its implications for work groups. *Research on Managing Groups and Teams, 4,* 235–266.

Bluedorn, A. C., Turban, D. B., & Love, M. S. (1999). The effects of stand-up and sit-down meeting formats on meeting outcomes. *Journal of Applied Psychology, 84*(2), 277–285.

Boh, W., Ren, Y., Kiesler, S., & Bussjaeger, R. (2007). Expertise and collaboration in the geographically dispersed organization. *Organization Science, 18*(4), 595.

Bourgeon, L. (2002). Temporal context of organizational learning in new product development projects. *Creativity & Innovation Management, 11*(3), 175–183.

Bredin, K., & Söderlund, J. (2006). Perspective on human resources management: An explorative study of the consequences of projectification in four firms. *International Journal of Human Resource Development & Management, 6*(1), 92–113.

Bresman, H. (2010). External learning activities and team performance: A multimethod field study. *Organization Science, 21*(1), 81–96.

Bresnen, M., Goussevskaia, A., & Swan, J. (2004). Embedding new management knowledge in project-based organizations. *Organization Studies (01708406), 25*(9), 1535–1555.

Brooks, F. P., Jr. (1975). *The mythical man-month.* Boston: Addison Wesley.

Bureau of Labor Statistics. (2005a). *Table A-10: Employed and unemployed persons by occupation.* Washington, DC: Author.

Bureau of Labor Statistics. (2005b). *Tomorrow's jobs.* Washington, DC: Author.

Chung, K. H., & Ross, M. F. (1977). Differences in motivational properties between job enlargement and job enrichment. *Academy of Management Review, 2*(1), 113–122.

Cohen, S. G., & Bailey, D. E. (1997). What makes teams work: Group effectiveness research from the shop floor to the executive suite. *Journal of Management, 23*(3), 239–290.

Crossan, M. M., Lane, H. W., & White, R. E. (1999). An organizational learning framework: From intuition to institution. *Academy of Management Review, 24*(3), 522–537.

Curris, B., Krasner, H., & Iscoe, N. (1988). A field study of software design process for large systems. *Communication of the ACM, 31*(11), 1268–1287.

DeMarco, T. (2002). *Slack: Getting past burnout, busywork, and the myth of total efficiency.* New York: Broadway.

DeMarco, T., & Lister, T. (1985). Programmer performance and the effects of the workplace. In *Proceedings of the 8th International Conference on Software Engineering* (pp. 268–272). Los Alamitos, CA: IEEE Computer Society Press.

Dennis, A., Fuller, R., & Valacich, J. (2008). Media, tasks, and communication processes: A theory of media synchronicity. *MIS Quarterly, 32*(3), 575–600.

Drucker, P. F. (1999). Knowledge worker productivity: The biggest challenge. *California Management Review, 41*(2), 79–95.

Dychtwald, K., Morison, R., & Erickson, T. (2006). *Workforce crisis: How to beat the coming shortage of skills and talent.* Boston: HBS Press.

Earley, P. C., & Mosakowski, E. (2000). Creating hybrid team cultures: An empirical test of transnational team functioning. *Academy of Management Journal, 43*(1), 26–49.

Edmondson, A. (1999). Psychological safety and learning behavior in work teams. *Administrative Science Quarterly, 44*(2), 350–383.

Edmondson, A., Bohmer, R., & Pisano, G. (2001). Speeding up team learning. *Harvard Business Review, 79*(9), 125–132.

Ellis, A. P. J., Hollenbeck, J. R., Ilgen, D. R., Porter, C. O. L. H., West, B. J., & Moon, H. (2003). Team learning: Collectively connecting the dots. *Journal of Applied Psychology, 88*(5), 821–834.

Engwall, L. (1998). The project concept(s): On the unit of analysis in the study of project management. In R. A. Lundin & C. Midler (Eds.), *Projects as arenas for renewal and learning processes.* Boston: Kluwer.

Eriksson, T., & Ortega, J. (2006). The adoption of job rotation: Testing the theories. *Industrial & Labor Relations Review, 59*(4), 653–666.

Faniel, I., & Majchrzak, A. (2007). Innovating by accessing knowledge across departments. *Decision Support Systems, 43*(4), 1684–1691.

Fitzgerald, B., & Wynn, E. (2004, May 30–June 2). *Innovation for adaptability and competitiveness: IFIP TC8/WG8.6* (Proceedings of the Seventh Working Conference on IT Innovation for Adaptability and Competitiveness). Leixlip, Ireland: Kluwer Academic.

Fuller, R., & Dennis, A. (2004). Does fit matter? The impact of fit on collaboration technology effectiveness over time, *Proceedings of the 37th annual Hawaii International Conference on System Sciences* (p. 10). Manoa: Shidler College of Business, University of Hawai'i.

Gevers, J. M. P., Rutte, C. G., & van Eerde, W. (2006). Meeting deadlines in work groups: Implicit and explicit mechanisms. *Applied Psychology: An International Review, 55*(1), 52–72.

Gillie, T., & Broadbent, D. (1989). What makes interruptions disruptive? A study of length, similarity and complexity. *Psychological Research & Development, 50*, 243–250.

Grabher, G. (2002a). Cool projects, boring institutions: Temporary collaboration in social context. *Regional Studies, 36*(3), 205–214.

Grabher, G. (2002b). The project ecology of advertising: Tasks, talents and teams. *Regional Studies, 36*(3), 245–262.

Grant, R. M. (1996). Toward a knowledge-based theory of the firm. *Strategic Management Journal, 17*, 109–122.

Gratton, L., & Ghoshal, S. (2003). Managing personal human capital: New ethos for the "volunteer" employee. *European Management Journal, 21*(1), 1–10.

Griffin, R. W. (1982). *Task design: An integrative approach*. Glenview, IL: Scott Foresman.

Gupta, A. (2009). The 24-hour knowledge factory: Can it replace the graveyard shift? *Computer, 42*(1), 66–73.

Hackman, J. R. (1990). *Groups that work (and those that don't): Creating conditions for effective teamwork*. San Francisco: Jossey-Bass.

Hackman, J. R. (2002). *Leading teams: Setting the stage for great performances*. Boston: Harvard Business School Press.

Hansen, M. T. (1999). The search-transfer problem: The role of weak ties in sharing knowledge across organization subunits. *Administrative Science Quarterly, 44*(1), 82–111.

Harrison, D. A., Mohammed, S., McGrath, J. E., Florey, A. T., & Vanderstoep, S. W. (2003). Time matters in team performance: Effects of member familiarity, entrainment, and task discontinuity on speed and quality. *Personnel Psychology, 56*(3), 633–669.

Harrison, D. D., & Klein, K. J. (2007). What's the difference? Diversity constructs as separation, variety, or disparity in organizations. *Academy of Management Review, 32*(4), 1199–1228.

Hinsz, V. B., Tindale, R. S., & Vollrath, D. A. (1997). The emerging conceptualization of groups as information processors. *Psychological Bulletin, 121*, 43–64.

Hirschfeld, L. A., & Gelman, S. A. (Eds.). (1994). *Mapping the mind: Domain specificity in cognition and culture*. Cambridge: Cambridge University Press.

Huber, G. P. (1991). Organizational learning: The contributing process and literatures. *Organization Science, 2*(1), 88–115.

Huey, B. M., & Wickens, C. D. (Eds.). (1993). *Workload transition: Implications for individual and team performance*. Washington, DC: National Academy Press.

Jett, Q. R., & George, J. M. (2003). Work interrupted: A closer look at the role of interruptions in organizational life. *Academy of Management Review, 28*, 494–507.

Kelly, J. R., & McGrath, J. E. (1985). Effects of time limits and task types on task performance and interaction of four-person groups. *Journal of Personality and Social Psychology, 49*(2), 395–407.

Kock, N. (2004). The psychobiological model: Towards a new theory of computer-mediated communication based on Darwinian evolution. *Organization Science, 15*(3), 327–348.

Kolodny, H. F. (1979). Evolution to a matrix organization. *Academy of Management Review, 4*(4), 543–553.

Latham, G. P., & Morin, L. (2005). Job rotation. In L. Peters, C. R. Greer, and S. Youngblood, (Eds.). *Blackwell encyclopedic dictionary of human resource management* (pp. 210–211). Malden, MA: Blackwell.

Leroy, S., & Sproull, L. S. (Forthcoming). When team work means working on multiple teams: Examining the impact of multiple team memberships. *Organizational Behavior & Human Decision Processes.*

Levine, J. M., Resnick, L. B., & Higgins, E. T. (1993). Social foundations of cognition. *Annual Review of Psychology, 44*(1), 585–612.

Lojeski, K., Reilly, R., & Dominick, P. (2007). Multitasking and innovation in virtual teams. In *Proceedings of the 40th Hawaii International Conference on System Sciences* (Vol. 40, 1–9). Piscataway, NJ: IEEE.

Lu, M., Wynn, E., Chudoba, K., & Watson-Manheim, M. B. (2003). Understanding virtuality in a global organization: Toward a virtuality index. In S. T. March, A. Massey, & J. I. DeGross (Eds.), *Proceedings of the International Conference on Information Systems* (pp. 1–7). Seattle, WA: Association for Information Systems.

Lundin, R. A., & Midler, C. (1998). *Projects as arenas for renewal and learning processes.* Boston: Kluwer Academic.

Mabrito, M. (2006). A study of synchronous versus asynchronous collaboration in an online business writing class. *American Journal of Distance Education, 20*(2), 93–107.

Malone, T. W., & Crowston, K. (1994). The interdisciplinary study of coordination. *ACM Computing Surveys, 26*(1), 87–119.

Mark, G., Gudith, D., & Klocke, U. (2008). The cost of interrupted work: More speed and stress. In *Proceedings of the 26th annual SIGCHI Conference on Human Factors in Computing Systems* (pp. 107–110). Florence, Italy: ACM.

Martin, A., & Bal, V. (2006). *The state of teams.* Greensboro, NC: Center for Creative Leadership.

Massey, A. P., Montoya-Weiss, M. M., & Hung, Y. T. (2003). Because time matters: Temporal coordination in global virtual project teams. *Journal of Management Information Systems, 19*, 129–155.

Masten, S. E., Meehan, J. W., & Snyder, E. A. (1991). The costs of organization. *Journal of Law, Economics, and Organization, 7*(1), 1–25.

Mayer, K. J. (2000, September). Transactional alignment and project performance: Evidence from information technology. Paper presented at the ISNIE Conference, Tübingen, Germany.

Maznevski, M. L., & Chudoba, K. M. (2000). Bridging space over time: Global virtual team dynamics and effectiveness. *Organization Science, 11*(5), 473–492.

McGrath, J. E. (1991). Time, interaction, and performance (TIP): A theory of groups. *Small Group Research, 22*(2), 147–174.

Mehra, A., Smith, B. R., Dixon, A. L., & Robertson, B. (2006). Distributed leadership in teams: The network of leadership perceptions and team performance. *Leadership Quarterly, 17*(3), 232–245.

Meyer, M. A. (1994). The dynamics of learning with team production: Implications for task assignment. *Quarterly Journal of Economics, 109*(4), 1157–1184.

Midler, C. (1995). "Projectification" of the firm: The Renault case. *Scandinavian Journal of Management, 11*(4), 363–375.

Milgrom, P. R., & Roberts, J. (1992). *Economics, organization, and management.* Englewood Cliffs, NJ: Prentice Hall.

Mohrman, S. A., Cohen, S. G., & Mohrman, A. M., Jr. (1995). *Designing team-based organizations: New forms for knowledge work.* New York: Jossey-Bass.

Montoya-Weiss, M. M., Massey, A. P., & Song, M. (2001). Getting it together: Temporal coordination and conflict management in global virtual teams. *Academy of Management Journal, 44*(6), 1251–1262.

Nobeoka, K. (1995). Inter-project learning in new product development. *Academy of Management Journal Best Papers Proceedings,* 432–436.

Ocker, R., Hiltz, S. R., Turoff, M., & Fjermestad, J. (1995). The effects of distributed group support and process structuring on software requirements development teams: Results on creativity and quality. *Journal of Management Information Systems, 12*(3), 127–153.

O'Conaill, B., & Frohlich, D. (1995). Timespace in the workplace: Dealing with interruptions. In *Proceedings of the Conference on Human Factors in Computing Systems* (pp. 262–263). Denver, CO: ACM Press.

O'Leary, M. B., Mortensen, M., & Woolley, A. W. (In press.) Multiple team membership: A theoretical model of its effects on productivity and learning for individuals and teams. *Academy of Management Review, 36*(3), XX–44.

Olson, J. S., Teasley, S., Covi, L., & Olson, G. M. (2002). The (currently) unique advantages of collocated work. In P. Hinds & S. Kiesler (Eds.), *Distributed work* (pp. 113–136). Cambridge, MA: MIT Press.

Orlikowski, W. J., & Yates, J. (2002). It's about time: Temporal structuring in organizations. *Organization Science, 13*(6), 684–699.

Ortega, J. (2001). Job rotation as a learning mechanism. *Management Science, 47*(10), 1361–1370.

Paese, P. W., Bieser, M., & Tubbs, M. E. (1993). Framing effects and choice shifts in group decision making. *Organizational Behavior and Human Decision Processes, 56,* 149–165.

Parkinson, C. N. (1955). Parkinson's law. *The Economist,* 635–637.

Parkinson, C. N. (1958). *Parkinson's law: The pursuit of progress.* London: John Murray.

Perlow, L. A. (1999). The time famine: Toward a sociology of work time. *Administrative Science Quarterly, 44*(1), 57–81.

Pierce, J. L., & Dunham, R. B. (1976). Task design: A literature review. *Academy of Management Review, 1*(4), 83–97.

Postrel, S. (2009). Multitasking teams with variable complementarity: Challenges for capability management. *Academy of Management Review, 34*(2), 273–296.

Quinn, R. W. (2005). Flow in knowledge work: High performance experience in the design of national security technology. *Administrative Science Quarterly, 50,* 610–641.

Roberts, K. H., & Glick, W. (1981). The job characteristics approach to task design: A critical review. *Journal of Applied Psychology, 66*(2), 193–217.

Ruuska, I., Artto, K., Aaltonen, K., & Lehtonen, P. (2008). Dimensions of distance in a project network: Exploring Olkiluoto 3 nuclear power plant project. *International Journal of Project Management, 27*(2), 142–153.

Savolainen, R. (2007). Filtering and withdrawing: Strategies for coping with information overload in everyday contexts. *Journal of Information Science, 33*(5), 611–621.

Schultz, M. (1991). Transitions between symbolic domains in organizations. *Organization Studies, 12*(4), 489–506.

Seers, A., & Woodruff, S. (1997). Temporal pacing in task forces: Group development or deadline pressure. *Journal of Management, 23*(2), 169–187.

Shore, J., & Warden, S. (2007). *Art of agile development.* Sebastopol, CA: O'Reilly Media.

Söderlund, J., & Bredin, K. (2006). HRM in project-intensive firms: Changes and challenges. *Human Resource Management, 45*(2), 249–265.

Sole, D., & Edmondson, A. (2002). Bridging knowledge gaps: Learning in geographically dispersed crossfunctional teams. In N. Bontis, & C. W. Choo (Eds.), *Strategic management of intellectual capital and organizational knowledge.* Oxford: Oxford University Press.

Stasser, G., Taylor, L. A., & Hanna, C. (1989). Information sampling in structured and unstructured discussions of three- and six-person groups. *Journal of Personality and Social Psychology, 57*(1), 67–78.

Stasser, G., & Titus, W. (1985). Pooling of unshared information during group decision making: Biased information sampling during discussion. *Journal of Personality & Social Psychology, 48,* 1467–1478.

Sundstrom, E., McIntyre, M., Halfhill, T., & Richards, H. (2000). Work groups: From the Hawthorne studies to work teams of the 1990s and beyond. *Group Dynamics, 4,* 44–67.

Svenson, O., & Maule, A. J. (Eds.). (1993). *Time pressure and stress in human judgment and decision making.* New York: Springer.

Thoits, P. A. (1986). Multiple identities: Examining gender and marital status differences in distress. *American Sociological Review, 51,* 259–272.

Thompson, J. D. (1967). *Organizations in action.* New York: McGraw-Hill.

Tindale, R. S., Sheffey, S., & Scott, L. A. (1993). Framing and group decision-making: Do cognitive changes parallel preference changes? *Organizational Behavior and Human Decision Processes, 55*(3), 470–485.

Tischler, L. (2005). Extreme jobs (and the people who love them). *Fast Company, 93,* 55–60.

Tucker, A. L., Nembhard, I. M., & Edmondson, A. C. (2007). Implementing new practices: An empirical study of organizational learning in hospital intensive care units. *Management Science, 53*(6), 894–907.

Waller, M. J., Conte, J. M., Gibson, C. A., & Carpenter, M. A. (2001). The effect of individual perceptions of deadlines on team performance. *Academy of Management Review, 26*(4), 586–600.

Waller, M. J., Zellmer-Bruhn, M. E., & Giambatista, R. C. (2002). Watching the clock: Group pacing behavior under dynamic deadlines. *Academy of Management Journal, 45*(5), 1046–1055.

Warkentin, M. E., Sayeed, L., & Hightower, R. (1997). Virtual teams versus face-to-face teams: An exploratory study of a Web-based conference system. *Decision Sciences, 28*(4), 975–996.

Wheelwright, S. C., & Clark, K. B. (1992). *Revolutionizing product development: Quantum leaps in speed, efficiency and quality.* New York: Free Press.

Wilson, J. M., Goodman, P. S., & Cronin, M. A. (2007). Group learning. *Academy of Management Review, 37*(4), 1041–1059.

Wittenbaum, G. M., Vaughan, S. I., & Stasser, G. I. (2002). Coordination in task-performing groups. In R. S. Tindale (Ed.), *Theory and research on small groups* (pp. 177–204). New York: Kluwer Academic.

Wong, S. (2004). Distal and local group learning: Performance trade-offs and tensions. *Organization Science, 15*(6), 645–656.

Yakura, E. (2001). Billables: The valorization of time in consulting. *American Behavioral Scientist, 44*(7), 1076–1095.

Zellmer-Bruhn, M. E. (2003). Interruptive events and team knowledge acquisition. *Management Science, 49*(4), 514–528.

Zika-Viktorsson, A., Sundstrom, P., & Engwall, M. (2006). Project overload: An exploratory study of work and management in multi-project settings. *International Journal of Project Management, 24*(5), 385–394.

7

Communication, Collaboration, and Identification as Facilitators and Constraints of Multiteam Systems

Joann Keyton
North Carolina State University

Debra J. Ford
University of Kansas Medical Center

Faye L. Smith
Missouri Western State University

Multiteam systems (MTSs) surround us. They are especially prevalent in government, military, and disaster relief settings. Multiteam systems have become common in other arenas as well, as problems are perceived as having become more challenging and complex, and the pace, scope, and scale of work have outgrown the skills, talents, and resources of any one group. This problem-focused work environment requires that teams and organizations become more interdependent, often in ways that are not planned for or in ways that arise from emergent situations. This type of boundary crossing has long existed, but this new environment develops at such a pace and in such a way that teams and organization may not be isomorphic in their interdependencies. That is, MTS as structures will require teams (and team members) who have specialized skills, knowledge, or resources, and the selection of team members and the organizations they represent may vary based on their organization's respective availability of resources. This is particular true as a new economy and complex social problems require greater fluidity and interdependence among public and private organizations.

As Zaccaro, Marks, and DeChurch (Chapter 1, this volume) note, these new forms of organizing and problem solving are different than team-based, virtual, or matrix organizations. Rather, multiteam systems are "tightly coupled constellations of teams, where the different teams may possess [and bring] very different core missions, expertise, structures, norms, and operating procedures to the collective effort" (Zaccaro et al., Chapter 1, this volume). Teams that comprise an MTS are labeled *component teams* whether teams are from the same organization (an internal MTS) or from different organizations (a cross-boundary MTS). In this chapter, we make a further distinction in describing and categorizing multiteam systems. Whereas Zacarro et al. and colleagues focus on the integration and interdependencies of intact or internal teams (we call these *integrating teams*), we have identified multiteam systems in which individuals from different organizations form teams to problem solve for a third-party organization (see Keyton, Ford, & Smith, 2008). In this different type of multiteam system, a number of teams composed of individuals who are not accustomed to working together create interdependencies to devise solutions that have macro and mutually beneficial outcomes. So, in this type of MTS, there is another layer of complexity. As relational and skill interdependencies must be created at the level of the individuals who comprise the team, they must also be developed at the level of the teams that are generating solutions for the third-party organization. Ultimately, the third-party organization acts as a facilitator across the teams in pursuit of a complex goal.

To avoid confusion and to make the distinction, we label this third type of multiteam systems *representative teams.* They are similar to integrative multiteam systems (DeChurch & Marks, 2006; DeChurch & Mathieu, 2009; Mathieu, Marks, & Zaccaro, 2001) in that they (a) are relatively new collective forms that (b) have emerged from collaborating rather than competing ways of organizing, and (c) have formed in response to environmental contingencies. (d) Two or more teams (e) are expected to work quickly and (f) interdependently, as they work toward (g) different proximal goals but a common distal goal.

Representative MTSs are distinguished from integrative MTSs in that teams in the former do not come intact to the collective system. Rather, representative teams are composed of individuals who have been recruited (or who have volunteered), and the individuals have little or no relational (personal or professional) or organizational history. In essence, each team member represents a different constituency or stakeholder. Also important is that the individuals who form the teams may come from environments in which they may think of their new team colleagues as competitors rather than collaborators. As a result, the individual–team–organization structure is not isomorphic, as individuals, not teams, are from different organizations. The representative type of MTS is similar to, but extends, Mathieu et al.'s (2001) cross-boundary MTS. For example, Keyton et al. (2008) described a collaborative organization in which a third-party organization created six teams composed of just over 100 people representing slightly fewer organizations. Thus, the entire collaborative system is doubly embedded: first in each of the teams, and, second across the teams. This type of organizing creates a greater degree of complexity and potentially creates a situation in which teams are not as well integrated or interdependent as they might be if teams, rather than individuals, represented different organizations.

We broaden the conceptualization of multiteam systems purposely, as we argue that there are multiteam systems that have characteristics of both MTSs as defined by Zaccaro et al. (Chapter 1, this volume) and representative teams as just described. For example, two recent and very public examples are the organizational and team responses to the September 11, 2001, disaster at the World Trade Center and to Hurricane Katrina. Whereas operational teams were more characteristic of Zaccaro et al.'s definition, the teams at the executive policy and problem-solving level were more characteristic of representative teams.

Thus, this chapter focuses on representative team MTSs. Our perspective is grounded in observation and analysis of such a system (see Keyton et al., 2008); our theorizing is primarily based on the communication literature. In the remainder of the chapter, we draw attention to task differences that will influence MTSs, and examine the role of communication, collaboration, and identification in MTSs. Propositions are presented.

TASK TYPE MAKES A DIFFERENCE

A different type of distinction must also be drawn between integrative and representative MTSs. MTSs can differ in the type of tasks to be accomplished. Moreover, this task type distinction may further differentiate integrated teams from representative teams. Routine or procedural tasks have been the focus of most studies of MTSs (see Mathieu et al. 2001; Marks, DeChurch, Mathieu, Panzer, & Alonso, 2005). It appears that integrated teams are more likely to be charged with performance-oriented tasks. But MTSs can also be tasked with more abstract, creative, inventive cognitive tasks. In these task situations, communication among team members is necessary to share ideas, critique information shared, and develop innovative ideas for which the team has little basis for assessing its effectiveness. This type of cognitive task is more likely connected to representative teams. As DeChurch and Marks (2006) noted, MTSs are abundant in organizations, but little is known, including how and if task types would moderate their interactions. We believe that the tasks for which MTSs are designed or assigned have the potential to make a difference both in the interactions of teams and team members, and in how component teams of MTSs are composed. These differences make extending the previous work on MTSs (DeChurch & Marks, 2006; Marks et al., 2005) difficult, as generally one type of MTS (e.g., performance oriented or mission specific) has been examined.

By definition, *routine tasks* are more easily learned, trained, and/or transferred across teams because the routine has a generative structure that exists within the social relationships of team members (Hodgson, 2008). Contingencies can be identified, and exceptions to the routine can be practiced. This is especially true when performance and organizational roles are associated with routines and when external stimuli trigger performance. Alternately, cognitive tasks are more open ended, less predictable, and more influenced by the interaction of team members. That is, this type of task carries little information from one instance to the other—thus, no routine exists.

Ironically, these differences allow such groups to work toward *greater good*, or public good (Savas, 2000), goals. In other words, the teams' work is inventive and creative, and not performance oriented. Someone else will take on the responsibility for implementing the teams' innovative ideas. The only performance expected is the generation of innovative solutions to the problem presented. Thus, the teamwork–goal accomplishment relationship is more abstract than that of many of the other multiteam systems that have been reported. Although both types of tasks require that teams do their work quickly (see Lipman-Blumen & Leavitt, 1999), the performance evaluation of work on cognitive tasks is more distal and often not easily observable. Despite the lower level of integration and interdependency among component teams in representative team MTSs, teams' outputs still comprise the higher order MTS goal (Marks et al., 2005). This is particularly evident in greater good goals in which team goals can be enacted in a parallel rather than sequential or ordered fashion.

DeChurch and Marks (2006) acknowledged that governments, municipalities, and agencies are the site of the integrative type of organizing structure. In contrast, policy-making and planning tasks are quite different from mission-specific team tasks. In addition, organizations that must respond to organizational exigencies (such as an economic downturn) may temporarily turn a more traditional organizational structure into an MTS. Thus, the difference in context may be a primary criterion for different types of MTSs. Although other characteristics may hold true across both types of MTSs, differences in context-driven end-goal states may distinguish between MTSs with integrating teams and those with representative teams.

> Proposition 1: Context-driven end-goal states will influence how teams emerge to comprise multiteam systems.
>
> Proposition 2: Cognitive, creative, and inventive tasks will require greater team member, and potentially greater organizational, variation in multiteam systems.
>
> Proposition 3: Multiteam systems charged with the integration of routine, trainable, and performance-oriented tasks are more likely to be composed of intact groups.
>
> Proposition 4: Multiteam systems charged with the generation of innovation or policy are more likely to be composed of zero-history groups.

COMMUNICATION, COLLABORATION, AND IDENTIFICATION

In this section, we explain why the communication, collaboration, and identification linkage attributes of Zaccaro et al.'s (Chapter 1, this volume) model were selected as our focus in this chapter and how we conceptualize their relationships among them. In any MTS system, *collaboration* is required, as the goal is outside the scope of one team, one organization, or a smaller embedded or integrated team structure. *Communication* is required to bring teams into existence and to create interdependencies with other teams. Communication is the essence of what it means to collaborate (Hardy, Lawrence, & Grant, 2005; Keyton et al., 2008; Robichaud, Giroux, & Taylor, 2004), as collaboration cannot occur if team members do not interact with one another. Thus, communication is the broader concept.

Both communication and collaboration are social processes, and, as such, are moderated by *identification*. Other reviews of the teamwork literature (Rousseau, Aube, & Savoie, 2006) acknowledge the central presence of communication and collaboration. These concepts—communication, collaboration, and identification—*together* specify to a greater degree the team processes that Mathieu, Marks, and Zaccaro (2001) described as necessary to achieve collective goals.

In sum, three principles are central. First, collaboration is the process that MTS teams need to move toward to achieve MTS goals. Second, collaboration can only happen through communication. Third, team and MTS identification influence if and how team members communicate. If team and MTS identification are not established, communication will be weakened such that collaboration is less likely to occur.

> Proposition 5: Communication, collaboration, and team and organizational identification are necessary processes to the successful execution of MTS tasks.

Communication

Often in literature outside the communication studies discipline, communication is reduced to information flow or information exchange. For example, Williams and Mahan (2006) described communication as having four major functions in MTS: (a) controlling behavior through norms and policy; (b) motivating and teaching through performance feedback that is linked to scripted or routine performances; (c) expressing emotions, especially those related to conflict management; and (d) supplying information. Undoubtedly, communication fulfills these functions. However, we believe a more compelling view of communication is the broader conceptualization of communication as the processes of (a) developing and sending messages, and (b) creating shared meaning. By taking this broader conceptualization of communication into account, researchers and observers reduce the risk of (a) focusing on one type of communication (i.e., interaction or talk) at the exclusion of other types, (b) using quantity of communication over quality of communication as the evaluation criterion, and (c) confusing meaning (what the receiver interpreted) with message (what the sender said). Dougherty, Kramer, Klatzke, and Rogers (2009) recently demonstrated how language can converge, giving the illusion of shared meanings. Their findings corroborate the position that meanings are derived from messages by examining their functionality in sequence (Beck & Keyton, 2009; Keyton & Beck, 2009). Finally, this broader view acknowledges both the task and relational qualities (see Keyton, 1999; Keyton & Beck, 2009) of communication that are inherent in team members' conversations (pretask, task, and post task), and that influence goal accomplishment and evaluation.

Proposition 6: Task and relational talk are necessary for successful completion of MTS tasks.

In MTSs, how teams are constructed and who serves in teams have important implications. Despite training and role assignments, individuals use unique qualities (style, experience, and information) in their communication with other team members. Although training and role assignment can bring a degree of uniformity in task performance, it cannot guarantee the substitution of one team member for another. Fluidity regarding what team members represent which organizations works against constancy. Thus, changing team membership transforms not only a team but also the MTS system (see Zaccaro et al., Chapter 1, this volume). One way of expressing these differences in team settings is to consider differences as residing between or among team members.

Here, we introduced the concept of relational distance, an extension of Lau and Murnighan's (1998) faultline concept. *Relational distance* is the relative degree of interaction difficulty that team members face in negotiating differences among team members. Differentiating one's self among other team members is natural in social contexts, including groups, and can be observed through roles or role performances (see Poole, 1999). Although formal roles are assigned, group members also negotiate informal roles through their communication with one another.

Faultline differences can be expected in MTS teams because heterogeneity (DeChurch & Mathieu, 2009) is characteristic of MTSs. Faultlines can be based on a number of real or perceived structural attributes: authority or superiority, degree of importance or centrality to the task or problem, access to resources, and location. Faultlines among team members are also based on demographic diversity, but personal characteristics, such as perceived honesty and trustworthiness, and personal style can create faultlines. Team members use faultlines to assess their differences from one another.

With that social categorization, interaction is affected as team members communicate to either construct or overcome these differences. Whereas a faultline characterizes divisions between or among team members, relational distance is the way in which faultlines are revealed in team members' interactions. As reported, faultlines can negatively influence communication (Lau & Murnighan, 2005), which in turn reinforces differences among team members (Polzer, Crisp, Jarvenpaa, & Kim, 2006).

Proposition 7: Greater relational distance among component team members is negatively related to the quality and quantity of communication within the component team.

Common across all group development literature is the notion that groups develop through stages in which first formation issues (e.g., identity or role distinctions) and then dependency issues (e.g., power struggles) are negotiated. Models differ in the way they address how task issues develop with respect to relational issues. But all models acknowledge relational development (for reviews, see Keyton, 1999; Wheelan, 2005).

Teams with more rigid and formal role structures heavily influence who communicates to whom, when, and how. Other teams have less defined structures and rely more heavily on the emerging interaction among team members to negotiate task and relational roles. Even in the former, however, team member differences are being revealed and negotiated (key communicative processes) as they perform in their roles, as well as through informal interactions outside the task. Thus, communication among team members can heighten or weaken relational distances.

Similar to work and professional contexts, team member relationships are generally nonvoluntary, as we do not select our coworkers or teammates. Thus, teammates can develop negative, neutral, or positive views of one another and relationships with one another. Thus, *which* organizations are represented and *who* organizations send to represent them have consequences for the development of the MTS.

> Proposition 8: Communication can either facilitate or constrain team interaction as group members negotiate their formal and informal task roles and relational roles.

From a communicative frame, another distinction strikes us. Multiteam systems are most often described as *structures*, whereas we view these systems as *processes*. Keyton et al. (2008) made this distinction and argued that a structural view cannot explain how interaction at the team or organizational level occurs. In simple terms, integrative MTSs focus on organizations or teams, whereas representative MTSs focus on individuals who comprise teams and organizations. This shift is subtle but provides a perspective that is both micro and macro. Integrative MTSs focus on how teams function together; representative MTSs focus on how individuals in teams function together. This shift allows us to consider how individual action creates team interaction. More recent conceptualizations of organizing (e.g., Bengtsson, Mullern, Soderholm, & Wahlin, 2007; Taylor, 2006) support this extension. As a result, we propose two levels of communication as important to MTSs: face-to-face communication of organizational representatives within the component group, and communication and collaboration among the teams. Thus, MTSs are by their very nature collaborative.

Collaboration

Keyton et al. (2008) defined *interorganizational collaboration* as "the set of communicative processes in which individuals representing multiple organizations or stakeholders engage when working interdependently to address problems outside the spheres of individuals or organizations working in isolation" (p. 381). This definition is consistent with Zaccaro et al.'s definition of multiteam systems (see Chapter 1, this volume), but it does not restrict MTSs to being composed of intact or existing teams. Taking this approach extends Mathieu et al.'s (2001) view of input and process interdependence. The difference is that both types of interdependence must be first addressed at the within-team level and before output interdependence can be addressed at the across-team level. Finally, this approach highlights the linkages described by Zaccaro et al., especially the within- and across-team communication processes.

Collaboration is often (especially outside the communication literature) conceptualized as a structure (i.e., a collaboration). Two literature reviews (Keyton et al., 2008; Lewis, 2006), however, highlight collaboration as a process. Lewis (2006) argued, "We don't have a collaboration, nor are we a collaboration; we engage in collaboration" (p. 213); her literature review further described collaboration as a process with a beginning, middle, and end. We propose that the middle is larger than its beginning or end, and that the middle is where the greatest amount of MTS work is accomplished. We also propose that collaboration is a moving target. That is, collaboration is also not an end state, but simultaneous processes within and across teams. Thus, our focus should be on *collaborating*, not collaboration (Keyton et al., 2008). Applying Giddens's (1979, 1984) theory of structuration to collaboration, we posited that "the process of collaborating creates and then reifies or modifies structural elements of collaboration (roles, rights, and resources)" (Keyton et al., 2008, p. 382). When there is a structural focus on collaboration, attention shifts to organizations or teams as entities rather than individuals in teams. Thus, we believe that the role of talk in collaboration has been undervalued.

> Proposition 9: The process of collaboration in an MTS requires that teams manage the process at both team and organizational levels.
> Proposition 10: Collaboration processes can be observed as the interdependencies within and across teams in an MTS.
> Proposition 11: MTS collaboration is a form of organizing that both creates and reifies roles, norms, and structures within and across teams.

Part of the difficulty that team members and organizations face in the collaboration process can be attributed to creating new communication relationships in dynamic environments. Communicating and collaborating with new partners will stimulate issues of identification. Problematic for integrative component teams is the requirement that team members manage their existing parent organizational and team identifications relative to a new and emergent organizational (or cross-team) identification. For representative teams, these team members, who hold some degree of identification with their parent organization, must create identification with their team and then again with the larger multiteam system.

Identification

From a communication perspective, identification is the feeling of attachment between the individual and organization, often based on a perceived linkage of the individual to the organization (Burke, 1969; Cheney, 1983; Scott, Corman, & Cheney, 1998). Identity is a set of rules and resources for creating identification that produce identity structures. Thus, identification "is the process of emerging identity" (p. 304). Identity and identification are not *thought* into being. Rather, they are communicatively constructed and jointly produced (Kuhn & Nelson, 2002). More specifically,

> [I]t is through communication with others that we express our belongingness (or lack thereof) to various collectives, assess the reputation and image of those collectives, that various identities are made known to us, and the social costs and rewards of maintaining various identities are revealed. (Scott, 2007, p. 124)

As Russo (1998) argued, the process and the product of identification are ongoing as individuals reevaluate identification "based on messages about the group from other individuals and from the actions of the group itself" (p. 77).

This view is slightly different than the view of identification anchored in the management literature. However, the two are more similar than different. From a management perspective, organizational identification occurs when members view the organization as self-defining, or when a member's self-concept contains the same attributes as those of the organization (Ashforth, Harrison, & Corley, 2008; Dutton, Dukerich, & Harquail, 1994; Pratt, 1998). Both communication and management perspectives acknowledge that individuals do hold multiple identifications simultaneously.

Identification is also fluid. Once the MTS tasks are completed, members will revert to daily work norms as they reenter their home organization routines, but identification with the MTS may not be severed just as organizational identification will not necessarily be severed when a member joins a component team (Kuhn & Nelson, 2002). Maintaining both identities is more likely when values that are central, distinctive, and relatively enduring for a parent organization are more or less shared with the MTS. It is well documented that lack of value alignment is a core obstacle when organizations merge (Kramer, Dougherty, & Pierce, 2004). This same obstacle can occur when new team members come together, as in the case of representative teams. If core values within the MTS are or become shared, characteristics of organizational identity become embedded in the MTS identity.

Particularly for members of representative component teams, we would initially posit that their strongest organizational identification will be with their parent organizations, and that this saliency will endure even when members engage in MTS tasks. However, experimental findings have demonstrated that strong identification with the home organization does not preclude team members from developing strong identification with their teams (Rockmann, Pratt, & Northcraft, 2007). Parent organization and team identification could both be relatively and simultaneously high, because team members are integrated in close proximity to one another (emphasizing team identification), whereas team members are similar to those from their home organization (emphasizing organizational identification). Thus, the degree to which the MTS and its component teams can develop identification with team members is especially important given that component teams are together for short periods of time.

This suggests that the membership spread (i.e., differences in and the number of organizations represented) and organizational value alignment of the parent organizations represented within an MTS will likely influence the degree of organizational and MTS identification overlap. In MTSs, each of the parent organizations was engaged in achieving organizational goals that may or may not have been tightly connected with the goals of other organizations. But, presumably, some goal overlap is construed or valued, or organizations would not assign their human resources to MTSs.

Identification is also temporal. MTS activity of short duration may result in *identity tension* (Pepper & Larson, 2006; Tompkins & Cheney, 1985) for MTS members as they are pulled toward the culture of their parent organization and toward the emerging culture of their component team or MTS. Because individuals may actively choose which identifications will be most influential (Bisel, Ford, & Keyton, 2007), it is not uncommon for employees in merged organizations to resist cultural integration by trying to negotiate or reshape the resulting communication environment and organization culture (Trethewey & Ashcraft, 2004).

Proposition 12: The direction and source of value alignment between team members and their home organization and team will influence organization and team identification, respectively.

As team members negotiate organizational and team roles and identities, analysis of roles may provide a reconciliation of different or contested cultures (e.g., the parent organization vs. the MTS). Two possibilities exist.

First, organizational identity may be influenced to some degree by role identity (see Hogg, Abrams, Otten, & Hinkle, 2004) such that MTS members' positions in their home organization may be more salient and prestigious than their role within the MTS. Second, the role differentiation that MTSs embrace may positively influence identification in a component team, especially in the case when individuals' roles are interdependent and valued as necessary to complete the component team task. For example, being in a unique role in the component team as compared to being in a role similar to many others in the parent organization may enhance identification with the component team. Finally, the duration of time together in an MTS component team is likely to interact with role specificity. That is, the more specific the role (and the better known a role is by other component team members), the less time it may take for component team members to develop team identification. Alternatively, the less specific the role, the greater the time it may take for the same degree of team identification to develop. When MTSs are composed of representative teams, taking time to develop team identification within a short horizon task can be especially difficult.

Proposition 13: A team member's role identity will influence with which system (home organization, team, or MTS) identification is highest.

The competing or parallel nature of identities could be detrimental or disastrous for MTS component teams. The stronger the identification with an identity, the more likely that one's communication will be shaped by it, or "understanding how individuals behave requires consideration of both the target of their identities and the relative strength of their identification with each" (Hillman et al., 2008, p. 443). We would expect, then, that members of an MTS with a strong organizational identity would elicit strong identification, which would result in more frequent communication and messages that are more meaningful and valuable to other members. Identification may be strengthened if members are from home organizations or existing teams that share common language norms (e.g., industry or professional norms, or common vernacular; see Keyton et al., 2008). In this case, communication among MTS members is more likely to also reflect norms and meanings that are common and useful. Teams form identity through their discourse. And the degree to which identification with a team is developed depends on competing or parallel identifications.

> Proposition 14: Differences among and the greater the number of organizations represented in a representative team MTS will influence the degree of overlap in parent organization, representative team, and MTS identification.
> Proposition 15: Higher identification (with home organization, team, or MTS) will result in more frequent communication with individuals in that entity.
> Proposition 16: Shared language norms with the home organization, team, or MTS will be positively related to identification with the home organization, team, or MTS, respectively.

RESEARCH AGENDA

The aims of this chapter were (a) to bring more attention to the underlying communication, collaboration, and identification processes of multiteam systems; and (b) to theorize how these processes can facilitate and constrain MTSs' goal accomplishment. A secondary aim was to introduce a different form (i.e., representative teams) of MTS and distinguish between it and the type traditionally conceptualized as MTS (i.e., integrative teams). Although the two types are similar in many respects, they differ in how the MTS is structured and in their end-goal state. Acknowledging greater variety in MTS structures allows us to describe this relatively new organizing form more fully and demonstrate in a more nuanced way how communication, collaboration, and identification are pivotal processes.

Essentially, comparing the two types has the potential to illuminate where processes in either are vulnerable.

Propositions about communication, collaboration, and identification and their relationships are presented throughout this chapter. These could be developed into testable hypotheses to examine and evaluate to assess MTS effectiveness as part of an MTS research agenda.

As Keyton et al. (2008) described, interorganizational collaboration occurs at the team level: "That is the level at which relationships among individuals and organizations are revealed and acted upon, as it is the level at which strategic communication can be observed" (p. 402). Because the heart of an MTS is the capacity of its teams, we ask several research questions that cannot be answered by an analysis of the existing literature:

RQ1: What communication anchors are associated with different types of MTS team goals?

RQ2: What are the observable communication indicators of collaboration and identification in MTSs?

What methodological tools are required to answer these questions and test the propositions? Automated capture of team conversations is widely available. But automated coding has a considerable time horizon to move beyond identifying patterns of communication to identify *what messages resulted in which meanings* and looking for the influence of these message-meaning relationships upon team performance.

When automated analysis does become available, researchers need to be sensitive to not being overly narrow in what they are looking for or to select one attribute to stand in for the whole of communication. Foltz and Martin (2009) described how latent semantic analysis may be a useful tool. One caution in the use of any coding (hand or machine) or analysis is that nonverbal symbols are largely ignored, including cases in which team members are silent.

In any new organizing form, there is a tendency to rush to describe how the system should work without first clarifying *how it does work*. For that reason, this chapter focuses on processes that influence and lead to goal accomplishment. Our choice of the three processes—communication, collaboration, and identification—was deliberate in that they are inter-related and especially relevant when team members and/or teams must develop new working relationships and work together across existing organizational structures. For an MTS, if the teams fail, the MTS structure falls apart. Thus, exploring how connections within and across teams can either facilitate or constrain is key.

REFERENCES

Ashforth, B. E., Harrison, S. H., & Corley, K. G. (2008). Identification in organizations: An examination of four fundamental questions. *Journal of Management, 34*, 325–374.

Beck, S. J., & Keyton, J. (2009). Perceiving strategic meeting interaction. *Small Group Research, 40*, 223–246.

Bengtsson, M., Mullern, T, Soderholm, A., & Wahlin, N. (2007). *A grammar of organizing.* Northampton. MA: Elgar.

Bisel, R. S., Ford, D. J., & Keyton, J. K. (2007). Unobtrusive control in a leadership organization: Integrating control and consent. *Western Journal of Communication, 71,* 136–158.

Burke, K. (1969). *The rhetoric of motives.* Berkeley: University of California Press.

Cheney, G. (1983). The rhetoric of identification and the study of organizational communication. *Quarterly Journal of Speech, 69*, 143–158.

DeChurch, L. A., & Marks, M. A. (2005). Leadership in multiteam systems. *Journal of Applied Psychology, 91*, 311–329.

DeChurch, L. A., & Mathieu, J. E. (2009). Thinking in terms of multiteam systems. In E. Salas, G. F. Goodwin, & C. S. Burke (Eds.), *Team effectiveness in complex organizations: Cross-disciplinary perspectives and approaches* (pp. 267–292). New York: Routledge.

Dougherty, D. S., Kramer, M. W., Klatzke, S. R., & Rogers, T. K. K. (2009). Language convergence and meaning divergence: A meaning centered communication theory. *Communication Monographs, 76*, 20–46.

Dutton, J., Dukerich, J., & Harquail, C. V. (1994). Organizational images and member identification. *Administrative Science Quarterly, 39*, 239–263.

Foltz, P. W., & Martin, M. J. (2009). Automated communication analysis of teams. In E. Salas, G. F. Goodwin, & C. S. Burke (Eds.), *Team effectiveness in complex organizations: Cross-disciplinary perspectives and approaches* (pp. 411–431). New York: Routledge.

Giddens, A. (1979). *Central problems in social theory: Action, structure, and contradiction in social analysis.* Berkeley: University of California Press.

Giddens, A. (1984). *The constitution of society: Outline of the theory of structuration.* Berkeley: University of California Press.

Hardy, C., Lawrence, T. B., & Grant, D. (2005). Discourse and collaboration: The role of conversations and collective identity. *Academy of Management Review, 31*, 58–77.

Hillman, A. J., Nicholson, G., & Shropshire, C. (2008). Directors' multiple identities, identification, and board monitoring and resource provision. *Organization Science, 19,* 441–456.

Hodgson, G. M. (2008). The concept of a routine. In M. C. Becker (Ed.), *Handbook of organizational routines* (pp. 15–28). Northampton, MA: Elgar.

Hogg, M. A., Abrams, D., Otten, S., & Hinkle, S. (2004). The social identity perspective: Intergroup relations, self-conception, and small groups. *Small Group Research, 35,* 246–276.

Keyton, J. (1999). Relational communication in groups. In L. R. Frey, D. S. Gouran, & M. S. Poole (Eds.), *The handbook of group communication theory and research* (pp. 192–222). Thousand Oaks, CA: Sage.

Keyton, J., & Beck, S. J. (2009). The influential role of relational messages in group interaction. *Group Dynamics, 13*, 14–30.

Keyton, J., Ford, D. J., & Smith, F. L. (2008). A meso-level communicative model of interorganizational collaboration. *Communication Theory, 18*, 376–406.

Kramer, M. W., Dougherty, D. S., & Pierce, T. A. (2004). Managing uncertainty during a corporate acquisition: A longitudinal study of communication during an airline acquisition. *Human Communication Research, 30*, 71–101.

Kuhn, T., & Nelson, N. (2002). Reengineering identity: A case study of multiplicity and duality in organizational identification. *Management Communication Quarterly, 16*, 5–38.

Lau, D. C., & Murnighan, J. K. (1998). Demographic diversity and faultlines: The compositional dynamics of organizational groups. *Academy of Management Review, 23*, 325–340.

Lau, D. C., & Murnighan, J. K. (2005). Interactions within groups and subgroups: The effects of demographic faultlines. *Academy of Management Journal, 48*, 645–659.

Lewis, L. K. (2006). Collaborative interaction: Review of communication scholarship and a research agenda. In C. S. Beck (Ed.) *Communication Yearbook 30*, (pp. 197–247). Mahwah, NJ: Erlbaum.

Lipman-Blumen, J., & Leavitt, H. J. (1999). *Hot groups: The rebirth of individualism.* New York: Oxford University Press.

Marks, M. A., DeChurch, L. A., Mathieu, J. E., Panzer, F. J., & Alonso, A. (2005). Teamwork in multiteam systems. *Journal of Applied Psychology, 90*, 964–971.

Mathieu, J. E., Marks, M. A., & Zaccaro, S. J. (2001). Multiteam systems. In N. Anderson, D. Ones, H. K. Sinangil, & C. Viswesvaran (Eds.), *Handbook of industrial, work and organizational psychology* (Vol. 2, pp. 289–313). London: Sage.

Pepper, G. L., & Larson, G. S. (2006). Cultural identity tensions in a post-acquisition organization. *Journal of Applied Communication Research, 34*, 49–71.

Polzer, J. T., Crisp, C. B., Jarvenpaa, S. L., & Kim, J. W. (2006). Extending the faultline model to geographically dispersed teams: How collocated subgroups can impair group functioning. *Academy of Management Journal, 49*, 579–692.

Poole, M. S. (1999). Group communication theory. In L. R. Frey, D. S. Gouran, & M. S. Poole (Eds.), *The handbook of group communication theory and research* (pp. 37–70). Thousand Oaks, CA: Sage.

Pratt, M. G., (1998). To be or not to be: Central questions in organizational identification. In D. A. Whetten & P. C. Godfrey (Eds.), *Identity in organizations: Building theory through conversation* (pp. 171–207). Thousand Oaks, CA: Sage.

Robichaud, D., Giroux, H., & Taylor, J. R. (2004). The metaconversation: The recursive property of language as a key to organizing. *Academy of Management Review, 29*, 617–634.

Rockmann, K. W., Pratt, M. G., & Northcraft, G. B. (2007). Divided loyalties: Determinants of identification in interorganizational teams. *Small Group Research, 38*, 727–751.

Rousseau, V., Aube, C., & Savoie, A. (2006). A review and an integration of frameworks. *Small Group Research, 37*, 540–570.

Russo, T. C. (1998). Organizational and professional identification: A case of newspaper journalists. *Management Communication Quarterly, 12*, 72–111.

Savas, E. S. (2000). *Privatization and public-private partnerships.* New York: Chatham House.

Scott, C. R. (2007). Communication and social identity theory: Existing and potential connections in organizational research. *Communication Studies, 58,* 123–138.

Scott, C. R., Corman, S. R., & Cheney, G. (1998). Development of a structurational model of identification in the organization. *Communication Theory, 8,* 298–336.

Taylor, J. R. (2006). Coorientation: A conceptual framework. In F. Cooren, J. R. Taylor, & E. J. Van Every (Eds.), *Communication as organizing: Empirical and theoretical explorations in the dynamic of text and conversation* (pp. 141–156). Mahwah, NJ: Erlbaum.

Tompkins, P. K., & Cheney, G. (1985). Communication and unobtrusive control in contemporary organizations. In R. D. McPhee & P. K. Tompkins (Eds.), *Organizational communication: Traditional themes and new directions* (pp. 179–210). Beverly Hills, CA: Sage.

Trethewey, A., & Ashcraft, K. L. (2004). Practicing disorganization: The development of applied perspectives on living with tension. *Journal of Applied Communication Research, 32,* 81–88.

Wheelan, S. A. (2005). The developmental perspective. In S. A. Wheelan (Ed.), *The handbook of group research and practice* (pp. 119–132). Thousand Oaks, CA: Sage.

Williams, C. C., & Mahan, R. P. (2006). Understanding multiteam functioning. In. W. Bennett, Jr., C. E. Lance, & D. J. Woehr (Eds.), *Performance measurement: Current perspectives and future challenges* (pp. 205–224). Mahwah, NJ: Erlbaum.

Section III

Linkages

8

Conceptualizing the Multiteam System as an Ecosystem of Networked Groups

Marshall Scott Poole
University of Illinois Urbana-Champaign

Noshir Contractor
Northwestern University

This chapter will consider the multiteam system (MTS) as part of a larger ecology of networked groups and individuals that the MTS acts within and that, in turn, shapes the MTS itself. The original description of the multiteam system by Mathieu, Marks, and Zaccaro (2001) treated the MTS largely as a self-contained entity composed of several interacting teams, such as firefighters, emergency medical technicians (EMTs), and the surgical and recovery teams at the hospital. According to them, the MTS has a hierarchy of goals, stretching from the overall goal of the MTS (e.g., patient survival) down to the subgoals of each of the constituent teams (e.g., extract the victim from the wreck, or transport the victim to the hospital). Task and goal interdependencies lend the MTS its coherence as a system and provide a degree of closure for the system. Mathieu et al. noted that the MTS is situated within two types of environments, the embedding organization and the external environment, both of which include other groups that the MTS must relate to. This implies the existence of a group ecology for the MTS, though Mathieu et al. did not develop this idea much further.

This chapter will undertake to develop this line of thought more fully by advancing a model of an ecology of networked groups that compete for members and for tasks. This model was originally developed to fill a gap in our knowledge of human organization. We have a great deal of theory and knowledge about individuals, dyads, and isolated small groups, on the one hand, and about large aggregates such as markets, societies, and organizations, on the other, but there is remarkably little understanding of the behavior of intermediate to large groups composed of between 8 and 200 members in natural contexts. Recent developments in theory and research on small groups and networks position us to develop a theory to fill this gap. This theory, network ecosystems theory, takes the form of a dynamic, evolving set of groups that exchange members as they organize around various task foci. Evolution of the network of groups is driven both by microlevel network and group processes and by macrolevel network processes.

Multiteam systems operate in group ecosystems, and although not all group ecosystems are multiteam systems, many are. Multiteam systems are composed of networks of teams that must interact with an environment that includes other teams and individuals, many of whom are at least temporarily networked with the teams that comprise the MTS. As such, the MTS can be viewed as part of a larger dynamic network that is constantly evolving and exchanging information, assistance, and other resources with other actors and groups in the network. Hence, considering MTSs in group ecologies allows us to highlight group environment interactions in a more specific way than current theories of MTSs.

This chapter will be organized as follows. First, we develop a statement of the problem that motivates network ecosystems theory and a canonical description of the group ecosystem that will serve as the reference point for development of the theory. Second, we develop the theoretical framework as a series of propositions about the network ecosystem. Following this, we discuss the MTS in the context of network ecosystems and present an example illustrating how an MTS might operate in a network ecosystem. Finally, we discuss the implications of network ecosystems theory for MTS theory and research.

THE PROBLEM

Most previous research on small groups and teams has operated under a restrictive model that treats groups as well-defined, clearly bounded entities with a stable set of members. The vast majority of experiments on groups and teams take as their unit of analysis a single, small, isolated group whose members are assigned by the researchers. Studies of workgroups and other groups in natural settings, too, overwhelmingly focus on well-bounded, relatively small and stable groups, relying on managers or members to define the groups for study, and assuming that the group remains more or less stable and well bounded throughout the study. Viewing groups in this way makes conducting research on groups straightforward, because researchers have a well-defined unit of analysis that can be observed relatively easily. It is a simple matter to videotape a five-person group gathered around a table in the experimenter's laboratory. It is straightforward to administer a survey to a well-defined work unit (e.g., a nursing unit in a hospital) and the results of the survey clearly apply to this unit.

However, groups in their actual settings are much more complex entities than the small, stable sets of people considered in most previous group research (Putnam & Stohl, 1996). Although small, insulated groups can be found in many hierarchical organizations and traditional small businesses, it is more often the case that groups and teams must coordinate with other groups, and most members of a given group belong to other groups. Consider two examples:

- A nursing floor in a hospital runs two 12-hour shifts a day with two different sets of nurses (each working three to four 12-hour days) for each shift. Nurses during each shift work in flexible teams to coordinate care for patients; these teams reconfigure depending on the specific mix of patients and their needs. Nurses working the two shifts must coordinate patient care at the handoff time, and nurses in one set must coordinate with those in another when a new set comes on. Nurses from the floor also serve on several committees, including five who comprise a quality improvement committee whose members also include a couple of physicians and a facilitator from human resources; a patient safety committee of five nurses; and two who serve as liaisons to the General Nursing Management Committee, which sets general policy for all floors in the hospital. This hospital floor can be viewed as one large team, as four teams composed of nurses in the same shift and set, or as seven teams if the three additional committees are added. The nurses also have to coordinate on an ad hoc basis with physicians and physical therapists to deliver care, improvising small groups "on the fly."
- An emergency response management team composed of two city fire chiefs, a county fire chief, city and county police chiefs, a city

manager, and the director of the local Red Cross convene in the county response center to coordinate response to a train derailment that has resulted in a chemical spill and fire. The emergency management team must gather data from multiple sources, make sense of the situation, and plan a response, including assignment of personnel to teams, task assignment, supervision of responder teams, updating plans as new information comes in, and communication with the public about the incident. As the group works, its members will reconfigure into subgroups that deal with different aspects of the situation and work out elements of response. Some members will go out into the field to supervise response teams or coordinate different teams, effectively creating multiteam complexes that greatly expand the size of the team. The operative management team will decompose, then recompose as the response unfolds. Additional members with needed expertise will be added temporarily or permanently.

These groups differ in significant ways from the simple small group that is the focus of most extant research on groups. They "burst" the boundaries of the traditional idealized small group in several respects:

- They are large and are composed of subgroups that may be functionally and hierarchically differentiated.
- Their membership shifts over time, not only as a function of turnover, but also because the shifts are necessary to enable the group to do its work. A group may have core members, but other members who join the group temporarily to advance its work must be considered to have some status in the group.
- Their boundaries are ill defined, because their work requires them to adapt rapidly to changing demands. Like the nursing floor or the emergency response team, groups are nested within other groups, and in some cases two or more groups must coordinate so closely that they seem to merge into a larger working unit.
- Some subgroups (and, in some cases, the entire large group) form for limited-term projects and go out of existence when the project is complete. Members of these project teams are drawn from a pool of available personnel.
- Different subgroups within the larger group may have different goals, agendas, or concerns and may be subject to different influences.

Hence, there is a diversity of generative mechanisms in operation in the ensemble of groups. These may also shift over time as groups develop or confront different contexts.

- The members may be spread spatially and temporally so that a particular "location" (such as an office) for the group cannot be specified. Instead, the group members come together in different patterns of subgroups as they need to collaborate. These subgroups are often temporary and improvisational, but the members act as a group when they convene and then disband to rejoin the larger group.

- Context, including the demands of task and environment, and the pool of individuals who are potential members of these groups and organizations exert a strong influence on the dynamics discussed in this list. In a real sense, these systems of groups are interdependent with their context.

- Because the groups are large and spatially dispersed, contextual influences may vary within the ensemble of subgroups and individuals that makes up the large group.

- The groups often deal with highly complex problems involving a large amount of diverse information. This requires expertise beyond that of its core members and necessitates external linkages to other groups and units.

This list of properties suggests several ways in which MTSs as described by Mathieu et al. (2001) are similar to large groups. They are dynamic in terms of tasks, goals, and team structure. They are dispersed over space. They are differentiated in terms of the goals of the teams making up the MTS and in terms of how the teams operate. They are networks of groups in particular relationships of interdependence. Although not all network ecosystems are MTSs, it seems that all MTSs could be analyzed in terms of group ecosystems.

The network ecosystems model is also designed to tackle an important problem that exists in research on social networks, though in this case it is turned on its head. Most previous research on social networks has primarily focused on entire networks with much less attention accorded to subgroups or parts of networks as autonomous units, except in relation to larger network generative mechanisms that generally operate at the level of the individual member, the dyad, or at most the triad. In this research, groups are regarded as cliques within the encompassing network, and their formation and existence are explained in terms of the overall mechanisms generating the network, such as balance or exchange. Network research does not usually acknowledge that individual groups within the network may have their own local concerns or generative mechanisms that drive the group's formation and behavior, or that various groups may have different concerns or generative mechanisms. This prevents network models from capturing the internal diversity that is characteristic of the ensembles of groups just discussed.

Network ecosystems theory attempts to integrate theories of small-group behavior with theories of networks. This integration has the potential to capture the effects of network contexts on small groups and to extend the reach of theories of social networks. This would also enable us to understand and to explain the behavior of a set of critically important groups that is currently inadequately studied.

THE NETWORK ECOSYSTEM

A broader picture of groups and networks that takes their dynamic and variegated nature into account views them as part of a complex system of groups and individuals operating as an "ecosystem." A canonical description of groups in complex ecosystems constituted by networks would offer the following picture:

> A large set of N individuals is organized into M groups that undertake long-term projects that require them to carry out various tasks (McGrath, 1984). The membership of these units shifts over time as members enter and exit them. Units themselves form, develop, and disband or decay subject to the demands of the task and other group-level processes. Within the units, members take on specialized roles and accumulate experience and skills that can be brought to bear on various tasks that the unit must carry out. Tasks vary from relatively simple and contained ones that can be done by a single person to more complex ones that require a small group to very complex tasks that require MTSs. The members take on tasks as they arise, and at any given time there is a mix of tasks being carried out in the unit, some by individuals, some by small groups, and some, less often, by large groups or by assemblages of small groups.

Some of the groups have relatively stable membership, whereas others are crews, which have a specific set of roles that can be filled by whatever qualified personnel are available to assign to them (operating room and airline crews are examples). Still other groups are special project teams composed of members specifically assembled for a particular task. For some tasks, groups are formed that include members from multiple units. Their success in these tasks is an important determinant of the overall effectiveness of the unit in its larger project and of the units standing among other units. Effectiveness also has consequences for individual members such as learning, reputation, and morale that make them more or less fit to serve in their groups in the future (and differentially attractive as members of groups).

The ecosystem is composed of a dynamic network of individuals and units. Units are formed by networks of individuals whose structure reflects the demands of tasks and other group dynamics such as status sorting. Multiunit structures are formed by networks of units whose structure reflects the demands of higher order or more complex tasks and intergroup dynamics. Viewed longitudinally, we would see links forming and breaking in a temporal trajectory determined by workflows, task demands, changes in task, and endogenous network processes.

In this basic model, the MTS would be viewed as organizing itself around various tasks and forming a multilayered network of teams based on task, communication links, and authority links. The model would assume that teams are not necessarily fixed units, but may dynamically reorganize themselves, as reflected in the different kinds of interdependence discussed by Mathieu et al. (2001).

NETWORK ECOSYSTEM THEORY

The theory is stated in the form of a series of propositions that characterize the dynamics of a network ecosystem. These propositions assume that (a) the individual-level processes that generate networks and groups, (b) group-level processes, and (c) higher order endogenous network processes form a heterarchy in which each operates autonomously and in which each influences the other two. The interaction of individual-, group-, and network-level generative mechanisms, as well as the impact of exogenous structural variables such as base rates and environmental "shocks," explains the network ecosystem.

Generative Mechanisms for the Network Ecosystem

Both group-level and network-level generative mechanisms operate in the network ecosystem. The network mechanisms are primary drivers, and once groups form, they take on a life of their own and generative mechanisms at the small-group level come into play.

The network generative mechanisms include both individual-level network generative mechanisms and endogenous network–level generative mechanisms. Monge and Contractor (2003) distinguished eight families of theoretical mechanisms that explain the formation, configuration, and dynamics of networks. One important individual-level generative mechanism defined in their analysis is *homophily*, which accounts for the emergence of links on the basis of trait similarity (McPherson, Smith-Lovin, & Cook, 2001). A second relevant individual-level network generative mechanism is *exchange*, which explains the emergence of networks on the basis of the distribution of information and material resources among network members (Cook, 1982). People seek ties with those whose resources they need and who in turn seek resources they possess. In this view, people would join a network so that they can exchange resources they need with resources they can offer. A third mechanism at the individual level is balance, which (Heider, 1958; Holland & Leinhardt, 1975) posits a consistency toward relations. That is, individuals are more likely to create transitive ties. For example, this would predict that people are more likely to form linkages with friends of their friends.

Each of these network-generative mechanisms represents individual-level motivations—toward realizing personal benefits and reducing costs, toward achieving cognitive consistency, toward finding others like oneself, toward building social capital, toward engaging in collective action, and so on—that generate and sustain network linkages. The aggregate of these individual behaviors yields the network. Most network theories, such as those that McPherson and colleagues (McPherson et al., 2001) have developed around the principle of homophily, presume that a single motivation predominates or can serve as a conduit for other motivations (e.g., homophilic bonding with others might serve one's self-interests and help to achieve balance). More complex theories such as Monge and Contractor's

(2003) multitheoretical network model argue that certain sets of generative mechanisms are compatible because they function to realize higher order goals. For example, in a network dedicated to exploiting resources, the collective action, balance, and contagion generative mechanisms would work together to drive network formation and maintenance.

The other network dynamic is driven by endogenous network–level generative mechanisms. Once a network becomes a going concern, higher order connectivity among members sets in motion downward-acting generative mechanisms that are independent of individual-level and group-level generative mechanisms. There are multiple ways in which this might occur (Kontopoulos, 1993), of which two common examples will be given here. First, network-level generative mechanisms may set up a preference for certain dyadic, triadic, and group-level linkage patterns that influence lower-level processes. For example, once a homophilic network attains a certain critical mass of linkages, it becomes self-sustaining in that new members and new linkages that are homophilic are preferred over those that are not. This occurs because of structural properties of the network as a whole, independent of individual-level choices. With many members interconnected by homophilic bonds, for instance, bonds of other types become "dispreferred." Forming bonds on other principles, such as connecting to someone different from oneself to build social capital, runs against current network organization, which is reinforced by the prevalence of preexisting homophilic linkages. This is a type of the autocatalysis often observed in complex systems.

Second, the higher order network may create "spatial" inhomogeneities such that individuals and groups are separated by different partitions of the network in which certain dynamics are forced on occupants. For instance, once a homophilic network is set up, different regions of the network may be reserved for different social groups (e.g., different races), in essence forcing members to leave one area of the network and enter another.

A second level of generative mechanisms in network ecosystems operates at the small-group level, in groups of three to seven (and sometimes more) members. When small, cohesive groups form in a network, they operate as a semiautonomous unit driven by their particular group dynamics. These groups are self-organizing systems within the network that are influenced by individual-level network generative mechanisms, but once they form they support independent generative mechanisms. For example, a set of individuals linking on the basis of homophily that achieves sufficient connectivity and multiplex interdependence among members to form a densely connected group is likely to develop social identity dynamics. Research on social identity in small groups suggests that in addition to sustaining and reproducing homophily as a basis for grouping, other more complex dynamics develop, including a tendency to differentiate members according to status or role within the homogeneous group (Abrams, Hogg, Hinkle, & Otten, 2005). This dynamic toward differentiation, which will be discussed in more detail under subsequent propositions, serves as an autonomous generative mechanism within the network.

All three generative mechanisms—individual-level network generative mechanisms, network-level generative mechanisms, and group-level generative mechanisms—interact to affect individual outcomesgroup formation; and network formation, maintenance, and change. They are related in a heterarchy in which each affects the others, but each also has autonomy. The relative strength of the generative mechanisms at different levels, how they relate to each other, and the impact they have on individuals, groups, and the network vary. In subsequent propositions, we discuss some ways in which they relate.

Because individual network generative mechanisms are the initial drivers of group formation, group-level generative mechanisms are initially homologous to the network generative mechanisms. The group mechanism homologous to homophily is social identity (Abrams et al., 2005). The specific social identity formulation that most closely matches the homophily principle is social categorization theory. The dynamics of social categorization—an emphasis on distinctive social categories, the valorization of one's own group compared to other groups, the stereotyping of other groups, and the development of distinctive group ideologies—offer explanations for the enactment of homophily at the microlevel that are consistent with McPherson et al.'s (2001) discussion. There are two homologues to exchange, group exchange (Thibaut & Kelley, 1959) and functional mechanisms in which there is a division of labor among members and member behavior functions to enable the group to achieve its goals (Hollingshead et al., 2005). Finally, balance principles operate in both networks and small groups. Taylor (1970) developed a rigorous theory of balance in small groups that can easily be linked with the balance formulations of networks that were developed in the 1970s and 1980s.

Interactions Among Generative Mechanisms at Different Levels

Once a network becomes a going concern, its structure at the macrolevel may autocatalyze the formation and maintenance of future links according to the individual-level generative mechanism drivers that constituted it. This counteracts the ability of competing generative mechanisms to get started to some extent. This downward influence is imperfect and does not wholly determine what happens at the individual and group levels.

The strength of the autocatalysis varies depending on the structural immediacy of the network generative mechanism and network carrying capacity. Autocatalysis is promoted by individual network generative mechanisms that have a high degree of *structural immediacy*, defined as the degree to which link generation and maintenance are based on node-to-node processes. The generative mechanism of homophily, for example, is high in structural immediacy because nodes associate based on a direct evaluation of their similarity in an immediate one-to-one fashion that results in growing networks of homophilous linkages. Other generative mechanisms with high levels of structural immediacy include contagion, simple exchange, and self-interest in market economies (Monge & Contractor, 2003). Generative mechanisms lower in structural immediacy and therefore likely to result in weaker autocatalysis include balance, collective action, and generalized exchange, which all generate links based on multinodal patterns.

Autocatalysis will be limited by network carrying capacity. Monge, Heiss, and Margolin (2009) argued that intra- and interorganizational communication networks have carrying capacities, that is, maximum numbers of linkages that they can sustain. It is well known that the number of potential linkages in a communication network can increase geometrically with linear increases in the number of nodes. For example, if everyone were to connect to everyone else, a network of 10 people would have 90 links, whereas a network of 11 people has the potential for 110 links. But the individuals and groups in a network have limits on their time and energy that constrain the number of actual linkages they can create and sustain to a value well below the number of potential linkages. The nearer the network gets to its network carrying capacity, the weaker the autocatalysis should be.

As the network ecosystem initially forms, individual members try to link to others based on motivators such as homophily, exchange, and balance. These represent competing "bids" for network formation. The fitness of these bids is determined by the various foci that the network is forming around (Feld, 1981) and also by exogenous shocks to the system.

Two aspects of foci can be defined, their purpose and their physical locations. Purposes for foci can be differentiated into task, social, and normative ones. Some foci attract members on the basis of the tasks they require them to do, whereas others attract members based on the need to socialize (e.g., bars or playing fields), whereas still others attract members based on normative considerations (e.g., churches or courts). To use the example of the MTS developed by Mathieu et al. (2001), when there has been a severe accident, firefighters, police, and EMTs converge on the location of the accident and each organizes around tasks, such as controlling the perimeter, keeping gawkers at a distance, putting out any fires, extracting the victims, stabilizing them on the spot, loading them into the ambulance, and transporting them to the hospital, a different location where other task foci organize the work of the surgical and recovery teams in different places within the hospital (ER, operating room, recovery room, intensive care, etc.). In this case, the foci will tend to favor network organization based on functional and exchange principles where each member gathers at the task focus that is suited to his or her skills and operating routines, which will result in a distribution of members across various locales according to task assignments. This will result in preservation of the reticulation mechanisms of exchange and homophily by profession (because firefighters, EMTs, and surgical teams are typically organized into coherent practiced units of members of a single profession).

Exogenous shocks to the system, such as a power struggle between a police commander and the fire chief who has ultimate control over the accident scene, or a sudden escalation of the emergency to a much larger disaster (e.g., the accident involved a fuel truck that suddenly exploded, razing adjacent buildings and starting fires in them), also shape the fitness of generative mechanisms. The power struggle between police and fire chiefs would tend to favor reticulation according to homophily. On the other hand, sudden expansion of the disaster would likely favor functional division of labor, because the different professionals would have to help each other on common tasks (e.g., carrying wounded colleagues to safety).

Once groups form around a generative mechanism, they exhibit a property of self-closure and become self-organizing systems. When small groups form self-organizing systems, they serve as powerful "amplification devices" for network generative mechanisms, because they represent densely connected regions of the network that have the potential to sustain a generative mechanism by virtue of the interdependent action systems they represent. Pressures toward conformity in small groups are powerful (and sometimes repressive) forces reinforcing homophily, because once in place these pressures tend to be self-reinforcing and self-sustaining. In the same vein, once a system has been set up, exchange in small groups creates a self-perpetuating system that rewards similarity and withholds rewards from those different from the group, thus providing another mechanism for enacting homophily and for regulating the flows of information, advice, and help among members of the network.

Group-level processes are also complex and have their own internal dynamics that introduce additional "twists" into the network processes. These have the potential to explain network dynamics in much more detail than individual-level network generative processes allow. For example, in networks formed in terms of exchange principles, another functional theory, the collective information-sharing model (Hollingshead et al., 2005), would specify which information would be most likely to be shared with the group. This model presumes that information is distributed among members and specifies mechanisms that govern which information is most likely to be activated in the discussion; information shared by several members of the group is more likely, for example, to be contributed than is information held by only one member. Sharing of information at the group level is likely to influence group outcomes, which provide value to members in return for their exchange of information. To the extent that the members do not share information adequately and the group is less effective, other network ties are likely to be more attractive to members and the group is likely to dissolve, thus changing the overall network topology.

What determines the fitness of a given group that forms in the network ecosystem? First, the *constraint* of the focus determines the coherence of the group. Constraint refers to the degree to which the focus requires participation by members. For example, in an emergency situation, a fire in the vehicle that has victims trapped in it is strongly constraining and almost demands participation (Corman & Scott, 1994). Second, the degree of *activation* of the focus determines whether it actually gets attention. Activation is triggered by events that make the focus salient to members. In a disaster situation in which a fire suddenly breaks out in a damaged vehicle, the focus is activated and likely to attract the group. So long as it remains activated (e.g., until the fire is put out), it is likely to retain members (Corman & Scott, 1994). Third, foci vary in *strength*, with some having stronger organizing properties than others. In the disaster just described, if a propane tank nearby suddenly explodes into flame, the burning vehicle becomes a much less strong attractor for group formation than the propane tank. *Group performance* also contributes to fitness. If the group is performing well, there are rewards for members and an incentive to stay in the group. Groups that meet their members' *needs* are also likely to be fitter, as their members will remain as well.

There is an interesting twist on fitness in the preceding discussion. In evolutionary theory, *fitness* is generally defined as surviving to reproduce. However, in the network ecosystem, groups come into and pass out of existence as their foci are activated and deactivated, so there is no reproduction. Instead, fitness is determined by comparative ability to cohere compared to other possible groups that might form in the space.

A complex mix of generative mechanisms operates at the group level, generative mechanisms that are often self-reinforcing and self-perpetuating due to the nature of the group system. These mechanisms can influence the formation and quality of linkages in the network and the interactions that occur in the network. From this, it follows that one or more generative mechanisms other than those engendering the encompassing network may come into operation at the group level.

For example, assume that homophily is the major organizing principle in a network. As noted, homophily at the network level is likely to engender and be generated by social identity processes at the local level. However, although social identity dynamics do create a tendency toward sorting on similarity in the network, once this has occurred, a countervailing process is likely to result. Within any group of similar people arise forces leading to differentiation; once people are comfortable that they are with "their kind" and no longer feel threatened, they begin to wish to differentiate themselves. This is reflected in the "optimal distinctiveness" model within the social identity perspective (Abrams et al., 2005). This complexity at the local level reflects the dialectic between wishing to be part of a larger collective and wishing to be independent (Smith & Berg, 1987). This countervailing process sets in motion an alternative generative mechanism that is different from that fostered by the network generative mechanism.

Networks also affect the composition of groups. People in the ecosystem are limited in terms of the time and energy they have to put into relationships of various types and also in terms of their opportunities to form linkages with others. The topology of the network determines who has open time to form new links and who is currently not available due to saturation of possible involvements or simply due to base rate demographics in the network. If, for example, most people similar to person X are already "taken" in the network, this may cause X to seek out partners on bases other than homophily. If there are only two people in the entire network with a particular skill or expertise, then the number of linkages that can form based on complementarity is necessarily limited.

Multiple Generative Mechanisms in Networks

The foregoing implies that different generative mechanisms may be in operation in the same network ecosystem. The simplest case is when the network is segmented into two or more relatively independent regions. In this case, different generative mechanisms may be in operation in different parts of the network.

A second case was implied in the previous section: A variation may begin to take hold within a region of the network previously dominated by a particular generative mechanism. In this case, the new generative mechanism grows within the existing one, carving out its own space in the network. It could be either beneficial or a "cancer" depending on one's point of view.

It is also possible for two or more network generative mechanisms to be compatible with each other and operate simultaneously within the same network space. Contractor and colleagues (Contractor, Wasserman, & Faust, 2006) describe empirical tests of multi-theoretical multi-level (MTML) model predictions in over four dozen networks, using recent advances in exponential random graph-modeling techniques. Their findings across the networks indicate that the individuals' motivations to create, maintain, and dissolve ties with other individuals or knowledge repositories are a complex combination of multitheoretical motivations. No one theoretical motivation is consistently superior or inferior to others. Instead, they tend to work in ensembles.

Contractor et al. (2006) proposed that variation across networks reflects the diverse tasks that are being accomplished in these networks.

The contingency framework proposes that the likelihood of a theoretical mechanism explaining the network will depend on the goals of the group. They identified five goals commonly found in the networks they investigated:

- *Exploring* refers to networks whose members are in search of new information or undiscovered resources. Theories of self-interest, cognition, and contagion are more influential in explaining networks whose goal is exploring.
- *Exploiting* refers to networks in which the major impetus is to maximize members' ability to exploit the resources that already exist in the networks. Collective action, cognition, and exchange generative mechanisms are most influential in exploiting networks.
- *Mobilizing* refers to networks whose members are trying to organize toward some collective action. Collective action, balance, and contagion are the generative mechanisms that explain these networks best.
- *Bonding* refers to networks in which the main objective is to provide social support. The generative mechanisms of balance, exchange, homophily, and proximity are more influential in the formation of networks whose goal is bonding.
- *Swarming* refers to networks where the ability to gear for a rapid response is a high priority. Collective action, cognition, and proximity best explain these networks.

Each of these goals defines configurations of compatible and complementary generative mechanisms for networks or subnetworks. Obviously, different configurations could also operate in different regions of the network, as in the first two cases discussed in this section.

Variation in the Mix of Generative Mechanisms in the Network Ecosystem

There are two major sources of variation in generative mechanisms in network ecosystems. First, group-level generative mechanisms may produce variations that compete with existing generative mechanisms in the network ecosystem. The self-organizing and autonomous nature of small groups within networks gives alternative generative mechanisms a space to develop in for a time.

For a local-level generative mechanism that differs from the prevailing generative mechanism(s) at the global network level to gain a foothold depends in the first instance on the nature and robustness of local-level processes. Consider the example of optimal distinctiveness mentioned in this chapter. If the group in which this differentiation occurs is secure and free from outside threat via contact with another social group that is putatively more powerful or superior, then the differentiation will proceed apace and a differentiated social structure will develop in the group. If this differentiated structure develops complementary roles—for example, task and socioemotional leaders, procedural experts, and followers—that are rewarding to members because they help it operate more effectively and bring success (and rewards) to the group, then a competing generative mechanism of exchange may be set into motion. On the other hand, if the group is confronted by a threatening outside group, distinctiveness dynamics are likely to be dampened, whereas in-group and out-group processes that reinforce homophily are fostered. In this case, the alternative generative mechanism is not likely to develop fully or to persist. Local conditions provide the materials that enable a small fire to get started from the tinder, so to speak. Whether this fire spreads depends on selection processes in the network to be discussed in this chapter.

A second source of variation is factors exogenous to the network ecosystem. Interventions by external authorities that change assigned tasks or goals or that impose norms on the network ecosystem may give rise to variations in generative mechanisms. Each of these represents a "perturbation" in the existing network. The nature of the new task or norm may be such that it organizes members of the network system according to a generative mechanism currently in operation, but it may set up a competing generative mechanism. For example, if the emergency takes an unanticipated direction, as with the chemical explosion mentioned previously, this may also lead to wholesale reorganization of the network system. In cases where there are regular sequences or cycles of tasks, networks may undergo periodic reorganization. Organizations that must design new products and then put them into production typically require two types of networks, one densely connected and easily reconfigured for innovation, and a second that is more hierarchically and tightly configured for production (Zaltman & Duncan, 1977). In some organizations, these two networks are achieved by partitioning the organization, whereas in other smaller organizations there would be oscillations from decentralized to hierarchical networks over time.

Other exogenous factors that influence network systems include the entry of new individuals or organizations into the larger organizational set in which the network ecosystem is embedded, changes in the network's environment due to factors such as new technologies, changing legal requirements, or a financial crisis. Some of these exert continuous pressure on the network, whereas others are "shocks" to the network system, but all present opportunities for the introduction of novel generative mechanisms into the network.

Once a novel generative mechanism takes hold, it can spread to other nodes in the network, and ultimately (a) it may be extinguished by the existing dynamics; (b) it may create its own space of operation, thus partitioning the network; (c) it may enter into a commensalistic relationship with existing network mechanisms; or (d) it may outcompete existing mechanisms and take over the network.

Selection of Generative Mechanisms in the Network Ecosystem

Selection among the various generative mechanisms is influenced by six factors: (a) characteristics of the niches in the ecosystem, (b) base rates of individual role types in the network ecosystem, (c) autocatalysis, (d) dissipative structure, (e) emergence, and (f) overall network configuration.

The niches in any ecosystem of task groups correspond to *activity foci*, sites at which members assemble around a common activity or to garner resources (or both). Just as tasks can be layered—one task may be broken into subtasks, and the subtasks into component tasks, and so on—so too are foci layered. The characteristics of a task focus include the following:

- Its location: proximity to and distance from other foci
- Subtasks: foci embedded within foci (if any)
- Within-unit interdependencies: the various roles involved and how these roles relate to one another
- Between-unit interdependencies: the roles that different units within the focus undertake and how these units relate to one another; also the relationships between foci if there are multiple foci
- Task difficulty and complexity of the task and its subtasks (if any)

- The tools required

This corresponds to the multitiered task and goal hierarchies discussed by Mathieu et al. (2001) for MTS. Together these characteristics influence how reticulation of groups and the networks occurs and the particular generative mechanisms that are supported.

The foci in group ecosystems vary in terms of stability. Some are quite stable, as would be the case in a factory in which work stations are set out systematically for a continuous, stabilized workflow. Other group ecosystems may have foci that rearrange dynamically as components of the task are completed and new aspects develop. Product development departments often are organized around tasks that shift and change as the product evolves, problems emerge, and different stages of the development process unfold.

Following Thompson (1967), within-unit, between-unit, and between-foci interdependencies may be of three general types: pooled, sequential, and reciprocal. *Pooled interdependencies* are cases in which the work can be distributed to different individuals or units who work in parallel and independently and then pool their work after completing it. *Sequential interdependencies* are cases in which one person or unit finishes its work, passes it on to the next, and so on until the work is finished. *Reciprocal interdependencies* are cases in which the units must coordinate their efforts and pass the work back and forth among them, often in a very complex pattern. Types of interdependence—and combinations or sequences of them—will shape the nature of the interaction in the network and thus the selection of generative mechanisms. For instance, pooled interdependence among subtasks in a focus would encourage a sparse network by dampening the tendencies to create links based on social capital or exchange between those working on different subtasks.

A second factor influencing selection in a network ecosystem is the number of individuals capable of filling the various roles required by the task, the base rates of individuals in the population. In a day care center with 60 children and an ideal teacher–child ratio of one to six, the center can function at its best only if at least 10 teachers are in the center on any given day. If fewer teachers are available, then a network system premised on setting up quality exchanges between children and teacher may be reoriented to one in which those teachers who are thought by their colleagues to be excellent at dealing with difficult situations would be allocated additional children (a system based on cognition about the network and exchange).

A third factor that governs selection in network ecosystems is the auto-catalysis discussed previously. Structural immediacy will promote auto-catalysis and thus favor the selection of generative mechanisms similar to those already ascendant in the network. Autocatalysis will dampen as the network carrying capacity is approached, thus lessening selection pressure on different generative mechanisms.

A fourth factor in selection is the formation of dissipative structures. As we noted under a previous proposition, group-level processes give the variation "energy," and, if sufficiently robust, they can form a strong foundation for the persistence and spread of the generative mechanism, much as the dissipative structures described by Prigogine and colleagues are able to maintain themselves in part through the expenditure of localized energy (e.g., Nicolis & Prigogine, 1977). Certain types of network generative mechanisms may also generate the resources or energy required to sustain themselves. The self-interest, mutual interest, exchange, and coevolutionary network generative mechanisms seem particularly likely to have this characteristic, because they confer material or intangible reward on participants.

Fifth, selection is influenced by the type of emergence through which groups emerge from individual-level network processes and clusters of groups from groups. The nature of emergence shapes how well established the competing generative mechanisms are.

Kozlowski and Klein (2000) distinguished two ways in which higher level phenomena can emerge from lower level phenomena, composition and compilation. In *composition*, the higher level property emerges from the convergence of similar lower level properties that add together to yield a whole that has the same property as the sum of its parts. Homophily is one such process; lower level members and dyads choose those like themselves, and the sum of these choices yields a homophilous network. Other network generative mechanisms that seem compatible with composition are balance and contagion. When emergence occurs through *compilation*, the lower level units have different properties, and it is the relationships among them and their complementarities that result in the emergence of the higher level property. So in exchange lower level members, dyads, and groups develop distinct competencies or resources and link to other units that have complementary ones, yielding a whole that is distinct from its parts. Other network generative mechanisms that seem to work on a complementary basis are self-interest, mutual interest, cognitive mechanisms, and collective action.

Composition occurs more quickly and is more straightforward than compilation, because it operates via enlistment, that is, through individual unit changes where units are more or less independent to make changes. However, emergents based on composition are also relatively fragile, because members can be taken off or "de-enlist" one by one with little consequence for the whole emergent. Compilation is slower and requires more effort than composition, because members form interdependencies. Compilation thus requires coordination among lower level units. Once established, emergents based on compilation are relatively durable, precisely because they are constructed of interdependent units that mutually support one another's adherence. Members cannot leave or be taken off the assemblage without upsetting the interdependencies, so the network is likely to mobilize resistance or to rapidly seek out replacements. So the nature of emergence affects the speed with which networks organized around different generative mechanisms emerge and their durability in the face of counterpressures that might erode them. Hence, in very new networks, those formed by composition are likely to be more robust than equally new networks formed by compilation and also to find it easier to penetrate existing networks than compilation-based networks. In more established networks, however, the obverse is likely to be true: Compilation networks are more likely to be sustainable in competition with composition networks and also in competition with preexisting established networks.

Finally, the structure of the global network also influences selection. If the global network is segmented into relatively independent portions, these may support different mechanisms or configurations of mechanisms in a sort of peaceful coexistence. On the other hand, if the development of the network brings the competing generative mechanisms into contact, then one or the other is likely to spread and prevail in the network.

Different individual-level network generative mechanisms are also likely to foster overall configurations with differential selection strengths. Some of the generative mechanisms are more likely to leave "gaps" in which they do not operate strongly, enabling local variations to persist and grow. For example, balance is likely to leave gaps in the network, because balancing processes are subject to incompatibilities in relationships that "block" the balance process. Taylor (1970) noted that long cycles of relationships that must be balanced have less effect on target persons, making them less likely to change to restore balance. A network with many long and complex cycles will have weaker tendencies toward balance. Taylor also observed that there were tendencies toward unbalance in networks governed by balance, which suggests that gaps will form. In these gaps, where the impact of the generative mechanism is relatively weak, there is an opportunity for variations to take hold and spread. Homophily, on the other, hand, has a high level of structural immediacy. It is likely to be more difficult for variations to take root and spread in a network governed by homophily than in one governed by balance.

Then too, some network generative mechanisms are likely to spread variations. In a network with strong contagion processes, the behaviors, values, and attitudes underlying variations are likely to spread. Indeed, contagion can act as a mesolevel process in the respect that it enables the group-level generative mechanism to "jump" to other portions of the network. A network organized according to balance principles is also likely to propagate variations, because this generative mechanism assumes that links and nodes change in order to become more consistent.

Coevolution of Generative Mechanisms

The evolution of networks occurs during episodes, each of which consists of a period of instability and change followed by a temporary equilibrium in which the network ecosystem stabilizes. The instability represents a transition to the new stable state, which could consist of a single network governed by a uniform generative mechanism, a set of compatible generative mechanisms, or a partition of the network ecosystem into subnetworks governed by competing generative mechanisms.

The temporary equilibria vary in terms of their stability and durability. Overall, we would expect networks organized around a single generative mechanism or a set of compatible mechanisms to be more stable and durable than those in which there are two or more incompatible and competing generative mechanisms. Further, as noted previously, depending on whether they are constituted through composition or compilation, networks may vary in their robustness and durability.

The development of the network system over time occurs through a series of episodes in which the network ecosystem moves from temporary equilibrium to temporary equilibrium, shifting its mix of generative mechanisms over time. Group-level processes and exogenous factors continue to introduce variation into the network system, which destabilizes the existing equilibrium and initiates a new episode, which ends in another equilibrium.

From this, it follows that networks may reconfigure if one network generative mechanism outcompetes the prevailing mechanism. When this occurs, a new set of network influences is introduced, and this may change which generative mechanisms are able to operate at the group level. This in turn creates new possibilities for variation at the local level that then influence the global level in a continuous loop of influence.

AN ILLUSTRATION OF A MULTITEAM SYSTEM AS A NETWORK ECOLOGY

The MTS of emergency responders in Collegeville, U.S.A., offers an illustration of a network ecosystem. At the outset, the fire, police, EMT, and college police operated relatively independently of one another, as is the case in most communities. Although they were capable of coordinated response similar to that in the MTS example from Mathieu et al. (2001), which has been used throughout this chapter, their network was organized primarily by the homophily mechanism. Each profession largely kept to itself, and teams were organized separately for fire, police, EMT, and university police. Within these teams, as might be expected, social identity processes were strong and members were differentiated according to status hierarchies based on optimal distinctiveness in terms of seniority, skill, and "manliness" (Desmond, 2007). As in most towns in the state in question, if a large disaster occurred, the fire chief was authorized to take charge of the situation and exert command and control over the other units.

A major crisis occurred when a historic downtown building that was being remodeled caught on fire. It went up in flames much faster than anyone expected and burned much more fiercely, probably because some wood-refinishing supplies served as accelerants. The fire was so severe that several adjoining buildings were threatened. The fire chief coordinated the response of the Collegeville firefighters, police, and EMTs. The three groups worked in parallel and largely kept to their own tasks. In several cases, fire teams found themselves tangled with police personnel who were trying to make sure that the crowd at the scene was under control and safe, and this was the source of some friction, both at the scene and afterward in the after-action review.

Cognizant of the shortcomings of the previous response, the fire chief invited officers from the fire department, police, EMT, and college police to the yearly training offered by the state Fire Service Institute in the National Incident Management System (NIMS). This training focuses on preparing participants to fulfill the various roles involved in planning for and carrying out incident management, including those of incident commander, operations chief, safety officer, logistics chief, and communications officer. The team prepares an incident management plan, and the various officers then take charge of their sphere of duty. The incident management team is multidisciplinary, and participants may cross-train to fulfill multiple roles. Just as important as the training itself, stress Fire Service instructors, is the development of relationships and trust among participants. As one instructor commented, "We really cannot prepare them for any specific disaster, because every one is different, but we can help participants understand their roles and build relationships among them, so that when a disaster does occur, they can work together smoothly as a team."

Ranking officers from the fire department, police department, EMT services, and college police department were assigned to an incident command team and engaged in planning in response to a simulated disaster. The team used the NIMS forms to guide their work and developed an incident management plan. A fire captain served as the incident commander, an assistant police chief the operations manager, an EMT the safety officer, a college police sergeant the communications officer, and a police lieutenant the logistics officer. Because the entire team had been trained in NIMS and planning, members could take on any of these roles. The planning exercise built trust across the professions and gave them some practice in working together. The NIMS process provided a structure for the team's interaction. In this workshop, networking among participants was based on the task focus of the exercise, and members networked based on role interdependencies, rather than homophily or social identity. At the group level, team processes were driven by functional interdependencies.

When the next big disaster struck, the incident management team network formed around the task focus of planning in an incident command truck, and networking was based on functional interdependence. The action teams in the field still worked as cohesive units with their own profession (e.g., fire teams or EMT teams), but due to the planning and coordination among their supervisors, there was much less confusion and interference among the teams. In this network, the seed for functional interdependency as an organizing principle has been planted in a portion of the network, which has partitioned itself off from the rest of the network of actors who link according to the principle of homophily.

IMPLICATIONS FOR RESEARCH

Empirical research on this framework requires longitudinal designs that capture data on links among individuals in the ecosystem and also on generative mechanisms relevant to the local level, such as social identity. This research will require a large data set with multiple measures of constructs at both the network and group levels and large numbers of observations at successive time points. Fitting successive network models that change over time requires significant amounts of data.

The study of a network ecosystem requires researchers to collect network data either continuously or at regular intervals. Continuous data collection would require either automated recording of information relevant to inducing linkages or a continuous record such as video recordings of the ecosystem. Automated records of the network ecosystem could be obtained by monitoring message traffic over radio frequencies used by participants. Another way of obtaining automated records would be to access information systems that record participants' behavior. Williams, Contractor, Poole, Srivastava, and Cai (2009) described a research project that uses the databases of massive multiplayer online games to study dynamic networks that include group ecosystems. The databases record every major movement and transaction made by the players and so enable researchers to follow networks of dynamic groups over time. An additional advantage of game databases is that they preserve information about characteristics of participants (that is, of their avatar characters), task difficulty, and objectively measured outcomes and so allow discrimination between links formed on the basis of exchange, social identity, and some other network generative mechanisms.

A continuous record of the ecosystem can also be obtained by video and audio recording the ecosystem over time. This poses a challenge for data management and analysis, because network ecosystems are composed of many actors spread around a large space, unlike the nice, neat groups in labs that can be recorded with a single video camera. Recording an MTS at work requires multiple cameras and personal audio recording for each member, and might also involve other types of sensors (e.g., infrared cameras in the case of firefighters) and instruments. Managing and analyzing this massive body of data pose a major challenge. In a separate project (Poole et al., 2009), we are developing GroupScope, an observational and analytic system for large groups distributed over large physical areas. GroupScope, currently under development, uses IT to manage retrieval, annotation, and coding of large numbers of videos and audios. Developing it requires developing a suite of tools to identify automatically the best segments for human analysis, map networks from video data, and capture text from audio.

A key problem facing analysts of data gathered either automatically or through continuous recording is how to identify network connections from data that are not relational in nature. Various algorithms have been developed to extract network information from databases (see a high-level description in Williams et al., 2009). Mathur, Poole, Pena-Mora, Contractor, and Hasegawa-Johnson (2009) described an algorithm for identification of network linkages from video data. It is presently partially automated, and when fully automated should allow accurate link detection when combined with transcriptions of interactions.

In addition to records or observational data, it is also important to have subjective responses of the members of the MTS and network ecosystem. It is not practical to collect repeated measures of network ties from members. However, members can provide valuable information on why they selected partners, what the characteristics of foci are, and other information that can be used to validate measures based on records or observation.

In terms of analysis of the network data, Contractor et al. (2006) have developed procedures to test for the various generative mechanisms based on signatures of the mechanisms, particular patterns of links that signal that the operation of a specific generative mechanism. In order to test the framework, it is necessary to find ways to partition the network into portions in which different generative mechanisms prevail and to track shifts in generative mechanisms over time. Poole et al. (2009) are currently working on methods suitable for undertaking these tasks. They involve (a) identification of groups from the bottom up in terms of member–member relationships, member–group relationships, and group–group relationships using group cohesiveness thresholds; and (b) tracking the movements into and out of groups via sparse matrix techniques and parallelized Markov chains.

At the group level, we must specify the particular group processes expected to be in operation, because the set of possible dynamics is much too large to inductively sort through them. This can be done deductively by specifying which group theories are likely to hold in a given context; previous research in the context of choice can provide guidance as to which group dynamics are most likely to be in play. It could also be done inductively by making an initial determination of the generative mechanisms governing the network for a portion of the longitudinal data and selecting homologous group theories. The deductive approach seems preferable, because it gives some a priori guidance as to what to measure.

DISCUSSION

In this chapter, we have discussed a theoretical framework that unifies global network theory and theories of groups, dyads, and individuals at the local level. There are at least two potential benefits of this integration. First, it provides a foundation for the study of a behavior in a class of social phenomena that has hitherto been largely neglected, the large networks of groups with membership between 8 and 200. Network systems of this type perform many important functions, and careful study of how they form, operate, and dissolve has both theoretical and practical significance, particularly for networked MTSs. For instance, we do not have good theories of what makes groups of this size effective, and study of their behavior could lead to improved understanding.

A second benefit of this integration is its potential to lead to a more general theory of group and network behavior. By conceptualizing networks as ecosystems of groups and individuals and groups as embedded within larger network ecosystems, we begin to be able to see what seem to be two disparate phenomena as part of a greater, multifaceted whole. Including local-level group dynamics as a factor in network dynamics allows us to move away from uniform, relatively simple explanations of network phenomena, and toward recognition of the complexity underlying network generative mechanisms. Including the impact of global network genera-tive mechanisms with local group dynamics allows us to emphasize the context of the group, including its competition with other groups for members and its position in the larger network, just as bona fide group theory recommends.

A third benefit (though one with possible dangers as well) is that the framework recognizes the complexity of human behavior and attempts to build it into the explanation of network systems. The forces driving individual behavior are much more variegated and multiplicitous than is acknowledged in most network and group research. Simply put, people are complicated. People's motives tend to change over time, over context, and according to the people they are interacting with. An individual may well feel a desire for the comfort of familiarity and similarity (homoph-ily), but in almost the same breath desire to differentiate him or herself from others who suddenly seem boringly the same. Furthermore, people are reflexive, and they can come to know larger dynamics that are shap-ing them and choose other grounds of action that can be locally insulated from the wider influence of the network.

The relative simplicity of most current group and network explanations is in part a product of the desire for parsimony. Although a case can be made for parsimony, it can also be argued that our theories can be too par-simonious and ignore human nature. A balance between parsimony and realism must be struck. Simple models are also in part a methodological artifact of fitting the prevalent explanation to a large sample of individuals and "averaging" across them and controlling out the "error" due to other explanations. In this case, other explanations represent perturbations in the prevalent model that could be detected using more sensitive method-ologies. Simplicity may also be a real property of networks that only a few drivers can hold at any given point in time if the system is to be stable. It may well be the case that one or a few generative mechanisms must hold for a coherent system to exist and that too much diversity in genera-tive mechanisms undermines the grounds of the system and breaks it into smaller systems.

The great diversity of generative mechanisms for human behavior has two implications for network ecosystems. First, generative mechanisms other than those driving a network system may "erupt" due to human agency. This introduces variation into the system. Second, the multiple lev-els of generative mechanisms offer one way of incorporating this diversity into the system. Although one level may operate in one mode, other levels offer the opportunity for diverse generative mechanisms to emerge. The group level is particularly diverse in terms of the generative mechanisms it offers, because group dynamics often feature multiple factors.

Research within this framework requires the development of new methods for studying networks and their linkage to local group processes. As noted, it requires methods for dynamically identifying groups, network configurations, and network generative mechanisms. It also requires methods to measure other variables related to group generative mechanisms coordinated with the network analysis.

The framework also suggests some interesting future directions. One is to explore developmental sequences for network generative mechanisms. For example, one might posit that the homophily generative mechanism at the global level would foster and be sustained by social identity dynamics at the local level. Social identity dynamics would promote the emergence of homogeneous groups, which in turn would give rise to a tendency toward differentiation within these groups at the local level. If this differentiation occurred via a process of special and eventually generalized exchange, then the exchange generative mechanism would be established at the local level and would compete with homophily as an organizing principle. If exchange led to more effective groups, then eventually it may supplant homophily as the organizing principle for the network. This can be described in terms of a developmental sequence in the network, from homophily (global) and social identity (local) as the first stage to exchange (global) and exchange (local) as the second stage. With sufficient data, developmental models for networks could be defined.

A second important goal is to work out the various ways in which generative mechanisms at global and local levels might be related. In the previous paragraph, we gave an example of a competitive relationship in which one generative mechanism supplanted the other. However, other relationships are possible. It might also be the case that homophily may define large-scale groupings at the network level, and exchange may be the prevalent mechanism within these large-scale groupings. In this case, there is a hierarchical or heterarchical relationship between the two generative mechanisms. It is important to work out the types of possible relationships among generative mechanisms and the factors that promote them.

The theory also suggests some implications for the study of MTSs. First, it suggests that MTSs must be understood in the context of the larger organization and group network in which they are embedded. It also suggests that MTSs are embedded in an ongoing temporal process in which they may persist in multiple incarnations as teams add to and leave the MTS. For instance, the emergency response MTS described by Mathieu et al. (2001) may add a utility worker team, if an accident involves downed power lines. This "natural history" of the MTS suggests that we can also study it, not as a predefined structure with set goals, but in terms of ongoing behavior. This allows us to discern slippage in the goals of the MTS and how it interacts with other teams and MTSs in its environment.

The network ecosystem model also implies that there may be more generative mechanisms operating in the MTS than simply functional interdependence based on goal hierarchies, as assumed by Mathieu et al. (2001). Social identity dynamics may also intrude on all or parts of an MTS through homophily-generated networks, and other generative mechanisms may also come into play. To greater or lesser extent, these may interfere with the functioning of the MTS and reduce its effectiveness.

Though not every network ecosystem is an MTS, every MTS is part of a network ecosystem. Considering the dynamics in operation in the network ecosystem promises to provide a richer understanding of MTSs.

ACKNOWLEDGMENTS

Preparation of this chapter was supported by the National Science Foundation (IIS-0729421), the Army Research Institute (W91WAW-08-C-0106, and the U.S. Army Research Laboratory (ARL) Cooperative Agreement No. W911NF-09-2-0053, Network Science Collaborative Technology Alliance. The authors would like to thank Kees Boersma, Peter Groenewegen, Michelle Shumate, and Pieter Waagenar for discussions and comments about the model.

REFERENCES

Abrams, D., Hogg, M., Hinkle, S., & Otten, S. (2005). The social identity perspective on small groups. In M. S. Poole & A. H. Hollingshead (Eds.), *Theories of small groups: Interdisciplinary perspectives* (pp. 99–138). Thousand Oaks, CA: Sage.

Contractor, N., Wasserman, S., & Faust, K. (2006). Testing multi-theoretical multilevel hypotheses about organizational networks: An analytic framework and empirical example. *Academy of Management Review, 31,* 681–703.

Cook, K. S. (1982). Network structures from an exchange perspective. In P. V. Marsden & N. Lin (Eds.), *Social structure and network analysis* (pp. 177–218). Beverly Hills, CA: Sage.

Corman, S. R., & Scott, C. R. (1994). Perceived communication relationships, activity foci and observable communication in collectives. *Communication Theory, 4,* 171–190.

Desmond, M. (2007). *On the fireline: Living and dying with wildland firefighters.* Chicago: University of Chicago Press.

Feld, S. L. (1981). The focused organization of social ties. *American Journal of Sociology, 86,* 1015–1035.

Heider, F. (1958). *The psychology of interpersonal relations.* New York: Wiley.

Holland, P. W., & Leinhardt, S. (1975). The statistical analysis of local structure in social networks. In D. R. Heise (Ed.), *Sociological methodology, 1976* (pp. 1–45). San Francisco: Jossey-Bass.

Hollingshead, A. B., Wittenbaum, G., Paulus, P. B., Hirokawa, R. Y., Ancona, D. G., Peterson, R., et al. (2005). A look at groups from the functional perspective. In M. S. Poole & A. B. Hollingshead (Eds.), *Theories of small groups: Interdisciplinary perspectives* (pp. 21–63). Thousand Oaks, CA: Sage.

Kontopoulos, K. (1993). *The logics of social structure.* Cambridge: Cambridge University Press.

Kozlowski, S. W. J., & Klein, K. J. (2000). A multilevel approach to theory and research in organizations: Contextual, temporal, and emergent processes. In K. J. Klein & S. W. Kozlowski (Eds.), *Multilevel theory, research, and methods in organizations* (pp. 3–90). San Francisco: Jossey-Bass.

Mathieu, J. E., Marks, M. A., & Zaccaro, S. J. (2001). Multiteam systems. In N. Anderson, D. Ones, H. K. Sinangil, & C. Viswesvaran (Eds.), *International handbook of work and organizational psychology* (pp. 289–313). London: Sage.

Mathur, S., Poole, M. S., Pena-Mora, F., Contractor, N., & Hasegawa-Johnson, M. (2009). Detecting interaction links in a collaborating group using manually annotated data (Working paper). Urbana: National Center for Supercomputing Applications, University of Illinois Urbana-Champaign.

McGrath, J. E. (1984). *Groups: Interaction and performance.* Englewood Cliffs, NJ: Prentice Hall.

McPherson, M., Smith-Lovin, L., & Cook, J. M. (2001). Birds of a feather: Homophily in social networks. *Annual Review of Sociology, 27,* 415–444.

Monge, P. R., & Contractor, N. (2003). *Theories of communication networks.* New York: Oxford University Press.

Monge, P. R., Heiss, B., & Margolin, D. (2009). Communication network evolution in organizational communities. *Communication Theory, 18,* 449–477.

Nicolis, G., & Prigogine, I. (1977). *Self-organization in non-equilibrium systems: From dissipative structures to order through fluctuations.* New York: Wiley.

Poole, M. S., Bajcsy, P., Contractor, N., Espelage, D., Fleck, M., Forsyth, D., et al. (2009). GroupScope: Instrumenting research on interaction networks in complex social contexts (Working paper). Urbana: National Center for Supercomputing Applications, University of Illinois Urbana-Champaign.

Putnam, L. L., & Stohl, C. (1996). Bona fide groups: An alternative perspective for communication and small group decision making. In R. Y. Hirokawa & M. S. Poole (Eds.), *Communication and group decision making* (2nd ed., pp. 179–214). Thousand Oaks, CA: Sage.

Smith, K. K., & Berg, D. N. (1987). *Paradoxes of group life: Understanding conflict, paralysis and movement in group dynamics.* San Francisco: New Lexington Press.

Taylor, H. F. (1970). *Balance in small groups.* New York: Van Nostrand Reinhold.

Thibaut, J. W., & Kelley, H. H. (1959). *The social psychology of groups.* New York: Wiley.

Thompson, J. D. (1967). *Organizations in action.* New York: Harper.

Williams, D., Contractor, N., Poole, M. S., Srivastava, J., & Cai, D. (2009). The virtual worlds exploratorium (Working paper). Urbana: National Center for Supercompting Applications, University of Illinois Urbana-Champaign.

Zaltman, G., & Duncan, R. (1977). *Strategies for planned change.* New York: Wiley.

9

Cognitive Similarity Configurations in Multiteam Systems

Joan R. Rentsch
The University of Tennessee

Melissa J. Staniewicz
The University of Tennessee

Piracy off the coast of Somalia was recently brought to public awareness when pirates held a U.S. merchant captain hostage in a lifeboat after his crew had successfully regained control of their ship, the *Maersk Alabama*. Reports of rescue efforts revealed a complex system of multinational and interagency teams with a mission to thwart piracy and protect shipping routes within a 1.1 million-square-mile region (Gilmore, 2009). The U.S. Navy, European Union, and NATO coalition forces, devoted to protecting the region, coordinate and support each other to combat piracy (U.S. Second Fleet Public Affairs, 2009). In the case of the merchant captain, the coalition ships synchronized actions to achieve the common objective of neutralizing the pirates. The coalition ships played interference and deterred other pirates from reaching the lifeboat (Mount & Starr, 2009), which supported forces, including Navy SEAL teams, that neutralized the pirates holding the captain. Together these efforts resulted in a successful rescue. In addition, other coalition ships focused on recapturing merchant ships that had been recently hijacked by pirates and on protecting other merchant ships from new hijacking attempts.

This example represents a system containing multiple teams that function interdependently to achieve collective goals. It is a multiteam system (MTS) because it contains teams that coordinate activities to achieve common goals, and it emerged from or was formed in response to a dynamic and turbulent environment (Mathieu, Marks, & Zaccaro, 2001). The strength of MTSs is their adaptability. Their challenge is to develop coordinating mechanisms to support adaptability. Coordinating mechanisms need to function at the team, interteam, and system levels in order for MTSs to utilize their available capacity fully.

As team members and teams interact, they socially construct similar understandings regarding relevant domains, including the task, members, leaders, and work context. Organizational research has produced several conceptualizations for the development of common understanding, such as "schema similarity, climate, culture, sensemaking, and collective climate" (Rentsch, Small, & Hanges, 2008, p. 130). These conceptualizations are types of cognitive similarity, and they can exist at multiple levels of analysis (e.g., team, interteam, and system). The development of functional, similar understandings of system members, tasks, team process, and other aspects of collaboration within a team are needed to adapt to and to perform in dynamic environments (Rentsch, Delise, & Hutchison, 2008). Thus, the examination of cognitive similarity and its configurations within MTSs should provide insight into the processes that enable MTSs to function efficiently and effectively in dynamic environments.

The purpose of this chapter is to present cognitive similarity configurations as coordinating mechanisms available to MTSs. In this discussion, we point out the relevance of cognitive similarity configurations for the team, interteam, and system levels and highlight the need to develop an MTS typology with respect to patterns of interdependencies. Points of intervention that can influence the development of useful cognitive similarity configurations are discussed. We begin this chapter by summarizing the core features of MTSs and by discussing interdependencies that exist at the team, interteam, and system levels. Next, we describe specific forms of cognitive configurations that can serve as coordinating mechanisms for MTSs. Then, we discuss the points of intervention.

FEATURES OF MULTITEAM SYSTEMS

Mathieu et al. (2001) defined MTSs as being composed of "two or more teams that interface directly and interdependently in response to environmental contingencies toward the accomplishment of collective goals" (p. 290). An important component of the definition is interdependence. According to Mathieu et al. (2001), component teams comprising a MTS share at least one input, process, or outcome functional interdependency with one other team in the system. These component teams have functional interdependencies whereby their activities are accomplished through "mutual reliance, determination, influence, and shared vested interest" (Mathieu et al., 2001, p. 293). Input interdependence refers to the degree to which component teams share such resources as equipment, personnel, and training in efforts to achieve proximal goals. Process interdependence is the scope and manner in which component teams must interact with each other while completing a task. Outcome interdependence refers to the extent to which teams' outcomes, including rewards, are contingent upon the performance of another team (Mathieu et al., 2001). The nature of interteam interdependence is closely associated with another component of the definition, MTS goals.

Although component teams in a MTS share at least one distal goal, they may pursue different proximal goals that contribute to the achievement of that distal goal. Goal hierarchies within MTSs demonstrate the collective effort to reach distal system goals. Component teams are primarily focused on proximal goals that lead to the system's distal goal (DeChurch & Mathieu, 2008). Interteam-level interdependencies are related to combining team-level task performance in order to achieve distal goals. Within the team, team members' interdependent activities are related to completing the tasks required to meet team-level proximal goals. At the system level of a MTS, the coordination of the interteam and team activities reflects the effort to reach the system's distal goal(s) (Mathieu et al., 2001). Overall, interdependent processes must be coordinated within and between teams to reach proximal and distal goals successfully. In addition, interdependence is influenced by performance episodes that exist within the MTS.

Performance episodes contain identifiable actions and transitions in which input–process–outcome cycles are nested (Marks, Mathieu, & Zaccaro, 2001). During action phases, team activities include monitoring systems (e.g., environment or resources), monitoring team actions, backing up teammates, coordinating (e.g., managing the sequencing and pacing of goal-driven tasks), and monitoring progress. During transition phases, teams focus on mission analysis (e.g., interpreting, evaluating, and identifying their overall mission, abilities, resources, and constraints), goal specification (e.g., prioritizing goals and subgoals), and strategy formulation and planning (e.g., developing an initial plan, contingency plans, and reactive strategies for completing tasks) (Marks et al., 2001). The timing of performance episodes tends to vary within and across component teams, which demands that coordination within an MTS depends in part on managing these rhythms (DeChurch & Marks, 2006). Coordination at the team, interteam, and system levels is required to manage the rhythms contained in the overall system (Mathieu et al., 2001; Williams & Mahan, 2006). For example, coordination becomes important when the outcomes from one team in the system are inputs for more than one other team, especially when the teams' tasks are dictated by differential pacing. A component team must also accommodate its internal performance episodes in order to coordinate its internal interdependencies among team members that are needed to achieve its proximal goals. In doing so, it must simultaneously account for relevant performance episodes of the teams with which it shares interdependence in order to contribute to the system's distal goals.

MTSs tend to work in dynamic environments, because they present the advantage of being able to respond and adapt rapidly to complex, novel, changing, and uncertain situations (Mathieu et al., 2001; Williams & Mahan, 2006). Coordinating mechanisms are essential for component teams to accurately monitor and interpret environmental changes, identify and enact contingency and reactive strategies, compensate for constraints, and provide needed backup functions. In order to synchronize interteam collaboration toward collective goals, teams need to coordinate, communicate, and transfer knowledge related to the task, environmental contingencies, team processes, timing, and goals. Coordination, communication, and knowledge transfer within and among teams may vary due to the nature and degree of interdependence within the MTS. For example, in loosely coupled systems with few interdependencies among teams, teams may be more concerned with timing information flow and knowledge transfer than with sequencing simultaneous activities (Mathieu et al., 2001), whereas in more tightly coupled systems, highly interdependent teams may spend most of their time synchronizing activities (Williams & Mahan, 2006).

COORDINATING MECHANISMS IN MTSs

The structure of MTSs necessitates effective coordinating mechanisms for communication, knowledge transfer, and collaboration to synchronize goal-directed efforts in dynamic environments. Coordinating mechanisms are "methods for attaining system integration" (DeChurch & Mathieu,

2008, p. 284) and include leadership, technology, and cognitive similarity. For example, leaders within MTSs should focus on team and interteam processes and interactions (DeChurch & Marks, 2006; DeChurch & Mathieu, 2008; Mathieu et al., 2001) to manage within- and between-team performance episodes effectively. Similarly, such technological coordination mechanisms as well-designed computer interfaces displaying environmental and task information can facilitate communication between and within teams.

Although technology and leadership can function as coordinating mechanisms for MTS performance, these coordinating mechanisms are effective due to the *cognitive similarity* they establish among interdependent parties. Cognitive similarity provides team members with the capability to anticipate, to appreciate, and to compensate for the actions of other team members and of other teams. Cognitive similarity is the key driving component of coordinating mechanisms for MTSs.

FEATURES OF COGNITIVE SIMILARITY

Cognitive similarity refers to "forms of related meanings or understandings attributed to and utilized to make sense of and interpret internal and external events including affect, behavior, and thoughts of self and others" (Rentsch, Small, et al., 2008, p. 130). Collaborative interactions, negotiation processes, and life experiences are antecedents associated with organizational and team members developing cognitive similarity with respect to a variety of content domains. Various types of cognitive similarity influence team and organizational processes and outcomes (Rentsch, Delise, et al., 2008). For example, cognitive congruence among team members has been found to be positively associated with team performance (e.g., Mathieu, Heffner, Goodwin, Salas, & Cannon-Bowers, 2000; Naumann & Bennett, 2002; Rentsch & Klimoski, 2001; Smith-Jentsch, Mathieu, & Kraiger, 2005), presumably because cognitive congruence increases a team's efficiency and the quality of its processes. When team members possess accurate cognitions regarding their teammates (another type of cognitive similarity), they are able to correctly understand team members' domain expertise, abilities, preferences, and/or roles. Therefore, they can identify when to compensate or help team members who need backup.

Most teams are expected to benefit from a combination of cognitive similarity types, which form cognitive similarity configurations.

Cognitive similarity types are distinguished by the intersections of form of similarity, form of cognition, and cognitive content domain. Cognitions among individuals may be similar in several ways, including being congruent, accurate, or complementary. Each form of similarity defines the nature of how the cognitions among individuals correspond. Congruent cognitions exist when cognitions between individuals match, although there is no "correct" value, true score, or target. For example, team members may have congruent cognitions about how team meetings are conducted. Cognitions among individuals are accurate to the extent they reflect the degree of match to a "true score" or target value. For example, a team member's cognitions about the team leader will be accurate to the extent that the team member understands the leader's preferences. Complementary cognitions refer to the unique cognitions that team members contribute to the team that fit together like puzzle pieces. For example, team members with differing expert domains may have complementary understandings of task components. Sharing, integrating, and merging the unique cognitive contributions of each team member are indicative of cognitive complementarity.

Just as there are multiple forms of cognitive similarity, there are also various forms of cognition, including perceptual, structured, and interpretive cognitive forms. Perceptual cognition refers to meaning "reflected in descriptions or expectations constructed on the basis of patterns identified from accumulated observations" (Rentsch, Delise, et al., 2008, p. 149) and includes attitudes, values, beliefs, prototypes, and expectations (Rentsch, Small, et al., 2008). Perceptual meaning, as it is typically assessed, provides little information about deep understanding of causal, relational, or explanatory links, and is more closely related to content nodes in schemata. Structured cognition refers to organized meaning and incorporates causal, relational, and explanatory links. Within the team research literature, structured cognition has been conceptualized as mental models and schemata. Structured cognition provides the foundation for the interpretive processes of ascribing value-laden explanations and meaning to events. Interpretative forms of cognition are rooted in the individual's experience and environmental, biological, and cultural influences, but more importantly, the interaction with others helps frame the meanings of events and thus interpretive cognitions. Interpretative cognition is studied primarily in organizational science.

Type of cognitive similarity is also distinguished by *cognitive content domains*, which are the topics or subject matter areas for which individuals develop understanding. Particularly relevant to teams are content domains such as self, team members, leadership, tasks, team context, team goals, system goals, and so on. Team members may develop cognition with respect to an infinite number of domains. Researchers must identify those most relevant for team performance while keeping in mind that specific domain contents may vary by situation (or by MTS type).

CONFIGURATIONS OF COGNITIVE SIMILARITY

A type of cognitive similarity is defined by a similarity form, a cognitive form, and a cognitive content domain. For example, a team may have a congruent (form of similarity) mental model (form of cognition) for client needs (domain). Defining the types of cognitive similarity most relevant to specific teams should increase the prediction of team processes and performance in terms of qualitative and quantitative differences. Due to the complexity of team functioning and many team tasks, configurations of cognitive similarity are likely to exist.

Cognitive similarity configurations are combinations of cognitive similarity types. For example, a cognitive similarity configuration that includes complementary schemata of the task, accurate perceptions of team members' areas of expertise, and congruent interpretations of team members' interaction may increase a cross-functional team's effectiveness. Members of cross-functional teams likely have different areas of expertise causing their schemata of the task to differ in complementary ways. This type of cognitive similarity may be functional to the extent that team members develop accurate perceptions of team members' area of expertise. Understanding who knows what enables the team to extract and use the expertise of its members knowing that each member is focusing on a different but relevant aspect of the task, thereby enabling the team to evaluate potential solutions, opportunities, and obstacles to success. Congruent interpretations regarding how team members interact with one another should lead to a smooth, efficient process of integrating expertise between team members.

COGNITIVE SIMILARITY CONFIGURATIONS AS COORDINATING MECHANISMS IN MULTITEAM SYSTEMS

Figure 9.1 represents the notion that cognitive similarity configurations (CS configurations) exist at the team, interteam, and system levels and influence coordination within and between levels of MTSs. Configurations at each level may also influence configurations at the other levels. As coordinating mechanisms, CS configurations support the functioning of team, interteam, and system levels in the MTS. Therefore, they should be aimed at the linkages (e.g., functional I–P–O interdependences, goal hierarchies, and performance episodes) between and within the three levels. Shown in Table 9.1 are sample linkage points among MTS components that require coordination. The representation in Table 9.1 is a simplification of the potential intricate networks of linkages in MTSs that can be described by complex patterns of interdependencies. By way of example, consider the issues associated with potential patterns of task interdependencies in MTSs.

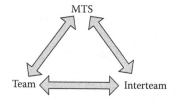

FIGURE 9.1
Cognitive similarity configurations influence coordination within and between levels of MTSs.

TABLE 9.1

Linkage Points Requiring Coordination at Each Level

Linkage Point Requiring Coordination	Constituent Level		
	Team	**Interteam**	**System**
Outcome interdependence			
Process interdependence			
Input interdependence			
Proximal goals			
Distal goals			
Performance episodes			

Patterns of Task Interdependencies

Past research has focused primarily on such task interdependencies as sequential, reciprocal, or intensive arrangements between component teams. By definition, component teams are interdependent, and the nature and intensity of these interdependencies are associated with the degree of complexity of goal hierarchies (Marks, DeChurch, Mathieu, Panzer, & Alonso, 2005), the rhythms of performance episodes, and the nature of the functional relationships that influence the manner of interactions and processes mandatory for teams to meet system goals.

The nature of interdependencies within the overall system forms *patterns of interdependencies* that should be considered in a serious typology of multiteam systems. Weights (i.e., representing the degree of required coordination), timing, criticality and importance, and ease or difficulty of establishing and maintaining the linkages are some definitional features of the patterns. We focus here on the qualitative aspect of the patterns regarding task interdependence. At the system level, interdependency patterns are potentially dynamic and contain embedded cross-level interdependencies within and between team and interteam levels.

Shown in Figure 9.2 is an example in which, within the system, goal-directed work requires Team A to engage in an intensive interdependent relationship with Team B, but Team A has no direct relationship with Team C. Rather, Team A has an indirect relationship with Team C through Team B's sequential interdependence with Team C. Not shown explicitly in the figure is the notion that the degree or intensity of the coordination required varies depending on the nature of the proximal goals and the resulting task interdependencies between teams. Of the three teams shown in Figure 9.2, Team B has the greatest coordination challenge, because it has interdependencies with two teams and the nature of the interdependencies are different for each team. Team B will benefit from a coordinating mechanism (or mechanisms) that can accommodate this

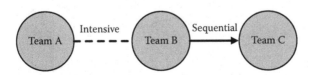

FIGURE 9.2
Mixed sequential pattern at the interteam level.

complexity. A MTS containing these types of interdependencies may be referred to as having a *mixed intensive* or *sequential pattern.*

Similarly, as shown in Figure 9.3, a pattern may exist in which Team A has sequential interdependencies with Team B, Team B has reciprocal interdependencies with Team C, and Teams B and C have intensive interdependencies with Team D. This pattern of interdependencies is clearly more complex than that shown in Figure 9.2. MTSs may be characterized by interteam interdependency patterns that might be referenced by the global, majority of, or most critical interdependencies that exist between component teams.

Furthermore, the potentially shifting nature of the pattern of interdependencies should not be ignored. It is likely that the degree and nature of interdependencies shift at various action and transition phases of goal completion. For example, most of the time teams' interdependence may be characterized by reciprocal arrangements, but at other times their interdependence may be characterized by intensive interdependency. An example of this type of pattern exists in product development teams, which are typically embedded in turbulent and dynamic operating environments (Brown & Eisenhardt, 1997), as are most MTSs. These teams must manage changing types and levels of interdependencies throughout the product development cycle (e.g., Hoegl & Weinkauf, 2005).

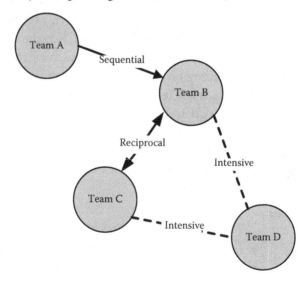

FIGURE 9.3
Dynamic pattern of interdependencies at the interteam level.

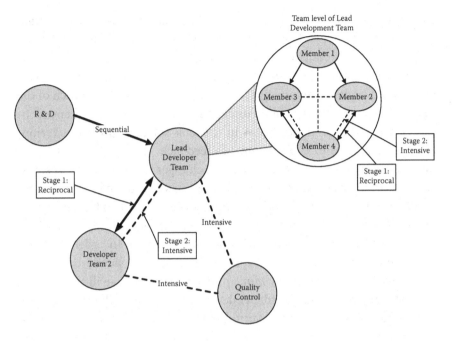

FIGURE 9.4
Dynamic pattern of interdependencies at the team and interteam levels.

See Figure 9.4 for an example of a MTS in a product development cycle within a high-tech software development company that is characterized by the following pattern of interdependency. The research and development team (R&D) generates concepts for new programs that it forwards to the lead program developer team. This creates a sequential interdependency between R&D and the lead developer team, because R&D's output serves as an input to the lead developer team. The lead program developer team cannot begin work on the program until the product concept has been handed off by the R&D team. The lead program developer team works in tandem with Developer Team 2 to develop singular modules (or components) of the overall program. During the initial transition phase, the developer team's activities include portioning out responsibilities and communicating technical requirements. It will delegate activities to Developer Team 2. Both teams create additive components for the overall product, interacting to clarify, hand off, or test the functionality of the software as the components are pulled together. This creates a reciprocal arrangement in the initial stages of product development between the developer teams. Once the software program is completed, the quality control team reviews and tests the product. Quality control then engages in intensive interdependency with each of the developer teams to work out bugs and improve functions. Quality control explains the potential flaws of the product and assists the developer teams in finding solutions. This process can occur simultaneously between quality control and each of the developer teams, forcing a more intensive arrangement of interdependencies between the developer teams in the later stages of product development. In response to quality control's feedback, the development teams must coordinate and collaborate to make changes to the program. A single change to the program can initiate a surging series of changes throughout the program. Therefore, although the developer teams had reciprocal interdependencies during the initial stages of product development, in the later stages their interdependencies become intensive in order for them to create a viable product. Perhaps this type of MTS should be referred to as a *reciprocal-intensive dynamic pattern*. This example illustrates that a variety of *patterns* of interdependencies may exist at the system level, and these patterns may shift over time due to such factors as task evolution, environmental changes, or performance rhythms. A full articulation of the interdependencies in a MTS also includes the dynamic patterns of interdependencies occurring at the *team* level.

In Figure 9.4, the team-level interdependencies for the lead developer team are shown. Of course, each team has its own set of interdependencies. Figure 9.5 offers a representation of the interdependencies in each team depicted in Figure 9.4. At the team level, key interdependencies are related to goal hierarchies, and to action and transition processes (Marks et al., 2001, 2005). Information-sharing and knowledge transfer requirements are also likely to affect interdependencies at the team level, especially in teams where members possess specific unique task-related knowledge that contributes to the team's performance. Teams are also subject to temporally related constraints or rhythms (e.g., Ancona & Chong, 1996, 1999) that can impact the coordination of individual team member actions. Similar to the shifts in interdependencies that are seen between teams, shifts can occur at different stages at the team level between teammates. Furthermore, cross-level interdependencies may exist. For example, highly interdependent goal hierarchy teams require more cross-team transitions and action processes to reach goals, although team action processes are more important with less interdependent goal hierarchy teams (Marks et al., 2005).

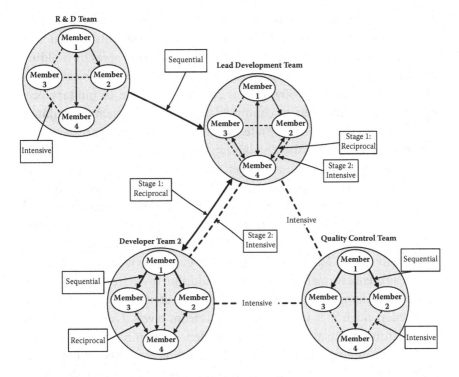

FIGURE 9.5
Dynamic pattern of interdependence at the system level.

Figure 9.5 shows the patterns of task interdependencies within a product development multiteam system composed of the team and interteam level patterns of interdependencies. All of the interdependencies require coordination, and CS configurations aimed at patterns of interdependencies at the system, interteam, and team levels serve as coordinating mechanisms. Cognitive similarity configurations that operate as coordination mechanisms will depend on where coordination is needed and the pattern of associated interdependence. Below, an illustrative example of cognitive similarity configurations as coordinating mechanisms in an MTS is presented.

Illustrative Example of Cognitive Similarity Configurations as Coordinating Mechanisms in MTSs

An illustrative example of a provincial reconstruction team (PRT) will be used to demonstrate the role of cognitive similarity configurations as coordinating mechanisms in a MTS. A PRT consists of joint civilian–military teams "whose mission is to promote governance, security, and reconstruction" (Perito, 2005, p. 1). PRTs have been used in Afghanistan and Iraq to decrease insurgency and increase stability in volatile areas by building infrastructure and supporting the development and scope of governments (Malkasian & Meyerle, 2009; Perito, 2007). In addition to military personnel, PRTs in Iraq are also composed of leaders from such nonmilitary units as USAID and the U.S. State Department, Justice Department, and Department of Agriculture (Malkasian & Meyerle, 2009; Perito, 2007). Each leader represents a much larger team, and these larger teams must work together to complete the mission (Linda Pierce, personal communication, May 12, 2009). PRTs operate in highly dynamic environments and have a great deal of latitude in reaching distal goals. Because they consist of interdependent component teams, PRTs represent a form of MTS.

Not unlike other MTSs, PRTs experience gaps as to when certain members are present and member rotation. In addition to environmental uncertainties and changes, these membership inconsistencies require flexibility in interdependence at the team and interteam levels. Due to these and other features, the patterns of interdependencies within this type of MTS are complex and dynamic. Using and expanding elements characteristic of PRTs, we developed an illustrative example intended to provide a point of departure for discussing cognitive similarity configurations as coordinating mechanisms in MTSs in which patterns of interdependencies are complex and vigorous.

This example PRT consists of four component teams. The health team's primary role is to work with local health officials to develop healthcare initiatives (e.g., a vaccination program and family medical kits), create and improve health care facilities, and attract and retain physicians and specialists to the region. The engineering team provides expertise to assess and perform construction projects, develop engineering skills within the local populace, and enlist contract agreements with local construction agencies. The State Department team supplies the administrative coordination of projects, schedules activities, facilitates obtaining project funding from multiple sources, and is responsible for building effective relations with the provincial government. The State Department team is also the primary contact for the U.S. Embassy and the national PRT coordination team. The military team contributes to the PRT by providing protection for convoys, escorts for other teams that are in the field, intelligence on insurgency and potential security risks, and emergency response in the event of an attack.

For purposes of this example, the MTS's distal goal is to develop a healthcare system in a foreign war-torn province. This is a simplified example, because increasing access to healthcare facilities and the resulting improvement of the overall health of the population comprise only one factor that contributes to the stability of the region. Furthermore, not all of the density, intricacies, and complexities of the patterns of interdependencies are included in the example. The intention is not to present a study of PRTs, but rather to provide a point of discussion for the purposes of illustrating CS configurations in MTSs. Examples of CS configurations that could serve as coordinating mechanisms for this MTS at the system, interteam, and team levels with respect to task interdependencies are described.

System Level

One type of cognitive similarity likely to be important at the system level is complementary perceptions of required resources. The system requires resources to reach its distal goal, and when each team understands its resource needs and how to acquire the resources needed to meet its own goal(s), then the entire system can access what it needs. For example, when the State Department team's understanding of its needs for outside funding is complemented by the military team's understanding of its resource needs in terms of Soldier availability, mission schedules, and vehicles, then the system "understands" its resource needs. With respect to process interdependence, the system will have better internal coordination if teams have accurate schemata regarding the expertise and roles of other teams. Knowing which teams are responsible for specific functions, for example, that the military team provides escorts for missions and the State Department team negotiates with locals, coordinates system actions so that teams are not "stepping on each other," causing process loss (cf. Steiner, 1972) or embarrassment. This type of cognitive similarity also aids in coordinating backup functions, because when members understand the system's structure, they will know better who to turn to for assistance to meet the distal system goal and where they might be able to contribute backup to other members of the system.

Because each team understands and experiences different aspects of the region, at the system level, these types of MTSs should possess complementary interpretations of environmental changes. For example, the State Department team interfaces with the local government officials and is the primary contact for the U.S. Embassy and the national PRT coordination team (which coordinates all the PRTs within the country). Therefore, it may have much more information regarding the political and diplomatic climate of the region, whereas the military team will have detailed information on safety, the likelihood of insurgent attacks, areas to avoid, intelligence reports, and other strategic information regarding the security of the region. Each of these domains of knowledge represents the dynamic nature of the environment in which the MTS is operating. To the extent that members of the system interpret different elements of the environment in complementary ways, the system is better positioned to be aware of environmental turbulence.

All teams should develop an accurate schema of the distal goal. This cognitive similarity type will focus team and interteam actions toward the common objective and serves as a standard for self-regulatory assessments. Thus, at the system level, at least four types of cognitive similarity form a CS configuration for this example MTS. A system-level CS configuration composed of several CS types is expected to facilitate system functioning above and beyond any one type alone. Furthermore, CS configurations at the interteam level will also contribute to the system-level coordination.

Interteam Level

CS configurations also exist at the interteam level, particularly among those teams with direct interdependencies. The nature of the coordination needs (and therefore the CS types) will be associated with the type of task interdependence that exists between the teams. For example, teams with intensive task interdependence will likely benefit from congruent perceptions of resources requisite for fulfilling their interdependent objectives, because this common understanding will help them to coordinate their connected efforts. Teams with multiple interdependent relationships (such as Team B in Figures 9.2 and 9.3) must develop different types of cognitive similarity for resources depending on the nature of the interdependence with each team. For example, the State Department team would need to develop one form of similar perceptions for resources with the health team to achieve their interdependent goal of developing the healthcare system, and another form of similar perceptions of resources with the engineering team involved with rebuilding schools (their interdependent goal).

In addition to different forms of similarity, the specific cognitive content related to resources may vary by sets of interdependent teams. For example, if the engineering team encounters a shortage of skilled labor and it and the health team had congruent schemata for the causal relationships between resources and their interdependent goals, then both teams would understand that the construction of the health clinic will be delayed and the health team will not be able to occupy the clinic when originally scheduled. This type of cognitive similarity will likely reduce affective conflict between teams that is likely to result when teams do not fully understand each other's positions (cf. Baron, 1988) and facilitate coordination among the teams to adapt to the resource shortage (e.g., by creating their own workforce) to avoid any additional delays.

Complementary interpretations of the team's joint task will also serve to coordinate teams with process interdependence. Each team contributes unique expertise to the joint task, and each has different interpretations of the task and the functions that contribute to the mission. This type of cognitive similarity will be functional for the interdependent teams to the extent that they also develop accurate schemata of each team's expertise. Although team members will approach the task from complementary perspectives, members from neither team would know how to fulfill the other team's function. However, with accurate schemata of the other team's expertise, they will understand the other's contributions to and role in the mission. Together these types of cognitive similarity form a CS configuration that coordinates team activities, thereby increasing the teams' efficiency. For example, when a health team goes into the field to interact with provincial health officials, it understands that the military team escorting it has the expertise to avoid any counter attacks. The health team does not have the expertise to spot potential security risks or to initiate appropriate evasive or combat maneuvers. Therefore, the health team will not attempt to fulfill that security role. Likewise, the military team does not have the expertise to discuss medical issues or to negotiate with the local health officials, but understands that the health team does. Therefore, it leaves that role to the health team. The coordinating effect of these two cognitive similarity types may be increased when teams also possess congruent interpretations of the proximal interteam goal (e.g., arriving at and returning from the meeting safely and on schedule), and congruent schemata for interteam interaction processes. The latter pertains to the expectation and understanding of

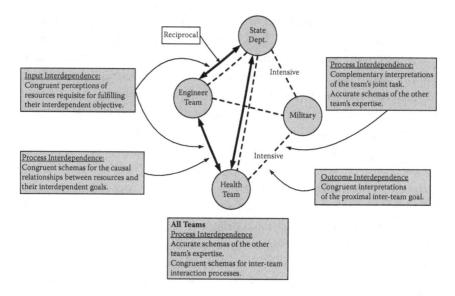

FIGURE 9.6

Illustrative example of a cognitive similarity configuration as a coordination mechanism at the interteam level.

how the teams will interact as they accomplish their interdependent proximal goal. It should contain information related to the performance episode rhythms of each team. For example, the health team and the military team should envision their interaction for a daily escort mission to proceed in a similar way. Congruent cognitions regarding interaction processes are likely to be related to interteam performance, as has been found in the within-team research (e.g., Mathieu et al., 2000).

As with the system level, an interteam CS configuration composed of several CS types, as illustrated in the above paragraphs and shown in Figure 9.6, is expected to facilitate interteam coordination and functioning above and beyond any one type alone. Furthermore, CS configurations at the interteam level will contribute to system-level coordination, and team-level CS configurations will contribute to interteam coordination.

Team Level

At the team level, the locus of interdependencies shifts from being between teams to being between members within each component team. The nature of the interdependence among team members will dictate the types of CS similarity that will serve each team's coordination needs. For example, complementary task schemata may serve to coordinate team members who have reciprocal or sequential process interdependence, such that team members are able to make unique contributions to the task. Perhaps one member of the engineering team builds health facilities (builder), another member trains the local workers on constructions skills (T&D), and another member allocates workers to specific projects (HR). Their work may be characterized by reciprocal handoffs. For example, the T&D member trains workers who the HR member assigns to work with the builder. Each member likely has a unique understanding of how to reach the team's goal (e.g., building construction). However, the effects of complementary cognitions will be useful to the extent they are coordinated by team members also possessing congruent schemata regarding the teamwork process (e.g., agreeing on how to work effectively with others on the team) and congruent schemata of the causal relationships between team member performance and reaching team goals. (See Figure 9.7.)

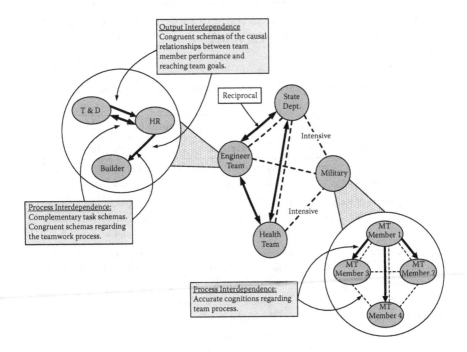

FIGURE 9.7

Illustrative example of a cognitive similarity configuration as a coordination mechanism at the team level.

Congruent task schemata combined with accurate cognitions regarding team process (e.g., knowing standard procedures, and knowing what they offer to and need from their teammates to complete the task) may serve to coordinate members who work together intensively. For example, in the event of an insurgent attack during an escort mission, the military team members need to adapt to the situation and implement well-trained procedures to achieve their goal (to protect the escort). If a member is injured, other members must compensate for his or her functions (i.e., utilize congruent task schemata) and be able to cope swiftly with these kinds of problems with minimal discussion or debate (cf. Dyer, 1984) by utilizing information contained in accurate process schemata.

Summary

In summary, the above examples suggest that MTSs contain many CS types. In combination, these types form CS configurations at the team, interteam, and system levels to serve as coordinating mechanisms for the entire MTS. An example set of CS configurations for the illustrative sample MTS is presented in Table 9.2. A MTS should benefit from many CS

TABLE 9.2

Sample Cognitive Similarity Types at the System, Interteam, and Team Levels Forming a Cognitive Similarity Configuration in a MTS

	Constituent Level	
System	**Interteam**	**Team**
Complementary perceptions of required resources	Congruent perceptions of task resources	Accurate perceptions of task resources
Accurate schema of teams' expertise and roles	Accurate schemata of interacting teams' expertise and roles	Congruent task schemata or complementary task schemata
Complementary interpretation of environment	Complementary interpretations of the teams' joint task	Congruent schemata for within team processes
Accurate schemata of the distal system goal	Congruent interpretations of the joint goal(s)	
	Congruent schemata for interteam processes (for the specific set of interacting teams)	

types that indicate points of coordination and points of intervention for improving coordination. As noted above, the nature and intensity of the interdependencies within MTSs depend on more than task interdependence. Interdependencies may be dominated by goal systems, performance rhythms, environmental changes, and so on. In addition, the dynamic aspect of these interdependencies must be handled by the coordination mechanisms. For example, cognitive similarity configurations at the team and interteam levels should accommodate the dynamic nature of process interdependence within and between teams such as those shown in Figure 9.5. CS configurations must be managed in order to serve effectively as coordination mechanisms in MTSs.

MANAGING COGNITIVE SIMILARITY CONFIGURATIONS

Cognitive similarity configurations are important coordinating mechanisms in MTSs. A single type of cognitive similarity (e.g., accurate understanding of complementary expert knowledge) may not be effectively utilized (cf. Levesque, Wilson, & Wholey, 2001) without the existence of some other type of cognitive similarity (e.g., congruent understandings communicating expert knowledge). Cognition in MTSs must be actively managed to assure that beneficial cognitive similarity configurations develop; otherwise, they may not develop or they may not develop functionally. Evidence suggests, for example, that accurate schemata for what expertise others possess may not develop naturally (e.g., Zhang, Hempel, Han, & Tjosvold, 2007). Although lack of beneficial CS configurations may impede MTS effectiveness, dysfunctional cognitive similarity (e.g., countercultures, dysfunctional team processes, and toxic climates) may develop that will destroy the functioning of the MTS. Organizational and team climates and cultures, leadership, and informal relationships and networks are points of intervention for managing CS configurations.

Aspects of climate and culture associated with congruent interpretations and perceptions of events represent forms of cognitive similarity. Cognitive domains are represented by various "climates for" (e.g., justice, safety, absence, and teamwork). Organizations, organizational units, and teams develop cultures and climates (e.g., Glisson & James, 2002) whether or not efforts are aimed at managing their development and maintenance. Congruent interpretations represented by climate and culture at the team or organizational level can be managed by effectively socializing newcomers. Socialization to a unit may occur through formal sources such as selection, training, or formal mentoring programs (e.g., Schneider, 1987) or through informal sources such as on-the-job or social interactions among members (e.g., Louis, 1980). Properly socialized members will possess cognitions congruent with those of "old-timers;" therefore, they will interpret organizational events in ways that are consistent with other members' interpretations, behave as expected in the system, and be able to make valued performance contributions. Furthermore, they will perpetuate the set of similar cognitions by socializing other new members, correcting deviants, and enacting the interpretations (e.g., Daft & Weick, 1984; Schneider, 1987). Cognitive congruence in the form of climate and culture is also achieved through social construction processes (e.g., Berger & Luckmann, 1966; Schneider & Reichers, 1983) and negotiation processes (Walsh, Henderson, & Deighton, 1988).

MTSs located in organizations with strong functional organizational climates and cultures with respect to teamwork, goal hierarchies, and interdependence may be characterized by smooth and efficient work processes. MTSs that consist of teams located in different organizations may be served by efforts aimed at developing cognitive congruence by managing climate and culture at the system level. These types of MTSs should establish policies, practices, and procedures (Schneider, 1975) for "rules of engagement" within the system, which will result in cognitive congruence regarding how to handle input, process, and outcome interdependencies. Attention should be given at the team level to new members to the MTS to assure that they are properly socialized. MTSs without a formal leadership structure may have to rely on informal networks to support these efforts.

Leadership has been noted as a key coordinating mechanism that forms linkages in MTSs (Hoegl & Weinkauf, 2005; Mathieu et al., 2001) with the most critical responsibility being the coordination of actions within and between teams. A leader's coordination role is primarily related to creating CS configurations within and across teams. For example, leaders should attend to building team members' cognitive accuracy (e.g., regarding other team members' and other teams' areas of expertise), congruence (e.g., regarding work process), and complementarity (e.g., professional perspectives) in domains relevant for internal team functioning, while also developing CS configurations with other teams with which direct interdependencies are shared. In addition, having some level of accuracy with respect to the roles of other teams whether there is a direct or indirect interdependency would seem important.

Leaders have a key responsibility to develop and maintain cultures (e.g., Yukl, 1989) by developing and reinforcing policies, practices, and procedures that form consistent messages to guide team, interteam, and system functioning. These efforts can be aimed at creating CS configurations for predictable MTS elements and events. However, because most MTSs are expected to operate in turbulent environments, adaptability, including flexible CS configurations, is essential. Another major role of leaders is to be interpreters of organizational events (e.g., Smircich & Morgan, 1982), which is especially important for MTSs that frequently encounter unexpected situations that require interpretation.

Leaders should aid MTS members in developing meaningful interpretations of system goal hierarchies (an important content domain that should be included in a CS configuration) in terms of priority, importance, and time frames in order to coordinate action directed toward the system's goal hierarchies. Members within teams need cognitive congruence regarding their own proximal goals, and in some cases they may need to develop accuracy regarding the proximal goals of teams with which they are directly interdependent. As Mathieu et al. (2001) stated, "Effective MTSs have component teams that not only work in a nested goal hierarchy, but also have awareness of the cooperative nature of proximal goals" (p. 303).

Leaders as liaisons (Zaccaro & Marks, 1998) also have a major role in developing CS configurations that coordinate across teams, particularly in MTSs that involve leader teams in which members are leaders (or regular members who perform the liaison function) for other component teams. A leader team is in a good position to influence CS configurations throughout the system. These team members might develop CS configurations, pieces of which will be relevant to their constituent teams. They can develop accurate cognitions with respect to what other teams know, need, and do; their performance episode rhythms; proximal goals (to the extent they are relevant); and communication preferences. To the extent that interdependence is intensive, they should develop, test, or negotiate congruent process schemata. Then they can take this information back to their teams, educate team members about the relevant domains, and guide them in developing relevant CS types (i.e., some may need to have accurate cognitions with respect to a particular domain, whereas others may need to develop congruent interteam cognitions with respect to the same domains). The leader must manage the mutual relationships by taking the team's cognition needs to the leadership team so that they may be integrated and passed along to influence the other teams. In this way, the MTS develops and maintains its CS configurations. A strong emphasis should be placed on being mindful and conscious about this process and to avoid inadvertently creating mixed messages.

In addition to avoiding mixed messages, leaders should monitor multiteam interactions for potential miscommunications or deviations that could derail team performance, and intervene by facilitating communication between teams or by coordinating the multiteam actions (DeChurch & Marks, 2006). Miscommunications and deviations present clues as to where CS configurations need to be managed or maintained. Leaders need to be aware of changing features of CS configurations. This also highlights training as another technique for managing CS configurations.

Informal relationships and networks also serve to create functional CS configurations. In MTSs, particularly those located in a single organization, component team members may have informal relationships with one another by which they can share information about the CS needs. Individuals who interact develop similar meaning for interpreting events (Rentsch, 1990), and if they understand the essential aspects of the MTS they will be more effective in creating similar understandings by conversing about those aspects and developing CS with key others about relevant content domains (e.g., goals, timing, and task). In this way, informal networks may serve to link different aspects of the system and be more effective than or serve to augment leaders' efforts to develop CS configurations.

The location of the MTS components being in either a single organization or several organizations should be considered when managing CS configurations. When component teams are from different organizations, teams may benefit from understanding aspects of other component teams' home organizations. For example, members of an Army team and a State Department team working together in a PRT will likely benefit from accurate perceptions about the organizational values, procedures, and structure of the other's home organization. Leadership (e.g., interlocking directorates), alliance arrangements, and informal networks may serve to support CS configurations in these types of MTSs.

FUTURE RESEARCH

Future research on CS configurations in teams is needed. We have provided illustrative examples of how CS configurations will serve as coordination mechanisms in MTSs. However, future research must be aimed at determining the precise nature of these configurations. Descriptive research and theoretical development are needed. As a starting point, we offer the following propositions.

Proposition 1: Types of MTSs may be characterized by patterns of interdependencies defined by a variety of features (e.g., criticality, timing weighting, and ease or difficulty of establishing and maintaining linkages).

Proposition 2: Patterns of interdependencies in MTSs are complex, containing potentially dynamic and cross-level interdependencies within and between the team and interteam levels.

Proposition 3: The functionality of interdependencies is influenced by coordinating mechanisms.

Proposition 4: Cognitive similarity is a driving component of coordinating mechanisms for MTSs.

Proposition 5: Cognitive similarity (CS) configurations serve as coordination mechanisms and support the functioning of team, interteam, and systems levels in MTSs.

Proposition 6: Cognitive similarity configurations must accommodate the complexity of the patterns of interdependence in the MTS. Therefore, unique CS configurations may be required for each team.

Proposition 7: The nature of CS types forming CS configurations that serve as coordinating mechanisms in MTSs will depend on features of the goal; environmental features; performance episodes; and input, process, and outcome functional interdependencies.

Proposition 8: At the system level, some CS types may serve as coordinating mechanisms in most MTSs (e.g., accurate schemata regarding the expertise and roles of each team, complementary interpretations of environmental features, and accurate schemata of distal system goals).

Proposition 9: At the interteam level, some CS types may serve as coordinating mechanisms in most MTSs depending on the nature of the interdependencies.

Proposition10: At the team level, some CS types may serve as coordinating mechanisms in most MTSs depending on the nature of the interdependencies.

Proposition 11: CS configurations serving as coordinating mechanisms for MTSs will depend on the MTS type.

In summary, MTSs will take many forms depending in part on the nature of interdependencies embedded in the system. Cognitive similarity configurations are one type of coordinating mechanism that will sustain MTS effectiveness. MTSs must manage and maintain their CS configurations. A key aspect of increasing the efficiency, performance, adaptability, and flexibility of a MTS is locating at which points in the MTS's structure, timeline, and team interactions, interventions can develop, create, or enhance CS configurations. Organizational and team-level climate, culture, leadership, and informal networks should be used to manage CS configurations mindfully. Future research should focus on identifying a model or typology of MTSs with respect to patterns of interdependencies (and/or based on function, goal hierarchies, structure, or operating environment) so that specific CS configurations relevant to each type of MTS can be identified. Some CS configurations may be MTS specific, but other CS configurations are likely to be core and apply generally to all MTSs.

ACKNOWLEDGMENT

The authors' work on this chapter was funded in part by a grant to the first author from the Office of Naval Research (Award Number N00014-09-1-0021).

REFERENCES

Ancona, D., & Chong, C. L. (1996). Entrainment: Pace, cycle, and rhythm in organizational behavior. *Research in Organizational Behavior, 18,* 251–284.

Ancona, D., & Chong, C. L. (1999). Cycles and synchrony: The temporal role of context in team behavior. *Research on Managing Groups and Teams, 2,* 33–48.

Baron, R. A. (1988). Attributions and organizational conflict: The mediating role of apparent sincerity. *Organizational Behavior and Human Decision Processes, 41,* 111–127.

Berger, P. L., & Luckmann, T. (1966). *The social construction of reality.* New York: Doubleday.

Brown, S. L., & Eisenhardt, K. (1997). The art of continuous change: Linking complexity theory and time-paced evolution in relentlessly shifting organizations. *Administrative Science Quarterly, 42,* 1–34.

Daft, R. L., & Weick, K. E. (1984). Toward a model of organizations as interpretation systems. *Academy of Management Review, 9*(2), 284–295.

DeChurch, L. A., & Marks, M. A. (2006). Leadership in multiteam systems. *Journal of Applied Psychology, 9*(2), 311–329.

DeChurch, L. A., & Mathieu, J. E. (2008). Thinking in terms of multiteam systems. In E. Salas, G. F. Goodwin, & C. S. Burke (Eds.), *Team effectiveness in complex organizations: Cross-disciplinary perspectives and approaches* (pp. 267–292). New York: Routledge.

Dyer, D. J. (1984). Team research and team training: A state-of-the-art review. In F. A. Muckler (Ed.), *Human factors review: 1984* (pp. 285–323). Santa Monica, CA: Human Factors Society.

Gilmore, J. (2009, April 9). Navy crew arrives to assess pirate situation. *American Forces Press Service.* Retrieved from http://www.navy.mil/search/display.asp?story_id=44210

Glisson, C., & James, L. R. (2002). The cross-level effects of culture and climate in human service teams. *Journal of Organizational Behavior, 23,* 767–794.

Hoegl, M., & Weinkauf, K. (2005). Managing task interdependencies in multiteam projects: A longitudinal study. *Journal of Management Studies, 42*(6), 1287–1308.

Levesque, L. L., Wilson, J. M., & Wholey, D. R. (2001). Cognitive divergence and shared mental models in software development project teams. *Journal of Organizational Behavior, 22,* 135–144.

Louis, M. R. (1980). Surprise and sense making: What newcomers experience in unfamiliar organizational settings. *Administrative Science Quarterly, 25,* 226–251.

Malkasian, C., & Meyerle, G. (2009). Provincial reconstruction teams: How do we know that they work? Strategic Studies Institute, U.S. Army War College. Retrieved from http://www.strategicstudiesinstitute.army.mil/Pubs/Display.Cfm?pubID=911

Marks, M. A., DeChurch, L. A., Mathieu, J. E., Panzer, F. J., & Alonso, A. (2005). Teamwork in multiteam systems. *Journal of Applied Psychology, 90*(5), 964–971.

Marks, M. A., Mathieu, J. E., & Zaccaro, S. J. (2001). A temporally based framework and taxonomy of team processes. *Academy of Management Review, 26*(3), 356–376.

Mathieu, J. E., Heffner, T. S., Goodwin, G. F., Salas, E., & Cannon-Bowers, J. A. (2000). The influence of shared mental models on team process and performance. *Journal of Applied Psychology, 85,* 273–282.

Mathieu, J. E., Marks, M. A., & Zaccaro, S. J. (2001). Multiteam systems. In N. Anderson, D. S. Ones, H. K. Sinangil, & C. Viswesvaran (Eds.), *Handbook of industrial, work and organizational psychology* (Vol. 2, pp. 289–313). Thousand Oaks, CA: Sage.

Mount, M., & Starr, B. (2009, April 10). More pirates searching for lifeboat, official says. CNN.com. Retrieved from http://www.cnn.com/2009/WORLD/africa/04/10/somalia.u.s.ship/index.html?iref=newssearch

Naumann, S. E., & Bennett, N. (2002). The effects of procedural justice climate on work group performance. *Small Group Research, 33,* 361–377.

Perito, R. M. (2005, October). *The U.S. experience with provincial reconstruction teams in Afghanistan* (Special Report No. 152). Washington, DC: United States Institute of Peace. Retrieved from http://www.usip.org/pubs/specialreports/sr152.html

Perito, R. M. (2007, March). *Provincial reconstruction teams in Iraq* (Special Report No. 185). Washington, DC: United States Institute of Peace. Retrieved from http://www.usip.org/pubs/specialreports/sr185.html

Rentsch, J. R. (1990). Climate and culture: Interaction and qualitative differences in organizational meanings. *Journal of Applied Psychology, 75*, 668–681.

Rentsch, J. R., Delise, L. A., & Hutchison, S. (2008). Cognitive similarity configurations in teams: In search of the Team MindMeld™. In E. Salas, G. F. Goodwin, & C. S. Burke (Eds.), *Team effectiveness in complex organizations: Cross-disciplinary perspectives and approaches* (pp. 241–266). New York: Routledge.

Rentsch, J. R., & Klimoski, R. J. (2001). Why do great minds think alike? Antecedents of team member schema agreement. *Journal of Organizational Behavior, 22*, 107–120.

Rentsch, J. R., Small, E. E., & Hanges, P. J. (2008). Cognitions in organizations and teams: What is the *meaning* of cognitive similarity? In B. Smith (Ed.), *The people make the place: Exploring dynamic linkages between individuals and organizations* (pp. 127–156). New York: Erlbaum.

Schneider, B. (1975). Organizational climates: An essay. *Personnel Psychology, 28*, 447–479.

Schneider, B. (1987). The people make the place. *Personnel Psychology, 40*, 437–453.

Schneider, B., & Reichers, A. E. (1983). On the etiology of climates. *Personnel Psychology, 36*, 19–39.

Smircich, L., & Morgan, G. (1982). Leadership: The management of meaning. *Journal of Applied Behavioral Science, 18*, 257–273.

Smith-Jentsch, K. A., Mathieu, J. E., & Kraiger, K. (2005). Investigating linear and interactive effects of shared mental models on safety and efficiency in a field setting. *Journal of Applied Psychology, 90*, 523–535.

Steiner, I. D. (1972). *Group process and productivity.* New York: Academic Press.

U.S. Second Fleet Public Affairs. (2009, April 2). Two dozen nations and maritime security conference enhance interoperability. Retrieved from http://www.navy.mil/search/display.asp?story_id=43978

Walsh, J. P., Henderson, C. M., & Deighton, J. (1988). Negotiated belief structures and decision performance: An empirical investigation. *Organizational Behavior and Human Decision Processes, 42*, 194–216.

Williams, C. C., & Mahan, R. P. (2006). Understanding multiteam system functioning. In W. Bennett, Jr., C. E. Lance, & D. J. Woehr (Eds.), *Performance measurement: Current perspectives and future challenges* (pp. 205–224). Mahwah, NJ: Erlbaum.

Yukl, G. A. (1989). *Leadership in organizations* (2nd ed.). Englewood Cliffs, NJ: Prentice Hall.

Zaccaro, S. J., & Marks, M. A. (1998). The roles of leaders in high-performance teams. In E. Sundstrom & Associates (Eds.), *Supporting work team effectiveness: Best management practices for fostering high performance* (pp. 95–125). San Francisco: Jossey-Bass.

Zhang, Z. X., Hempel, P. S., Han, Y. L., & Tjosvold, D. (2007). Transactive memory system links work team characteristics and performance. *Journal of Applied Psychology, 92*(6), 1722–1730.

10

Leadership Forms and Functions in Multiteam Systems

Stephen J. Zaccaro
George Mason University

Leslie A. DeChurch
University of Central Florida

Multiteam systems (MTSs) exist to join the efforts of complex systems of teams toward the accomplishment of ambitious goals too large to be tackled by a single team. These systems have boundaries that differ substantially from those of teams and organizations; they span teams, functions, and geography, and stretch across organizations, industry sectors, and, quite often, nations (Mathieu, Marks, & Zaccaro, 2001; Zaccaro, Marks, & DeChurch, Chapter 1, this volume). For example, BP's Deepwater Horizon oil spill required an MTS to develop the engineering solution that ultimately stopped oil from gushing into the Gulf of Mexico; this MTS included teams with divergent complementary expertise located in corporate and public sectors in the United States and United Kingdom.

The mantra of MTS researchers is that MTSs are complex organizational forms. To be more precise, the nature of the complexity stems from the fact that unlike teams governed by forces toward uniformity (Festinger, 1950), these systems are often characterized by a powerful force toward disorder and intergroup conflict. The particular challenge this presents to leadership is not to understand how leaders create large teams but, rather, to understand how multiple leaders working within a complex system of interconnected goals jointly strike a balance between these competing forces so that the system can succeed.

As defined by Mathieu et al. (2001) and Zaccaro et al. (Chapter 1, this volume), MTSs are organization forms with components (i.e., teams) that can exist within and across organizational boundaries, and with goal hierarchies that can create complex arrangements among these components. The systems aspect of this form means disparate teams are bound through goal hierarchies. Influences on one team, or the actions of one team, reverberate through multiple other teams. Moreover, MTSs form mostly in response to dynamic environmental contingencies and face challenges that cannot be easily addressed by more traditional organizational forms (Mathieu, et al., 2001; Zaccaro et al. Chapter 1 this volume). These qualities—the complexity of MTSs as organizational forms, the importance of boundary functions in such systems, their sensitivity to contextual dynamics, and the interconnectivity of component activity—mean that leadership processes become particularly crucial drivers of MTS effectiveness.

THE SYSTEMS PERSPECTIVE: CHALLENGES FOR LEADERSHIP

Katz and Kahn's (1978) classic formulation of organizations as open systems provides the conceptual foundation for this assertion regarding the particular importance of leadership for multiteam systems. They argued that managerial subsystems in organizations have two primary functions. First, they facilitate the coordination of activities across other subsystems within the organization. Second, they have primary responsibility for monitoring and managing relationships across the boundary between the organization and its environment. To elaborate, Katz and Kahn offered four specific requirements for leadership around these two core functions. These requirements appear even more prominently in MTSs, particularly those that are composed of teams from different organizations (called *external MTSs* by Mathieu et al., 2001). The first of these requirements follows from "the incompleteness of organizational design" (Katz & Kahn, 1978, p. 530). The actual ongoing interactions of organizational units and members do not nearly resemble formalized or written rules for such activities. Instead, normative processes arise that govern the real nature of transactions among members. These processes are often derived and reinforced through leadership activities (Feldman, 1984). Moreover, Katz and Kahn argued that leadership requirements deriving from the incompleteness of organizational designs are most apparent in determining how different organizational subsystems are to relate to one another, and how the system as a whole is related to its embedding environment. They noted that "the articulation of parts or of the whole with its surround is not necessarily specified in the programmed arrangements. Leadership emerges as individuals take charge of relating a unit or subsystem to the external structure or environment" (Katz & Kahn, 1978, p. 532).

These issues abound exponentially in MTSs. Because teams in many MTSs can come from different organizations, the gulfs represented by their boundaries may be broader than those between subsystems or components in more traditional organizations. Moreover, what Katz and Kahn (1978, p. 532) referred to as the system's "surround," meaning its embedding context, has multiple and nuanced layers in MTSs. The MTS as a whole has a boundary with an external environment much as more traditional organizations do, and this relationship gives rise to the boundary spanning leadership requirements articulated by Katz and Kahn. However, the nature of boundary dynamics and relationships will differ across organizations—how one organization interprets and manages its environmental surround will differ in both subtle and obvious ways from those processes in another organization. Such differences will filter into the processes and activities of external MTSs, where component teams come from these separate organizations, and bring with them the different boundary relationships that characterize their parent organizations. These differences exacerbate the requirement for leadership in such MTSs.

Katz and Kahn's (1978) second leadership requirement is perhaps most directly related to MTSs because it derives from the observation that the "organization as a system ... functions in a changing environment" (p. 533). Here, the role of leadership is to help organizations react to, or even anticipate, changing environmental contingencies. We have noted the argument by Mathieu et al. (2001) that "MTSs are usually formed or develop naturally to deal with highly turbulent environments that place a premium on the ability to transform work units and to respond rapidly to changing circumstances" (p. 290). The formation of an MTS reflects a process of helping connected organizations and their work units to realign with shifting environmental contingencies. Such transformation and realignment are not likely to be initiated, much less succeed, without the input of strong leadership processes. Organizational leadership would focus on (a) making sense of environmental changes, (b) determining that the formation of an MTS (external or internal) is an effective and warranted response, (c) facilitating or directing the emergence of the MTS, and (d) monitoring the subsequent actions of the MTS to determine that the organization or organizations involved are indeed realigned with the changed environment (cf. Zaccaro, Banks, Kiechel-Koles, Kemp, & Bader, 2009).

Katz and Kahn (1978) argued that a third requirement for organizational leadership follows from a tendency of organizations to grow and undergo structural changes as they try to absorb those aspects of their environment most influential to their operating and production processes. This dynamic may not be as prevalent in MTSs as they would not be expected to become permanent and expanding organizations in their own right (Mathieu et al., 2001). However, as environmental forces that gave rise to the emergence of the MTS shift, MTSs may need to remove existing component teams and/or add new ones. They may need to seek alliances with additional organizations and/or break off relationships with existing partners. These types of changes spark greater need for what Katz and Kahn called the processes of "coordination and adjudication" and "persisting organizational change" (p. 536) that are the province of organizational leaders.

The final leadership requirement articulated by Katz and Kahn (1978) pertains to the observation that organizational members are "above all not members of only one organization. Human membership in an organization is segmental in nature; it involves only a part of the person" (p. 534). They noted that influences from other activities and memberships outside the organization could affect work behavior to the point where adjustive or adaptive responses from leaders become necessary. Such extracurricular influences would also exist for all MTS members; however, if these members come from different organizations, demands and forces from those participating organizations can raise unique disruptions within the MTS. Indeed, Zaccaro et al. (Chapter 1, this volume) noted that external MTSs

> confront a degree of complexity of a magnitude greater than their wholly internal counterparts because they need to integrate demands not only from the environmental context common to all of the component teams, but also from their respective and different embedding organizations.

These possible conflicts, disruptions, and integration needs prime more forcefully the need for strong MTS leadership.

These arguments support our contention that leadership processes are particularly potent factors in the effectiveness of MTSs. This point was also articulated by DeChurch et al. (2011), who noted that "mission critical multiteam situations represent a point on the organizational environment continuum precisely where leaders are most needed" (pp. 152–153). Despite the importance of leadership for MTS effectiveness, however, there has been limited attention in the nascent MTS literature to those functions of leaders that optimize MTS success (for exceptions, see DeChurch et al., 2011; DeChurch & Marks, 2006). Moreover, we would argue that the qualities and characteristics of different forms of MTSs described by Zaccaro et al. (Chapter 1, this volume) will prescribe different types and functions of leadership within and across component teams. In this chapter, we describe the pathways by which leaders improve system functioning among teams in an MTS. We use functional leadership models (Fleishman et al., 1991; Hackman & Walton, 1986; McGrath, 1962; Morgeson, DeRue, & Karam, 2009; Mumford, Zaccaro, Harding, Jacobs, & Fleishman, 2000) to articulate these leadership processes. Researchers have noted that such models are particularly well suited to describing MTS leadership (DeChurch et al., 2011; DeChurch & Marks, 2006).

LEADERSHIP FORMS IN MTSs

Leadership in MTSs can be exhibited through either vertical or shared forms, depending upon a number of MTS characteristics. Thus, in this chapter, we will articulate the different structures of leadership, including three forms of shared leadership—rotated, distributed, and simultaneous—that can emerge in different types of MTSs. Our central argument here is that the form of leadership that is most effective is likely to be determined by the particular compositional, linkage, and developmental characteristics of the MTS. Accordingly, we complete the chapter with a description of such moderated relationships, detailing a set of research propositions. As noted, our underlying conceptual frame rests in functional theories of leadership. We describe this perspective in the next section.

FUNCTIONAL LEADERSHIP PROCESSES IN MULTITEAM SYSTEMS

Functional leadership theory emerged as an effort to describe the generic activities of leaders that support or enhance team effectiveness (McGrath, 1962; Roby, 1961; Schutz, 1961). The particular focus of this approach is on how leadership processes in collectives (e.g., teams, groups, or organizations) foster the emergence of effective *synergy* (Zaccaro, Heinen, & Shuffler, 2009), defined by Larson (2010) as occurring when members of an aggregate can "accomplish collectively something that could not reasonably have been achieved by any simple combination of individual member efforts" (p. 4). Larson distinguished "weak synergy" ("group performance that exceeds the performance of the typical group member"; p. 6) from the exceedingly rare "strong synergy" ("group performance that exceeds the solo performance of even the *best* group member"; p. 7). Leadership functions would then be defined as those processes that help teams establish and maintain at least a level of weak synergy across team members.

Several researchers have identified and offered generic categories of leadership functions in teams. Hackman and Walton (1986) argued that team leaders need to monitor team conditions and, when necessary, take action around fostering five conditions for team effectiveness—a clear engaging direction, a facilitating group structure, a supportive context, available expert coaching, and sufficient material resources. Fleishman et al. (1991) offered a taxonomy of leadership functions that summarized 13 sets of activities around four superordinate dimensions—information search and structuring, information use in problem solving, managing personnel resources, and managing material resources. Although their taxonomy was not explicitly about leaders fostering team synergy, the dimensions easily applied to such leadership (Zaccaro, Rittman, & Marks, 2001). Both Hackman and Walton; and Fleishman et al. highlighted two basic facilitating functions of leaders, setting direction or purpose for team action and managing or facilitating collective actions around that purpose (Burke et al., 2006; Gardner & Schermerhorn, 1992; Jacobs & Jaques, 1990; Zaccaro, 2001). Zaccaro, Heinen et al. (2009) elaborated these functions, and added as a separate set several activities related to developing the team's leadership capacity (cf. Day, Gronn, & Salas, 2004; Hackman & Wageman, 2005;

Kozlowski, Gully, McHugh, Salas, & Cannon-Bowers, 1996; Kozlowski, Watola, Jensen, Kim, & Botera, 2009).

Another recent contribution is also noteworthy. Morgeson et al. (2009) examined team leadership functions from the perspective of the team's performance cycle in which members move reciprocally through transition and action phases (Marks, Mathieu, & Zaccaro, 2001). In the transition phase, members focus on defining the direction and goals for team action, and developing plans for achieving those goals (e.g., mission analysis, goal specification, and strategy formulation; Marks et al., 2001). Functional leadership behaviors focus then on helping team members successfully navigate this performance phase. Morgeson et al. defined seven transition phase leadership functions. In the action phase of team performance cycles, members are conducting integrated activities that drive goal accomplishment (e.g., coordination, monitoring progress toward goals, systems monitoring, and backup behavior; Marks et al., 2001). Again, the functional role of team leadership is to foster the effective occurrence of these activities. Morgeson et al. defined eight leadership functions that facilitate team action phases. Their taxonomy integrated the earlier specifications of leadership functions from several researchers (Burke et al., 2006; Fleishman et al., 1991; Hackman & Walton, 1986; Kozlowski et al., 2009; McGrath, 1962; Zaccaro et al., 2001; Zaccaro, Heinen et al., 2009) within the team performance cycle model offered by Marks et al. (2001).

DeChurch and Marks (2006) and DeChurch et al. (2011) extended functional leadership models to MTSs. In essence, the role of leadership processes within an MTS is to help team members and component teams attain levels of synergy necessary to accomplish the goals and missions of the overall system. Note that the emphasis here is on achieving process effectiveness at two levels of interaction: *within* each component team and *across* component teams (DeChurch & Marks, 2006). As DeChurch et al. noted, studies of MTSs in laboratories found that effective processes can occur within teams, but fail between teams, resulting in a breakdown of the overall MTS (DeChurch & Marks, 2006; Marks, DeChurch, Mathieu, Panzer, & Alonso, 2005). What is different about leading in a MTS is that such leadership needs to attend to multiple foci of integration. Thus, DeChurch and Marks (2006) noted that "effective *team* leadership requires synchronization of interdependent team members' action. Effective *multiteam* leadership balances the management of internal teamwork with a significant emphasis on cross-team interdependencies in response to task and performance demands" (p. 312).

DeChurch and Marks (2006) and DeChurch et al. (2011) both used the transition–action performance cycle to articulate leadership functions that would enable collective functioning within and between component teams in MTSs. DeChurch et al. added those functions that pertain to boundary-spanning activities between the MTS and external stakeholders. Table 10.1 presents a set of leadership functions that (a) enable a clear direction for the MTS, and (b) foster coordinated actions among component teams, as well as between the MTS and external stakeholders. These functions were derived and adapted from several sources (DeChurch et al., 2011; DeChurch and Marks, 2006; Marks et al., 2001; Morgeson et al., 2009; Zaccaro et al., 2009). Following DeChurch and Marks (2006) as well as DeChurch et al. (2011), leadership functions are separated into those that enable within-team processes, between-team processes, and interactions across the boundary of the MTS. They are also separated into those functions that would facilitate team transition processes and those that facilitate action processes.

Within-Team MTS Leadership Functions

Leadership functions that enable the development of component team synergy toward goal accomplishment closely reflect those offered by Hackman and Walton (1986), Fleishman et al. (1991), Morgeson et al. (2009), Zaccaro, Heinen et al. (2009), and DeChurch et al. (2011), as well as the team processes described by Marks et al. (2001).

Transition Processes

In the transition phase of component team performance cycles, leaders help team members establish team objectives and develop a plan to meet those objectives. If necessary, leaders staff the team and train and develop team members. However, because the component team is embedded within a network of other component teams, team leaders also need to help the team establish its direction and plan tasks in concert with the dynamics and plans of the overall MTS. Indeed, a defining feature of MTSs is the degree of interdependence among component teams (Mathieu et al., 2001; Zaccaro et al., Chapter 1, this volume). The mutuality that exists among

TABLE 10.1

Leadership Functions in Multiteam Systems

	Within Teams	Between Teams	External

Transition Processes	• Interpreting and framing component team proximal goals within the context of distal goals and overall MTS strategy
	  ○ setting team objectives
	  ○ specifying team tasks
	  ○ identifying necessary member resources and capabilities
	• Staffing of the team
	• Developing team capabilities necessary for MTS functioning
	• Acquiring material resources for task accomplishment
	• Communicating MTS norms, standards, and expectations to team members
	• Developing team plan to meet goals and objectives
	  ○ assigning members to task roles
	  ○ specifying priority and synchronization of member actions and task accomplishment
	• Communicating team plans and expectations to team members
	• Communicating team plans to other component teams in the MTS
		• Identifying component teams resources and capabilities
		• Developing shared MTS standards, norms, and expectations
		• Specifying goal hierarchy for the MTS
		  ○ delineating distal and proximal goals
		  ○ specifying priority and synchronization of proximal and distal goals
		• Developing action plan for how component teams will work together to accomplish MTS strategy
		  ○ assigning component teams to positions within goal hierarchy
		  ○ clarifying how teams need to work interdependently (i.e., pooled, sequential, intensive)
		• Communicating mission, MTS strategy, and plans across component teams
			• Environmental scanning and analysis
			  ○ identifying and making sense of problem event and its parameters
			  ○ identifying dynamic situational contingencies and constraints
			  ○ specifying MTS mission
			• Strategy formulation
			  ○ developing action plans, including contingent courses of action, for MTS
			  ○ identifying and selecting of necessary component teams
			• Acquiring resources and support from external stakeholders
			• Intergrating MTS strategy with external constituents and stakeholders
			  ○ sense-giving: providing mission frame and plan to stakeholders
			  ○ integrating MTS strategy with those of constituents

(continued)

TABLE 10.1 (continued)

Leadership Functions in Multiteam Systems

	Within Teams	Between Teams	External

Action Processes	• Monitoring of the sequential and synchronous coordination of member actions
	  ◦ providing feedback to team members
	  ◦ facilitating necessary backup behaviors by team members
	• Tracking use of material resources in task accomplishment
	• Monitoring of team goal progress
	  ◦ tracking of progress and identification of goal blockages
	  ◦ developing plans to resolve goal blockages
	  ◦ communicating goal progress to team members
	• Monitoring and calibrating team task accomplishment relative to actions of MTS component teams
	• Communicating of team actions and progress to other component teams
		• Monitoring of the sequential and synchronous coordination of component teams
		  ◦ providing feedback to component teams
		  ◦ facilitating necessary backup by behaviors by component teams
		• Monitoring of distal goal progress (i.e., joint goal progress by two or more component teams)
		  ◦ tracking progress and identifying goal blockages
		  ◦ developing plans to resolve goal blockages
		  ◦ communicating goal progress to relevant component teams
		• Managing communications about team actions and goal progress across all component teams
			• Managing communications between MTS and external stakeholders
			  ◦ communicating MTS actions and goal progress to external stakeholders
			  ◦ communicating concerns and feedback from stakeholders to MTS
			• Monitoring and maintaining alignment of MTS actions with external contingencies
			• Coordinating and monitoring the sequential and synchronous actions of the MTS with those of other external stakeholders

Note: The functions and activities specified in this table were derived and adapted from the following sources: DeChurch et al. (2011); DeChurch and Marks (2006); Marks, Mathieu, and Zaccaro (2001); Morgeson, DeRue, and Karam (2009); and Zaccaro, Heinen et al. (2009).

component teams is represented (a) in the MTS's hierarchy of proximal and distal goals, and (b) in the nature of the interdependencies among component teams (reciprocal or intensive, and input, process, and/or outcome; for more details, see Mathieu et al., 2001; Zaccaro et al., Chapter 1, this volume). When team leaders help members form task objectives and plans, they do so in terms of how planned activities need to contribute to the accomplishment of both proximal and distal goals.

For example, in an MTS established to respond to and treat accident victims (see Mathieu et al., 2001; Zaccaro et al., Chapter 1, this volume), the firefighters and EMTs have the proximal goals of extracting victims and transporting them to the hospital. Functional leadership actions center on enabling such team actions. However, these actions also need to reflect the distal goal of patient survival and recovery. Thus, several activities of the firefighters and EMTs may be geared not only toward extracting victims from the accident scene but also toward doing so in ways that enhance their physical condition and prepare them for delivery to the surgical and recovery teams. When team leaders help component teams establish task objectives and action plans, they account for the accomplishment of the teams' proximal goals, as well as their contribution to the accomplishment of shared distal goals.

External MTSs, where component teams come from different organizations, pose additional challenges to the team that call for leadership intervention. A component team will likely reflect the culture, mission, and operating norms and standards of its parent organization. When these team qualities are dissonant to those of other component teams in the MTS, then team leaders need to facilitate a better understanding and acceptance among team members of alternate cultures, norms, and standards. This is not the same as changing those aspects of the team; attempts at such change are likely to be too disruptive and generally unnecessary. Instead, team leadership processes focus on helping members respond effectively and professionally when their team culture, norms, and standards clash with those of other teams.

Action Processes

In the action phase of task accomplishment, leadership processes within component teams center on ensuring and monitoring the effective coordination of member actions. Thus, they include such activities as providing feedback to the team when needed, facilitating member backup behaviors, monitoring the progress of the team toward proximal goal accomplishment, and tracking the use of team resources in task accomplishment (DeChurch et al., 2011; DeChurch & Marks, 2006). However, because the component team is acting within a goal hierarchy, team leadership processes also need to focus on two team boundary functions. One function entails monitoring and ensuring that the team's task accomplishment is occurring as planned in sequential or synchronous coordination with the actions of other component teams. If team actions are occurring "out of turn," then team leaders need to calibrate and adjust member actions accordingly. The second boundary function pertains to the communication of team actions and progress to other component team and MTS leaders.

Between-Team MTS Leadership Functions

The purpose of between-team leadership functions is to facilitate a degree of effective synergy and coordination among component teams in the MTS (DeChurch et al., 2011; DeChurch & Marks, 2006). The focus of leadership moves from within the individual teams to interactions occurring between and across teams. Accordingly, functional leadership processes are geared more toward enabling the smooth enactment of team interdependence as multiple teams work to accomplish distal goals. These leadership processes can also be divided into those that occur in MTS transition phases and those that occur in action phases.

Transition Phase

In the transition phase of MTS performance cycles, leadership processes focus on helping component teams define objectives within the context of the MTS goal hierarchy. To do so, MTS leaders must be fully cognizant of several interdependence demands that may be posed by the MTS's mission and task environment (DeChurch & Marks, 2006). Mathieu et al. (2001) defined three forms of functional interdependence that could exist among component teams in MTSs (see also Zaccaro et al., Chapter 1, this volume). The first, *input interdependence*, refers to shared use by at least two component teams of the resources necessary to accomplish a common (i.e., proximal) goal. In such instances, MTS leaders need to help component teams identify necessary resources and ensure that a system is in place for their coordinated sharing. Note that the emphasis here is on shared resources, not on resources that are the sole province of a single component team. The identification of such resources for use by a single team would be the responsibility of leadership processes within that team. They become the concern of leadership at the higher MTS level at those nodes of goal hierarchy where input interdependence exists.

Process interdependence is defined as "the amount of *interteam* interaction required for goal accomplishment, and refers to the degree to which teams depend on each other to perform the tasks at hand" (Mathieu et al., 2001, p. 294). Such interdependence can take the form of sequential, reciprocal, and intensive arrangements (for a description of these forms of interdependence, see Tesluk, Mathieu, Zaccaro, & Marks, 1997; for how these forms may occur in MTSs, see Mathieu et al., 2001; Zaccaro et al., Chapter 1, this volume). The existence of process interdependence in MTSs means that MTS leaders need to help component teams develop action plans for how they will work together, including the development of necessary shared norms, standards, expectations, and interaction mental models (cf. Cannon-Bowers, Salas, & Converse, 1993). Because different combinations of component teams that share proximal goals may have different forms of interdependence, MTS leaders may need to foster the development of multiple action plans across the MTS. Thus, MTS leaders may need to develop one action plan for teams engaged in sequential interdependence to accomplish a proximal goal, but a different action plan for component teams working in intensive interdependence to achieve another proximal goal. Moreover, because these two subunits within the MTS may share a distal goal, MTS leaders also need to help them combine their respective accomplishments.

Output interdependence refers to "the extent to which personal benefits, rewards, costs, or other outcomes received by team members [in one component team] depend on the performance or successful goal attainment of [other component teams]" (Mathieu et al., 2001, p. 294). Such interdependence will reflect—and influence—the shared motivational dynamics that are occurring within the MTS (see Kanfer & Kerry, Chapter 4 this volume). MTS leadership processes in the transition phase of MTS performance cycles may entail the identification of shared benefits and outcomes, as well as the development of a plan for their equitable distribution among relevant component teams. Although we list such leadership interventions under transition processes, they probably more likely reflect what Marks et al. (2001) referred to as *interpersonal processes*, which included "conflict management," "motivation and confidence building," and "affect management" (p. 363). As MTSs exhibit greater forms of organizational, functional, and cultural diversity among component teams, as well as greater geographic dispersion (see Zaccaro et al., Chapter 1, this volume, for a description of these MTS attributes), higher levels of outcome interdependence may result in more conflict and negative affect between teams. Thus, in such instances, MTS leaders may be required to help component teams resolve these issues.

Mathieu et al. (2001) noted that the multiple interdependencies operating among component teams are reflected in the MTS goal hierarchy. Although teams may work either independently or interdependently on lower level proximal goals, distal goals at higher levels entail the combined actions of multiple component teams, until, at the top level, all team actions contribute indirectly or directly to goal accomplishment. This quality of MTSs requires their leaders to help component teams accomplish several activities during transition phases of performance cycles. First, they must use their understanding of functional interdependencies among component teams, and their knowledge of the MTS's mission to delineate proximal and distal goals within the hierarchy. Once the goal hierarchy is established, the nature of extant interdependencies will determine the assignment of component teams to positions within the hierarchy. However, MTS leaders may still need to ascertain the best fitting arrangement of component teams, and perhaps acquire other teams to replace those that are not the most appropriate fit for a particular position within the goal hierarchy. MTS leaders also need to specify the priority and synchronization of proximal and distal goal achievement, helping component teams develop an action plan or overall strategy for goal accomplishment. Finally, MTS goal strategies and plans needed to be coordinated across all component teams (DeChurch et al., 2011).

Action Phase

In the action phase of MTS performance cycles, MTS leadership processes focus on helping component teams coordinate their actions to reach proximal and distal goals. This entails at minimum monitoring the sequential and synchronous integration of team activities as they strive toward proximal and distal goal attainment (DeChurch et al., 2011; DeChurch & Marks, 2006). In the course of such monitoring, MTS leaders may provide feedback to component teams and facilitate necessary backup behaviors to help any faltering teams. Because distal goals will entail greater levels of interdependence, leaders will need to attend more closely to progress toward such goals, identifying impending and actual blockages to goal accomplishment, and developing coordinated plans to resolve such blockages. Finally, MTS leaders need to manage the communications across component teams to facilitate the timely and accurate exchanges of information at appropriate points in MTS action cycles (DeChurch et al., 2011).

Along these lines, DeChurch and Marks (2006) found that in laboratory-based MTSs where leaders were trained in specific behaviors to foster interteam coordination, component teams exhibited greater behavioral synchronization than teams in MTSs where leaders did not receive such training. DeChurch et al. (2011) examined critical incidents of MTS functioning in more realistic settings (e.g., Hurricane Katrina, or provincial reconstruction teams [PRTs] in Afghanistan), and found support for the leadership functions related to "orchestrating action and managing the flow of information" (p. 163). As an example, they cited that when large crowds began to pack the New Orleans Convention Center in the aftermath of Hurricane Katrina, contrary to expectations of MTSs on the ground, units from the U.S. Departments of Defense and Transportation, as well as state and local leaders coordinated efforts to deliver food and water. Note that this incident reflects not only the facilitation of coordinated action among teams but also an integrated reaction of MTS leaders to potential distal goal blockage (i.e., the safety and welfare of local residents). Note also that the emphasis here remains on interteam coordination. The action cycles of individual teams remain the province of team leaders, with the proviso that they convey appropriate information about their actions to MTS leaders, who in turn manage the flow of such information to other relevant component teams.

External MTS Leadership Functions

Mathieu et al. (2001) argued that "a primary reason for the existence of MTSs is their responsiveness and adaptability to challenging performance environments" (p. 296). They noted that such environments were characterized by a greater diversity of elements and stakeholders, a higher rate of change and volatility, more unfamiliar and novel problem situations, and greater levels of ambiguity and unpredictability. They also argued that what made MTSs effective for work in such environments was their "ability to reconfigure themselves to best align with environmental demands" (p. 296). That is, the interdependent arrangements among component teams can be adjusted to accommodate changes in the MTS's operating environment. We would add that the composition of the MTS may change as well, with the addition or subtraction of particular teams to respond to new emergent challenges. This ability to be responsive to a dynamic environment places a premium on environmental scanning, sense making, and communication processes that leaders perform across the boundary of the MTS (Ancona & Caldwell, 1988, 1992; Katz & Kahn, 1978).

DeChurch et al. (2011) noted that prior studies on MTSs have focused solely on the interaction processes occurring within and between component teams, but not on those occurring across the boundary of the MTS (DeChurch & Marks, 2006; DeChurch & Mathieu, 2009; Marks et al., 2005; Mathieu et al., 2001). They argued that a "point of impact" (p. 160) for MTS leaders was the management of alignment between the MTS and its challenging external environment. Indeed, they found that half of the leadership-critical incidents they derived from the activities of Hurricane Katrina–related MTSs and military-based PRTs in Afghanistan and Iraq represented such boundary-spanning processes. Following their arguments and listing of leadership functions, we have treated external processes as a category of MTS leadership functions separate from those operating within and between component teams (see Table 10.1). We also separated these processes into those that occur in the transition and action phases of MTS performance cycles.

Transition Processes

Because transition processes are directed at developing plans for collective action (Marks et al., 2001), externally focused activities in this domain pertain to the acquisition and interpretation of information necessary to derive the appropriate mission for the MTS (DeChurch et al., 2011). Such environmental scanning and analysis would also extend to identifying the situational contingencies and constraints that would likely influence mission accomplishment (Joshi, Pandey, & Han, 2009). These activities also contribute to another MTS leadership function, the formulation of a strategic plan that aligns MTS capabilities, resources, and actions with emergent dynamics in its operating environment. The quality of the strategic plan depends upon how well it fosters and maintains this alignment. The strategic plan also provides the basis for determining the best combination of component teams, as well as the relationships among them, to accomplish the mission.

External MTS boundary spanning also requires MTS leaders to represent their constituents to outside stakeholders often for the purpose of acquiring necessary support and resources, negotiating on their behalf, defending them against unwarranted interference, and communicating (even extolling) their progress and accomplishments (Ancona & Caldwell, 1992; DeChurch et al., 2011; Joshi et al., 2009). As part of this "ambassador" role (Ancona & Caldwell, 1992, p. 640), MTS leaders also provide to stakeholders a preview of the MTS strategic plan and ensure that this plan is integrated with those of other units and collectives in its operating environment (DeChurch et al., 2011). Finally, MTS leaders need to stay attuned to their network of stakeholders to anticipate impending environmental disruptions, shifts in alliances, or other changes that may require alterations to MTS plans and actions.

Action Processes

According to DeChurch et al. (2011), boundary-spanning processes that occur during the action phase of MTS performance cycles entail in part managing communications to and from external stakeholders. This includes information to stakeholders regarding goal progress, as well as feedback conveyed from them about concerns and issues raised by MTS actions. Also, MTS leaders need to foster the continuing alignment of the overall MTS with the changing context as the component teams engage in their actions. This includes coordinating and synchronizing the activities of the MTS with those of other MTSs and external stakeholders.

FORMS OF MTS LEADERSHIP

We have noted several leadership functions that should help MTSs accomplish their goals and overall mission. Researchers have been careful to note that the responsibilities for functional team leadership do not necessarily reside in single team leaders; they can be shared across team members (Hackman & Walton, 1986; McGrath, 1962; Morgeson et al., 2009). Conger and Pearce (2003) summarized several of the conditions or factors that would facilitate the emergence of shared leadership, most of which operate in many MTSs. One such factor refers to the degree of task competence and expertise possessed by team members. When members possess higher degrees of expertise, they are more able to contribute to situational analysis, mission specification, and the development of team action plans, prompting their greater participation in or contribution to team decision making (Cox, Pearce, & Perry, 2003; Hersey & Blanchard, 1988; Kerr & Jermier, 1978; Vroom & Yetton, 1973). This may be especially true when (a) members possess high but diverse levels of expertise (e.g., distributed expertise, informational diversity, and functional heterogeneity) (Conger & Pearce, 2003; Hollenbeck et al., 1995; Mayo, Meindl, & Pastor, 2003), and (b) the team task is highly interdependent (Cox et al., 2003; Pearce & Sims, 2000; Perry, Pearce, & Sims, 1999). Both conditions are likely to be common to many types of MTSs.

Other factors in MTSs that may support (or moderate) shared leadership factors include dispersion of power across component teams; social, cultural, and demographic diversity; geographic dispersion; shared team goals; and MTS size (Carson, Tesluk, & Marrone, 2007; Conger & Pearce, 2003; Cox et al., 2003; Yukl, 2010). Later in this chapter, we will offer propositions regarding when different forms of shared or vertical (i.e., centralized) leadership are likely to dominate, either at different nodes in the MTS's network of component teams, or in the MTS as a whole. However, before articulating these propositions, we need to delineate these various forms of leadership as they have been described in the extant literature. Note that we are describing leadership at the MTS level, or between component teams, not in the teams themselves. These forms, as described in the next sections, are summarized within Table 10.2.

TABLE 10.2

Forms of Leadership in Multiteam Systems

Forms of Leadership	Description
Vertical: Fully Centralized	Leadership responsibilities, decisions, and actions are conducted by a single individual in a formal leader role (Mehra, Smith, Dixon, & Robertson, 2006).
Vertical: Multilevel	Leadership in the MTS is organized formally in a multitier structure, in which lower level leaders are subordinated to higher level leaders (Jaques, 1990, 1996).
Shared: Rotated	The full responsibilities of leadership functions are cycled among different individual members of the MTS (Erez, LePine, & Elms, 2002).
Shared: Distributed	Different component team leaders, or members of the leadership team (DeChurch & Marks, 2006), in the MTS are individually responsible for separate leadership functions (Gronn, 2002; Hulpia, Devos, & Rosseel, 2009).
Shared: Simultaneous	All component team leaders, or members of the leadership team, are mutually engaged in leadership activities throughout phases of the MTS performance cycle (Fletcher & Käufer, 2003; Mehra et al., 2006).

Forms of Vertical Leadership in MTSs

Vertical leadership reflects the traditional form of "top-down" leadership that has been the prime focus in the leadership literature (Day et al., 2004; Hiller, Day, & Vance, 2006; Pearce & Conger, 2003). In the prototypic version of this form, "leadership [originates] from a higher level in the organizational hierarchy," and "power and authority are invested in a single appointed leader who serves as the primary source of influence, wisdom, and guidance for team members" (Houghton, Neck, & Manz, 2003, p, 125). A core assumption is that one individual, or perhaps a few individuals nested hierarchically, are considered "accountable" to stakeholders for collective functioning and goal accomplishment (Friedrich, Vessey, Schuelke, Ruark, & Mumford, 2009, p. 935). We suggest that vertical leadership can occur in MTSs in two ways. The first is a fully centralized model (Mehra, Smith, Dixon, & Robertson, 2006), in which all component team leaders are subordinate to a single MTS leader. That leader would be fully responsible for enacting the leadership functions described in Table 10.1, when conditions in the MTS warranted such intervention. Such leadership structures may sometimes be found in military-based MTSs, where there is usually a commanding officer who is ultimately responsible for unit decisions. For example, DeChurch et al. (2011) described provincial reconstruction teams in Afghanistan as

> led by an Army commanding officer who is supported by Army Civil Affairs Teams, Military Police Units, and civilian representatives from the Department of State, the Agency for International Development (USAID), and the Department of Agriculture (USDA; Dorman, 2007). Local Afghan Ministry representatives and interpreters are also usually a part of the PRT. (p. 155)

Fully centralized vertical leadership refers to the formal decision-making structure of the MTS. However, of course, central leaders may still choose to share the responsibility and power of decision making among their subordinates (Vroom & Yetton, 1973); in such instances, leadership processes may reflect more of the shared arrangements described below.

Zaccaro, Heinen et al. (2009) articulated several formal leadership roles that can exist even when team members share leadership responsibilities. These teams can have internal leaders, external leaders, and/or executive coordinators (see also Cohen, Chang, & Ledford, 1997; Druskat & Wheeler, 2003; Morgeson et al., 2009). We suggest that these types of leaders can all exist in an MTS having a *multilevel* hierarchical structure (e.g., Jaques, 1996). Thus, the component teams may be led as a collective by an internal leader who is heavily involved in the transition and action processes of the MTS. However, the MTS may also have an external leader that is more oriented toward the boundary-spanning activities of the MTS (Druskat & Wheeler, 2003; Manz & Sims, 1987). Such leaders may also help staff the MTS and provide its overall direction in line with a superordinate strategy, but they are still fairly disconnected from typical MTS performance cycles (Morgeson et al., 2009; Zaccaro, Heinen et al., 2009). According to Zaccaro, Heinen et al., executive coordinators often work outside of the team and have responsibility for establishing the superordinate strategic framework for collective action. Thus, in MTSs such leaders would establish the MTS itself, including its component teams, but then give MTS leaders and component teams significant responsibility for the subsequent structure, objectives, and plans of the MTS. For example, DeChurch et al. (2011) described disaster response MTSs that would form at the direction of an affected state's governor, including decisions about what units were to be included in the MTS, and whether federal agencies were to be invited as well. However, planning and facilitating the structured interactions of component teams in the course of their performance cycles were more likely the province of MTS internal and external leaders.

Forms of Shared Leadership in MTSs

Pearce and Conger (2003) defined shared leadership as

a dynamic, interactive influence process among individuals in a groups for which the objective is to lead one another to the achievement of group or organizational goals or both. This influence process often involves peer, or lateral, influence and at other times involves upward or downward hierarchical influence.... Leadership is broadly distributed among a set of individuals instead of centralized in hands of a single individual who acts in the role of a superior. (p. 1)

Friedrich et al. (2009) offered several assumptions for a framework of collective leadership that are particularly applicable to MTSs. The first is that effective collective leadership rests on a distribution of expertise and skills in the network of potential leaders. As MTSs are generally composed of teams each having a particular expertise necessary for overall MTS functioning, this assumption would likely be common to most such collectives.

Second, teams (and MTSs) need to have the mechanisms in place to foster the exchange of information necessary for effective collective leadership. As seen in Table 10.1, both transition and action processes entail significant communications of information and knowledge within and among component teams, as well as with external stakeholders. Effective functional leadership of MTSs would accordingly center on enabling such information flow (DeChurch et al., 2011). Once such exchanges are enabled, they in turn become, according to Friedrich et al. (2009), the grease for the operations of collective leadership.

Friedrich et al.'s third assumption is that collective leadership does not mean the absence of formal leadership (see also Zaccaro, Heinen et al., 2009). They argued that collectives still require persons in positions of accountability as well as those who have responsibility for functions related to staffing and constructing the team. Studies have shown that forms of shared and vertical leadership are both necessary for team effectiveness (Ensley, Hmieleski, & Pearce, 2006; Pearce & Sims, 2002). As a final assumption, Friedrich et al. noted that forms of collective leadership are not static, and as the nature of the problems confronting the team change, members may shift their patterns of leadership. Thus, they suggested that in the course of collective responses to different situations, "there may be shifts in the need for a single leader, multiple individuals sharing the leadership role, or even a shift in the roles that each individual engages in" (Friedrich et al., 2009, p. 935).

This last assumption suggests that shared leadership can occur in several different forms, a point argued by other theorists as well (Carson et al., 2007; Erez, LePine, & Elms, 2002; Gronn, 2002; Mehra et al., 2006; Pearce & Conger, 2003). However, these different forms are not often clearly delineated. In MTSs, we suggest that shared leadership processes can take at least three forms, *rotated*, *distributed*, and *simultaneous*. Indeed, sometimes all three forms can operate within the same MTS at the same or different points in its performance cycle.

Rotated leadership refers to situations in which "different individuals provide leadership at different points in the team's life cycle and development" (Carson et al., 2007, p. 1220). Such an arrangement represents in essence a structurally hierarchical or vertical form of leadership, but one in which the responsibility for leadership is shared sequentially or serially among team members. At any point in time, the focus of leadership remains on a single individual, but over the life span of the collective, some or all members engage in leadership activities. Erez et al. (2002) argued that such leadership allows all team members to feel responsibility for collective leadership, a feeling that "should translate into a greater likelihood that members do their fair share of the team's work" (p. 933). They also reported that such leadership increased the degree to which members offer suggestions for change in the team, and the overall level of cooperation within the team.

The structure of rotated leadership, and specifically who occupies the leadership role at a particular time, can be set formally, or can depend upon who has the primary expertise and resources to solve the problem confronting the team at that point in its performance cycle (Friedrich et al., 2009). In MTSs, rotated forms of shared leadership can occur when different component team leaders assume the MTS leader role at different times, or when the role is rotated among members of an MTS external leader team.

Distributed leadership refers to arrangements in which members of a collective take on different leadership functions (Gronn, 2002; Hulpia, Devos, & Rosseel, 2009). Thus, one or a few members may be primarily responsible for strategy development, others for boundary-spanning activities, and still others for coordination and monitoring during the action phase of performance cycles. This kind of shared leadership arrangement may arise when members have varied skills that make each of them more suited to a subset of leadership functions. They may also occupy particular role positions (e.g., at the boundary of the group, or within the portion of the collective most responsible for ongoing action) that favor particular leadership functions over others (Gronn, 2002).

Simultaneous shared leadership refers to those instances when all members of the collective are mutually engaged in leadership activities throughout all phases of a performance cycle (Fletcher & Käufer, 2003; Mehra et al., 2006). In such instances, "every person is a leader and a follower" in the same performance cycle (Mehra et al., 2006, p. 235). Fully realized versions of this arrangement are relatively rare, as not all members of the collective will have the skills, knowledge, or inclination to engage in leadership (Friedrich et al., 2009; Mehra et al., 2006). However, MTSs may contain a leadership team that includes all component team leaders, where leadership functions are equally shared among these individuals (e.g., DeChurch & Marks, 2006). Such shared leadership arrangements are likely to be best suited to collective tasks that are highly interdependent and in which those who share leadership functions have full access to information flows within the team or MTS (Friedrich et al., 2009).

MTSs may be characterized by either vertical or shared forms of leadership, and, if the latter, rotated, distributed, or intensive forms. Because levels of interdependencies can vary at different nodes within the MTS goal hierarchy (Mathieu et al., 2001), alternate forms of shared leadership may operate at separate nodes. We suggest that several attributes of MTSs as described by Zaccaro et al. (Chapter 1, this volume) will likely determine which form of leadership is best suited for maximum system effectiveness. We elaborate on this premise in the next section of this chapter.

MTS ATTRIBUTES AND FORMS OF LEADERSHIP

Zaccaro et al. (Chapter 1 of this volume) offered a classification of attributes that distinguish different types of MTSs. They divided these attributes into three categories: compositional attributes, linkage attributes, and developmental attributes (see Table 1.1, Chapter 1, this volume). *Compositional attributes* refer to demographic characteristics of the MTS as well as the attributes of the component teams. *Linkage attributes* refer to the different kinds of attachments and relationships teams have with one another within the MTS. *Developmental attributes* refer to differences in how MTSs are initiated and grow as a collective; they also refer to the tenure and maturity of the MTS. Based on research from the shared leadership literature, we would argue that many of the attributes defined by Zaccaro et al. are likely to determine the degree to which collective forms of leadership will occur in MTSs and lead to overall effectiveness. In this section, we offer some propositions that we hope will encourage future research on MTS leadership and its moderating conditions.

Compositional Attributes and Leadership Forms

For this chapter, we have focused on how three compositional attributes defined by Zaccaro et al. (Chapter 1, this volume) might influence the degree of shared leadership likely to be displayed in the MTS. These attributes are (a) the number of component teams in the MTS, (b) the degree of diversity (organizational, cultural, and functional) present among component teams, and (c) the geographic dispersion of component teams.

MTS Size

Research on the size of the collective and the emergence of shared leadership has been limited and somewhat mixed. The lack of clarity in the literature may stem from the countervailing influences of two conditions for effective shared leadership—the need for a sufficient number of leadership partners with requisite levels of knowledge and expertise (Conger & Pearce, 2003), and cohesive and supportive relationships among members (Carson et al., 2007). Several researchers have argued that as the size of the collective grows, it is more likely to contain multiple individuals capable of sharing leadership functions

(Conger & Pearce, 2003; Cox et al., 2003). That is, more members will likely possess the skills, knowledge, and expertise required to successfully engage in leader problem-solving activities (Friedrich et al., 2009). Accordingly, we can expect that as the number of component teams in an MTS grows, there will be more team leaders that can participate in MTS leadership. However, other studies have shown that increases in team and organizational size can interfere with the development of cohesion and coordinated working relationships (Hambrick, 1994; Seers, Keller, & Wilkerson, 2003). The lack of such support and mutuality across team members is likely to impair the display of shared leadership (Carson et al., 2007; Kirkman & Rosen, 1999). This argument suggests that increases in MTS component teams will lessen such leadership.

Tests of the relationship between team size and shared leadership have been mixed. Several studies have reported nonsignificant correlations between size and shared leadership (Boone & Hendricks, 2009; Ensley et al., 2006, sample 2; Kirkman, Rosen, Tesluk, & Gibson, 2004; Pearce and Sims, 2002), whereas others found a positive relationship (Campion, Medsker, & Higgs, 1993; Carson et al., 2007; Ensley et al., 2006, sample 1). Thus, there is not a consistent finding that can be extrapolated to MTSs. However, based on the conceptual arguments outlined in this chapter, we would argue that MTSs need to contain enough component teams (with leaders) so that there is a sufficient reserve of expertise to engage in leadership; however, as the number of teams increases to the point where coordination and social support begin to suffer, the positive relationship between team size and displayed shared leadership will likely asymptote at a particular level and then become more negative.

Proposition 1. A curvilinear relationship will exist between MTS size and displays of shared leadership, such that increases in the number of component teams will be associated with greater shared leadership to a point at which further increases will be associated with less shared leadership.

MTS Diversity

The influence of MTS diversity on the display of shared leadership may vary with different kinds of diversity. Mayo et al. (2003) differentiated social and informational diversity and their effects of shared leadership in teams (see also the summary by Conger & Pearce, 2003). Social diversity reflects heterogeneity in such demographic variables as age, gender, race, and status. Teams characterized by higher levels of social diversity may find it more difficult to develop the degree of cohesion, trust, and support necessary for effective shared leadership (Cox et al., 2003; Jackson, 1992; Jackson, Joshi, & Erhardt, 2003; Knight et al., 1999; O'Reilly, Caldwell, & Barnett, 1989; Phillips, Rothbard, & Dumas, 2008; Smith et al., 1994; Van Knippenberg, De Dreu, & Homan, 2004). Based on Zaccaro et al.'s (Chapter 1, this volume) dimensions of MTS characteristics, such social diversity can occur when (a) component teams come from different organizations (organizational diversity), especially when represented organizations differ themselves on demographic and industry characteristics; and/or (b) component teams come from different nations and cultures (cultural diversity). Accordingly, we propose the following:

> Proposition 2. MTSs with higher levels of organizational diversity will display less shared forms of leadership.
> Proposition 3. MTSs with higher levels of cultural diversity will display less shared forms of leadership.

Informational diversity generally reflects heterogeneity in members' experiences, skills, abilities, expertise, and educational and functional background (see "cognitive diversity" by O'Bannon & Gupta, 1992). Such diversity would presumably bring a greater array of cognitive and informational responses to the collective, fostering better collective leadership. Several studies have shown that such diversity does indeed lead to a broader range of ideas and perspectives in teams (Joshi et al., 2009; Van Knippenberg et al., 2004), particularly in those at the top of the organization (Bantel, 1993; Wiersema & Bantel, 1992). Greater numbers of ideas should contribute richer cognitive resources to shared leadership (Conger & Pearce, 2003; Friedrich et al., 2009; Mayo et al., 2003; Pearce & Ravlin, 1987).

Informational diversity, however, may also likely increase the degree of interpersonal conflict in collectives, resulting in lower cohesion and therefore less displays of such leadership (Knight et al., 1999; Van Knippenberg et al., 2004). This suggests that when collectives possess higher levels of informational diversity, the effects of such heterogeneity on social processes may need to be offset by those team attributes that minimize such conflict. Indeed, several studies have offered support for this premise. For example, Carmel (1995) found that effective product innovation teams were characterized by *heterogeneity* in educational backgrounds (i.e., high informational diversity) but *homogeneity* in age, gender, and home country (i.e., low social diversity). Phillips, Mannix, Neale, and Gruenfeld (2004) reported that diverse groups were better able to use information from members under conditions of higher social support. Boone and Hendricks (2009) reported that the relationship between functional diversity in top management teams and organizational performance was much higher in teams with higher levels of collaborative behavior than in teams not characterized by such behavior. Based on this research line, we expect that MTSs with higher levels of functional diversity among component teams may not use forms of shared leadership unless they were characterized by higher levels of cohesion and cooperation among the teams.

Proposition 4. The effects of MTS functional diversity on displays of shared leadership and MTS effectiveness will be moderated by interteam cohesion and social support, such that these effects will be more positive under higher levels of cohesion and support.

Geographic Dispersion

MTSs can be characterized by component teams that are either physically co-located or geographically dispersed (Zaccaro et al., Chapter 1, this volume). Research on dispersed teams indicates that greater levels of physical distance between members decrease the development of trust (Jarvenpaa & Leidner, 1999), group cohesion (Straus, 1996; Warkentin, Sayeed, & Hightower, 1997), and the quantity and quality of communications and information exchanges among team members (Cramton, 2001; Straus, 1997). These impairments in team social and information dynamics will likely reduce the degree of shared leadership in the system.

Proposition 5. MTSs with greater geographic dispersion among component teams will display less shared leadership.

Linkage Attributes and Leadership Forms

Linkage attributes refer to the task and goal characteristics that connect component teams to one another (Zaccaro et al., Chapter 1, this volume). We consider the influences of two such attributes, interdependence and power distribution, on adopted forms of leadership within the MTS.

Interdependence

One of the necessary conditions for an MTS—interdependence among component teams (Mathieu et al., 2001; Zaccaro et al., Chapter 1, this volume)—in turn increases the likelihood of displayed shared leadership among these teams (Cox et al., 2003). Cox et al. argued that shared leadership was more effective under conditions of high interdependence because it fostered greater information exchange and coordinated the effort that such conditions required. Accordingly, Campion et al., (1993) found that members' ratings of the amount of task, goal, and feedback interdependence required by their work were significantly correlated with their rated degree of self-management and member participation in the team. Other studies have shown that collective leadership emerged more readily from a shared purpose and common objectives among team members (Carson et al., 2007; Seers, 1996; Yukl, 2010).

Mathieu et al. (2001) noted that not all component teams in an MTS are linked functionally with all other teams. Accordingly, we would expect that the higher the degree of functional interdependence among component teams, the more likely they will display between-team shared leadership.

> Proposition 6. Those component teams linked by higher degrees of functional interdependence will display higher levels of shared leadership between them.

Mathieu et al. (2001) also contrasted sequential, reciprocal, and intensive forms of interdependence among component teams. Sequential and reciprocal forms reflect situations where particular teams take the lead at different points in the MTS performance cycle. Intensive forms entail more simultaneous and synchronous forms of coaction among teams. Each form is likely to foster a different type of shared leadership.

Proposition 7. Component teams that are linked by sequential and reciprocal forms of interdependence are more likely to use rotated forms of shared leadership than less interdependent teams, or teams with more intensive forms of interdependence.

Proposition 8. Component teams that are linked by intensive forms of interdependence are more likely to use simultaneous forms of shared leadership than less interdependent teams, or teams with more sequential and reciprocal forms of interdependence.

Power Distribution

Zaccaro et al. (Chapter 1, this volume) suggested that MTSs may differ in the power arrangements among component teams. According to them, factors that may increase the power accrued by a component team include higher placement within the MTS goal hierarchy, the larger size of the team, their higher functional necessity for the core purpose of the MTS, and the granting of formal authority to them by external MTS leaders. When power is concentrated among few members or component teams, shared leadership is less likely to occur (Conger & Pearce, 2003; Seers et al., 2003).

Proposition 9. MTSs that are characterized by limited or centralized power distributions will display lower levels of shared leadership.

Developmental Attributes and Leadership Forms

Zaccaro et al. (Chapter 1, this volume) argued that MTSs can also be distinguished by such attributes as how they came into being (e.g., appointed by eternal leaders, or emergent), their duration, and their stage of development (e.g., their maturation). Several models of organizational growth have suggested that as organizations mature, decision making becomes more decentralized (Griener, 1972; Quinn & Cameron, 1983; Smith, Mitchell, & Summer, 1985). In such instances, the leadership responsibilities become so numerous and varied that no single individual can handle them all (Ensley et al., 2006). These models, however, may be confounding size and maturity. Other researchers have argued that as collectives mature in terms of their time together, members become more familiar with collective capabilities, and form more effective working relationships (Conger & Pearce, 2003; Cox et al., 2003; Kozlowski et al., 2009), factors that promote shared leadership. We would expect to see the same dynamics appear in MTSs as they mature.

> Proposition 10. More mature MTSs will display greater levels of shared leadership than less mature MTSs.

Additional Leadership Dimensions

Although this chapter advances thinking about leadership in multiteam systems by first classifying leadership in terms of forms and functions (two dimensions), and then considering the interplay of forms and functions with the attributes of MTSs to advance a contingency perspective of MTS leadership, we also wish to spark the idea that perhaps there is an additional dimension of leadership in MTSs stemming from the inherent complexity of these systems. Such a 3D conceptualization may begin with thinking about how these forms serve these functions when component teams are in nonoverlapping performance episodes, and when multiple forms of leadership are being simultaneously enacted at different locations within the system. Two necessary aspects of such a 3D view will be (a) the temporal evolution of leadership dynamics within the system; and (b) MTS leadership as a patterned, compilationally emergent phenomenon.

SUMMARY

We have focused in this chapter on leadership processes in MTSs. We have argued that the particular qualities of MTSs—their attunement and adaptability to dynamic and turbulent environments, the complexity of their boundary relationships, their complex compositional arrangements and need for interdependence, and the multiple identities of their members—especially increase the need for strong leadership processes. Leadership in MTSs has multiple levels, including within component teams, between component teams, and across the external boundary of MTSs. We have therefore articulated sets of functional leadership processes that pertain to these levels. Because different functional leadership activities will be necessary at different points in the MTS performance cycle, we also segmented leadership processes by their primary occurrence in the transition and action phases of these cycles. We believe that different forms of vertical and shared leadership can occur in MTSs, and their display will vary according to the attributes of the MTS. We have accordingly offered several propositions about how MTS attributes influence the display of shared leadership.

There have been a fairly limited number of empirical studies on leadership in MTSs. We can think of only two (DeChurch et al., 2011; DeChurch & Marks, 2006). Because we believe that leadership processes are particularly important drivers of MTS success, additional research will be necessary to further our understanding of MTS dynamics and effectiveness. We hope this chapter stimulates such research.

REFERENCES

Ancona, D. G., & Caldwell, D. F. (1988). Beyond task and maintenance: Defining external functions in groups. *Group and Organization Studies, 13,* 468–494.

Ancona, D. G., & Caldwell, D. F. (1992). Bridging the boundary: External activity and performance in organizational teams. *Administrative Science Quarterly, 37*(4), 634–665.

Bantel, K. A. (1993). Strategic clarity in banking: Role of top management team demography. *Psychological Reports, 73,* 1187–1201.

Boone, C., & Hendricks, W. (2009). Top management team diversity and firm performance: Moderators of functional-background and locus of control diversity. *Management Science, 55,* 165–180.

Burke, C. S., Stagl, K. C., Klein, C., Goodwin, G. F., Salas, E., & Halpin, S. (2006). What types of leadership behaviors are functional in team? A meta-analysis. *The Leadership Quarterly, 17,* 288–307.

Campion, M. A., Medsker, G. J., & Higgs, A. C. (1993). Relations between work group characteristics and effectiveness: Implications for designing effective work groups. *Personnel Psychology, 46,* 823–850.

Cannon-Bowers, J. A., Salas, E., & Converse, S. (1993). Shared mental models in expert team decision making. In N. J., Castellan, Jr. (Ed.), *Current issues in individual and group decision making* (pp. 221–246). Hillsdale, NJ: Erlbaum.

Carmel, E. (1995). Cycle time in packaged software firms. *Journal of Product Innovation Management, 9,* 140–147.

Carson, J. B., Tesluk, P. E., & Marrone, J. A. (2007). Shared leadership in teams: An investigation of antecedent conditions and performance. *Academy of Management Journal, 50,* 1217–1234.

Cohen, S. G., Chang, L., & Ledford, G. E. (1997). A hierarchical construct of self-management leadership and its relationship to quality of work life and perceived work group effectiveness. *Personnel Psychology, 50,* 275–308.

Conger, J. A., & Pearce, C. L. (2003). A landscape of opportunities: Future research on shared leadership. In C. L. Pearce & J. A. Conger (Eds.), *Shared leadership: Reframing the hows and whys of leadership* (pp. 285–303). Thousand Oaks, CA: Sage.

Cox, J. F., Pearce, C. L., & Perry, M. (2003). Toward a model of shared leadership and distributed influence in the innovation process: How shared leadership can influence new product development team dynamics and effectiveness. In C. L. Pearce & J. A. Conger (Eds), *Shared leadership: Reframing the hows and whys of leadership* (pp. 48–76). Thousand Oaks, CA: Sage.

Cramton, C. D. (2001). The mutual knowledge problem and its consequences for dispersed collaboration. *Organization Science, 12,* 346–371.

Day, D. V., Gronn, P., & Salas, E. (2004). Leadership capacity in teams. *The Leadership Quarterly, 15,* 857–880.

DeChurch, L. A., Burke, C. S., Shuffler, M., Lyons, R., Doty, D., & Salas, E. (2011). A historiometric analysis of leadership in mission critical multiteam environments. *The Leadership Quarterly.*

DeChurch, L. A., & Marks, M. A. (2006). Leadership in multiteam systems. *Journal of Applied Psychology, 91,* 311–329.

DeChurch, L. A., & Mathieu, J. E. (2009). Thinking in terms of multiteam systems. In E. Salas, G. F. Goodwin, & C. S. Burke (Eds.), *Team effectiveness in complex organizations: Cross-disciplinary perspectives and approaches* (pp. 267–292). New York: Taylor & Francis.

Druskat, V., & Wheeler, J. V. (2003). Managing from the boundary: The effective leadership of self-managing work teams. *Academy of Management Review, 46,* 435–457.

Dorman, S. (2007). Iraq PRTs: Pins on a map. *Foreign Service Journal,* March, 2007, 21–39.

Ensley, M. D., Hmieleski, K. M., & Pearce, C. L. (2006). The importance of vertical and shared leadership within new venture top management teams: Implications for the performance of startups. *The Leadership Quarterly, 17*(3), 217–231.

Erez, A., LePine, J. A., & Elms, H. (2002). Effects of rotated leadership and peer evaluation on the functioning and effectiveness of self-managed teams: A quasi-experiment. *Personnel Psychology, 55,* 929–948.

Feldman, D. C. (1984). The development and enforcement of group norms. *Academy of Management Review, 9,* 47–53.

Festinger, L. (1950). Informal social communication. *Psychological Review, 57,* 271–282.

Fleishman, E. A., Mumford, M. D., Zaccaro, S. J., Levin, K. Y., Korotkin, A. L., & Hein, M. B. (1991). Taxonomic efforts in the description of leader behavior: A synthesis and functional interpretation. *The Leadership Quarterly, 2,* 245–287.

Fletcher, J. K., & Käufer, K. (2003). Shared leadership: Paradox and possibility. In C. L. Pearce & J. A. Conger (Eds.), *Shared leadership: Reframing the hows and whys of leadership* (pp. 21–46). Thousand Oaks, CA: Sage.

Friedrich, T. L., Vessey, W. B., Schuelke, M. J., Ruark, G. A., & Mumford, M. D. (2009). A framework for understanding collective leadership: The selective utilization of leader and team expertise within networks. *The Leadership Quarterly, 20*(6), 933–958.

Gardner, W. L., III, & Schermerhorn, J. R., Jr. (1992). Strategic operational leadership and the management of supportive work environments. In R. L. Hunt & J. G. Hunt (Eds.), *Strategic leadership: A multiorganizational-level perspective*. Westport, CT: Quorum.

Griener, L. E. (1972). Evolution and revolution as organizations grow. *Harvard Business Review, 50*(4), 37–46.

Gronn, P. (2002). Distributed leadership as a unit of analysis. *The Leadership Quarterly, 13*, 423–451.

Hackman, J. R., & Wageman, R. (2005). A theory of team coaching. *Academy of Management Review, 30*, 269–287.

Hackman, J. R., & Walton, R. E. (1986). Leading groups in organizations. In P. S. Goodman & Associates (Eds.), *Designing effective work groups* (pp. 72–119). San Francisco: Jossey-Bass.

Hambrick, D. C. (1994). Top management groups: A conceptual integration and reconsideration of the "team" label. In D. C. Hambrick, *Research in organizational behavior* (Vol. 16, pp. 171–213). Greenwich, CT: JAI.

Hersey, P., & Blanchard, K. H. (1988). *Management of organizational behavior: Utilizing human resources* (5th ed.). Englewood Cliffs, NJ: Prentice Hall.

Hiller, N. J., Day, D. V., & Vance, R. J. (2006). Collective enactment of leadership roles and team effectiveness: A field study. *Leadership Quarterly, 17*, 387–397.

Hollenbeck, J. R., Ilgen, D. R., Sego, D. J., Hedlund, J., Major, D. A., & Phillips, J. (1995). Multilevel theory of team decision-making: Decision performance in teams incorporating distributed expertise. *Journal of Applied Psychology, 80*, 292–316.

Houghton, J. D., Neck, C. P., & Manz, C. C. (2003). Self-leadership and superleadership: The heart and art of creating shared leadership in teams In C. L. Pearce & J. A. Conger (Eds.), *Shared leadership: Reframing the hows and whys of leadership* (pp. 123–139). Thousand Oaks, CA: Sage.

Hulpia, H., Devos, G., & Rosseel, Y. (2009). Development and validation of scores on the distributed leadership inventory. *Educational and Psychology Measurement, 69*, 1013–1034.

Jackson, S. E. (1992). Team composition in organizational settings: Issues in managing a diverse work group. In S. Worchel, W. Wood, & J. Simpson (Eds.), *Group process and productivity*. Newbury Park, CA: Sage.

Jackson, S. E., Joshi, A., & Erhardt, N. L. (2003). Recent research on team and organizational diversity: SWOT analysis and implications. *Journal of Management, 29*, 801–830.

Jacobs, T. O., & Jaques, E. (1990). Military executive leadership. In K. E. Clark & M. B. Clark (Eds.), *Measures of leadership* (pp. 281–295). Greensboro, NC: Center for Creative Leadership.

Jaques, E. (1990, January–February). In praise of hierarchy. *Harvard Business Review*, 127–133.

Jaques, E. (1996). *Requisite organization: A total system for effective managerial organization and managerial leadership for the 21st century*. Arlington, VA: Cason Hall.

Jarvenpaa, S. L., & Leidner, D. E. (1999). Communication and trust in global virtual teams. *Organization Science, 10*(6), 791–815.

Joshi, A., Pandey, N., & Han, G. (2009). Bracketing team boundary spanning: An examination of task-based, team-level, and contextual antecedents. *Journal of Organizational Behavior, 30*, 731–759.

Katz, D., & Kahn, R. L. (1978). *The social psychology of organizations*. New York: Wiley.

Kerr, S., & Jermier, J. M. (1978). Substitutes for leadership: Their meaning and measurement. *Organizational Behavior and Human Performance, 22*, 375–403.

Kirkman, B. L., & Rosen, B. (1999). Beyond self-management: The antecedents and consequence of team empowerment. *Academy of Management, 42*, 58–74.

Kirkman, B. L., Rosen, B., Tesluk, P. E., & Gibson, C. B. (2004). The impact of team empowerment on virtual team performance: The moderating role of face-to-face interaction. *Academy of Management Journal, 47*, 175–192.

Knight, D., Pearce, C. L., Smith, K. G., Olian, J. D., Sims, H. P., Smith, K. A., et al. (1999). Top management team diversity, group process, and strategic consensus. *Strategic Management Journal, 20*, 445–465.

Kozlowski, S. W. J., Gully, S. M., McHugh, P. P., Salas, E., & Cannon-Bowers, J. A. (1996). A dynamic theory of leadership and team effectiveness: Developmental and task contingent leader roles. *Research in Personnel and Human Resources Management, 14*, 253–305.

Kozlowski, S. W. J., Watola, D. J., Jensen, J. M., Kim, B. H., & Botero, I. C. (2009). Developing adaptive teams: A theory of dynamic team leadership. In E. Salas, G. F. Goodwin, & C. S. Burke (Eds.), *Team effectiveness in complex organizations* (pp. 113–156). New York: Psychology Press.

Larson, J. R., Jr. (2010). *In search of synergy in small group performance.* New York: Taylor & Francis.

Manz, C. C., & Sims, H. P. (1987). Leading workers to lead themselves: The external leadership of self-managing work teams. *Administrative Science Quarterly, 32*, 106–128.

Marks, M. A., DeChurch, L. A., Mathieu, J. E., Panzer, F. J., & Alonso, A. A. (2005). Teamwork in multi-team systems. *Journal of Applied Psychology, 90*(5), 964–971.

Marks, M. A., Mathieu, J. E., & Zaccaro, S. J. (2001). A temporally based framework and taxonomy of team processes. *Academy of Management Review, 26*(3), 356–376.

Mathieu, J. E., Marks, M. A., & Zaccaro, S. J. (2001). Multi-team systems. In N. Anderson, D. Ones, H. K. Sinangil, & C. Viswesvaran (Eds.), *International handbook of work and organizational psychology* (pp. 289–313). London: Sage.

Mayo, M., Meindl, J. R., & Pastor, J. C. (2003). Shared leadership in work teams: A social network approach. In C. L. Pearce & J. A. Conger (Eds.), *Shared leadership: Reframing the hows and whys of leadership* (pp. 193–212). Thousand Oaks, CA: Sage.

McGrath, J. E. (1962). *Leadership behavior: Some requirements for leadership training.* Washington, DC: U.S. Civil Service Commission, Office of Career Development.

Mehra, A., Smith, B. R., Dixon, A. L., & Robertson, B. (2006). Distributed leadership in teams: The network of leadership perceptions and team performance. *The Leadership Quarterly, 17*(3), 232–245.

Morgeson, F. P., DeRue, D. S., & Karam, E. P. (2009). Leadership in teams: A functional approach to understanding leadership structures and processes. *Journal of Management, 36*, 5–39.

Mumford, M. D., Zaccaro, S. J., Harding, F. D., Jacobs, T. O., & Fleishman, E. A. (2000). Leadership skills for a changing world: Solving complex social problems. *Leadership Quarterly, 11*, 11–35.

O'Bannon, D. P., & Gupta, A. K. (1992, August). The utility of homogeneity versus heterogeneity within top management teams: Alternate resolutions of the emerging conundrum. Paper presented at the annual meeting of the Academy of Management, Las Vegas, NV.

O'Reilly, C. A., III, Caldwell, D., & Barnett, W. (1989). Work group demography, social integration, and turnover. *Administrative Science Quarterly, 34*, 21–37.

Pearce, C. L., & Conger, J. A. (2003). All those years ago: The historical underpinnings of shared leadership. In C. L. Pearce & J. A. Conger (Eds.), *Shared leadership: Reframing the hows and whys of leadership* (pp. 1–18). Thousand Oaks, CA: Sage.

Pearce, C. L., & Sims, H. P. (2000). Shared leadership: Toward a multi-level theory of leadership. In M. M. Beyerlein, D. A. Johnson, & S. T. Beyerlein (Eds.), *Advances in interdisciplinary studies of work teams: Team leadership* (Vol. 7, pp. 115–139). Greenwich, CT: JAI.

Pearce, C. L., & Sims, H. P. (2002). Vertical versus shared leadership as predictors of the effectiveness of change management teams: An examination of aversive, directive, transactional, transformational and empowering leader behaviors. *Group Dynamics: Theory, Research, and Practice, 6*, 172–197.

Pearce, J. A., & Ravlin, E. C. (1987). The design and activation of self-regulating work groups. *Human Relations, 40*(11), 751–782.

Perry, M. L., Pearce, C. L., & Sims, H. P., Jr. (1999). Empowered selling teams: How shared leadership can contribute to selling team outcomes. *Journal of Personal Selling and Sales Management, 19*, 35–51.

Phillips, K. W., Mannix, E. A., Neale. M. A., & Gruenfeld, D. H. (2004). Diverse groups and information sharing: The effects of congruent ties. *Journal of Experimental Social Psychology, 40*, 497–510.

Phillips, K. W., Rothbard, N. P., & Dumas, T. L. (2008). To disclose or not to disclose? Status distance and self-disclosure in diverse environments. *Academy of Management Review, 34*(4), 710–732.

Quinn, R. E., & Cameron, K. (1983). Organizational life cycles and shifting criteria of effectiveness: Some preliminary evidence. *Management Science, 29*, 33–51.

Roby, T. B. (1961). The executive function in small groups. In L. Petrullo & B. Bass (Eds.), *Leadership and interpersonal behavior.* New York: Holt, Rinehart & Winston.

Schutz, W. C. (1961). The ego, FIRO theory and the leader as completer. In L. Petrullo & B. M. Bass (Eds.), *Leadership and interpersonal behavior* (pp. 48–65). New York: Holt, Rinehart & Winston.

Seers, A. (1996). Better leadership through chemistry: Toward a model of emergent shared team leadership. In M. M. Beyerlein & D. A. Johnson (Eds.), *Advances in the interdisciplinary study of work teams: Team leadership* (Vol. 3, pp. 145–172). Greenwich, CT: JAI.

Seers, A., Keller, T., & Wilkerson, J. M. (2003). Can team members share leadership? Foundations in research and theory. In C. L. Pearce & J. A. Conger (Eds.), *Shared leadership: Reframing the hows and whys of leadership* (pp. 77–101). Thousand Oaks, CA: Sage.

Smith, K. G., Mitchell, T. R., & Summer, C. E. (1985). Top level management priorities in different stages of the organizational life cycle. *Academy of Management Journal, 28*(4), 799–820.

Smith, K. G., Smith, K. A., Olian, J. D., Sims, H. P., O'Bannon, D. P., & Scully, J. A. (1994). Top management team demography and process: The role of social integration and communication. *Administrative Science Quarterly, 39*, 412–438.

Straus, S. G. (1996). Getting a clue: The effects of communication media and information distribution on participation and performance in computer-mediated and face-to-face groups. *Small Group Research, 27*(1), 115–142.

Straus, S. G. (1997). Technology, group process, and group outcomes: Testing the connections in computer-mediated and face-to-face groups. *Human-Computer Interaction*, *12*(3), 227–266.

Tesluk, P., Mathieu, J. E., Zaccaro, S. J., & Marks, M. A. (1997). Task and aggregation issues in analysis and assessment of team performance. In M. T. Brannick, E. Salas, & C. Prince (Eds.), *Team performance assessment and measurement: Theory, methods, and applications*. Mahwah, NJ: Erlbaum.

van Knippenberg, D., De Dreu, C. K. W., & Homan, A. C. (2004). Work group diversity and group performance: An integrative model and research agenda. *Journal of Applied Psychology*, *89*(6), 1008–1022.

Vroom, V. H., & Yetton, P. W. (1973). *Leadership and decision-making*. Pittsburgh, PA: University of Pittsburgh Press.

Warkentin, M. E., Sayeed, L., & Hightower, R. (1997). Virtual teams versus face-to-face teams: An exploratory study of a web-based conference system. *Decision Sciences*, *28*, 975–996.

Wiersema, M. F., & Bantel, K. A. (1992). Top management team demography and corporate strategic change. *Academy of Management Journal*, *35*, 91–121.

Yukl, G. (2010). *Leadership in organizations* (7th ed.). Upper Saddle River, NJ: Prentice Hall.

Zaccaro, S. J. (2001). *The nature of executive leadership: A conceptual and empirical analysis of success*. Washington, DC: APA Books.

Zaccaro, S. J., Banks, D., Kiechel-Koles, L., Kemp, C., & Bader, P. (2009). *Principles and strategies for developing skills that promote adaptive performance*. Arlington, VA: U.S. Army Research Institute for Behavioral and Social Sciences.

Zaccaro, S. J., Heinen, B., & Shuffler, M. (2009). Team leadership and team effectiveness. In E. Salas, G. F. Goodwin, & C. S. Burke (Eds.), *Team effectiveness in complex organizations: Cross-disciplinary perspectives and approaches* (pp. 83–111). New York: Routledge.

Zaccaro, S. J., Rittman, A. L., & Marks, M. A. (2001). Team leadership. *Leadership Quarterly*, *12*, 451–483.

11

Conflict in Multiteam Situations

Verlin B. Hinsz
North Dakota State University

Kevin R. Betts
North Dakota State University

Task success in modern organizations often requires that multiple teams work in concert. Multiple teams often bring with them additional resources that allow them to outperform individual teams. However, multiple-team situations may also lead to conflict. Examples of conflict in multiple-team situations may include coordination difficulties, role conflicts, competition, and antagonism between teams. Conflict in teams involves perceived differences between parties about things that matter to them (e.g., beliefs and resources) (De Dreu & Gelfand, 2008). From this perspective, conflict can be seen as potentially arising within and between teams in multiple-team situations. We begin this chapter by describing "Multiple Teams Working in Concert," which encompasses both multiteam systems and teams-of-teams. We then describe the inherent potential for conflict when multiple teams work in concert, identify sources of conflict, and discuss potential remedies for reducing this conflict.

MULTIPLE TEAMS WORKING IN CONCERT

Mathieu, Marks, and Zaccaro (2002) provided the widely accepted definition of *multiteam systems* (see DeChurch & Mathieu, 2009; Zaccaro, Marks, & DeChurch, Chapter 1, this volume). Perhaps the critical element of multiteam systems is to consider them as "tightly coupled networks of teams" (DeChurch & Mathieu, 2009, p. 271). In that regard, a multiteam system is one example of multiple teams working in concert. Zaccaro et al. (Chapter 1, this volume) provide a more elaborate conceptualization of multiteam systems. Much of this conceptualization is consistent with our view of multiteam systems. However, we see multiteam systems as just one type of multiple-team situation. We use the global term of *multiple teams working in concert* to describe situations in which more than one team interact while performing tasks. We specifically define two types of multiple-team situations: teams-of-teams and multiteam systems.

We refer to a *team-of-teams* as a situation in which multiple teams perform a similar function in conjunction. The teams have a common set of task goals, they perform very similar or identical tasks, and they are interdependent in their achievement of task goals. In contrast, a *multiteam system* is defined by teams that perform different functions in pursuit of a common, often superordinate goal. For a multiteam system, the teams might each have task goals, but the teams in conjunction have a superordinate goal that directs the teams' activities. Also, the different teams may have some similar tasks, but the teams have other unique tasks that help differentiate their functions. The teams are interdependent in how they act to achieve the team and superordinate goals.

Emergency medical dispatch (EMD) teams in London provide an example of both a team-of-teams and a multiteam system. EMD teams are responsible for the "reception and management of requests for emergency medical assistance" (Clawson & Dernocoeur, 1998). EMD teams stabilize and transport persons suffering from medical emergencies (Furniss & Blandford, 2006). EMD teams consist of allocators, radio operators, telephone dispatchers, and ambulance crews. Call takers acquire the details of emergency calls and enter them into a computer to which the appropriate EMD team responds. Allocators decide which ambulance crews should be directed to which location. Radio and telephone operators communicate directions to ambulance crews, and ambulance crews locate and provide medical services to persons in need. Additionally, all EMD teams are supported by individuals providing helicopter emergency medical services, and support services such as vehicle maintenance and paramedic advice.

EMD teams act as both a team-of-teams and a multiteam system, depending on their needs. During a slow shift, EMD teams are more likely to act as a team-of-teams. Each EMD team has the same proximal goal, to provide medical services to persons in need. Each EMD team is assigned to a different sector of the city. On a busy shift, EMD teams become more like a multiteam system as they mobilize units across typical region boundaries. For example, if few calls are received in one sector of the city, available units in this region may be asked to provide assistance in a neighboring sector. Each EMD team continuously works toward its proximal goal of providing medical services to needy individuals in their respective region, and occasionally coordinates with teams assigned to neighboring regions. By acting as both a team-of-teams and a multiteam system, these actions serve to ensure that a superordinate goal of providing medical services to needy individuals in the entire city of London is met.

From our definitions and example of multiteam systems and teams-of-teams, a number of characteristics arise upon which they are similar or differ. The two types of multiple-team situations differ in the nature of their functions, the tasks performed, and the task goals. Moreover, these multiple-team situations involve two critical psychological processes: interdependence and coordination. As noted above and in the literature, multiteam systems and teams-of-teams both have sets of interdependencies among the teams (DeChurch & Mathieu, 2009; Zaccaro et al., Chapter 1, this volume). In a broad sense, the interdependencies focus on the goals being pursued and the way the tasks are performed. Teams in a team-of-teams situation generally have the same task goals (i.e., proximal and distal) because they have very similar functions. Teams in multiteam systems generally have different proximal task goals, but might also have similar or identical superordinate goals or system goals (i.e., distal goals). A problem inherent with these multiple goals is how to orchestrate or coordinate the teams' actions to achieve the goals.

Coordination is considered one of the emergent processes of team interaction (Arrow, McGrath, & Berdahl, 2000; Wiltermuth & Heath, 2009). Coordination is the way that members, resources, tasks, and situations are orchestrated to achieve goals through team action. Consequently, coordination is one of the critical features of multiple-team situations (Hinsz, Wallace, & Ladbury, 2009). Generally, we consider coordination as who does what, when, where, and how (Hinsz et al., 2009; Park, Hinsz, & Ladbury, 2006). Within teams, this coordination would focus on how members coordinate their actions. However, in multiple-team situations, coordination occurs between teams as well. Coordination in multiple teams involves which team does what, when, where, and how in addition to the within-team coordination. Consequently, multiple-team situations involve coordination at both the team and multiple-team levels, which introduces another level of complexity. Therefore, planning, organizing, and executing the actions of multiple teams working in concert involve more coordination and interdependencies than individuals interacting, even as a single team.

CONFLICT IN MULTIPLE-TEAM SITUATIONS

There are many advantages to multiple-team collaboration (Marks, DeChurch, Mathieu, Panzer, & Alonso, 2005), several of which are described in the chapters of this volume. Certainly, collaboration between multiple teams should not be discouraged. However, there is an inherent potential for conflict when multiple teams work in concert. This potential for conflict in multiple-team situations merits recognition. Many of the conflicts we discuss are common to both individual teams and multiple teams working in concert. Importantly, though, the chances of these conflicts emerging and their severity appear to increase in multiple-team situations. We intend to show that multiple-team collaboration includes additional complexities that generate additional opportunities for conflict. We also describe how these additional opportunities for conflict in multiple-team situations may be overcome with known techniques and strategies.

We describe six sources of conflict that may emerge when multiple teams work together. These sources of conflict are summarized in Table 11.1 and discussed in depth below. These six reflect diverse sources of conflict, but they are not inclusive. Rather, they represent examples of ways in which conflict might result from actions and interactions in multiple-team situations. First, we describe how conflict arises when multiple teams have different identities. Second, we discuss how structural contingencies for teams can produce conflict as well as more competitive or cooperative interteam actions. Third, we describe problems associated with failed and faulty shared representations within and between teams. Fourth, we describe conflicts resulting from role violations and redundancy. Fifth, the conflict that can arise from the way information is exchanged within and between teams is considered with reference to transactive knowledge systems. Sixth, the conflict that can arise from divergent decision preferences of team members and teams is discussed. For each source of conflict, we offer brief examples of potential solutions for their occurrence. We

TABLE 11.1

Features of Conflict in Multiple-Team Situations

Sources of Conflict	Processes That Lead to Conflict	Example(s) of Conflict	Remedies for Conflict
Intergroup relations	Divergent identities of teams and team members	Ingroup favoritism, outgroup hostility	Promote superordinate goals without deemphasizing team goals.
Structural contingencies	Situational constraints and environmental contingencies	Inappropriate adaptation to situational demands	Construct or constrain contingencies so that appropriate responses will be more forthcoming.
Shared representations	Failed or faulty shared understanding about team-relevant concerns	Failure to agree on expected patterns of interaction and coordination	Ensure team and team member responsibilities are clearly specified and understood by all involved.
Role violations and redundancy	Violations of role assignment or overly similar roles being performed by different teams or team members	Performing responsibilities assigned to other teams or team members	Determine role assignments early in multiple-team situations, and periodically restate or redefine these roles.
Information exchange	Communication failures and inefficient transactive knowledge systems	Failure to share information relevant to proximal team goals	Train multiple teams to work in concert. Consider appointing linking pins and/or boundary spanners.
Divergent decision preferences	Disagreements between teams or team members about appropriate responses to team-relevant concerns	Underrepresentation of minority viewpoints	Form subgroups by taking members from different teams to discuss the issue and propose a recommended course of action.

conclude the descriptions of each source of conflict with directions for future research concerning conflict in multiple-team situations. Following our discussion of sources of conflict, we discuss the different patterns of cross-level effects (e.g., within teams versus between teams) that can arise for multiple-team situations.

Conflict From Intergroup Relations

Conflict appears to occur naturally when two or more teams having separate identities and unique goals interact with each other (Hogg & Terry, 2000). These teams do not have to be in competition for resources for this conflict to arise (Hogg & Abrams, 2003). Research has shown that when teams emerge or are defined, they are ascribed or acquire an identity (Hogg & Terry, 2001). Research related to social identity theory and self-categorization theory has revealed much about intergroup behavior (Hogg & Terry, 2000). What is important for our considerations is that when these teams with different identities interact, a number of phenomena occur that indicate that the teams see themselves as in conflict with one another.

There is ample evidence that members of different teams that are constructed for unique purposes respond to their own group differently than they do to outgroups. For instance, ingroup favoritism reflects a tendency to ascribe better attributes to one's ingroup relative to an outgroup (Tajfel & Turner, 1986). Similarly, if team members are asked to allocate resources to their ingroup and to an outgroup, they are biased to favor their ingroup even in the face of known differential inputs (Brewer, 1979). This ingroup favoritism can even spill over to instances of outgroup hostility (Hogg & Terry, 2000). There is evidence that members of one group are willing to derogate an outgroup and its members. It is important to recognize that these differences in responses to ingroups and outgroups do not result from provocation, but apparently from processes associated with one's own ingroup having a different identity from an outgroup.

Other research demonstrates this hostility toward outgroups under other circumstances. Research by Insko, Schloper, and colleagues (see Wildschut, Pinter, Vevea, Insko, & Schopler, 2003, for a review) indicates that teams are likely to compete with each other without prior interaction. In this research, individuals play a prisoner's dilemma game with other individuals, and groups play the game with other groups. In the game, a party can choose a competitive or a cooperative response. In the first trial of the game, results indicate that groups are much more likely to compete with the other group, whereas individuals are much more likely to cooperate with other individuals. This pattern continues even when groups and individuals undergo numerous trials of the game. This finding, known as the *interindividual–intergroup discontinuity*, shows a dramatic cross-level effect because the pattern observed at the individual level is strikingly different from that observed at the group level.

The interindividual–intergroup discontinuity suggests that compared to single teams, multiple teams working in concert may be more likely to anticipate noncooperative behavior from other teams (Cohen & Insko, 2008). Members of single teams typically work closely with one another and may develop trust easier than multiple teams working in concert. However, both trust within teams and between teams may be important for task success in multiple-team situations. For example, the ability to trust other team members and teams to achieve their proximal goals allows one to focus more exclusively on one's own goals (Ellis, Porter, & Wolverton, 2008; Worschel & Austin, 1986).

Because the interindividual–intergroup discontinuity can occur before groups even have an interaction, it appears that group members perceive other groups differently from individuals (Wildschut et al., 2003). In particular, Insko and his colleagues suggested that group members distrust other groups, they implicitly perceive other groups negatively (Pinter & Insko, 2003), and they are more motivated by greed in the presence of other groups (Wildschut et al., 2003). Related research suggests that groups are more likely to act competitively in a negotiation than individuals (Morgan & Tindale, 2002). Additionally, in a study of aggressive responses, Meier and Hinsz (2004) found that groups assigned other groups to consume twice as much hot sauce as individuals assigned to other individuals. Again, it is important to note that these patterns of effects occurred before the groups or individuals had interaction with the other party. Clearly, the research on intergroup relations demonstrates that groups are predisposed to perceive other groups as hostile and as opposing parties rather than as collaborators with whom they would cooperate. Such findings have important implications for multiple teams working in concert. In particular, it should be expected that the different teams will inherently see their team as being in conflict with other teams without the necessity of evidence to support that belief.

Numerous techniques have been developed to reduce intergroup conflict (Cohen & Insko, 2008). The contact hypothesis is probably the best known (Amir, 1969). The contact hypothesis suggests that intergroup contact reduces conflict. However, contact alone does not reduce conflict between teams. In competitive situations, contact between teams may even exacerbate conflict (Worschel & Austin, 1986). Rather than promoting simple contact between teams, the most appropriate solution for multiple-team situations may be to redirect the attention of teams and their members to superordinate goals. As mentioned, teams form social identities around the functions they perform (Hogg & Terry, 2000), and these social identities may lead teams to perceive and treat ingroup members differently from outgroup members (Wildschut et al., 2003). However, when multiple teams work in concert, a common identity that is supported by shared superordinate goals may also develop (Gaertner & Dovidio, 2000). Periodically redirecting the attention of teams and their members to these superordinate goals may encourage cooperation between teams.

Importantly, when promoting superordinate goals among multiple teams working in concert, the value of component team functions and goals should not be ignored (Fiol, Pratt, & O'Connor, 2009). In contrast to single teams, teams involved in multiple-team situations have dual identities. One identity develops based on their team-specific function, and another identity develops based on their function in the multiple-team situation. Focusing only on superordinate goals deemphasizes the importance of team proximal goals. If a team feels that their function is not valued, they may seek to affirm themselves by derogating the importance of other teams (Fein & Spencer, 1997). Placing value on both the superordinate and proximal goals of teams in multiple-team situations may be most effective for reducing intergroup conflict.

There are many potential directions for research concerning intergroup conflict in multiple-team situations. Our analysis suggests that in multiple-team situations, conflict between teams should be more profound than conflict within teams. However, much of our support for this conclusion comes from research concerning conflict between distinct groups rather than conflict among multiple teams working in concert. Importantly, it is possible that conflict among multiple teams working in concert may be greater or less than conflict between distinct teams. For example, the greater awareness of a superordinate goal may reduce conflict among multiple teams working in concert as they strive to meet that goal.

Alternatively, multiple teams working in concert may become especially competitive if they are concerned about threats to the perceived importance of their role among fellow teams. Future research should investigate the potential differences between conflict among distinct groups and conflict among multiple teams working in concert.

Conflict From Structural Contingencies

An alternative conception of how teams in a multiple-team situation might relate to each other can be seen from implications of structural contingency theory (Hollenbeck et al., 2002). When considering teams in organizations, structural contingency theory suggests that there is no best way for teams to be most effective. Rather, teams will be most effective if they adapt to situational constraints and environmental contingencies that exist in the contexts the teams face. For example, teams that are defined in functional terms (e.g., emergency medical dispatch teams) are best able to respond to dynamic task environments in which the application of skills, knowledge, and abilities changes rapidly. In contrast, in more stable environments, teams that are designed along divisional lines are likely to be most effective (Hollenbeck et al., 2002). An implication of structural contingency theory for teams would be that teams will respond to the task environments when they act and interact with other teams in multiple-team situations. If resources are scarce and resource distribution is uncertain, then teams would be likely to compete for the resources and conflict among teams would be likely to develop. Alternatively, if the component teams have shared goals and high interdependence for goal attainment with strong training that fosters collaboration, more cooperative responses would be expected in multiple-team situations.

The clear implication of structural contingency theory for multiple-team situations is that the component teams will be responsive to the environmental contingencies that confront them. So, to reduce the conflict among the teams, it is important to construct or constrain the contingencies so that the appropriate responses will be more forthcoming (e.g., collaboration) and undesirable actions will be limited (e.g., competition). Substantial research shows how teams are likely to respond to environmental contingencies. In particular, there appears to be an asymmetry in how well teams can change from functional to divisional structures (Moon et al., 2004). Moreover, there is also an asymmetry making it easier to switch from a collaborative response posture than a competitive one (Johnson et al., 2006). This research demonstrates the two implications that (a) teams respond to structural contingencies, and (b) conflict can be amplified or ameliorated in multiple-team situations as a function of how the environment is constructed to influence the teams.

One way that future research could more closely examine conflict resulting from structural contingencies is by drawing connections between structural contingencies in the environment and research on situation awareness. *Situation awareness* refers to an awareness of important elements in one's environment (Endsley & Garland, 2000). Situation awareness is important for teams to perceive, understand, and predict what is going on in the environment (Endsley & Jones, 2001). For structural contingencies to influence teams, the teams must perceive, comprehend, and anticipate those contingencies. As a consequence, teams that have more situation awareness would also be more responsive to contingencies that reduce conflict among teams. That is, team situation awareness could be a moderator of contingencies that influence conflict. Moreover, training that enhances situation awareness in team members (Endsley & Garland, 2000) should similarly moderate the effect of contingencies on conflict in multiple-team situations. This research would show how conflict results from the structural contingencies that affect teams and that the members' situation awareness would influence their sensitivity to these contingencies.

Conflict From Shared Representations

Mathieu et al. (2002) identified shared mental models as critical levers for multiteam system effectiveness. A *shared mental model* refers to a common understanding among teams and team members regarding expected behavior patterns (Cannon-Bowers, Salas, & Converse, 1993; Hinsz, 1995). Multiteam systems develop expected behavior patterns about (a) task procedures, (b) component team and member characteristics, (c) expected patterns of interaction and coordination, and (d) strategies (Mathieu et al., 2002). Teams-of-teams likely develop shared mental models in a similar manner. A related construct, *shared representations*, has been used to describe "any task/situation-relevant concept, norm, perspective or cognitive process that is shared by most or all of the group members" (Tindale, Smith, Thomas, Filkins, & Sheffey, 1996). Similarities between shared mental models and shared representations suggest that they should lead to similar outcomes, so we use the term *shared representation* to refer to both.

Generally, the formation of shared representations among component teams and team members should aid the performance of multiple teams working in concert. For example, a shared representation about the functions of component teams in a multiteam system or team-of-teams allows for understanding of what is and is not expected of each team. A shared representation about a superordinate goal ensures different teams are working toward the same outcome. Shared representations aid component teams as they attempt to perform their responsibilities and coordinate with one another. Conflict can occur when a shared representation fails to develop or when a faulty shared representation develops.

A shared representation fails to develop when different teams or team members perceive aspects of a situation differently. In London, different emergency medical dispatch teams are assigned to unique sectors. It could be said that a shared representation failed to develop if different teams perceive boundaries that divide these sectors differently. Variation in perception between teams may be explicit or implicit. Explicitly, teams may disagree about where these boundaries should lie and respond based on their perceptions rather than actual agreed upon boundaries. Implicitly, teams may misunderstand agreed upon boundaries. There may be severe consequences if a shared representation fails to develop. If emergency medical dispatch teams perceive sector boundaries differently, they may send multiple units to the same incident, leaving other incidents unaided. Similarly, if the teams believe another team is responsible for a certain location, individuals in an emergency may not be attended to by any medical dispatch teams.

A shared representation is considered faulty when teams or team members perceive something similarly but incorrectly. That is, the team members agree on a representation, but that representation is inaccurate, inappropriate, or otherwise faulty. A superordinate goal of emergency medical dispatch teams is to stabilize and transport persons suffering from medical emergencies. If emergency medical dispatch teams begin to perceive themselves as transportation units exclusively, then they may have developed a faulty shared representation because they have lost track of the important goal of medical aid. This example illustrates that the consequences of a faulty shared representation may also be severe. A failure to stabilize a person suffering from a medical emergency before transporting may result in that person's death. Nevertheless, if the team members agree that they serve only a transport function, then the general tendency of teams to correct errors (Hinsz, 2004) may be overridden. Other teams would then have their expectations about the emergency medical dispatch team unfulfilled, and there would be conflict about the expected behavior from the emergency medical dispatch team. Consequently, the degree to which task representations are shared can influence the effectiveness of teams in a multiple-team situation in a variety of ways.

Failed and faulty shared representations may interfere with the ability of multiteam systems and teams-of-teams to reach important goals. For example, if team members are performing their responsibilities incorrectly or inefficiently, other members will need to compensate for this. They may do so by instructing these team members in the correct fashion of performing their responsibilities, or simply by performing the responsibilities themselves. If team members are devoting time and energy toward responsibilities that their function does not require, they will necessarily be devoting less time and energy toward responsibilities that their function does require. Each of these possibilities makes reaching important goals more difficult. Thus, whenever multiple teams work in concert, attempts should be made to encourage the development of appropriate shared representations.

Appropriate shared representations should develop when team and team member responsibilities are clearly specified and understood by all involved. Presumably, emergency medical dispatch systems attempt to clearly specify the responsibilities and proximal goals of each team and member in their system, as well as the superordinate goals of the larger collective. Specification of these expectations should help to ensure that an appropriate shared representation develops. Without the specification of expectations, teams and team members may think they share an understanding of their responsibilities when in fact they do not. These gaps in shared representations can be harbingers of conflict in functionally diverse teams (Cronin & Weingart, 2007).

Further research concerning shared representations and conflict in multiple-team situations may prove fruitful. We can hypothesize that if appropriate shared representations reduce conflict in multiple-team situations, then teams may benefit from accelerating the process by which shared representations develop. That is, if teams were provided training or received an intervention so that they reach a shared representation faster, then those teams should be able to address task concerns sooner. This training may be particularly potent for new team members. Techniques, strategies, and technology that could hasten the development of shared task representations (e.g., Letsky, Warner, Fiore, & Smith, 2008) would provide valuable tools to those involved in multiple-team situations.

Conflict From Role Violations and Redundancy

Generally, teams and their members in multiple-team situations play specific roles that contribute to the success of common goals. The roles assigned to component teams and their members in emergency medical dispatch systems allow for effective and efficient emergency medical services in London (Furniss & Blandford, 2006). Each member plays a unique role that contributes to the success of the team, and each team plays a unique role that contributes to the success of the larger system (Humphrey, Morgeson, & Mannor, 2009). The result is a quick response to medical emergencies in London. Further, emergency medical dispatch teams and their members likely identify with these roles, define themselves largely in terms of their team membership, and derive psychological benefits by fulfilling these roles (Cargile, Bradac, & Cole, 2006; Fiol et al., 2009). For these reasons, the assignment of specific roles in any multiple-team situation is important (Beauchamp, Bray, Eys, & Carron, 2005; Jackson & Schuler, 1985), and failure to assign specific roles to teams and their members may result in role conflict. Specifically, role conflict may occur because of role violations or role redundancy.

Role violations occur when expected role assignments are fulfilled by teams or members not assigned to those roles. In the emergency medical dispatch example, allocators are responsible for determining where ambulance crews should be directed, whereas radio and telephone operators communicate these directions to ambulance crews. A role violation may emerge in this situation if allocators begin to communicate with ambulance crews directly, making assigned radio and telephone operators unnecessary for task success. In addition to any inefficiency associated with such a role violation, such an action may also threaten the social identity of teams and their members. This threatened social identity may lead to resentment between teams or team members. Resentment and other forms of relationship conflict have been shown to have negative effects on task performance (De Dreu & Weingart, 2003), and may even affect team member psychological and physical well-being (Emmons & King, 1988; Spector & Bruk-Lee, 2008).

Conflict may also emerge when multiple teams or team members are assigned similar or identical roles. A team-of-teams consists of multiple teams with similar goals. Therefore, teams-of-teams are often assigned identical roles. Likewise, some redundancy in role assignment may occur in multiteam systems when teams become large. If teams and team members form their social identity around these roles, then the action of assigning similar roles may be perceived as threatening. This perceived threat may lead teams and their members to become competitive. Competition between teams may then lead to conflict between teams and distract from superordinate goals (Surowiecki, 2005).

Role redundancy is not solely associated with negative outcomes. In many systems contexts, redundancy is common. One benefit of redundancy in multiple-team situations is that it allows more than one team or member to perform a function. The purpose of this redundancy is to prevent failure in fulfilling that function. Similarly, role redundancy in multiteam situations increases the likelihood that all roles will be adequately fulfilled. If a team or team member fails to fulfill a role, redundancy allows for other teams or team members to fulfill that role.

The fulfillment of role responsibilities by teams and team members is important for task success. Consequently, task success is more likely if role conflicts do not emerge. Role conflict may be avoided by determining role assignments early in multiple-team situations and periodically restating and/or redefining these roles. This is particularly true in dynamic situations in which teams and their members may need to take on a variety of roles and switch in and out of role behaviors quickly. For example, when a team reaches a proximal goal, their role may become obsolete. At this time, it may be advantageous to assign new roles to this team.

It may also be necessary to identify appropriate levels of role redundancy. Teams in team-of-teams contexts inherently seek to fulfill similar or identical roles, and thus are redundant by their nature. In contrast, multiteam systems attempt to fulfill more diverse roles. In both contexts, role redundancy may lead to positive outcomes, negative outcomes, or both. The issue with role redundancy seems to be that it can result in conflict if the redundancy is not appropriately managed. An important task of team leaders may be to consider the potential outcomes of role redundancy and identify what level of redundancy is appropriate.

There are many potential directions for future research concerning role violations and redundancy and their relation to conflict in multiple-team situations. One potential avenue suggested by the interindividual–intergroup discontinuity concerns the hypothesis that conflict between teams may be more profound than conflict within teams. In line with this research, we hypothesize that role violations and redundancy may be more profound when they occur between teams than when they occur within teams. If a team violates another team's role (i.e., performs that team's responsibilities), resulting conflict may be more profound than if a team member violates another team member's role. Because leaders play an instrumental role in multiple-team situations (DeChurch & Marks, 2006), they may be able to manage roles so the conflict is reduced. If the leader frames performing a fellow team member's role as a helping behavior, it may reduce the tendency of teams and team members to react negatively. Future research should investigate the impact that team leaders can have on concerns about role violations and role redundancy, which can contribute to conflict in multiple-team situations.

Conflict From Information Exchange

When multiple teams work in concert, they often exchange critical information. In dynamic task environments such as emergency medical dispatch, this information may be essential for attaining proximal and distal team goals (Hinsz et al., 2009). Research on teams shows how information exchange is important for effectiveness on numerous dimensions of task performance (Ellis et al., 2008; Hinsz, Tindale, & Vollrath, 1997; Hinsz et al., 2009; Mesmer-Magnus & DeChurch, 2009). Therefore, it should be expected that information exchange within multiple-team situations would influence their effectiveness as well. Nevertheless, just as information hoarding and strategic information (non)sharing can hamper the effectiveness of teams (Wittenbaum, Hollingshead, & Botero, 2004), similar problems can occur for multiple teams working in concert.

One way that information exchange in teams has been conceptualized is in terms of a transactive memory system (Ellis et al., 2008; Hollingshead, 2001; Moreland, 1999; Wegner, 1987, 1995) or transactive knowledge system (Austin, 2003; Brauner & Becker, 2006). We prefer the term *knowledge system* because cognitive processes in addition to memory are applied in teams that face cognitive tasks (e.g., inference, evaluation, and judgment; Wallace & Hinsz, 2010). A transactive knowledge system within a team reflects the way information is encoded, remembered, retrieved, and utilized for a cognitive task (Hinsz et al., 1997; Hollingshead, 2001; Wegner, 1987). Like much of team interaction, the information exchange in a transactive knowledge system requires and builds upon interdependence of the members.

A transactive knowledge system involves a number of mechanisms that contribute to efficient and effective information exchange (DeChurch & Mesmer-Magnus, 2010). In some regards, the transactive knowledge system reflects a division of mental labor in a team such that the members collectively have all the knowledge necessary to meet the challenges of the cognitive task. One mechanism is *specialization*, which reflects individual members of the team having responsibility for remembering or knowing specific information needed for the cognitive task. For example, the driver of the emergency medical dispatch knows where the medical facilities are located and the most efficient route to them under different traffic conditions. Similarly, the ambulance crews include people who know how to assess various medical conditions and their significance within the context of what might be a life-threatening emergency. Consequently, the team is made up of members having specialized memory and knowledge, and they interact together to solve the problem or achieve some resolution to the cognitive task they face.

The specialization of knowledge can be compared to teams in which the knowledge is integrated. That is, all members have common knowledge, and it is integrated into the members' understanding of the situation. We could see that it might be effective for specific task information to be specifically allocated to a particular team member (e.g., the ambulance driver knows where the entrance to a medical facility will be). However, we might also hope that all members of the ambulance crew know that the driver retains this specialized knowledge. For a transactive knowledge system to be effective, the responsibility for knowing specific knowledge needs to be allocated to a particular member, and that member has to take that responsibility for knowing that information. But also, the other team members need to know where the knowledge is located in the team and to have accurate information about who retains that knowledge.

Another mechanism implicated by a transactive knowledge system is coordination in the way the desired knowledge is accessed and retrieved. For effective coordination, team members have to share the understanding of who knows what, and how they can get that knowledge when they need it. So, the knowledge needs to be divided among members, the members need to know of this knowledge allocation, the members must share an integrated view of the distribution of the knowledge, and the members need to be able to access or retrieve this information from the appropriate team member when it is needed. So, a transactive knowledge system involves the specialization, distribution, allocation, and coordination of information exchange within a team.

Important efficiencies can be derived from an appropriately structured transactive knowledge system in teams (Austin, 2003; Hollingshead, 2001; Moreland, 1999). However, there is some evidence that these achievements in efficiencies are not robust (Moreland, 2005) and that they may be limited to specific circumstances (Wallace & Hinsz, 2010). Moreover, an improperly structured transactive knowledge system can bring about inefficiencies and poor cognitive task performance. Research on tacit and implicit coordination has uncovered similar inefficiencies (Rico, Sánchez-Manzanares, Gil, & Gibson, 2008; Wittenbaum, Stasser, & Merry, 1996). Somewhat like a faulty shared task representation, a problem may arise when team members assume agreement but in reality don't share the same representation about how knowledge will be distributed in the team. If individuals inappropriately believe other teammates will have the specific knowledge or assume teammates will take responsibility for aspects of the cognitive task, then conflicting expectations and ineffectiveness may result.

Conflicts may arise whenever teammates do not meet one another's expectations. Unshared distribution or specialization rules can result in unmet expectations that lead to ineffective performance and conflict within the team. For example, emergency medical dispatch teams responding to an emergency might determine that a patient has a special problem that requires transport to a medical facility, implying a facility specializing in a specific disorder. In contrast, the ambulance driver may take this statement to mean that the condition is serious, and transports the patient to the nearest medical facility, which is not one with specialized expertise.

Multiple teams working in concert can also be considered as transactive knowledge systems. However, for multiple-team situations, each team might be considered to have specialized information that is effectively distributed and allocated among a set of teams. In a team-of-teams that is working in a specific divisional structure, one team might focus on one type of knowledge and the other teams would be responsible for other knowledge. For example, emergency medical dispatch teams in London are responsible for knowing about and responding to medical emergencies in different sectors of the city. By focusing the resources of each team on specific sectors of the city, knowledge about the most appropriate routes to victims and hospitals may develop more quickly.

There is more resemblance between multiple teams in transactive knowledge systems and multiteam systems than for a team-of-teams. In a multiteam system, such as a combined operations center (Marks, Mathieu, & Zaccaro, 2004), a transactive knowledge system could arise such that different teams serve different functions and, as such, have a different distribution of specialized knowledge. In this case, information is located within teams rather than held by team members. Consequently, teams and their members rely on the particular team to get the information that might be necessary to resolve the problem. Beyond this knowledge distribution, a multiteam system also allocates functions to and anticipates actions of other teams in the system. In this way, a multiteam system is more general and extensive than a multiple-team transactive knowledge system. However, a number of similarities remain. Division of labor is central to both a transactive knowledge system and a multiteam system. In both multiteam and transactive knowledge systems, specification, allocation, and taking responsibility for actions or knowledge are involved. Therefore, a multiple-team transactive knowledge system would be a special case of a multiteam system that focuses on task knowledge rather than particular functions that each team would pursue. However, unlike a single team, a multiple-team transactive knowledge system provides unique opportunities for conflict among the teams involved.

Because of the inherent nature of distrust, hostility, and ingroup favoritism among multiple teams working in concert, the exchange of information as part of a multiple-team transactive knowledge system may be hindered. Moreover, because information may be seen as a resource to be hoarded or for which one may restrict access (i.e., information as power; Wallace & Hinsz, 2010), teams may not easily exchange information with other teams (e.g., animosity between police and firefighters). There may be strategic (un)sharing of information among these multiple teams, just as there may be with interacting individuals (Toma & Butera,

2009; Wittenbaum et al., 2004). The analysis in this chapter suggests that conflict among parties may be more likely for multiple-team situations compared to intrateam situations having a transactive knowledge system.

Case studies of multiple-team situations are replete with stories of situations in which information needed by one team is not forthcoming from another team in a multiteam system (e.g., Kean et al., 2004). One often hears that police and firefighters do not share information. Military forces also claim that one force (e.g., the Marines) does not share important information with another force (e.g., the Army) in multiple-force operations. One of the prompts for research on multiteam systems was to overcome these apparent inefficiencies in information exchange. Our analysis suggests that such information hoarding and failure to share critical information may be inherent to multiteam systems. One issue that is yet to be more fully explored is how to overcome the problems of information exchange among multiple teams working in concert.

In the preceding discussion, ways in which information exchange may act as a source of conflict in multiple-team situations (e.g., hoarding information) were identified. The information exchange advantages that multiple teams working in concert have over single teams were also considered and illustrated with regard to transactive knowledge systems. In many ways, remedies for information exchange conflict may be similar to those outlined above for intergroup conflict and shared representations. For example, if conflict results from team efforts to hoard information, it may be beneficial to emphasize the common identity and superordinate goals shared among the multiple teams. If conflict results from the application of an improper transactive knowledge system, then clear specification about which teams are expected to do what, how, and where may be helpful. An important leadership function may be to insure that the multiple-team transactive knowledge system is effectively organized.

Training of multiple teams to work in concert may be one of the best ways to reduce conflict from information exchange. Just as team training is expected to enhance the coordination of interactions within a team (Salas et al., 2008), training of multiple teams to coordinate and interact effectively should enhance how multiple teams work in concert. One feature of this training may include using individual team members to bridge the gaps between teams that need to work together. Specific individuals may be identified to serve as linking pins (Likert, 1967) or boundary spanners (Ancona & Caldwell, 1992) and function to enhance the information exchange between teams and facilitate their communication. That is, to overcome conflict related to information exchange, it may be necessary to structure multiple-team situations so that some individuals are members of multiple teams and provide these individuals with specific training so that they function as conduits for exchanging critical information among the teams. In this fashion, the potential benefits of multiple teams working in concert may be achieved by reducing the conflicts of multiple-team situations.

There are numerous research questions that need to be addressed to gain a better understanding of how information exchange would influence conflict in multiple-team situations. One, noted above, concerns how transactive knowledge systems might differ for single-team and multiple-team situations. Given the ways in which outgroup hostility, ingroup favoritism, and distrust emerge in multiple-team situations, it was proposed that teams might be more likely to inhibit the exchange of information and hoard critical information. As a consequence, if a transactive knowledge system was imposed on a multiple-team situation, deleterious consequences might result. Although transactive knowledge systems have been found to enhance information processing and performance in single teams (DeChurch & Mesmer-Magnus, 2010), the opposite might be likely to arise because of the potentially negative nature of intergroup relations. An empirical test of this speculation with single-team and multiple-team situations is necessary to determine if effective information exchange suffers from the conflict that can arise in multiple-team situations.

Conflict From Divergent Decision Preferences

Research on decision making in teams also demonstrates how conflict might arise for multiple teams working in concert. Team decision making involves a number of processes involved in getting a team to resolve the divergent preferences among its members (Guzzo, Salas, & Associates, 1995). These processes include information and normative social influence, among many others (Hinsz, 1999; Stasser, Kerr, & Davis, 1989). The purpose of most team decisions is to arrive at a consensus position as a result of the team members discussing the issue and bringing to bear their individual preferences, which often differ from those of other team members. Consequently, when teams come together to make a decision, the members may already be arrayed in factions, have clearly demarcated majority and minority positions, and appreciate the conflict that arises from the team members endorsing divergent preferences.

Divergent decision preferences could also result in conflict for multiple-team situations. When a team embraces a particular position regarding an issue, by the nature of the agreement within the team, the team members might feel that their team is correct in its judgment (Janis, 1982). The members might believe that because they all agree, members of other teams will also agree with them (e.g., false consensus effect; Ross, Greene, & House, 1977). In reality, however, members of different teams are likely to have differing experiences and knowledge, so they are likely to hold somewhat different positions on issues that might be relevant to the teams and their interaction. Consequently, not only will there be divergent preferences, but also members will likely believe that other teams are in agreement with them. These false expectations of agreement could result in animosity and conflict among teams in a multiple-team situation.

Another feature of multiple-team situations is that hierarchical decision making may hide and misrepresent the underlying preference distribution of the team members in the hierarchy. That is, in hierarchical decision making involving teams (Ilgen, Major, Hollenbeck, & Sego, 1995), the single decision that is made at the top of the hierarchy may not represent the opinions of the team members in the lower echelon of the hierarchy (Ono, Tindale, Hulin, & Davis, 1988). Let us illustrate how this might arise with a decision to launch a space shuttle by the teams at the NASA Space Center. Although we are not representing their actual decision-making process (Gehman et al., 2003; Rogers et al., 1986), these teams would be examples of multiple teams working in concert.

The decision to launch the space shuttle reflects the input of many teams having different functions, expertise, and knowledge (NASA, 1995). Let us assume that there are five teams of five members each that make up the decision-making hierarchy. Each team makes a decision to approve a specific launch time and date or rejects that launch. A representative from each team then meets with representatives from the other four teams, and they make a recommendation to launch. This recommendation then is forwarded to the launch commander, who makes the ultimate decision to launch the space shuttle at the specified time and date. Let us assume that the preferences of the members of one team (medical) are 4–1 in favor of launching. A second team (atmospherics and meteorology) has a preference distribution of 0–5 and opposes the launch. A third team (rocket engines) favors launch with a simple majority of member preferences (3–2). The fourth team (telemetry) recommends launch, also with a simple majority (3–2). The fifth team (ground support) opposes launch with a 1–4 preference distribution. The teams each apply a majority rule to determine their recommendation. Consequently, three teams recommend launch, and two oppose launch. If the representatives from the five teams then meet and forward a recommendation based on a majority rule, the recommendation to the launch commander from the five teams would be to launch. However, that recommendation would belie the underlying member preference distribution of 11 in favor of launching and 14 opposing launch. In this example, a hierarchical decision structure that may exist in multiple-team situations (e.g., Ilgen et al., 1995) could conceal the preference distribution of the set of team members and produce a response that was opposed by more than a majority of the members of the multiple teams.

This illustration shows just one of the ways that preference factions in teams may be arranged such that the system response does not represent the team member preferences. In these cases, team members may not perceive the multiple-team decision process to be fair. Conflict may be likely because the decision outcome is perceived as biased. Moreover, even if the teams accept a majority rule as a consensus procedure, members of the minority faction may still feel slighted because the weight of their position was not fully considered. Again, factions are likely in multiple-team situations, and with these factions there will be preferences that are supported by the system and preferences that are not adopted by the system decisions. These factions will clearly be in conflict, showing just one of the many ways in which conflict can arise from divergent decision preferences among multiple teams working in concert.

The preceding discussion shows that conflict may be native to the processes involved in decision making by multiple teams. There are a number of ways of addressing this conflict from multiple-team decision making. Many of the potential remedies can be derived from recommendations for reducing groupthink (Janis, 1982). The remedies for overcoming groupthink are intended for single-team situations but should also be useful for multiple-team situations. As we have discussed roles in this chapter, one way to prevent some of the pressures and perceptions of uniform opinion would be to assign the role of a critical evaluator to each team member (cf. Postmes, Spears, & Cihangir, 2001). This changes the focus from interpersonal or intergroup conflicts to one of achieving the best decision for all involved. Another method of reducing the conflict in multiple-team decision making is to form several subgroups by taking members from the different teams and asking these unique subgroups to discuss the issue and propose a recommended course of action. By forming these decision-making subgroups, the members will come to realize that there are different decision preferences and the bases for the divergent preferences. In this fashion, each team might focus on achieving the right decision rather than representing their team's position. Consequently, the subgroups may arrive at novel solutions while overcoming the conflict that might inherently reside in the teams. These remedies for overcoming conflict from divergent decision processes are similar to many of the other remedies for the sources of conflict in that they reflect structural, behavioral, and process approaches to changing the ways that multiple teams can work in concert.

There are important effects of divergent preferences on decision making in multiple-team situations that warrant further research. One point of this discussion is that individuals or teams with a specific preference can form an identity. This identity can arise within and between different teams and result in conflict. Nevertheless, important decisions still need to be reached with multiple teams. One interesting and important question that deserves investigation is how the different sizes of teams and factions might influence how multiple teams reach a collective decision. With regard to this decision situation, preferences may be arrayed in factions with minority and majority teams having specific factions. From the research on group decision making, it is clear that faction size has an influence on which preferences are likely to dominate in the decision reached (Hinsz, 1999; Stasser et al., 1989) and the persuasion strategies that are likely to be used (Hinsz et al., 1997). Majority factions use normative influence to push for consensus based on strength in numbers. In contrast, minority factions are more likely to use informational influence in an attempt to persuade others to their position. One could speculate that this pattern of influence strategies would be replicated in multiple-team situations where teams of different sizes favoring different positions attempt to resolve their divergent preferences to reach a collective decision. Alternatively, if the different identities of the teams lead the team members to distrust others and anticipate conflict, then the teams may not use informational influence to persuade. For example, teams may perceive other teams as unwilling to listen to information-based arguments. In such cases, teams may use normative or political (e.g., procedural maneuvers) strategies to gain the desired collective decision. The effects of faction size in multiple-team situations illustrate just one of the research questions that might be addressed in future research relating to conflict arising from divergent preferences.

CROSS-LEVEL EFFECTS AND CONFLICT WITH TEAMS

The previous descriptions of potential conflicts that can arise for multiple-team situations highlight a number of patterns of relationships. One of the most striking aspects of the descriptions was that the pattern of an effect at one level (within a team) seemed not to arise at another, higher level (between teams). The differences between processes and mechanisms at two or more levels are considered cross-level effects (Chan, 1998). Most often, cross-level effects have focused on individual versus team or individual versus organizational effects (Klein & Kozlowski, 2000). In this chapter, cross-level effects have been noted for single-team versus multiple-team situations. A number of phenomena reflecting these cross-level effects were considered in the preceding analysis of conflict in multiple-team situations.

Cross-level effects reflect patterns of phenomena or responses at two or more levels of analysis (Hitt, Beamish, Jackson, & Mathieu, 2007; Klein & Kozlowski, 2000). The development of multilevel modeling techniques has facilitated the understanding of cross-level effects (Raudenbush & Bryk, 2002). The study of behavior and processes in teams and organizations has been greatly influenced by advances in multilevel modeling. Moreover, this research has also led to the elucidation of cross-level effects as well as new theoretical approaches (Hitt et al., 2007; Klein & Kozlowski, 2000). For our purposes, it is of interest to understand the different patterns of cross-level effects. In this regard, we discuss patterns of homology, asymmetry, and discontinuity.

Although multilevel approaches have generally reflected on differences between levels, research and theorizing have also focused on patterns of responding that are similar across levels. That is, homology (Chen, Bliese, & Mathieu, 2005; Kozlowski & Ilgen, 2006) and parallelism (Chen & Kanfer, 2006) arise for phenomena across levels (Hinsz et al., 2009). For multiple teams working in concert, this implies that response patterns observed within teams would also be observed in multiple-team situations. There is often a strong similarity between the responses at two levels. Conceptually, it can be argued that similarities in patterns of responding across levels should be the default assumption (e.g., Kerr, Niedermeier, & Kaplan, 2000). Yet, this is a default assumption that needs to be verified for the cross-level comparisons. For this reason, it is frequently necessary to collect data at both levels to discern whether there are similarities or differences between the levels.

In cross-level comparisons, the general approach is to assume that the pattern observed in the lower level would be found at the higher level. The individual–group comparison tradition (Davis, 1969) exemplifies this type of research by using the lower level as a baseline for comparison with the higher level. (For an example of cross-level comparisons with individual and group decision making, see Hinsz, 1999.) Because of the frequent similarities observed between levels, it is easy to accept a false assumption that research on multiple-team situations is not necessary because we understand how teams respond, and multiple teams would respond in the same way. However, if the same reductionism was applied to teams, the argument would be made that there is no need to investigate teams because of the research conducted on individuals. Extensive research on groups and teams demonstrates that this is a fallacy (Ilgen, Hollenbeck, Johnson, & Jundt, 2005; Kerr & Tindale, 2004). Consequently, in spite of the homologies of response patterns observed within and between teams, much research has focused on cross-level differences.

One type of difference in the pattern of responding observed for cross-level effects is the asymmetries that are found. As an example of a cross-level asymmetry, individuals are likely to have less impact on team responses than the team would have on its members (Chen & Kanfer, 2006). This asymmetrical pattern is consistent with longstanding research showing that norms have more influence on team members than team members have on the norms (Hackman, 1992). Yet, asymmetries of the opposite sort show that individuals can have more influence on the teams than the teams have on individuals.

Research often considers levers that can be introduced among team members to influence the response patterns of the team as a whole (Kozlowski & Ilgen, 2006). To achieve other types of changes, it may be necessary to intervene at the higher level of the organization to influence how multiple teams interact. The research on structural contingencies described in this chapter showed that asymmetries exist in the way teams can take on different response patterns as a function of structures put in place. Based on these asymmetrical patterns of responses, it will be of interest to further explore the asymmetries in patterns of responses within and between teams that are imbedded in multiple-team situations.

The most striking form of differences in the patterns in responding across levels is that of a discontinuity. This pattern has been referred to repeatedly in our consideration of conflict in multiple-team situations. A discontinuity occurs when the pattern at one level is distinct from, and not likely to be predicted by, an examination of the pattern of responding at another level. The interindividual–intergroup discontinuity is a good example of this discontinuity. The pattern of responding at the individual level (cooperation) is distinct from that of the team level (competition). The difference between the underlying distribution of decision preferences and an eventual hierarchical decision illustrates another discontinuity because different alternatives are chosen from an examination of majority decision processes across levels. We also speculate that conflict will emerge for a transactive knowledge system between teams that might not exist within a team.

These various discontinuity patterns of responding raise perplexing issues for theoretical efforts on multiple-team situations because they are difficult to predict from underlying patterns. That is, theories of multilevel effects in teams need to propose that unique processes exist at different levels. Consequently, the theories also have to explain how different mechanisms and processes emerge at one level, and others disappear at a different level. Such explanations require sophisticated understanding of team phenomena at different levels as well as how they do and do not arise. These efforts of multilevel theorizing will require conceptualizations of teams that differ dramatically from past conceptualizations. However, it is the discontinuities—and, to a lesser extent, the asymmetries in patterns of responding—that capture our attention because of the novel phenomena they reveal about multiple teams working in concert.

It is cross-level effects that often lead researchers to investigate teams and multiple-team situations. Researchers hope that homologies exist such that theories of teams can be applied to multiple-team situations.

However, in contrast to theoretical efforts, research often uncovers asymmetries and discontinuities in patterns of responding across levels. These differences in patterns of responding challenge theories of multiple-team situations that are based on homologies with theories of team process and effectiveness. It is these asymmetries, discontinuities, and homologies in patterns of responding across levels that require the development and adaptation of theories to account for the phenomena that are observed in multiple-team situations. Regardless of whether a similarity or difference in the pattern of responding across levels is observed, our understanding of multiple-team situations benefits.

SUMMARY

The objective of this chapter is to consider the ways in which conflict may result from, and influence the activities of, multiple-team situations. Conflict can occur between and within teams when the parties perceive differences with regard to things important to them such as beliefs and resources (cf. De Dreu & Gelfand, 2008). Conflict in these multiple-team situations can reflect cognitive, emotional, or behavioral differences for teams and team members. We describe multiple teams working in concert to include both multiteam systems and teams-of-teams. These multiple-team situations have similarities in tasks, goals, and interdependencies but also have important differences in functions. Similar to other chapters in this volume, we note that coordination and interdependence are two of the consistent yet unique processes that emerge in multiple-team situations. Cross-level effects also arise as an issue when teams embedded in multiple-team situations are considered.

This chapter discussed six sources of conflict that can arise for multiple-team situations. These six do not include all sources of conflict that can emerge for multiple-team situations, but rather a sample representing features of conflict. We also describe possible remedies for addressing the conflict, but not all potential remedies are considered. Rather, the discussion of conflict and potential remedies is meant to be illustrative of the nature of conflict in multiple-team situations. It is important to note that our discussion of conflict in multiple-team situations is only loosely based on empirical evidence. Much of our discussion is speculative and derives from analysis and generalizations from existing research on teams and groups. As such, we offer more hypotheses than claims about how conflict would arise in multiple-team situations.

Identifying and addressing conflict in multiple-team situations are important because conflict may reduce the ability of teams to work together and accomplish important goals. In the complex and dynamic task environments that organizations face, this conflict may hinder teams in contributing to the organization reaching critical goals. Consequently, it is important for researchers to continue the investigation of conflict in multiple-team situations. Clearly, research should seek to identify sources of conflict in multiple-team situations beyond those that we have described. Future research should also examine additional strategies for reducing conflict in multiple-team situations. We have identified several common and unique strategies for addressing various sources of conflict in multiple-team situations (e.g., training, and emphasizing superordinate goals). Future investigation into the identification of strategies for reducing conflict in multiple-team situations may lead to desirable performance outcomes for multiple teams working in concert. We encourage researchers to conduct empirical investigations of strategies that may reduce the types of conflict described as well as for other potential sources of conflict.

One of the major claims implied by our analysis is that multiple-team situations are likely to arouse more conflict than teams that act alone. Consequently, when multiple teams are working in concert, they may perceive themselves as being in conflict. Based on research on intergroup relations and other sources of conflict, it appears that conflict is inherently more likely between team interactions than within them. This difference is an example of a cross-level effect in patterns of responding between and within teams. We suggest that three types of cross-level effects can be found for similarities and differences between and within teams: homologies, asymmetries, and discontinuities. These different patterns of responding demonstrate that at this time, research provides few clear expectations for how team behavior may differ from that of the actions of multiple teams working in concert. Consequently, there is much fruitful ground for future investigation, speculation, and analysis about how teams and team members are influenced by, and contribute to, multiple teams working in concert.

ACKNOWLEDGMENT

Preparation of this chapter was supported by a grant from the National Science Foundation (BCS 0721796).

REFERENCES

Amir, Y. (1969). Contact hypothesis in ethnic relations. *Psychological Bulletin, 71,* 319–341.

Ancona, D. G., & Caldwell, D. F. (1992). Bridging the boundary: External activity and performance in organizational teams. *Administrative Science Quarterly, 37,* 634–665.

Arrow, H., McGrath, J. E., & Berdahl, J. L. (2000). *Small groups as complex systems.* Newbury Park, CA: Sage.

Austin, J. R. (2003). Transactive memory in organizational groups: The effects of content, consensus, specialization, and accuracy on group performance. *Journal of Applied Psychology, 88,* 866–878.

Beauchamp, M. R., Bray, S. R., Eys, M. A., & Carron, A. V. (2005). Multidimensional role ambiguity and role satisfaction: A prospective examination using interdependent sport teams. *Journal of Applied Social Psychology, 35,* 2560–2576.

Brauner, E., & Becker, A. (2006). Beyond knowledge sharing: The management of transactive knowledge systems. *Knowledge and Process Management, 13,* 62–71.

Brewer, M. B. (1979). Ingroup bias in the minimal inter-group situation: A cognitive motivational analysis. *Psychological Bulletin, 86,* 307–324.

Cannon-Bowers, J. A., Salas, E., & Converse, S. A. (1993). Shared mental models in team decision making. In N. J. Castellan, Jr., (Ed.), *Individual and group decision making* (pp. 221–246). Hillsdale, NJ: Erlbaum.

Cargile, A. C., Bradac, J. J., & Cole, T. (2006). Theories of intergroup conflict: A report of lay attributions. *Journal of Language and Social Psychology, 25,* 47–63.

Chan, D. (1998). Functional relations among constructs in the same content domain at different levels of analysis: A typology of composition models. *Journal of Applied Psychology, 83,* 234–246.

Chen, G., Bliese, P. D., & Mathieu, J. E. (2005). Conceptual framework and statistical procedures for delineating and testing multilevel theories of homology. *Organizational Research Methods, 8,* 375–409.

Chen, G., & Kanfer, R. (2006). Toward a systems theory of motivated behavior in work teams. *Research in Organizational Behavior, 27,* 223–267.

Clawson, J. J., & Dernococur, K. B. (1998). *Principles of emergency medical dispatch* (2nd ed.). Salt Lake City, UT: Priority Press.

Cohen, T. R., & Insko, C. A. (2008). War and peace: Possible approaches to reducing intergroup conflict. *Perspectives on Psychological Science, 3,* 87–93.

Cronin, M. A., & Weingart, L. R. (2007). Representational gaps, information processing, and conflict in functionally diverse teams. *Academy of Management Review, 32,* 761–773.

Davis, J. H. (1969). *Group performance.* Reading, MA: Addison-Wesley.

DeChurch, L. A., & Marks, M. A. (2006). Leadership in multiteam systems. *Journal of Applied Psychology, 91,* 311–329.

DeChurch, L. A., & Mathieu, J. E. (2009). Thinking in terms of multiteam systems. In E. Salas, G. F. Goodwin, & C. S. Burke (Eds.), *Team effectiveness in complex organizations: Cross-disciplinary perspectives and approaches* (pp. 267–292). New York: Routledge.

DeChurch, L. A., & Mesmer-Magnus, J. R. (2010). The cognitive underpinnings of effective teamwork: A meta-analysis. *Journal of Applied Psychology, 95*, 32–52.

De Dreu, C. K. W., & Gelfand, M. J. (2008). Conflict in the workplace: Sources, functions, and dynamics across multiple levels of analysis. In C. K. W. De Dreu & M. J. Gelfand (Eds.), *The psychology of conflict and conflict management in organizations* (pp. 3–54). New York: Erlbaum.

De Dreu, C. K. W., & Weingart, L. R. (2003). Task versus relationship conflict, team performance, and team member satisfaction: A meta-analysis. *Journal of Applied Psychology, 88*, 741–749.

Ellis, A. P. J., Porter, C. O. L. H., & Wolverton, S. A. (2008). Learning to work together: An examination of transactive memory system development in teams. In V. I. Sessa & M. London (Eds.), *Work group learning* (pp. 91–115). New York: Erlbaum.

Emmons, R. A., & King, L. A. (1988). Conflict among personal strivings: Immediate and long-term implications for psychological and physical well-being. *Journal of Personality and Social Psychology, 54*, 1040–1048.

Endsley, M. R., & Garland, D. J. (2000). *Situation awareness: Analysis and measurement.* Mahwah, NJ: Erlbaum.

Endsley, M. R., & Jones, W. M. (2001). A model of inter- and intrateam situation awareness: Implications for design, training and measurement. In M. McNeese, E. Salas, & M. Endsley (Eds.), *New trends in cooperative activities: Understanding system dynamics in complex environments* (pp. 46–67). Santa Monica, CA: Human Factors and Ergonomics Society.

Fein, S., & Spencer, S. J. (1997). Prejudice as self-image maintenance: Affirming the self through derogating others. *Journal of Personality and Social Psychology, 73*, 31–44.

Fiol, C. M., Pratt, M. G., & O'Connor, E. J. (2009). Managing intractable identity conflicts. *Academy of Management Review, 34*, 32–55.

Furniss, D., & Blandford, A. (2006). Understanding emergency medical dispatch in terms of distributed cognition: A case study. *Ergonomics, 49*, 1174–1203.

Gaertner, S. L., & Dovidio, J. F. (2000). *Reducing intergroup bias: The common ingroup identity model.* Philadelphia, PA: Psychology Press.

Gehman, H. W. (Chair), et al. (2003). *Columbia Accident Investigation Board final report.* Retrieved from http://caib.nasa.gov

Guzzo, R. A., Salas, E., & Associates. (1995). *Team effectiveness and decision making in organizations.* San Francisco: Jossey-Bass.

Hackman, J. R. (1992). Group influences on individuals in organizations. In M. D. Dunnette & L. M. Hough (Eds.), *Handbook of industrial and organizational psychology* (Vol. 3, pp. 1455–1525). Palo Alto, CA: Consulting Psychologists Press.

Hinsz, V. B. (1995). Mental models of groups as social systems: Considerations of specification and assessment. *Small Group Research, 26*, 200–233.

Hinsz, V. B. (1999). Group decision making with responses of a quantitative nature: The theory of social decision schemes for quantities. *Organizational Behavior and Human Decision Processes, 80*, 28–49.

Hinsz, V. B. (2004). Metacognition and mental models in groups: An illustration with metamemory of group recognition memory. In E. Salas & S. M. Fiore (Eds.), *Team cognition: Understanding the factors that drive process and performance* (pp. 33–58). Washington, DC: American Psychological Association.

Hinsz, V. B., Tindale, R. S., & Vollrath, D. A. (1997). The emerging conceptualization of groups as information processors. *Psychological Bulletin, 121*, 43–64.

Hinsz, V. B., Wallace, D. M., & Ladbury, J. L. (2009). Team performance in dynamic task environments. In G. P. Hodgkinson & J. K. Ford (Eds.), *International review of industrial and organizational psychology* (Vol. 24, pp. 183–216). New York: Wiley.

Hitt, M. A., Beamish, P. W., Jackson, S. E., & Mathieu, J. E. (2007). Building theoretical and empirical bridges across levels: Multilevel research in management. *Academy of Management Journal, 50*, 1385–1399.

Hogg, M. A., & Abrams, D. (2003). Intergroup behavior and social identity. In M. A. Hogg & J. Cooper (Eds.), *Sage handbook of social psychology* (pp. 407–431). Thousand Oaks, CA: Sage.

Hogg, M. A., & Terry, D. J. (2000). Social identity and self-categorization processes in organizational contexts. *Academy of Management Review, 25*, 121–140.

Hogg, M. A., & Terry, D. J. (2001). *Social identity processes in organizational contexts.* New York: Psychology Press.

Hollenbeck, J. R., Moon, H., Ellis, A. P. J., West, B. J., Ilgen, D. R., Sheppard, L., et al. (2002). Structural contingency theory and individual differences: Examination of external and internal person-fit. *Journal of Applied Psychology, 87*, 599–606.

Hollingshead, A. B. (2001). Cognitive interdependence and convergent expectations in transactive memory. *Journal of Personality and Social Psychology, 81*, 1080–1089.

Humphrey, S. E., Morgeson, F. P., & Mannor, M. J. (2009). Developing a theory of the strategic core of teams: A role composition model of team performance. *Journal of Applied Psychology, 94*, 48–61.

Ilgen, D. R., Hollenbeck, J. R., Johnson, M., & Jundt, D. (2005). Teams in organizations: From input-process-output models to IMOI models. *Annual Review of Psychology, 56*, 517–543.

Ilgen, D. R., Major, D. A., Hollenbeck, J. R., & Sego, D. J. (1995). Decision making in teams: Raising an individual decision making model to the team level. In R. A. Guzzo & E. Salas (Eds.), *Team effectiveness and decision making in organizations* (pp. 113–148). San Francisco: Jossey-Bass.

Jackson, S. E., & Schuler, R. S. (1985). A meta-analysis and conceptual critique of research on role ambiguity and role conflict in work settings. *Organizational Behavior and Human Decision Processes, 36*, 16–78.

Janis, I. L. (1982). *Groupthink* (2nd ed.). Boston: Houghton Mifflin.

Johnson, M. D., Hollenbeck, J. R., Ilgen, D. R., Humphrey, S. E., Meyer, C. J., & Jundt, D. K. (2006). Cutthroat cooperation: Asymmetrical adaptation of team reward structures. *Academy of Management Journal, 49*, 103–120.

Kean, T. H. (Chair), et al. (2004). *The 9/11 Commission report.* Downloaded from http://govinfo.library.unt.edu/911/report/index.htm

Kerr, N. L., Niedermeier, K. E., & Kaplan, M. F. (2000). On the virtues of assuming minimal information processing in individuals and groups. *Group Processes and Intergroup Relations, 3*, 203–217.

Kerr, N., & Tindale, R. S. (2004). Group performance and decision making. *Annual Review of Psychology, 55*, 623–655.

Klein, K. J., & Kozlowski, S. W. J. (2000). *Multilevel theory, research, and methods in organizations: Foundations, extensions, and new directions.* San Francisco: Jossey-Bass.

Kozlowski, S. W. J., & Ilgen, D. R. (2006). Enhancing the effectiveness of work groups and teams. *Psychological Science in the Public Interest, 7,* 77–124.

Letsky, M. P., Warner, N. W., Fiore, S. M., & Smith, C. A. P. (2008). *Macrocognition in teams: Theories and methodologies.* Hampshire, UK: Ashgate.

Likert, R. (1967). *The human organization: Its management and value.* New York: McGraw-Hill.

Marks, M. A., DeChurch, L. A., Mathieu, J. E., Panzer, F. J., & Alonso, A. (2005). Teamwork in multiteam systems. *Journal of Applied Psychology, 90,* 964–971.

Marks, M. A., Mathieu, J. E., & Zaccaro, S. J. (2004). Using scaled worlds to study multiteam systems. In S. G. Schiflett, L. R. Elliott, E. Salas, & M. D. Coovert (Eds.), *Scaled worlds: Development, validation, and applications* (pp. 279–296). Hampshire, UK: Ashgate.

Mathieu, J. E., Marks, M. A., & Zaccaro, S. J. (2002). Multiteam systems. In N. Anderson, D. S. Ones, H. K. Sinagil, & C. Viswesvaran (Eds.), *Handbook of industrial, work, and organizational psychology: Vol. 2. Organizational psychology* (pp. 289–313). Thousand Oaks, CA: Sage.

Meier, B. P., & Hinsz, V. B. (2004). A comparison of human aggression committed by groups and individuals: An interindividual-intergroup discontinuity. *Journal of Experimental Social Psychology, 40,* 551–559.

Mesmer-Magnus, J. R., & DeChurch, L. A. (2009). Information sharing and team performance: A meta-analysis. *Journal of Applied Psychology, 94,* 535–546.

Moon, H., Hollenbeck, J. R., Humphrey, S. E., Ilgen, D. R., West, B., Ellis, A. P. J., et al. (2004). Asymmetric adaptability: Dynamic team structures as one-way streets. *Academy of Management Journal, 47,* 681–695.

Moreland, R. L. (1999). Transactive memory: Learning who knows what in work groups and organizations. In L. Thompson, J. Levine, & D. Messick (Eds.), *Shared cognition in organizations: The management of knowledge* (pp. 3–31). Mahwah, NJ: Erlbaum.

Moreland, R. L. (2005). The strategic use of transactive memory systems in groups. In E. S. Park, T. Reimer, & V. B. Hinsz (Orgs.), *Symposium: Strategies of information processing in groups.* Paper presented at the annual meeting of the Midwestern Psychological Association, Chicago.

Morgan, P. M., & Tindale, R. S. (2002). Group vs. individual performance in mixed motive situations: Exploring an inconsistency. *Organizational Behavior and Human Decision Processes, 87,* 44–65.

NASA. (1995). The Space Shuttle launch team. Retrieved from http://science.ksc.nasa.gov/shuttle/countdown/launch-team.html

Ono, K., Tindale, R. S., Hulin, C. L., & Davis J. H. (1988). Intuition vs. deduction: Some thought experiments concerning Likert's linking-pin theory of organization. *Organizational Behavior and Human Decision Processes, 42,* 135–154.

Park, E. S., Hinsz, V. B., & Ladbury, J. L. (2006). A theoretical perspective on enhancing coordination and collaboration in remotely operated vehicle (ROV) teams. In N. J. Cooke, H. Pringle, H. Pederson, & O. Connor (Eds.), *Human factors of remotely operated vehicles* (pp. 301–312). North Holland: Elsevier.

Pinter, B., & Insko, C. A. (2003). *Implicit distrust in the absence of context: Generality of the negative outgroup schema.* Unpublished manuscript, University of Washington.

Postmes, T., Spears, R., & Cihangir, S. (2001). Quality of decision making and group norms. *Journal of Personality and Social Psychology, 80,* 918–930.

Raudenbush, S. W., & Bryk, A. S. (2002). *Hierarchical linear models: Applications and data analysis methods* (2nd ed.). Thousand Oaks, CA: Sage.

Rico, R., Sanchez-Manzanares, M., Gil, F., & Gibson, C. (2008). Team implicit coordination processes: A team knowledge-based approach. *Academy of Management Review, 33,* 163–184.

Rogers, W. P. (Chair), et al. (1986). *Report of the Presidential Commission on the Space Shuttle Challenger Accident.* Retrieved from http://science.ksc.nasa.gov/shuttle/missions/51-l/docs/rogers-commission/table-of-contents.html

Ross, L., Greene, D., & House, P. (1977). The false consensus effect: An egocentric bias in social perception and attribution processes. *Journal of Experimental Social Psychology, 13,* 279–301.

Salas, E., DiazGranados, D., Klein, C., Burke, C. S., Stagl, K. C., Goodwin, G. F., et al. (2008). Does team training improve team performance? A meta-analysis. *Human Factors, 50,* 903–933.

Spector, P. E., & Bruk-Lee, V. (2008). Conflict, health, and well-being. In C. K. W. De Dreu & M. J. Gelfand (Eds.), *The psychology of conflict and conflict management in organizations* (pp. 267–288). New York: Erlbaum.

Stasser, G., Kerr, N. L., & Davis, J. H. (1989). Influence processes and consensus models in decision-making groups. In P. Paulus (Ed.), *Psychology of group influence* (2nd ed., pp. 279–326). Hillsdale, NJ: Erlbaum.

Surowiecki, J. (2005). *The wisdom of crowds.* New York: Anchor.

Tajfel, H., & Turner, J. C. (1986). The social identity theory of inter-group behavior. In S. Worchel & W. G. Austin (Eds.), *Psychology of intergroup relations* (2nd ed., pp. 7–24). Chicago: Nelson-Hall.

Tindale, R. S., Smith, C. M., Thomas, L. S., Filkins, J., & Sheffey, S. (1996). Shared representations and asymmetric social influence processes in small groups. In E. Witte & J. H. Davis (Eds.), *Understanding group behavior: Consensual action by small groups* (pp. 81–103). Mahwah, NJ: Erlbaum.

Toma, C., & Butera, F. (2009). Hidden profiles and concealed information: Strategic information sharing and use in group decision making. *Personality and Social Psychology Bulletin, 35,* 793–806.

Wallace, D. M., & Hinsz, V. B. (2010). Teams as technology: Applying theory and research to model macrocognition processes in teams. *Theoretical Issues in Ergonomic Science, 11,* 359–374.

Wegner, D. M. (1987). Transactive memory: A contemporary analysis of the group mind. In B. Mullen & G. R. Goethals (Eds.), *Theories of group behavior* (pp. 185–208). New York: Springer-Verlag.

Wegner, D. M. (1995). A computer network model of human transactive memory. *Social Cognition, 13,* 319–339.

Wildschut, T., Pinter, B., Vevea, J. L., Insko, C. A., & Schopler, J. (2003). Beyond the group mind: A quantitative review of the interindividual-intergroup discontinuity effect. *Psychological Bulletin, 129,* 698–722.

Wiltermuth, S. S., & Heath, C. (2009). Synchrony and cooperation. *Psychological Science, 20,* 1–5.

Wittenbaum, G. M., Hollingshead, A. B., & Botero, I. (2004). From cooperative to motivated information sharing in groups: Going beyond the hidden profile paradigm. *Communication Monographs, 71,* 286–310.

Wittenbaum, G. M., Stasser, G., & Merry, C. J. (1996). Tacit coordination in anticipation of small group task completion. *Journal of Experimental Social Psychology*, *32*, 129–152.

Worschel, S., & Austin, W. G. (1986). *The psychology of intergroup relations* (2nd ed.). Chicago: Nelson-Hall.

12

Boundary Spanning in the Domain of Multiteam Systems

Robert B. Davison
Michigan State University

John R. Hollenbeck
Michigan State University

Mathieu, Marks, and Zaccaro (2001) were among the first to identify that although the environment external to the team has been featured in several theoretical frameworks (Gladstein, 1984; Hackman & Morris, 1975; Tannenbaum, Beard, & Salas, 1992), little is actually known about the influence of teams on other teams (i.e., how teams interact as a distinct activity system in the coordinated performance of tasks aimed at achieving a set of common outcomes). Their groundbreaking work, appearing in the *Handbook of Industrial, Work, and Organizational Psychology,* Volume 2, established the theoretical underpinnings of multiteam systems research and serves as the foundation for a growing body of empirical work. As described by the authors, "To date, no conceptualization has addressed a configuration of tightly coupled teams, contained either within a single organization or across organizations, working interdependently as a unique entity towards a single superordinate goal" (Mathieu et al., 2001, p. 293). We add a further caveat to this statement: To date, no conceptualization has holistically addressed boundary spanning in the specific domain of multiteam systems (MTSs). Thus, the objective of this chapter is to do just that.

Boundary spanning is a concept that encompasses a wide variety of activities, located at the interface between organizational units both within and across formal (e.g., legal) boundaries, from simple information exchange to complex and real-time behavior integration and coordination. As pointed out by Faraj and Yan (2009),

> Research on team boundaries falls into two major traditions. One group of researchers takes an external perspective, viewing teams through an open systems lens and focusing on issues of demarcation with environment and system frontiers (e.g., Scott, 1998). A second group of researchers adopts a teamwork perspective based on small group research, emphasizing the importance of processes for team effectiveness (e.g., Marks, Mathieu, & Zaccaro, 2001). (P. 605)

Our read of the extant literature leads us to the conclusion that although it may appear that these two traditions have approached research on team boundaries from distinctly different points of view, in fact, they collectively form a naturally holistic perspective firmly rooted in an open systems perspective. This is especially true when one considers that *process*, as defined by Marks and colleagues, encompasses interdependent team activities that serve the purpose of integrating task work. What is missing from the literature, then, is a framework that illuminates this holistic perspective. Thus, a key goal of this chapter is to offer a framework informed by the open systems perspective from organizational theory (e.g., Thompson, 1967).

To accomplish this goal, we discuss the boundary-spanning construct as conceptualized in the organizational sciences literature, and present an overarching conceptual framework aimed at providing the reader with an all-encompassing, bird's-eye view of the boundary-spanning landscape that is both helpful and informative when thinking about boundary-spanning activities and roles. Leading up to the presentation of our framework is a discussion of three key attributes—the type of boundary being spanned, the purpose or function served by a particular boundary-spanning activity, and the degree to which the units on the two sides of the boundary are coupled (i.e., degree of task interdependence). These attributes serve as the underpinnings of the *boundary-spanning landscape framework*, defined primarily by the first two attributes (i.e., boundary type and purpose of the boundary-spanning activity), with the third acting to subcategorize the first; and the *behavioral integration framework*, a more focused look at a subsection of the first framework presented further on in this chapter. We use these two frameworks throughout to organize and direct our discussion.

The latter sections of the chapter focus on that portion of the literature most essential to an understanding of the boundary-spanning activities and roles attributable to MTSs, specifically, versus more generally to all teams and organizations. This includes an important discussion of the pivotal boundary-spanning roles that, due to the size of their membership and the complex and reciprocally interdependent nature of MTSs, fall upon the shoulders of their leaders. Although all the activities discussed in this chapter are relevant to the MTS domain, what differentiates multiteam systems most from all other organizational environments is the need for clear separation between intrateam and interteam horizontal coordination, a requirement demanded by both the size of system membership and the tight coupling inherent in the complex, real-time, and highly interdependent nature of their task environment. We will discuss these specifically in the final section of this chapter by drawing out inferences from extant research in the specific context of multiteam systems. We end with a brief discussion of levels of analysis in the domain of multiteam systems and some closing comments.

OVERVIEW OF BOUNDARY SPANNING

Our review of the extant literature has identified over 70 articles in the organizational sciences literature, spread across the last 4 decades, that pertain to the topic of boundary spanning. In addition, several of the early works in the organizational theory literature make important and foundational contributions to the topic (e.g., March & Simon, 1958; Thompson, 1967).

Boundary spanning is a construct encompassing a wide range of activities that have been conceptualized in the literature and found through empirical study to be contingent on the nature of the system's work (Tushman, 1977). The contingent and overlapping nature of these activities has made categorization a challenge, and thus the literature is replete with conceptual schemata. For example, Adams (1976) originally identified five categories of boundary-spanning activities—filtering, transacting, buffering, representing, and protecting—yet categorized them slightly differently 4 years later as the acquisition of organizational inputs, the disposal of outputs, searching for and collecting information, representing the organization to outsiders, and buffering it from external threat and pressure (Adams, 1980). More recently, Faraj and Yan (2009) conceptualized boundary work to be boundary spanning (engaging the environment), boundary buffering (disengaging from the environment), or boundary reinforcing (establishing the boundary, maintaining it, and adapting it to shifts in the environment) in nature.

Due to the broad-ranging and contingent nature of activities, it is important to be cognizant of the primary objective of the boundary-spanning activities being considered, whether they are, for example, primarily aimed at knowledge acquisition, assimilation, and transfer across communications boundaries or specifically aimed at efficacious real-time mutual adjustment between subunits in a complex organization. Although there are clearly differences across conditions, there are also many similarities. Thus the boundary-spanning literature is ripe with information pertinent, to a greater or lesser degree, to the condition of interest, which is, in our case, boundary-spanning activities specifically aimed at real-time, mutual adjustment between subunits in an MTS. Therefore, it is useful and informative to consider, at least at a cursory level, the breadth of our understanding of this topic.

From our review of the extant literature, we suggest that it is best to conceptually categorize the specific contributions that each of these articles makes to the literature, and thus to our understanding of boundary spanning, based on three key attributes: the type of boundary being spanned, the purpose or function served by a particular boundary-spanning activity, and the degree to which the units on the two sides of the boundary are coupled (i.e., the degree of task interdependence). Additionally, it is important to recognize a fourth attribute, the degree to which a particular boundary-spanning activity is universally applicable across the others, or is more localized to some subset of conditions. One edifying way to think about this fourth attribute is that it is, in essence, a reflection of the moderating effect of boundary type and degree of coupling on the purpose of the boundary-spanning activity. That is, some activities are carried out across all organizational boundaries (e.g., information flow in and out of the focal unit) and thus occur at the boundary defined by any two organizational units, whereas others are only necessarily carried out by a subset of organizational units (e.g., real-time mutual adjustment); this latter distinction is driven by the type of boundary being spanned and the degree of task interdependence. For ease of understanding, we have chosen to discuss these attributes utilizing two frameworks to organize the literature; we refer to these as the *boundary-spanning landscape framework* and the *behavioral integration framework*.

BOUNDARY-SPANNING LANDSCAPE FRAMEWORK

Figure 12.1 is a depiction of the *boundary-spanning landscape frame-work*. The two ordinates of this first framework incorporate the first three attributes previously discussed. Whereas closed system perspectives envisioned a relatively distinct boundary between the organization and its environment, the open systems perspective views organizations as interconnected with their environment through interdependencies and boundary-spanning relationships (Katz & Kahn, 1966). Scott (1998) defined this perspective as consisting of "coalitions of shifting interest groups that develop goals by negotiations; the structure of coalitions, its activities, and its outcomes are strongly influenced by environmental factors" (p. 23). The degree to which the work of two organizational units is interdependent defines the tightness of their coupling and the requisite permeability of their boundary. The boundary being spanned can be conceptualized as existing somewhere along a continuum representing the degree of coupling and the degree to which the boundary is thus, by necessity, permeable (i.e., open versus closed); the higher the degree of coupling required, the more permeable the boundary. Thus, we have further subdivided the boundary-spanned dimension in our first framework into categories loosely representing the degree of coupling (see Figure 12.1).

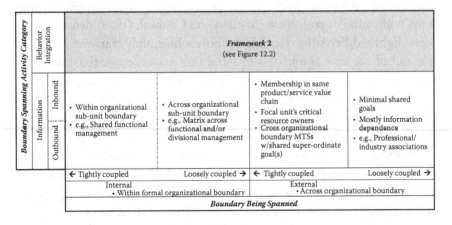

FIGURE 12.1
Boundary-spanning landscape (Framework 1).

It is useful to further subdivide the purpose and function of boundary-spanning activities into three subcategories: outbound information flow, inbound information flow, and behavioral integration. Many of the early studies concerned themselves with information boundary spanning, the import and export of information across the organizational boundaries between a focal unit and units both internal and external to the broader organization, often in support of the process of innovation (e.g., Aldrich & Herker, 1977; Coleman, Katz, & Menzel, 1966; Tushman, 1977), and the characteristics of individuals tasked with these roles (e.g., Tushman & Scanlan, 1981a, 1981b).

Outbound Information Flow

Outbound information flow refers to communications activities aimed specifically at representing the unit to outsiders, such as resource owners upon which the team is critically dependent and other external constituencies that hold power and influence over the unit, for example senior management. These activities are undertaken in an attempt to represent and identify the unit to its environment (Ahearne, Bhattacharya, & Gruen, 2005), to manage impressions of the unit, to buffer it from external threat and pressure, and to position issues and initiatives of importance to the unit (i.e., issue selling; Dutton, Ashford, O'Neill, Hayes, & Wierba, 1997). Tushman (1977) referred to individuals who perform these duties on behalf of the unit as *liaisons*, and drew a distinction between liaisons that span the boundary between tightly coupled and more loosely coupled units within the organization. Ancona and Caldwell (1988) defined these roles slightly differently, referring to those who simply transmit information out of the unit as *ambassadors* and those who censor the outflow of information as *guards*. Individuals tasked with representing the organization to its environment and with interorganizational relations (van de Ven, 1976), for example sales representatives and other output roles (Thompson, 1962), have been referred to as *agents* in the literature.

Several of the articles in our review investigated specific aspects of outbound information flow. For example, in an exploratory study based on her previous assertion (Gladstein, 1984) that members of teams conceptualize group process as two distinct sets of activities, intragroup or cross-boundary, Ancona (1990) conducted an exploratory study to investigate the strategies adopted by five newly formed internal-consulting teams when interacting with their organizational environment. She found that team leaders adopted one of three different strategies: remaining relatively isolated from their environment, pursuing high levels of passive observation, and actively engaging the environment (denoted as *informing, parading*, and *probing*, respectively). Although we believe these represent the set of strategies adopted by teams and are, therefore, informative, because the measure was reported as an analysis of team leader plans, it should be noted that it could be confounded with the previously discussed characteristics of boundary spanners (e.g., *guards* in the case of informing).

Two studies conducted by Dutton and colleagues (Dutton et al., 1997) investigated the contextual influences that act as determinants of the degree to which middle managers sell issues to top management, and the role of issue selling in the creation of strategic change initiatives. Dutton et al. found that the perceived willingness of top managers to listen, and an overall supportive culture, signaled favorable contexts for issue selling, whereas fear of negative consequences, downsizing, and general uncertainty signaled that the context was unfavorable. They also found that middle managers risked their image when they attempted to sell issues in ways that violated norms, when their relationship with executives was distant, or when the selling effort was undertaken in politically vulnerable ways.

Inbound Information Flow

Inbound information flow encompasses the set of communications activities specifically associated with informing the focal unit about the environment, both external and internal to the organization to which the unit belongs (e.g., environmental scanning and monitoring). These activities are aimed at keeping the unit abreast of new or emerging developments and trends in the marketplace and in key or related technologies (e.g., organizational learning), and in shifts or changes to the organization's strategy, goals, and objectives. Further, these activities establish and maintain the unit's boundary, thus serving to build the unit's identity, intraunit bonds, and commitment to both the unit itself and the broader organization, and act as a source of information for sense making (Weick, 1995). In his studies of research and development (R&D) organizations and innovation, Tushman (1977) referred to individuals who perform these duties on behalf of the unit as *gatekeepers*, whereas Ancona and Caldwell (1988, 1990), studying new product development teams, drew a finer distinction between such individuals, referring to those who bring information into the team as *scouts* and those who police the inbound information flow as *sentries*. Later work by Tushman and Scanlon (1981a) draws a more detailed distinction between gatekeepers that spans the boundary between tightly coupled versus more loosely coupled units within the organization.

As with outbound information flow, there were articles in our review that investigated specific aspects of inbound flows. As an example, Maitlis (2005) employed a longitudinal qualitative study of three British symphony orchestras, across 27 issue domains, to investigate the social processes of sense making among large groups of diverse organizational stakeholders. She found that high levels of sense giving by leaders led to highly controlled and systematic sense-making processes, whereas sense-making processes were less controlled when leaders exhibited lower levels of sense giving and employed fewer mechanisms to organize sense-giving activities (e.g., more public forums and fewer private meetings). In addition, when organizational stakeholders engaged in extensive sense giving, sense-making processes were characterized by an intense flow of information and were highly animated, whereas the opposite was also true. Bartel (2001) investigated how community outreach and the ensuing process of social comparison affected perceptions of organizational identity and individuals' identification with it. She found that boundary-spanning activities of this type have both attitudinal and behavioral implications. Cross, Yan, and Louis (2000) investigated the use of boundary-spanning activities, specifically spanning, buffering, and the creation and maintenance of boundaries, in an organization during and after a shift from a functional form of organizing to a more team-based structure. In a case study, these authors found that boundary-spanning activities of this sort actually increased in significance and their enactment shifted to lower levels in the organization.

Importantly, when one considers the studies associated with outbound and inbound information flow together, common, underlying themes begin to emerge. Collectively, these studies indicate that contextual factors and uncertainty are key moderators of information boundary spanning—the more task or environmental uncertainty a unit faces, the greater the need for these activities (Faraj & Yan, 2009)—and point to the central role that domain-specific knowledge plays in information boundary spanning. Boundary spanners are the "linking pin" (Organ, 1971) between the organization and its environment, and the effectiveness of the link is highly dependent on competence. Due to the interaction between idiosyncratic language and coding schemes, and the localized conceptual frameworks that exist within different organizational units, boundary spanners must be competent in both domains to effectively transfer meaning across the boundary.

Interestingly, one mechanism used by boundary spanners to effectively transfer meaning across a boundary is *boundary objects*, artifacts that "are plastic enough to adapt to local needs and constraints of the several parties employing them, yet robust enough to maintain a common identity across sites" (Star & Griesemer, 1989, p. 393). For example, business analysts typically create a specification document, stipulating both business requirements and program architecture in enough detail, to insure that software development meets the needs of the end user. Neither the business user nor the software developer is required to be fluent in the other's domain; the specification document serves as a facilitating bridge, transferring just the right amount of information across the boundary to effectively convey meaning. This concept, originating in the social studies of science literature, has been effectively employed in the information systems literature (e.g., Levina & Vaast, 2005) and others, and we suggest that it would be a useful concept to import into the organizational sciences literature.

A key implication of this discussion is that although individuals may be effective at spanning the boundary between unit A and unit B, they are not thereby de facto effective at spanning the boundary between unit A and unit C. Research has indicated that dissimilar boundary-spanning roles are often undertaken by different individuals, and that the practices of these different roles may be task or goal dependent. Evidence of this can be found in the work of Ancona (e.g., 1990), Tushman (e.g., 1977), and others. For example, in a longitudinal study of labor negotiations, Friedman and Podolny (1992) found that some individuals on the negotiating team brokered ties to bring information into their unit, others brokered ties to send information out of the unit, and others still brokered more task or socioemotional ties across the boundary. A recent study investigated the role that communications technology choice plays in efforts to collaborate and share information across organizational boundaries. This study of communications patterns of administrative and technical personnel belonging to a large telecommunications firm found that over 50% of employees' communication was across departmental boundaries, that the majority of communications was horizontal, that first-level managers were more likely to communicate across departmental lines and diagonally upward than were technical personnel, and that the majority of both lateral and cross-boundary communications still occurred by telephone (Hinds & Kiesler, 1995). Hinds and Kiesler suggested that these differential findings can be partially explained by the flatter structure of the technical groups and the nonlocal search efforts of administrators, driven by factors such as resource scarcity, and that organizations should strengthen both horizontal structures and the use of old and new technology to encourage communication flows across organizational boundaries.

Importantly for our discussion of MTSs, this research, in combination with research from several other disciplines, strongly suggests that informational boundary spanning is more than a function of formal status. Although formal position facilitates communications, perceived domain-specific competence appears to be the fundamental determinant of boundary role status and, ultimately, effectiveness (Tushman & Scanlan, 1981a). In line with these studies, we suggest that hierarchical position is a necessary but not sufficient condition for effectively spanning the boundaries within an MTS; MTS leaders must be competent in the domains specific to their boundary-spanning responsibilities. We will return to this in our discussion of the critical boundary-spanning role played by middle mangers in MTSs.

Before turning to a discussion of our second framework, it is incumbent upon us to note that a great deal of discussion regarding information flow has occurred in other literatures and thus lies beyond the more focused scope of this chapter. For example, numerous studies have been conducted in the context of new product development, software development, and innovation, and there is a further wealth of information regarding boundary-spanning activities and roles available in the literatures dedicated to these particular topics. Further, the knowledge management and interorganizational relations literatures also explore the acquisition and dissimulation of information and knowledge across organizational boundaries. Because our goal was to establish a conceptual framework for thinking about boundary spanning while providing a bird's-eye view of the boundary-spanning landscape, followed by a more detailed look at behavioral integration specifically, with the exception of a few specific studies, we were unfortunately only able to touch on the richness of these literatures in this review. Thus, readers deeply interested in these topics may want to look further into these literatures to gain a more thorough understanding of boundary-spanning activities and roles in these specific contexts. We turn now to a discussion of our second framework, *behavioral integration*.

BEHAVIORAL INTEGRATION FRAMEWORK

We again draw on the open systems perspective from the organizational theory literature, generally, and more specifically Thompson's (1967) concepts of technical core, managerial, and institutional levels, and pooled, sequential, and reciprocal interdependence. It is important to note that in the case of behavioral integration, the key determinant of boundary-spanning activities employed becomes the degree to which tasks are interdependent (i.e., degree of coupling). In recognition of this, Figure 12.2 employs the first (type of boundary spanned) and the third (degree of coupling) attributes of our conceptualization.

Parsons (1960) was among the first to suggest that three nested levels of distinctive responsibility and control exist with an organization: the technical core, managerial, and institutional. Conceiving complex organizations to be "open systems, hence indeterminate and faced with uncertainty, but at the same time as subject to criteria of rationality and hence needing determinateness and certainty" (Thompson, 1967, p. 10), Thompson argued that organizations seek strategies to manage the inherent conflicts that arise due to these realities. Both Parsons and Thompson, hinting at distinctive boundaries between levels, argued that the functions at each of the three levels are qualitatively different. The technical core is concerned with the efficient performance of the technical function (e.g., the production of a product, and service offerings) and is the most nested level. It is within the technical core that the need for determinateness and certainty is the greatest. The two higher levels, managerial and institutional, service the technical core, buffering it from those elements over which it has no formal authority or control (i.e., sources of uncertainty and other influences external to it). Interestingly, one of the early studies of boundary-spanning activities across external boundaries suggested that the frequency of boundary-spanning activity might mediate the relationship between perceived environmental uncertainty and structure (Leifer & Huber, 1977).

Boundary Type Being Spanned		Pooled (Low Tempo)	Sequential	Reciprocal (High tempo)
Institutional	External • Across formal organizational boundary • Inter-organization	• Shared institutional goals • Mostly information dependence • e.g., Professional/industry associations	• Membership in same product/service industry value chain • e.g., Focal unit's critical resource owners	Cross organization MTS • Shared super-ordinate goal • Some form of governing board • e.g., Emergency response team
Managerial	Internal – Across sub-unit • Within formal organizational boundary (e.g., legal entity) • Across organizational sub-unit boundary	Unrelated diversification • Across multiple product/service value chains, conglomerates • Shared TMT/senior management • Relationship defined at corporate strategy level • e.g., Businesses at G.E.	Related diversification • Within same product or service value chain • Shared divisional/middle management • Relationship defined at business strategy level • e.g., Captive supplier	Within organization MTS • Shared super-ordinate goal • Vertical coordination required • e.g., Aircraft carrier flight deck
Technical Core	Internal – Within sub-unit • Within formal organizational boundary (e.g., legal entity) • Within organizational sub-unit boundary	Component teams across departments within the same function • Functionally equivalent • Product/service differentiated • Little to no shared goals or horizontal coordination • e.g., R&D teams		Component teams across areas of specialization • Often functionally differentiated • Same product/service • Shared lower level goals • Horizontal coordination · MTS Component Teams · e.g., Action Teams
		← Loose	Degree of coupling/task interdependence	Tight →
			Behavior Integration	

FIGURE 12.2

Behavioral integration (Framework 2).

Note: In line with Thompson's (1967) conceptualization of pooled, sequential, and reciprocal, activities undertaken by organizational units with only a pooled relationship are also carried out by units with a sequential relationship, and those undertaken by both pooled and sequentially related units are also carried out by organizational units with a reciprocal relationship. The reverse is not true.

Units within the same technical core (e.g., cross-functional new product development units) share a common goal hierarchy (Bateman, O'Neill, & Kenworthy-U'Ren, 2002) and thus are the most tightly coupled. Organizations connected at the managerial level (e.g., a product division) are more loosely coupled, sharing only a set of superordinate goals (Bateman et al., 2002), and those at the institutional level (e.g., a multiproduct corporation or an industry association) are coupled the least. Although alternative organizational structures, such as strategic alliances and cross-organizational multiteam systems, that have emerged in the literature blur the administrative and legal distinctiveness of the boundaries implicit in Thompson's (1967) original conception, we retain a semblance of it in our frameworks as it serves a useful purpose for conceptually structuring our discussion. Thus, we have further subdivided the *boundary type being spanned* dimension of our framework into Thompson's three categories (see Figure 12.2).

Interdependence has been conceptualized in the literature as a multifaceted construct composed of task interdependence, goal interdependence, and outcome interdependence requiring interaction between multiple organizational entities (Morgeson & Humphrey, 2008; Saavedra, Earley, & Van Dyne, 1993). *Task interdependence* refers to the extent to which jobs mutually interrelate and thereby require each other (Kiggundu, 1981), *goal interdependence* refers to the extent to which goals overlap (Saavedra et al., 1993), and *outcome interdependence* refers to the degree to which rewards and feedback are linked (Campion, Medsker, & Higgs, 1993; Guzzo & Shea, 1992). Although these latter two categories of interdependence are not depicted in our framework, one can think of them as continuums across both of the framework's dimensions, increasing as one moves from left to right on the horizontal axis and from top to bottom on the vertical axis.

Thompson (1967) also conceived of different degrees to which the work of organizational units is interdependent. As described by Thompson, *pooled interdependence* is one in which "each part renders a discreet contribution to the whole and each is supported by the whole" (pp. 54–55). He defined *sequential interdependence* as situations where the output of one organizational unit is an input to another, in other words, there is a direct but asymmetrical interdependence between them. The speed with which the output of one organization becomes the input of the other defines the tempo of the relationship. Finally, those organizational units most interdependently coupled, where the work activities of each are mutually dependent on the other, have a *reciprocal interdependence* with each other; the tighter the coupling, the more these exchanges occur in real time. Further, in line with Thompson's conceptualization of pooled, sequential, and reciprocal, activities undertaken by organizational units with only a pooled relationship are also carried out by units with a sequential relationship, and those undertaken by both pooled and sequentially related units are also carried out by organizational units with a reciprocal relationship. The reverse is not true. Thus, we have noted this continuum along the task interdependence dimension of our second framework (see Figure 12.2). We turn now to a brief discussion of the left side of this second framework.

Loosely Coupled Behavioral Integration Across External Boundaries

The upper left-hand corner of this framework represents boundary-spanning activities undertaken across the boundary separating distinct legal entities. Such organizations run the gamut from professional and industry or trade associations to members of the same industry's product or service value chain. Along with being legally distinct, what most typify the boundary between these organizations are that goals and norms are shared at only the broadest and highest of levels, and the central role played by power dependence (Emerson, 1962). Further, activities undertaken include those aimed at the management of external stakeholder relations, generally, and resource owners, in particular, and task-specific organizational learning among others.

Noting that norms often differ across organizational boundaries, Caldwell and O'Reilly (1982) hypothesized that the performance of boundary-spanning agents would be higher if they were adept at reading social cues and tailoring their behavior to fit the situation. Using a scale of self-monitoring to measure attention to social cues, self-reported by a sample of 93 field representatives working for a large franchise organization in the same geographic region, the authors found that a significant relationship existed between the ability of these individuals to adjust their self-presentation based on social cues and their job performance. Splitting the sample into high- and low-tenured groupings, a second analysis suggested that this relationship was moderated by job tenure. The authors speculated that this latter result is related to knowledge of the job. High-tenured individuals rely on competence, whereas low-tenured individuals must be more attuned to social cues in order to be successful. In addition, a study of 119 buyer–supplier relationships found that organizational agents, in this case purchasing managers, who were free from constraints that limit their ability to interpret their boundary-spanning role (i.e., role autonomy) were better able to develop relationships based on trust (Perrone, Zaheer, & McEvily, 2003).

Several of the studies we reviewed investigated boundary spanning in the context of health care organizations. Fennell and Alexander (1987) tested hypotheses concerning the differences in three boundary-spanning strategies—(a) boundary redefinition, when an organization formally joins a multiorganizational system; (b) buffering, augmenting either internal administrative structures or buffering external organizations, such as industry trade groups, in order to protect itself from disturbing environmental influences (Thompson, 1967); and (c) bridging, when an organization creates external linkages to other organizations rather than developing internal structural buffers (Pfeffer & Salancik, 1978)—employed by freestanding hospitals and hospitals that are members of multihospital systems. Of perhaps the greatest interest to our discussion of MTSs, this study found a relationship between size and boundary-spanning strategy employed: Specifically, large hospitals were more likely to buffer by augmenting their governing board (i.e., leadership structure). We will develop this point more completely in the section specifically dedicated to MTSs.

In a study of the relationship between managed care organizations (e.g., HMOs) and health care providers (e.g., physicians, clinics, and hospitals), Callister and Wall (2001) identified that three factors are most influential in determining the degree to which interorganizational conflict arises: the power of the managed care organization in relation to the health care provider (suggestive of Emerson's 1962 power dependence theory), differences in personal status between the individuals on the two sides of the boundary, and the previous interactions between these individuals. Results of a second study suggest that organizations with power use it, influencing behavioral responses, whereas differences in status and previous negative interactions influence emotions.

Although most of the boundary-spanning studies have looked at more traditional organizations and institutional settings, Dollinger (1984) investigated the boundary-spanning activities of very small firms. Importantly, this study found that the percentage of time spent by entrepreneurs on boundary-spanning activities (intensity) of all types, both strategic and operational in nature, was positively and significantly related to several measures of financial performance. This study also found that just like their larger counterparts, effectively engaging the environment to capture opportunities and ward off risks is an important factor in the success of small firms. A study of two new biotechnology firms (NBFs), conducted by Liebeskind, Oliver, Zucker, and Brewer (1996), found that the exchange of scientific knowledge was rarely governed by formal market contracts. Instead, these authors found that scientists in these firms enter into large numbers of collaborative research efforts, employing their professional social network to source knowledge from external scientist-collaborators at numerous other institutions (e.g., universities). In a study of 127 strategic alliances, Luo (2007) found that the distributive, procedural, and interactional justice perceptions of executives in these relationships had an effect on the actions of their parent company. Further, the author found that procedural and distributive forms of justice interact to jointly influence alliance performance in situations where a high degree of goal conflict exists.

Drawing upon 16 years of archival data from an open innovation community, the Internet Engineering Task Force (IETF), Fleming and Waguespack (2007) conducted an investigation of leadership emergence in voluntary communities as compared to the process by which individuals are promoted to management in for-profit organizations. The authors contended that a key difference in the contexts specific to these two situations is that succeeding to a position of leadership in a voluntary community requires an even greater and more effective use of human capital, as measured by the degree of one's technical contribution to the community, and social capital, as measured by the frequency and effectiveness of one's boundary-spanning and brokering activities, than the equivalent rise to leadership in a for-profit organization. The authors argued further that those who attain leadership positions in open innovation communities are exceedingly adept at building and leveraging these capital resources to mobilize efforts across a broad spectrum of peers, friends, and colleagues. The authors found that fears of cooption by commercial interests make trust building exceedingly hard in these communities, and thus aspiring leaders use physical attendance at community meetings to build strong relationships. This creates somewhat of a paradox, though, as trust was found to be negatively related to boundary-spanning activity. Lastly, boundary spanning was found to have a greater influence on becoming a leader than brokerage.

Employing a more traditional organizational sample, Geletkanycz and Hambrick (1997) investigated the external boundary-spanning role played by executives in two contrasting industries, one facing a relatively stable and certain external environment, the branded foods industry, and one facing a high degree of environmental uncertainty and dynamism, the computer industry. These authors found that executives of both industries undertake a broad set of boundary-spanning roles; that intraindustry ties are related to strategies that conform to the industry norm, whereas extraindustry ties are associated with the adoption of deviant strategies; and that one of the key linkages leading to nonconforming strategies was memberships in professional associations whose membership consisted of participants from diverse market environments. Finally, organizational performance is enhanced when executives' external boundary-spanning activities and the informational needs of the firm's strategy are closely aligned.

One study in particular looked at the emerging network form of organizations, reporting on a case study of the British government's "mainstreaming genetics" policy initiative. These authors (Currie, Finn, & Martin, 2008) pointed out that "professional hierarchy and traditional power relationships, combined with marketization and a strong centralized performance regime focused upon the organizational level, adversely impact upon policy aspirations for transcendence of professional and organizational boundaries through implementing network forms of organizing" (p. 544). This has important implications for this chapter's discussion of cross-organizational MTSs, and the crucial role played by its governing board.

Loosely Coupled Behavioral Integration Across Internal Subunit Boundaries

The center left cell in Framework 2 captures organizations whose relationship is defined at either the corporate or business strategy level. These organizational units are loosely coupled, related primarily through synergistic value-creating activities undertaken at the management levels. Organizations that fit most appropriately to the far left of this cell enjoy the benefits of unrelated diversification, such as corporate parenting, corporate restructuring, and portfolio management, whereas those that fall toward the right enjoy the benefits of related diversification activities such as economies of scope and market power. Thus, these latter organizations share either a product or service value chain (e.g., captive supplier) or channel. According to March and Simon (1958), coordination can be accomplished through standardization (e.g., the establishment of routines or rules), planning (e.g., the establishment of schedules), or mutual adjustment (e.g., the direct transmission of job-related information from person to person during the process of action). In the case of pooled interdependence, coordination by standardization is most appropriate, whereas coordination by plan is most appropriate for sequential interdependence (Thompson, 1967). A key implication of this coordination schema is that the volume of boundary-spanning-related activities is small, as one would expect based on the low amount of coupling.

Although this is still generally true, in response to environmental turbulence, organizational structures are increasingly shifting from hierarchical to more modular forms in an attempt to achieve greater organizational flexibility (Schilling & Steensma, 2001). Part and parcel with this shift, Balogun and Johnson (2004) noted that "[r]esponsibility, power, and resources are decentralized to semi-independent units based around a set of core activities and coordinated through contractual and 'mutually beneficial' relationships (Child & McGrath, 2001, p. 1137)" (p. 523). We suggest that these new, emerging organizational forms sit at the far right boundary of this cell.

In a longitudinal, qualitative study that examined middle management sense making, these authors found that the process of sense making consequentially moved from shared through clustered to shared but differentiated. Importantly for our discussion, Balogun and Johnson (2004) found that middle managers' lateral social interactions (i.e., boundary spanning) were key in effecting change. In a separate article, Balogun and colleagues (Balogun, Gleadle, Hailey, & Willmott, 2005) pointed out that there is fairly little research that addresses the boundary-spanning activities and practices of internal change agents associated with implementing boundary-shaking change initiatives across internal organizational boundaries. Balogun et al. (2005) found that boundary shakers use their knowledge of their organization's political context and the motivations of other organizational members to identify and enlist networks consisting of individuals sharing a degree of common interest. This, in turn, allows boundary shakers to create both new networks and new meanings within old networks in support of their change objectives.

Only a few of the studies from the boundary-spanning literature that we reviewed for this chapter fit squarely into this cell. For example, in a study of R&D project teams, Hirst and Mann (2004) found that project leaders performed the vast majority of boundary-spanning activities, and suggested that project leaders are more effective at performing inter-unit boundary-spanning activities with other units, for example project customers, than were individual members of the team. Representing an example of boundary-spanning task coordination in this cell, other than operational coordination, are strategic initiatives undertaken by middle managers. Middle managers often take the initiative to push strategic agendas, coordinating parallel activities across areas, and building both awareness and commitment to the new strategy, up, down, and across the organization (Floyd & Wooldridge, 1997). Combing the findings of three studies (Floyd & Wooldridge, 1992, 1997; Wooldridge & Floyd, 1990), Floyd and Wooldridge argued that the involvement of middle managers in both the definition and execution of strategy is significant.

Although this finding is somewhat surprising at first, after further reflection a plausible explanation arises. We argue that a rich cache of studies concerning issues associated with behavior integration across organizational boundaries within the same legal entity exists elsewhere in other literatures, for example the literatures on leadership, teams, and groups. We refer the reader to these literatures for further insight.

Behavioral Integration Within Internal Subunits

The bottom two cells of Framework 2 concern the boundary-spanning activities of lower level, component teams. What differentiates these cells is the degree to which the coupling of task work drives the need for horizontal coordination of task work. At the extreme bottom right of Framework 2 are teams such as cross-functional task groups and MTS component teams, and action teams (Klein, Ziegert, Knight, & Xiao, 2006). What all of these teams have in common is that they consist of a blend of functional specialists working together to achieve a shared goal set; they all require, to a greater or lesser degree, real-time task coordination; they all are small enough in membership to be able to coordinate horizontally within the team; and they have the authority to do so. As with information boundary spanning, competence is key to the effective performance of horizontal coordination by boundary spanners at this level. Among specialists, network centrality is a reflection of the degree to which an expert is held in high regard, and this, in turn, defines the extent to which the boundary spanner is endowed with a source of informal power (Ibarra, 1993).

The last two attributes, small enough membership to allow horizontal coordination and the authority to do so, are what fundamentally separate the organizational forms that fit the bottom-right cells from those in the two upper-right cells. Due to team size and the time-dependent nature of the task, effective vertical coordination emerges as a key necessity for organizations that fit into these latter two cells, as will be discussed in the "Behavioral Integration Boundary Spanning in Multiteam Systems (MTSs)" section. (*Note:* It can be argued that the need for horizontal coordination and mutual adjustment occurs earlier along the task interdependence continuum, moving from loosely coupled to the direction of tightly coupled [i.e., left to right], for component teams than does the need for horizontal coordination at the higher levels in the organization. In other words, in practice, close coupling typically occurs first at lower levels. For ease of illustration, we chose not to make this finer aspect of horizontal coordination distinct in Framework 2.)

Loosely Coupled Behavioral Integration Within Internal Subunit Boundaries

By far and away, the vast majority of the boundary-spanning activities undertaken by loosely coupled or decoupled, pooled, and low-tempo sequential organizational subunits, represented by the lower left cell of Framework 2, fall into the previously discussed categories of outbound and inbound information flow. Thus, we refer the reader to our discussion of Framework 1 in this chapter for further details. Before turning to our discussion of the far right side of Framework 2, which includes the MTS domain, we will briefly discuss two articles that provide additional and useful insight into more tightly coupled and higher tempo sequential organizational subunits.

Tightly Coupled Behavioral Integration Within Internal Subunit Boundaries

Although more a study of intrateam leadership than of boundary-spanning activities, specifically, the grounded theory–based study conducted by Klein et al. (2006) provides numerous valuable insights into the workings of extreme action teams. Based on observations of medical action teams in an emergency trauma center and interviews with team members, the authors found that the key to the success of teams faced with a task environment that is "uncertain, unpredictable, urgent, complex, interdependent, and tightly coupled" (Klein et al., 2006, pp. 590–591) is "dynamic delegation," informally enacted leadership that is shared, hierarchical, and deindividualized. We highlight this study as an informative example of real-time mutual adjustment within teams.

In an examination of interactive marketing organizations facing high uncertainty and rapid change, Kellogg, Orlikowski, and Yates (2006) employed the concept of "trading zones" (Galison, 1999) from the social studies of science literature to study the structure of coordination across organizational boundaries characterized by fast-paced and volatile working conditions (i.e., postbureaucratic organizations), through the use of a common digital space. Reminiscent of Lawrence and Lorsch's (1967) concept of integrative devices and this chapter's discussion of boundary objects, Galison developed

> the metaphor of a *trading zone* to highlight how the local coordination of ideas and actions may take place despite differences in community purposes, norms, meanings, values, and performance criteria. Importantly, this metaphor is not intended to evoke the commodified transactions of efficient markets, but the complex interactions of distinct communities encountering each other for purposes of exchange. (Kellogg et al., 2006, p. 39)

Of additional importance to our discussion of MTS boundary spanning, specifically vertical coordination, Kellogg and associates suggested that although trading zone practices act as key enablers of temporary, local, ongoing, and dynamic coordination across horizontal boundaries, they do not eliminate jurisdictional conflicts, and are often the source of problematic consequences.

BEHAVIORAL INTEGRATION BOUNDARY SPANNING IN MTSs

One of the first discussions of a complex suborganization (i.e., a multiteam system) appeared in a technical report about a medium bomb wing of the

Strategic Air Command of the U.S. Air Force written by James Thompson in 1953. Thompson subsequently used this multiteam system as an example in his 1967 seminal work, *Organizations in Action*, to illustrate the concepts of reciprocal interdependence (complex organizational situations in which the outputs of each group become inputs for other groups), mutual adjustment, and hierarchy as a mechanism specifically introduced into an organization to inclusively cluster or combine component groups in order to cope with those aspects of coordination that are beyond the capability or scope of any individual component group. These three concepts—functional interdependence, mutual adjustment, and hierarchy—form the theoretical underpinnings of boundary spanning in multiteam systems.

The notion of functional interdependence, a form of reciprocal interdependence, is a critical feature of MTSs introduced by Mathieu and colleagues (2001). Stemming from the activities performed by each of the component teams, "Functional interdependence is *a state by which entities have mutual reliance, determination, influence, and shared vested interest in processes they use to accomplish work activities*" (Mathieu et al., 2001, p. 293, emphasis in original). In the case of systems of teams, *process interdependence*, defined as the amount of interteam interaction required to accomplish the collective goal (Mathieu et al., 2001), can be conceptualized as comparable to the concept of task interdependence (van de Ven & Ferry, 1980, p. 966). Importantly in the specific case of interdependence between teams, issues regarding the sharing and coordination of information and other resources often arise (Ancona & Caldwell, 1988). Thus, the importance of process in general, and boundary-spanning activities specifically, for the coordination and sharing of information and other resources increases as a positive function of the functional interdependence between teams. In short, due to the high degree of functional interdependence within MTSs, *MTS effectiveness depends heavily on how well the component teams coordinate their activities.*

As mentioned earlier, coordination can be accomplished through standardization, planning, or mutual adjustment (March & Simon, 1958). Further, situations involving high degrees of variability and unpredictability (prototypical characteristics of situations faced by a multiteam system) demand a greater reliance on coordination by mutual adjustment (March & Simon, 1958). A key to the effectiveness of mutual adjustment as a coordination mechanism is that every member of a group must have the capacity to interact with every other member, but as size increases this becomes not only increasingly difficult but also exceedingly costly, inefficient, and prone to bias and distortion (March & Simon, 1958). Further, the degree of uncertainty in the task environment exacerbates the problems associated with mutual adjustment across reciprocally interdependent organizations. Research conducted by Tushman (1977) serves as an illustration of this issue. In a study of an R&D organization, Tushman found evidence that suggests a curvilinear relationship between project performance and the number of boundary-spanning roles for projects facing higher degrees of work-related uncertainty due to either task environment uncertainty or increased task interdependence.

One of the earliest papers in the organizational science literature (Caplow, 1957), drawing upon prior work in sociology (Bossard, 1945; Kephart, 1950), demonstrated that the complexity of interpersonal relations increases rapidly with small increases in size. Bossard's Law of Family Interaction states,

> With the addition of each person to a family or a primary group, the number of persons increases in the simplest arithmetical progression in whole numbers, while the number of personal interrelationships within the group increases in the order of triangular numbers. (Bossard, 1945, p. 292)

The number of interpersonal relationships (i.e., dyadic links) within a group is given by the following formula:

$$\frac{N(N-1)}{2}$$

where
N = the number of persons in the group.

The number of dyadic links that can arise in a small group is clearly manageable; for example, 10 for a group consisting of 5 members. However, as Figure 12.3 clearly illustrates, the number of linkages grows in a nonlinear fashion as group size increases such that when group size is increased from our earlier example of 5 to 15, the number of dyadic links grows from 10 to 105, or by more than a multiple of 10. Consequently, the sheer number of potential links makes mutual adjustment a nonviable option for large social units.

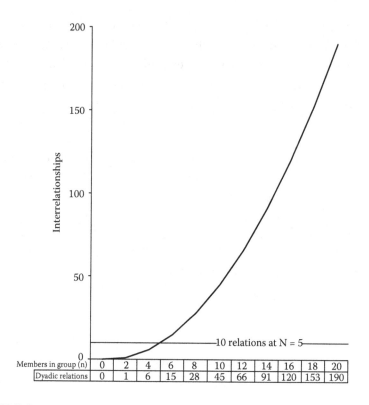

Members in group (n)	0	2	4	6	8	10	12	14	16	18	20
Dyadic relations	0	1	6	15	28	45	66	91	120	153	190

FIGURE 12.3
Dyadic interpersonal relations by group size.

Expanding this discussion to include all the intrateam relations that members of a team can have with each other (i.e., dyadic, individual with subgroups of other members, and subgroups of members with subgroups of other members) only serves to further exacerbate the issue (e.g., in our example, a group of 5 could have 90 such linkages, whereas a group of 15 could have over 7 million; see Caplow, 1957, for a thorough discussion). Because complex MTSs tend to be large by definition, and often require action in real time, it is important to note that a core and defining characteristic of MTSs is that *unlike more traditional work units, an MTS is too large to permit direct mutual adjustment among all its members.*

The obvious solution to this apparent dilemma is to break the larger unit into smaller subunits, capable of mutual adjustment across their smaller memberships, which are then linked together through some form of coordinating mechanism. The introduction of hierarchy, or

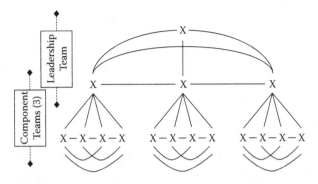

FIGURE 12.4
Multiteam system consisting of 16 members organized into four teams.

vertical differentiation (i.e., managerial layers), acts as just such a coordinating mechanism. Consider a work group consisting of 16 members. Applying the formula discussed earlier, a group of 16 could have upward of 120 dyadic communications links to manage. However, breaking this group into three lower level subgroups charged with the performance of specialized tasks and one higher level subgroup charged with integration and coordination reduces the number of dyadic links dramatically while reestablishing the ability of the group to mutually adjust and coordinate. As illustrated in Figure 12.4, with the introduction of vertical differentiation, the maximum number of communication links that have to be managed by any one individual is seven as opposed to the original 15, and the number of dyadic linkages that have to be managed in totality is reduced from 120 to 36. Thus, an undifferentiated group of 16 people is converted into a multiteam system consisting of four distinct teams, each capable of mutual adjustment and horizontal coordination within their subgroup.

Understandably, increases in problems of communication and coordination related to organizational size, the implications of size for patterns of control and affiliation, and the consequences of size for certain aspects of organizational structure, for example the number of levels in the hierarchy of authority and the span of control, have occupied a significant place in the literature for quite some time (Blau, 1970; Kimberly, 1976; Weick, 1969). Thompson (1967) discussed the need for hierarchical structure to facilitate effective mutual adjustment within complex organizations, noting,

On occasion, reciprocal interdependence is so extensive that to link all of the involved positions into one group would overtax communication mechanisms. When this occurs, organizations [subject to norms of rationality] rank-order interdependent positions in terms of the amount of contingency each possess for the others. Those with the greatest intercontingency form a group, and the resulting groups are then clustered into an overarching second-order group (p. 59).

Multiteam systems fit Thompson's conception of intercontingent clustered groups perfectly. They consist of differentiated (specialized) yet reciprocally interdependent subsystems, each performing a portion of the superordinate task, that need to be integrated to achieve effective performance of the overall system. This high degree of subsystem differentiation, combined with the fact that the members of each subsystem develop a primary concern with the goals of their own subsystem (Dearborn & Simon, 1958), gives rise to a need for an integrative subsystem (Lawrence & Lorsch, 1967) to coordinate the activities of the various subsystems and to provide a formal mechanism for discussing and resolving mutual problems, making decisions, and insuring that the superordinate goals of the MTS are ultimately achieved. In an MTS, the integrative subsystem, or second-order group as argued by Thompson, is the leadership team. The leadership team depicted in Figure 12.2 consists of four members, the maximum number of communication links that have to be managed by any one individual is three, and the number of dyadic linkages that have to be managed in totality is six. Thus, whereas an MTS is too large to support mutual adjustment among all of the members of the system, *an MTS has clusters that are small enough to allow for mutual adjustment among the leaders or managers of the system.*

Thus, for an MTS to be effective, teams must be large and specialized enough at the lowest level to succeed in a complex task environment, but fluid and adaptable enough at the managerial level to respond quickly to environment dynamism. It must be structured such that the most reciprocally interdependent positions are grouped together into component teams sized to allow effective intrateam mutual adjustment, employing hierarchy as a mechanism to inclusively cluster component teams such that MTS management can cope with those aspects of coordination that are beyond the capability or scope of any individual component team. This leaves the component teams undistracted, unencumbered, and thereby able to focus their attention on the complex task at hand. For these reasons, the lion's share of the cross-unit boundary-spanning responsibilities falls firmly onto the shoulders of the managers. Thus, MTS leadership enacts pivotal integrative boundary-spanning roles linking each component team to the other units within the MTS, establishing strategic and operational directions for both team and MTS actions, and facilitating within- and between-team cooperation to accomplish the objectives of both the component teams and the MTS.

Within- and Cross-Organizational MTS Behavioral Integration

Although the literature on boundary spanning reviewed in this chapter is of relevance to the context of MTSs, few extant studies shed light specifically on the question of boundary spanning in the domain of multiteam systems. Still, there are a few that we have endeavored to present in greater detail than those reviewed up to this point in the chapter. Finally, the plain fact is that aside from anecdotal stories, such as the illustrative description of an emergency response MTS provided by Mathieu and colleagues (Mathieu et al., 2001), we simply didn't identify any studies that could truly be classed as cross-organizational MTS behavioral integration. Thus, we decided it was not possible to break within- and cross-organizational boundary MTS behavioral integration, the two most upper right cells in Framework 2, into two sections, but, rather, it was most prudent to cover these collectively in one.

Hoegl, Weinkauf, and Gemuenden (2004) employed a 36-month longitudinal research design involving 39 cross-functional product development teams in the European automotive industry, with an average size of nine members, to investigate collaboration within and between teams. The 39 teams were divided into eight subprojects, with each subproject under the leadership of a project manager responsible, in turn, to an overall project director. Individual teams were led by a formal team leader, were responsible for specific project deliverables, and had authority to make task-related decisions within the boundaries of their predetermined task domain. Decisions that involved changes affecting a number of teams, however, required the approval of their project manager. The leadership team thus was composed of the team leads and the project managers, who, collectively, were accountable to the project director for ensuring that product specifications were met.

The study design employed multi-informant process measures for within-team coordination (a 5-item Teamwork Quality Scale), between-team coordination (a 5-item Interteam Coordination Scale), and a cross-MTS measure of project commitment (20 items measuring six facets). Outcome measures included a 5-item scale assessing overall performance (superordinate goal) along with measures of several important dimensions of performance (e.g., product quality, adherence to schedule, and adherence to budget). All ratings of performance were provided by the project managers.

This study showed a positive main effect relationship between the measure of interteam coordination and the measures of overall team performance and adherence to schedule, no significant relationship between the measures of interteam coordination and quality, and a negative main effect relationship between measures of interteam coordination and adherence to budget. A further exploratory analysis showed that interteam coordination was particularly critical for highly task-interdependent teams. In addition, the study showed that early measures of within-team coordination positively predicted both later overall performance and schedule performance, but had no influence on later quality and budget performance. Finally, the authors commented that "while interteam coordination may have both positive and negative effects on individual module quality, it seems safe to assume that the exchange of important technical data ultimately helps to optimize quality on the system or project level" (Hoegl et al., 2004, p. 49).

Utilizing a PC-based flight simulation, Marks and colleagues (Marks, DeChurch, Mathieu, Panzer, & Alonso, 2005) examined "how transition process-action process-performance relationships operate within and between teams in the context of an MTS performing under different goal hierarchies" (p. 970). *Action processes* encompass the set of activities that can broadly be defined as monitoring process toward goals, systems monitoring, team monitoring, and coordination activities (Marks et al., 2001). Included in systems monitoring are those activities involved in the tracking of team resources and the monitoring of environmental conditions relevant to the team. Marks and colleagues (2001) defined coordination activities as "the process of orchestrating the sequence and timing of interdependent actions" (pp. 367–368). Both the monitoring of environmental conditions and the sequence and timing of interdependent action *across team boundaries within the MTS* represent boundary-spanning activities that occur in real time. *Transition processes* encompass the set of boundary-spanning activities that can broadly be defined as mission analysis, goal specification, and strategy and planning (Marks et al., 2001), and they represent a key form of "integrative device" (Lawrence & Lorsch, 1967) of critical importance in the MTS domain.

Working together in dyads (a pilot and a weapons specialist), a total of 184 psychology students participated in the study. Each simulated mission consisted of two "live" dyads, one tasked with air-to-air combat and the other tasked with air-to-ground combat, and six computer-controlled allied aircraft. The pilot of the aircraft assigned responsibility for air-to-air combat was designated the MTS (mission) leader. All aircraft could be destroyed by both air and ground enemy assets, and team score was based on destroying enemy targets and the degree to which allied assets survived the mission intact. Thus, teams had to work cooperatively in order to maximize their combined score. A mission entailed 20 minutes of pre-flight planning, designated the *transition process phase*, and a 15-minute flight, designated the *action phase*. Interviews conducted prior to the mission with the air-to-air pilot were coded independently by two raters and subsequently used to create a composite measure of the effectiveness of the transition phase, whereas ratings by two subject matter expert observers and two additional subject matter experts reviewing videotapes of the mission were combined to measure action process effectiveness. Teams of eight aircraft (two live and six computer controlled) flew three experimental missions; the three missions were conducted under different experimental conditions, with one constructed to model a pooled goal hierarchy condition, one a sequential goal hierarchy condition, and one an intensive (reciprocal) goal hierarchy condition. A manipulation check later showed that the first two conditions did not differ statistically, and thus these were combined, yielding two experimental conditions dummy coded as more or less interdependent.

Of interest, analysis of the results indicated that teams performed worse in the more interdependent mission condition, and that a positive relationship existed between cross-team action processes and performance in this condition. As could logically be expected, cross-team action processes did not significantly influence collective performance in the less interdependent condition. This study found no evidence that transition processes directly influenced team-level action processes, but transition process effectiveness did predict cross-team action process effectiveness. Marks et al. (2005) also concluded that cross-team action processes, but not team-level action processes, partially mediated the influence of transition processes on combined performance. Most interesting, no significant relationship was found for the more interdependent condition; however, a positive relationship between transition processes and collective performance was found to exist for missions with less interdependent goal hierarchies. This last result was contrary to the authors' hypothesis, but, unfortunately, this study did not parse transition processes into finer detail, so it is unclear what mechanism(s) underlie these results.

Importantly, in their discussion of limitations, Marks et al. (2005) pointed out that MTSs composed of more and larger teams may function differently and engender different processes than collectives of dyadic teams, and that although they

> operated under the assumption that teamwork processes are homologous at the MTS level of inquiry … it may be the case that the types of teamwork processes differ at the team and MTS levels. By definition, MTSs are more complex entities because they contain multiple teams that must work cooperatively and interdependently toward a common set of goals. This demands both vertical and horizontal alignment of subgoals and synchronized actions with other teams in the MTS. Depending on the nature of the process interdependencies and the temporal pressures, the sequencing of MTS interactions may be highly complex and require more sophisticated boundary management processes (Kozlowski, Gully, McHugh, Salas, & Cannon-Bowers, 1996, p. 971).

We agree, and will return to this observation later in the chapter.

DeChurch and Marks (2006) conducted a study to investigate the effects of leader strategizing and leader coordination processes on functional leadership, interteam coordination, and MTS performance: 384 undergraduates forming 64 six-person MTSs participated in an experimental simulation utilizing a modified version of the Air Combat Effectiveness Simulation (ACES; Mathieu, Cobb, Marks, Zaccaro, & Marsh, 2004). Each six-person MTS was divided into a two-person team tasked with air-to-air combat, a two-person team tasked with air-to-ground combat, and a two-person leadership team individually tasked with directing the efforts of one component team while collectively charged with ensuring MTS success. Similar to the Marks et al. (2005) study, all aircraft could be destroyed by both air and ground enemy assets, and the teams were assigned points based on both destroying enemy targets and the degree to which their assets survived the mission intact. Thus, teams had to work cooperatively in order to maximize their combined score. Operationalization of performance measures was an important difference between this study and the Marks et al. (2005) study. Although the scores of the two flight teams were combined in the Marks et al. (2005) study into an MTS-level performance measure, in this study each team's score was employed as an individual team-level measure of performance, and the superordinate MTS goal of disabling four enemy bases on the battlefield was assigned to the three component teams (i.e., air, ground, and leader) constituting the MTS in this study in place of combined score.

MTS functional leadership was assessed both via a scale rated by the four nonleader members of the MTS and via subject matter expert (SME)–rated Behaviorally Anchored Rating Scales (BARS). Both interteam and intrateam coordination processes were measured using SME-rated BARS. In the specific case of interteam coordination, this measure was designated a rating of explicit coordination. In addition, an experimenter's assessment of the quality of the coordination used during the completion of acts that require interteam coordination provided a rating deemed a measure of implicit interteam coordination. This study found that MTS leader behavior and interteam coordination processes are positive predictors of MTS performance, and that better MTS functional leadership and interteam coordination resulted, in general, from the training of MTS leaders in the development of strategy and coordinating behaviors that facilitate MTS-level processes. Further, this research indicates that functional MTS leadership behavior mediates the influence of leadership training on interteam coordination, and that interteam coordination mediates the relationship between MTS leadership and MTS performance.

A recent field study reported by Mathieu and colleagues (Mathieu, Maynard, Taylor, Gilson, & Ruddy, 2007) employed a longitudinal cross-level design to investigate the relationships between a set of organizational and team contextual variables, measuring aspects of MTS coordination and team processes, and MTS performance. Participating in the study were 94 teams of customer service technicians that ranged in size from 3 to 10 individuals. The teams were embedded across 10 operational districts within the Canadian division of a multinational corporation that sells, services, and maintains large office equipment.

Contextual variables at the organizational level included a two-item measure of MTS coordination, whereas team-level variables included a measure of team interdependence consisting of two dimensional measures, one for input interdependence and one for process interdependence (outcome interdependence was measured but not included in the consolidated measure because it was constant across teams), and an index of nine items measuring team process. Team performance was operationalized as the index of three archival measures for machine reliability, response time, and parts expense.

This study found that the relationship between degree of team interdependence and team performance was partially mediated by team process, and that a direct relationship existed between MTS coordination and team performance. Interestingly, Mathieu et al. (2007) had hypothesized that MTS coordination and team processes would be positively related, and that the relationship between MTS coordination and team performance would be mediated by team processes; however, neither of these hypotheses was supported. In a supplemental analysis, the authors found a significant negative moderating effect of MTS coordination on the relationship between team processes and team performance, and this relationship was stronger for districts reporting less MTS coordination.

By way of summary, these studies collectively illustrate the central importance of MTS boundary-spanning activities, specifically interteam coordination and transition processes, to MTS performance. Further, these studies seem to suggest that transition processes may moderate the effects of some intrateam and interteam processes on MTS performance; however, the findings in this regard are somewhat contradictory and thus are in need of further study. We turn next to a discussion of an investigation, conducted by a group of researchers that includes the authors of this chapter, that may shed some light on this important and previously unresolved issue.

A study conducted by Davison and colleagues (Davison, Hollenbeck, Ilgen, Barnes, & Sleesman, 2010) differs from earlier studies in that it employs larger and more complex MTSs in terms of (a) the number of subteams, (b) the size of membership in the subteams, (c) the vertical differentiation between subteams, and (d) the number of levels constituting the leadership team. The results of this study give every indication that the astute observation made by Marks and colleagues (2005) that "it may be the case that the types of teamwork processes differ at the team and MTS levels" (p. 971) is correct. Through the use of a task complex enough that an MTS structure was a necessity and not simply a somewhat artificially imposed experimental constraint, the results emerging from this work suggest a somewhat complicated picture, as suggested by Marks and colleagues (2005). In particular, the antecedents of effective MTS performance appear to vary depending upon whether one is referring to the component teams or the leadership team.

Two hypotheses explored the effects of horizontal coordinated action within and between component teams. The results of this analysis indicated that horizontal coordinated action within component teams were significant and *positively* related to overall MTS performance, as predicted, whereas horizontal coordinated action between component teams was significant and *negatively* related to overall MTS performance ($\beta = -.14$, $p < .05$), also as predicted. This latter finding is counter to previous research, and was attributed by Davison et al. (2010) to differences in the overall size of the MTS and the effects of component team specialization associated with larger MTSs. A third hypothesis, which predicted that coordinated actions between the leaders of the two component teams would be positive, was significant and in the direction predicted ($\beta = .13$, $p < .05$). Finally, in a post hoc analysis, the authors found that the key contingency that determines whether or not effective transition processes accentuate the effects of coordinated actions seems to be the *nature of the work done* by the subunit, rather than the hierarchical level at which the work takes place.

Importantly for our discussion of MTS behavior integration is that although the results of all the studies appear to be relatively unequivocal with regard to intrateam coordination at the component team level, and in line with the reported results from other studies of lower level teams, the case is not the same at the level of the leadership team. In this latter case, the picture is more complex. Leadership is tasked with simultaneously managing both the vertical coordination of their respective component teams and horizontal interteam coordination, in real time, making their task domain much more demanding than is often the case in non-MTS environments.

LEVELS OF ANALYSIS CONCERNS IN THE CONTEXT OF BOUNDARY SPANNING

Before closing our discussion of boundary spanning, there is one other topic of importance we would like to briefly comment on. Multiteam systems in general, and boundary-spanning activities in the context of MTSs in particular, give rise to methodological concerns regarding level of analysis. Multilevel analysis has been a topic of interest to researchers in many fields over the last decade (Klein, Dansereau, & Hall, 1994), yet we were unable to find any research in the MTS literature that begins to address this important topic. We did find an article, however, that addressed this topic from a broader perspective than the MTS domain.

Marrone and colleagues (Marrone, Tesluk, & Carson, 2007) applied a multilevel approach to the investigation of boundary-spanning behavior, noting that contrary to the more recent research findings of Ancona and others (e.g., Ancona, 1990; Ancona & Caldwell, 1992),

> [E]arlier findings from social-psychological research conducted at the individual level have demonstrated that those who carry out boundary-spanning responsibilities, although gaining status and influence through access to unique knowledge, also experience significant role overload as a result of facing simultaneous and often conflicting pressures (Kahn, Wolfe, Quinn, Snoek, & Rosenthal, 1964; Katz & Kahn, 1978, p. 1423).

Marrone et al. (2007) developed a model, consisting of variables at both the individual and team levels of analysis, to test the consequences of boundary-spanning behavior on team performance and team viability. Interesting, the authors found that greater boundary-spanning behaviors at the team level actually reduce role overload of team members—in other words, the benefits of boundary spanning outweighed the costs— and that variables resident at both the individual and team levels, along with interactions across these levels, predict the boundary-spanning behaviors of team members.

IN CLOSING

As we mention in the introduction to this chapter, boundary spanning is a concept that encompasses a wide variety of activities from simple information exchange to complex and real-time behavior integration and coordination. Whereas all the activities discussed in this chapter are relevant to the MTS domain, what differentiates multiteam systems most from all other organizational environments is that the tight coupling inherent in the complex, real-time, and highly interdependent nature of their task environment demands a clear separation between intrateam and interteam horizontal coordination. Key to MTS effectiveness is that the subdivision of work into meaningful and manageable task activities at the component team level reduces the requirement for direct contact among the members at the component team level. Due to the small size of the component teams, coordination requirements are reduced while, at the same time, accountability is promoted. The work of these teams can still be coordinated, however, because they are linked by a leadership team purposefully responsible for interteam coordination (i.e., leaders are formally tasked with this boundary-spanning function). Moreover, because the size of the leadership team is small enough to support mutual adjustment, the MTS as a whole can be flexible and react to a dynamic task environment despite its overall relatively large size.

As we indicated at the beginning of this chapter, it was our intent to present the reader with a comprehensive look at the literature pertaining to boundary spanning, employing two organizing frameworks aimed at providing a useful structure both for facilitating our discussion and for thinking about this complex area, followed by a look at the research in the MTS domain as seen through the lens of boundary spanning in an attempt to tease out aspects of boundary spanning most critically important to this domain. We hope that this chapter has, in some way, added to our collective understanding. Our much loftier hope is that it will serve to inspire additional and more detailed investigations of boundary-spanning activities in the specific context of multiteam systems.

REFERENCES

Adams, J. S. (1976). The structure and dynamics of behavior in organizational boundary roles. In M. D. Dunnette (Ed.), *Handbook of industrial and organizational psychology* (pp. 1175–1199). New York: Rand McNally.

Adams, J. S. (1980). Interorganizational processes and organization boundary activities. In B. M. Staw & L. L. Cummings (Eds.), *Research in organizational behavior* (Vol. 2, pp. 321–355). Greenwich, CT: JAI.

Ahearne, M., Bhattacharya, C. B., & Gruen, T. (2005). Antecedents and consequences of customer-company identification: Expanding the role of relationship marketing. *Journal of Applied Psychology, 90*(3), 574–585.

Aldrich, H., & Herker, D. (1977). Boundary spanning roles and organization structure. *Academy of Management Review, 2*(2), 217–230.

Ancona, D. G. (1990). Outward bound: Strategies for team survival in an organization. *Academy of Management Journal, 33*(2), 334–365.

Ancona, D. G., & Caldwell, D. F. (1988). Beyond task and maintenance: Defining external functions in groups. *Group & Organization (Management) Studies, 13*(4), 468–494.

Ancona, D. G., & Caldwell, D. F. (1990). Beyond boundary spanning: Managing external dependence in product development teams. *Journal of High Technology Management Research, 1*(2), 119–135.

Balogun, J., Gleadle, P., Hailey, V. H., & Willmott, H. (2005). Managing change across boundaries: Boundary-shaking practices. *British Journal of Management, 16*(4), 261–278.

Balogun, J., & Johnson, G. (2004). Organizational restructuring and middle manager sensemaking. *Academy of Management Journal, 47*(4), 523–549.

Bartel, C. A. (2001). Social comparisons in boundary-spanning work: Effects of community outreach on members' organizational identity and identification. *Administrative Science Quarterly, 46*(3), 379–413.

Bateman, T. S., O'Neill, H., & Kenworthy-U'Ren, A. (2002). A hierarchical taxonomy of top managers' goals. *Journal of Applied Psychology, 87*(6), 1134–1148.

Blau, P. M. (1970). A formal theory of differentiation in organizations. *American Sociological Review, 35*(2), 201–218.

Bossard, J. H. S. (1945). The law of family interaction. *American Journal of Sociology, 50*(4), 292–294.

Caldwell, D. F., & O'Reilly, C. A. (1982). Boundary spanning and individual performance: The impact of self-monitoring. *Journal of Applied Psychology, 67*(1), 124–127.

Callister, R. R., & Wall, J. A. (2001). Conflict across organizational boundaries: Managed care organizations versus health care providers. *Journal of Applied Psychology, 86*(4), 754–763.

Campion, M. A., Medsker, G. J., & Higgs, A. C. (1993). Relations between work group characteristics and effectiveness: Implications for designing effective work groups. *Personnel Psychology, 46*(4), 823–850.

Caplow, T. (1957). Organizational size. *Administrative Science Quarterly, 1*(4), 484–505.

Child, J., & McGrath, R. G. (2001). Organizations unfettered: Organizational form in an information-intensive economy. *Academy of Management Journal, 44*(6), 1135–1148.

Coleman, J. S., Katz, E., & Menzel, H. (1966). *Medical innovation: A diffusion study.* New York: Bobbs-Merrill.

Cross, R. L., Yan, A. M., & Louis, M. R. (2000). Boundary activities in "boundaryless" organizations: A case study of a transformation to a team-based structure. *Human Relations, 53*(6), 841–868.

Currie, G., Finn, R., & Martin, G. (2008). Accounting for the "dark side" of new organizational forms: The case of healthcare professionals. *Human Relations, 61*(4), 539–564.

Davison, R. B., Hollenbeck, J. R., Ilgen, D. R., Barnes, C. M., & Sleesman, D. J. (April 2010). The role of action and transition processes in large multiteam systems: Why size matters. Symposium at the 25th Annual Meeting of the Society for Industrial and Organizational Psychology, Atlanta, GA.

Dearborn, D. C., & Simon, H. A. (1958). Selective perception: A note on the departmental identifications of executives. *Sociometry, 21*(2), 140–144.

DeChurch, L. A., & Marks, M. A. (2006). Leadership in multiteam systems. *Journal of Applied Psychology, 91*(2), 311–329.

Dollinger, M. J. (1984). Environmental boundary spanning and information processing effects on organizational performance. *Academy of Management Journal, 27*(2), 351–368.

Dutton, J. E., Ashford, S. J., O'Neill, R. M., Hayes, E., & Wierba, E. E. (1997). Reading the wind: How middle managers assess the context for selling issues to top managers. *Strategic Management Journal, 18*(5), 407–423.

Emerson, R. M. (1962). Power-dependence relations. *American Sociological Review, 27*(1), 31–41.

Faraj, S., & Yan, A. M. (2009). Boundary work in knowledge teams. *Journal of Applied Psychology, 94*(3), 604–617.

Fennell, M. L., & Alexander, J. A. (1987). Organizational boundary spanning in institutionalized environments. *Academy of Management Journal, 30*(3), 456–476.

Fleming, L., & Waguespack, D. M. (2007). Brokerage, boundary spanning, and leadership in open innovation communities. *Organization Science, 18*(2), 165–180.

Floyd, S. W., & Wooldridge, B. (1992). Middle management involvement in strategy and its association with strategic type: A research note. *Strategic Management Journal, 13*, 153–167.

Floyd, S. W., & Wooldridge, B. (1997). Middle management's strategic influence and organizational performance. *Journal of Management Studies, 34*(3), 465–485.

Friedman, R. A., & Podolny, J. (1992). Differentiation of boundary spanning roles: Labor negotiations and implications for role-conflict. *Administrative Science Quarterly, 37*(1), 28–47.

Galison, P. (1999). Trading zone: Coordinating action and belief. In M. Biagioli (Ed.), *The science studies reader* (pp. 137–160). New York: Routledge.

Geletkanycz, M. A., & Hambrick, D. C. (1997). The external ties of top executives: Implications for strategic choice and performance. *Administrative Science Quarterly, 42*(4), 654–681.

Gladstein, D. L. (1984). Groups in context: A model of task group effectiveness. *Administrative Science Quarterly, 29*(4), 499–517.

Guzzo, R. A., & Shea, G. P. (1992). Group performance and intergroup relations in organizations. In M. D. Dunette & L. M. Hough (Eds.), *Handbook of industrial and organizational psychology* (2nd ed., pp. 269–313). Palo Alto, CA: Consulting Psychologists Press.

Hackman, J. R., & Morris, C. G. (1975). Group tasks, group interaction process and group performance effectiveness: A review and partial integration. In L. Berkowitz (Ed.), *Advances in experimental social psychology* (Vol. 8, pp. 47–99). New York: Academic Press.

Hinds, P., & Kiesler, S. (1995). Communication across boundaries: Work, structure, and use of communication technologies in a large organization. *Organization Science, 6*(4), 373–393.

Hirst, G., & Mann, L. (2004). A model of R&D leadership and team communication: The relationship with project performance. *R & D Management, 34*(2), 147–160.

Hoegl, M., Weinkauf, K., & Gemuenden, H. G. (2004). Interteam coordination, project commitment, and teamwork in multiteam R&D projects: A longitudinal study. *Organization Science, 15*(1), 38–55.

Ibarra, H. (1993). Network centrality, power, and innovation involvement: Determinants of technical and administrative roles. *Academy of Management Journal, 36*(3), 471–501.

Kahn, R. L., Wolfe, D. M., Quinn, R. P., Snoek, J. D., & Rosenthal, R. A. (1964). *Organizational stress: Studies in role conflict and ambiguity.* New York: Wiley.

Katz, D., & Kahn, R. L. (1966). Common characteristics of open systems. In D. Katz & R. L. Kahn, *The social psychology of organizations.* New York: Wiley.

Katz, D., & Kahn, R. L. (1978). *The social psychology of organizations.* New York: Wiley.

Kellogg, K. C., Orlikowski, W. J., & Yates, J. A. (2006). Life in the trading zone: Structuring coordination across boundaries in postbureaucratic organizations. *Organization Science, 17*(1), 22–44.

Kephart, W. M. (1950). A quantitative analysis of intragroup relationships. *American Journal of Sociology, 55*(6), 544–549.

Kiggundu, M. N. (1981). Task interdependence and the theory of job design. *Academy of Management Review, 6*(3), 499–508.

Kimberly, J. R. (1976). Organizational size and structuralist perspective: Review, critique and proposal. *Administrative Science Quarterly, 21*(4), 571–597.

Klein, K. J., Dansereau, F., & Hall, R. J. (1994). Levels issues in theory development, data collection, and analysis. *Academy of Management Review, 19*(2), 195–229.

Klein, K. J., Ziegert, J. C., Knight, A. P., & Xiao, Y. (2006). Dynamic delegation: Hierarchical, shared and deindividualized leadership in extreme action teams. *Administrative Science Quarterly, 51*(4), 590–621.

Kozlowski, S. W. J., Gully, S. M., McHugh, P. P., Salas, E., & Cannon-Bowers, J. A. (1996). A dynamic theory of leadership and team effectiveness: Developmental and task contingent leader roles. In G. R. Ferris (Ed.), *Research in personnel and human resource management* (Vol. 14, pp. 253–305). Greenwich, CT: JAI.

Lawrence, P. R., & Lorsch, J. W. (1967). Differentiation and integration in complex organizations. *Administrative Science Quarterly, 12*(1), 1–47.

Leifer, R., & Huber, G. P. (1977). Relations among perceived environmental uncertainty, organization structure, and boundary-spanning behavior. *Administrative Science Quarterly, 22*(2), 235–247.

Levina, N., & Vaast, E. (2005). The emergence of boundary spanning competence in practice: Implications for information systems' implementation and use. *MIS Quarterly, 29*(2), 335–363.

Liebeskind, J. P., Oliver, A. L., Zucker, L., & Brewer, M. (1996). Social networks, learning, and flexibility: Sourcing scientific knowledge in new biotechnology firms. *Organization Science, 7*(4), 428–443.

Luo, Y. D. (2007). The independent and interactive roles of procedural, distributive, and interactional justice in strategic alliances. *Academy of Management Journal, 50*(3), 644–664.

Maitlis, S. (2005). The social processes of organizational sensemaking. *Academy of Management Journal, 48*(1), 21–49.

March, J. G., & Simon, H. A. (1958). *Organizations.* New York: Wiley.

Marks, M. A., DeChurch, L. A., Mathieu, J. E., Panzer, F. J., & Alonso, A. (2005). Teamwork in multiteam systems. *Journal of Applied Psychology, 90*(5), 964–971.

Marks, M. A., Mathieu, J. E., & Zaccaro, S. J. (2001). A temporally based framework and taxonomy of team processes. *Academy of Management Review, 26*(3), 356–376.

Marrone, J. A., Tesluk, P. E., & Carson, J. B. (2007). A multilevel investigation of antecedents and consequences of team member boundary-spanning behavior. *Academy of Management Journal, 50*(6), 1423–1439.

Mathieu, J. E., Cobb, M. G., Marks, M. A., Zaccaro, S. J., & Marsh, S. (2004). Multiteam ACES: A low-fidelity platform for studying multiteam systems. In E. Salas (Ed.), *Scaled worlds: Development, validation and applications* (pp. 297–315). Burlington, VT: Ashgate.

Mathieu, J. E., Marks, M. A., & Zaccaro, S. J. (2001). Multiteam systems. In N. Anderson, D. Ones, H. K. Sinangil, & C. Viswesvaran (Eds.), *Handbook of industrial, work and organizational psychology: Vol. 2. Organizational psychology* (pp. 289–313). Thousand Oaks, CA: Sage.

Mathieu, J. E., Maynard, M. T., Taylor, S. R., Gilson, L. L., & Ruddy, T. M. (2007). An examination of the effects of organizational district and team contexts on team processes and performance: A meso-mediational model. *Journal of Organizational Behavior, 28*(7), 891–910.

Morgeson, F. P., & Humphrey, S. E. (2008). Job and team design: Toward a more integrative conceptualization of work design. In J. Martocchio (Ed.), *Research in personnel and human resource management* (Vol. 27, pp. 39–92). London: Emerald Group.

Organ, D. W. (1971). Linking pins between organizations and environment. *Business Horizons, 14*(6), 73–80.

Parsons, T. (1960). *Structure and process in modern societies.* New York: Free Press of Glencoe.

Perrone, V., Zaheer, A., & McEvily, B. (2003). Free to be trusted? Organizational constraints on trust in boundary spanners. *Organization Science, 14*(4), 422–439.

Pfeffer, J., & Salancik, G. R. (1978). *The external control of organizations: A resource dependence perspective.* New York: Harper & Row.

Saavedra, R., Earley, P. C., & Van Dyne, L. (1993). Complex interdependence in task-performing groups. *Journal of Applied Psychology, 78*(1), 61–72.

Schilling, M. A., & Steensma, H. K. (2001). The use of modular organizational forms: An industry-level analysis. *Academy of Management Journal, 44*(6), 1149–1168.

Scott, W. R. (1998). *Organizations: Rational, natural, and open systems.* Englewood Cliffs, NJ: Prentice Hall.

Star, S. L., & Griesemer, J. R. (1989). Institutional ecology, "translations" and boundary objects: Amateurs and professionals in Berkeley's Museum of Vertebrate Zoology, 1907–39. *Social Studies of Science, 19*(3), 387–420.

Tannenbaum, S. I., Beard, R. L., & Salas, E. (1992). Team building and its influence on team effectiveness: An examination of conceptual and empirical developments. In K. Kelley (Ed.), *Issues, theory, and research in industrial/organizational psychology* (pp. 117–153). New York: Elsevier Science.

Thompson, J. D. (1953). *The organization of executive action* (Air Force Base Project, Technical Report No. 12). Chapel Hill: Institute for Research in Social Science, University of North Carolina.

Thompson, J. D. (1962). Organizations and output transactions. *American Journal of Sociology, 68*(3), 309–324.

Thompson, J. D. (1967). *Organizations in action.* New York: McGraw-Hill.

Tushman, M. L. (1977). Special boundary roles in the innovation process. *Administrative Science Quarterly, 22*(4), 587–605.

Tushman, M. L., & Scanlan, T. J. (1981a). Boundary spanning individuals: Their role in information transfer and their antecedents. *Academy of Management Journal, 24*(2), 289–305.

Tushman, M. L., & Scanlan, T. J. (1981b). Characteristics and external orientations of boundary spanning individuals. *Academy of Management Journal, 24*(1), 83–98.

van de Ven, A. H. (1976). On the nature, formation, and maintenance of relations among organizations. *Academy of Management Review, 1*(4), 24–36.

van de Ven, A. H., & Ferry, D. L. (1980). *Measuring and assessing organizations.* New York: Wiley.

Weick, K. E. (1969). *The social psychology of organizing.* Reading, MA: Addison-Wesley.

Weick, K. E. (1995). *Sensemaking in organizations.* Thousand Oaks, CA: Sage.

Wooldridge, B., & Floyd, S. W. (1990). The strategy process, middle management involvement, and organizational performance. *Strategic Management Journal, 11*(3), 231–241.

Section IV

Development

13

Adaptation in Multiteam Systems: The Role of Temporal Semistructures

Sjir Uitdewilligen
Maastricht University

Mary J. Waller
York University

INTRODUCTION

Mathieu, Marks, and Zaccaro (2001) suggested that one of the main benefits of a multiteam system (MTS) is its responsiveness and adaptability to challenging performance environments. The constellation-like nature of MTSs, which consist of separate self-contained teams, fosters adaptability as the teams can be shifted, reordered, dismissed, and prioritized contingent on the demands of the situation. Particularly in emergency situations, characterized by high levels of ambiguity, uncertainty, and rapidly changing environmental dynamics, these flexible structures are crucial for rapid organizational adaptation in an unknown and developing environment. High adaptive capacity makes these systems particularly suitable for quickly bringing together collections of people to deal with emergent nonroutine events. For example, public health organizations employ systems of laboratory, research, clinical, logistics, and evacuation teams to contain outbreaks of infectious diseases (World Health Organization, 2009). During large fire outbreaks, fire departments make use of highly integrated team structures in order to quickly and accurately assess and control the situation (Bigley & Roberts, 2001; Myers & McPhee, 2006). And in the case of major oil spills, networked constellations of teams from various organizations coordinate their activities into a collective containment and clean-up response (Harrald, Cohn, & Wallace, 1992; Hunter, 1993; Kurtz, 2008).

In general, adaptability in such situations depends on rapid information gathering and communication, the development of situation awareness, and sound decision making (Bigley & Roberts, 2001; Weick & Sutcliffe, 2001). The adaptability of MTSs is fostered by their structural form, in particular by their loose coupling and the modular nature of their components. *Modularity* refers to the "degree to which a system's components can be separated and recombined" (Schilling, 2000, p. 312). Scholars of adaptation at the team and organizational levels have indicated, however, that adaptation to changing circumstances depends on more than structural flexibility alone. In their conceptual model of team adaptation, Burke, Stagl, Salas, Pierce, and Kendall (2006) depicted team adaptation as a recursive, cyclical process in which teams pass through phases of situation assessment, plan formulation, plan execution, and team learning to adapt to their changing contexts. On the organizational level, Daft and Weick (1984) reasoned that organizations proceed through three consecutive stages—scanning, interpretation, and learning (action taking)—in order to stay aligned with complex and continuously changing environments. These models imply that adaptation of systems on both the higher (organizational) and the lower (team) levels depends on a sequence of phases or functions that have to be successfully completed by the system.

In line with this reasoning, a number of recent studies indicate how more temporal characteristics of adaptive performance manifest in the interaction and knowledge integration processes of organizational members (Bigley & Roberts, 2001; Brown & Eisenhardt, 1997; Faraj & Xiao, 2006; Klein, Ziegert, Knight, & Xiao, 2006). According to this view, it is not so much the stable structural foundation of the system but instead the more dynamic structural mechanisms and practices that enable organizations to function reliably and act rapidly in the face of unexpected events. For instance, Faraj and Xiao identified coordination practices that reduce the need for formal structural coordination while guaranteeing effective management of interdependencies; similarly, Bigley and Roberts found that, within incident command systems, adaptive and improvisational capability is achieved by combining traditional bureaucratic role-based structures with flexibility-enhancing processes.

In an extension of these recent studies, we examine here several temporary MTSs as they form, work, and disband, and explore the role of a temporal semistructure—a particular, rhythmic shift in team focus—in the MTS's performance (Okhuysen & Eisenhardt, 2002). The goal of the MTSs is to enact the interorganization crisis management response in one of the world's biggest ports: the Port of Rotterdam in the Netherlands. In general, these MTSs consist of teams representing various emergency response organizations (e.g., fire brigade, police force, emergency medical services, and others) and become operational each time a crisis occurs that requires immediate action and extensive collaboration among the organizations involved.

In our analysis of these MTSs, we found evidence for cyclical adaptation on two separate levels. First, at the MTS level, each system adapts by reshaping and optimally aligning its structure and processes to the immediate demands posed by the crisis it faces. Our work reveals the importance of temporal pacing in the central command teams' meetings on adaptation at this level. Second, our work suggests that in order to understand system-wide MTS adaptation in the long run—beyond single instantiations of a MTS—one must look to the organizational structures and processes that facilitate the transfer of knowledge from one crisis to another. We begin with a description of these MTSs within their context, and then discuss both types of adaptation.

TEMPORARY MTSs, PARENTS, AND COMMAND TEAMS

Although embedded within multiple permanent organizations, the type of MTSs we focus on is temporary. Upon the emergence of a crisis situation, teams are formed by separate organizations from individuals pulled from their daily operations or from their homes, and an MTS is rapidly assembled according to previously established protocols. As soon as the crisis has been resolved or contained and the temporary MTS is no longer needed, its members are debriefed and the system is disbanded or reduced to units that finalize the aftermath of the crisis.

Goodman and Goodman (1976) defined *temporary systems* (or organizations) as "a set of diversely skilled people working together on a complex task over a limited period of time" (p. 494). Temporary response organizations such as the MTSs we describe here can be distinguished from emergency response organizations—spontaneously formed civilian initiatives providing disaster relief—by the existence of preexisting structural blue-prints and procedures, and because organizations and members generally have previous experience working together (Drabek & McEntire, 2003; Majchrzak, Jarvenpaa, & Hollingshead, 2007). Although the functional existence of temporary response organizations is momentary, the "parent" organizations that supply them with individuals and teams often spend substantial amounts of effort and time in training employees and establishing structures and procedures to prepare for events that infrequently occur.

The parent organizations provide a key source of contingencies that make up an important part of the context of the type of MTSs that we studied. They provide MTSs with resources, structures, and practices, and they install specific cultures, knowledge, and languages within their separate teams. Often, a collection of parent organizations conjointly designs the blueprint of the MTS and commits to providing the required resources for MTSs necessary in the future. For instance, the parent organizations of the MTSs we describe in this chapter not only provide resources but also have established a permanent interorganizational task force that is responsible for training the members, developing protocols, and integrating new technologies into the MTS blueprint.

However, the most crucial contingencies of these MTSs are not the organizations they stem from but the dynamic task environments they face during an emergency. When faced with an emergency, their immediate task environment is defined by the development of fires, the condition of victims, and the diffusion of hazardous material. During the response, the primary demands on the MTS stem from the incident environment. Based on an assessment of the incident, it is determined which structures will be applied and what practices will be followed, while the parent organizations remain flexible and in the service of the MTS. So, although the organizational context enables and constrains MTS functioning during an emergency, the dynamic task context is the primary context in which the MTS is embedded (Kozlowski & Ilgen, 2006).

Although the MTSs we studied consist of a collection of teams, each of which is indispensable for the functioning of the overall system, one team within the MTS was more central to the communication flows, information processing, and the coordination of interdependencies. In an extensive laboratory study, DeChurch and Marks (2006) demonstrated the pivotal role of leader functions in a multiteam setting. The results of their study indicate that effective leadership behaviors, which shape the interaction processes among the interdependent component teams based on a thorough assessment of the environment, task, and team members, positively influence interteam coordination and multiteam system performance. Similar to the design of this experiment, the MTSs we studied have a "team leading teams" structure in which a command team—consisting of members from each of the component teams of the multiteam system—is responsible for ensuring that the MTS functions as an integrated entity. Given the crucial role of this command team in the emergency response operations, we pay special attention to processes occurring within the command team and between this team and the other teams in the MTSs.

In the "Emergency Management in the Port of Rotterdam Region" section, we provide a brief overview of the context in which these MTSs operate at the Port of Rotterdam.

EMERGENCY MANAGEMENT IN THE PORT OF ROTTERDAM REGION

The Port of Rotterdam, located in the Netherlands, is annually visited by more than 37,000 seagoing vessels, and between 130,000 and 140,000 inland vessels. With a yearly throughput of more than 400 million tons of goods, it is the biggest seaport in Europe and the third biggest seaport in the world. The port and its adjacent industrial area stretch over a length of 40 kilometers and cover 10,500 hectares. The port contains five oil refineries, 44 chemical and petrochemical companies, three industrial gas producers, six raw oil producers, 19 independent tank terminals for oil and chemical products, and four independent terminals for edible oils and fats. The companies in the harbor are interconnected with an extensive network of over 1500 kilometers of pipelines, through which each year about 60 million tons of various oil and chemical products are transported (Havenbedrijf Rotterdam N.V., 2007). Almost half of the total transhipment of the port consists of oil and chemical products; this together with the sheer volume of interdependent activities taking place within a relatively confined location close to a densely populated residential area—1.2 million people living on 30,000 hectares—makes the port region vulnerable to both human and environmental disasters.

The emergency response organization (ERO) in the Rotterdam port region must be prepared for a wide variety of incidents, such as fires in warehouses filled with hazardous materials, chemical leakages causing gas clouds to threaten residential areas, or sinking ships containing contaminating or toxic materials. Apart from human and environmental hazards, even slight discontinuities in the shipping traffic and the logistic channel will immediately result in substantial losses for the companies involved, as well as for the port and its region. Because of these large commercial interests, there is a strong incentive to handle each incident as rapidly and with as little intrusion for commercial activities as possible. Moreover, increasingly tight coupling between manufacturers and suppliers and the relatively recent addition of terrorist attacks to the collection of potential hazards create new challenges to security and safety. Altogether, the immense complexity of the environment in which they operate, the preoccupation with speed, and the uniqueness of each emergency incident put heavy requirements on the emergency management system to be extremely flexible, adaptive, and fast responding. One of the most important tools available to the ERO is the formation of temporary interorganizational MTSs charged with containing crisis situations.

The ERO at the Rotterdam port region is an organization that is cooperatively established by a number of emergency management organizations in order to ensure rapid and effective multidisciplinary reactions to unexpected emergencies in a densely populated area. The organizations contributing to the ERO are the regional fire brigade, the medical emergency organization, the regional police department, the municipal emergency services, the environmental protection service, and the Rotterdam port authority. These organizations constitute the "parent" organizations that contribute teams to temporary MTSs for emergency responses to crises.

In the Netherlands, regional EROs have a hierarchical multilevel structure in which, depending on the scale and severity of the incident, the operation is "scaled up" to a higher level involving a wider group of stakeholders at higher levels of authority (Trijselaar, 2006). During day-to-day routine situations that do not require extensive coordination among the various services, incidents are dealt with locally by monodisciplinary response teams, and minor coordination requirements are dealt with on an ad hoc basis via the communal dispatch center or by means of so-called hood meetings during which operational personnel gather (literally) over the hood of their vehicles to make bilateral operational decisions. In such routine operations, each organization functions rather autonomously, and only limited interorganizational coordination is required; thus, no multidisciplinary MTS is needed.

The severity of emerging crisis situations is rated as Grip 1 (locally contained incident requiring interorganizational coordination), Grip 2 (poses a threat to the surrounding area outside the incident), Grip 3 (severe threat to the community requiring extensive coordination), and Grip 4 (disaster with consequences beyond the municipality's borders). As soon as an incident occurs that is considered local but requiring extensive coordination between the various emergency management organizations, the first emergency operation level (Grip 1) is declared. At the Grip 1 level, an operational command team (Command Place Incident, or CoPI) is mobilized by the ERO to manage the operational processes at the location of the incident and to coordinate the actions of the operational field teams from the various emergency organizations that constitute the MTS. This CoPI team assembles in a specially equipped vehicle at or near the location of the incident. The team is headed by (a) the fire brigade commander, and in addition comprises the officers on duty of (b) the fire brigade, (c) the police force, and (d) the port authority; (e) a chemical specialist from the medical protection service; (f) a representative of the medical emergency service; (g) a representative of the municipality; (h) an information manager; and (i) a public relations official of the police department. In addition to these standard members, representatives of a number of auxiliary organizations (transport organizations and companies) can be asked to attend the team's meeting in case their organizations are involved in the incident. When an MTS is activated during a crisis, these teams are highly functionally interdependent in terms of inputs, processes, and outcomes, exemplifying a defining characteristic of MTSs (Mathieu et al., 2001).

The component teams of this crisis management organization are interdependent regarding each of these dimensions. First, the component teams have interdependent outcomes not only because they share the distal goal of containing the incident and optimizing care for victims, but also because they have more proximal goals that depend on the combined action of the various services. For instance, whereas during a fire related incident, the fire brigade is in charge of the overall management of the incident, close collaboration with the port authority is a necessity, as the port authority has at its disposal a number of boats with powerful water pumps as well as an elaborate water supply network for the firefighters on the ground to use. Second, the teams have interdependent inputs as they require similar resources for their task execution. For example, they must apportion access roads to and from the incident location and divide space for placement of equipment and crisis centers. Third, process interdependence in the form of sequential interdependence occurs when police personnel must clear routes for the transportation of casualties that the other departments need for driving to the incident location.

Process interdependence also manifests as reciprocal interdependence in the close collaboration of the fire brigade and the emergency services during the rescue of casualties. For incidents that involve fires or hazardous materials, firefighters are the only emergency personnel that are equipped—and allowed—to enter the actual incident location, and hence they are responsible for the actual rescue of the victims. However, this happens in close collaboration with emergency service personnel who advise the fire brigade on how to initially treat the victims and who take charge of the victims after the rescue. Thus, these teams engage in a constant exchange of information and resources while saving victims from the incident location.

Finally, given the idiosyncratic nature of many incident situations, team interdependence is required for complex diagnoses and decisions about issues in which different services are involved, such as general decisions about how the incident should be approached, the determination of the area that is considered safe, and the location of the CoPI team and the center for the reception of casualties.

Given the scope of this chapter, we focus on the functioning of the MTS as it becomes effective under conditions of Grip 1 and Grip 2. Under these emergency levels, the MTS has a particular "team leading teams" structure as enunciated by Mathieu and colleagues (Mathieu et al., 2001). In "The Start-Up" section, we describe the process whereby these safety levels are declared and the MTS is formed.

THE START-UP

When an incident is reported to the dispatch center of one of the parent organizations, a first responder team of one of the organizations (e.g., fire brigade, police department, or port authority) is dispatched to the incident location to assess the situation and initiate actions toward the containment of the incident. If the officer in charge of the operation, or an executive official, judges the situation to require a multidisciplinary crisis response, it is declared a Grip 1 incident, and the members of the CoPI team are summoned by the ERO to report at the incident location. Alternatively, staff members of the dispatch center can declare the Grip 1 status based on an assessment of the calls they receive, as is illustrated by this description from a staff member of the communal dispatch center:

> Then we are sitting there with a limited number of people, and these people do a fire, an accident, another fire, another accident, a substantive fire, you know it may rumble a bit at the dispatch center. Or a lot of skating accidents, all small ones—that all stays with us. Until somebody says, "It smells like chloride here, and I see a woman collapse on the street, and back there some more." That is not an incident; it is going to grow. At a subway station, for example, and then it appears that at another station, somebody has the same complaints and the REV [the regional public transport organization] is missing a metro. Then you think, this is big, this is over our heads. Then these people have to manage this stream of 112 calls [European version of 911] and ensure that a staff officer is bleeped, and the officers of the fire department, and the head officer and commander. The public emergency servant has to be bleeped. We alarm for a Grip 1.[1]

Already en route to the incident location, CoPI members will start gathering and sharing information by means of mobile phones and radiotelephones. As soon as they arrive at the incident location, they will physically come together in the mobile vehicle in order to commence with a first assessment of the situation, to demarcate the incident area, and to formulate initial tactics. Based on the outcomes of these meetings, the CoPI members will summon the additional field teams (e.g., fire engines, police cars, medical units, and fire floats) that constitute the MTS. In order to allow the dispatch centers to take incident calls from other incidents that may be simultaneously emerging, the police force, ambulance service, fire brigade, and environmental service will each set up a specific action center for the incident. These action centers gather and communicate information, and manage the dispatch of additional units and resources. Figure 13.1 depicts the structure of the MTS responsible for managing the

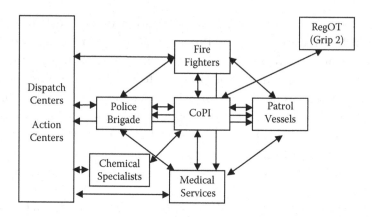

FIGURE 13.1

The crisis management system at the Port of Rotterdam region (arrows indicate direct communication channels).

crisis management operation at the Port of Rotterdam under Grip levels 1 and 2.

In sum, the context for the temporary CoPI teams and MTSs at the Port of Rotterdam is complex and dynamic, with unexpected crisis events emerging and a high level of coordination among teams necessary to effectively manage the events. In the "Data Collection" section, we describe how we collected data from these teams in order to better understand how they effectively adapt to and operate under these extreme circumstances.

DATA COLLECTION

Data for this study were collected in three consecutive phases: an interview phase, a behavioral observation data collection phase, and a training exercise observation phase. The first phase involved unstructured interviews with three key persons from the ERO. These interviews were conducted with the goal of gaining a primary understanding of the overall organization in light of our goal to understand how the MTS adapts to the crisis as it changes and emerges over time, with particular attention paid to information gathering and communication, situation awareness, and decision making. In addition to their verbal explanations, these contact persons supplied us with protocols and internal reports that provided a general understanding of the process of forming and using MTSs.

In the second phase of our research, the first author attended six multidisciplinary crisis management training exercises in order to better understand the functioning of a CoPI team and its MTS in action, and to gain a more thorough understanding of the coordination requirements among the various parent organizations involved. The purpose of these exercises is to prepare members of the various organizations for their roles as members of a CoPI team during actual crises. These exercises take place in a large room equipped with computers through which participants can receive information and communicate with each other, a central screen on which general information is displayed, and a meeting area for the CoPI teams. Each exercise lasts approximately 3 hours. The exercises simulate crisis events at the Port of Rotterdam and involve the activation of a CoPI team and a multiteam system charged with the responsibility of managing the crisis. As part of an ongoing research project, we collected data from these exercises in the form of video-recordings of command team member interactions during the exercises; in addition, team members completed questionnaires and answered our numerous questions informally after each exercise.

The third phase of the research consisted of 14 semistructured face-to-face interviews with members from the various parent organizations who participated in the MTSs we video-recorded. During these interviews, we collected additional details and tested our preliminary conceptualizations of the multiteam system. Nine of the interviewees were members who played roles during a crisis management exercise, whereas the other interviewees were involved in organizing and assessing training sessions for the ERO and had ample experience working in the MTSs. Interviews covered communication, coordination, and shared cognition requirements during emergency situations, and interviewees were asked to recount an incident during which the MTS performed particularly well and an incident during which the performance of the MTS was low. All interviews were tape-recorded for later analyses, and all interviewees agreed to the recording.

We compiled the data collected from the initial unstructured interviews, video observations, questionnaires, and semistructured follow-up interviews and categorized data in terms of our focus on understanding more about MTS adaptive processes. Initially, we focused chiefly on categorizing information based on situation assessment, situation interpretation, and adaptation processes. These three processes certainly have ample support in existing literature regarding their importance in team responses to unexpected events, and we were not surprised to find that much of the behavior represented by our data could be categorized in terms of these processes. We were surprised, however, as we later figuratively "stepped back" and watched the data with a more holistic lens as to the rhythm and timing of events during the crisis exercises. We found that behaviors fitting into our three categories were embedded within a temporal semistructure that facilitated MTS adaption during emergent and unpredictable events. In the next section, we describe this temporal semistructure, and then illustrate how the structure facilitates MTS adaptive efforts in terms of information gathering, situation awareness, and decision making.

TEMPORAL SEMISTRUCTURE AND RHYTHM OF THE MTS

Previous scholars have indicated the pivotal role of information gathering and communication, and the formation of an understanding of the situation as crucial for deliberate adaptive performance (Burke et al., 2006; Waller, 1999). The MTSs we observed at the Port of Rotterdam applied a temporal semistructure (Okhuysen & Waller, 2002) that enabled them to successfully gather information and communicate, develop situation awareness, and make decisions in order to adapt to changing task situations. A *semistructure* is a structure that is "sufficiently rigid so that change can be organized to happen, but not so rigid that it cannot occur" (Brown & Eisenhardt, 1997, p. 29). The temporal semistructure we observed consisted of a rhythmic shift in focus—either local or general—of all teams comprising the MTS. We describe this facilitation in the sections below, beginning with an elaboration of the pivotal role of the CoPI meetings.

CoPI Meetings

Participants in the CoPI meetings fulfill the dual role of team leader and interteam decision maker. In the field, they lead their own functional component teams, provide them with directions, implement decisions, and collect information, whereas in the CoPI meetings they share information, assess the situation, make decisions, and discuss possible courses of action with the other CoPI members. This dual function of the CoPI members provides an important element in bridging the interdisciplinary understanding of the crisis situation and implementing multidisciplinary decisions. By physically coming together and exchanging information at the very onset of a crisis, the CoPI engages in "thick" information exchange, including the possibility to assess if one has been understood by others and to directly ask questions in case questions arise. Previous studies have indicated the importance of physically coming together and actively engaging in collective situation assessment for adaptive performance during nonroutine task situations (Waller, Gupta, & Giambatista, 2004). Moreover, the structure whereby CoPI members themselves function as the leaders of the functional component teams facilitates the implementation of decisions and action plans that have been formulated in the CoPI meetings.

The regular meetings of the CoPI teams provide the emergency response organization with a temporal structure that links together planning and action, mono- and multidisciplinary perspectives, and present and future thinking. The first CoPI meeting takes place immediately when all CoPI members have arrived at the incident location. Following the first meeting, CoPI teams reassemble at regular intervals during the crisis management operation. At the end of each meeting, the CoPI leader sets the start time for the next meeting generally at about 15 minutes from then. However, the period in between meetings is not fixed a priori but will be determined based on an estimation of the time it will take to issue commands and gather information in the intermediate phase. As described by an officer of the fire brigade,

> A CoPI does not gather to have a conference. A CoPI gathers to solve a problem, so they must be brief and to the point, and then out of that vehicle and back to work, communicate results, discuss again, and yet again out of that vehicle. And that must be a well-tuned rhythm in which all the services have sufficient time to do the things they have to do. And that will depend, on the one hand, on the location of the CoPI and, on the other hand, on the location of the incident. Most of the time, this is determined by the time the fire officer or the medical advisor needs, after the first meeting, to go back to the incident and talk to their colleagues in the field and come back for a next plenary meeting. That determines the time in between. So if it is close, you have to be able to be back in 5 or maximum 10 minutes,

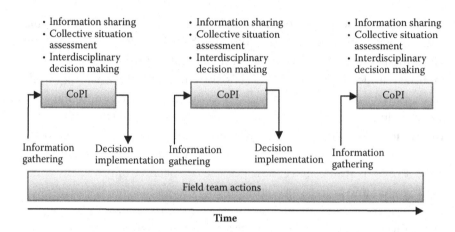

FIGURE 13.2
A depiction of the temporal structure of the MTS and its adaptive processes.

because also with these colleague officers in the field you are not going to have a nice group discussion. So there it also is to the point. But if you have to drive up the terrain of Company X and you are located at the gate with your CoPI, then it may be possible that you first have to drive for 10 minutes over this terrain before you are with your colleague officer. Well, that means 10 minutes there, talking for 5 minutes, and 10 minutes back, then 25 minutes passed.

In this way, the team engages in a phased temporal structure of alternating stages of engaging in operations and collective sense making. Literature on entrainment (e.g., Ancona & Chong, 1996) has emphasized the importance of rhythms in coordinating related processes. The temporal attunement of the synchronized rhythms of separate entities creates temporal windows in which coordination can take place. As can be seen in Figure 13.2, the rhythms created by the repetitive meetings of the CoPI teams create natural moments for attuning multiteam actions. In the "Information Gathering and Communication" section, we detail how this temporal pattern of assembling and disjoining facilitates the adaptive processes of information gathering and communication, the development of situation awareness, and collective decision making.

INFORMATION GATHERING AND COMMUNICATION

The first requirement for functional adaptation is the ability to quickly recognize and communicate cues that signal the need for adaptive reactions (Burke et al., 2006). On both the team and organizational levels, scholars have indicated the importance of information collection behaviors for keeping attuned to dynamic environments (Aguilar, 1967; Ancona, 1990). The division of MTSs into component teams, each with its specific roles and functions, creates a highly distributed information-gathering system in which the different component teams are likely to collect and contribute a wide variety of information; the chemical advisors keep track of chemical substances located in the area, firefighters attend to information about the development of the fire, and medical personnel gather cues about the amount and severity of casualties.

Having timely dispersion of crucial information is pivotal to the effective management of nonroutine situations. In order to facilitate the rapid dispersion of information throughout the system and minimize the amount of time that elapses before information travels among different teams and across various hierarchical layers, the Rotterdam ERO has adopted a *netcentric* approach to information sharing. This approach implies that information is immediately made available to all teams independent of the organization they stem from or their hierarchical level. This contrasts with more traditional approaches of information sharing in which information is transferred mainly within divisions and only upward or downward through the direct chain of command. A correctly applied netcentric information-sharing approach sharply decreases the time it takes for relevant information to reach the appropriate person. For example, measurement outcomes from the chemical advisor regarding the type and amount of materials involved in the incident will be directly made available to other teams on a shared information system. In this way, the firefighters in the field will be able to act upon this information much more rapidly than if this information had first gone through an intermediary link of commanding officers.

However, simply making information available throughout the system does not guarantee that this information will be successfully interpreted and the right conclusions will be drawn from it. Collective integration and interpretation of information require communication structures of high media richness (Daft & Lengel, 1986). Daft and Lengel suggested that communication media can be considered rich to the extent that they "can overcome different frames of reference or clarify ambiguous issues to change understanding in a timely manner" (p. 560). Hence, whereas netcentric communication channels may facilitate rapid and effective dispersion of information throughout the system, richer communication channels are required to facilitate the integration and interpretation of this information within the system.

Although highly functional for sampling a wide variety of information, the diversity of the component teams may also have detrimental effects by hampering effective interteam communication (Zaccaro et al., Chapter 1, this volume). Whereas each component team often requires its own specific information, at the collective level it is crucial for MTS adaptation that important information from the separate fields is combined and integrated into system-level knowledge (Grant, 1996). Laboratory studies on group information sharing are often designed around the idea that it is important for the group task that all information is shared among the group members (Larson, Christensen, Abbott, & Franz, 1996; Stasser, Stewart & Wittenbaum, 1995; Stasser & Titus, 1985). However, in MTSs, sharing all available information is likely to lead to a situation in which team members become overloaded with details and unable to distinguish relevant from irrelevant information. Moreover, given the diversity in functional backgrounds of team members from the various teams, raw information sent by an expert member may not directly make sense to the other members. As Cronin and Weingart (2007) indicated, functional diversity may lead to representational gaps—differences in how the collective task is viewed that may make it more difficult to integrate one another's information and that may lead to conflict.

The regular CoPI meetings constitute a mechanism that facilitates these MTSs in overcoming information-sharing difficulties. Two processes appear to play an important role in the pooling of information within the CoPI teams: *filtering* and *explaining*.

Filtering refers to the process of selecting which information elements will be shared with the other team members (Ancona & Caldwell, 1992). As previous scholars have indicated, not all members need to have a complete understanding of the task situations, nor do they all need to have the same understanding about all aspects of that situation (e.g., Endsley,

1995; Wellens, 1993). Given the limited amount of time during the CoPI meetings for sharing and explaining information, CoPI members weigh the importance of each piece of information for the overall understanding of the team. Although it is important for the team members to share a general understanding of the incident, more specific information often is important to only one or two of the services, and there is a strong norm for such information to be shared outside of the CoPI meetings in bilateral conversations. So team members are very sensitive to the relevance of the information that is shared within the CoPI meetings and they expect from each other to judge the information they bring in on the relevance it has for the overall understanding of the incident by the team. This filtering of information before they share it with the team allows for an efficient balance between distribution and overlap of information. As a police officer described the ideal situation,

> The ideal picture is: everyone has sufficient information from his own service and they know how to filter this information—what to share and what is simply your own expertise that you do not have to shout. For example, it only has very little additional value to inform the CoPI team where you have placed all your enclosures. You have to say what has been enclosed but that can be quite globally, so from east to west we do not allow any traffic to pass there. Well, that is clear for everyone ... and that is what one has to be very good at, filtering.

Similarly, a medical officer indicated,

> I would say that people would know themselves what little unimportant details are, which they do not have to take with them. So, they will restrict themselves to the main lines. Placing that clearly and forming a shared image and strategy and possibly think in scenarios, and that happens collectively.

Explanation refers to the transformation of information into a form that is comprehensible by the other team members and makes sense within their frames of reference. Without explanation, field-specific technical information will not make sense to all team members. For example, if the chemical advisor notifies that gaseous chlorine is involved in the accident, the other team members will not be able to ascertain what this information means for their understanding of the situation. However, when explained that chlorine is not flammable but causes irritation of the airways and eyes and burns on the skin, the medical officer and fire officer will be able to fit this information into their understanding of the situation. Thus, each CoPI member takes a gatekeeping and boundary-spanning role, monitoring the environment and translating technical information from his or her field of expertise into a form understandable to the members of the group (Cohen & Levinthal, 1990; Tushman, 1977).

Whereas these processes facilitate information exchange from the component teams to the system level, similar processes take place when CoPI team members return to their own component teams. They also decide what information should be communicated back to the team in the field and translate the outcomes of the CoPI meetings into the terminology of their own teams.

THE DEVELOPMENT OF SITUATION AWARENESS

The construction of a collective understanding of the dynamic task situation is a consistently resurfacing theme in a wide variety of field studies on teams and organizations functioning in challenging environments (e.g., Bigley & Roberts, 2001; Faraj & Xiao, 2006; Roberts, 1990; Roth, Multer, & Raslear, 2006). For systems faced with a dynamic and shifting environment, the ability of members to rapidly assess and update an understanding of the situation is crucial for adaptation and reliable performance (Burke et al., 2006; Reason, 1997; Weick, Sutcliffe, & Obstfeld, 2005; Woods & Shattuck, 2000). Various labels have been used to denote this understanding of the situation, including having the "bubble" (Roberts & Rousseau, 1989), team situation models (Rico, Sánchez-Manzanares, Gil, & Gibson, 2008), and team situation awareness (Endsley, 1995; Endsley & Jones, 2001). Situation awareness is important for system adaptiveness for two main reasons. First, sensitivity to changes in the task environment enables rapid detection and the formulation of appropriate responses to environmental jolts. Second, a shared understanding of the task situation enables members from various system components to ensure the systems functions together as an integrated entity (Endsley, 1995; Rico et al., 2008; Salas, Prince, Baker, & Shrestha, 1995).

A number of factors make it particularly difficult for an MTS to develop and maintain shared situation awareness in emergency situations. First, the actual execution of the tasks needed to manage the incident may require so much attentional resources from individuals that no spare capacity is available to develop situation awareness. In their study on the Incident Command System, Bigley and Roberts (2001) found that due to the cognitively demanding nature of their tasks, many individuals in the system were not able to uphold an awareness of the system around them. When this was the case, responsibility for situation awareness was shifted to another member of the organization who was in a better position to uphold a representation of the task environment. Second, the multifaceted nature of an incident management operation makes it almost impossible for any single individual to encompass all elements that are relevant for an overall understanding. Third, the unfolding nature of the incident makes situation assessment a challenging and highly dynamic process in which an understanding of the situation may become rapidly outdated. Not only do dynamic aspects of the incident—such as fires and the condition of casualties—change over time, but also information about the incident becomes available over time. For example, the CoPI team may have to wait until the manager of a private firm arrives before they get the blueprints of a burning warehouse. In addition, in complex real-life situations, the formation of an understanding of the situation often is not an instant revelation, but instead may constitute an iterative process of conceptualizing and adjusting previous understandings based on reasoning and new insights (Klein & Thordsen, 1989; Waller & Uitdewilligen, 2009). For example:

Chemical advisor: An incident is an incident; it is a dynamic thing that changes all the time. So, then you think you have the image, but your information is not complete. So, if you hear from a company that Benzene is burning and after three quarters of an hour you hear that some other chemical is burning, then you suddenly have a completely different picture. So, theoretically it is difficult to say that you have an image in the CoPI and it is "the image"; that is nonsense. It changes every 10 minutes—and, if you have tough luck, every minute, particularly with a fire.

Police officer: It is always difficult [to form an understanding of the situation]. You get such fragmented information. So, already when you are driving toward the incident you are called by everyone.

> If I look at my service: by the dispatch center, by colleagues that are already at the location, by the (supervisor on duty). So you get so much information that you hardly have time to form an image yourself, and then of course you have the others that join in. Yes, in the beginning it simply is difficult to form a good image. And that practically is the case in any situation, although sometimes it will go quicker than at other times.

Therefore, in the ERO, the main responsibility for developing an overall understanding of the situation lies within the CoPI teams. During the CoPI meetings, the team members share and collectively make sense of the wide variety of information they receive about the incident. Endsley (1995) posed that the ability to project the future status of the environment constitutes the highest level of situation awareness. Whereas an appropriate understanding of the current situation is required to effectively deal with direct demands, insight into the potential development trajectories of the situation enables the system to prepare and plan for future contingencies. For instance, knowledge about the development trajectories of a fire enables an emergency management organization to order and dispatch required resources, such as fire trucks and support systems, and to issue timely warnings. Brown and Eisenhardt (1997) associated the transitions inherent in temporal rhythms with the ability to couple the present to the future. Comparing transitions with the "routinized pit stop in car racing" that "quickly brings competitors back to the race," they argued that such rhythmic transformations bring together managers focusing on developing current products and others creating a sense of the future.

In the MTS under investigation here, future and present perspectives are not divided between persons but rather vary within individuals over time. Transformations between field and CoPI phases link the present perspective forced upon them by the immediate call for attention of the field operations, in which CoPI members stand—sometimes literally—with their feet in the mud, to the more abstract perspective taken in the CoPI meetings, where future contingencies are assessed and possible future scenarios are developed. Okhuysen and Eisenhardt (2002) suggested that formal interventions in teams work by stimulating a cognitive switch between completing the principal activity of the group and attending to a second agenda inherent in the intervention. They indicated that this cognitive switch creates a "window of opportunity" for team process improvement and adaptation. Similarly, Waller and colleagues (Waller et al., 2004) found that in nuclear power plant control teams, so-called tailboard meetings, during which team members momentarily left their ongoing activities and came together to discuss the current or possible future status of the systems and outline plans of actions, positively related to team adaptation and performance under nonroutine circumstances.

COLLECTIVE DECISION MAKING

An important aspect that was explicitly mentioned by all interviewees at the port was an extreme emphasis on speed. Although an accurate and shared understanding of the crisis situation is crucial for effective performance, time spent in the CoPI meeting is time not spent in the field. And time not spent in the field implies that CoPI members do not have the latest updates about the situation and cannot issue appropriate commands. Incidents often develop and escalate rapidly, and therefore the system is impregnated with a sense of urgency. There simply is not sufficient time to exchange and discuss information until all team members' understanding of the situation is complete and accurate. At times, actions must be taken despite this fact. As Weick (1995) indicated, "We might expect that speed, rather than a 'constant and close look,' would dominate whenever anyone has to adapt to complex cue patterns" (p. 58). As one police officer cogently put it,

> What particularly is lethal is lack of speed. When you are not able to form an image in within 10 to 15 minutes, to cut it and to accept that your image is not yet complete ... but "come on" split up and after 10 or 15 minutes you come back with revised information ... because the world out there does not stand still.

This extreme emphasis on speed also changes the traditional dichotomy between decision making and action execution. As an incident unfolds, the immediate pressure to contain the incident leaves individuals with little time to stop and think about the best course of action, let alone consider the ramifications of the actions of their own team on the other component teams. Therefore, CoPI meetings provide brackets of time away from the field that can be devoted to collective decision making.

Marks, Mathieu, and Zaccaro (2001) posed that teams cycle through identifiable periods of action and transition periods between actions. During transition phases, team members make decisions regarding goals, strategies, and contingency plans, whereas in subsequent action phases, team members engage in the acts that directly contribute to goal accomplishment. In these MTSs, *transition processes* include the planning, decision making, and coordination of joint actions of teams from different organizations, whereas *action processes* refer to the actual extinguishing of fires or the transportation of casualties. In the port MTSs, we find that although the CoPI teams do engage in recurrent phase patterns—as the members toggled between multidisciplinary coordination processes and monodisciplinary action processes—at the system level, transition and action phases are executed by different teams. Whereas the CoPI teams periodically engage in the transition behaviors of situation assessment and decision making, field teams are more or less continuously engaged in action processes directly related to combating the incident.

Finally, the switch from the field to the CoPI meeting engenders a switch not only between action and decision making but also between mono- and multidisciplinary reasoning. Because the officers on duty in this MTS have a dual role as members of the multidisciplinary CoPI team and as leaders of their own functional team, they continuously switch between monofunctional and multifunctional reasoning and decision making. In the field they give commands and solve problems for their own teams, whereas in the CoPI meetings they look beyond their monodisciplinary problems toward the broader picture of what their actions mean for the other teams and how the actions of the other teams impact the situation they are facing.

ADAPTATION AT THE ORGANIZATIONAL LEVEL

While the previous discussion focused on adaptation within single MTSs, adaptation also occurs in the overall organization over time, as various crises erupt and multiple MTSs are formed and disbanded. Although each crisis situation is unique, some elements may be shared across crises.

Changes in the general environment of the crisis management organization—such as changes in traffic patterns, new safety threats, technological developments—that are noticed within one instantiation of an MTS should be transferred to future MTSs. For example, knowledge of shortcuts to rapidly reach hospitals, the development of a more efficient system for categorizing victims, or especially efficient interaction patterns among different emergency services may be developed by an MTS during a crisis management operation. However, given that MTSs are staffed based on the work schedules of individual employees, there is no guarantee that future MTSs will be identically staffed for a similar type of crisis.

Therefore, the organization must ensure that any generalizable insights and processes developed within one crisis management operation—one MTS—are captured so that they can be adequately retrieved and applied in future crisis operations. It is this ability to generate, maintain, and transfer knowledge over crises and time that drives MTS adaptive performance in the long run.

How might an organization glean such knowledge over time from temporary MTSs? Scholars of organizational memory have identified several forms in which knowledge can be retained and transferred within organizations, including organizational culture, beliefs, norms, and values, routines, procedures, and scripts, and artifacts and technologies (Moorman & Miner, 1997; Walsh & Ungson, 1991). Similarly, scholars of organizational learning have argued that an important part of organizational memory lies in the translation of experience into formal and informal routines (Nelson & Winter, 1982). Formal routines may be encoded in standard operating procedures or protocols. Informal routines may be reflected in scripted interactions (Poole, Gray, & Gioia, 1990). However, the development and transfer of routines is particularly challenging for temporary inter-organizational systems such as MTSs because their discontinuous nature causes interruptions in their learning cycle (Defillipi & Arthur, 1998; Gann & Salter, 2000).

At the Port of Rotterdam, we found that this transfer of knowledge occurs through two different pathways: a procedural approach and an informal community of practice approach. The emergency response organization (ERO) plays a role in both approaches by installing processes aimed at the elicitation and codification of knowledge and by actively encouraging and facilitating the construction of inter-organizational networks and the exchange of knowledge within these networks. We will shortly describe each approach below.

In the procedural approach, the organization makes use of knowledge elicitation—anchoring knowledge obtained during crises in procedures—and dissemination of this knowledge through meetings and training. At the end of the last CoPI meeting of a crisis, all members of the CoPI team are asked if they would like to have a formal evaluation of the crisis management operation. If one of the members answers affirmative, a date will be set on which the members will come together and collectively discuss and evaluate the management of the previous crisis. Evaluations are not only requested when something went wrong but may also be conducted to better understand why some operations proceeded remarkably well. As a fire officer indicated:

> This does not only take place when the situation went awry, not at all. It could also be because many things went very well in an unusual situation. Then you have a kind of learning document. So, in case something like it does happen again we know at least we have to think in that direction. These documents are then presented in meetings of the regional officers and head officers. [There we say] "guys if you encounter this kind of situation then take into account that...".

In addition to learning from actual crises, crisis simulations used for training are an important source for process improvements, as is indicated by the statements of this police officer:

> During an exercise at Rotterdam Airport there was a pre-alarm in case there may be a possible crash. But it appeared that during this pre-alarm phase, everyone was there except our CoPI-member, because nobody thought about that before. Our CoPI member is not called in until the situation is declared a Grip situation and a Grip situation is only declared when the plane has crashed. So, I was at that exercise and I thought, this is not right; this is not in accordance with practice. So, I make a phone call and they say "no problem," and I did already hear them typing.

The procedural approach described above constitutes a rather formal way in which insights that are acquired during actual or simulated crisis management operations are elicited and transferred through the organization. These are processes of codification; knowledge is converted into messages that can easily be stored, retrieved, and transferred to others (Cowan & Foray, 1997). However, while codified knowledge may form a solid basis for proactive training and planning, given the time pressure inherent in most crisis situations, MTSs may not have the time necessary to peruse organizational stores of knowledge for potentially relevant information during an active incident.

Thus, at the Port of Rotterdam, the codification approach is supplemented by a community of practice approach via devices such as transactive memory systems (Majchrzak, Jarvenpaa, & Hollingshead, 2007) and interpersonal networks (Borgatti & Cross, 2003) that provide platforms for knowledge storage and transfer. Communities of practice are a method to promote organizational learning through information sharing in informal networks of members who have a shared domain of interest (Lave & Wenger, 1991). At the emergency response organization of the Port of Rotterdam, members of MTSs principally belong to communities of specialists from their own emergency service area—police, medical, fire brigade. However, in addition to professional networks within these specific services, MTS members also indicated to us the existence of an overlapping community of practice; they not only identify with their own organization and profession but also to their more general occupation as "emergency management workers" (see Nelson, 1997). The formation of this community of practice is strengthened by shared norms and values of safety and rescuing people and facilitated by frequent interaction between members of the various services. Not only during crises but also during "normal operations," contact between members of different emergency services is quite frequent; many daily operations involve the cooperation between at least two services—such as medical services and police force working together during car accidents. In addition, there are also practices of the inter-organizational emergency response organization that seem to be aimed at the facilitation of socialization and the development of an inter-organizational community of practice. For example, several interviewees indicated that one of the most important goals of inter-organizational training exercises is to develop an inter-organizational network in which members know each other and share cross-functional knowledge. Many of these training exercises, therefore, take several days and include hotel stays so that members receive ample time to socialize.

CONCLUSION

We investigated a single case study of a repeatedly enacted MTS with the goal of identifying structures and processes that enable this system to adapt to a wide variety of situational circumstances and demands. Based on existing literature from the team and organizational levels, we investigated how the system's information-gathering and communication, situation assessment, and decision-making processes facilitated the system's ability to adapt to emergent crisis situations. What most struck us in our observations of this specific type of MTS, however, was that behaviors fitting into these three categories were embedded within a temporal semistructure that facilitated system adaption during emergent and unpredictable events. The momentary yet rhythmic pattern of CoPI meetings, during which members of the component teams assembled to exchange information, discuss the development of the incident, and develop scenarios and plans, served as a bridging mechanism between immediate and future demands, present and future orientation, and mono- and multidisciplinary approaches. It enabled the MTS to continuously engage in fighting the incident while at the same time taking care of the transition processes required for adaptive performance.

This temporal structure is an inherently multilevel phenomenon, as it bridges the lower level component teams and the higher level CoPI team. Zaccaro and colleagues (Chapter 1, this volume) discuss the linking mechanisms that connect component teams as an important aspect for distinguishing MTSs. The present study indicates that we should think of linking mechanisms not only in terms of fixed, static structures but also in terms of temporal structures, unfolding and rearranging component teams over time as multiteam systems adapt and realign with their external environments.

In addition to adaptation at the MTS level we found that adaptation also takes place at the organizational level as knowledge is transferred over different instantiations of the MTS. The discontinuous nature of temporary response organizations and the constant reshuffling of membership poses specific challenges for eliciting and reproducing knowledge within such organizations. In response to this challenge and to facilitate adaptation at this level, the emergency response organization at the Port of Rotterdam applied and actively facilitated both a procedural and a community of practice approach. Thus, researchers and practitioners interested in MTS adaptation should consider adaptation not only at the level of the MTS itself but should also address how adaptation occurs beyond single instantiations of an MTS in order to identify process that will lead to long-term continuous improvement.

NOTE

1. All excerpts in this chapter have been translated from Dutch by the first author. In the translations, we have attempted to keep the content and tone of the excerpts as close to the original Dutch version as possible.

REFERENCES

Aguilar, F. J. (1967). *Scanning the business environment.* New York: Macmillan.

Ancona, D. G. (1990). Outward bound: Strategies for team survival in an organization. *Academy of Management Journal, 33*(2), 334.

Ancona, D. G., & Caldwell, D. F. (1992). Bridging the boundary: External activity and performance in organizational teams. *Administrative Science Quarterly, 37*(4), 634–661.

Ancona, D. G., & Chong, C. L. (1996). Entrainment: Pace, cycle, and rhythm in organizational behavior. In B. Staw & T. Cummings (Eds.), *Research in organizational behavior* (Vol. 18, pp. 251–284). Greenwich, CT: JAI.

Bigley, G. A., & Roberts, K. H. (2001). The incident command system: High-reliability organizing for complex and volatile task environments. *Academy of Management Journal, 44*(6): 1281–1299.

Borgatti, S. P., & Cross, R. (2003). A relational view of information seeking and learning in social networks. *Management Science, 49*(4), 432–445.

Brown, S. L., & Eisenhardt, K. M. (1997). The art of continuous change: Linking complexity theory and time-paced evolution in relentlessly shifting organizations. *Administrative Science Quarterly, 42*(1), 1–34.

Burke, C. S., Stagl, K. C., Salas, E., Pierce, L., & Kendall, D. (2006). Understanding team adaptation: A conceptual analysis and model. *Journal of Applied Psychology, 91*(6), 1189–1207.

Cohen, W. M., & Levinthal, D. A. (1990). Absorptive capacity: A new perspective on learning and innovation. *Administrative Science Quarterly, 35*(1), 128–152.

Cowan, R., & Foray, D. (1997). The economics of codification and the diffusion of knowledge. *Industrial and Corporate Change, 6*(3), 595–622.

Cronin, M. A., & Weingart, L. R. (2007). Representational gaps, information processing, and conflict in functionally diverse teams. *Academy of Management Review, 32*(3), 761–773.

Daft, R. L., & Lengel, R. H. (1986). Organizational information requirements, media richness and structural design. *Management Science, 32*(5), 554–571.

Daft, R. L., & Weick, K. E. (1984). Toward a model of organizations as interpretation systems. *Academy of Management Review, 9*(2), 284.

DeChurch, L. A., & Marks, M. A. (2006). Leadership in multiteam systems. *Journal of Applied Psychology, 91*(2), 311–329.

DeFillippi, R. J., & Arthur, M. B. (1998). Paradox in project-based enterprise: The case of film making. *California Management Review, 40*(2), 125–139.

Drabek, T. E., & McEntire, D. A. (2003). Emergent phenomena and the sociology of disaster: Lessons, trends and opportunities from the research literature. *Disaster Prevention and Management, 12*(2), 97–112.

Endsley, M. R. (1995). Measurement of situation awareness in dynamic systems. *Human Factors, 37*(1), 65–84.

Endsley, M. R., & Jones, W. M. (2001). A model of inter- and intrateam situational awareness: Implications for design, training, and measurement. In M. McNeese, E. Salas, & M. Endsley (Eds.), *New trends in cooperative activities: Understanding system dynamics in complex environments* (pp. 46–67). Santa Monica, CA: Human Factors and Ergonomics Society.

Faraj, S., & Xiao, Y. (2006). Coordination in fast-response organizations. *Management Science, 52*(8), 1155–1169.

Gann, D. M., & Salter, A. J. (2000). Innovation in project-based, service-enhanced firms: The construction of complex products and systems. *Research Policy, 29*(7–8), 955–972.

Goodman, R. A., & Goodman, L. P. (1976). Some management issues in temporary systems: A study of professional development and manpower—the theater case. *Administrative Science Quarterly, 21*(3), 494–501.

Grant, R. M. (1996). Prospering in dynamically-competitive environments: Organizational capability as knowledge integration. *Organization Science, 7*(4), 375–387.

Harrald, J. R., Cohn, R., & Wallace, W. A. (1992). We were always reorganizing: Some crisis management implications of the Exxon *Valdez* oil spill. *Industrial Crisis Quarterly, 6,* 197–217.

Havenbedrijf Rotterdam N.V. (2007). *Haven in Cijfers.* http://www.portofrotterdam.com/nl/Over-de-haven/havenstatistieken/Documents/Haven_in_cijfers_2009.pdf

Hunter, S. (1993). The oiling of ICS. In *Proceedings of the 1993 Oil Spill Conference* (pp. 25–30). Washington, DC: American Petroleum Institute.

Klein, G., & Thordsen, M. L. (1989). *A cognitive model of team decision making.* Yellow Springs, OH: Klein Associates.

Klein, K. J., Ziegert, J. C., Knight, A. P., & Xiao, Y. (2006). Dynamic delegation: Shared, hierarchical, and deindividualized leadership in extreme action teams. *Administrative Science Quarterly, 51*(4), 590–621.

Kozlowski, S. W. J., & Ilgen, D. R. (2006). Enhancing the effectiveness of work groups and teams. *Psychological Science in the Public Interest, 7*(3), 77–124.

Kurtz, R. S. (2008). Coastal oil spill preparedness and response: The Morris J. Berman incident. *Review of Policy Research, 25*:2.

Larson, J. R., Christensen, C., Abbott, A. S., & Franz, T. M. (1996). Diagnosing groups: Charting the flow of information in medical decision-making teams. *Journal of Personality and Social Psychology, 71*(2), 315–330.

Lave, J., & Wenger, E. (1991). *Situated learning: Legitimate peripheral participation.* Cambridge, UK: Cambridge University Press.

Majchrzak, A., Jarvenpaa, S. L., & Hollingshead, A. B. (2007). Coordinating expertise among emergent groups responding to disasters. *Organization Science, 18*(1), 147–161.

Marks, M. A., Mathieu, J. E., & Zaccaro, S. J. (2001). A temporally based framework and taxonomy of team processes. *Academy of Management Review, 26*(3), 356–376.

Mathieu, J., Marks, M. A., & Zaccaro, S. J. (2001). Multiteam systems. In N. Anderson, D. Ones, H. K. Sinangil, & C. Viswesvaran (Eds.), *International handbook of work and organizational psychology* (Vol. 2, pp. 289–313). London: Sage.

Moorman, C., & Miner, A. S. (1997). The impact of organizational memory on new product performance and creativity. *Journal of Marketing Research, 34*, 91–106.

Myers, K. K., & McPhee, R. D. (2006). Influences on member assimilation in workgroups in high-reliability organizations: A multilevel analysis. *Human Communication Research, 32*(4), 440–468.

Nelson, B. J. (1997). Work as a moral act: How emergency medical technicians understand their work. In S.R. Barley & J.E. Orr (Eds.), *Between craft and science: Technical work in U.S. settings*, pp. 154–186. Ithaca, NY: Cornell University Press.

Nelson, R. R. & Winter, S. (1982). *An evolutionary theory of economic change.* Cambridge, MA: The Belknap Press of Harvard University.

Okhuysen, G. A., & Eisenhardt, K. M. (2002). Integrating knowledge in groups: How formal interventions enable flexibility. *Organization Science, 13*(4), 370–386.

Okhuysen, G., & Waller, M.J. (2002). Focusing on midpoint transitions: An analysis of boundary conditions. *Academy of Management Journal, 45*: 1056–1065.

Poole, P. P., Gray, B., & Gioia, D. A. (1990). Organizational script development through interactive accommodation. *Group Organization Management, 15*(2): 212–232.

Reason, J. (1997). *Managing the risks of organizational accidents.* Aldershot, UK: Ashgate.

Rico, R., Sánchez-Manzanares, M., Gil, F., & Gibson, C. (2008). Team implicit coordination processes: A team knowledge-based approach. *Academy of Management Review, 33*(1), 163–184.

Roberts, K. H. (1990). Some characteristics of one type of high reliability organizations. *Organization Science, 1*(2), 160–176.

Roberts, K. H., & Rousseau, D. M. (1989). Research in nearly failure free high reliability organizations: Having the bubble. *IEEE Transactions on Engineering Management, 36*, 132–139.

Roth, E. M., Multer, J., & Raslear, T. (2006). Shared situation awareness as a contributor to high reliability performance in railroad operations. *Organization Studies, 27*(7), 967–987.

Salas, E., Prince, C., Baker, D. P., & Shrestha, L. (1995). Situation awareness in team performance: Implications for measurement and training. *Human Factors, 37*(1), 123–136.

Schilling, M. A. (2000). Toward a general modular system theory and its application to interfirm product modularity. *Academy of Management Review, 25*(2), 312–334.

Stasser, G., Stewart, D. D., & Wittenbaum, G. M. (1995). Expert roles and information exchange during discussion: The importance of knowing who knows what. *Journal of Experimental Social Psychology, 31*(3), 244–265.

Stasser, G., & Titus, W. (1985). Pooling of unshared information in group decision making: Biased information sampling during discussion. *Journal of Personality and Social Psychology, 48*(6), 1467–1478.

Trijselaar, J. (2006). *Gecoördineerde Regionale Incidentenbestrijdingsprocedure Rotterdam-Rijnmond* (Version 4.2). Retrieved from http://www.rhrr.nl/eCache/DEF/1/956.pdf

Tushman, M. L. (1977). Special boundary roles in the innovative process. *Administrative Science Quarterly, 22*, 587–605.

Waller, M. J. (1999). The timing of adaptive group responses to nonroutine events. *Academy of Management Journal, 42*(2), 127–137.

Waller, M. J., Gupta, N., & Giambatista, R. C. (2004). Effects of adaptive behaviors and shared mental models on control crew performance. *Management Science, 50*(11), 1534–1545.

Waller, M., & Uitdewilligen, S. (2009). Talking to the room: Collective sensemaking during crisis situations. In R. A. Roe, M. J. Waller, & S. R. Clegg (Eds.), *Time in organizational research* (pp. 186–203). London: Routledge.

Walsh, J. P. & Ungson, G. R. (1991). Organizational memory. *Academy of Management Review, 16*(1): 57.

Weick, K. E. (1995). *Sensemaking in organizations.* Thousand Oaks, CA: Sage.

Weick, K. E., & Sutcliffe, K. M. (2001). *Managing the unexpected: Assuring high performance in an age of complexity.* San Francisco: Jossey-Bass.

Weick, K. E., Sutcliffe, K. M., & Obstfeld, D. (2005). Organizing and the process of sensemaking. *Organization Science, 16*(4), 409–421.

Wellens, A. R. (1993). Group situation awareness and distributed decision making: From military to civilian applications. In N. J. Castellan, Jr. (Ed.), *Individual and group decision making* (pp. 267–291). Hillsdale, NJ: Erlbaum.

Woods, D. D., & Shattuck, L. G. (2000). Distance supervision: Local action given the potential for surprise. *Cognition, Technology and Work, 2*, 86–96.

World Health Organization. (2009). Global outbreak alert & response network. Retrieved from http://www.who.int/csr/outbreaknetwork/en/

14

The Emergence of Temporal Coordination Within Multiteam Systems

Rhetta L. Standifer
University of Wisconsin–Eau Claire

Imagine you were to discover your grandfather's pocket watch in the attic. You see it still working, so you turn it over and look into the back of the watch to find out how it runs. What you observe is a series of individual moving gears, large and small. They appear to be interconnected, but they are all moving at seemingly random paces; some gears move slowly, whereas others turn at a much faster rate. And yet, by their coordinated, unified effort, one collective goal is effectively reached—namely, you can tell the time. Multiteam systems (MTSs) work in much the same way: Individual units, each performing their own tasks that involve unique episodic durations, cycles, and pace, interconnect their activities in order to achieve a collective superordinate goal. Whether or not this goal is achieved effectively, however, depends on how successfully these individual teams can coordinate with one another, and successful coordination involves the element of *timing*.

In this chapter, I explore the temporal aspect of coordination, known as *entrainment*, within MTSs: how entrainment manifests and how it impacts coordinative efforts within such relationships. I begin with an overview of entrainment and its elements. Next, I use the "core elements" of MTS outlined in Mathieu, Marks, and Zaccaro (2001) as a conceptual basis to describe ways in which temporal coordination is exhibited through entrainment in MTSs. One element of particular interest is the impact that shared temporal perspectives of MTS leadership have on the success of these endeavors. Having presented these concepts within a temporal perspective, I provide an overarching description of *strategic entrainment* to illustrate how mindful, effective temporal coordination may benefit MTSs. Finally, I suggest ways in which researchers may contribute to the MTS literature through future temporal research.

ENTRAINMENT AND ITS ELEMENTS

The theoretical concept of entrainment was first introduced in the biological sciences as far back as the 17th century (Ancona & Chong, 1999; Minorsky, 1962) and was eventually adopted by social science researchers such as Edward Hall (1983) and McGrath and Rotchford (1983). *Entrainment*, as it is defined in the organizational literature, is the "adjustment of the pace or cycle of an activity to match or synchronize with that of another activity" (Ancona & Chong, 1996, p. 253). Entrainment is about rhythmic patterns of activity and how they interact with one another, specifically how interconnected rhythmic patterns of activity are adjusted to correspond with one primary rhythm. This one particular rhythm, whether consciously designated or naturally selected, "captures" or entrains other interdependent rhythmic activity. This rhythm is known as a *dominant rhythm*, and it entrains other rhythmic activities into an aggregated pattern, becoming a coordinative mechanism for all parties involved (Ancona & Chong, 1999; Standifer & Bluedorn, 2006). As such, entrainment is a systemwide process, pulling related parties into an "interdependent temporal web" (Zellmer-Bruhn, Waller, & Ancona, 2004). Because of this, the key unit of analysis when studying entrainment is the aggregated rhythmic pattern of this temporal web that encompasses all related parties (Ancona & Chong, 1996).

The basic elements of rhythmic activities are *cycle* and *pace*. The term *cycle* refers to one complete execution of a systematic, recurrent event or incident (Ancona & Chong, 1996; McGrath & Tschan, 2004). In fact, the notion that endogenous cycles exist at all levels of analysis (e.g., individual, group, and organization) is a primary principle of entrainment (Ancona & Chong, 1999). Cyclical, repetitive activity is evident in such societal norms as the standard 7-day pattern of weekdays and weekend, the frantic push of rush hour, and the relative calm of summer vacation (Ancona & Chong, 1999; McGrath & Rotchford, 1983). The entrainment of cycles within a business context is exemplified in the way that activities are predictably (and repeatedly) altered over the course of the year in response to fiscal quarterly deadlines (Ancona & Chong, 1999, p. 37).

Pace involves the rate of speed at which an activity occurs (Bluedorn, 2002). With regard to entrainment, the focus lies in the pace alignment of multiple activities (Ancona & Chong, 1996); in other words, it is the pace or rate of speed in which activities from interconnected entities occur relative to each other that is important. For example, decisions made by strategic alliance partners such as when resources should be made available and when activities are started or completed are all influenced by pace (Harbison & Pekar, 1998). Similarly, Eisenhardt and Brown (1998) referred to "time pacing" with regard to entering new markets or creating new products. The impact of pace is also evident when a company increases the speed in which it completes its development cycle to match the pace of a competitor (Ancona & Chong, 1999).

One other temporal concept related indirectly to entrainment is time orientation. *Time orientation* concerns how far ahead or behind a person, group, or organization considers the past or future (Lawrence & Lorsch, 1967; Schein, 1992). As the definition implies, time orientation denotes a subjective interpretation; what one person (team or organization) considers to be "long-term future" might be vastly different from another's understanding of the concept. In a multiheaded entity like an MTS, this has implications for such interteam processes as goal specification and prioritization, strategic formulation, and the interpretation of communication between teams.

In summary, cycle and pace combine to create rhythmic activity. These rhythms intermingle, and in so doing one rhythm exerts a greater influence than others, "capturing" or entraining the other interconnected rhythmic activity to it and thus becoming a dominant mechanism of coordination (Ancona & Chong, 1999; Standifer & Bluedorn, 2006). These three elements of entrainment (e.g., cycle, pace, and dominant rhythm) are in turn tangentially affected by the temporal element of time orientation.

With a better understanding of the phenomenon of entrainment, I can now turn to a description of how entrainment appears in MTSs and consider ways in which it can impact coordinative efforts among the component teams that constitute the aggregated system.

ENTRAINMENT WITHIN MTSs

An MTS consists of two or more component teams that are directly and interdependently working toward one or more distal (or superordinate) goals (Mathieu et al., 2001). These distal goals sit atop a goal hierarchy and facilitate the coordinative efforts of each component team's lower level proximal goals (Mathieu et al., 2001). These component teams are distinct entities in and of themselves; each has its own set of goals and related activities, including activities that may be unrelated to the MTS. In addition, these component teams might be embedded solely within one organization or, more likely, act as cross-boundary representative units from a number of organizations. Regardless of its makeup, an MTS can exist only if all of its component teams recognize their interdependence and come together to coordinate their activities in such a way as to collectively work toward the superordinate goal (Bateman, O'Neill, & Kenworthy-U'Ren, 2002; DeChurch & Mathieu, 2009; Marks, Mathieu, DeChurch, Panzer, & Alonso, 2005).

Coordination involves sequencing or the element of timing (Marks, Mathieu, & Zaccaro, 2001; Waller, Zellmer-Bruhn, & Giambatista, 2002; Zalesny, Salas, & Prince, 1995). At the MTS level, coordinating behavior requires component teams to effectively sequence their interdependent rhythmic activities according to the needs of each party and the composite whole (Ancona & Caldwell, 1992; DeChurch & Marks, 2006; Marks et al., 2001; Nelson, Armstrong, Buche, & Ghods, 2000; Standifer & Bluedorn, 2006). Each team completes work toward its goals by engaging in cyclic, goal-directed periods of rhythmic activity called "episodes" (Marks, et al, 2001, p. 298); in addition, the means by which teams work interdependently to convert inputs to outcomes to achieve the superordinate goals of the MTS are known as "processes" (Mathieu, Heffner, Goodwin, Cannon-Bowers, & Salas, 2005, p. 40). These processes often include "temporal coordinating mechanisms" to direct the pattern, timing, and content of communication (Montoya-Weiss, Massey, & Song, 2001, p. 1252).

Aspects of entrainment influence each of the core elements of an MTS. These elements include (a) goal hierarchies, (b) the nature of task interdependence and complexity, (c) intra- and interteam processes, (d) performance episodes, and (e) environmental elements. In this section, I delineate ways in which entrainment manifests and influences each of these core elements, beginning with goal hierarchies.

Goal Hierarchies

Component teams within MTSs must orchestrate their interrelated actions and responses in order to achieve a mutual, higher order goal (Standifer & Bluedorn, 2006, p. 10). However, this superordinate goal must be identified and agreed upon. Furthermore, any of the component teams' lower order subgoals that are related to the higher order goal must complement and align to that goal. Put another way, the relevant subgoals (or *proximal goals*) of component teams need to be entrained in order for the higher order goal (or *distal goal*) to be successfully achieved (Marks et al., 2001). That said, all goals have a temporal component (Marks et al., 2001, p. 303), and it is important for MTS leadership to recognize this and work proactively to entrain interconnected objectives.

Within an MTS, each component team will have proximal goals, each with its own time demands (Latham & Locke, 1975). This drives the pace in which work is done relative to that goal (Latham & Locke, 1975; Marks et al., 2001). These proximal goals will also entail cyclic activity of various tasks; some tasks will involve more cyclic repetitions than others, influencing overall goal duration. Therefore, variation exists across proximal goals in terms of pace, cycle, and duration. This has implications for the way in which these proximal goals may be entrained to one another and to any respective distal goals of the MTS, which we will discuss later. Moreover, some teams will share certain proximal goals within MTSs, whereas others will not. Teams will also have unique proximal goals, some related to distal goals of the MTS, some related to other initiatives of the team outside of the MTS. It is also important to note in terms of entrainment that although component teams of an MTS often do not share proximal goals, they must share at least one distal goal in order to be part of the system.

Such distal goals make two essential processes of MTSs possible (Marks et al., 2001, p. 297). First, higher order goals aid in the selection and generation of strategic plans and subsequent proximal goals for the overall system and for component teams; and, second, they allow for collective coordination (Marks et al., 2001, p. 298). Here, we see a direct influence of entrainment in the form of dominant rhythms. As mentioned above, a dominant rhythm "captures" or entrains other interdependent rhythmic activity to it and becomes a coordinative mechanism for all interconnected parties involved (Ancona & Chong, 1999; Standifer & Bluedorn, 2006). These dominant rhythms may be consciously generated by MTS leadership or occur naturally among the various rhythmic activities related to the system. Additionally, dominant rhythms may originate from a source either internal or external to the MTS. This represents a difference from traditional, stand-alone teams or other entities concerned with entrainment; because MTSs are often composed of multiple, boundary-spanning parties, these systems embrace more of the macroenvironment within themselves (Standifer & Bluedorn, 2006, p. 11). As such, what qualifies as an "internal" source must be more broadly conceptualized.

To be clear, distal MTS goals and dominant rhythms are not the same thing. Rather, the dominant rhythm represents an important temporal influence upon the goal. For example, in April 2009, the drug discovery and development company Galapagos announced a multiyear strategic alliance with Merck & Co. to develop new treatments in inflammatory diseases (Marketwire, 2009). The product development of specific treatments will certainly be among the distal goals for this two-party MTS. As such, the developmental cycle is likely to act as a dominant rhythm for lower level goals within the two companies, in terms of cycle, pace, and duration. Now consider the MTS created by several consumer goods companies that align themselves with a distributor for the purposes of decreasing logistical costs. The distal goal may focus on efficiency and cost; however, the rhythmic activity of these component units will be severely affected by the cyclic phenomenon of the holiday shopping season (Standifer & Bluedorn, 2006). In this case, the dominant rhythm that is the seasonal event is not in and of itself part of the distal goal; nevertheless, it exerts tremendous influence on this goal and, by extension, the rhythmic activity related to component units' proximal goals.

Just as dominant rhythms are related to distal goals, so are they related to the proximal goals of component teams. These lower order goals will entrain to a rhythm as well; it may be the same one to which the distal goal is entrained, or it may be to another, subdominant rhythm. The dominant rhythm of the distal goal remains paramount in terms of task completion; component team leaders must still be mindful of the influence of the distal goal and its temporal influence. However, in the minute details related to the implementation of their proximal goals, subdominant rhythmic influences can and will exist. The important thing is to identify essential goals within each component team, determine their relevance to the distal goal(s) of the MTS, and distinguish rhythmic activity relative to each goal. There will almost certainly be discrepancies among the rhythmic activity across these goals; for example, teams may realize that the rhythmic activity of one goal constrains the rhythmic activity of another. In such cases, it is the job of MTS leadership to prioritize rhythmic activity and make decisions related to these temporal elements: the pace in which activities occur, the cyclic form and duration, and the like. It is imperative that goal and temporal alignment be achieved at the team level in order for the goal hierarchy to work at the MTS level.

One key aspect of dominant rhythms that illustrates this point is the fact that when a change occurs within a dominant rhythm (i.e., the pace in which the cyclic activity occurs is shortened or lengthened), any entity entrained to that dominant rhythm will likewise have to change (Ancona & Chong, 1996). Let's return to the consumer goods and seasonal-shopping example. As the holiday shopping season has extended over the years, this has changed the dominant rhythm. According to entrainment theory (Ancona & Chong, 1996), this change necessitates a subsequent change in all entrained rhythmic activity of each of the component units in order for the activity to remain entrained. This demonstrates the need for component teams to understand and align their efforts internally at the lower levels of the MTS goal hierarchy to better maintain temporal coordination among each other if changes occur at higher levels.

Such coordination between hierarchical goal levels is essential; in fact, the success of the superordinate goal at the top of this hierarchy is dependent upon the success of proximal goals below it (Marks et al., 2005). Naturally, these coordinative efforts will exert more force upon teams that are deeply embedded in the MTS goal hierarchy (DeChurch & Mathieu, 2009), meaning the team's actions are highly interdependent with other component teams in the system and/or are directly tied to one or more distal goals. One reason for this effect is temporal: If the cycle or pace of a component team's rhythmic activities is closely entrained to the activities of one or more other component teams and/or is strongly entrained to the dominant rhythm of a distal goal, then the forces of entrainment are a constant influence. This would be in contrast to a component team whose activities are only distantly aligned to others in the system or weakly affected by a distal goal's dominant rhythm. It is also crucial to remember that teams rarely pursue one goal (and its accompanying "bundle" of activities) in a vacuum; usually, teams are required to work on multiple goals simultaneously at any specific point in time (McGrath, 1991, p. 163). Marks et al. (2001) extended this idea by suggesting that time is linked to goal accomplishment and goal-related activity is performed within an "episodic framework" (p. 359).

It should be noted, however, that proximal goals need not unfold over comparable episodic durations; rather, the focus should be on timing the rhythmic activities of these goals to more effectively and collectively meet the distal goals of the MTS (Marks et al., 2001, p. 291). Specifically, the relationship among rhythmic activities may be entrained in one of three ways: (a) *leading*, where the "captured" or entrained activities occur *before* the activity of the more dominant rhythm; (b) *lagging*, where the entrained cycles occur *after* the cycle of the more dominant rhythm; or (c) *synchronic*, where various cycles occur exactly at the same time (Ancona & Chong, 1996; Aschoff, 1979; Bluedorn, 2002). Also, as Zaccaro, Marks, and DeChurch stated in Chapter 1 of this book, the duration (or time horizon) of distal goals will typically be longer than that of any one proximal goal. This is reasonable to suggest given the above statement, namely, distal goals are dependent upon proximal goals for successful completion. If so, there are implications here in terms of time orientation within component teams. Such teams must familiarize themselves with the distal goal(s) of the MTS and be comfortable with the implied time horizon of these higher order goals in order to effectively create, implement, and align their proximal goals within the hierarchy. This also speaks to the temporal ordering of goal creation and selection, which will be discussed in this chapter.

An example of the relationship that exists between an MTS's rhythmic activities and its goals is provided in Figure 14.1. In this example, the dominant and subdominant rhythms of an MTS's distal goal and two proximal goals are represented in a linear way, showing a beginning and endpoint for each rhythmic pattern. (It is assumed that this rhythmic pattern could repeat.) Note that the duration of the distal goal's overall cyclic pattern is longer than that of the two proximal goal's rhythms, as discussed in this chapter. There are two shaded areas within the dominant rhythm's timeline; these represent crucial points in that rhythm's cycle. (For this example, those points occur at the midpoint and endpoint of the cycle.) At three unique points along the dominant rhythm, tasks are to be performed from proximal goals in order to achieve the higher order goal—these are represented by the crosses along the dominant rhythm's line coming out from the two proximal goals. Tasks 1 and 2 are part of Proximal Goal I; Task 3 is part of Proximal Goal II. As illustrated in Figure 14.1, Task 3 is the sole responsibility of Component Team II. However, Tasks 1 and 2

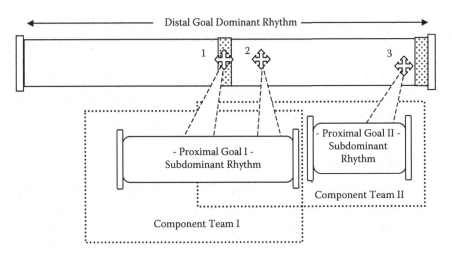

FIGURE 14.1
The relationship among rhythmic activities and MTS goals (distal and proximal).

represent shared, interdependent tasks between Component Teams I and II. This has implications for the degree of coordination and interaction that will be required between the two units. This example also illustrates the three ways in which entrainment may emerge. Task 1 exemplifies a "synchronous" relationship; in other words, Component Teams I and II must complete this task *at the same time* as the crucial midpoint in the dominant rhythm. In contrast, Task 2 represents a "lagging" relationship; in this case, the activities must be completed by the two component teams *after* the crucial midpoint. Task 3 is an example of "leading" entrainment, whereby the task is completed *before* the crucial endpoint in the dominant rhythm. For MTS and component team leadership, each entrainment type represents a unique set of challenges. For Team III, the "leading" task requires that team to *anticipate* activities prior to the endpoint. If changes occur to the dominant rhythm, changes will likewise be required of the proximal goals (and, by extension, possibly the tasks involved in the proximal goals) to maintain entrainment. Team III will need to coordinate and communicate with other teams to ensure that any necessary adaptations are made. For "lagging" Task 2, Component Teams I and II must *react* to the dominant rhythm; if change occurs in the dominant rhythm between that midpoint and the lagging event, these teams have little time to adapt, making coordination efforts between them even more vital. Likewise, pertinent information from Task 2 needs to be utilized by Team II when they complete Task 3. Finally, the synchronous nature of Task 1 means Component Teams I and II will have no time to adapt at the point the task occurs; this implies prior coordination and scanning to ensure that the task and proximal goal are accurately entrained to the dominant rhythm.

Another aspect of timing relates to the nature of task interdependence and complexity, to which we will now turn.

Task Interdependence and Complexity

Thompson (1967) denoted three forms of interdependence: (a) pooled, (b) sequential, and (c) reciprocal. The first form, *pooled*, represents the least interdependent state, followed by sequential, then reciprocal. At each state, the extent to which interdependence exists and coordinative mechanisms are required increases. Other researchers (Bell & Kozlowski, 2002; Van de Ven, Delbecq, & Koenig, 1976) have described an additional state of interdependence known as *intensive interdependence*, wherein teams must diagnose, problem solve, and/or collaborate simultaneously to accomplish the task (Bell & Kozlowski, 2002, p. 19). With higher levels of interdependence (e.g., reciprocal or intensive), teams must integrate activities, exchange work products more often, and engage in greater sharing of knowledge and information (Marks et al., 2001; Tesluk, Mathieu, Zaccaro, & Marks, 1997). However, it is likely that not every component unit will be equally interdependent with each other in an MTS (Standifer & Bluedorn, 2006).

Again, this core element of MTSs has connotations for entrainment. First, pace is governed in part by the degree of interdependence among the component teams (Standifer & Bluedorn, 2006). Put another way, the greater the interdependence between two teams, the greater the need for entrained pacing and cyclic activity. For example, component teams that are reciprocally interdependent require a more complex response in terms of pacing than two teams that are sequentially interdependent (Gerwin, 2004; Thompson, 1967). Pacing can also involve more than the sequencing of specific tasks; the rate in which component teams generate information and communicate it to one another is likewise influenced by their degree of interdependence (Standifer & Bluedorn, 2006). Cyclical activity, too, is affected by the extent of interdependency between teams; the greater the interdependence, the greater the need for coordinated activity (Mathieu et al., 2001). The pace and extent of information sharing will likely increase as the degree of interdependence increases. This is because with more complex states of interdependence such as reciprocal and intensive states, the cyclic activity of the interconnected teams becomes integrated to such a degree that the teams find it difficult, if not impossible, to carry out their goals without frequent, almost constant interaction.

Interdependency and entrainment efforts are also influenced by task complexity. If task complexity is low, then loose coupling between teams is allowable. This, in turn, means minimal entrainment efforts are required, as team linkages are fewer and/or less synchronous (Ancona & Chong, 1999; Bell & Kozlowski, 2002; McGrath, 1991). However, when task complexity is high, tighter coupling and a greater level of collaboration and communication among team members are required (Bell & Kozlowski, 2002; Kozlowski, Gully, Nason, & Smith, 1999). As such, greater entrainment efforts are likewise needed. In MTSs, high task complexity is more the norm; often, these systems are situated in dynamic, uncertain environments. As one portion of the system adapts to environmental changes, tightly coupled component teams must alter their actions and processes in order to maintain coordination (Mathieu et al., 2001, p. 297) and to remain entrained. From a temporal perspective, greater degrees of task complexity demand a tighter relationship between the dominant rhythm and those rhythms entrained to it (Standifer & Bluedorn, 2006).

As the above discussion implies, greater interdependence and complexity also demand a greater reliance upon intrateam and interteam processes and coordinative mechanisms by component teams if entrainment (and the MTS) are to be successful. In fact, Mathieu et al. (2001) defined the amount of team interaction necessary to achieve the proximal and distal goals of an MTS as "process interdependence" and stressed the importance of timing in such interaction. It is to these processes and their relationship to MTS entrainment efforts that I now turn.

Processes Within MTSs

In the context of MTSs, researchers (LePine, Piccolo, Jackson, Mathieu, & Saul, 2008; Marks et al., 2001) have listed three distinct forms of teamwork processes: transition, action, and interpersonal. Although Marks and colleagues (2001) considered interpersonal processes to be an ongoing activity within and across component teams, transition and action processes are presented as cyclically triggering one another over episodic intervals (LePine et al., 2008, p. 277). Given this, the focus here will be on these two forms.

First, transition processes involve actions of planning, preparation, and interpretation. When component teams engage in transition processes, it is to assess environmental conditions, to analyze recently completed tasks, to strategize, and to formulate and prioritize goals (LePine et al., 2008). Action processes, on the other hand, represent actions that teams take while working to achieve set goals and may include interpreting, attending to, and communicating information (Marks et al., 2001). More importantly with regard to entrainment, action processes also include coordinative efforts, specifically the aligning of team member activities with respect to their sequence and timing (LePine et al., 2008; Marks et al., 2001; Wittenbaum, Vaughan, & Stasser, 2002). Such temporally oriented processes could include creating timetables and schedules, communicating (i.e., when to generate and provide information), the pace of action sequencing, and when resources are shared, delivered, and so on (Standifer & Bluedorn, 2006, pp. 20–21).

Within MTSs, these processes are evident at the aggregated level, as well as within each component team. In both the MTS and the component teams, transition and action processes cyclically occur within what Marks and her colleagues (2001) referred to as "episodes." These episodes are measurable periods of time, with durations determined largely by the goals they are meant to achieve and the tasks and activities involved therein (Marks et al., 2001, p. 359).

Performance Episodes

Performance episodes within MTSs represent temporal cycles of goal-directed activity, and these episodes constitute the rhythms of task performance for teams and the manner in which team members complete work (Mathieu et al., 2001, p. 298). To become effectively entrained, MTS leadership must recognize and interpret this cyclic activity relevant to the achievement of their distal goals and respond appropriately. Using the earlier example of the Galapagos–Merck alliance, the consistent, repetitive activity related to the development of a new inflammatory treatment drug constitutes a recurrent cycle that reflects a superordinate goal for the alliance as a whole. Given its significance to the superordinate goal, this development cycle is likely to become the dominant rhythm for this alliance. In addition, the episodic activity that is related to that product's development and that is embedded in each component team represents rhythmic proximal goal activity. The extent to which the cyclical workflow occurring within each organizational team in the alliance must be entrained will vary depending on the extent to which partners are interdependent (Standifer & Bluedorn, 2006, p. 11).

It becomes readily apparent that the alignment of episodic activity among multiple teams, and at multiple hierarchical levels within MTSs, can quickly become a formidable task. Teams generate input–process–outcome cycles within each transition or action process phase; the outcome from a transition phase becomes the input for the next action phase (Marks et al., 2001). However, the lines demarcating the phases can be blurry—phases can blend into each other (Marks et al., 2001). Furthermore, what constitutes activities commonly associated with the transition phase (e.g., planning and goal setting) and what constitutes actual task work activities associated with an action phase can also be murky depending on the role of the team (Marks et al., 2001). It is here that entrainment theory may provide some parsimonious clarity.

As Marks et al. (2001) indicated, multiple performance episodes may occur together within a single component team at any given point in time, and each episode will have its own duration, start time, and pace of cyclic activity (p. 360). Within each episode, the cyclic back and forth of transition and action processes will happen, and the pace in which that cyclic triggering occurs will vary as well. According to Mathieu et al. (2001), the primary challenge for teams is to develop and execute a strategy that not only manages performance gaps in each of the important episodes but also devises strategies for episodic action by each component team enabling the aggregate whole to work toward the accomplishment of both proximal and distal goals over time (pp. 299–300). I would suggest that the key lies in the dominant rhythms of an aggregated system's distal goals, not in the myriad of rhythmic patterns that comprise the temporal web of the MTS. Identification by MTS leadership of these ascendant rhythms (which are linked or embedded in the top-tier goals of the system) provides a roadmap by which component teams may guide the episodic phase models of their own rhythmic activities.

Remember the mechanical gear clock—it does not work by forcing all gears to match one synchronized pace or cyclic duration. Its system's success does not rest in the herculean task of devising a system that accounts for each phase of each episode of each component's activities. Rather, each distinct component is allowed to perform its cyclic tasks at its own pace, perhaps with its own naturally occurring subdominant rhythm, so long as these episodic tasks remain entrained to the superordinate goal's dominant rhythm. Within an MTS, it is a matter of perspective: Just as the system has a hierarchical arrangement of goals, the system's participants can perceive its entrainment in hierarchical levels as well. First, it is essential that leaders at the aggregated level of an MTS identify and communicate these superordinate goal dominant rhythms to each component team's leadership. In · turn, team leaders would need to understand the key performance episodes their team must perform, determine the processes required in each episode, and decide how multiple episodes will be accomplished internally with the superordinate goal dominant rhythm as the guiding force. Once each team has entrained its own episodic activities, it can turn its attention to interteam entrainment at the dyadic level, in effect linking one gear to another, and always with a distal goal's dominant rhythm at the forefront of any discussion. Teams that are highly interdependent will naturally need to work more closely with each other when making these determinations than teams of a less interdependent status. Leaders at the macrolevel of the MTS can oversee the overall entrainment of the system, knowing that entrainment at lower levels of the goal hierarchy has been accomplished.

As mentioned previously, the dominant rhythms that influence MTSs so strongly may originate from inside or outside of the system. This leads to a discussion of the final MTS core element, environmental elements.

Environmental Elements of MTSs

MTSs are situated in two primary environments: the organizations of the component teams and the general external environment (Mathieu et al., 2001). Included in the component teams' embedded organizational environment are other teams, departments, and so on that may not be associated with the MTS at all, but with which the component team must interact as part of its responsibilities to the organization (Mathieu et al., 2001, p. 296). The latter environment consists of phenomena outside the participating organizations that impact the MTS such as major stakeholders (e.g., customers and governmental bodies) (Mathieu et al., 2001, p. 296). Each environment wields an effect on the actions of component teams and, by extension, efforts to temporally coordinate them; however, the level of subtlety involved in that effect is greater within the embedded environment. Put another way, facets of the external environment apply a fairly straightforward degree of temporal influence regardless of the type of MTS (e.g., internal or cross-boundary). By contrast, the temporal effect from the embedded environment involves the inner workings of the organization, the team, and the MTS to varying extents.

To explain, component teams must often interact and coordinate tasks that are unrelated (*external*) to the goals of their MTS in order to perform their function within the embedded organizational environment. The extent to which these "outside" efforts require a team's attention will impact that team's ability to effectively entrain with MTS partners. In order for entrainment efforts to be successful, MTS and home organizational leadership must consider a team's roles from both perspectives. In terms of their organizational role, component team leaders must work in tandem with organizational top management to temporally coordinate their activity in such a way as to minimize conflicts between the episodic activity of the MTS and other activity. As stated earlier, teams are capable of enacting multiple episodes concurrently; the key is to manage these episodes so as to time their cyclic duration and pace for maximum efficiency and minimum conflict between MTS proximal goal activity and other organizational activity. For the MTS, recognizing a component team's positioning and role(s) within the organization will be beneficial; however, as mentioned previously, component teams that have effectively entrained their activity at the team level with the MTS's distal goals in mind should enable MTS leadership to focus their entrainment efforts at the higher order system level. Even so, MTS leadership must work with component team leadership to recognize and balance the influence of these two environments upon intra- and interteam goals as well as maintain a focused awareness of the (macro) MTS level in order to effectively entrain episodic activity.

One potential difference between internal and cross-boundary MTSs that should be of primary concern to this leadership is dominant rhythms' environmental points of origin. Cross-boundary MTSs engage the external environment to a greater extent than internal MTSs completely embedded in their organizations. This means that internal MTSs are protected to varying degrees (depending on their proximity to their organization's boundaries) by the organizational system that acts as a "buffer of influence" between the MTS and the external environment (Mathieu et al., 2001, p. 296). If this is the case, then the rhythmic activity of cross-boundary MTS component teams stands a greater likelihood of direct exposure to dominant rhythms from external sources than do internal MTS component teams. That is not to say that internal MTSs are completely impervious to external dominant rhythms; it is possible that a recurrent cyclic activity or environmental pacer may emerge within an industry wielding so much influence that it penetrates the buffer of organizational barriers. To illustrate, mandatory technological changes due to federal regulatory legislation could subsequently influence the pace of an MTS's rhythmic activity, internal or otherwise. However, because cross-boundary MTSs lack buffers such as those of internal MTSs, their level of exposure to the forces of outside dominant rhythms is apt to be greater. Other temporal aspects of entrainment are influenced by the presence (or absence) of buffers as well. The pace in which information can be assimilated and communicated among component teams may vary depending on the type of MTS in which these processes are carried out (Standifer & Bluedorn, 2006). This would be due to differences in unit proximity and/or the presence of organizational buffers (Standifer & Bluedorn, 2006, p. 15).

Not only are cross-boundary MTSs more likely to be affected by environmental demands, but also it is reasonable to suggest that their level of complexity will be higher than that of internal MTSs. Leaders of cross-boundary MTSs must consider and coordinate the demands of both the external environment (affecting all component teams) and the environmental elements indicative of each respective embedding organization such as are discussed in this chapter (Mathieu et al., 2001). Given this, entrainment efforts for cross-boundary MTSs should reflect that complexity more so than the efforts of internal MTSs that primarily involve the factors of the component teams' home organization. Consider the difference in complexity between the two types of MTSs if a shift occurs within a dominant rhythm. As mentioned earlier, a change in a dominant rhythm precipitates changes among all entrained rhythmic activity in order for this activity to remain temporally coordinated. For internal MTSs, this realignment will happen among component teams nested within the same organization. In contrast, the realignment of cross-boundary MTS teams requires adaptation and collaboration from parties across different organizations. If teams are tightly coupled, highly interdependent, and faced with multiple proximal goals, temporal realignment becomes even more important within cross-boundary MTSs (and more multifaceted).

In addition, the size of the MTS will influence the level of complexity and subsequently the level of intricacy for entrainment efforts. The size of an MTS is determined by the number of component teams involved as well as the total number of individuals working within these teams. As DeChurch and Mathieu (2009) indicated, size is an inherent characteristic of an MTS that makes temporal issues even more critical (p. 281). In terms of entrainment, with greater size (e.g., more component teams, or more individuals) comes greater complexity. With every addition of a component team (and the individuals within them), the temporal complexity increases as leaders attempt to map and sequence episodic activity, identify proximal goals, determine levels of interdependence, and so on.

On a related note, Zaccaro and his colleagues use the terms *organizational diversity* and *proportional membership* (Chapter 1, this volume) to refer to the number of different organizations with component teams involved and to the number of teams that each participating organization brings into the MTS, respectively. Both will impact entrainment. In fact, one sees the subtle temporal influence of the embedded organizational environment at play with regard to these two concepts. For instance, an MTS consisting of three organizations, one of which is contributing half of the component teams, will face a distinctly different entrainment challenge than an MTS of four organizations that are contributing one team each, due in large part to the way in which organizational activity unrelated to the MTS influences component team work.

Finally, there is the matter of time orientation. Within an internal MTS, there is a greater chance that component teams share a congruent perspective with regard to this concept. In contrast, component teams of a cross-boundary MTS represent a variety of organizations, each with its own distinct view of past and future. The consequences of such diversity of temporal perspective may be particularly salient during transition phases of episodic activity, when strategic planning and goal setting are undertaken. The issue of temporal perspective is a crucial factor in MTS success, and it is one I will discuss in the next section.

IMPACT OF MTS LEADERSHIP ON ENTRAINMENT

The role of leadership on effective temporal coordination in MTSs is crucial. This is because time is a subjective concept; what is *long-term future* to one may be *short-term future* to another. What is the "appropriate" pace for a particular cyclic activity? What is (or should be) the dominant rhythmic force that will guide the activity of those involved for a particular distal goal? These decisions are in the hands of those who lead and make such determinations on behalf of component teams and the MTS as a whole. Because of this, awareness of temporal perspective among these leaders is important. Similarly, the degree to which these leaders share certain temporal cognitions and perspectives will have an inevitable effect on the success of MTS coordinative efforts. In this section, I discuss the idea of shared temporal views in greater detail.

Shared Temporal Cognitions and Perspectives

An MTS is composed of a collection of teams that must interact directly and interdependently with each other in response to environmental demands as they work to accomplish one or more shared goals (Mathieu et al., 2001). To achieve this mutual objective requires varying degrees of cooperative and interdependent action among its members as they utilize various processes (e.g., coordination) to convert inputs to outcomes within cyclic episodic activity (Marks, Sabella, Burke, & Zaccaro, 2002). Mathieu and his colleagues (Mathieu et al., 2001) suggested that a shared understanding among MTS teams promotes more efficiency within these processes (e.g., collective information processing and coordinated actions) (p. 304). If so, it is vital that the members of this collective system, and particularly its leadership, share common, functional perspectives with regard to key concepts affecting coordination. Furthermore, effective coordination is greatly enhanced if members also work to build and sustain shared cognitions with regard to coordinative efforts. Although these shared mental representations may entail a large range of topics, for the purposes of this discussion my focus will be on shared perspectives and cognitions as they relate to *temporal* matters.

As envisioned by Bluedorn and Standifer (2004), a shared temporal perspective would involve shared meanings about time and temporal matters among team members and constitute a range of temporal concepts (Standifer & Bluedorn, 2006, p. 6). For specific strategic temporal considerations as they relate to coordination, these shared temporal perspectives would need to include an understanding of entrainment itself and its components (Standifer & Bluedorn, 2006). Other temporal researchers have promoted the importance of shared temporal perspectives; in particular, Ancona and Chong (1999) maintained that a shared temporal perspective (with regard to pace, cycle, and dominant rhythms) aids coordinative processes.

Theories regarding shared cognitions assert that cognitive congruence enhances team performance by improving processes (Gevers, Rutte, & van Eerde, 2006, p. 54). For instance, researchers studying shared mental models stated that the degree to which correct team-related mental models are common among all members influences coordination efforts (Cannon-Bowers, Salas, & Converse, 1993; Klimoski & Mohammed, 1994). In their 2001 article, Mathieu et al. specifically identified "team interaction" mental models among component teams as essential to effective coordinated action within MTSs. These models include shared conceptualizations about how units coordinate their responses with other units in the MTS, allowing each team to know what it must do when interacting with other teams. Standifer and Bluedorn have suggested extending this particular mental model to explicitly include a temporal perspective (2006).

Another theory refers to *shared temporal cognitions*. This idea of shared cognitions on time has been defined as the degree to which members have similar mental representations about temporal demands and specific temporal aspects of team tasks (e.g., deadline awareness, and pacing of task activity) (Bartel & Milliken, 2004; Gevers et al., 2006; Mohammed, Hamilton, & Lim, 2009). According to Gevers and her colleagues (Gevers et al., 2006), such mutual cognitions allow members to anticipate and comprehend each other's actions, create compatible patterns of interaction, and coordinate more effectively (p. 54). These cognitions may emerge without conscious effort or may be developed through proactive action such as leaders employing temporal reminders (Gevers, Rutte, & van Eerde, 2004; Mohammed et al., 2009). However, it should be noted that shared temporal cognitions can bring about positive results within team processes (and, by extension, entrainment efforts) only if they are accurate and functional (Gevers et al., 2006). For instance, if the leadership of an MTS makes an incorrect identification of a particular dominant rhythm for a distal goal due to flawed shared cognitions, then these mental representations act as a hindrance rather than an aid.

Functional shared cognitions regarding entrainment within MTSs would allow MTS and component team leadership to better recognize and acknowledge important internal and external cyclic activities of the system. During transition phases when leaders were engaged in goal-setting processes, shared temporal cognitions could aid in the planning, sequencing, and implementation of cyclic activity and workflow occurring within and between component teams. Additionally, a shared temporal model would help both the component teams' leadership and that of the overall MTS to determine each partner's degree of "process interdependence" (Mathieu et al., 2001) in terms of the cyclic activity needed to achieve the collective goal (Standifer & Bluedorn, 2006, p. 21). One vital way in which shared temporal cognitions aid entrainment within MTSs is by enabling MTS leadership to better reach consensus with regard to what constitutes dominant rhythms for the system.

If MTS leaders share functional and accurate temporal cognitions, it should be possible to reach consensus with regard to the dominant rhythms of distal goals faster and with greater accuracy. This raises a key issue in entrainment efforts, namely, the extent to which time and temporal matters is passively (and mistakenly) assumed to be a foregone conclusion among MTS leaders and not in need of consideration or discussion. In this chapter, the point was made that time is a subjective concept; this should not be forgotten when strategic coordinative processes are engaged. When the MTS has agreed-upon distal goals and accompanying dominant rhythms, they serve as a "specific central temporal mechanism" around which unified action and consensus about subsequent decisions may revolve (Standifer & Bluedorn, 2006, p. 22). Moreover, MTS leadership that identifies dominant rhythms in the *early* stages of the system's development may have the benefit of some unique advantages. Distinguishing the dominant rhythm of an MTS's distal goal early allows leadership at every level of the goal hierarchy to use this knowledge in their own entrainment efforts. Component teams may address the influence of this higher order dominant rhythm relative to their own proximal goals; specifically, the pace of important internal cycles can be set, interdependency among various component teams can be determined and mapped, and so on (Standifer & Bluedorn, 2006). Admittedly, change can and will occur over the life of the MTS; as discussed in this chapter, dominant rhythms occasionally shift. However, this does not eliminate the benefits of proactive planning and consensus building. In addition, with shared temporal cognitions, MTS leaders stand a better chance of responding faster and more accurately to changes during unexpected, time-constrained events (Standifer & Bluedorn, 2006, p. 22).

Shared temporal cognitions are also crucial to effective MTS entrainment with regard to time orientation. Although not a direct element of entrainment, time orientation exerts a significant influence on temporal coordination due to the fact that each MTS partner comes to the system with a unique conceptualization of past and future. Given this, Standifer and Bluedorn (2006) suggested that shared temporal cognitions should include a mental representation of the overall time horizon (duration) that MTS members expect the MTS to be in existence. Again, it is better for MTS leadership to arrive at a shared perspective with regard to the overall duration of the MTS earlier rather than later in the life of the system. Although an exact end date might not be possible, is the MTS to be ongoing or of a definite length of time? Also, is the purpose of the MTS *one-cycle* or *multicycle* in nature? In other words, is the MTS intended for one isolated distal goal, after which the system will be disbanded, or will the system conceivably be engaged in multiple distal goals? Here, it is important to distinguish between the one-cycle or multicycle characteristic and the overall *duration* of the MTS, or what Das and Teng (2002) referred to as the "exchange horizon." As Standifer and Bluedorn (2006) illustrated, a one-cycle strategic alliance might involve a research and development project spanning many years, whereas a multicycle alliance might be formed to expedite several short, month-long projects (p. 14). A shared temporal perspective will ease the progress of this decision.

In summary, MTS leaders are better prepared with shared temporal cognitions to strategically plan and carry out the goals of the system at all levels of the goal hierarchy.

STRATEGIC ENTRAINMENT: EMERGENCE AND ADAPTATION OF MTSs

Within multiteam systems, entrainment manifests as coordinated cyclic activity originating from the tasks and processes associated with the proximal goals of component teams and entrained to the unifying, dominant rhythm of an overarching distal goal. In this section, I outline ways in which the factors described in previous sections may come together in the development of effective, or *strategic*, entrainment of emerging MTSs.

On a related note, some might question whether the process of entraining, with its focus on synchronizing activity into an organized, rhythmic pattern, might routinize the interactions of an MTS in such a way as to inhibit or decrease adaptation. This would be problematic inasmuch as MTSs are conceptualized as adaptive mechanisms. However, I will also argue in this section that effective (*strategic*) entrainment promotes and encourages adaptation and flexibility within MTSs rather than inhibits it.

Developing Strategic Entrainment in Emerging MTSs

As mentioned by Zaccaro et al. in Chapter 1 of this book, MTSs may differ in their genesis or method of origination. An MTS might be proactively created by the organizations that will contribute component teams, or it may emerge more organically through repeated interactions among teams that will eventually constitute the system. The reason for which the MTS is developed may vary as well; it may emerge informally as a result of a specific event and formalize over time or commence as a more formal entity (Zaccaro et al., Chapter 1, this volume). Regardless of the nature of its beginnings, however, there are factors that can positively influence the extent to which MTS leadership creates an effective, more strategic entrainment process as the MTS emerges and evolves.

Early in the strategic entrainment process (and at the aggregated level of leadership), shared temporal cognitions will be beneficial. For instance, an understanding of the subjective nature of time will sensitize MTS leaders to the need for communication and clarification of temporally oriented concepts such as the time horizon of distal goals and the time orientation of each involved unit. Congruency of goals is a well-established benefit in team literature; similarly, strategic entrainment can occur only if MTS leadership is of similar minds with regard to crucial timelines, deadlines, and so on, which are influenced by time horizon and time orientation. An awareness and shared appreciation for the importance of temporal indicators or influencers such as dominant rhythms are similarly important. All MTS leadership must perceive, acknowledge, agree upon, and incorporate the impact of the dominant rhythm into the planning and implementation of distal goals if a strategically oriented entrainment process is to occur. Entrainment at the lower levels of the MTS hierarchy will be effective only inasmuch as consensus and proactive planning are utilized at the aggregate level.

With the distal goal(s) firmly set and related aspects of the dominant rhythm(s) incorporated into the strategic plan of the MTS, it is possible for leadership at the component team level to more strategically align their temporal efforts to those of the overall MTS. Component team leadership should determine the relevance of proximal goals and their tasks to the distal goal, including a similar evaluative process for the subdominant rhythm of each proximal goal as exhibited at the aggregate level. (Bear in mind that the subdominant rhythm of a particular proximal goal may or may not be identical to the dominant rhythm of the distal goal.) As mentioned in an earlier section, component leaders must decide on the pace of activities, cyclic form, and duration. Each team is a gear in the clock; as such, the temporal alignment of each proximal goal should be achieved at the team unit level with the objective to ultimately achieve the overarching distal goal. Where potential discrepancies or conflicts constrain activity, component team leaders should work collaboratively (and interdependently) with MTS leadership to prioritize rhythmic activity across the component units. Team leaders must also determine their unit's degree of embeddedness within the MTS—again, these determinations should be made collaboratively with MTS leadership. Similarly, team leaders must identify proximal goals that entail activities involving higher levels of interdependency with other component teams. Consensus on such linkage points is essential, as it has implications for transition and action processes among MTS leadership, component team leadership, and component team interactions.

An example of strategic entrainment and linkages among MTS and component team leadership is provided in Figure 14.2, in which MTS leadership is shown to be responsible for the development of distal goals and the identification of dominant rhythms. The collaborative and interdependent relationship between MTS leadership and the leadership of each component team is also illustrated by the double-headed arrow lines between the parties. In Figure 14.2, three component teams are depicted. Component Teams I and II each have two proximal goals, whereas Component Team III has one proximal goal. Each of these component teams is responsible for using the information obtained from MTS leadership regarding distal goals and dominant rhythms to plan and implement proximal goals in such a way as to aid in the achievement of collective, distal goals and to minimize conflicts between the episodic activity within its own boundaries and among the other teams. In addition, there is an example of a shared

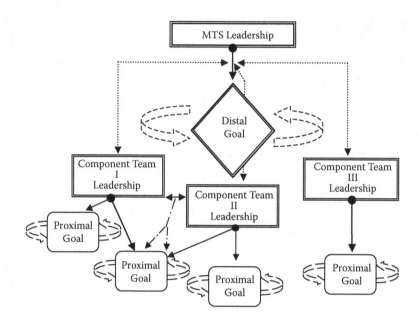

FIGURE 14.2
Strategic entrainment and linkages among MTS and component team leadership.

proximal goal between Component Teams I and II. For this shared goal, each team must maintain its own strategy and implementation relative to its other tasks and goals; however, team leadership must also ensure the effective pacing of cyclic activity related to the goal shared with its team partner. Figure 14.2 provides a visual interpretation of particular linkage points where effective interaction processes are especially crucial.

A U.S. provincial reconstruction team (PRT) in Afghanistan provides an example of how strategic entrainment could be applied. PRTs are joint civilian–military organizations; because they consist of small, fairly independent units working on a collective mission, PRTs constitute a type of MTS. One of the primary missions of a PRT is to promote reconstruction in Afghanistan (Perlito, 2005). The successful completion of such reconstruction projects represents a distal goal for the PRT, if these reconstruction projects were to have an ongoing, cyclical schedule (i.e., completion every 6 months) that could represent the dominant rhythm of that distal goal. Ideally, there would be leadership at the MTS level to identify this goal and its dominant rhythm, and communicate this information to the leadership of each component unit of the PRT. Each unit participating in the PRT would then identify the proximal goals it needs to complete in order to achieve the project and key temporal identifiers such as subdominant rhythms, relevant cyclic activities, and their pace. These leaders should also work collaboratively on shared proximal goals to ensure entrained activity between them with minimal redundancy or episodic constraint.

One such proximal goal for U.S. PRTs is known as *village improvement projects*. At least two units share in this proximal goal: the U.S. Army Civil Affairs Team conducts assessment needs within the villages and contracts with Afghan construction firms (Perlito, 2005). Another unit—the U.S. Agency of International Development Representatives—participates in a review committee to monitor such projects. Given their shared interest and interdependency relative to this proximal goal, the leadership of these units need to work together to entrain their activities, mindful of the temporal conditions of each unit. A third unit—the U.S. Department of Agriculture Representatives—works on a separate aspect of reconstruction, providing agricultural services to the rural population (Perlito, 2005). In this unit, members were brought in on a 6-month rotation; this could possibly act as a subdominant rhythm when units are trying to complete the goal.

Adaptability Through Strategic Entrainment

Although entrainment emphasizes synchronized activity into organized, rhythmic patterns, this does not necessarily translate into a decrease in the flexibility of the MTS; in fact, strategic entrainment should create the foundation for increased adaptability in MTSs, rather than a decrease. First, the process of entrainment does not involve stagnant routinization. Effective entrainment creates coordinative efficiencies; it minimizes redundancies and constrains episodic conflicts, making it easier to adapt to changes in the environment. Also, if independent units are sequencing their activities around a unified rhythm, it enables those units to respond more intuitively and as a unified whole when changes to that rhythm occur. In addition, the strategic entrainment process described here clearly delineates the roles of each party in the MTS; adaptation and flexibility should be improved as roles are clarified and tasks are allocated relative to the goal hierarchy. Finally, strategic entrainment allows those entrained to one another to work collaboratively from a shared perspective. The benefits of such a shared understanding is well established in the research on shared cognitions and shared mental models, particularly as it relates to the ability to adapt. As mentioned earlier, shared cognitions allow members to anticipate and understand each other's actions and coordinate more effectively (Mohammed et al., 2009). This remains the case with regard to shared temporal cognitions and entrainment-oriented factors.

In summary, it is possible for emerging MTSs to develop strategic entrainment processes that not only improve the system's effectiveness but also provide the foundation for increased adaptability. The ways in which MTSs develop provide just one of many potential and exciting avenues for study. In the next section, I suggest other ways in which temporal researchers may both extend the temporal literature and contribute to our understanding of these multiteam systems.

ENTRAINMENT AND MTSs: FUTURE RESEARCH DIRECTIONS

The concept of temporal coordination, or entrainment, is not a new one. However, past entrainment research largely focused on the group level of analysis (e.g., Blount & Janicik, 2002; Kelly & McGrath, 1985; McGrath & Tschan, 2004), with some work done on entrainment at the organizational level (Bluedorn & Denhardt, 1988; Pettigrew, 1985; Zerubavel, 1979). Although this research certainly remains important, many businesses, military forces, and governmental service units today find themselves situated in competitive, networked environments where it is increasingly necessary to work within the MTS context in order to be effective. This presents temporal researchers with a timely, fresh challenge, namely, the need to study the nature of entrainment within the context of these multiheaded entities. In this section, I present research questions based on the concepts discussed above that are intended to promote the study of temporal coordination at the MTS level of analysis.

To begin, it is perhaps fair (and interesting) to ask a rather fundamental research question: whether performance is improved by entrainment efforts within MTSs. Are the results of such entities improved through shared temporal cognitions, through increased awareness of pertinent entrainment issues and/or effective use of temporal coordinating mechanisms, or the like? To date, the extant literature is primarily conceptual. To determine whether entrainment efforts are as beneficial to MTSs as they have proven to be at other levels of analysis, further study is warranted.

Along these lines, it is prudent to reexamine the basic elements of rhythmic activities as they unfold in the context of MTS. Specifically, how do the elements of pace and cycle manifest in MTSs? Although each MTS will entail unique activity indicative of its purpose and the tasks involved in achieving that purpose, I suggest there are patterns of temporal activity that may be generalized and studied across MTSs. For example, do MTSs of a particular size tend to exhibit similar pacing and cyclic duration in terms of their episodic, interteam communication specific to transition or action processes, or is task complexity a greater determinant? Another avenue of study with regard to these basic elements relates to MTSs and their identification of cyclic activity relevant to goals. It is worth studying the extent to which, and the method by which, MTS leaders and members identify, react, and adapt key cyclical activity related to both proximal and distal goals.

In terms of pace, one possible avenue of study would be to examine the impact of different pacing choices made by MTSs implementing activities of similar interdependence. To what extent does pace matter among interdependent units, and what wields influence in the selection of pace? For instance, consider two MTSs: In the first, two component teams engaged in tasks for a mutual proximal goal requiring intensive interdependence do not pace their activities at a similar frequency. In the other MTS, two component teams involved in a relationship under similar circumstances make a conscious effort to use congruent pacing for their interdependent activities. What is the impact? To what extent do task complexity and the nature of the interdependent tasks between the two component teams allow for flexibility as long as interdependence (and general temporal coordination) is maintained and the proximal goal achieved? Or does the high level of interdependence in and of itself require congruent pacing between two aligned (yet essentially independent) units?

Related to the above question is the use of temporal coordinating mechanisms among component teams, as described by Montoya-Weiss and colleagues (Montoya-Weiss et al., 2001). If these devices are intended to direct coordinative efforts (particularly with regard to communication), these mechanisms serve as the type of "linkage attribute" described by Zaccaro et al. (Chapter 1, this volume). As such, they represent a crucial tool in the effective entrainment of goal-related efforts among MTS units. An exploration of which temporal mechanisms work best in certain contexts, for example among MTSs of certain sizes, organizational diversity, or proportional membership, would therefore be meaningful.

Dominant rhythms within MTSs represent another area worthy of study. How do MTS leaders perceive the impact or influence of dominant rhythms as they relate to superordinate (distal) goals? If a particular MTS's leadership are aware of a distal goal's dominant rhythm and are cognizant of its potential impact, how does that affect their decisions and strategies relative to the implementation and achievement of that goal? What happens when MTS leadership cannot reach consensus or is unaware of a distal goal's dominant rhythm? The nature of dominant rhythms within an MTS is worth noting as well. For example, do the dominant rhythms of MTSs experience periods of stability similar to those of traditional teams, or are the dominant rhythms of MTSs more (or less) stable by virtue of the different relationship most MTSs have to their environment (as described in this chapter)?

Turning to shared temporal cognitions once again, further insights could be gained by examining whether temporal coordination within an MTS is improved by a shared understanding of key entrainment constructs such as the dominant rhythm example given in this chapter. In addition, other temporal constructs tangential to entrainment, but potentially beneficial if included in a shared temporal model, might be studied. Such constructs include polychronic traits among component teams, time urgency, and attention to scheduling and deadlines. These constructs have been classified by researchers as elements of *temporal diversity* or *temporal profile* (Bluedorn & Standifer, 2006; Mohammed et al., 2009; Standifer, Halbesleben, & Kramer, 2009).

Entrainment researchers (Ancona, Okhuysen, & Perlow, 2001; Arrow, Poole, Henry, Wheelan, & Moreland, 2004) have used the term *social entrainment* to describe the temporal coordination of multiple actions of involved parties (Arrow, McGrath, & Berdahl, 2000, p. 255). In fact, Hall (1983) stated that all social phenomena (including teams, organizations, etc.) occur in a temporal context (Bluedorn, 1998, p. 110), and other temporal researchers have explicitly characterized time as a socially constructed experience (Ancona et al., 2001; Bluedorn & Standifer, 2006). As discussed in this chapter, shared temporal cognitions may emerge naturally or deliberately, but if they happen, they will be as a result of interaction. One potential avenue of research, therefore, is to determine how a socially constructed view of temporal issues or matters materializes at this aggregated level as MTS partners plan, work, and communicate with each other.

A last research suggestion involves the study of organizations involved in multiple MTSs. In some cases, organizations are finding it necessary to engage in more than one MTS concurrently. For example, business organizations are sometimes finding it necessary to engage in multiple strategic alliances simultaneously to maintain a competitive advantage; this means the leaders responsible for making their business (and, by extension, a host of alliances) successful are faced with the real challenge of coordinating not just one MTS but many. Businesses are not alone in this challenge, however. In the military arena, the United States has maintained 13 PRTs in Afghanistan similar to the type discussed in this chapter (Perlito, 2005). In these situations, there is a tendency among leadership to view each MTS as a stand-alone, independent system, which can lead to a short-term mind-set, limiting the ability to extract and utilize value across multiple MTSs (Lavie, 2009, p. 32). A preferable method would be to visualize all of an organization's multiteam system activity from a "portfolio" standpoint, much the same way as alliance researchers study alliance networks. From this perspective, an organization's leadership may consider how each partnership in the MTS portfolio influences the organization's interactions within other partnerships (Lavie, 2009, p. 32).

In their 2003 article, Parise and Casher delineated a way in which organizations may manage multiple strategic alliances using this portfolio technique. Based on their conceptualization, I propose the idea of *temporal portfolio management*. This concept would involve a method by which an organization simultaneously involved in more than one MTS could temporally coordinate these systems in such a way as to maximize effectiveness for each MTS and for the collective MTS "portfolio." I suggest that by determining areas of *temporal synergy* (e.g., MTSs with congruent or temporally aligning dominant rhythms, episodic cyclic activity, etc.) and areas of *temporal constraint* (e.g., MTSs with dominant rhythms, episodic cyclic activity, etc., that do not temporally align well), then by charting the resultant designations as a visual representation of the entire MTS portfolio, organizations can vastly improve their entrainment efforts. I suggest such proactive temporal management will facilitate improved interdependence, reduce redundancy, and create a more centralized temporal strategy that enriches the information available to each MTS and enables the organization to adapt more quickly and accurately to environmental fluctuations (Ozcan & Eisenhardt, 2009). In essence, I expect this technique to allow MTS leadership to strategically entrain more effectively. This research will most likely begin as conceptual work in which models of such a method may be delineated; however, I hope that eventually a multiple MTS situation might be located and temporal portfolio management be tested for its usefulness and practical application.

Finally, the work related to entrainment at this macrolevel of analysis so far has been largely conceptual; this is a meaningful step that lends tremendous insight into a phenomenon that is both rich and complex. However, a logical (and necessary) next step involves further study of actual MTSs in the field and in lab studies through the use of both quantitative and qualitative methodology.

CONCLUSION

Multiteam systems represent a unique way for teams to come together and work collaboratively toward a mutually beneficial goal. To achieve this, however, effective coordination among participating teams is essential. Entrainment, as the temporal element of coordination, makes such interdependent efforts possible. MTS leadership must work to build shared temporal cognitions with regard to the fundamental aspects of entrainment, and strive for temporal alignment of episodic activity both within and among component teams. If a multiteam system is successful, it works much the same way as the mechanical watch from the attic, outwardly appearing to work as one, unified entity. But if you examine the inner workings closely, what you'll see is a set of independent units, each functioning at its own internal pace, yet able to work collectively through the coordinative mechanism of one overarching, dominant rhythm reflecting a collective goal that is indicative of entrainment.

REFERENCES

Ancona, D. G., & Caldwell, D. F. (1992). Bridging the boundary: External activity and performance in organizational teams. *Administrative Science Quarterly, 37*, 634–665.

Ancona, D. G., & Chong, C. (1996). Entrainment: Pace, cycle, and rhythm in organizational behavior. *Research in Organizational Behavior, 8*, 251–284.

Ancona, D. G., & Chong, C. (1999). Cycles and synchrony: The temporal role of context in team behavior. *Research on Managing Groups and Teams, 2*, 33–48.

Ancona, D. G., Okhuysen, G. A., & Perlow, L. A. (2001). Taking time to integrate temporal research. *Academy of Management Review, 26*, 512–529.

Arrow, H., McGrath, J. E., & Berdahl, J. L. (2000). *Small groups as complex systems.* Thousand Oaks, CA: Sage.

Arrow, H., Poole, S. P., Henry, K. B., Wheelan, S., & Moreland, R. (2004). Time, change, and development: The temporal perspective on groups. *Small Group Research, 35*, 73–105.

Aschoff, J. (1979). Circadian rhythms: General features and endocrinological aspects. In D. R. Krieger (Ed.), *Endocrine rhythms* (pp. 1–61). New York: Raven Press.

Bartel, C. A., & Milliken, F. J. (2004). Perceptions of time in work groups: Do members develop shared cognitions about their temporal demands? In S. Blount (Ed.), *Research on managing groups and teams: Time in groups* (Vol. 6, pp. 87–109). New York: Elsevier.

Bateman, T. S., O'Neill, H., & Kenworthy-U'Ren, A. (2002). A hierarchical taxonomy of top managers' goals. *Journal of Applied Psychology, 87*, 1134–1148.

Bell, B. S., & Kozlowski, S. W. J. (2002). A typology of virtual teams. *Group and Organization Management, 27*, 14–49.

Blount, S., & Janicik, G. A. (2002). Getting and staying in-pace: The "in-synch" preference and its implications for work groups. *Toward Phenomenology of Groups and Group Membership, 4*, 235–266.

Bluedorn, A. C. (1998). An interview with anthropologist Edward T. Hall. *Journal of Management Inquiry, 7*, 109–115.

Bluedorn, A. C. (2002). *The human organization of time: Temporal realities and experience.* Stanford, CA: Stanford University Press.

Bluedorn, A. C., & Denhardt, R. B. (1988). Time and organizations. *Journal of Management, 14*, 299–320.

Bluedorn, A. C., & Standifer, R. L. (2004). Groups, boundary spanning, and the temporal imagination. *Research on Managing Groups and Teams, 6*, 159–184.

Bluedorn, A. C., & Standifer, R. L. (2006). Time and the temporal imagination. *Academy of Management Learning & Education, 5*, 196–206.

Cannon-Bowers, J. A., Salas, E., & Converse, S. (1993). Shared mental models in expert team decision making. In N. J. Castellan, Jr. (Ed.), *Individual and group decision making* (pp. 221–246). Hillsdale, NJ: Erlbaum.

Das, T. K., & Teng, B.-S. (2002). Alliance constellations: A social exchange perspective. *Academy of Management Review, 27*, 445–456.

DeChurch, L. A., & Marks, M. A. (2006). Leadership in multiteam systems. *Journal of Applied Psychology, 91*, 311–329.

DeChurch, L. A., & Mathieu, J. E. (2009). Thinking in terms of multiteam systems. In E. Salas, G. F. Goodwin, & C. S. Burke (Eds.), *Team effectiveness in complex organizations: Cross-disciplinary perspectives and approaches* (pp. 267–292). New York: Psychology Press.

Eisenhardt, K. M., & Brown, S. L. (1998). Time pacing: Competing in markets that won't stand still. *Harvard Business Review, 76*, 59–69.

Gerwin, D. (2004). Coordinating new product development in strategic alliances. *Academy of Management Review, 29*, 241–257.

Gevers, J. M., Rutte, C. G., & van Eerde, W. (2004). How project teams achieve coordinated action: A model of shared cognitions on time. In S. Blount (Ed.), *Research on managing groups and teams: Time in groups* (Vol. 6, pp. 67–85). New York: Elsevier.

Gevers, J. M., Rutte, C. G., & van Eerde, W. (2006). Meeting deadlines in work groups: Implicit and explicit mechanisms. *Applied Psychology: An International Review, 55*, 52–72.

Hall, E. T. (1983). *The dance of life: The other dimension of time.* Garden City, NY: Anchor.

Harbison, J. R., & Pekar, P. L. (1998). *Smart alliances: A practical guide to repeatable success.* San Francisco: Jossey-Bass.

Kelly, J. R., & McGrath, J. E. (1985). Effects of time limits and task types on task performance and interaction of four-person groups. *Journal of Personality and Social Psychology, 49*, 395–407.

Klimoski, R., & Mohammed, S. (1994). Team mental models: Construct or metaphor? *Journal of Management, 20*, 403–437.

Kozlowski, S. W. J., Gully, S. M., Nason, E. R., & Smith, E. M. (1999). Developing adaptive teams: A theory of compilation and performance across levels and time. In D. R. Ilgen & E. D. Pulakos (Eds.), *The changing nature of work and performance: Implications for staffing, personnel actions, and development* (pp. 240–294). San Francisco: Jossey-Bass.

Latham, G. P., & Locke, E. A. (1975). Increasing productivity and decreasing time limits: A field replication of Parkinson's law. *Journal of Applied Psychology, 60*, 524–526.

Lavie, D. (2009). Capturing value from alliance portfolios. *Organizational Dynamics, 38*, 26–36.

Lawrence, P. R., & Lorsch, J. W. (1967). *Organization and environment: Managing differentiation and integration.* Cambridge, MA: Harvard University Press.

LePine, J. A., Piccolo, R. F., Jackson, C. L., Mathieu, J. E., & Saul, J. R. (2008). A meta-analysis of teamwork processes: Tests of a multidimensional model and relationships with team effectiveness criteria. *Personnel Psychology, 61*, 273–308.

Marketwire. (2009, April 20). Galapagos enters strategic alliance in inflammatory diseases with Merck & Co., Inc. Mechelen, Belgium: Author. Retrieved from http://www.marketwire.com/press-release/Galapagos-Nv-LSE-GLPG-976380.html

Marks, M. A., Mathieu, J. E., DeChurch, L. A., Panzer, F. J., & Alonso, A. (2005). Teamwork in multiteam systems. *Journal of Applied Psychology, 87*, 964–971.

Marks, M. A., Mathieu, J. E., & Zaccaro, S. J. (2001). A temporally based framework and taxonomy of team processes. *Academy of Management Review, 26*, 356–376.

Marks, M. A., Sabella, M. J., Burke, C. S., & Zaccaro, S. J. (2002). The impact of cross-training on team effectiveness. *Journal of Applied Psychology, 87*, 3–13.

Mathieu, J. E., Heffner, T. S., Goodwin, G. F., Cannon-Bowers, J. A., & Salas, E. (2005). Scaling the quality of teammates' mental models: Equifinality and normative comparisons. *Journal of Organizational Behavior, 26*, 37–56.

Mathieu, J. E., Marks, M. A., & Zaccaro, S. J. (2001). Multiteam systems. In N. Anderson, D. S. Ones, H. K. Sinangil, & C. Viswesvaran (Eds.), *Handbook of industrial, work, and organizational psychology* (Vol. 2, pp. 289–313). London: Sage.

McGrath, J. E. (1991). Time, interaction, and performance (TIP): A theory of groups. *Small Group Research, 22*, 147–174.

McGrath, J. E., & Rotchford, N. L. (1983). Time and behavior in organizations. *Research in Organizational Behavior, 5*, 57–101.

McGrath, J. E., & Tschan, F. (2004). *Temporal matters in social psychology: Examining the role of time in the lives of groups and individuals.* Washington, DC: American Psychological Association.

Minorsky, N. (1962). *Nonlinear oscillations.* Princeton, NJ: Van Nostrand.

Mohammed, S., Hamilton, K., & Lim, A. (2009). The incorporation in team research: Past, current, and future. In E. Salas, G. F. Goodwin, & C. S. Burke (Eds.), *Team effectiveness in complex organizations: Cross-disciplinary perspectives and approaches* (pp. 321–348). New York: Psychology Press.

Montoya-Weiss, M. M., Massey, A. P., & Song, M. (2001). Getting it together: Temporal coordination and conflict management in global virtual teams. *Academy of Management Journal, 44,* 1251–1262.

Nelson, K. M., Armstrong, D., Buche, M., & Ghods, M. (2000). Evaluating the CMM Level 3 KPA of intergroup coordination: A theory-based approach. *Information Technology and Management, 1,* 171–181.

Ozcan, P., & Eisenhardt, K. M. (2009). Origin of alliance portfolios: Entrepreneurs, network strategies, and firm performance. *Academy of Management Journal, 52,* 246–279.

Parise, S., & Casher, A. (2003). Designing and managing alliance networks. *Academy of Management Executive, 17,* 25–39.

Perlito, R. M. (2005). *The US experience with provincial reconstruction teams in Afghanistan: Lessons identified* (US Institute of Peace Special Report 152). Washington, DC: US Institute of Peace.

Pettigrew, A. M. (1985). *The awakening giant: Continuity and change in Imperial Chemical Industries.* New York: Blackwell.

Schein, E. H. (1992). *Organizational culture and leadership* (2nd ed.). San Francisco: Jossey-Bass.

Standifer, R. L., & Bluedorn, A. C. (2006). Alliance management teams and entrainment: Sharing temporal mental models. *Human Relations, 59,* 903–927.

Standifer, R. L., Halbesleben, J., & Kramer, J. A. (2009, April). The impact of temporal differences on team process and effectiveness. Paper presented at the SIOP Conference, New Orleans, LA.

Tesluk, P., Mathieu, J. E., Zaccaro, S. J., & Marks, M. A. (1997). Task and aggregation issues in the analysis and assessment of team performance. In M. Brannick, E. Salas, & C. Prince (Eds.), *Team performance assessment and measurement: Theory, methods, and applications* (pp. 197–224). Hillsdale, NJ: Erlbaum.

Thompson, J. D. (1967). *Organizations in action.* Chicago: McGraw-Hill.

Van de Ven, A. H., Delbecq, A. L., & Koenig, R., Jr. (1976). Determinants of coordination modes within organizations. *American Sociological Review, 41,* 322–338.

Waller, M. J., Zellmer-Bruhn, M., & Giambatista, R. C. (2002). Watching the clock: Group pacing behavior under dynamic deadlines. *Academy of Management Journal, 45,* 1046–1055.

Wittenbaum, G. M., Vaughan, S. I., & Stasser, G. I. (2002). Coordination in task-performing groups. In R. S. Tindale (Ed.), *Theory and research on small groups* (pp. 177–204). New York: Kluwer Academic.

Zalesny, M. D., Salas, E., & Prince, C. (1995). Conceptual and measurement issues in coordination: Implications for team behavior and performance. In G. R. Ferris (Ed.), *Research in personnel and human resources management* (Vol. 13, pp. 81–115). Greenwich, CT: JAI.

Zellmer-Bruhn, M. E., Waller, M. J., & Ancona, D. (2004). The effect of temporal entrainment on the ability of teams to change their routines. *Research on Managing Groups and Teams, 6,* 135–158.

Zerubavel, E. (1979). *Patterns of time in hospital life.* Chicago: University of Chicago Press.

Section V

Methods and Conclusion

15

Research Methodology for Studying Dynamic Multiteam Systems: Application of Complexity Science

Juliet R. Aiken
University of Maryland

Paul J. Hanges
University of Maryland

Our fellow authors in this book have discussed the nature of multiteam systems (MTSs) and have explained what makes these systems unique. As noted by several authors, multiteam systems are both *dynamic* and *complex*. Although such systems are sometimes deliberately formed by some external body, more often than not, these teams *emerge* as a function of environmental pressures, and the nature of these teams develops and evolves over time (Hoegl & Weinkauf, 2005; Marks, DeChurch, Mathieu, Panzer, & Alonso, 2005; Zaccaro, Marks, & DeChurch, Chapter 1, this volume).

The question that will be addressed in the present chapter is how research on such teams should be conducted. It is our contention that research designs and statistical methods that are currently popular are simply not up to the challenge of revealing the true story embedded in the dynamic phenomena exhibited by multiteam systems. For example, the frequently employed factorial research design basically assumes that observations (e.g., those produced by individuals, teams, or organizations) within the same experimental condition are fungible. Although this might be an appropriate assumption when exploring static systems, this assumption is completely inappropriate when studying dynamic phenomena. It is well known in the dynamic systems literature that two equivalent systems at the beginning of a study can diverge into completely different stable states at the end of an experiment despite the fact that both systems encountered the same exact environmental and experimental stimuli (Hanges, Braverman, & Rentsch, 1991; Hanges, Lord, Godfrey, & Raver, 2002). In other words, dynamic phenomena are inherently inconsistent with the basic assumptions of traditional experimental methodology and the statistical techniques used to understand it. This intrinsic inconsistency between research design, statistical method, and processes of the underlying phenomenon potentially produces uninterpretable results due to the inevitable reduction of the study's internal validity and statistical conclusion validity (Shadish, Cook, & Campbell, 2001).

Clearly, serious exploration of multiteam systems requires us to rethink our current research paradigm. In this chapter, we discuss some of the methodologies being developed in the growing field of complexity science. We suggest that these approaches can be used as a framework for addressing the measurement, design, and analysis of multiteam systems. In the next section, we will review the basic framework of complexity science, and briefly detail how it conceptually applies to multiteam systems. We then provide suggestions with regard to measurement, research methods, and data analysis of the dynamic phenomena inherent in multiteam systems.

COMPLEXITY SCIENCE

Rather than referring to a single, unified discipline, the term *complexity science* can actually be thought of as a superordinate category that covers a number of interdisciplinary research streams. For example, systems theory, nonlinear dynamical systems theory, network theory, synergetics, and complex adaptive systems theory all inform and can be rightfully categorized under the general label of complexity science (Goldstein, 2008). Given these different approaches to complexity science, it is important to first identify a subdiscipline whose model best fits the phenomenon of interest. In our opinion, multiteam systems are closely related to complex adaptive systems, and thus we focus on this complexity science approach in our chapter.

Complex adaptive systems are said to be complex because they are composed of multiple, richly interconnected elements (Hanges et al., 2002).

They are adaptive because they can change and learn from their own experience (Vallacher & Nowak, 1994). Examples of complex adaptive systems can be readily seen in the world. For example, the behavior of the stock market, the central nervous system, the immune system, social communities, businesses, and social cultural systems are all examples of complex adaptive systems in that they are composed of multiple elements (e.g., people) that are richly interconnected (e.g., face-to-face communication, blogs, email, phone, written letters, Twitter, Facebook, and YouTube). These elements are influenced by one another, and they learn from their interactions. This learning is reflected throughout the entire system over time such that the system starts to self-organize. That is, the interactions among the elements tend to become more hierarchically organized over time (Morel & Ramanujam, 1999). This self-organization results in emergent behavior (e.g., leadership or culture) that is seen only at a system level of analysis (Dooley & Lichtenstein, 2008; Vallacher & Nowak, 1994).

As discussed by other authors in this volume, multiteam systems are composed of multiple interconnected elements. These elements include team members, team leaders, and the teams themselves. The team members are richly interconnected within their teams, and one or more team members within a team are likely to span boundaries between teams. Multiteam systems adapt in multiple ways. First, the initial structure within each component team changes as team members adapt their behavior in response to environmental contingencies and the unique competencies of their fellow team members. Second, the behavior of the multiteam system itself emerges as the individual teams interact and build new interconnections to accomplish one or more shared goals.

In summary, we argue that complex adaptive systems are a good model for understanding the behavior of multiteam systems. Given this framework, we can now consider the implications of viewing multiteam systems as complex adaptive systems with regard to measurement, methods, and analytic techniques. Specifically, in the following sections, we highlight three critical issues that can be clearly traced back to complexity science: (a) the role of time (emergence and dynamism), (b) the level of the phenomenon of interest (emergence), and (c) interconnections between units in the system (dynamism). We start with a discussion on measurement.

MEASUREMENT

Framing multiteam systems as complex adaptive systems requires the incorporation of time and levels of analysis into measurement. Due to the natural change and growth that occur in multiteam systems, the common practice of measuring a phenomenon at a single level at one or two time periods simply doesn't work. We propose that adequate measurement of dynamic phenomena demands attention to three temporal issues and to two levels of analysis concerns. Specifically, the measurement imperatives pertaining to temporal concerns are (a) the necessity for moving beyond single observation time periods, (b) the need to move beyond self-report measures, and (c) the need to consider the relevant time scale for the phenomenon of interest. Correspondingly, the two critical issues relevant to levels are (a) the actual level of measurement (e.g., individual, team, or multiteam system) for the phenomenon of interest, and (b) the extent to which the phenomenon of interest reflects a compilation or composition model. We will first address the three concerns relevant to the role of time.

Multiple Observation Time Periods

The first concern that researchers must address in the dynamic measurement of multiteam systems is to obtain multiple observations. As stated previously, multiteam systems researchers must accept that *single observation time periods are unacceptable.* Work by Eiser (1994a, 1994b) has revealed multiple deficiencies that stem from single time point measurement. Borrowing from the physical sciences approach to studying dynamic phenomena, Eiser (1994a, 1994b) recommended repeatedly measuring the phenomena of interest over time in order to overcome such deficiencies. Measuring a dynamic system by taking only one observation is similar to taking a picture of a dancer with a still camera. The still picture does not provide information about the beauty or intricacies of the entire dance. Indeed, the picture might even be a blurred representation of the part of the dance that was captured. Rather, its emergent beauty can be captured only in the projection of at least 30 still pictures per second for the entire length of the dance.

Although the former approach can intuitively be applied to objective measurement, the issue of repeated attitude measurement remains a challenge. One solution was proposed by Vallacher, Nowak, and Kaufman (1994), who developed a dynamic measure of attitudes. In developing this measure, they applied Hovland, Janis, and Kelley's (1953) hypothesis that the distance between a person and a target stimulus indirectly reflects that person's feelings toward the target. Vallacher et al. had participants manipulate a computer mouse to vary the distance between the computer's cursor and some target symbol. The location of the cursor was recorded 10 times per second, and the distance between the cursor and the target symbol was calculated. This distance was used as an inverse measure of attitude favorability. The Vallacher et al. study provided support for Eiser's (1994a, 1994b) arguments on attitude measurement, and the study demonstrated the viability of this dynamic measurement methodology. This dynamic attitude measurement has since been successfully applied in a number of leadership research studies (Foti, Knee, & Backert, 2008; Hanges et al., submitted). These latter studies demonstrated that this repeated measurement approach captured the dynamic properties of leadership perceptions in a way that static measurement could never accomplish.

Moving Beyond Self-Report

As previously discussed, researchers of multiteam systems must move beyond single observation measurement. Indeed, in moving toward repeated measurement, another concern is likely to arise for the multiteam systems researcher: *the need to move beyond traditional self-report measurement.* Naturally, this particular concern may be more applicable to certain types of multiteam systems relative to others.

For example, Zaccaro et al. (Chapter 1, this volume) and Mathieu, Marks, and Zaccaro (2001) reviewed an emergency response multiteam system example in which the team was composed of firefighters, emergency medical technicians (EMTs), a surgical team, and a recovery team. Clearly, it would not be practical to ask the members of this multiteam system to complete self-report measures or move a computer mouse in the middle of an emergency. In addition to these limitations, other considerations may make it difficult for the members of such teams to accurately recall their feelings and experiences after the emergency is over.

Specifically, for members of these teams, the pressures of the moment may overtake rational thought and response. Indeed, research consistently reveals that individuals working in situations where they experience stress tend to have more difficulty accurately recalling details of these experiences, especially those that are emotionally charged (Smeets, Otgaar, Candel, & Wolf, 2008). Moreover, research has repeatedly affirmed the tendency for an individual to recall information more accurately when he or she is in the same mood as when the event actually occurred (Gupta & Khosla, 2006; Parrott, 1991). Indeed, this so-called mood-congruent recall effect has been found to hold even for autobiographical memories (Bullington, 1990). Thus, because individuals in emergency response multiteam systems will likely experience stress while dealing with an event, but not afterward, it is unlikely that self-report measures after the fact will provide accurate information about what transpired while this multiteam system responded to the prior emergency.

Accuracy of information is a large concern with self-report measurement, but not the only concern. A one-time self-report measure after the event transpired will likely not only be inaccurate but also fail to satisfy the previously discussed imperative: the need for repeated measures. In summary, self-report measures may not provide the kinds of information required by multiteam systems researchers. The more dynamic the multiteam system, and the more critical the environmental contingency to which they respond, the less useful self-report measures will be. Thus, researchers interested in multiteam systems must move beyond self-report. Moving beyond reliance on self-report may require researchers to get creative in data collection. For instance, researchers may have to rely on observational measurement, if they can get the cooperation of the teams they are studying (e.g., Tesluk & Mathieu, 1999). Otherwise, researchers may be able to record team members' conversations throughout the day, or may be able to utilize archival data to procure additional information (e.g., Dooley & Lichtenstein, 2008).

Time Scale

The final temporal measurement concern is that of the time scale. That is, choices of measurement that satisfy the previous two conditions (i.e., repeated measures and moving beyond self-report) must also be suited to the time scale on which the phenomenon of interest is expected to function. Dooley and Lichtenstein (2008) discussed three general time scales that demand different types of measurement: micro-, meso-, and macrolevel. These three levels of time address different periods over which certain phenomena emerge or are exhibited. Microlevel time measurement is designed toward capturing minute-by-minute interactions. Mesolevel measurement assesses daily or weekly changes, and macrolevel measurement assesses long-term changes.

Different methods of measurement satisfy different time scale requirements. The Vallacher et al. (1994) mouse measure is a good example of a microlevel measure. Also, Dooley and Lichtenstein (2008) discussed the merits of audio-recording individuals to catch second-by-second interactions. On the mesolevel, Tesluk and Mathieu (1999) recorded daily and weekly changes in the conditions of road workers. Another mesolevel measurement example is provided by Dooley and Lichtenstein, in that they collected social network data weekly. Finally, macrolevel measurement can be obtained through the use of archival data (Dooley & Lichtenstein, 2008).

Although research conducted on any single level of time may be illuminating, Dooley and Lichtenstein (2008) posited that the strongest research will assess multiple levels of time. Specifically, they draw distinctions between these time scales using the framework of fractal time ecology (Koehler, 2001). According to fractal time ecology, patterns of interaction at any given level are linked to emergent behavior at other levels (Koehler, 2001). Said differently, all levels of time are interconnected. This suggests that researchers should strive to collect data on multiple time levels for the same project. Focusing on and measuring social network data on a weekly basis will not reveal how the day-by-day interactions among team members cause the network structures to change. Reflecting back on the dance example discussed in this chapter, although the microlevel measurement of 30 pictures per minute captures a smooth representation of the movement of the dancer's limbs, unless you consider the full length of the dance (a meso- or macrolevel issue), you will miss or get a biased representation of its emergent story.

In sum, multiteam systems researchers need to address the role of time in their research. First, they must strive for repeated measurements, as a single time measurement will not yield enough information to capture the dynamism of multiteam systems. Second, these researchers must move beyond single-source data. Specifically, single-source data may be unreliable, especially for multiteam systems under pressure. Finally, researchers need to consider the level of time that they are interested in examining (i.e., micro, meso, or macro). Measurement tools should be evaluated and systematically selected for their usefulness in answering researchers' questions.

Next, we discuss issues surrounding levels of analysis. Two issues in particular will be highlighted. Specifically, we address issues concerning the level of the emergent phenomena and whether the phenomenon of interest emerges through a compilation or composition process.

Levels of Emergent Phenomenon

As discussed earlier, the structure of complex adaptive systems becomes more orderly and hierarchical over time. As a consequence, new behavior emerges at the system level. Thus, it is apparent that researchers interested in multiteam systems must attend to both lower and higher level phenomena. The first issue that researchers must address is the deceptively simple question of the level on which any given phenomenon of interest resides. This question becomes difficult to answer because the units within a multiteam system might be simultaneously nested within several different levels. In other words, an individual is a member of his or her individual team as well as a member of the broader multiteam system. Likewise, the teams within multiteam systems have membership both within the multiteam systems and within their parent organization. Thus, researchers must answer the following two questions: (a) Is the unit of analysis primarily an individual, team, or multiteam system? And (b) is this unit of analysis embedded in the team, multiteam system, and/or parent organization? Answering these two questions will aid researchers in determining the correct referent to use in measurement.

In addressing these questions, researchers interested in multiteam systems can begin by referring to guidelines outlined by Klein, Dansereau, and Hall (1994) regarding the assumptions underlying the specification of constructs at any given level. Specifically, Klein et al. indicated that these assumptions include (a) homogeneity of subgroups within higher level units (e.g., individuals within the team, or teams within the multiteam system, are homogeneous); (b) independence from higher level units (e.g., individuals within the team, or teams within the multiteam system, are independent of the higher level's influence); or, alternatively, (c) heterogeneity within higher level units (e.g., the relationship between an individual's or team's characteristics and some outcome of interest is dependent on the composition of the higher level unit). Thus, if the researcher holds the first assumption, the unit of analysis might be the multiteam system. If the researcher holds the second assumption, the unit of analysis might be the teams within the multiteam system. Finally, if the researcher holds the third assumption, the unit of analysis might be the individual within the team.

Although a useful starting point, it is critical to note that the Klein et al. (1994) guidelines were developed under the assumption that group phenomena are static at the time of measurement. Researchers interested in multiteam systems need to employ these guidelines flexibly, as multiteam systems exhibit dynamic processes where the level of analysis of phenomena of interest may change over time. For example, assume that there are 600 individuals at the beginning of a study and that these individuals are randomly assigned to 100 teams. Further assume that each team is instructed to pursue one goal and that there are only four different goals for all the teams in this study. At the beginning of a study, the various individuals and the teams would operate independently of each other. The level of analysis of any construct would be at the individual level of analysis during this time. However, as time passes the individuals within each group will form common mental models and begin to work as a team. At this point, the construct that was determined to be operating at the individual level earlier in this study would be operating at the team level of analysis. As more time passes, the teams that are pursuing a common goal may start cooperating. As they do, the level of analysis changes once again to the multiteam level of analysis. Thus, as illustrated by this thought experiment, levels of analysis issues for dynamic systems are more complex than for static systems, and they require the researcher to be aware of timing issues within the dynamic process itself.

Determining the level of analysis of a construct can be helpful for developing appropriate and meaningful measures. As outlined by Klein et al. (1994), researchers interested in teams within the multiteam system as the unit of analysis should measure their constructs at the team level, whereas researchers interested in individuals as the unit of analysis should measure their constructs at the individual level of analysis. Finally, researchers interested in the individual within the group should use measures that highlight the relative position of the individual within the group (e.g., forced-choice ranking). Although these recommendations are readily applied when measuring static constructs, researchers studying dynamic phenomena such as multiteam systems need to take extra steps. We recommend that researchers include multiple measures of their primary construct at different levels of analysis (e.g., individual self-efficacy, or group potency). This allows researchers to study how system-level (e.g., team or organizational) constructs emerge over time. For example, the inclusion of individual-level measures might identify specific patterns among lower level units (e.g., individuals within teams, or teams within organizations) that facilitate the development or destruction of those system-level constructs.

Another guideline to consider is that of which level is more salient for a given phenomenon. As discussed by Zaccaro et al. (Chapter 1, this volume), multiteam systems are composed of teams that share at least one goal in common. Thus, if the researcher is interested in the shared goal, it is likely that the appropriate unit of analysis for that researcher would be the overall multiteam system. However, if the researcher was interested in a goal that differs across individual teams, the appropriate unit of analysis would be the team level and not the multiteam system.

In summary, the level of analysis of a phenomenon of interest will determine the level of measurement used to capture that phenomenon. The final concern in the area of measurement that multiteam systems researchers should consider pertains specifically to instances where the level of analysis is higher than the individual—that is, at the team, multiteam system, or organizational level. This concern is whether the phenomenon emerges through compilation or composition processes.

Compilation or Composition

In levels research, there are two general classifications for how upper level processes develop. One way is through compilation processes, and the other through composition. The latter case of development is one more frequently discussed in the literature, and it emphasizes similarity amongst lower level units. For instance, Chan (1998) delineated a typology of composition models that can be applied to understanding higher level phenomena. Amongst these, we will briefly review two, the direct consensus and the referent shift models, in order to highlight potential measurement issues associated with the composition model believed to underlie the phenomenon of interest. Direct consensus composition models assume that the phenomenon of interest resides on the individual level, and that it is shared amongst individuals. Referent shift composition models assume that the phenomenon of interest resides at the higher level, and that it is shared amongst individuals. Both of these models require that the phenomenon be shared at the higher level—thus, treatment of these models in terms of analysis will not be different. Both will require that researchers justify aggregation (via interagency coordinating committees [ICCs] and regional working groups [RWGs]) prior to analysis at the level on which they are expected to operate. However, the assumptions behind each of these models will influence the measurement: Direct consensus models will need to be measured with a lower level referent (e.g., "I feel ..."), whereas referent shift models will need to be measured with a higher level referent (e.g., "The team feels ...").

Although the underlying assumption of the composition model is the similarity of lower level units, the underlying assumption of the compilation model is that lower level units vary meaningfully. Moreover, the compilation model assumes that there are distinct differences between unaggregated and aggregated data for these models. In other words, the whole is different from the sum of the parts. With these models, there is no need to assess agreement amongst lower level units, as they are expected and desired to vary (Bliese, 2000). Although the use of a compilation model does not immediately seem to greatly impact measurement, it is clearly tied to the dynamism proposition of complexity science. That is, complex adaptive systems are characterized by dynamic, nonlinear emergence that corresponds to the process of compilation just discussed. Thus, the determination of the level of analysis, and the way in which the phenomenon develops, should affect the way in which data are collected.

In summary, we have argued that multiteam systems researchers must address two overarching issues in measurement: time and levels. With respect to time, we have proposed that researchers must obtain repeated measures from multiple sources on the time scale desired to measure the phenomenon of interest. With respect to levels, we have proposed that researchers decide not only the level of measurement for the phenomenon of interest but also the process through which this phenomenon emerged in order to measure it more accurately. Although measurement concerns are clearly a priority for multiteam system researchers, they are not the only methodological and statistical issues that researchers interested in these unique systems face. Next, we discuss salient methodological concerns relevant to research on multiteam systems.

METHODS

In addition to measurement issues, researchers must address methodological issues when designing multiteam system studies. The application of complexity science to the study of multiteam systems yields a number of key issues that researchers must address. These issues are linked to two aspects of complex adaptive systems: emergence and dynamism. Again, emergence takes time. Thus, time is a critical factor that researchers must include in their research designs. Additionally, emergent, dynamic data are, by nature, expansive and detailed. Thus, issues of the most appropriate way to measure these data (i.e., qualitatively for richness, and quantitatively for clarity) also arise. In this section, we review concerns related to design in general and conclude with a discussion of a few suggested methodologies that might be particularly useful when studying multiteam systems. First, we will address the need for the consideration of time in all multiteam system designs.

Longitudinal Research

Concerns with cross-sectional measurement abound. Traditionally, such designs are seen as subject to a number of measurement context effects (Podsakoff, MacKenzie, Lee, & Podsakoff, 2003). Two frequently discussed issues with cross-sectional methodologies are that biases introduced by measurement context may inflate apparent relationships between variables and that causality is more difficult, if not impossible, to ascertain. As previously stated, we believe that there is a third concern particularly relevant to the study of multiteam systems. Specifically, these systems are dynamic. Cross-sectional methodologies completely overlook the dynamism inherent in such systems. As such, researchers investigating multiteam systems through cross-sectional designs will be unable to discover and understand emergent and dynamic properties in the system and among its subunits.

Thus, researchers are urged to explicitly incorporate the role of time into their designs. Indeed, this chapter is not the first to mention this imperative. In their recommendations for research on complex adaptive systems, Dooley and Lichtenstein (2008) repeatedly emphasized the importance of time in design, regardless of the time frame. Next, we will briefly review another concern, the importance of rich data for the researcher's question and the subsequent influence they have on the choice of qualitative or quantitative designs.

Rich Data: Qualitative Versus Quantitative Designs

The use of longitudinal designs and repeated measures can result in a large body of extremely rich data. Dooley and Lichtenstein (2008) provided a vivid example of just how work intensive it can be to obtain rich qualitative data. In their study, these authors had their participants wear microphones at all times when they were at work for a 3-year period. These recordings not only had to be transcribed but also often had to be translated into English. Clearly, depending on the scope, qualitative longitudinal designs can result in a massive amount of data that are challenging to analyze.

When designing studies to assess complex phenomena, the researcher has three options. First, the researcher can focus on only quantitative data. Quantitative data might be easier to collect and will likely involve less time in terms of processing than qualitative data. On the downside, however, quantitative data lack the "richness" of information obtained through qualitative efforts. Thus, researchers employing quantitative methodologies may be able to complete their work more readily, but are likely to miss out on some subtle, dynamic issues that would be better detected through the use of a qualitative design.

Second, researchers could focus on qualitative methodology exclusively. Qualitative methodologies are useful in that the data collected are extremely rich and intensive. One of the tenets of complex adaptive systems is that subtle perturbations can result in dramatic system changes (Byrne, 1998). Thus, given the richness of the data, researchers employing these methodologies are more likely to pick up on these small, but significant, disruptions. However, these data tend to be cumbersome to process and analyze. Although data collected by qualitative methodologies may be richer, it will take longer and require more effort to prepare and analyze these data.

Finally, researchers may choose to employ both qualitative and quantitative methodologies simultaneously. This option provides the benefits of both designs while retaining the drawback of qualitative methodologies. Instead of incorporating an intensive qualitative analysis, researchers may wish to employ a "light" qualitative design in addition to their quantitative work. Doing so may enhance their ability to assess small perturbations without undue effort. Next, we will review different types of qualitative and quantitative designs that researchers may choose to employ. In the discussion of each design, issues relating to time, the richness of data, difficulty processing data, and other relevant concerns will be discussed.

Qualitative Designs: Real-Time Tracking of Events

Real-time tracking of events, also referred to as *real-time observation*, can be implemented in a number of ways. For example, researchers might employ recording devices (e.g., microphones or hidden cameras), event sampling (Reis & Gable, 2000), or active observation. Real-time tracking is consistent with Eiser's (1994a, 1994b) recommendation for the repeated measurement of a phenomenon. Although real-time tracking is generally considered time consuming, researchers can choose the level of involvement they wish to have in the course of the study. For example, in the Dooley and Lichtenstein (2008) case study discussed in this chapter, the researchers not only recorded all conversations at work but also photographed the facility every 5 minutes, and conducted periodic field observations to supplement the photographic and recorded data. Leonard-Barton (1990) also conducted a 3-year real-time observation study. However, she visited the research site only once or twice a week, and ran a series of interviews about recent events to capture what occurred when she was not onsite. In sum, researchers employing real-time observation and tracking can mitigate some of the labor-intensive nature of this approach by employing less constant observational methods.

Real-time tracking clearly affords researchers the ability to watch events unfold and record dynamic interactions as they happen. Several limitations to this kind of research should be remembered. The first has already been mentioned. It is time consuming and work intensive. The second is that real-time observation may introduce a *Hawthorne effect*. That is, employees may become distracted or may react differently when the researcher is onsite or if they know they are being recorded.

The role of time in real-time tracking is substantial. Indeed, the consideration of time and change over time is inherent in the implementation of real-time tracking methodologies. However, researchers may control the level of time on which they conduct their measurement. For instance, the methodology employed by Dooley and Lichtenstein (2008) was able to capture phenomena on a microlevel (second by second). Conversely, because Leonard-Barton (1990) was on site only a few times a week and used interviews to "fill in" for missing time, she was able to capture the phenomenon of interest on a more mesolevel (day by day, or week by week). Thus, although time is by necessity a consideration in real-time observation, researchers have control over the level on which they collect and analyze the resultant data.

Qualitative Designs: Retrospective Case Studies

Another way through which case studies can be conducted is through retrospective data collection. For example, Leonard-Barton (1990) supplemented her real-time observation with additional information gleaned from nine retrospective case studies. Specifically, she conducted over 100 interviews with programmers. These interviews assessed users' and developers' views on recently implemented technology.

Although the data gleaned from retrospective case studies can be quite rich, there remain some drawbacks to this method. First, the data from interviews can still be time consuming to process and prepare for analysis. Second, the data collected are all after the fact. That is, by using retrospective methods of collecting data, researchers cannot watch events unfold. Instead, they must hope to correctly assess what happened historically given the "end" result. Thus, it is more difficult to capture subtle dynamics.

Likewise, the role of time is more difficult to pinpoint in such studies. Even if data are collected from multiple sources, if the interviews are conducted at the same time, much information is lost. This method also runs the risk of producing static results. Thus, researchers employing retrospective analysis may want to combine them with methodologies that better capture changes as they occur, such as real-time tracking. Otherwise, researchers may wish to employ several waves of retrospective analyses in the same organization to get a more longitudinal view, if only on a macroscale.

Qualitative Designs: Ethnographic Methods

A third study design that researchers can employ in studying longitudinal data is ethnographic methodology. Barley (1990) employed this methodology in investigating technological change in radiology. In the course of this work, he employed three different methods of ethnographic data collection. These methods were called the *synchronic*, the *diachronic*, and the *parallel*. The first of these three, the synchronic, assumes that "old" and "new" technologies are concomitant at the moment of change. Moreover, this approach assumes that there are distinct social orders that support the use of these "old" and "new" technologies. In other words, the researcher takes the frame of reference that events are static and that two end states can exist at the same time. This frame of reference forces the researcher to focus on the present moment.

In contrast to the synchronic method, the diachronic method also treats time as static but looks at the developmental path of one specific technology's use. Thus, this approach requires the researcher to use both a past and present time perspective in his or her ethnography. Finally, the parallel method requires researchers to conduct synchronic and diachronic analyses in numerous sites in an attempt to tease out the unique effects of context-specific and more universal issues.

In summary, like other qualitative designs discussed in this chapter, the use of ethnographic methods can be time consuming. Additionally, such methods are labor intensive. Moreover, because much of it must be pursued at the site, the researcher runs the risk of potentially inducing the Hawthorne effect. Finally, these kinds of analyses are easier when there are objects to measure. Without concrete objects, the difficulty of ethnography increases.

As discussed, certain approaches to ethnography can be used to capture dynamic phenomena. Although synchronic analysis freezes time, diachronic analysis captures time-variant phenomena such as those apparent in dynamic systems. As illustrated by the Barley (1990) study, it can be used to track the emergence of new technology or other objects through time.

Qualitative Designs: Event History Analysis

Finally, researchers employing qualitative designs can use event history analysis to study dynamic phenomena. Event history analysis involves acquiring retrospective reports from key players to determine what occurred and changed at a given organization or site. Glick, Huber, Miller, Doty, and Sutcliffe (1990) employed this methodology in assessing 100 different organizations over 2 years. In this time, four structured interviews, one every 6 months, were conducted with the top managers in each organization. In these interviews, managers were asked to describe design and nondesign changes and specify which were most important. Likewise, Dooley and Lichtenstein (2008) conducted event history analysis on a macrolevel for one organization. These authors gathered, coded, and analyzed macrolevel data reflecting company leadership.

The use of retrospective event history analysis, as in the examples briefly discussed in this chapter, has both advantages and disadvantages (Glick et al., 1990). One advantage is that actual dates of change, as best as can be remembered by managers, can be obtained. Also, event history data collected via interviews provide a variety of rich data describing the events and change. However, there are also several drawbacks. First, informants across organizations may pay attention to different issues or may discuss the same construct using different language—both of which can affect coding. Second, informants may not recall situations accurately. Third, according to complexity science, large shifts in organizations are thought to result from small perturbations. Thus, informants are only likely to report shifts after they occur and are more likely to identify the causes of such shifts to salient features of the environment, regardless of their true causal nature.

The role of time in retrospective reports is moderate. Although dates can be obtained from informants, it is unlikely that all dates provided are accurate. Thus, it may not be possible to map the rich data onto a narrow timeline. However, although micro- and mesolevel times may not be captured by this technique, it is possible to analyze macrolevel time changes through retrospective event history analysis.

Quantitative Designs: Simulations

One way through which researchers may choose to study multiteam systems, especially initially, is through the use of simulations. With simulations, researchers can model the way such systems are expected to operate given certain constraints and parameters. For instance, Marks et al. (2005) conducted a simulation on how cross- and within-team processes relate to the performance of multiteam systems over time. Their simulation showed that cross-team processes were more important for multiteam performance than within-team processes. Further, cross-team processes were more predictive in conditions of high cross-team interdependence.

Simulations provide many advantages for multiteam system researchers. First, multiteam systems may be difficult to study en masse. Simulations provide the tools to assess many systems at once, or a single system over time. Second, simulations are reflections of the researchers' theory. As such, they permit the researcher to see hidden implications of their theory that reveal themselves only as the system operates over time. One principal drawback of using simulations is that they, by dint of being specified by the researchers, cannot fully capture the complexity of the multiteam systems they are designed to model. That is, one central tenet of complexity science's stance on emergence is that it is affected by what is called "sensitivity to initial conditions" (Byrne, 1998). Essentially, complex systems will evolve in radically different ways given slight changes in inputs. Complexity scientists often cite this phenomenon as why meteorologists cannot accurately predict the weather past 5 days (Byrne, 1998; Marion, 1999). As such, small "details" that may be left out of the simulation, if included, might introduce profound and otherwise unexpected effects.

The role of time in the use of simulations is, in fact, one of the key components of this methodology that makes it useful. Specifically, researchers can dictate the time frame on which they wish to observe multiteam systems. If desired, simulations can be run on a second-by-second basis (micro), on a day-by-day basis (meso), or over long stretches of time (macro). Thus, simulations are ideal for preliminary analyses of multiteam systems over any time frame. However, because they are not "natural," such simulations need to be followed up with real-world studies.

Quantitative Designs: Laboratory Studies

Laboratory studies are yet another option for the multiteam systems researcher. Work by DeChurch and Marks (2006) employed a three-team laboratory simulation to assess leadership in multiteam systems. Likewise, Mathieu, Cobb, Marks, Zaccaro, and Marsh (2004) also advocated the use of laboratory simulations in the study of multiteam systems, which they deemed Air Campaign Effectiveness Simulations (ACES).

There are advantages and disadvantages to the use of laboratory methodology. One primary advantage is the ability to control the environment, the threats, and the composition of the systems. Thus, it is easier to distill the underlying processes impacted in such systems, all else being equal. The primary disadvantage is that these simulations may not provide insight into all kinds of multiteam systems. For instance, not all multiteam systems are necessarily as fast paced as those that operate through

ACES. Thus, for multiteam systems whose environmental contingencies are less immediate, critical processes and inputs may vary compared to those systems whose environmental contingencies come in short bursts.

Correspondingly, the role of time in ACES is somewhat limited. That is, it is truly difficult to run day-by-day or week-by-week analyses in the lab, and quite impossible to do a several-year study using these methods. Thus, largely, the use of ACES will provide information on a microlevel of time more than on a meso- or macrolevel.

Quantitative Designs: Daily Diaries

Another type of methodology researchers can employ is daily diary research. In these studies, participants are provided with technology that indicates when and how they need to respond to a series of questions. Daily diary studies have been conducted to assess a number of issues, including stress and alcohol consumption (Armeli, Carney, Tennen, Affleck, & O'Neil, 2000), affective responses to psychological contract breach (Briner, 2002), and even organizational citizenship behaviors (Ilies, Scott, & Judge, 2006).

Daily diary studies pose a number of benefits for the multiteam systems researcher. First, they provide a large number of quantitative observation points by which multiteam systems researchers can assess changes over time. As such, they allow for observation of dynamic change and small perturbations. However, it should be noted that most daily diary studies have been conducted on affective phenomena, as affective issues are the most likely to fluctuate daily. Thus, for the study of performance criteria, this methodology may not be ideal. Additionally, these methodologies tend to be best suited for *intra*individual study, not *inter*individual study. Thus, they may not always be ideal for assessing an entire multiteam system, or even its subunits, unless adapted explicitly for this purpose.

The role of time is fairly apparent in the name of this methodology. Specifically, these studies are generally conducted *daily*, which puts their measurement on a mesolevel time scale. As such, they are suited largely for the measurement of mesolevel phenomena, not micro- or macrolevel phenomena. Moreover, these studies are generally limited in duration (only a few months), so it may be difficult to assess larger changes that take longer amounts of time to manifest.

Quantitative Designs: Social Network Analysis

A final quantitative methodology multiteam system that researchers may employ is social network analysis. Social network analysis is the third technique discussed by Dooley and Lichtenstein (2008). By analyzing team social networks, it is possible to examine individuals, teams, and the entire multiteam system, as well as connections outside of these systems. Although Dooley and Lichtenstein used social network analysis to retrospectively assess which events made networks change within the organization, it is possible to conduct social network analysis in a more prospective fashion.

As with all previously discussed methodologies, social network analysis has both advantages and disadvantages. One advantage, as discussed earlier, is that social network analysis can allow for the simultaneous analysis of a number of levels. Moreover, with repeated collection of data, researchers can watch these networks change and evolve over time.

The primary disadvantage associated with social network analysis is that missing data can be prevalent, which disrupts the researcher's ability to accurately map the existing networks. This is likely compounded when networks are collected daily or weekly. Additionally, it is possible that, because of repeated observations, the methodology interferes with the reality. Specifically, if individuals are affirming their networks weekly, they may be less likely to go beyond the usual people they have in their network. Finally, it should be noted that social network data are all self-report, which may artificially inflate the appearance of stability over time.

The role of time in social network studies is fairly limited. These networks cannot be collected second by second, and they cannot reasonably be collected over a course of many years. Instead, social network analysis is best suited for mesolevel phenomena that may change weekly or daily.

In summary, we have argued that there are a number of qualitative and quantitative methodologies that may be adapted to suit the needs of multiteam system researchers. In making these recommendations, we have further emphasized the time level for which each methodology is best suited. Only simulations are likely to be useful for all time levels. For microlevel phenomena, the ideal qualitative methodology is real-time tracking of events, and the ideal quantitative methodology is laboratory experiments. For mesolevel phenomena, researchers may employ the qualitative design of ethnographic methods, and the quantitative designs of daily diaries and social network analysis. Finally, the qualitative designs of retrospective case studies, ethnographic methods, and event history analysis are best employed to assess macrolevel change.

As a final note, we remind researchers that complex adaptive systems are inherently linked across time and levels (Dooley & Lichtenstein, 2008). As such, the use of only one of these methodologies may be limited in its ability to truly capture the dynamism inherent in multiteam systems. Next, we will briefly review the data analysis techniques that are particularly well suited to examine complex phenomena.

DATA ANALYSIS

In addition to the measurement and research design issues previously discussed, dynamic systems also pose a number of data analysis challenges for researchers. In this section, we discuss some unique data analytic tools that have been developed to handle dynamic data.

Catastrophe Analysis

Catastrophe mathematical models, originally derived by René Thom (1975) and popularized by E. Christopher Zeeman (1971, 1976, 1977), are useful for describing the behavior of an entire system as it shifts from one equilibrium point or goal to another (Casti, 1979). Dynamic systems usually exhibit continuous behavior when under the influence of one goal, but they exhibit discontinuous or erratic behavior when the system is under the influence of two or more goals (Casti, 1979). In catastrophe theory, there are seven elementary catastrophe models that are hypothesized to be useful for describing almost all discontinuous behavior (Hanges et al., 2002; Stewart & Peregoy, 1983). These seven models differ in terms of the number of independent parameters, the number of dependent parameters, and, more importantly, the number of goals assumed to be influencing the overall system (Saunders, 1990). Of these seven models, the cusp catastrophe model has received the most attention in the psychology literature (e.g., Golembiewski, 1986; Hanges et al., 1991).

The cusp catastrophe model is appropriate to analyze systems that are influenced by two stable goals. It is composed of one dependent and two independent parameters (Stewart & Peregoy, 1983). The two independent parameters, called the *asymmetry* and the *bifurcation* parameters, have different effects on the dependent variable (Hanges et al., 2002). The asymmetry parameter is a factor that separates the two goals on some conceptual domain (e.g., the importance of customer service). The second independent parameter (i.e., the bifurcation parameter) moderates the relationship between the asymmetry and dependent parameters. Specifically, the bifurcation parameter determines whether the system's behavior exhibits continuous change (i.e., when the system is operating under the influence of one goal) or discontinuous change (i.e., when the system moves from one goal to another; Stewart & Peregoy, 1983). Cusp catastrophe modeling has most commonly been conducted using second-by-second data (Foti et al., 2008; Hanges et al., submitted). However, it could be employed on day-by-day or week-by-week data as well. As such, it is suitable for both micro– and meso–time scales.

One way by which cusp catastrophe models can be used to detect dynamic properties in data is to look for several unique characteristics that Gilmore (1981) referred to as "catastrophe flags." The presence of one or more of these flags in the sampling distribution of a dependent variable signals that an underlying cusp catastrophe model might be operating (Gilmore, 1981). Among the flags mentioned by Gilmore are (a) the presence of bimodality in the dependent variable, (b) discontinuous change in the value of the dependent variable, and (c) anomalous variance (i.e., heteroskedasticity).

A second analytic procedure that allows for formal hypothesis testing was developed by Loren Cobb (1980, 1981). The reader can think of this procedure as similar, but not identical, to structural equation modeling. In particular, the cusp catastrophe model is conceptualized as a latent model with the researcher specifying the manifest variables that load on the asymmetry, bifurcation, and dependent latent variables. The fit of the latent cusp catastrophe model to the empirical data is compared to the fit of the data to a linear model and a logistic model. A version of the Cobb program that can be run in R is available, along with a manual describing the output of the program (see http://cran.r-project.org/web/packages/cusp/vignettes/Cusp-JSS.pdf ; Grasman, van der Maas, & Wagenmakers, n.d.).

Neural Network Models

Another technique that has proven useful for analyzing dynamic systems is neural network analysis. The kinds of analyses produced by this analytic tool are closely related to traditional statistical analyses (Abdi, Valentin, & Edelman, 1999). Indeed, traditional statistical tools such as ordinary least squares regression analysis, logistic analysis, and cluster analysis can be thought of as special cases of neural networks. In their most general form, neural networks are systems of highly interconnected information nodes that combine information from manifest input variables to either capture underlying patterns or maximally predict one or more dependent variables. Unlike traditional statistical methodology, neural networks use computational brute force to identify the optimal weights among the information nodes in order to maximize discovery of the underlying regularity in the data. Organizational researchers have used neural network analysis to capture regularities in decision-making processes (Lord, Hanges, & Godfrey, 2003), as well as identify how attitudes form and change over time (Monroe & Read, 2008).

Neural networks are useful for modeling team- and multilevel system behavior. Indeed, neural network analysis could be conducted on different levels of time, depending on the nature of the research question. For example, if split-second decisions are required, microlevel data might be analyzed using neural network analysis to understand how they are made. If longer term decisions made over days or weeks are of interest, neural network analysis could also be used to analyze mesolevel data.

Social Network Analysis

Earlier in this chapter, we discussed the use of social networks as a methodology for use in data collection. The information collected using a social network methodology generally reflects ties between individuals in a larger group, whether these ties are relationship ties, influence ties, or simply communication ties. Indeed, consistent with the shift toward thinking of external factors and broader systems, recent network studies have begun to examine interteam ties (e.g., Baldwin, Bedell, & Johnson, 1997; Hansen, Morse, & Lovas, 2005). As discussed, social network analysis as a methodology stands to contribute greatly toward the understanding of multiteam system phenomenon on the meso–, or week-by-week, time scale.

As an analysis technique, social network analysis both provides insight into how individuals stand relative to their team and provides information on team-level phenomena. Take, for example, a study on influence within teams. Social network analysis would allow a researcher to understand who is the most influential person within a team (centrality), as well as whether influence within a team is dispersed or concentrated on one person (centralization). Although issues of centrality (Balkundi & Harrison, 2006; Klein, Lim, Salz, & Mayer, 2004) and density (Balkundi & Harrison, 2006; Tenkasi & Chesmore, 2003) are generally employed in current organizational research, many other network measures are available. For example, integration of networks (Valente & Foreman, 1998) and domination within networks (van den Brink & Gilles, 2000) may also be of interest to the network researcher. Multiteam system researchers may be particularly interested in how network measures within teams and the broader multiteam system may converge or diverge. For example, do central individuals in teams become central in the multiteam system, or do boundary spanners of individual teams become crucial in understanding multiteam system influence? Likewise, do centralized teams become central to the broader system? Issues of convergence in measures across levels of network analysis such as these may prove fruitful for researchers of multiteam systems. Analytic tools (e.g., ORA and Construct) developed and freely shared by Carnegie Mellon University's Center for Computational Analysis of Social and Organizational Systems (see http://www.casos. cs.cmu.edu/index.php; Center for Computational Analysis, 2011) provide researchers with the tools to perform dynamic network analysis.

CONCLUSIONS AND IMPLICATIONS

Researchers interested in the study of multiteam systems face a number of unique methodological challenges. In this chapter, we have applied the principles of complexity science to multiteam systems in order to highlight these challenges and offer ways to address them. First, we introduced and discussed the critical roles of time and levels in multiteam system research, based on the principles of complex adaptive systems theory (Goldstein, 2008). Second, we specifically reviewed three time scales on which such phenomena can be measured—the micro-, meso-, and macrolevel (Dooley

& Lichtenstein, 2008)—and emphasized the interconnections between the different levels of time. Measurement concerns, such as the need for repeated measurement, the need to move beyond self-report measurement, and issues concerning the appropriate level and model of emergence, were discussed. Qualitative and quantitative methodologies suited for the study of multiteam systems were then reviewed. These methodologies were discussed with respect to their strengths and limitations as well as with respect to the time scale they are most appropriate to capture. Finally, the implications of the use of these methodologies and measurement techniques on data analysis were discussed.

REFERENCES

Abdi, H., Valentin, D., & Edelman, B. (1999). *Neural networks*. Thousand Oaks, CA: Sage.

Armeli, S., Carney, M. A., Tennen, H., Affleck, G., & O'Neil, T. P. (2000). Stress and alcohol use: A daily process examination of the stressor-vulnerability model. *Journal of Personality and Social Psychology, 78,* 979–994.

Baldwin, T. T., Bedell, M. D., & Johnson, J. L. (1997). The social fabric of a team-based M.B.A. program: Network effects on student satisfaction and performance. *Academy of Management Journal, 40,* 1369–1397.

Balkundi, P., & Harrison, D. A. (2006). Ties, leaders, and time in teams: Strong inference about network structure's effects on team viability and performance. *Academy of Management Journal, 49,* 49–68.

Barley, S. R. (1990). Images of imaging: Notes on doing longitudinal field work. *Organization Science, 1,* 220–247.

Bliese, P. D. (2000). Within-group agreement, non-independence, and reliability: Implications for data aggregation and analysis. In K. J. Klein & S. W. J. Kozlowski (Eds.), *Multilevel theory, research, and methods in organizations: Foundations, extensions, and new directions* (pp. 349–381). San Francisco: Jossey-Bass.

Briner, R. B. (2002). A daily diary study of affective responses to psychological contract breach and exceeded promises. *Journal of Organizational Behavior, 23,* 287–302.

Bullington, J. C. (1990). Mood congruent memory: A replication of symmetrical effects for both positive and negative moods. *Journal of Social Behavior & Personality, 5,* 123–134.

Byrne, D. (1998). *Complexity theory and the social sciences: An introduction*. New York: Routledge.

Casti, J. (1979). *Connectivity, complexity, and catastrophe in large-scale systems*. New York: Wiley.

Center for Computational Analysis of Social and Organizational Systems. (2011). [Home page]. Carnegie Mellon University. Retrieved from http://www.casos.cs.cmu.edu/index.php

Chan, D. (1998). Functional relations among constructs in the same content domain at different levels of analysis: A typology of composition models. *Journal of Applied Psychology, 83,* 234–246.

Cobb, L. (1980). Estimation theory for the cusp catastrophe model. In *Proceedings of the Section on Survey Research Methods*. Washington, DC: American Statistical Association.

Cobb, L. (1981). Parameter estimation for the cusp catastrophe model. *Behavioral Science, 26*, 75–78.

DeChurch, L. A., & Marks, M. A. (2006). Leadership in multiteam systems. *Journal of Applied Psychology, 91*, 311–329.

Dooley, K. J., & Lichtenstein, B. (2008). Research methods for studying the dynamics of leadership. In M. Uhl-Bien & R. Marion (Eds.), *Complexity leadership, part I: Conceptual foundations* (pp. 269–290). Charlotte, NC: Information Age.

Eiser, J. R. (1994a). *Attitudes, chaos, and the connectionist mind*. Cambridge: Blackwell.

Eiser, J. R. (1994b). Toward a dynamic conception of attitude consistency and change. In R. R. Vallacher & A. Nowak (Eds.), *Dynamical systems in social psychology* (pp. 198–218). New York: Academic Press.

Foti, R. J., Knee, R. E., Jr., & Backert, R. S. G. (2008). Multi-level implications of framing leadership perceptions as a dynamic process. *Leadership Quarterly, 19*, 178–194.

Gilmore, R. (1981). *Catastrophe theory for scientists and engineers*. New York: Dover.

Glick, W. H., Huber, G. P., Miller, C. C., Doty, D. H., & Sutcliffe, K. M. (1990). Studying changes in organizational design and effectiveness: Retrospective event histories and periodic assessments. *Organization Science, 1*, 293–312.

Goldstein, J. (2008). Conceptual foundations of complexity science: Development and main constructs. In M. Uhl-Bien & R. Marion (Eds.), *Complexity leadership, part I: Conceptual foundations* (pp. 17–48). Charlotte, NC: Information Age.

Golembiewski, R. T. (1986). Contours in social change: Elemental graphics and a surrogate variable for gamma change. *Academy of Management Review, 11*, 550–566.

Grasman, R. P. P. P., van der Maas, H. L. J., & Wagenmakers, E.-J. (N.d.). Fitting the cusp catastrophe in R: A cusp-package primer. Retrieved from http://cran.r-project.org/web/packages/cusp/vignettes/Cusp-JSS.pdf

Gupta, A., & Khosla, M. (2006). Effect of affective state: Is mood congruency an effect of affective state? *Psychological Studies, 51*, 269–274.

Hanges, P. J., Braverman, E. P., & Rentsch, J. R. (1991). Changes in raters impressions of subordinates: A catastrophe model. *Journal of Applied Psychology, 76*, 878–888.

Hanges, P. J., Lord, R. G., Day, D. V., Sipe, W. P., Gradwohl-Smith, W. C., & Brown, D. J. (submitted). Dynamic modeling of social perceptions: The role of gender in leadership perceptions.

Hanges, P. J., Lord, R. G., Godfrey, E. G., & Raver, J. L. (2002). Modeling nonlinear relationships: Neural networks and catastrophe analysis. In S. Rogelberg (Ed.), *Handbook of research methods in industrial and organizational psychology* (pp. 431–455). Malden, MA: Blackwell.

Hansen, M. T., Morse, M. L., & Lovas, B. (2005). Knowledge sharing in organizations: Multiple networks, multiple phases. *Academy of Management Journal, 48*, 776–793.

Hoegl, M., & Weinkauf, K. (2005). Managing task interdependencies in multiteam projects: A longitudinal study. *Journal of Management Studies, 42*, 1287–1308.

Hovland, C. I., Janis, I. L., & Kelley, H. H. (1953). *Communication and persuasion: Psychological studies of opinion change*. New Haven, CT: Yale University Press.

Ilies, R., Scott, B. A., & Judge, T. A. (2006). The interactive effects of personal traits and experiences states on intraindividual patterns of citizenship behavior. *Academy of Management Journal, 49*, 561–575.

Klein, K. J., Dansereau, F., & Hall, R. J. (1994). Levels issues in theory development, data collection, and analysis. *Academy of Management Review, 19*, 195–229.

Klein, K. J., Lim, B., Saltz, J. L., & Mayer, D. M. (2004). How do they get there? An examination of the antecedents of centrality in team networks. *Academy of Management Journal, 47*, 952–963.

Koehler, G. (2001). *A framework for visualizing the chronocomplexity.* Sacramento: California Research Bureau and Time Structures.

Leonard-Barton, D. (1990). A dual methodology for case studies: Synergistic use of a longitudinal single site with replicated multiple sites. *Organizational Science, 1*, 248–266.

Lord, R. G., Hanges, P. J., & Godfrey, E. G. (2003). Integrating neural networks into decision-making and motivational theory: Rethinking VIE theory. *Canadian Psychology, 44*, 21–28.

Marion, R. (1999). *The edge of organization: Chaos and complexity theories of formal social systems.* Thousand Oaks, CA: Sage.

Marks, M. A., DeChurch, L. A., Mathieu, J. E., Panzer, F. J., & Alonso, A. A. (2005). Teamwork in multiteam systems. *Journal of Applied Psychology, 90*, 964–971.

Mathieu, J. E., Cobb, M. A., Marks, M. A., Zaccaro, S. J., & Marsh, S. (2004). Multiteam ACES: A research platform for studying multiteam systems. In S. G. Schiflett, L. R. Elliott, E. Salas, & M. Coovert (Eds.), *Scaled worlds: Development, validation and applications* (pp. 297–315). Burlington, VT: Ashgate.

Mathieu, J. E., Marks, M. A., & Zaccaro, S. J. (2001). Multiteam systems. In N. Anderson, D. Ones, H. K. Sinangil, & C. Viswesvaran (Eds.), *International handbook of work and organizational psychology* (pp. 289–313). London: Sage.

Monroe, B. M., & Read, S. J. (2008). A general connectionist model of attitude structure and change: The ACS (Attitudes as Constraint Satisfaction) model. *Psychological Review, 115*, 733–759.

Morel, B., & Ramanujam, R. (1999). Through the looking glass of complexity: The dynamics of organizations as adaptive and evolving systems. *Organization Science, 10*, 278–293.

Parrott, W. G. (1991). Mood induction and instructions to sustain moods: A test of the subject compliance hypothesis of mood congruent memory. *Cognition & Emotion, 5*, 41–52.

Podsakoff, P. M., MacKenzie, S. B., Lee, J., & Podsakoff, N. P. (2003). Common method biases in behavioral research: A critical review of the literature and recommended remedies. *Journal of Applied Psychology, 88*, 879–903.

Reis, H. T., & Gable, S. L. (2000). Event-sampling and other methods for studying everyday experience. In H. T. Reis & C. M. Judd (Eds.), *Handbook of research methods in social and personality psychology* (pp. 190–222). New York: Cambridge University Press.

Saunders, P. T. (1990). *An introduction to catastrophe theory.* New York: Cambridge University Press.

Shadish, W. R., Cook, T. D., & Campbell, D. T. (2001). *Experimental and quasi-experimental designs for generalized causal inference.* Boston: Houghton Mifflin.

Smeets, T., Otgaar, H., Candel, I., & Wolf, O. T. (2008). True or false? Memory is differentially affected by stress-induced cortisol elevations and sympathetic activity at consolidation and retrieval. *Psychoneuroendocrinology, 33*, 1378–1386.

Stewart, I. N., & Peregoy, P. L. (1983). Catastrophe theory modeling in psychology. *Psychological Bulletin, 94*, 336–362.

Tenkasi, R. V., & Chesmore, M. C. (2003). Social networks and planned organizational change: The impact of strong network ties on effective change implementation and use. *Journal of Applied Behavioral Science, 39,* 281–300.

Tesluk, P. E., & Mathieu, J. E. (1999). Overcoming road blocks to effectiveness: Incorporating management of performance barriers into model of work group effectiveness. *Journal of Applied Psychology, 84,* 200–217.

Thom, R. (1975). *Structural stability and morphogenesis: An outline of a general theory of models.* Reading, MA: Benjamin.

Valente, T. W., & Foreman, R. K. (1998). Integration and radiality: Measuring the extent of an individual's connectedness and reachability in a network. *Social Networks, 20,* 89–105.

Vallacher, R., & Nowak, A. (Eds.). (1994). *Dynamical systems in social psychology.* New York: Academic Press.

Vallacher, R. R., Nowak, A., & Kaufman, J. (1994). Intrinsic dynamics of social judgment. *Journal of Personality and Social Psychology, 67,* 20–34.

van den Brink, R., & Gilles, R. P. (2000). Measuring domination in directed networks. *Social Networks, 22,* 141–157.

Zeeman, E. C. (1971, December 10). Geometry of catastrophe. *Times Literary Supplement,* pp. 1556–1557.

Zeeman, E. C. (1976). Catastrophe theory. *Scientific American, 234,* 65–83.

Zeeman, E. C. (Ed.). (1977). *Catastrophe theory: Selected papers, 1972–1977.* Reading, MA: Addison-Wesley.

16

Complex Systems Methods for Studying Multiteam Systems

Corinne A. Coen
Case Western Reserve University

Andrew Schnackenberg
Case Western Reserve University

Multiteam researchers are interested in explaining and predicting behavior within and between teams. They are not concerned with simply providing a snapshot of multiple teams at one time. Rather, they wish to provide insight into how choices by individuals generate team behavior in a multiple team context, or how people grouped in teams coordinate, communicate, and share knowledge with people in other teams. They want to know what processes explain the correlations among inputs and outcomes and how people in teams using multiple processes interact. They are interested in how choices, behaviors, and results coevolve.

Studying these dynamic multiteam systems (MTSs) is demanding. MTSs include many heterogeneous actors. They involve multiple levels of analysis. Many processes occur at the same time, each affecting the other. Because of all these are departures from a simple reductionist treatment, it is difficult to theorize what is going on in MTSs, and even more difficult to test the theories. MTSs are complicated systems. New research techniques offer new hope in understanding dynamic processes in a small subset of these complicated systems. This chapter explores existing and new approaches that researchers can employ to understand the dynamics in MTSs.

Unfortunately, complicated systems are often resistant to study. How, for example, might one make sense of the effects of boundary-spanning behavior within and between multiple and interdependent social systems (Davison &

Hollenbeck, Chapter 12, this volume)? Or how might one measure the effects of shared managerial mental models on the success of strategic alliances (Standifer & Bluedorn, 2006)? Reductionist science has helped us understand complicated systems by allowing us to apply formal methods to study manageable parts of the whole, but these techniques generally only enlighten our analysis at a single level and a single point in time (Dooley, 1997). Longitudinally, our analyses are still constrained to specific input times and output times.

Alternatively, we might measure the inputs and outputs of groups-as-a-whole. But by doing so, we hide group processes in a black box. Some advanced statistical techniques allow us to look at multiple levels at a single point in time (e.g., hierarchical linear modeling). Yet, although these techniques allow us to find correlations, they are not truly satisfactory to researchers looking to understand complex dynamic phenomena. Most small-group researchers would argue that they are interested in the entire rich system of processes by which people interact freely in various structures over time.

There has been movement in small-group research toward focusing on input–process–output (I-P-O) models (e.g., Hackman, 1987; McGrath, 1984; Steiner, 1972). Yet, early attempts at adding processes tended to reduce processes to traits or conditions, analyzed as mediators and moderators. But mediators and moderators are not processes; rather, they are factors affecting processes (Ilgen, Hollenbeck, Johnson, & Jundt, 2005). In addition, simple I-P-O constructs with a single linear process connecting the inputs and outputs tend to miss the realities of team life that include multiple interacting processes and feedback between outcomes and processes iterating over time.

Researchers from a variety of disciplines are developing new methods for exploring dynamic processes interacting with other processes and variables and across levels of analysis. These new approaches cannot explore all complicated systems, but they are excellent at helping identify the effects of a small or medium number of people (or teams or firms) interacting with a few simply conceived processes and some simple rules that actors use to make decisions. We call this new approach the *study of complex systems*. Given the relatively simple inputs that often manifest as complicated outcomes, some have suggested that we call it *simplexity* instead!

We continue this chapter with a brief introduction and discussion of complex systems. Some current research approaches used to study the processes in MTSs are then explored. Next, we describe a number of common methods used to study complex systems dynamics. A promising subset of these methods, agent-based computational simulation, is offered as a potentially useful approach to study the dynamic in MTSs.

THE NATURE OF COMPLEX SYSTEMS

Interdependence is the heart of any complex system (Casti, 1994; Cowan, Pines, & Meltzer, 1994; Waldrop, 1992). Rather than assuming the independence of participants, which is a requirement of most of our linear statistical analytic techniques, the methods for studying complex systems assume that the participants (whether they are people, teams, departments, or firms) interact with one another. Although nearly all researchers of groups—those studying single teams or MTSs—acknowledge that the outcomes we observe result from interactions among the people and/or teams involved, our methods require us to assume away such critical interactions. We need methods that match the true nature of our systems (Arrow, McGrath, & Berdahl, 2000).

It is important to note that what is meant by interaction among people is not equivalent to the *interaction effects* we measure in general linear analysis. *Interaction* in statistical terms is interaction between variables, assuming that all observations are independent of each other. Interaction in a complex system is action between actors based on some type of interdependence. The basis of interdependence may be influence through conversations, direct behaviors that alter another's behavior, or more indirect actions that may, for example, affect a shared market (for labor, for resources, or in the products or services sold).

Another feature of complex systems is that they are responsive to changing conditions over time (Berkes, Colding, & Folke, 2003). For example, team members change their behavior to adjust to their teammates or to influence or control them. Teams of people change their behavior in response to the observed effectiveness of their outcomes compared to the outcomes of other teams. The interaction among people, goals, teams, and other configurations of hopes, beliefs, personalities, preferences, structures, and goals may set up observable patterns, for example virtuous or vicious cycles, among the actors (Macy, 1991; Masuch, 1985). On the other hand, the participants may continuously adjust to evolving conditions. In such cases, many interesting components are based on the observable pattern of responses by individuals across time and conditions.

Finally, in complex systems, the interactions among people, processes, and goals or structures lead to unpredictable outcomes. The interdependence among the participants and structures in MTSs generates nonlinear feedback processes. Each action of any person feeds back by creating a new context for the actions of other people. Actions meet or fall short of goals. Actions allow people or teams to succeed or fail. Success or failure leads people to calibrate their subsequent actions. The relative performance outcomes generated from early actions give feedback to people who then adjust their performance. *Nonlinearity* means that the feedback processes rarely lead to simple correlations between action and outcome. Indeed, dramatic changes may occur over some range of a variable and not over other ranges.

By identifying some MTSs as complex systems, we can both expand our research questions and alter our approaches to exploring those questions. For example, adopting methods used to study complex systems might allow us to explain outcomes, identify processes, or induce decision rules in new ways. Most studies of nonlinear systems find nonintuitive results. Although our intuition is useful for understanding more linear systems, it is less helpful in complex environments. By contrast, studies of complex systems preserve feedback processes across people in teams and firms over time to generate unexpected connections and results. They reveal contingencies that are not obvious at first blush.

EMERGENCE

For people trying to make sense of complex systems like MTSs, the most intimidating problem is the nonlinear or nonadditive nature of the processes within the system. The workings of the MTS as a whole may have patterns and structures that are not contained in any of the respective parts of the system. Rather, the workings of the MTS generate totally new properties. This characteristic of many complex systems is called *emergence* (see Corning, 2002).

A simple example of emergence is the standing flow of water over rocks in a streambed. Reductionist techniques cannot explain this phenomenon. Studying hydrogen atoms and oxygen atoms in isolation cannot account for the shape of the water. Even understanding the processes of attraction that hold each pair of hydrogen atoms with an oxygen atom cannot explain this property of the flowing water. Rather, a careful study of the changing interactions among H_2O molecules is necessary. The recurring pattern of rushing water cascading over rocks is a property of the dynamic interdependence among a number of molecules of water. Dauntingly, studying molecules is downright simpleminded compared to the challenge of studying heterogeneous people with intentionality who can alter the flow of their own behaviors in reaction to internal feelings or external events!

Emergent behavior arises in many systems because interactions among interdependent parts increase exponentially as the number of parts in a system increases. For example, as the number of team members and the number of teams increase in an MTS, the variety of opinions, preferences, influence styles, goals, and choices multiplies. Similarly, the number of potential targets of comparison increases, the competitive challenges change form, patterns of contacts vary, and so on and so forth. It is not just the number of interactions between team members or teams that generates emergence. The structure of interactions directs and focuses the feedback among the agents (e.g., people, teams, and organizations) and processes in the MTSs in ways distinct from what occurs in single-team systems. Outcomes from interactions, as in any complex interdependent system, often are surprising and unpredictable.

Complex systems tend to exhibit tipping points and threshold effects (Gladwell, 2000; Urry, 2004). Tipping points may change processes from spiraling upward to spiraling downward. For example, consider the relationship between asset-backed securities and the global economy in recent decades. Easy access to capital led banks to underwrite increasingly risky mortgages. These mortgages were then sold, split, and resold in the secondary market, which further added liquidity to the asset-backed securities system and created a sense that these high-return vehicles were standard and reliable. Once it became clear that the value of many classes of collateralized debt obligations were far removed from anything approximating their true market value (i.e., the tipping point), the system began to hemorrhage. This, coupled with problems associated with the structuring of mortgage agreements on the retail end of the system as well as a waning economy, led investors and other interested observers to demand that financial institutions face the realities of their balance sheets. The recognition that asset prices were inflated across the entire system sent the economy into a vicious circle exacerbated by fears of a global meltdown.

Threshold effects describe outcomes that change dramatically with a small change in behavior. For example, Schelling (1978) showed us that although segregation of neighborhoods had a linear correlation with the desire to live with some people like oneself when people have low levels of desire (wanting approximately 10–30% of neighbors to be like oneself), at a critical point (wanting approximately 33% of neighbors to be like oneself), the resulting neighborhoods were near 100% segregated. Both above and below the threshold, the outcomes are linear, but there is a complete disconnect between the behaviors on either side of the threshold.

With tipping points and threshold effects, the results of the actions of a group bear little resemblance to the outcomes intended by the individual actors involved. So, for example, as the economy slows down, a social dilemma arises. Firms lay off workers to protect their returns to shareholders and managers. The more firms that lay off workers, the more the economy slows and firms need to lay off more workers. What is good for the group (participants in the whole economy) is opposite what is good for the individual firm. The more individual firms help themselves, the more they hurt the economy.

Exploring dynamic behavior among interdependent actors is beyond the reach of traditional linear methods. Taking interdependence and adding within-team and cross-team processes, effects, and feedback loops make studying with linear methods stunningly difficult. Researchers can study only the most stripped-down conceptions of these moving parts. Great dexterity in multiple methods is necessary to extend research into this area. Indeed, Arrow et al. (2000) have issued a call for increased emphasis on field studies and comparative case studies in combination with computational simulations to build on research in complex systems. One important new way to begin to explore complex interactions is to imagine simple dynamic models that include interdependence. Then one can build a computational model that can simulate the processes of interaction among people, goals, and structures. Computational analysis offers some unique advantages to the study of MTSs. It can allow cross-level effects, for example, allowing team members to influence each other, which changes team performance, which leads to relative success or failure compared to other teams, which leads to altering team member behavior. Computational analysis can track the unique effects of heterogeneous actors. The actors can all use the same decision rules, or they can operate according to different decision rules. Simulations mimic real-world patterns of interaction, but the research can replay them, run them multiple times, and freeze-frame them as desired. This ability to run interactions repeatedly and map every action makes understanding patterns and processes much more tractable than observing the same teams in practice. Neither method is a substitute for the other, but the ability to combine the two can lead to substantially more understanding of the processes and effects of interdependence.

MULTIPLE-TEAM SYSTEMS AND TRADITIONAL STUDY METHODS

Other chapters in this book and early journal articles (e.g., Marks, DeChurch, Mathieu, Panzer, & Alonso, 2005) have defined MTSs. Essentially, they are systems with more than one team in which, at minimum, joint goals link the teams. The joint goals may be distal or proximate, meaning they may be as simple as sharing the organization's overall desired outcomes but not having any direct interactions, or tightly linked as two teams engage in constant handoffs of work.

Similar to general studies of teams (e.g., Deshon, Kozlowski, Schmidt, Milner, & Weichmann, 2004), some studies of MTSs are amenable to traditional quantitative research approaches. Studies of the effect of membership in multiple teams on the individual participant at one point in time (e.g., Mortensen, Woolley, & O'Leary, 2007) can be readily examined with general linear statistics. Similarly, studies of the effect of conditions on teams-as-a-whole can be studied using these traditional approaches (e.g., Hoegl & Weinkauf, 2005; Johnson, Korsgaard, & Sapienza, 2002). Of course, qualitative methods are always suitable to studying the multiple processes (i.e., social action; Dougherty, 2002) occurring within and between a *particular* sample of teams without reducing the processes to traits or conditions. Yet most qualitative work is restricted by the very small number of multiple-team situations that can be studied at one time in such a labor-intensive fashion.

There are still only a small number of empirical studies of multiple processes occurring within and between multiple teams. These studies examine coordination issues (Hoegl & Weinkauf, 2005; Marks et al., 2005), knowledge sharing (Caldwell, 2005), decision processes (Coen, 2006a), and justice and control (Johnson et al., 2002).

A quick examination of a couple of these studies gives a sense of how MTS scholars have coped with studying multiple interaction processes. Given the limits of traditional methods, figuring out how to capture these processes is highly challenging. For example, the following two studies demonstrate traditional approaches to understanding a complex multiteam system. In each, the authors needed to adopt reductionist approaches that hide the complexity of the system.

Study 1

Marks et al. (2005) employed a human simulation of team warfare to examine whether multiple within-team processes and multiple between-team processes had separate effects on the performance of more or less interdependent teams. To examine this complex structure with multiple processes, they made a series of simplifying assumptions. Though the researchers were interested in how processes affected outcomes, they measured the *quality* of multiple processes (on a scale of 1–5), turning the processes into traits. In addition, they created strict controls so that participants were engaged in either transition processes (i.e., planning, goal setting, and evaluation) or action processes (i.e., task work, coordination, and monitoring), but not both simultaneously. By changing processes to traits and controlling for the interaction of transition and action processes, the researchers were able to run repeated measures of multiple regression on the process or trait variables within each multiple-team unit. Each multiteam unit was treated as the unit of analysis. Although this was a rich study of a complex system, the researchers needed to consolidate data (and potential interplay) to perform statistical regression. As a consequence, we lost any knowledge about how the processes worked or about the iterative interaction of transition and action processes. In effect, our analytic methods restricted the questions that could be asked and answered.

Study 2

In another study of multiteam processes, which investigates cooperation in teams given competition with other teams, Coen (2006a) sorted the participants into 2 × 2 conditions (single team or multiteam, or cooperative or uncooperative teammates) and had them interact with teammates through computer terminals. Just like the researchers in the previous multiple-team study, Coen made simplifications. She simplified by eliminating human teammates, telling participants that they were interacting with others in the room but actually replacing the people with computer scripts. Participants' teammates and the members of other teams they compared themselves to were all virtual. Because teammates and members of other teams were virtual, they could not actively respond to the participants. Although the live participants took changing actions over multiple rounds and the computer software tracked each choice, the researcher summed the decisions over time, thus turning processes into a single performance variable. By creating controlled conditions, the researcher could aggregate all decisions and processes into features of each condition, and then compare the conditions. Unfortunately, the behavior of the multiteam system as a whole could not be evaluated because the virtual teammates operated strictly according to scripts. The participants' choices took place in the context of a fixed environment.

The approaches of the authors of these two studies are the orthodox approaches in the social sciences. As Ilgen et al. (2005) pointed out, we reduce processes to traits or conditions. Why did the authors make these simplifying assumptions? They did so because these assumptions allowed them to use a general linear model to analyze the results. The authors limited the number of variables in play and aggregated measures across individuals or to the team or multiteam level. They controlled away conditions that might be common in naturally occurring settings. They simplified even though their theory of the real processes among teams in a single goal hierarchy suggested that teams often operate without strict temporal division among activities, interact with one another, and generate feedback loops. Further, they knew that participants with some outlier traits might alter outcomes. These simplifications allow the researchers to draw conclusions about what conditions or processes are correlated with specific outcomes. What they do not allow us to understand is how the processes work or how individuals with behavior differing from the mean affect team- or multiteam-level results. We cannot tell how processes affect processes or interact with changing outcomes.

Clearly, alternative methods that allow MTSs scholars to relax any of these simplifying assumptions would add value. In the following pages, we explore one particularly appealing alternative to traditional methods known as *agent-based computational simulation.*

UNDERSTANDING COMPLEX SYSTEMS

All social science studies have their challenges. Nevertheless, the difficulties in achieving high-quality studies in dynamic MTSs are exponential compared to the challenges of studying individuals alone, the effect of a team on an individual, or the outcomes from groups or multiteam-units-as-a-whole. As in any study of teams, researchers have challenges finding sufficient numbers of participants and allowing team size and diversity in appropriate dimensions. Moreover, as in any study of processes, researchers struggle in tracking and measuring dynamics, identifying distinct processes, and controlling for the overlap of processes. Studying feedback effects among the processes is daunting. In addition, MTSs add more teams and thus more complex structures, more goals, more heterogeneity, more processes, and cross-level effects.

In other words, MTSs are complicated systems. Short of reductionism, there are few ways to study complicated systems. Nevertheless, over the past few decades, researchers have made pioneering efforts in studying the subset of complicated systems called *complex systems.*

Scientists have discovered that some systems that look complicated are made up of simple elements. These simple elements may interact in complex ways leading to unexpected and difficult-to-predict outcomes. Nonetheless, identifying the simple elements adds great explanatory power to the description of a system, a system whose functioning would otherwise be intractable.

An example may help. This example applies to a single-team system but can convey many key ideas about complex systems. In 1986, an artificial life expert named Craig Reynolds (1987) built a computer simulation to embody birds' flocking behavior. He called the simulation and the birds in it *Boids.* Reynolds programmed the boids in his model with three simple "steering rules," which described how the boid would maneuver and how it could match its velocity to that of other members of the flock. He based the rules on the ideas of separation, alignment, and cohesion. Each rule requires that the boids have the ability to monitor their neighbors. The first rule, separation, requires the boids to avoid crowding their neighbors. Alignment directs each boid to steer in the average direction taken by all of its neighbors. Cohesion has each boid steering into the average position of its neighbors. The model of flying birds is impressively realistic looking.

Intriguingly, no two simulated runs of the boids demonstrate the same flying pattern. In addition, the observable outcomes are quite complicated. Nevertheless, Boids is an example of the subset of complicated systems called *complex systems*. A group of interdependent agents, birds in this case, each using simple rules, generates unpredictable but patterned outcomes. Knowledge of the simple rules and the interaction structure are sufficient to understand the processes in the system. But, of course, knowing these features will not tell you where the birds will fly! The model is not predictive in that sense. It is important to emphasize here the underlying contribution of this study. Rather than explain correlations between variables, the boids simulation was able to explain the process by which birds flock together. The complex system (the combination of the number of birds and the rules) tells you *how* the flight patterns emerge.

Interestingly, Reynolds's early attempts at modeling flocking behavior involved more complicated decision rules. Eventually, he discovered that the simple rules were sufficient. For example, in the early models Reynolds programmed the boids to dodge physical obstacles. In addition, he gave the boids goals that sent them along a scripted path. Amazingly, the three simple rules were sufficient for lifelike behavior. In fact, the behavior appears so lifelike that the animation in several movies (e.g., the bats and the penguins in Tim Burton's *Batman* [1992]) uses Reynolds's simulation rules.

Of course, that the rules generate lifelike behavior is not proof that the cognitive process of birds follows these rules. That is an empirical question. Nevertheless, by identifying a few rules that are sufficient, Reynolds provided testable propositions for subsequent study of the cognitive functions of flocking animals.

Reynolds's model shares fundamental features with other complex system models. He identified a small number of decision rules that might direct the behavior of the boids. Each individual boid uses the rules. Each boid's choices are dependent on the choices of other boids. The choices are repeated over time with feedback effects (e.g., the choices of some boids affect other boids, whose choices affect neighboring boids). The outcomes that emerge are unpredictable—each boid flies a unique path—

but the flocking pattern that emerges looks suspiciously like the behavior observed in nature.

Like most studies of complex systems, the conclusions that are drawn generate propositions that can be tested in the field. Although Reynolds's model lends credence to the idea that birds flock by using three simple rules, biologists need to confirm separately that these are (or are not) the cognitive processes that birds employ to navigate and flock. Nevertheless, Reynolds's model helps biologists focus on a small set of possible processes that may explain a complex system of observed behavior.

STUDYING COMPLEX SYSTEMS

The study of complex systems is a relatively new approach to research (early examples include Cohen, March, & Olsen, 1972; Schelling, 1978). It is not a theory but an alternate conceptual view of how systems work with unique methods and tools. It is being used across the natural and social sciences, including but not limited to physics, biology, anthropology, epidemiology, economics, political science, and organization studies. Scientists across these areas work together on the development of the approach, both to hone improved methods and to seek general principles or at least common patterns of outcomes.

All of these sciences have their challenges. Nevertheless, the challenges in the study of complex systems have certain common features no matter what field of science. To communicate across disciplines, complex systems researchers call the *basic elements* (whether molecules, sand particles, germs, animals, people, political parties, or firms) in their models *agents*. In all complex systems, the agents are interdependent. Thus, the actions of one agent alter the context and often the subsequent actions of other agents iteratively over time. The systems are not static. The behaviors of the interdependent agents change the system over time.

Substantial debate still exists about the necessary or common features in complex systems. Thompson (1967), for example, has found systems complex when he identified interdependence of parts both within and between systems. Jennings (2001) and Simon (1996) have defined *complex systems* as those with a large number of parts exhibiting many interactions. Hacken (2006) has defined *complex systems* further by requiring interactions to occur in a well-regulated manner. We suspect that these definitions are too general. The behavior of a very large number of particles—especially homogeneous particles—interacting by fixed rules can be characterized quite simply by formal equations (think of particle physics). These systems also tend to be well regulated in the sense of being guided by the laws of physics, chemistry, or biology. In contrast, in human social systems, "parts" (i.e., humans) tend to be highly heterogeneous, with distinctive and changing preference and intentionality. Having a large number of parts makes the system complicated rather than complex and too difficult to analyze using formal methods. More commonly, complex systems researchers find systems with a small or medium number of heterogeneous parts (or, more particularly, agents) that are loosely regulated, at best, by laws, norms, standard operating procedures, or practices, most susceptible to analysis using complex systems research methods. Interdependence is clearly a feature of complex systems, but may play a greater or lesser role depending on the degree and types of interdependence, for example varieties of task interdependence (pooled, sequential, and reciprocal; Thompson, 1967) or interdependence in multiple categories (task, role, social, and knowledge; Pennings, 1974).

Many issues about complex systems remain unresolved. Not the least of these is the features of complex systems. John Holland, for example, in his book *Hidden Order: How Adaptation Builds Complexity* (1996) identifies seven components of complex adaptive systems: four properties and three elements. The four properties are aggregation, tagging, nonlinearity, and flows. The three elements are diversity, internal models, and building blocks. Although some people debate the components in his list, Holland is a MacArthur Genius Grant winner and explores structures creatively, usually to impressive effect. In creating his list of components, Holland tried to capture the essential features of these systems. His properties refer to how the things agents do "add up" given feedback and the ability of agents to keep track of others. The properties also include nonadditive relationships in the system and focus on the way things, actions, or concepts move through the system. His elements attempt to capture the features of heterogeneity, the way agents track the real or perceived system, and the way in which agents categorize and thus simplify their world in order to function in it.

In John Holland's terms, an MTS will include more than one team (where team assignment is one form of aggregation); some way to recognize individuals and their team membership (e.g., tagging); reciprocal action so that what one person does affects the others, whose response affects all the others, including the first actor (viz., causing nonlinearity); and flows of information, influence, or products or services. Like most complex systems, MTSs will have members (viz., teams and people) that are distinct in knowledge, skills, and abilities (viz., heterogeneous). Each individual will have internal models about the relationships and processes within and between the teams and their larger system (e.g., a firm). Finally, Holland suggested that some processes or tasks (e.g., agendas, meeting minutes, and other routinized activities) may be building blocks, used and reused systematically, to build larger processes.

Within our current discussion, nonlinearity is especially important to explain. Classic examples of nonlinearity can be found in predator-prey relationships. Even though a simple measure in time might suggest a balance—say, between the number of rabbits and the number of foxes who prey on them—a dynamic model would tell a different story. In the short term, one might suggest that the more rabbits in existence, the more foxes in existence—a linear relationship. This would likely be true for a while. Eventually, though, the more foxes we observe, the fewer rabbits we would expect to observe (another linear relationship). This scenario plays out at times when the foxes stalk their prey. Nevertheless, observed over a long enough time, one would observe cycles of increase among the rabbit population and then decreases in the rabbit population. There would be predictable, but delayed, changes in the fox population. (The model described here could be well understood by system dynamics simulation, but an agent-based model would be required if there was heterogeneity among the predator or among the prey.)

Where traditional quantitative analyses look at something or someone (expressed as traits or conditions) acting on a person and assume a linear correlation among independent events, complex systems researchers look at nonlinear systems in which, for example, the actions of one person influence a second person. The second person then responds, altering the environment and subsequent actions of the first person, and so on. The "actor" here could be represented by a thing (e.g., a hurricane) or a concept (e.g., a change in interest rates). Although in a complex system, an environment might change in any way, the simple addition of other actors responding to the focal actor creates the simplest form of changing environment. Without the assumption of linear relations, a general linear math is no longer a main tool (although it still has uses in understanding complex systems, especially the analysis of relationships at fixed time points).

Therefore, one result of the complexity is nonlinear behavior within the system (Mason, 2001). Because of the interdependence among people and processes, small changes in inputs in one area of the system may lead to large changes in outputs. For example, one person's change in behavior may so alter the reactions of everyone else that the system changes its nature. Box-and-arrow diagrams are not appropriate for modeling these types of systems. They have difficulty capturing feedback loops or changes in the system over time. The complex interdependencies especially found in dynamic situations are likely to be very complicated to map out (e.g., multiple arrows in the box-and-arrow diagrams would need to move backward and forward at changing rates and directions across time).

Tipping points and threshold effects are not unusual in these nonlinear systems. As discussed in this chapter, *tipping points* and *threshold effects* refer to the idea that at some critical point, the entire system changes. Although behavior on either side of the tipping point or threshold may be linear, applying linear analysis to data without identifying the tipping point will lead to poor fit. In contrast, identifying the critical change point and using general linear analysis on either side may generate high fit.

In complex systems models, variables are no longer the point of interest. The complex systems approach copes with the challenges of exploring nonlinear relationships by shifting the emphasis from variables to a focus on actors and processes. Instead of turning processes into traits and conditions, researchers using a complex systems approach retain the actions of people over time as they respond to a changing world. Because variables rarely exhibit a fixed and linear relationship to one another in the world when time passes and actors interact, the focus on processes, patterns, and even the influence of the actions of actors whose traits keep them far from the mean is more effective in defining the system. While describing the world in these naturalistic ways, researchers can identify simple rules that might generate the observed, complex outcomes.

Computational simulation, and agent-based modeling in particular, is the preferred method for understanding the dynamics of complex systems (or at least for making the first cut at finding areas to focus on). Agent-based simulations can be used in a variety of ways. They are typically approached not as a strict deductive tool or an inductive tool. Rather, researchers use simulations to reason abductively (Peirce, 1955), moving back and forth between deduction and induction. Researchers might ask questions, identify sometimes surprising results from a simulation, and use the simulation to explore how the surprising outcome emerged. The researcher might follow this back-and-forth approach many times while growing in understanding of how the system works. The purpose of these simulations can be prediction, proof, discovery, explanation, critique, prescription, or empirical guidance (Axelrod, 1997a; Harrison, Lin, Carroll, & Carley, 2007).

APPLYING AGENT-BASED COMPUTATIONAL SIMULATIONS TO MTSs

Computational simulation methods support the study of the inputs, processes, and outputs of interest to scholars working to understand MTSs (Gilbert, 2008). These methods allow us to investigate multiple interdependent processes, dynamic cross-level activities, effects of heterogeneous traits among individuals on processes, outcomes based on complex interactions, and more.

As in any scientific study, researchers first need to identify what they consider to be the most important relationships between agents. Unlike exploring traditional conceptual relationships that can be represented by box-and-arrow diagrams, the researcher must think about people engaged in multiple processes working with many other people in a variety of structures (e.g., within one team and across teams). The researcher does not focus on variables, but on the actors and their processes. So, for example, someone studying MTSs might consider people, perhaps in the role of team member or manager, as a unit of analysis in the study. The researcher would consider how the people interact. Do the actions of one person affect just one other person? Do team members' actions have the potential to affect all other team members? Could a team member's actions affect members of other teams as well? Next, the researcher may consider how a person makes decisions. These decisions might be captured in a mathematical equation, but they need not be. If fact, it is more common to capture these decision processes in if-then statements.

An illustration may help. In the study of social dilemmas, scholars have a long history of studying rules such as win-cooperate/lose-defect or win-stay/lose-shift (see Messick & Liebrand, 1995). The first rule, *win-cooperate/lose-defect*, is an affective rule. When people believe they are winning (i.e., outperforming targets of comparison), they feel good and will cooperate. When people feel they are losing, they are discouraged, and they will defect or withhold cooperation. The second rule, *win-stay/lose-shift*, posits that people do what is reinforced. So when they are succeeding, they repeat whatever they have done in the past (*win-stay*), but if they feel that their efforts are not paying off, they try an alternate behavior (*lose-change*). A modeler might create agents who are heterogeneous in their tendency to cooperate. Some do routinely. Some rarely do. Then the modeler decides whose behavior affects others' behavior (e.g., acts of cooperation affect the performance of everyone else within the team, and acts of comparison occur among people across teams). The modeler allows these agents to interact within the structure, with each agent acting according to its decision rule and its environment. Feedback processes arise as agents assess their standing (winning or losing) based on team performance or individual performance against target comparisons.

A researcher studying multiteam systems through agent-based models might pose questions asking how team or multiteam performance changes over time, or wonder what dynamics lie behind an observed behavior in team members trying to deal with teammates dealing with another team or in managing multiteam membership. A multiteam researcher could explore the processes that account for observed correlations. The effect of team members' choices could be explored to see how they affect team-level and multiteam-level outcomes. Any social interaction could be modeled dynamically to identify processes within and between teams. Such interaction might be modeled to capture how people in teams switch between processes to coordinate with each other or other teams, or to explore how the external environment composed of other teams changes based on people's choices within certain teams. Action at all levels (e.g., the individual, team, and multiteam unit) can be measured simultaneously to find connections at a point in time and across times. Delays between changes in inputs at the team or individual level and changes in outputs at the team or multiteam level could be identified.

Computational simulations are especially effective at ruling out proposed interpersonal and interteam processes that a modeler can show simply could not account over time for observed outcomes. A simulation might predict unexpected or unintended results of certain choices, such as when multiple actors in different organizations act independently to pursue separate but apparently rational goals. The extension of well-understood processes internal to a team or firm might lead to wholly new observations when each team or firm interacts with others who also apply these processes. Each group may vary their timing of similar choices in time or strength, leading to a rapidly changing environment for each other.

These multiteam models can tell us about a range of possible results, from those that on average are likely to appear to those that are unlikely yet might have a major impact if they occur. Human multiteam simulation is already a common method for military applications and emergency teams because it helps explore and explicate the within- and cross-team coordination, communication, and knowledge-sharing issues (e.g., Bond et al., 2007; Marks et al., 2005). Like human simulations, virtual simulations are especially helpful at exploring potentially dangerous situations in which errors can have catastrophic consequences.

AGENT-BASED COMPUTATIONAL SIMULATIONS AND TRADITIONAL ORDINARY LEAST SQUARES (OLS) METHODS

Following our previous analysis, we have identified a number of clear distinctions between traditional methods based on ordinary least squares analysis and agent-based computational simulations. Traditional methods generally average away heterogeneity, preventing unique actors (a powerful leader or an influential team member) from accounting for major changes in team or multiteam outcomes. Furthermore, traditional OLS methods focus us to consider behavior at a point in time, limiting the study of dynamics, delays between cause and effect, or cyclical changes. An assumption of OLS is that all observations are independent, limiting the ability to explore interdependent actions. Moreover, traditional methods are generally based on investigating the relationship between variable means. In contrast, agent-based computational simulations assume heterogeneity of instances, dynamic environments, and interdependence among actors. Instead of looking at variable means, agent-based computational simulations analyze people and decision rules, retaining actors whose behavior varies far from the mean as important factors that might

TABLE 16.1

Basic Parameters of General Linear Methods Relative to Those of Agent-Based Computational Simulations

	General Linear Methods	Agent-Based Computational Simulations
Observations	Independence	Interdependence
Participants and Agents	Homogeneity	Heterogeneity
Time	Static	Dynamic
Constructs	Variables	People and decision rules
Measurements	Means and variances	Actions of all, including outliers
Outcomes	Correlations	Emergence

carry the potential to sway overall systemic outcomes. Also, agent-based simulation reports can record actions at multiple levels across consecutive points in time, supporting the analysis of multilevel activities and dynamics spread over considerable time (see Table 16.1).

Although identifying the actors in teams and multiteam systems can be quite simple, scholars trying to explore the functioning of a complex system need to identify what "rules" these actors are using. Fortunately, descriptions may already exist within the experimental or theoretical literature in the form of if-then statements (see the cooperation rules discussed in this chapter), norms, mental models, schemata, and other decision criteria. Alternatively, a rule may have to be crafted from more general verbal explanations of a process available in the literature. The computational researcher will have to translate the verbal explanation into a simple decision rule (called an *algorithm* within a computer program).

Alternately, a computational simulation may be used to *derive* a rule from prior empirical or theoretical work. For example, the computational researcher may take an existing empirical study of dynamic processes and use a simulation to induce possible decision rules used by the participants. Any of a variety of rules might be tested in the simulation until it generates the type of outcomes seen in the empirical work. See, for example, the studies of team members' decision processes in a multiteam social dilemma that were found to be similar yet different in important ways from prior theoretical propositions about how people made their choices (Coen, 2006a, 2006b).

Although the design of nearly every agent-based model includes agents, structure, and decision rules, the multiple ways a modeler can arrange these is staggeringly large. In modeling a firm, a designer may have people as agents, teams as agents, departments as agents, and/or the firm itself as an agent. Traditionally, the basic actor—say, the worker in a model of the firm, or a firm in a model of industries—is called the *agent*. Yet, any number of agents of different types at the same level of analysis or nested across levels of analysis can be represented in an agent-based model. So, in a multiteam model, team members may be called the *agents*, but there could also be a *manager agent*. In addition, the team member agents may be nested in a team agent. There may also be multiple-team agents.

Agents generally have heterogeneous characteristics. These may be different personality traits, but they can be other differences. Consider the boids in Craig Reynolds's (1987) model. All of the boids are identical in their traits and in their decision rules. Yet they have different locations in space. (Note that their locations are a critical starting point, and their changing locations are the output measure of the model!) In studying teams of human beings, heterogeneity would be a commonly observed trait. To keep the agent-based model simple, most modelers identify only critical differences among agents. So, for example, in the model of social dilemmas, agents might only be heterogeneous along the dimension of their tendency to cooperate. A study focused on demographic fault lines, for example, might use a few demographic traits (e.g., race, gender, or age) to make their agents different. Although people differ in far more ways than these variables, making agents more complex makes the cause of the outcomes much more difficult to explain. Thus, complex systems models are actually models of relatively simple inputs that lead to complex outputs.

These homogeneous or heterogeneous agents interact in some sort of structure. The structure within the model represents the way the agents interact. Agents may make decisions in turn or simultaneously. They may use decision rules in which they observe their environment and choose a course of action. Their decision rules may consider their performance in a prior period or the performance of their team in a prior period. In models of team, individual team members might make choices or express preferences, and the structure is the process they use to make a joint decision. An MTS model might be built on this foundation, and then the relative performance of the teams in the environment in comparison to each other might add another layer of structured interaction.

Modelers spend a great deal of time in the design process. They try to identify the most stripped-down version of interactions of agents within structures that is true to the phenomena they are modeling. Most novice modelers err on the side of too much complexity. They want to consider the effects of too many processes at the same time. Although their intentions are good, the emergent outcomes are so complicated that they cannot understand them. Choosing the right level of simplicity is an art, but in general, a model requires two opposing processes. So, for example, a model of a social dilemma requires some process that rewards cooperation and some process that rewards defection.

Still, there remains debate in the field about how realistic versus how simple a model should be. All models present a tension between these extremes. Some advocate a KISS ("Keep it simple, stupid") approach. Classic examples of KISS models include the garbage can model (Cohen et al., 1972), the evolution of cooperation (Axelrod, 1984), and the housing segregation model (Schelling, 1978). Key examples of highly realistic models include work on how to destabilize the Al Qaeda network (Carley, Dombroski, Tsvetovat, Reminga, & Kamneva, 2003) and BioWar (Carley, Altman, Kaminsky, Nave, & Yahja, 2004; Carley et al., 2006).

In an article categorizing the types and strengths of various computational simulation approaches, Kathleen Carley (2009) discussed the trade-offs between simple models—typically thought experiments—and more veridical case studies. She observed that with all else held equal, increasing realism can be purchased by using fewer "agents." Yet, realism can exist at micro- and macrolevels. Models with fewer agents are better able to treat human thought processes and behaviors (i.e., they have more realistic actors), whereas models with more agents have more capacity for social and cultural interactions and learning (i.e., they have more realistic contexts to interact with) (see Carley, 2009, pp. 49–50). Discussing the same trade-offs, Steve Bankes (2009) identified "costs" associated with increasing realism. He pointed out that adding more details to a model has an economic cost in more labor, and a scientific cost in the time and cases required to support any one contention (Bankes, 2009, pp. 9–10). Given these trade-offs, Carley and Bankes, as well as many other computational simulation theorists, recommended making your model as realistic as necessary to represent your phenomena and as simple as possible to understand your results.

Building the Model

Software

Once modelers have designed their models, they must choose a computer software program to build it in. A variety of software packages exist, including Swarm (swarm.org), Repast (repast.sourceforge.net), Netlogo (ccl.northwestern.edu/netlogo/), and AnyLogic (xjtek.com). Several of these software packages are free (open source). Most use the Java programming language, but others work with Objective-C, C++, and other languages as well. The choice of software is dependent on the modelers' programming skill, the need for training and programming support, and resources. For a description of the features, strengths, and weaknesses of each primary software package currently available, see Gilbert (2008).

Build

Once a software environment is selected, the modeler must build the agents and structures, and write the decision rule algorithms. One of the great advantages of formal modeling, as opposed to verbal theorizing, is that every component has to be included and reasonably approximated (Gilbert, 2008). People describing their theories in works can often skip over key steps or relationships. Their absence may not be readily apparent to the reader (or the speaker, for that matter); however, when a person builds a formal model, it will not run if any element is unspecified. After carefully building each element of the model, going back to theory or empirical evidence to fill in any missing components, the modeler must see if the model works as designed.

Verify and Validate

After finishing coding a computer simulation, the modeler test runs the model. Commonly, there are some bugs (mistakes) in the code. Some bugs prevent the model from running at all. For example, a missing or incorrectly specified decision rule would cause problems. The modeler often runs a "base" model. All parameters are set to some neutral condition. Interdependence might be eliminated. The modeler examines the results of the base for odd or inappropriate results. Through these modeling practices, the modeler determines that the model is doing what it is intended to do (which is not the same as saying the outcomes are predictable.)

Run Data

Next, as an experimenter, the modeler begins asking questions, using the simulation to generate answers. First, questions tend to be quite simple. The experimenter will start with a logical progression (what if teammates are more or less cooperative? What if the structure, such as the number of teams, changes? What if team members use a different decision rule?). Slowly, the experimenter begins to build a map of a multidimensional decision space.

Analyze

The experimenter may begin to graph outcomes over time or across a key parameter. Some relationships will be simple and obvious. Others, especially those reliant upon interdependence of the agents, may show distinct behavior in some part of the parameter space. The experimenter will ask, "Why?" The experimenter will run further experiments attempting to find out which changes in which parameters or decision rules or structures cause the distinct behaviors.

Robustness Tests

Finally, the experimenter will run many additional experiments to see if an observed relationship holds over changes to any of the parameters, decision rules, or structures. If the observed relationship remains, it is considered "robust." Because simulations can be run thousands and tens of thousands of times or more, traditional tests for "statistical significance" cannot be used to determine the strength of a phenomenon. (They might be used to indicate that a phenomenon is not statistically significant, but the power available through so many runs of a simulation casts doubt on a claim of statistical significance.) Instead of tests of statistical significance, experimenters using computational simulation identify robustness.

CONCLUSION

There will be no simple solutions for finding adequate methodology to study multiple-team systems in all of their rich activity. Multiple methodological approaches will always be necessary to explore dynamic phenomena involved in a single-level analysis, and new methods are necessary to explore cross-levels of analysis as people in teams deal with other teams. Exploring the dynamics in multiteam systems will be challenging with any methodological approach.

So what can complex systems research do for the study of multiteam systems? The use of complex systems approaches allows researchers to consider the processes and decision rules pertaining to the subset of MTSs that are complex but not too complicated. Complex systems approaches can help us understand dynamic processes within and between teams. Rather than reduce processes to traits or conditions, it allows a robust examination and testing of the steps in a process. It lets us explore how actors' actions affect their team and teams around them and how this changing environment leads members and teams to alter their responses.

Complex systems is not a competing theory about multiple-team processes, but a third way of knowing how things work in the world (Axelrod, 1997b). Whereas verbal theorizing has predominated in the social sciences for centuries and in mathematical approaches for decades, theorizing with computational simulations is recent and expands on what we can know from the previous powerful approaches. When dynamic processes create intractable mathematical problems, simulations can guide our understanding of systems.

Generally, agent-based computational simulation is the favored method of complex systems researchers modeling adaptive agents in social systems (Harrison et al., 2005). Often these simulations are based on rich, detailed case studies or a strong existing theory. The simulations capture the structure and dynamics of a single system whether of interpersonal or interteam interaction. A computational simulation re-creates the system and extends it, allowing unlimited reenactments with endless variations of actors, exploring all parameters involved, and identifying processes and mapping out the "state space" of all possible outcomes, whether average or less common. Researchers may evaluate these processes and results to generate propositions for further testing. Or they may use the simulations to eliminate possible explanations, narrowing the number of alternatives that need to be explored experimentally or in the field. Decision rules-in-use can be induced by using a simulation to test whether rules can generate observed outputs or correlations. Whether used to predict, explain, explore, discover, or guide our thinking, computational simulation provides a new and powerful tool to examine the dynamics in multiteam systems.

REFERENCES

Axelrod, R. (1997a). *The complexity of cooperation: Agent-based models of competition and collaboration.* Princeton, NJ: Princeton University Press.

Axelrod, R. (1997b). Advancing the art of simulation in the social sciences. In R. Conte, R. Hegselmann, & P. Terna (Eds.), *Simulating social phenomena* (pp. 21–40). Berlin: Springer.

Axelrod, R. (1984). *The evolution of cooperation.* New York: Basic Books.

Arrow, H., McGrath, J., & Berdahl, J. (2000). *Small groups as complex systems: Formation, coordination, development, and adaptation.* Thousand Oaks, CA: Sage.

Bankes, S. (2009). Models and lab equipment: Science from computational experiments. *Computational & Mathematical Organization Theory, 15*(1), 1–59.

Berkes, F., Colding, J., & Folke, C. (2003). *Navigating social ecological systems.* Cambridge: Cambridge University Press.

Bond, W. F., Lammers, R. L., Spillane, L. L., Smith-Coggins, R., Fernandez, R., Reznek, M. A., et al. (2007). The use of simulation in emergency medicine: A research agenda. *Academic Emergency Medicine,* 1–11.

Caldwell, B. (2005). Multiteam dynamics and distributed expertise in mission operations. *Aviation, Space, and Environmental Medicine, 6,* 145–153.

Carley, K. M. (2009). Computational modeling for reasoning about the social behavior of humans. *Computational & Mathematical Organization Theory, 15*(1), 1–59.

Carley, K. M., Altman, N., Kaminsky, B., Nave, D., & Yahja, A. (2004). *BioWar: A city-scale multi-agent network model of weaponized biological attacks* (CASOS Technical Report: CMU-ISRI-04-101). Pittsburgh, PA: Carnegie Mellon University.

Carley, K. M., Dombroski, M., Tsvetovat, M., Reminga, J., & Kamneva, N. (2003). Destabilizing dynamic covert networks. In *Proceedings of the 8th International Command and Control: Research and Technology Symposium.* Washington, DC: National Defense War College.

Carley, K. M., Fridsma, D. B., Casman, E., Yahja, A., Altman, N., Chen, L.-C., et al. (2006). BioWar: A scalable agent-based model of bioattacks. *IEEE Trans Syst Man Cybern A, 36,* 252–265.

Casti, J. L. (1994). Recent developments and future perspectives in dynamical systems theory. *SEAM Review, 24,* 302–331.

Coen, C. A. (2006a). Seeking the comparative advantage: The dynamics of individual cooperation in single vs. multiple team environments. *Organizational Behavior and Human Decision Processes, 100,* 145–159.

Coen, C. A. (2006b). Mixing rules: When to cooperate in the multiple team context. *Simulation Modeling Practice and Theory, 14*(4), 423–437.

Cohen, M. D., March, J. G., & Olsen, J. P. (1972). A garbage can model of organizational choice. *Administrative Science Quarterly, 17*(1), 1–25.

Corning, P. A. (2002). The re-emergence of "emergence": A venerable concept in search of a theory. *Complexity, 7*(6), 18–30.

Cowan, G., Pines, D., & Meltzer, D. (1994). *Complexity: Metaphors, models, and reality.* Reading, MA: Addison-Wesley.

DeShon, R., Kozlowski, S., Schmidt, A., Milner, K., & Weichmann, D. (2004). A multiple-goal, multilevel model of feedback effects on the regulation of individual and team performance. *Journal of Applied Psychology, 6*, 1035–1056.

Dooley, K. (1997). A complex adaptive systems model of organization change. *Nonlinear Dynamics, Psychology, and Life Sciences, 1*, 69–97.

Dougherty, D. (2002). Grounded theory building: Some principles and practices. In J. A. C. Baum (Ed.), *Companion to organizations* (pp. 849–867). Oxford: Blackwell.

Gilbert, N. (2008). *Agent-based models.* Thousand Oaks, CA: Sage.

Gladwell, M. (2000). *Tipping points: How little things can make a big difference.* Boston: Little, Brown.

Hacken, H. (2006). *Information and self-organization* (3rd ed.). Heidelberg: Springer.

Hackman, J. R. (1987). The design of work teams. In J. W. Lorsch (Ed.), *Handbook of organizational behavior* (pp. 315–342). Englewood Cliffs, NJ: Prentice Hall.

Harrison, R., Lin, Z., Carroll, G., & Carley, K. (2007). Simulation modeling in organizational and management research. *Academy of Management Review, 32*, 1229–1245.

Hoegl, M., & Weinkauf, K. (2005). Managing task interdependencies in multiteam projects: A longitudinal study. *Journal of Management Studies, 6*, 1287–1308.

Holland, J. H. (1996). *Hidden order: How adaptation builds complexity.* New York: Helix.

Ilgen, D. R., Hollenbeck, J. R., Johnson, M., & Jundt, D. (2005). Team in organizations: From input-process-output models to IMOI models. *Annual Review of Psychology, 56*, 517–543.

Jennings, N. (2001). An agent-based approach to building complex software systems. *Communications of the ACM, 4*, 35–41.

Johnson, J., Korsgaard, M. A., & Sapienza, H. (2002). Perceived fairness, decision control, and commitment in international joint venture management teams. *Strategic Management Journal, 23*, 1141–1160.

Macy, M. (1991). Chains of cooperation: Threshold effects in collective action. *American Sociological Review, 6*, 730–747.

Marks, M. A., DeChurch, L. A., Mathieu, J. E., Panzer, F. J., & Alonso, A. A. (2005). Teamwork in multiteam systems. *Journal of Applied Psychology, 90*(5), 964–971.

Mason, S. (2001). Simplifying complexity: A review of complexity theory. *Geoforum, 3*, 405–414.

Masuch, M. (1985). Vicious cycles in organizations. *Administrative Science Quarterly, 1*, 14–33.

McGrath, J. E. (1984). *Groups: Interaction and performance.* Englewood Cliffs, NJ: Prentice Hall.

Messick, D. M., & Liebrand, W. B. G. (1995). Individual heuristics and the dynamics of cooperation in large groups. *Psychological Review, 102*(1), 131–145.

Mortensen, M., Woolley, A. W., & O'Leary, M. (2007). Conditions enabling effective multiple team membership. In K. Crowston, S. Sieber, & E. Wynn (Eds.), *IFIP International Federation for Information Processing: Vol. 236. Virtuality and virtualization* (pp. 215–228). Boston: Springer.

Peirce, C. (1955). *Abduction and induction*. New York: Dover.

Pennings, J. (1974). *Differentiation, interdependence and performance in formal organizations.* Paper presented at the American Sociological Association annual conference, Montreal.

Reynolds, C. (1987). Flocks, birds, and schools: A distributed behavioral model. *Computer Graphics, 21*, 25–34.

Schelling, T. C. (1978). *Micromotives and macrobehavior*. New York: Norton.

Simon, H. A. (1996). *The sciences of the artificial* (3rd ed.). Cambridge, MA: MIT Press.

Standifer, R., & Bluedorn, A. (2006). Alliance management teams and entrainment: Sharing temporal mental models. *Human Relations, 7*, 903–927.

Steiner, I. D. (1972). *Group process and productivity*. San Diego, CA: Academic Press.

Thompson, J. D. (1967). *Organizations in action*. New York: McGraw-Hill.

Urry, J. (2004). The "system" of automobility. *Theory, Culture & Society, 21*, 25–39.

Waldrop, M. (1992). *Complexity: The emerging science at the edge of order and chaos*. New York: Touchstone.

17

Multiteam System (MTS) Research in Laboratory Settings: A Look at the Technical and Practical Challenges

Christian J. Resick
Drexel University

C. Shawn Burke
University of Central Florida

Daniel Doty
University of Central Florida

Several types of multiteam systems (MTSs) have gained considerable attention of late in the media and popular press. One likely reason for this attention is that MTSs are often used to address large and complex challenges where the costs of failure are immense. For example, hurricane disaster response, provincial reconstruction, and corporate strategic alliances are just a few of the situations where MTSs are commonly employed. In some cases, these systems are able to integrate efforts smoothly and accomplish goals effectively; in many other instances, however, these systems are not able to perform effectively, or they even suffer from a complete failure. As MTSs are used to address extremely high-stake endeavors, managers and organizational scientists alike are seeking a better understanding of the antecedents, processes, and emergent states associated with the effectiveness of this complex organizational form.

Field research is often used to begin to form initial ideas and corresponding hypotheses for new and emerging constructs. However, MTSs frequently operate in conditions (i.e., complex, ambiguous, dynamic, and sometimes dangerous) that make it difficult to collect real-time data or to isolate key variables and relationships of interest. Laboratory research is one mechanism that can mitigate some of the difficulties in conducting field research in this area. In the laboratory, key variables can be isolated, and basic relationships can begin to be examined. Although some may argue that entities such as MTSs cannot be studied within a contrived setting, when properly designed, laboratory settings provide an important alternative to field research that enables researchers to test theoretically and practically meaningful questions in a controlled environment. These findings can then be used to augment findings from field research.

Laboratory research is likely to play a critical role in the evolution of MTS theory. However, laboratory settings present a number of challenges to researchers seeking to gain insights into the attributes and the affective, behavioral, and cognitive processes and emergent states that explain MTS effectiveness and generalize across settings. In this chapter, we examine the challenges that organizational researchers face when conducting MTS research in laboratory settings. One set of challenges focuses on the accuracy of inferences drawn from laboratory research studies, and the generalizability of findings to the various types of MTSs that are commonly found in both the private and public sectors. These challenges broadly address concerns about the validity of laboratory-based MTS research. Using the framework presented by Cook and Campbell (1979), and later refined by Shadish, Cook, and Campbell (2002), we examine the main threats to the validity of MTS laboratory research. A second set of challenges focuses on the practical concerns associated with establishing and running a laboratory devoted to MTS research, such as creating a simulation platform and ongoing management responsibilities. We conclude the chapter by examining some of the factors that mitigate these challenges, and discuss the role of laboratory-based research in the evolution of the MTS construct.

VALIDITY CONCERNS

The advancement of scientific knowledge in any field is predicated upon the ability to draw valid inferences from experimental research that generalizes across people, settings, and time (e.g., Cook & Campbell, 1979;

Sackett & Larson, 1990; Stone-Romero, 2002). Although laboratory-based research has played a critical role in the history of organizational science research, concerns about the validity of inferences drawn from laboratory-based experimental research are always present (for a discussion and defense of the importance of laboratory research, see Dipboye & Flanagan, 1979; Locke, 1986). MTSs are a particularly challenging organizational form to study as they frequently draw members from disparate organizations, are composed of units with some team boundary and identity ambiguities, and tackle large, multifaceted goals (DeChurch & Mathieu, 2008; Mathieu, Marks, & Zaccaro, 2001). Further, the range of MTS attributes that need to be considered, and the complex layering of affective, behavioral, and cognitive mediating forces and effectiveness criteria, present obstacles to adequately capturing the psychological realism of focal constructs in laboratory settings. These factors present challenges to conducting laboratory-based studies of MTS phenomena that enable researchers to draw valid, generalizable inferences.

To provide guidance on conducting research that enables accurate inferences to be drawn, Cook and Campbell (1979) presented four components of validity that impact the causal generalizations: *statistical conclusion validity, internal validity, construct validity,* and *external validity.* They went on to outline a series of factors that threaten the validity of inferences within each component. More recently, Shadish et al. (2002) presented an updated discussion of the four components of validity and their associated threats. For each component of validity, we now examine the four or five threats that present particular challenges to conducting valid MTS research in laboratory settings.

Statistical Conclusion Validity

Statistical conclusion validity addresses the accuracy of inferences about covariation among variables (Shadish et al., 2002). Inferences associated with this component of validity address the accurate identification of a relationship among variables, be that cause and effect or correlational in nature, as well as the accurate estimation of effect sizes. Among the nine threats to statistical conclusion validity discussed by Shadish et al., we suggest that four of these threats present particularly challenging obstacles for conducting MTS research in laboratory settings. These threats are *low statistical power, restriction of range, unreliable treatment implementation,* and *extraneous variance in the experimental setting.*

Although the potential for low statistical power is a challenge that all researchers must address, this threat is particularly germane to laboratory-based MTS research due to the complexity of the relationships that need to be modeled. As MTSs are composed of individuals nested within teams nested within larger systems (Mathieu et al., 2001), laboratory sessions will require four participants, composing two teams of two, at the very minimum. Substantially larger numbers of participants per session will be needed to model the more complex forms of MTSs common in natural settings. Further, sufficient statistical power is needed to isolate the level at which the MTS attributes and the affective, behavioral, and cognitive processes and emergent states that are critical to overall system success operate. Therefore, MTS researchers need access to large pools of participants to obtain necessary sample sizes. In addition, the relatively short duration of most laboratory studies may provide insufficient time for the true nature of many of the relationships to evolve. For example, the effects of a leader intervention or MTS compositional attribute on mediating factors such as information sharing or mental model similarity may evolve over time. These effects could be underidentified or misidentified in a cross-sectional laboratory study. Similarly, some mediating factors may impact longer term aspects of system performance and have little short-term impact. As a result, MTS researchers need to be cognizant of the factors that may restrict the range of variance and attenuate the strength of effects in laboratory research.

Characteristics of the laboratory settings, such as unreliable manipulations and extraneous factors, are also potential threats to the statistical conclusion validity of MTS laboratory-based research. Logistically, multiple experimenters will be needed to run the experimental sessions due to the large numbers of participants and component teams. The use of multiple experimenters increases the potential for the unreliable manipulation of variables and the introduction of extraneous variance due to experimenter differences. These factors may artificially inflate the amount of error in a study and decrease the magnitude of effects. Experimenter training and detailed protocols are needed to achieve consistency across sessions and minimize the potential for unreliability and extraneous variance.

Internal Validity

Internal validity addresses the accuracy of inferences about the causal relationship between focal study variables (Shadish et al., 2002). Because of the control that researchers have over the setting, the operationalization of variables, and the assignment of participants, internal validity should be an important strength of laboratory research (Marks, 2000; Sackett & Larson, 1990). We suggest that four of the nine threats to internal validity identified by Shadish and colleagues present challenges to the internal validity of MTS research conducted in laboratory settings. These threats are *selection, maturation, attrition,* and *testing.*

Selection biases may arise in the sampling and assignment of participants, leading to systematic differences in participant characteristics across conditions. Selection biases are problematic for laboratory-based MTS research for two reasons. First, laboratory research most often relies on undergraduate student subject pools. Participants within any particular experimental session will have varying levels of familiarity and experience working with their team- and system-mates, which may affect how individuals and teams interact, thereby adding a confounding effect. Additionally, undergraduate student participants are likely to have varying levels of motivation to participate and perform well in experimental scenarios. In studies where students fulfill course-related research requirements, those students who sign up at the beginning of a semester are likely to have different generalized levels of motivation reflecting different underlying traits than students who sign up at the end of the semester frantically trying to complete their requirements. As a result, selection biases may seep in, and impact the nature and magnitude of relationships between variables.

Maturation processes are natural changes that occur within participants with or without treatment effects. In laboratory settings, maturation occurs as participants learn their roles, and how to work with team- and system-mates during a study. Given the relatively short duration of many laboratory-based experiments, participants will naturally experience learning effects regarding their specific role responsibilities and the knowledge, capabilities, and working styles of their team- and system-mates. At the same time, experimental sessions can last as long as 5 hours (e.g., DeChurch & Marks, 2006; Marks, DeChurch, Mathieu, Panzer, & Alonso, 2005), which increases the likelihood for fatigue effects.

Ultimately, maturation may affect the relationships among study variables in laboratory-based MTS research.

Another important threat to internal validity involves the attrition of participants, which occurs when participants drop out of the study or fail to complete all measures. Attrition will be particularly problematic for MTS researchers needing large numbers of participants for a multihour experimental session, or for longitudinal studies that require participants to report to the laboratory on multiple occasions. These conditions increase the likelihood of participant attrition due to scheduling conflicts, fatigue, frustration, or general lack of interest. Attrition results in a situation where variables of interests are not collected from all study participants. When attrition levels vary systematically across study conditions, researchers are likely to draw erroneous conclusions about the effects of treatments. In addition, fatigue- or frustration-related attrition may point to serious design flaws in either the treatment manipulations or simulation platform.

Finally, testing threatens the internal validity of a study when self-report measures are administered repeatedly. Scores on these measures may change based on familiarity and practice with the questionnaires, and be mistaken for treatment effects. Testing may present a particular challenge to laboratory research when self-report measures of cognitive emergent states, such as mental models, transactive memory, or psychological safety, or affect states, such as conflict or social cohesion, are studied. Measures of one construct may have spillover effects on other constructs or affect the way participants interact after completing these measures. Testing effects may be particularly problematic when within-group designs are used or in situations where self-report measures are administered multiple times within a single session because later responses are likely to be affected by increased familiarity with the measures.

Construct Validity

Construct validity addresses the accuracy of operationalizations of the theoretical constructs they are designed to represent (Shadish et al., 2002). Construct validity is a concept of critical importance among organizational scientists because of its importance for theory building, theory testing, and the practical application of scientific knowledge to organizational problems (Cascio & Aguinis, 2005; Cronbach & Meehl, 1955).

For example, Binning and Barrett's (1989) seminal discussion of validity in personnel decision making placed construct validity in the center of their unified perspective on validity, suggesting that evidence of construct validity may be achieved from content-, construct-, or criterion-related strategies. We suggest that 4 of the 14 threats to construct validity discussed by Shadish and colleagues (2002) present particularly challenging obstacles for conducting MTS research in laboratory settings: *inadequate explication of constructs, confounding constructs with levels of constructs, reactivity to experimental situations,* and *experimenter expectancies.*

The first set of threats to the construct validity of MTS research conducted in laboratory settings addresses the inadequate explication of constructs and challenges in addressing the level of constructs. Phenomena operating at system, team, and individual levels of analysis are operating in MTS settings. Because of the complexity of MTS structures, goal hierarchies, and effectiveness criteria, construct explication and operationalization are critically important yet difficult tasks facing all MTS researchers. The difficulty of these tasks is heightened in laboratory settings as the operationalization of constructs will often be tied to characteristics of the experimental scenario or simulation platform; the challenge is to develop a valid measure of the conceptual construct within the setting that also has sufficient psychological fidelity to enable the generalization of findings.

Researchers need to identify the constructs important for success within and across levels, and provide clear conceptual and operational construct definitions. Within an MTS, some constructs will operate only at the system level, whereas other constructs will operate only at the team level, and still other constructs affect phenomena across levels. For example, within an MTS, between-team coordination processes are conceptually distinct from within-team coordination processes in terms of their referent levels, their emergence processes, and the criteria they are expected to be related to. Likewise, the leadership processes needed at the system level are likely to differ from the leadership processes needed at the team level in terms of direction setting, internal integration, and the creation of adaptive capacity. However, coordination or leadership processes operating at one level may directly or indirectly affect other mediating forces or effectiveness criteria at another level.

Two additional characteristics of the laboratory setting may also impact construct validity, including reactivity to experimental situations and experimenter expectancies. Participants' motivation, compliance, reactions, and responses may be affected by such things as apprehension to performing in situations where they are being evaluated. Demand characteristics, which occur when experimenters or conditions provide subtle cues to participants about expected reactions (Orne, 1962, 1970; Rosenthal & Rosnow, 1991) may also influence the performance or responses of participants. In addition, completing self-report measures of focal constructs may also provide cues to participants about expected behaviors. The potential for these effects is heightened in MTS laboratory studies because multiple participants are required to run each session, and any one participant's reactions could introduce bias into construct measurements for the entire session. In addition, experimenters may also act in a manner that provides cues to participants about the nature of different treatment conditions or expected results. Keeping experimenters blind to study hypotheses will help to reduce these concerns. However, this does not eliminate experimenters' knowledge of the manipulations that they will be administering within a particular session. Once again, these factors heighten the need for researchers to create detailed laboratory protocols and training programs.

External Validity

External validity addresses the accuracy of inferences about the generalizability of relationships within and across samples, populations, settings, treatments, outcomes, and periods in time (Shadish et al., 2002). Threats to external validity are among the toughest challenges associated with conducting organizational and behavioral science research in laboratory settings (Sackett & Larson, 1990). Shadish and colleagues framed the threats to external validity in terms of the interactions between causal relationships and (a) units, (b) treatment variations, (c) outcomes, and (d) settings, and also included context-dependent mediating variables. We discuss how these threats challenge the external validity of laboratory-based MTS research.

As noted in this chapter, laboratory research typically relies on samples of undergraduate students, who begin a study with little experience with their respective role responsibilities, no prior social identification with the particular team they are assigned to, and often little consequence for outstanding or poor performance in the experimental scenario. As a result, the magnitude and nature of relationships may be due, in part, to the characteristics of laboratory study participants. Researchers need to address questions about the generalizability of findings from laboratory samples to MTSs, because in the latter case members bring varying levels of role-specific experience, members have greater levels of social identification with their team or organizational unit, historical relationships between teams may exist, and there are important team- and system-level consequences for performance.

MTS researchers also face the challenge of creating realism in the experimental scenarios and conditions. One form of realism that laboratory researchers must consider is *mundane realism*, which represents the similarity of experimental conditions to conditions found in natural settings (Berkowitz & Donnerstein, 1982; Stone-Romero, 2002). Creating laboratory scenarios and simulations with high levels of mundane realism is a desired yet not necessary condition for conducting laboratory research with external validity (Berkowitz & Donnerstein, 1982; Colquitt, 2008; Marks, 2000). The important challenge facing MTS researchers is not to make participants in a laboratory study believe they are actually performing tasks identical to the tasks of an MTS in the field, but rather to create scenarios and manipulations that participants take seriously and believe in (Stone-Romero, 2002), and re-create the nomological network among the constructs of interest (Marks, 2000). This latter form of realism is referred to as *experimental realism* (Aronson & Carlsmith, 1968; Berkowitz & Donnerstein, 1982) or, more recently, as *psychological realism* by Colquitt (2008). Creating psychological realism is a key challenge to maximizing the external validity of laboratory-based MTS research.

MTS researchers conducting research in laboratory settings also face threats to external validity due to interactions of causal relationships across treatment variations. Due to the finite nature and brief duration of laboratory research, participants may respond differently than they would if they received exposure to conditions over an extended period of time. Further, some interventions may impact MTS effectiveness differently when used in conjunction with other interventions, or they may have a desired effect only for MTSs configured a certain way. Although laboratory research enables researchers to isolate effects, these same benefits may ultimately underestimate or overestimate treatment effects. Additionally, the briefings and training required to bring participants up to speed may differentially affect participants across treatment levels, specifically if either the training or treatments focus on multiple levels, thus changing relationships due to effects that would never be encountered outside of the laboratory.

Two additional important threats to the generalizability of MTS laboratory research include the interaction of the causal relationships with outcomes, and context-dependent mediation. MTS effectiveness outcomes are complex and involve multiple layers of goals (Mathieu et al., 2001; Zaccaro, Marks, & DeChurch, Chapter 1, this book). Researchers face a challenge in designing laboratory simulations that adequately model the complexity of these effectiveness outcomes, which could limit the generalizability of findings to the more complex phenomena that MTSs face in the field. As with team research (for reviews, see Kozlowski & Ilgen, 2006; LePine, Piccolo, Jackson, Mathieu, & Saul, 2008; Mathieu, Maynard, Rapp, & Gilson, 2008), a primary focus of much MTS research is the identification of affective, behavioral, and cognitive mediating factors through which various factors such as composition, structure, and leadership impact overall system effectiveness. The mediating factors identified in laboratory settings may be dependent on the types of effectiveness outcomes built into the simulation scenario. In addition, effect sizes associated with mediator variables may differ when contextual factors such as time pressures, important consequences, or disruptive events are factored into the situation. MTS researchers need to take these issues into consideration in designing laboratory studies.

PRACTICAL CONCERNS

Laboratory research is an enormous undertaking, and we turn our focus now to the practical challenges of designing and managing a research laboratory devoted to MTS research. To offer practical guidance to researchers contemplating a laboratory experiment, Aronson, Wilson, and Brewer (1998) presented a taxonomy of four areas of practical concern that researchers need to address, including (a) setting the stage for research, such as space layout and experimental scenarios; (b) constructing independent variables; (c) measuring dependent variables; and (d) planning postsession follow-up. Building on Aronson et al.'s (1998) categories, we discuss the practical challenges regarding (a) the establishment of simulation platforms and experimental scenarios (i.e., setting the stage for research), (b) the conceptual and operational definition of *variables* (combining the stages of constructing independent variables and measuring dependent variables), and (c) ongoing laboratory management. From our personal experiences of designing and conducting MTS and team research in laboratory settings, we suggest that the first two areas are among the most important, and also time-, labor-, and cognitively intensive aspects of conducing laboratory research. We can't stress enough the importance of due diligence during these phases to minimize the chance for unplanned issues to create threats to validity or result in fatal flaws.

Simulation Platforms and Experimental Scenarios

The first challenge that MTS researchers face is designing a simulation platform and experimental scenario that models the inherent complexity of the MTS compositional, linkage, and developmental attributes outlined by Zaccaro and colleagues in Chapter 1 of this book. Though a computer-based simulation isn't a necessity, we recommend using a simulation due to the complexity of scenarios that can be presented, and the potential to obtain unobtrusive and objective indices of mediating variables and effectiveness criteria. Further, computer-based simulations provide researchers with the unique ability to create manageable, defined environments that replicate the structure of systems they are modeling and capture the nomological networks of interest, thereby enhancing psychological realism (Marks, 2000).

The first challenge in setting up an MTS research laboratory is finding and customizing, or designing, a simulation platform or scenario that will adequately model the MTS attributes of interest. Although numerous simulation platforms have been identified as being useful for examining questions at the individual, team, and organizational levels, there has been little work done to systematically identify experimental platforms for use in MTS research (see Burke, Wooten, & Salas, 2009, for an exception). This, in turn, places a large burden on the experimenter in terms of time and resources. We recommend that researchers approach the task of establishing the simulation platform and experimental scenarios by first identifying the focal MTS attributes that need to be modeled to test the theoretical and practical issues of interest. At a minimum, researchers need to consider four questions when choosing a simulation platform. First, how many component teams can be represented by the platform?

The platform must be able to accommodate at least two teams. Second, what types of functional interdependence can be represented? Third, can the platform be structured to provide identifiable, independent team- and system-level performance outcomes? Finally, will the platform model distinct performance episodes?

During this stage, researchers must be cognizant of two factors that make MTSs unique. First, the definition of individual, team, and system roles needs to take into account the system's goal hierarchy. That is, individual tasks need to translate into individual goals, team tasks need to translate into team goals, and cross-team tasks need to translate into system-level goals. Further, the simulation platform will most closely align with MTSs found in natural settings if goals are not directly additive between levels and the success of component teams does not guarantee overall system success.

Second, component teams within an MTS must be identifiably separate not only through identification but also through resource, informational, task, and/or goal independence. Further, functional interdependence must exist on inputs, processes, and outcomes (Mathieu et al., 2001). Therefore, these factors must be identifiably separate between component teams, and each team must have influence on at least one other component team in some significant way for the MTS to be appropriately constructed. Though two teams may be designed to be separate, improper balancing of the MTS attributes may result in the two teams identifying and operating as a single functional unit, rather than as independent, yet tightly coupled, entities.

Another potential advantage of a computer-based simulation platform is customizability, which enables researchers to exercise a greater degree of experimental control over the setting and variable manipulations. A good platform should allow the researchers to change aspects of the task context, such as complexity, novelty, and dynamism. Such scenarios may also require the use of scripting, which is the creation of predefined events at specific points in time or in response to certain actions (Marks, 2000). A platform that is lacking customizability in the structure of the MTS, the task environment, or the scripting of events could lead to logistical challenges in the implementation of the research program.

Although computer-based simulation platforms provide a great deal of promise for the study of complex MTSs, we caution researchers to be cognizant of two major pitfalls when selecting or developing a research simulation: (a) do not be enamored by the platform's apparent capabilities, and (b) do not be constrained by the platform's apparent capabilities.

Many potential simulations will have features that extend far beyond what is actually needed and that may, in fact, interfere with the focus of the research. At the same time, it is very unlikely that an off-the-shelf simulation will be perfectly suited to answer a specific set of research questions. Through proper setup of the experimental area and framing of the scenario, even a largely constrained simulation may provide a useful platform from which to validly test theory.

Construct Manipulations and Measurements

In this section, we discuss challenges associated with the creation of experimental conditions, and the explication and measurement of input, process, emergent state, and performance-related variables. Internal and construct validity are particularly important factors to consider in designing and conducing laboratory studies to ensure the accuracy and generalizability of inferences (Stone-Romero, 2002). In laboratory settings, MTS researchers face the challenge of ensuring that variables being manipulated both truly capture the constructs of interest and target the desired level of analysis.

To create strong and robust manipulations, researchers need to (a) choose variables that can be appropriately and consistently manipulated, and (b) ensure that key features of the manipulation capture the conceptually important features of the construct. Compositional attributes and linkage attributes are MTS features most likely to be manipulated, and they can take the form of structural or behavioral characteristics. Structural characteristics include features such as MTS size, functional diversity, and independence–interdependence configurations. These features are objective, are easy to manipulate, and may have the most robust effects. However, behavioral characteristics such as leader sensemaking, structured briefings, and cross-training provide insights into interventions that may be useful across a wide range of types of MTSs and at various stages of their system life cycle. These manipulations may be more difficult to implement consistently across experimental sessions in a manner that provides appropriate psychological realism. For example, to study component team leadership processes, MTS researchers have several options, including (a) providing prerecorded messages from "leaders," (b) embedding confederate leaders, or (c) training participants to enact the leadership roles. The highest level of consistency is likely to be with the use of prerecorded leader messages. However, this approach is likely to yield the lowest psychological realism. In contrast, the use of trained participants is likely to have the greatest level of psychological realism, but also lead to variations across sessions due to factors not associated with the study such as personal abilities or motivation. Researchers need to carefully consider the trade-off among the alternatives when manipulating the behavioral characteristics of compositional and linkage attributes.

The multilevel nature of MTS phenomena is another challenge in the manipulation and measurement of focal constructs of interest. Specifically, individuals are nested within component teams, which are then nested within the MTS. The nature of construct emergence is important both in designing the instruments to use in collecting the data (e.g., questionnaires and observation) and in deciding the manner in which items should be aggregated when the information is collected at a lower level but references a higher level. When dealing with multilevel phenomena, constructs can become emergent in one of two ways: compositional or compilational (Kozlowski & Klein, 2000). *Composition* describes constructs that are "essentially the same as they emerge upward across levels" (Kozlowski & Klein, 2000, p. 16), whereas *compilation* describes constructs that "comprise a common domain but are distinctly different as they emerge across levels" (p. 16). Whereas constructs that emerge through composition represent shared properties at the lower and higher levels, those that emerge through compilation represent qualitatively different patterns across levels. Further, the manner in which constructs emerge will vary based on the situation, and the nature of this emergence will have measurement implications (e.g., what dispersion index should be used when aggregating).

MTS laboratory researchers, therefore, face the challenge of creating manipulations and measures of constructs that exist at multiple levels. Many of the important affective, behavioral, and cognitive mediating mechanisms and leadership functions in an MTS exist at both the team level and system level. For example, leadership processes will be needed at both the team and system levels. Similarly, cognitive states such as mental model quality and motivational intentions will operate at individual, team, and system levels. This poses several problems to researchers. First, researchers need to design manipulations to isolate the construct at the target level of analysis. Second, researchers need to ensure that measures capture the resulting mediating and effectiveness criteria at specific levels of analysis.

One key strength of laboratory experimentation is the ability to exercise control over the setting and variables of interest to isolate cause-and-effect relationships. The complexity of phenomena operating within and across multiple levels of analysis necessitates that researchers collect large amounts of data to capture these phenomena. It is important to note that the experimental scenarios, manipulation of variables, and measures of constructs of interest should be defined a priori and clearly aligned with theoretically and practically meaningful research questions. If self-report data are collected from participants at multiple intervals during experimental sessions, this may interfere with the study's psychological fidelity and even impact responses to questionnaires (Stone-Romero, 2002). These concerns may be minimized by using unobtrusive measurements of behaviors and processes that can be derived from the simulation platform or the coding of behaviors from trained observers (either live or via session recordings).

Ongoing Laboratory Management

The ongoing demands of managing a research laboratory devoted to MTS research are not vastly different from those of managing an organizational science research laboratory in general. However, the scale of complexity is somewhat larger. In this section, we discuss factors associated with managing participant pools, experimenters, and the simulation platform.

The first laboratory management challenge that MTS researchers face is obtaining the sheer number of participants needed to fulfill designed roles in each experimental session. In addition, to obtain adequate statistical power, a large enough sample of experimental sessions will need to be conducted. Researchers need access to a substantial pool of participants that are able to commit multiple hours of their time across one or more sessions. The logistics of recruiting and scheduling multiple participants per experimental session across several weeks or even months requires dedicated personnel. Moreover, as convenience samples of undergraduate students are often used in laboratory-based studies, universities need to offer access to large enough numbers of students willing to participate in the research. Laboratory personnel need to establish systems to recruit, schedule, remind, and track participation. In addition to the sheer number of participants needed, the inherent complexity of the MTS structure, and most likely also the simulation platform, will require that participants receive detailed and easily learnable training. Though computer-based platforms may require more comprehensive training, they also provide a more engaging task.

As noted previously, MTS researchers need to collect abundant amounts of data to reflect the complex, multilevel MTS phenomena. To minimize the drawbacks of self-report measures, observer behavioral ratings provide a useful measurement approach. However, observer ratings do not come without challenges due to the complexity of handling within- and cross-team processes simultaneously. In addition, some processes and emergent states are not readily observable (Marks, Mathieu, & Zaccaro, 2001; Sackett & Larson, 1990). Therefore, great care must be taken to ensure objective coding by providing frame-of-reference training, and measures that minimize subjective interpretations, such as critical behavior checklists, Behaviorally Anchored Rating Scales, and frequency counts.

Another challenge associated with managing an MTS research lab is the recruitment and training of laboratory personnel to conduct sessions and ratings of the system. Due to the length of sessions and number of participants needed, each session will likely require multiple experimenters to be actively involved. Experimenters can have a profound effect on the results of a research study if their actions and even demeanor are not consistent across both people and time. Therefore, researchers need to provide detailed training and comprehensive protocols to ensure standardization of conditions.

Finally, if a computer-based simulation platform is used, researchers need to continuously monitor system performance to minimize the potential for unforeseen interruptions. However, problems can and do arise with various pieces of equipment. It is important to have adequate supplies of backup equipment that can be used in the event of a system error or malfunction. This creates added expense to ongoing laboratory management. In addition, computer-based platforms provide the advantage of collecting various types of unobtrusive data. Researchers need to continuously monitor these indices to ensure they are working properly. A well-designed and well-maintained simulation platform will collect copious amounts of data unobtrusively that may be easily distilled to provide important information regarding team and system processes at specific points in time or across critical incidents.

OPPORTUNITIES AND MITIGATING FACTORS

Statistical Conclusion Validity

For the novice MTS researcher, statistical conclusion validity is extremely easy to violate, yet it is also fairly easy to mitigate given some systematic preparation. As this type of validity applies to the researcher's ability to talk about covariation (or lack thereof) between two variables, it is primarily impacted by low statistical power, restriction of range, unreliability of treatment implementation, extraneous variables in the experimental setting, and statistical knowledge. Of these threats, perhaps the most difficult to combat against are small sample sizes, which may hide the true relationship between two variables due to a *lack of power*. Mechanisms to combat low sample size primarily include being creative and diligent. The researcher must be creative in identifying mechanisms that can make the study appear attractive and appealing to research participants. One method is to do some homework and determine what is valued by the particular targeted population. We have found that this may differ by population and even discipline. Diligence is also required both in seeking out places to advertise or announce your need for participants and in reminding participants to show up for their assigned time slot. In MTS research, a "no show" can have a huge impact.

On a related note, *sampling procedures* can also impact statistical conclusion validity. Researchers need to ensure that the sample of participants is a representative sample and not skewed in some way. In addition, researchers could develop hypotheses during the design phase about individual characteristics that could introduce error into the study. These characteristics can later be used as a covariate to remove their effects.

Internal Validity

Although internal validity is often touted as a key strength of laboratory research, there are numerous inherent threats to internal validity. In this chapter, the threats of selection, maturation, attrition, and testing were briefly described in relation to MTS research. Here we offer a few strategies that can help mitigate the degree to which each of the aforementioned threats exists within a particular study.

Selection bias can occur when individuals are not randomly assigned across the treatment conditions, resulting in individuals in one condition differing significantly from those in the comparison condition prior to any treatment being delivered. The easiest way to combat selection bias is through randomization. When individuals are properly randomized, any bias that does exist is distributed equally throughout the various conditions. When considering randomization in an MTS study, there are more levels on which individuals should be randomized; individuals should be randomly assigned to team, MTS, and condition. In some extreme cases, randomization may not mitigate existing individual differences that were present prior to assignment to condition and the application of the treatment. To mitigate this situation, it is advisable to brainstorm prior to study implementation possible ways in which participants might covary, and then build a measure of the proposed instances such that data can be collected and, if there is a problem, can be controlled statistically.

Maturation is another threat that may impact internal validity. Given the amount of effort and resources it takes to conduct a study on MTS-related phenomena, researchers want to get as much possible data out of each study. As a result, MTS studies are often a bit longer than prototypic team studies. However, longer studies increase the potential for maturation or attrition to occur. We therefore advise researchers not to create "marathon" experimental sessions. In addition, the degree to which the participant is engaged in the task will decrease the tendency of attrition. Anecdotal evidence suggests that engagement is one of the benefits of using commercial-off-the-shelf testbeds as platforms for MTS research despite the slight modification they might need to become good experimental platforms.

Testing is a threat to validity that acknowledges the fact that merely taking a test or taking a test multiple times can influence someone's reaction. This threat to validity can be mitigated through item response theory and using a Solomon Four Group design. Additionally, within MTS research, as well as the larger body of research on collectives, there has been a push to make questionnaires and other testing tools less obtrusive. For example, although situation awareness is a key variable in team and MTS research, it is most often measured by stopping the task and asking the person about his or her task-related situation awareness (e.g., Situation Awareness Global Assessment Technique [SAGAT]; Endsley, 2000). This measurement approach is undesirable due to the disruption to individual and corresponding component teams. Conversely, there has been a recent move to create experimental platforms where the questions can be embedded as part of the ongoing task flow so as not to disrupt participants (see Situation Authorable Behavior Research Environment [SABRE]; Leung, Diller, & Ferguson, 2005). MTS researchers can also benefit from designing simulation platforms that allow the researcher to collect unobtrusive, objective, non-questionnaire-based indicators of constructs such as coordination or information sharing.

Construct Validity

In the development of simulations, MTS researchers need to provide clear conceptual definitions of the level at which a particular construct emerges, the level(s) at which that construct affects criteria of interest, and the meaning of that construct. Clearly defining *construct properties* will help to provide a conceptual and operational definition of *constructs*. In terms of properties, Klein and Kozlowski (2000) defined three forms of unit-level constructs: (a) global properties, (b) shared properties, and (c) configural properties. Within an MTS, constructs with global, shared, and configural properties exit at team and system levels. Global properties exist independently of member characteristics and are a product of the unit as a whole. Shared properties are a product of the collective affective, behavioral, or cognitive experiences among unit members. Shared properties may be measured by aggregating individual responses to the unit level of interest, in which case construct validity depends on substantial agreement among unit members or by third-party evaluations of unit-level phenomena. Configural properties represent the constellation of member characteristics across the unit of interest. These constructs can then be operationalized in a number of ways, including summing individual values, averaging individual values, and calculating indices of variability, the minimum values, or maximum values among team members.

Levels of analysis will again need to be taken into consideration in the measurement of focal constructs. When constructs are measured by observers, it is critical to provide clear indication of the referent level of analysis to which observations should be made. For constructs that involve shared or configural properties, and the aggregation of responses from individual members following composition models will help to clarify the measurement of the array of multilevel constructs. Chan (1998) presented a typology of composition models that identified five approaches to composing multilevel constructs from individual responses. These five composition models—additive models, direct consensus models, referent-shift models, dispersion models, and process models—should provide practical guidance to MTS researchers.

External Validity

In conducting laboratory research, the ultimate goal is to have findings that will generalize to the targeted setting, people, and time. Although some have argued that complex phenomena cannot be studied in a laboratory environment, others have argued that "laboratory research should not be evaluated by determining the extent to which it mimics organizational settings. Instead, it should be evaluated according to the extent that it increases our understanding of the processes in work behavior" (Dobbins, Lane, & Steiner, 1988, p. 282). The psychological realism of the setting and the psychological and environmental fidelity of the simulation are important factors to consider in maximizing external validity. One technique that can be used to foster both psychological realism and fidelity in the laboratory is to conduct a task and coordination demand analysis of the constructs of interest. For example, in examining MTS-related questions, researchers could interview subject matter experts who have worked as part of a strategic alliance or a disaster response team. In doing so, the researcher would need to sample from each level of the MTS such that a complete picture emerges of the environmental demands as well as the attitudinal, behavioral, and cognitive processes and emergent states involved.

Next, researchers need to ensure that the simulation platform matches the correct level of fidelity needed for the question. Rehmann, Mitman, and Reynolds (1995) argued for perhaps the most widely used fidelity taxonomy. Specifically, three types of fidelity were identified: equipment, environment, and psychological. The question that one is interested in drives the need for which of the three types needs to be represented within laboratory studies. In studies of MTSs, the one that we are the least concerned with, at this point, is *equipment fidelity*, or "the degree to which the simulator duplicates the appearance and feel of the real system" (Beubien & Baker, 2004, p. i52). This degree of fidelity is most important when the focus is on training or investigating psychomotor skills that must translate back to the equipment on the job. The second type of fidelity, *environmental fidelity*, refers to the "extent to which the simulator duplicates the motion cues, visual cues, and other sensory information from the environment" (Beubien & Baker, 2004, p. i52). The last type of fidelity is *psychological fidelity*, which refers to the degree to which a trainee would engage in similar affective, behavioral, and cognitive processes and emergent states as they would outside the simulated environment. As most of the questions that are examined within the emerging area of MTSs pertain to affective, cognitive, or behavioral dimensions, this is the level of fidelity that must be replicated within the laboratory.

Researchers then have two options. First, a researcher could search for an existing simulation that will allow many of the basic characteristics to be modeled at the desired level of psychological realism and fidelity. In many instances, this is possible with some modification to the existing program. For example, researchers have modified both SimCity as well as World in Conflict for use as MTS experimental platforms. As a second option, a researcher could build a synthetic task that mimics the desired MTS attributes.

CONCLUDING THOUGHTS

Although MTSs are commonly found in settings as diverse as military task forces, community disaster response settings, and management consulting engagements (DeChurch & Mathieu, 2008; Mathieu et al., 2001), theory and research advancing the scientific understanding of MTSs have emerged only within the last decade. As a unique organizational form in the organizational sciences, the MTS construct remains in the earlier stages of construct evolution.

To examine the state of the MTS construct and theory, we use the three stages of construct evolution proposed by Reichers and Schneider (1990). They referred to the first stage, *introduction and elaboration*. During this stage, researchers propose a new construct or adapt one from another field. Researchers attempt to legitimize the new construct by presenting articles that conceptually define the construct, and discuss its use as an independent and/or dependent variable. The second stage, *evaluation and augmentation*, begins when initial empirical studies and critical reviews of the construct appear. During this stage, researchers present empirical findings that attempt to clarify the construct and its usefulness, and critically review the use of the construct, suggesting better measurement techniques, and moderating and mediating variables. The final stage, referred to as *consolidation and accommodation*, begins when controversies surrounding the construct begin to diminish, one or two definitions come to be generally accepted, and antecedents, consequences, and boundary conditions are well established. With the publication of several important empirical studies (e.g., Coen, 2006; DeChurch & Marks, 2006; Marks et al., 2005) and the chapters of this book critically examining MTSs as an organizational form, we suggest that the MTS construct has progressed to the early part of Stage 2—evaluation and augmentation.

Much theory-driven empirical research is still needed to firmly establish the utility of the MTS as a unique organizational form. As Kaplan (1964) noted, science and theory develop through the description, prediction, and explanation of the phenomena of interest. Despite all of the challenges associated with laboratory-based MTS research that we discussed in this chapter, well-designed and well-executed laboratory experiments will play an essential role in the continued evolution of the MTS construct. Although the challenges are great, laboratory-based experimental research is essential for enabling researchers to draw valid inferences that describe, predict, and explain the relationships among the system attributes, leadership demands, and affective, behavioral, and cognitive forces that are important for system success. Well-designed and well-executed theory-driven laboratory research will help to bring to light the causal evidence that adds theoretical and practical value to this important organizational form.

REFERENCES

Aronson, E., & Carlsmith, J. M. (1968). Experimentation in social psychology. In G. Lindzey & E. Aronson (Eds.), *The handbook of social psychology* (Vol. 2, pp. 99–142). New York: McGraw-Hill.

Aronson, E., Wilson, T. D., & Brewer, M. B. (1998). Experimentation in social psychology. In D. Gilbert, S. Fiske, & L. Gardner (Eds.), *The handbook of social psychology* (Vol. 4, pp. 99–142). New York: McGraw-Hill.

Berkowitz, L., & Donnerstein, E. (1982). External validity is more than skin deep: Some answers to criticisms of laboratory experiments. *American Psychologist, 37,* 245–257.

Beubien, J. M., & Baker, D. P. (2004). The use of simulation for training teamwork skills in health care: How low can you go? *Quality Safety in Healthcare, 13,* i51–i56.

Binning, J. F., & Barrett, G. V. (1989). Validity of personnel decisions: A conceptual analysis of the inferential and evidential bases. *Journal of Applied Psychology, 74*, 478–494.

Burke, C. S., Wooten, S., & Salas, E. (2009). *A critical review of platforms for use in MTS research.* Unpublished manuscript.

Cascio, W. F., & Aguinis, H. (2005). *Applied psychology in human resource management.* Upper Saddle River, NJ: Prentice Hall.

Chan, D. (1998). Functional relations among constructs in the same content domain at different levels of analysis: A typology of composition models. *Journal of Applied Psychology, 83*, 234–246.

Coen, C. A. (2006). Seeking the comparative advantage: The dynamics of individual cooperation in single vs. multi-team environments. *Organizational Behavior and Human Decision Processes, 100*, 145–159.

Colquitt, J. A. (2008). From the editors: Publishing laboratory research in AMJ—a question of when, not if. *Academy of Management Journal, 51*, 616–620.

Cook, T. D., & Campbell, L. P. (1979). *Quasi-experimentation: Design and analysis for field settings.* Boston: Houghton Mifflin.

Cronbach, L. J., & Meehl, P. E. (1955). Construct validity in psychological tests. *Psychological Bulletin, 52*, 281–302.

DeChurch, L. A., & Marks, M. A. (2006). Leadership in multiteam systems. *Journal of Applied Psychology, 91*, 311–329.

DeChurch, L. A., & Mathieu, J. E. (2008). Thinking in terms of multiteam systems. In E. Salas, G. F. Goodwin, & C. S. Burke (Eds.), *Team effectiveness in complex organizations* (pp. 267–292). New York: Psychology Press.

Dipboye, R. L., & Flanagan, M. F. (1979). Research settings in industrial and organizational psychology: Are findings in the field more generalizable than in the laboratory? *American Psychologist, 34*, 141–150.

Dobbins, G. H., Lane, I. M., & Steiner, D. D. (1988). A note on the role of laboratory methodologies in applied behavioural research: Don't throw out the baby with the bath water. *Journal of Organizational Behavior, 9*, 281–286.

Endsley, M. R. (2000). Direct measurement of situation awareness: Validity and use of SAGAT. In M. R. Endsley & D. J. Garland (Eds.), *Situation awareness analysis and measurement* (pp. 147–174). Mahwah, NJ: Erlbaum.

Kaplan, A. (1964). *The conduct of inquiry.* San Francisco: Chandler.

Klein, K. J., & Kozlowski, S. W. J. (2000). From micro to meso: Critical steps in conceptualizing and conducting multilevel research. *Organizational Research Methods, 3*, 211–236.

Kozlowski, S. W. J., & Ilgen, D. R. (2006). Enhancing the effectiveness of work groups and teams. *Psychological Science in the Public Interest, 7*, 77–124.

Kozlowski, S. W. J., & Klein, K. J. (2000). A multilevel approach to theory and research in organizations: Contextual, temporal, and emergent processes. In K. J. Klein & S. W. J. Kozlowski (Eds.), *Multilevel theory, research, and methods in organizations: Foundations, extensions, and new directions* (pp. 3–90). San Francisco: Jossey-Bass.

LePine, J. A., Piccolo, R. F., Jackson, C. L., Mathieu, J. E., & Saul, J. R. (2008). A meta-analysis of teamwork processes: Tests of a multidimensional model and relationships with team effectiveness criteria. *Personnel Psychology, 61*, 273–307.

Leung, A. M., Diller, D. E., & Ferguson, W. (2005, September 18–23). A game-based testbed for studying team behavior. Paper presented at the 2005 Fall Simulation Interoperability Workshop, Orlando, FL.

Locke, E. A. (1986). Generalizing from laboratory to field settings. In E. A. Locke (Ed.), *Generalizing from laboratory to field settings: Research findings from industrial-organizational psychology, organizational behavior, and human resource management*. Lexington, MA: Lexington.

Marks, M. A. (2000). A critical analysis of computer simulations for conducting team research. *Small Group Research, 31*, 653–674.

Marks, M. A., DeChurch, L. A., Mathieu, J. E., Panzer, F. J., & Alonso, A. (2005). Teamwork in multiteam systems. *Journal of Applied Psychology, 90*, 964–971.

Marks, M. A., Mathieu, J. E., & Zaccaro, S. J. (2001). A temporally based framework and taxonomy of team processes. *Academy of Management Review, 26*, 356–376.

Mathieu, J. E., Marks, M. A., & Zaccaro, S. J. (2001). Multiteam systems. In N. Anderson, D. S. Ones, H. K. Sinangil, & C. Viswesvaran (Eds.), *Organizational Psychology: Vol. 2. Handbook of industrial, work and organizational psychology* (pp. 289–313). London: Sage.

Mathieu, J. E., Maynard, M. T., Rapp, T., & Gilson, L. (2008). Team effectiveness 1997–2007: A review of recent advancements and a glimpse into the future. *Journal of Management, 34*, 410–476.

Orne, M. T. (1962). On the social psychology of the psychological experiment: With particular reference to demand characteristics and their implications. *American Psychologist, 17*, 776–783.

Orne, M. T. (1970). From the subject's point of view, when is behavior private and when is it public: Problems of inference. *Journal of Consulting and Clinical Psychology, 35*, 143–147.

Rehmann, A., Mitman, R., & Reynolds, M. A. (1995). *A handbook of flight simulation fidelity requirements for human factors research* (Technical Report No. DOT/FAA/CT-TN95/46). Wright-Patterson AFB, OH: Crew Systems Ergonomics Information Analysis Center.

Reichers, A. E., & Schneider, B. (1990). Climate and culture: An evolution of constructs. In B. Schneider (Ed.), *Organizational climate and culture* (pp. 5–39). San Francisco: Jossey-Bass.

Rosenthal, R., & Rosnow, R. (1991). *Essentials of behavioral research: Methods and data analysis*. Boston: McGraw-Hill.

Sackett, P. R., & Larson, J. R. (1990). Research strategies and tactics in industrial and organizational psychology. In M. Dunnette & L. Hough (Eds.), *Handbook of industrial & organizational psychology* (Vol. 1, pp. 419–489). Palo Alto, CA: Consulting Psychologists Press.

Shadish, W. R., Cook, T. D., & Campbell, D. T. (2002). *Experimental and quasi-experimental designs for generalized causal inference*. Boston: Houghton, Mifflin.

Stone-Romero, E. F. (2002). The relative validity and usefulness of various empirical research designs. In S. Rogelberg (Ed.), *Handbook of research methods in industrial and organizational psychology* (pp. 77–98). New York: Blackwell.

18

Reflections on the Evolution of the Multiteam Systems Concept and a Look to the Future

John E. Mathieu
University of Connecticut

REFLECTIONS

It was roughly a decade or so ago, and my colleagues Michelle Marks and Steve Zaccaro and I were struck by a phenomenon that we continued to witness. Those were the heydays of the transformation from more traditionally designed organizations to team-based approaches. Organizations were delayering, right sizing, and so forth; globalization was seriously taking root; mergers and alliance arrangements were being leveraged; and the digital revolution was upon us. Internally, organizations were moving away from traditional top-down management philosophies and advocating empowerment, self-management, shared leadership, and team-based designs. The research frontier was paralleling this movement with team-focused research flourishing and moving away from sterile laboratory-based work and into the field.

It was an exciting time, and teams were the new wave. But, of course, teams were not a panacea, and they were implemented in many instances that were not appropriate. Naturally, many "team failures" ensued, and I was particularly taken aback when working with one organization where it was explained to me, "Team is a four-letter word around here!" But what Michelle, Steve, and I were struck by was not the inevitable backlash from the overzealous introductions of teams—what we were struck by were the unintended consequences and new problems that seemed to emerge, even in instances that were prime candidates for the application of teams. For example, shifting from top-down and centralized control to empowered teams, each conducting their work in a manner and time frame that best suited their needs, suddenly wreaked havoc with just-in-time delivery systems. Team-based incentives and rewards motivated people to maximize their personal benefits, not only by promoting their own team's functioning but also by undermining the operations of other teams. As teams became more focused and specialized, and operated on quickened yet varying schedules, coordinating activities across teams became harder and harder. As team selection, training, and motivation systems advanced, these cross-team coordination problems were only exacerbated. Add to the mix the fact that organizations were partnering more and reaching across the globe, often through digital technologies, and the silos surrounding individualized teams were hardening and problems involving cross-team functioning were becoming quite prevalent.

Whether it was friendly fire incidents such as the downing of Black Hawk helicopters by allied forces, or serious incidents in nuclear power plants during refueling when various contractors failed to coordinate their efforts, or building delays attributable to plumbers and electricians vying for the same spaces in a structure, performance problems and safety threats were frequently occurring in the "cracks" between teams. Team members were highly qualified and trained, had clear goals, were motivated, and worked well together. But problems kept occurring, and the consequences were often devastating—and it was not always clear who was responsible. In short, we saw the emergence of a new unit of inquiry and analysis, where teams-of-teams needed to coordinate their efforts to achieve one or more goals that were beyond the individual teams. We noticed that sometimes the teams in the system came from a single organization, but in many instances the system involved teams from different organizations, public and private, civilian and military, volunteer and paid, competitors and collaborators, foreign and nationals, and other nontraditional pairings. In many respects, these entities operated similar to "big teams," and in other respects, they were more like traditional organizations; but in all cases, they were a bit different and defied conventional logic and labels. We coined the term *multiteam systems* (MTSs) to refer to these entities, attempting to distinguish them from other forms of organizations and to describe their unique properties.

Although it was clear to us that a new form of collective was emerging in the field, defining exactly what "it" was proved elusive. Clearly, in our minds, the constituent entities were teams—what we came to refer to as *component teams*. Yet, developing rules for inclusion and exclusion of the boundaries of an MTS proved to be challenging. As astutely recognized by Poole and Contractor (Chapter 8, this volume), what we had in mind was a tightly coupled set of teams who needed to work together. But why did they need to work together? From where did they come? And what decision rules were there for determining whether a component team was part of the MTS or its environment? As noted by many of the authors in this volume, we defined an MTS as follows:

> [T]wo or more teams that interface directly and interdependently in response to environmental contingencies toward the accomplishment of collective goals. MTS boundaries are defined by virtue of the fact that all teams within the system, while pursuing different proximal goals, share at least one common distal goal; and in doing so exhibit input, process, and outcome interdependence with at least one other team in the system. (Mathieu, Marks, & Zaccaro, 2001, p. 290)

This definition was our attempt to sculpt the nature of MTS boundaries while not limiting the wide variety of MTSs that may exist. It was a functionally grounded definition in the sense that we relied on the existence of a superordinate goal as the answer to "why" the teams came and worked together. We highlighted the superordinate nature of this goal to acknowledge that teams may be performing quite similar activities (what Hinsz & Betts, Chapter 11, this volume, referred to as "teams-of-teams") or might be performing markedly different activities directed toward proximal goals, which collectively contribute to the achievement of the superordinate goal through a goal hierarchy (what Hinsz & Betts, Chapter 11, this volume, referred to as "MTS arrangements"). Now, a decade or more later, as many have grappled with the MTS concept, this notion of a superordinate goal as a defining characteristic of MTSs has been reified. In short, achieving the superordinate goal(s) is the reason that MTSs exist and a core feature of them.

Back in 2001 (Mathieu et al., 2001), as well as in Marks, DeChurch, Mathieu, Panzer, and Alonso (2005) and in Zaccaro, Marks, and DeChurch (Chapter 1, this volume), we have made the point that MTSs are not simply large teams. Their component teams are distinguishable entities capable of independent actions that may pursue different proximal goals. In other words, the relative interdependence of team members is *higher within component teams than between component teams* comprising an MTS, but there is a second layer of interdependence linking the teams within an MTS. Although the component teams are distinguishable entities, what defines the boundary for inclusion as an MTS is the fact that they share input, process, and outcome interdependence with at least another team in the MTS. It is the existence of the superordinate goal and the nature of team interdependencies that define MTS membership, not organizational boundaries. Component teams may be performing quite different operations, but their efforts are tied together by a goal hierarchy and the nature and variety of dependencies between them.

The interdependence portion of this definition was our attempt to operationalize a "tightly coupled" network of teams. In this sense, we faced the same dilemma as network researchers and scholars, in that drawing a line between entities or nodes that are in the network versus those outside of the network is somewhat arbitrary and a matter of choice. Any given node may have as many salient ties outside of the MTS as it does within the MTS network. Yet permitting all of those ties would lead to an infinite expansion of the MTS to the point where it is no longer meaningful to discuss. For sure, the functioning of MTS component teams are influenced both by aspects of the MTS, but also by the myriad of other ties that each component team has outside of the MTS. The nature of the component teams, along with the configuration of their network ties inside and outside of the MTS, is what defines differences among types of MTSs.

With the benefit of hindsight, it is debatable whether component teams must have all three forms of input, process, and outcome interdependence to be included in an MTS, or what the thresholds for those judgments might exactly be. I certainly believe that if all three forms of interdependence do exist to moderate or high degrees, an MTS exists. But there may be other ways to define *tightly coupled* besides this operationalization. What is clear, however, is that component teams must be tightly coupled on some basis in order to constitute an MTS. Looking forward, it is incumbent on future theorists and researchers to articulate, quite specifically, how they operationalize *tightly coupled* and thereby rules for inclusion and exclusion in an MTS. This will aid in the identification of MTSs and what distinguishes them from other forms of collectives, and permit the accumulation of knowledge. However, given the diversity of modern-day organizational forms, this "unit" problem is not at all unique to MTSs and must be addressed by all organizational theorists and researchers. For example, over 30 years ago Freeman (1980) submitted that

> the choice of unit is more problematic today than before because of the rise of open-systems approaches and because of the growing interest in longitudinal research. If we see boundaries as permeable to varying degrees, then we have more or less of a unit. And if the permeability of boundaries varies over time, we face the real possibility that a unit definition that seems useful at the beginning of a study will be inappropriate if not entirely misleading tomorrow. (P. 60)

These statements ring just as true today, and especially for MTSs which are complex open systems. Commenting on the unit problem in the context of multilevel management research, Mathieu and Chen (2011) argued that

> few management scholars endeavor to define why a particular collective is a salient grouping entity or to provide clear rules for inclusion and exclusion of membership. In short, despite their critical importance, complex issues surrounding the designation of the focal unit of an investigation are often minimized in current multi-level research. (P. 6)

Clearly, it is important to identify the boundaries of MTSs, just as it is important to define the boundaries of any unit of inquiry. Envisioned as networks of teams bound together for one or more superordinate purposes, MTSs do, in fact, represent distinguishable entities apart from teams or organizations. Pushed further, I envision each of the component teams (and their members) as potentially simultaneous members of multiple MTSs and other forms of collectives, and that the multiplicity of their ties will drive their team functioning (see O'Leary, Woolley, & Mortensen, Chapter 6, this volume). Accordingly, these network tie configurations will generate a host of factors that serve as *centrifugal forces* acting to pull MTS component teams apart, or alternatively as *bonding agents* helping to hold them together. I submit that developing a better understanding of these centrifugal forces and bonding agents represents one of the primary challenges involved in advancing a theory and science of MTSs, as well as effectively managing them.

LOOKING FORWARD

For this chapter, I will adopt the excellent template articulated by Zaccaro et al. in Chapter 1 of this volume and discuss MTS issues in terms of (a) compositional attributes, (b) linkage attributes, and (c) developmental attributes. I will also consider advances in ways to study and research MTSs. In so doing, I will refer to points raised in the preceding chapters, but I will not attempt to summarize the wealth of information and insights the authors of this volume have provided. Rather, I will try to illustrate how their work has influenced the evolution of the MTS concept and provided unique insights. I will close with some suggestions for future work in this area.

An Example

Before highlighting some of the issues that were raised in this volume, I wish to provide one quick example of a different MTS. When discussing MTSs, there seems to be a natural pull toward consideration of relatively large high-profile ones such as those involved in responding to Hurricane Katrina (DeChurch & Mathieu, 2006), humanitarian relief and reconstruction operations (Dziedzic & Seidl, 2005), operational control centers (Goodwin, Essens, & Smith, Chapter 3, this volume), piracy of the *Maersk Alabama* (Rentsch & Staniewicz, Chapter 9, this volume), and so forth (see DeChurch et al., in press). Although unquestionably applicable to MTS operations, these examples sometimes become too complex and unwieldy to make sharp points about the functioning of MTSs. Below, I provide a more confined example that may help to illustrate some of the points that follow.

A Local High School Development MTS

It was early in the 2000s, and a small New England town had seen substantial population growth of almost 20% over the past decade. The town high school was seriously overcrowded and in disrepair. An advantageous state bonding opportunity was available with matching funds yet had a fairly short time frame for eligibility. The question was "Should the town call for a vote on a bonding referendum to build a new high school?"

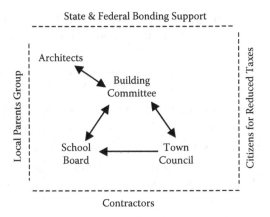

FIGURE 18.1
Functional interdependencies in the high school MTS.

To answer the question, the town needed to have a budget estimate for the school, which in turn required a detailed set of plans, cost analyses, and so forth. Although the town population was united in the superordinate goal of having a first-class educational system, there was a variety of other forces at play. Perhaps most notably, the town had recently experienced a large influx of affluent families with children that were putting a huge strain on the school system. These families, by and large, also applied political pressure to upscale the school facilities, which would necessitate huge tax increases. Long-time town residents were witnessing a change in the complexion of their hometown and facing tax increases the likes of which had never been seen before. Their preference was to enact short-term measures by using portable classrooms or expanding current school facilities. In short, there was a salient fault line in the town, and emotions ran high.

As shown in Figure 8.1, an MTS was formed to deal with the question of whether the town should vote on a bonding resolution for building the school, and if so, for how much. The town council was responsible for the town budget and was composed of elected officials who were attempting to balance the desires of the two subcultures. The town council itself was split across these constituencies with a one-person majority. The town council established a building committee to orchestrate the high school issue. This building committee became a highly centralized node in this MTS network and had to work closely with architects; the school board, which proscribed pedagogical facility requirements; the town council; and a host of external influences. Dueling political action committees were formed in the town. One was composed of people who sought to build a state-of-the-art facility that naturally drove up costs. The other group was opposed to increased taxes, and did everything in its power to derail the project. On one hand, the final budget proposal for the referendum needed to be sufficiently high to appease the former group and build a facility that would meet their desires. On the other hand, the final budget needed to be sufficiently low so that the latter group would not grow and vote down the proposal. All the while, the deadline for securing matching state funds was rapidly approaching.

At issue in this MTS is that the interdependencies were only somewhat functional in nature. As the school board suggested different options, such as laboratories or computer labs, they necessitated changes in the architectural plans, budget estimates, and so forth. However, the political ties dominated this MTS, motivations were mixed or sometimes contradictory, and individuals' identities were often torn. Again, the superordinate goal of providing high-quality education for the town's children was accepted by all. But what that meant in terms of this initiative, and the balancing acts with other concerns, was anything but agreed upon. In the end, a compromise budget and design were put before the voters, and in a town of over 13,000 with greater than 50% voter turnout, the bonding referendum passed by less than 250 votes. The MTS had succeeded in coming up with a building design and budget that met the superordinate goal while balancing a host of competing associated demands.

COMPOSITIONAL ATTRIBUTES

Zaccaro et al. (Chapter 1, this volume) and others in this volume describe the boundary status of MTS component teams in terms of *organizational representation* (Davidson & Hollenbeck, Chapter 12, this volume; Keyton, Ford, & Smith, Chapter 7, this volume; Marks & Luvison, Chapter 2, this volume), *functional heterogeneity* (Hinsz & Betts, Chapter 11, this volume; Poole & Contractor, Chapter 8, this volume), *geographic locations* (Gibson & Cohen, 2003), *cultural diversity* (Kirkman & Shapiro, 2005), *motive structures* (Connaughton, Williams,

& Shuffler, Chapter 5, this volume; Kanfer & Kerry, Chapter 4, this volume), and *temporal orientations* (Standifer, Chapter 14, this volume; Uitdewilligen & Waller, Chapter 4, this volume). Individually and in combination, these factors serve as centrifugal or bonding influences. Hinsz and Betts (Chapter 11, this volume) make the important point that, all else being equal, people are inclined to be cooperative within their group (i.e., component teams) while seeing other groups in a competitive light. So as a default, we can see that there are forces aligned against synergy in MTSs. To what extent do the factors listed above act to exacerbate or offset these defaults?

Organizational representation will likely play a powerful role, as I would surmise that homogeneous MTSs, where all component teams reside in the same organization, can more easily find common ground and coordinate their activities than can heterogeneous MTSs. In fact, it is not at all uncommon for there to be animosity between the parties from different organizations, whether that might be military branches, fire stations (see DeChurch & Mathieu, 2009), or organizations working on alliances (Marks & Luvison, Chapter 2, this volume). In the case of the high school MTS, component teams represented diverse groups with opposing views, and many of the teams themselves had mixed organizational representation. These factors did much to undermine their collective efforts.

Functionally homogeneous MTSs are likely to have enhanced cross-team synergy, unless their *motive structures* place them at odds with one another. In other words, to the extent that the component teams in an MTS are functionally similar (i.e., the teams-of-teams notion that Hinsz & Betts, Chapter 11, this volume, advanced), they will better understand one another, operate on similar temporal rhythms, know how to coordinate with one another, and so forth. If their reward structure reinforces cooperative cross-team relationships and the achievement of superordinate goals (e.g., overall mission success and profit sharing), then we can anticipate that they would work well together. Alternatively, if their reward structures place a premium on component team success (i.e., group-based rewards), then we would anticipate that they will view one another as close competitors and not help each other.

Functionally heterogeneous component teams are ripe for misunderstandings and breakdowns. Their differences will signal ingroup and outgroup distinctions, and temporal variations will reinforce their dissimilarities. For example, several of the politicians in the high school MTS got quickly agitated as they could not understand how minor changes in the proposed school structure necessitated delays and drastic design and cost adjustments. Their failure to understand engineering concepts led them to attributions that other groups were intentionally holding up the process. This also echoes an important temporal issue, in that cross-team collaboration and understanding will be strained to the extent that component teams operate under different temporal rhythms (Standifer, Chapter 14, this volume). The town council in the high school MTS example was focused on holding the bonding referendum within the next few weeks or months in order to secure matching funding, whereas the architects and school board were projecting out the needs and demands of an educational facility 20–40 years in the future. It's not surprising that each saw the other as naïve about temporal demands.

Generally, *geographic dispersion* would be viewed as a centrifugal force undermining MTS synergy. Yet it really depends on the nature of the MTS activities, *mediating technologies*, and the *temporal relations* among and between component teams. Normally, one would presume that co-located teams are likely to coordinate their efforts better than separated ones. Certainly, this would be the case in instances of reciprocal or intensive interdependence when teams need to mutually adjust and coordinate their actions in real time. However, in other instances this may not be the case. Consider the fact that many information technology (IT) and business solutions organizations align their component teams around the globe and pass off work packets across time zones (Zaheer, 2000). In other words, Team A may work on a project for 8 hours and then pass it off to Team B in another hemisphere. In turn, Team B may progress the project and pass it off later to Team C, who works on it and then hands it back off to Team A, who begins their work on a second day. In this sense, using various mediating technologies and a sequential form of interdependence, the MTS capitalizes on temporal differences and is far more efficient than it would be if teams were required to be co-located or even work at the same time.

In this brief review, we can see that the diversity of component teams, whether in terms of the home organizations, locations, functions, motives, cultures, time orientations, and no doubt a myriad of other factors, creates centrifugal forces that will undermine MTS synergies and effectiveness. In effect, these factors lead to mixed motives, multiple identities, and role confusion and conflicts for MTS members. Yet, paradoxically, those same diversities may be precisely what enable an MTS to successfully achieve its superordinate goals. Given the complexity of the challenges that MTSs are typically constituted to confront, the diversity of functions, organizational representations, temporal orientation, and so on represents the requisite human capital needed to succeed (Goodwin et al., Chapter 3, this volume). The challenge for effective MTS management, then, is to recognize what types of diversities are important for the MTS to succeed, and to compose it accordingly. On one hand, adding more diversity than is required will likely generate unnecessary process loss. On the other hand, overly homogeneous MTSs may not have the requisite human capital to successfully achieve their superordinate goals. In any event, to the extent that an MTS is composed of heterogeneous component teams, there will be a premium placed on their linkage attributes.

LINKAGE ATTRIBUTES

Zaccaro et al. (Chapter 1, this volume) identified the following as MTS linkage attributes: (a) interdependence, (b) hierarchical arrangements and power distribution, (c) communication modalities, and (d) communication networks. In short, linkage attributes describe the manner in which MTS work gets performed. Given the variety of centrifugal forces operating to drive MTS component teams apart, linkage attributes represent structural and process means of bringing them together and integrating efforts.

In their original chapter, Mathieu et al. (2001) suggested that (a) information technologies, (b) reward systems, (c) leadership, and (d) shared mental models (SMMs) could each aid in the coordination of MTS component teams. Generally speaking, IT, reward systems, interdependence, hierarchical and power arrangements, and communication modalities all represent *structural linkage mechanisms*, whereas SMMs and leadership represent *process linkage mechanisms*. However, I hasten to add that such distinctions are somewhat arbitrary, as, for instance, teams and MTSs may choose to use (or not) certain communication modalities (cf. Kirkman & Mathieu, 2005), and they may decide to operate in a highly differentiated versus interdependent manner (cf. Mathieu, Maynard, Rapp, & Gilson, 2008), among other choices. So the line between structural and process mechanisms is not that sharp.

Structural Linkage Mechanisms

Clearly, one of the key bonding agents for MTSs is the extent to which all members, and component teams, recognize and work toward a common superordinate goal. Whether component teams are highly similar or vastly different, to the extent that each is motivated to accomplish the same superordinate goal, it will be easier to coordinate their efforts. Superordinate goal achievement serves to align motives, provide a common identity, help to prioritize actions, and otherwise chart out common ground. The superordinate goal is one of the key defining aspects of MTSs and is their raison d'être. Although goals such as saving lives and protecting property clearly specify priorities for emergency response MTSs such as firefighters (DeChurch & Mathieu, 2009), disagreements as to whether to even build a new high school—and, if so, how elaborate it should be—generated numerous breakdowns in the high school MTS.

Beyond the superordinate goal, MTS structural features can enhance or deter linkages across teams. Davison and Hollenbeck (Chapter 12, this volume) evoked the behavioral integration framework and Thompson's (1967) concepts of technical core, institutional and managerial levels, mutual adjustment, and various forms of functional interdependence. This framework provides a useful means for examining the structural features of MTSs. Davison and Hollenbeck (Chapter 12, this volume) submit that the degree and nature of interdependence of MTS component teams place a premium on their boundary-spanning activities. Indeed, the degree and nature of team interdependencies were key defining features of our original conception of MTSs (Mathieu et al., 2001), and are also featured in the network perspective advanced by Poole and Contractor (Chapter 8, this volume).

As detailed by Davison and Hollenbeck (Chapter 12, this volume), Bossard's law of family interaction makes clear that the multitude of potential member-to-member interactions is daunting, even in relatively small MTSs. Some degree of differentiation will permit MTSs to capitalize on the diversity of human capital in the system, while also placing a high value on the mechanisms that integrate various efforts across component teams. IT systems, structural arrangements, power differentials, reward systems, and communication modalities can all serve to enhance cross-team communication and collaboration activities as proscribed by their interdependencies. The key is to create a structure that balances the degree to which communication channels are aligned with the nature of the task demands. For example, given the law of family interaction, it is clear that chaos will ensue if all members of an MTS can directly communicate with all other members. Equally clear, however, is that an MTS will come to a screeching halt if all communication is routed through some centralized mechanism, whether that is an IT knowledge portal or some high-ranking leader. To the extent that IT systems and communication modalities facilitate cross-team communication and collaborations, MTS synergy should be enhanced (Keyton et al., Chapter 7, this volume; Mathieu et al., 2001). When an MTS is designed such that the structural hierarchy and power are aligned with the most centralized nodes or component teams in the system (in terms of functional interdependence), cross-team collaboration should be facilitated. Moreover, to the extent that members and component teams are rewarded, formally and informally, for achieving the superordinate goal, it will reinforce its achievement (Mathieu et al., 2001). Of course, no set of structural features can guarantee MTS success, but it is equally certain that some structural arrangements are more advantageous than others for facilitating cross-team interdependent actions and accomplishing superordinate goals.

So what is the ideal structure? To answer the question, I first submit that few, if any, MTSs will exhibit a uniform structure. That is, there are likely to be portions of the system that are structured differently than others. In network terms, there may be cliques, structural holes, and other features. A *network clique* is a subset of a network in which the entities (in this case, some component teams) are more closely and intensely tied to one another than they are to other teams in the network. *Structural holes* refer to the gaps between these subsets or cliques in the overall network. I suspect that the overall MTS network structure should exhibit *requisite variety* (Goodwin et al., Chapter 3, this volume) and needs to parallel the nature and diversity of the task demands in the environment. I would expect to see the development of subsets, or cliques, where the communication channels between members of especially tightly coupled component teams are multifold and well established. This would necessitate bridging teams that span structural holes and serve to integrate different regions of the overall MTS network.

In short, this kind of MTS component team alignment will create pockets of activities and minimize the confusion stemming from the law of family interaction. Equally important, however, is that there will be a need to facilitate cross-team communication and coordination as teams or cliques need to synthesize their efforts toward the accomplishment or higher order goals in a goal hierarchy. In this way, a balance between within- and between-clique communications can be established. I want to emphasize, however, that this cross-clique communication need not always flow in a hierarchical fashion. Successful MTS operations often hinge on the coordination of low-ranking individuals dealing directly with one another and orchestrating mutual adjustments in real time. High-quality customer service often occurs where an employee ignores the formal structure and puts a buyer in direct contact with "the right person" elsewhere in the system who can actually help her. The back channel compromises and adjustments are what enabled the high school MTS to complete its task.

At issue is that I believe an MTS structure needs to support the development of an MTS-level transactive memory system (TMS; see Lewis, 2004). TMSs describe situations where members can confidently know where they can obtain valuable information and apply it to the task at hand. In this case, I would extend the TMS notion beyond merely the leveraging of information to also include the leveraging of action. In other words, the idea is to capitalize on specialization such that different component teams (or perhaps cliques of teams) are responsible for handling different portions of the MTS task. What is key, however, is that everyone in the MTS has a clear understanding of which teams are responsible for which portions, they have confidence that those teams will in fact deliver when called upon, and that work can be coordinated across teams when necessary. To the extent that the MTS structural linkage attributes such as IT, reward systems, interdependence arrangements, hierarchical and power arrangements, and communication modalities support the development and maintenance of an MTS-level TMS, it is more likely to be effective.

Process Linkage Mechanisms

No structural arrangements, no matter how well conceived, implemented, and maintained, can solve all of the cross-team coordination challenges in MTSs. Accordingly, process-linking mechanisms need to support the collective action of MTSs. Whereas there is a wide variety of such mechanisms, I will highlight two below: (a) shared mental models, and (b) leadership.

Mathieu et al. (2001) and Rentsch and Staniewicz (Chapter 9, this volume) highlighted the importance of MTS members sharing common mental models, or what Rentsch and Staniewicz referred to as "cognitive similarity." They defined *cognitive similarity* as "forms of related meanings or understandings attributed to and utilized to make sense of and interpret internal and external events including affect, behavior, and thoughts of self and others" (Rentsch, Small, & Hanges, 2008, p. 130). Cannon-Bowers, Salas, and Converse (1993), among others, argued that there are probably multiple mental models that must be shared among team members. These would include models of the task or technology, teamwork, how their teammates operate, and so forth. However, I submit that the importance of cognitive similarity differs in terms of *what* it is that is being shared, with *whom*, and *when*.

Previous research has shown that to the extent that members have a shared understanding of the task they are performing and how they will work as a team, their collective performance is enhanced (Mohammed, Ferzandi, & Hamilton, 2010). I would anticipate that these phenomena will continue to operate within MTS component teams, and perhaps across component teams that are especially tightly coupled within the system, such as members of a clique. In other words, shared task and team mental models among component team members, and among members of tightly coupled teams in a clique, should enhance their team and clique performance accordingly. However, for the entire MTS to succeed, all members should share a common vision of the overall purpose of the system. In other words, MTS success depends on establishing a shared *strategic* mental model that represents accomplishment of the superordinate goal(s). To the extent that members of different component teams, especially those vulnerable to centrifugal forces and structural holes, have a common understanding of the overall purpose and goals of the MTS, they should be better able to orchestrate cross-team coordination. This shared vision is a primary driver of the coordination of MTS component teams. In contrast, the lack of a shared understanding contributed to many of the breakdowns and frustrations seen in the high school MTS example.

Leadership is commonly evoked as a critical integrating mechanism for MTS success (e.g., DeChurch & Marks, 2006; Zaccaro & DeChurch, Chapter 10, this volume). Zaccaro and DeChurch (Chapter 10, this volume) argued that leadership processes in MTSs fall along four primary lines: (a) facilitating the coordination of activities across subsystems (or cliques) within the MTS; (b) monitoring and managing relationships across the MTS's environment boundary; (c) helping the MTS to anticipate and react to changing environmental contingencies; and (d) compensating for the fact that MTS members and component teams suffer distractions and conflicting demands stemming from their mutual memberships in other jobs, teams, and organizations (cf., O'Leary et al., Chapter 6, this volume). In short, Zaccaro et al. (Chapter 1, this volume) argued that leading MTSs is more challenging than leading traditional systems because of their complexity, fluid environments, time pressures, and multiple organizational representations.

I would echo these sentiments and simply add that MTS leadership is, indeed, better conceived of as a systemwide process rather than the actions of some high-level individual leader. In this sense, I am advocating a particular type of shared leadership system. At lower levels in an MTS, typical leadership designs are likely to be applicable within component teams (see Burke et al., 2006). Given the complexity of MTS environments, I would anticipate that some form of shared leadership design would be suitable for leading component teams, and perhaps cliques of teams (Millikin, Homa, & Manz, 2010; Pearce & Conger, 2003). More challenging is the leadership system that integrates the MTS and aligns various team efforts.

Notably, unlike teams embedded in a typical organizational design, there is often a very salient question as to who, in fact, has the leadership responsibility in many MTSs. In many instances, individuals or component teams in an MTS may be led by someone from a different organization, or receive mixed signals from different leaders. Many of the historic large-scale and highly visible MTS failures have been attributed to breakdowns in leadership, not only at one level but also across levels in the system (DeChurch et al., in press). In several of these instances it was not at all clear, to MTS members during the event, or even to historians after the fact, who was in charge during the event. In other words, given the array of centrifugal forces in many MTSs, particularly in terms of diverse organizational representation, who occupies the leadership roles at any given time is ambiguous and sometimes a contentious issue. This results in numerous MTS coordination problems and conflicts during their engagements, and much finger pointing following negative outcomes. To the extent that the MTS structure and power arrangements are clear, the lines of authority and responsibility should help to specify who are in leadership positions at any given time. But, given the complexity of MTS environments and pace of activities, as in *the fog of war*, confusion often reigns and emergent leadership is often called for. In some instances, the succession of leadership is predetermined and well entrenched in the culture (e.g., in military and paramilitary MTSs). In other instances, performance pressures lead to a contest for leadership and associated breakdowns and conflicts—or, worse yet, an abdication of leadership and a failure of the system (DeChurch et al., in press; DeChurch & Mathieu, 2009).

In sum, effective MTS leadership represents a combination of leadership forms. Millikin et al. (2010) recently illustrated the advantages of shared leadership designs for component teams. At higher levels in the MTS, different forms of leadership are likely to be called for as suggested by stratified system theory (Jaques, 1996). Top-level MTS management is primarily focused on strategy and coordinating functions that impact the entire MTS. They help to sculpt emergent states such as shared cognitions, identities, and motivation directed toward superordinate goal obtainment. These leaders act to fill structural holes and emphasize behavioral interaction processes across teams and cliques in the system. In so doing, they are influential in sculpting MTS linkage processes and thereby driving system effectiveness.

DEVELOPMENTAL ATTRIBUTES

MTSs are not static entities. They are constituted, evolve, and many times disband over time. Zaccaro et al. (Chapter 1, this volume) identified the genesis, direction of development, and transformation of system components (i.e., members and/or component teams) as critical maturation elements of MTSs. It may be useful to consider four different types of MTSs that underscore some of these salient temporal differences: (a) one-time entities, (b) long-term entities with fixed membership, (c) evolving MTSs with transformational composition, and (d) standing MTS networks. Below, I comment on these types and their import for the study and management of MTSs.

One-Time MTSs

One-time MTSs are similar to task forces, in that they are constituted to address a specific need and will be disbanded afterward with no expectation that they will be reconvened. My high school MTS is a prime example of this type. The component teams were selected on the basis of the needs of the particular circumstance, and once the decision was made to issue the school bond, their work—as an MTS—was completed. Although some elements of the MTS would, of course, work together again on other town matters, that particular configuration would not likely be brought together again.

In one-time designs, there is a premium on which teams are chosen to participate in the MTS and what their histories of working together are. Some teams will be on the MTSs to accomplish tasks, whereas other might be there as representatives of related constituents. The superordinate goal should be obvious in these instances, but as we saw in the high school MTS example, it may require reification if there are mixed motives or perspectives. Some of the component teams may have histories of working together (both good and bad), whereas some may be new to the mix. The focus of these MTSs is to sculpt a shared vision and commitment to the superordinate goal(s), and to align team efforts toward that end. Realistically, although it is always advantageous to build goodwill among component teams, attention can really be focused on goal accomplishment as these teams are not likely to work together in the future.

Long-Term Entities With Fixed Membership

Several MTSs represent fairly stable entities whereby the component teams, and even their memberships, remain intact over fairly long periods. Nuclear power plants, oil-drilling platforms, civil-planning efforts, and the like represent MTS operations where the participating teams and members remain fairly stable over time. In these instances, the MTS can operate with all the advantages and disadvantages of traditional organizations, even when their membership is heterogeneous. Shared vision, identity, motivations, and the like are well established over time, as are work routines and structures. Accordingly, maintenance or viability of the MTS itself is an important indicator of system effectiveness.

A slight variation within this type of MTS is where the team composition remains fixed but the membership is more fluid. For example, whereas the members participating in the civil-planning efforts are likely to be the same from one project to another, the membership of component teams in nuclear power plants and oil drilling plants is fluid. These 24-hour operations will have the same component teams in action over time, but who exactly staffs those teams will vary. In these situations, MTS coordination processes, such as shared cognitions, are focused on the nature of between-team interactions, no matter who is staffing the team in question. So, for example, the focus is on how radiological control, maintenance, and the control room teams interface with each other regardless of who is on duty. In safe air traffic MTSs, local and ground controllers, aircrews, baggage crews, and alike all have tightly orchestrated interdependencies. Teams represent a variety of different organizations, but are united toward the superordinate goals of safe and efficient passenger air travel. Structures, power relationships, entrainment processes, and so forth are well established and enduring over time.

Evolving MTSs With Transformational Composition

It is challenging to draw the boundaries around an MTS at any given point in time. It is even more challenging when one projects operations over time. This type of MTS has an important temporal lens, in that the MTS configuration changes as a function where the foci of work are. For example, Army aviation strike force MTSs are composed of a set of helicopters, each with its aircrew, who have the primary responsibility for destroying a target. Naturally the strike force itself has the qualities of an MTS. However, if extended back in time, one sees that the MTS operation has involved a series of MTS-type operations. Long before the mission commenced, maintenance, fueling, and ordnance teams combined their efforts to prepare the aircraft. Intelligence and planning functions involved numerous different teams, from ground forces to generals, integrating information and briefing the mission. Various front-area refueling platforms (FARPs) need to be established, secured, maintained, and operated in order to get the strike force to the target area. In and around the target area, allied forces work to jam enemy radar, provide protection, and offer information updates.

In one sense, the entire operation could be viewed as one very large, complex MTS. In another sense, this might be conceived of as a series of overlapping and interlocking MTSs that "hand off" a work package from one stage to another. I prefer this latter interpretation, and would argue that the planning and preparation activities constitute one MTS, operations surrounding refueling efforts represent a second MTS, and operations near the target area represent a third MTS. In essence, I am arguing that MTSs should have a temporal feature as part of their identification. Whether one conceives of this as one evolving MTS or a series of interlocking MTSs is probably arbitrary and matters little. What does matter is how interconnected different teams are at different stages, and how well they orchestrate their collective activities. In this case, the strike package is being handed off from one phase to another. How well this is done represents the superordinate goal for that phase, and also defines the component teams involved. Naturally the operations of later phases depend, in part, on how well earlier ones were accomplished. But I feel that it is valuable to identify coherent units of work, and to parse the overall operations into more manageable phases or periods, each constituting an MTS, than it is to consider the entire enterprise as a single MTS. I believe that such parsing permits both theorists and practitioners to focus on a manageable set of activities, driven by the attainment of a superordinate goal that in turn guides the inclusion of component teams.

Parsing ongoing MTSs into temporally defined ones introduces yet another unit of analysis to consider—the composition of an MTS *at a given time*—which then raises questions about higher level coordination. For example, parsing an ongoing MTS into temporal units then underscores the critical "handoff periods" where work is transitioned from one MTS phase to another. However, I think that the emphasis is well placed. For example, many of the errors seen in health care occur as patients are transferred from one MTS (e.g., emergency care or surgery) to another (e.g., recovery, long-term care, or rehabilitation). In continuous operations, such as power plants and oil platforms, problems often occur during shift changes or when transitioning from one stage to another (e.g., from normal operations to planned refueling outages). In sum, I would argue that many of the MTSs discussed by the authors in this volume might be better conceived of as a series of overlapping and interlocking MTSs. Of course, the challenge is to identify when one ends and another begins, but I believe that in so doing, we will distinguish more manageable units of inquiry that will enable us to better understand and to manage these complex entities. It is also true that in so doing, component teams that link the different temporal MTSs by spanning structural holes in the system across phases will be members of both of the MTSs. This represents another form of multiple-team (in this case, MTS) membership (see O'Leary et al., Chapter 6, this volume) and highlights the multiple identity, motivation, entrainment, and other pressures that teams in such positions experience.

Standing MTSs

As I alluded to earlier, sculpting the boundaries for inclusion and exclusion of component teams in an MTS is a challenging task. This is perhaps easier done once the system is activated and one can observe the component teams that are participating in functional exchanges. What I would like to propose, however, is that in many instances there may be a larger network that is called upon, depending on circumstances, which may populate an MTS on any particular occasion. My point, however, is that although this larger network of potential MTS component teams may exist, for purposes of the study, a given MTS is composed of the teams that exhibit the tight coupling as related to a superordinate goal achievement, as I discussed earlier.

For example, let us assume that a couple engages a "wedding-planning service" that serves as the hub or leadership team for an MTS. Depending on the couple's desires and the planning service network, other teams of participants need to be secured and their action coordinated. These might include teams from religious organizations, caterers, hotel or facility teams, florists, transportation, entertainment, and so forth. Some of these teams will have worked together in the past, whereas others may be doing so for the first time. Although every ceremony will be somewhat unique, many elements will be similar from one to another. In-home hospice care and general contractors, who orchestrate the construction of neighborhoods, represent but a couple of other MTSs that operate in this fashion. Notice that the "prime" source (i.e., the wedding or hospice service coordinators, or the general contractors) may have several teams as part of their organization, while also having to partner or "subcontract" out parts of the operation. So these MTSs will likely be hybrid entities mixing teams from different organizations, with a variety of histories of working together, who must coordinate their efforts for a given event. Some number of these teams, in different configurations, can be expected to be working together again in the future.

At issue for standing MTSs is that they have the costs and benefits associated with a diverse set of ties. On one hand, an organizing entity has a history of interactions with several teams and can leverage (or compensate for) their known qualities and expectations. In other words, they may be confident that they share a common mental model about how their interactions will go and how they each will help to achieve the superordinate goal. In other instances, however, new teams will need to be incorporated, necessitating the development of a shared vision, collective identity aligned with the superordinate goal attainment, entrainment to temporal cycles, and so forth. In short, MTSs that are constituted from a larger standing network will face a variety of integration challenges. In some cases, they can capitalize on histories of cooperation and collective understandings. In other instances, they may need to spend some development time at the beginning to address coordination problems that they have experienced in the past. And, in other instances, new component teams need to be integrated—sometimes by assimilating them into "how the MTS does things" while at other times needing to accommodate the MTSs to the unique capabilities of the new team. In any case, recognition of these challenges should facilitate not only how the MTS functions but also the selection of component teams at the onset.

In summary, the value of identifying different types of MTSs and their temporal qualities is that we move closer to a taxonomy of forms that should help in the accumulation of knowledge and identification of points of leverage for managing MTSs. Accumulating a coherent body of knowledge about MTSs is difficult, and I believe it is hindered by commingling discussions of many different types. Naturally categorizing MTSs as one type or another, or defining when one stops and another begins, and similar distinctions are somewhat subjective and artificial. But I do believe that they will enable us to develop a language and means of discussing MTSs and accumulating knowledge about them. How such knowledge can be gathered and analyzed, however, is a topic that I turn to next.

STUDYING MTSs

As like any other organizational entity, MTSs can be studied using a variety of research methods. These would include passive observational methods, various types of simulations, quasi-experimental and experimental methods, and action research methodologies. Each approach offers some unique advantages and has associated limitations. Notably, to the extent that various manipulations and interventions can be introduced and random assignments leveraged in any setting, causal inferences will be strengthened. Similarly, longitudinal methods and analyses are also beneficial in this regard. Below, I briefly review five major approaches: (a) cross-sectional field studies, (b) simulations, (c) longitudinal field investigations, (d) complexity models, and (e) case studies, and I discuss their relative advantages and disadvantages.

Cross-Sectional Field Studies

Cross-sectional field studies have a number of known limitations, most notably the inability to unpack developmental phenomena or any basis for specifying causal order (see Aiken & Hanges, Chapter 15, this volume). However, cross-sectional studies do provide some comparative insights. For example, Kirkman and Rosen (1999); de Jong, de Ruyter, and Lemmink (2004); and Mathieu, Gilson, and Ruddy (2006) all found MTS processes related positively to important team mediators (e.g., team empowerment, processes) and outcomes. Elsewhere, in a cross-level field study with lagged outcome measures, Mathieu, Maynard, Taylor, Gilson, and Ruddy (2007) found that MTS processes interacted with team processes to influence team performance. Specifically, team processes exhibited a stronger relationship with team performance to the extent that MTS-level processes were less, rather than more, cooperative. These findings paralleled those obtained by Marks et al. (2005) in a laboratory investigation. Interestingly, MTS coordination enhanced the performance of teams who reported poor team processes in our field study.

Millikin et al. (2010) recently tested a homologous model of self-management influences in the context of MTSs. They found support for positive relationships between individual self-management scores indexed at the individual, team, and MTS levels, and a variety of important outcomes associated with each level of analysis. An innovative variation on this theme was published by DeChurch and colleagues (DeChurch et al., in press). They performed a historiometric analysis whereby they coded secondary accounts of MTS functioning during extreme events (e.g., hurricane response) and analyzed leadership influences. Although subject to the same limitations as cross-sectional surveys, as well as those associated with secondary accounts of events, this approach enabled the authors to conduct a comparative study of complex MTS forms. The historical nature of the accounts also enabled them to infer cause–effect relationships more so than would have been afforded by a cross-sectional design.

As the above and a few other studies have shown, correlation field studies provide some insights as to how current MTS states relate to other variables of interest. However, they tell us little about how those MTS states evolved, nor do they permit strong cause–effect inferences. Moreover, cross-sectional studies can serve a diagnostic function—if practitioners are able to see reports that some MTSs are functioning well, whereas others are experiencing problems, they can better target their limited resources and attention accordingly.

Simulations

If you haven't seen them firsthand, you would be amazed at the current state of the art in simulations these days. From relatively simple four-person, two-team combat flight simulations that run for 4–5 hours with undergraduates (e.g., Mathieu, Cobb, Marks, Zaccaro, & Marsh, 2004), to large-scale, 14-person, three-team training platforms run over the course of 5 weeks with active duty Air Force captains (e.g., Davison, Hollenbeck, Ilgen, Barnes, & Sleesman, 2010), modern-day simulations for studying MTSs come in a wide variety of configurations and can be played by a variety of sample populations.

Resick, Burke, and Doty (Chapter 17, this volume) provide an excellent analysis of the strengths and weakness of laboratory-based simulations in terms of threats to various forms of validity inferences. I concur with their assessments and insights. I would like to extend that discussion, however, to note some of the unique aspects of simulations that may not be apparent to all. These simulations enable one to fully script scenarios yet have computer-controlled entities respond intelligently to evolving circumstances. The scripting feature ensures that all teams will initially confront identical performance conditions and thereby affords a high degree of experimental control. Because the number and actions of various units are fully controllable, one can create anywhere from a very simple, slowly evolving scenario to an exceptionally complex and demanding environment to test the influence of factors such as workload, environmental complexity, stress, and so forth on individual, team, and MTS behaviors and performance outcomes. Although in an experimental sense, MTSs may be placed in identical "starting positions" in different conditions or scenarios, the exact nature of the engagement they confront will evolve and be somewhat unique to each. This is because computer artificial intelligence

(AI) guided entities will respond to MTS actions in a dynamic fashion. In this sense, the participating MTS members work to enact the nature of the environment that they confront by virtue of how they respond to events. *Experimentally*, they are in a given condition. *Experientially*, every MTS confronts a unique environment.

The ability to script simulation features also allows one to embed various "critical events" or "triggers" designed to elicit or test particular team or MTS processes and responses within each scenario. These instances are designed to provide particularly informative windows within the ongoing flow of events. In this fashion, these scripted triggers permit what amounts to preprogrammed event history analyses (see Aiken & Hanges, Chapter 15, this volume). The fact that computer-controlled units respond adaptively to changing circumstances but in adherence to their programmed "strategies or rules of engagement" means that the scenario will remain realistic to events as they unfold, even if the live participating teams take actions that were never anticipated by research designers. This creates an interesting balance of experimental control and realistic emergent phenomena, in response to player actions, which has not been available in previous simulations.

Simulations also permit the testing of hybrid MTSs that combine live and AI-controlled component teams. For example, whereas early versions of an air combat simulation focused exclusively on the actions and results of two live flights teams (Mathieu et al., 2004), later versions of the simulation included AI-controlled allied flight teams (DeChurch & Marks, 2006; Marks et al., 2005). In these later versions, the live participating teams needed to interact with their computer-controlled allied flight teams to accomplish the superordinate goal, while also confronting an enemy force of 15–20 AI-controlled teams. In current-day simulations, whether an allied or enemy team is controlled by AI or real people is often indiscernible to players. This permits greater experimenter control over the simulation, reduced costs, and the introduction of computer agents into live experiments.

Finally, these simulations are not limited to use with the typical undergraduate subject pool participants. For example, Davison et al. (2010) have used complex simulations to study MTSs composed of Air Force captains participating in a midcareer training exercise. Although they are playing a simulated engagement, their performance therein has serious implications for their future career opportunities. At issue is that the participant sample can enhance the validity and generalizability of simulated MTS engagements. Complex business simulations are commonly used in business schools as capstone experiences for undergraduates in an effort to get them to work across functions and to see the integrative nature of organizations. They could easily be used to study MTS phenomena, albeit with student populations. However, these same simulations are also used in evening MBA classes and executive education programs where participants often have years or decades of real-life business experience. Again, it is still a simulated environment, but the generalizability inferences are enhanced by sampling a managerial population.

Sophisticated simulation platforms are both highly engaging and generate scads of data. They permit researchers to introduce various manipulations that would never be available in the real world, yet preserve the dynamic and evolving nature of MTSs. In short, I see these as extremely valuable testbeds for studying the more fundamental processes underlying MTS effectiveness.

Longitudinal Field Studies

Longitudinal field investigations are often held up as a gold standard (along with experiments) but are difficult to conduct and rarely conducted. No doubt, this stems from the difficulty of gaining access, the ability to gather data consistently over time, and the lack of experimental control. MTSs, particularly multiorganizational ones with transformational composition, are almost impossible to sample adequately. Both Aiken and Hanges (Chapter 15, this volume) and Coen and Schnackenberg (Chapter 16, this volume) well chronicle such challenges. With the challenges inherent in these types of designs, are they really a viable option? I think so, but in a limited set of circumstances.

Modern-day organizations, including MTSs, often coordinate their actions primarily, if not exclusively, through digital means. Whether we are considering voice over Internet protocol (VoIP), videoconferencing, knowledge portals and repositories, global positioning systems, or the like, there are quite often digital traces of within- and between-team actions (what Aiken and Hanges, Chapter 15, this volume, referred to as "real-time tracking methods"). As with any archival trace measure, these data are not always suitable for use in process analyses. However, they do signal who is interfacing with whom else, when they are interfacing, and how often those interactions occur, and they may well be suitable for content coding. In other words, secondary data sources and archival records may provide some unique insights into MTS operations. Undoubtedly these will not be at the depth of, say, a detailed qualitative study, but they may afford the opportunity to track a high volume of interactions and model them and their influences over time.

I should note the potential applicability of new forms of analyses that would be suitable for both simulation and longitudinal field studies. I and others (e.g., Poole & Contractor, Chapter 8, this volume) have argued that MTSs are complex networks of members and component teams. Moreover, these networks have multiple salient compositional attributes and linkage processes. What this suggests is that MTSs would be highly suitable for multidimensional (i.e., multiplex) network analysis applications (cf. Borgatti & Foster, 2003; Contractor, 2009). Multiplex network analyses simultaneously model the impact of network properties along several dimensions (e.g., identity, cooperation, and communication) and analyze their unique and combined influences (Xi & Tang, 2004). Further still, longitudinal applications of multiplex networks would help to identify which features, of which networks, at what times, are most influential in the evolving effectiveness of an MTS (Carley, 2003; Contractor, Wasserman, & Faust, 2006). These techniques are still evolving and are extremely complex to apply, but they offer a promising avenue for future MTS research, particularly if they can be combined with meaningful digital archival trace data.

Complexity Approaches

Coen and Schmackenberg (Chapter 16, this volume) and Aiken and Hanges (Chapter 15, this volume) make strong cases for the adoption of complexity approaches for studying MTSs. They emphasize that MTSs are complex systems that evolve over time. They note the primacy of actors (both individual members and component teams) in MTSs, and how processes unfold over time in nonlinear, nonadditive fashions. Their ideas are intuitively appealing, and I believe, ultimately, where the field needs to go. These are complex methods that are not familiar to most social scientists, who are trained in the positivist reductionist tradition and who employ mostly linear-modeling and experimental techniques. But we need more flexible and complex tools to understand complex systems such as MTSs.

Catastrophe and neutral networks models, among other approaches, permit researchers to use data that they customarily collect in more complex and nonlinear or additive fashions. Clearly, these provide some advantages in terms of processing data inductively to identify underlying patterns. They are data and computationally intensive, but provide mechanisms to look beyond ordinary least squares–style estimates. They also permit the uncovering of complex interactions that result from the confluence of a number of factors (see Coen & Schnackenburg, Chapter 16, this volume).

The beauty of complexity analyses is that they assume interdependence among "actors" (or nodes, aka MTS members and component teams), dynamic and emergent processes, and nonlinear functions such as tipping points and threshold effects. From what we know of MTS operations, these are inherent characteristics of the systems. The greatest strength of complexity-based methods, such as agent-based computational modeling (Coen & Schnackenburg, Chapter 16, this volume), is probably also their greatest weakness. Agent-based approaches require researchers to identify actors in the system and to articulate their process rules. These requirements force agent-based modelers to be very explicit about the systems that they are examining and their underlying assumptions. But therein lies the greatest challenge.

As discussed previously, most MTS forms are fluid entities, Even if component teams remain consistent over time, within-team memberships may vary over time. Some types of MTSs have dynamic component team compositions, and evolve into different configurations in response to environmental factors. In short, it is quite challenging to identify who exactly the MTS actors are at any point in time. More challenging still, however, is specifying their "rules" of interaction. Coen and Schnackenburg (Chapter 16, this volume) acknowledge that such rules may have to be developed from a general understanding of the processes available in the literature. Therein lies the conundrum, however, as no such general understanding of MTSs processes yet exists. Of course, we can extrapolate from related phenomena, but their application to MTS processes remains an open question. If the entire reason for doing complexity analyses is that they can model nonlinear and nonadditive effects, and thereby represent complex phenomena more accurately than traditional methods, then it seems antithetical to populate their key underlying parameters with values derived from traditional methods. We may well have to rely on subject matter experts' input- and qualitative-based approaches to generate initial estimates that can then be refined in cyclical inductive and deductive fashion.

In other words, in order to fully exploit insights from agent-based modeling techniques, we need to provide a clear set of actors and reasonable starting values for underlying processes—neither of which exists for most MTS applications. So we need to leverage many insights from other research methodologies before the promise of complexity techniques can be realized. Nevertheless, I believe that complexity techniques will play an important role in the evolution of our understanding of MTSs. Used in an iterative abduction fashion, alternating between indicative and deductive applications, agent-based modeling permits one to examine the dynamics underlying MTS configurations that may not readily appear in the field. They also enable a far more detailed and nonlinear examination of processes than could reasonably be simulated and observed with live-person MTSs. They are not a panacea, nor do I anticipate that they will replace more traditional social science methods in the near future. But, I do believe that these techniques will prove valuable going forward as they force scholars to be explicit about their underlying assumptions, and can test nonlinear and nonadditive relationships that would simply be obscured in the ordinary least squares and experimental paradigm.

Case Studies

My impression from reading the chapters of this volume is that the authors generally express a preference for quantitative research methodologies. My own tendencies gravitate in that direction as well—but we need to appreciate and take seriously the insights that qualitative methodologies offer for the study of MTSs. I strongly encourage the use of case studies for advancing our understanding of MTSs. Case study methodologies are often misunderstood and, arguably, underappreciated. Yin (1989) defined the *case study method* as an "empirical inquiry that investigates a contemporary phenomenon within its real-life context, addresses a situation in which the boundaries between phenomenon and context are not clearly evident, and uses multiple sources of evidence" (p. 23). This appears perfectly suitable for understanding MTSs.

I intentionally referred to *case study methodologies* in the plural as they come in many varieties. Yin (1993) outlined a 3 × 2 matrix of case study types. On one axis, he distinguishes the nature of case studies as *exploratory, descriptive,* or *explanatory,* whereas he noted that any of these may be based on *single* or *multiple* samples as the second axis. Yin (1993) further argued that "the exploratory case study has perhaps given all case study research its most notorious reputation … [as] in this type of case study, fieldwork and data collection are undertaken prior to the final definition of study questions and hypotheses" (pp. 4–5). In short, *exploratory case studies* are fine for generating hypotheses but not for testing them. Given the nascent stage of our understanding of MTSs, I believe that there remains a place for exploratory case studies with rich descriptions of the phenomena.

Descriptive case studies are efforts to categorize the nature and dimensions of a given phenomenon within its natural context. In this sense, descriptive case studies would be useful for building a taxonomy of MTSs and categorizing their similarities and differences. Finally, *explanatory case studies* seek to present data bearing on cause–effect relationships— in short, to illustrate how certain MTS attributes relate to one or more linkage processes and outcomes. Whereas exploratory case studies can be a theoretical (and, indeed, are intended to help develop applicable theory), descriptive and explanatory case studies rely on the use of a priori theories to categorize and then tie certain dimensions to outcomes, respectively.

Yin (1993) also distinguished between single and multiple case studies and argued that the latter offer the opportunity to replicate, and thereby validate, researchers' inferences. He submitted that for multiple case studies, researchers should attempt to sample replicated instances of the phenomenon being examined to minimize extraneous influences on the results. Certainly this would be the case if we sample multiple MTSs of a similar type. But I would add that if MTSs were selectively sampled from across the taxonomic categories (following descriptive-style work), then we can accelerate the learning that explanatory case studies provide by making comparisons both within and across types. In sum, much can be learned from case study investigations, and the MTS topic is ripe for such work. I strongly encourage their use in future MTS investigations.

FUTURE DIRECTIONS

Summing up, I am impressed by the amount of theorizing, research, and application that has been devoted to MTSs over the past decade. This topic began from an observation: a sense by Michelle, Steve, and I that something was missing from research that focused on intrateam functioning rather than interteam operations. Now, 10+ years later, there remain more questions than answers. But, the questions are better framed now than they were at the turn of the 21st century. The authors of the chapters in this volume have each identified an important theme, chronicled what is known about that theme from other domains of inquiry, and then extended its application to MTSs. In so doing, every author has identified something different, some unique twist or aspect of their ideas, that was unique to MTSs. Accordingly, I think that the jury has rendered its verdict—*MTSs are something different from teams, organizations, or other organizational entities.* That is not to say that identifying them is easy—in fact, it isn't—but that challenge is not unique to MTSs. I'll repeat here what I have said elsewhere (see Mathieu & Chen, 2011): Clearly identifying units of inquiry is one of the greatest burdens that is often swept under the rug by organizational theorists and researchers. But MTSs are one such unit of inquiry, and we should endeavor to clarify what they are, distinguish different types or forms, and then learn more about them.

One clear step toward a coherent science of MTSs is to develop a taxonomy of types. I believe that this is best accomplished by focusing first on their compositional attributes. The attribute profiles generate the stress points for different MTSs and will allow us to accumulate knowledge. Sometime in the future we may well determine that certain attributes have little consequence for MTS effectiveness, but in lieu of any categorization schemes, we will not be able to make such comparisons. In any event, developing a taxonomy of MTSs will also serve to accelerate our understanding of their key features and the critical drivers of their effectiveness. This will enable more predictive and explanatory work, whether it is done in simulated environments, in longitudinal field investigations, or using complexity approaches. All have a place in the evolving science of MTSs.

It is encouraging to see the energy and interest in the MTS topic. Future research will be challenging, but I believe that newer technologies will enable us to study these entities like never before. In any event, my sincere hope is that we continue to learn about these entities and how to improve their effectiveness, as I believe that MTSs will become only more prevalent in the years to come.

REFERENCES

Borgatti, S. P., & Foster, P. (2003). The network paradigm in organizational research: A review and typology. *Journal of Management, 29*, 991–1013.

Burke, C. S., Stagl, K. C., Klein, C., Goodwin, G. F., Salas, E., & Halpin, S. (2006). What types of leadership behaviors are functional in team? A meta-analysis. *The Leadership Quarterly, 17*, 288–307.

Cannon-Bowers, J. A., Salas, E., & Converse, S. A. (1993). Shared mental models in expert team decision making. In N. J. Castellan, Jr. (Ed.), *Individual and group decision making: Current issues* (pp. 221–246). Hillsdale, NJ: Erlbaum.

Carley, K. M. (2003). Dynamic network analysis. In R. Breiger, K. Carley, & P. Pattison (Eds.), *Dynamic social network modeling and analysis: Workshop summary and papers* (pp. 133–145). Washington, DC: Committee on Human Factors, National Research Council, National Research Council.

Contractor, N. (2009). The emergence of multidimensional networks. *Journal of Computer-Mediated Communication, 14*, 743–747.

Contractor, N., Wasserman, S., & Faust, K. (2006). Testing multi-theoretical multilevel hypotheses about organizational networks: An analytic framework and empirical example. *Academy of Management Review, 31*, 681–703.

Davison, R., Hollenbeck, J. R., Ilgen, D. R., Barnes, C. M., & Sleesman, D. J. (2010, April). Role of action and transition processes in large multiteam systems. In L. DeChurch (Chair), *Multiteam imperatives for leadership and organization.* Symposium presented at the annual meeting of Society for Industrial and Organizational Psychology, Atlanta, GA.

DeChurch, L. A., Burke, C. S., Shuffler, M., Lyons, R., Doty, D., & Salas, E. (In press). A historiometric analysis of leadership in mission critical multiteam environments. *Leadership Quarterly.*

DeChurch, L. A., & Marks, M. A. (2006). Leadership in multiteam systems. *Journal of Applied Psychology, 91*, 311–329.

DeChurch, L. A., & Mathieu, J. E. (2009). Thinking in terms of multiteam systems. In E. Salas, G. F. Goodwin, & C. S. Burke (Eds.), *Team effectiveness in complex organizations: Cross-disciplinary perspectives and approaches* (pp. 267–292). New York: Taylor & Francis.

de Jong, A., de Ruyter, K., & Lemmink, J. (2004). Antecedents and consequences of the service climate in boundary-spanning self-managing service teams. *Journal of Marketing, 68*(2), 18–35.

Dziedzic, M., & Seidl, M. (2005). *Provincial Reconstruction Teams and Military Relations with International and Nongovernmental Organizations in Afghanistan.* Washington, DC: United States Institute of Peace.

Freeman, J. H. (1980). The unit problem in organizational research. In W. M. Evan (Ed.), *Frontiers in organization and management* (pp. 59–68). New York: Praeger.

Gibson, C. B., & Cohen, S. G. (2003). *Virtual teams that work: Creating conditions for virtual team effectiveness.* New York: Wiley.

Jaques, E. (1996). *Requisite organization: A total system for effective managerial organization and managerial leadership for the 21st century.* Arlington, VA: Cason Hall.

Kirkman, B. L., & Mathieu, J. E. (2005). The dimensions and antecedents of team virtuality. *Journal of Management, 31*, 700–718.

Kirkman, B. L., & Rosen, B. (1999). Beyond self-management: Antecedents and consequences of team empowerment. *Academy of Management Journal, 42*(1), 58–74.

Kirkman, B. L., & Shapiro, D. L. (2005). The impact of cultural value diversity on multicultural team performance. In T. Devinney, T. Pedersen, & L. Tihanyi (Eds.), *Managing multinational teams: Global perspectives* (Advances in International Management No. 18, pp. 33–67). Bingley, UK: Emerald Group.

Lewis, K. (2004). Knowledge and performance in knowledge-worker teams: A longitudinal study of transactive memory systems. *Management Science, 50*, 1519–1533.

Marks, M. A., DeChurch, L. A., Mathieu, J. E., Panzer, F. J., & Alonso, A. A. (2005). The importance of goal hierarchies and teamwork processes for multiteam effectiveness. *Journal of Applied Psychology, 90*, 964–971.

Mathieu, J. E., & Chen, G. (2011). The etiology of the multilevel paradigm in management research. *Journal of Management, 37*, 610–641.

Mathieu, J. E., Cobb, M. A., Marks, M. A., Zaccaro, S. J., & Marsh, S. (2004). Multiteam ACES: A research platform for studying multiteam systems. In S. G. Schiflett, L. R. Elliott, E. Salas, & M. Coovert (Eds.), *Scaled worlds: Development, validation and applications* (pp. 297–315). Burlington, VT: Ashgate.

Mathieu, J. E., Gilson, L. L., & Ruddy, T. M. (2006). Empowerment and team effectiveness: An empirical test of an integrated model. *Journal of Applied Psychology, 91*(1), 97–108.

Mathieu, J. E., Marks, M. A., & Zaccaro, S. J. (2001). Multiteam systems. In N. Anderson, D. S. Ones, H. K. Sinangil, & C. Viswesvaran (Eds.), *Organizational psychology: Vol. 2. Handbook of industrial, work and organizational psychology* (pp. 289–313). London: Sage.

Mathieu, J. E., Maynard, M. T., Rapp, T. L., & Gilson, L. L. (2008). Team effectiveness 1997–2007: A review of recent advancements and a glimpse into the future. *Journal of Management, 34*, 410–476.

Mathieu, J. E., Maynard, M. T., Taylor, S. R., Gilson, L. L., & Ruddy, T. M. (2007). An examination of the effects of organizational district and team contexts on team processes and performance: a meso-mediational model. *Journal of Organizational Behavior, 28*(7), 891–910.

Millikin, J. P., Homa, P. W., & Manz, C. C. (2010). Self-management competencies in self-managing teams: Their impact on multiteam system productivity. *The Leadership Quarterly, 21*, 687–702.

Mohammed, S., Ferzandi, L., & Hamilton, K. (2010). Metaphor no more: A 15-year review of the team mental model. *Journal of Management, 36*, 876–910.

Pearce, C. L., & Conger, J. A. (2003). *Shared leadership: Reframing the hows and whys of leadership.* Thousand Oaks, CA: Sage.

Rentsch, J. R., Small, E. E., & Hanges, P. J. (2008). Cognitions in organizations and teams: What is the *meaning* of cognitive similarity? In B. Smith (Ed.), *The people make the place: Exploring dynamic linkages between individuals and organizations* (pp. 127–156). New York: Erlbaum.

Thompson, J. D. (1967). *Organizations in action.* New York: McGraw-Hill.

Xi, Y., & Tang, F. (2004). Multiplex multi-core pattern of network organizations: An exploratory study. *Computational & Mathematical Organization Theory, 10*(2), 179–195.

Yin, R. (1989). *Case study research: Design and methods* (Rev. ed.). Beverly Hills, CA: Sage.

Yin, R. (1993). *Applications of case study research.* Beverly Hills, CA: Sage.

Zaheer, S. (2000). Time-zone economies and managerial work in a global world. In P. C. Earley & H. Singh (Eds.), *Innovations in international management* (pp. 339–354). Thousand Oaks, CA: Sage.

Author Index

Subject Index